D1462184

MYTHS OF THE CHEROKEE

James Mooney

DOVER PUBLICATIONS, INC.
New York

Published in Canada by General Publishing Company, Ltd., 30 Lesmill Road, Don Mills, Toronto, Ontario.
Published in the United Kingdom by Constable and Company, Ltd., 3 The Lanchesters, 162–164 Fulham Palace Road, London W6 9ER.

Bibliographical Note

This Dover edition, first published in 1995, is an unabridged and slightly altered republication of the work originally published by the Government Printing Office, Washington, D.C., in 1900, as part of the *Nineteenth Annual Report of the Bureau of American Ethnology to the Secretary of the Smithsonian Institution, 1897–98: in Two Parts—Part I.* For the Dover edition the administrative report (*Report of the Director*, James Powell) has been omitted. Also, the maps, originally in color, appear in black and white and the plates have been rearranged for reasons of space.

Library of Congress Cataloging-in-Publication Data

Mooney, James, 1861–1921.
    Myths of the Cherokee / James Mooney.
        p.   cm.
    ". . . unabridged and slightly altered republication of the work originally published by the Government Printing Office, Washington, D.C., in 1900, as part of the nineteenth Annual report of the Bureau of American Ethnology to the Secretary of the Smithsonian Institution . . . the administrative report (report of the director, James Powell) has been omitted"—T.p. verso.
    Includes bibliographical references and index.
    ISBN 0-486-28907-9 (pbk.)
    1. Cherokee Indians—Folklore. 2. Cherokee mythology. 3. Tales—Southern States. 4. Legends—Southern States. 5. Cherokee Indians—History. I. Title.
E99.C5M763   1995
398.2'089975—dc20   95-22350
                                                                     CIP

Manufactured in the United States of America
Dover Publications, Inc., 31 East 2nd Street, Mineola, N.Y. 11501

CONTENTS

ILLUSTRATIONS

9

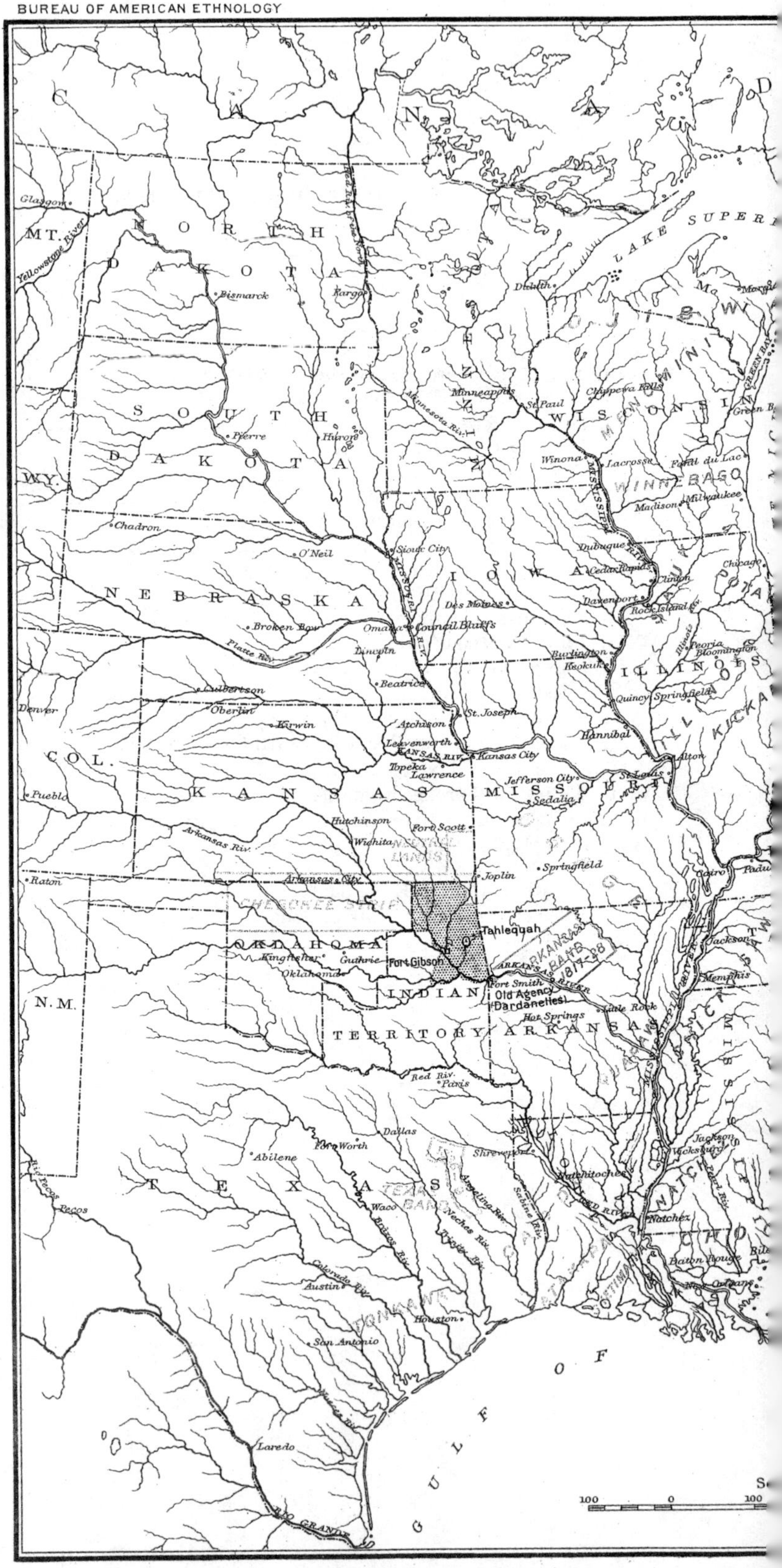
NORTH DAKOTA
SOUTH DAKOTA
NEBRASKA
KANSAS
MISSOURI
IOWA
ILLINOIS
WISCONSIN
ARKANSAS
INDIAN TERRITORY
OKLAHOMA
TEXAS
COL.
N.M.
WY.
MT.
LAKE SUPERIOR
GULF OF
CHEROKEE STRIP
NEUTRAL LANDS
ARKANSAS BAND 1817-38
TEXAS BAND
Tahlequah
Fort Gibson
Old Agency
(Dardanelles)
Fort Smith
Arkansas River
Red Riv.
Platte Riv.
Rio Grande
Bismarck
Fargo
Pierre
Huron
Duluth
Minneapolis
St. Paul
Chadron
O'Neil
Sioux City
Omaha
Council Bluffs
Lincoln
Broken Bow
Des Moines
Beatrice
St. Joseph
Atchison
Leavenworth
Kansas City
Topeka
Lawrence
Culbertson
Oberlin
Kirwin
Hutchinson
Wichita
Fort Scott
Joplin
Springfield
Jefferson City
Sedalia
St. Louis
Alton
Hannibal
Quincy
Burlington
Keokuk
Peoria
Bloomington
Chicago
Clinton
Davenport
Rock Island
Dubuque
Cedar Rapids
Madison
Milwaukee
Winona
Lacrosse
Fond du Lac
Chippewa Falls
Cairo
Memphis
Jackson
Little Rock
Hot Springs
Arkansas City
Kingfisher
Guthrie
Oklahoma
Paris
Dallas
Fort Worth
Abilene
Waco
Austin
Houston
San Antonio
Shreveport
Natchitoches
Natchez
Vicksburg
Baton Rouge
New Orleans
Laredo
Pecos
Denver
Pueblo
Raton
Glasgow
Yellowstone River
Minnesota Riv.
Sabine Riv.
Neches Riv.
Brazos Riv.
Colorado Riv.
WINNEBAGO
MENOMINI
OJIBWA
DAKOTA
KICKAPOO
100 0 100

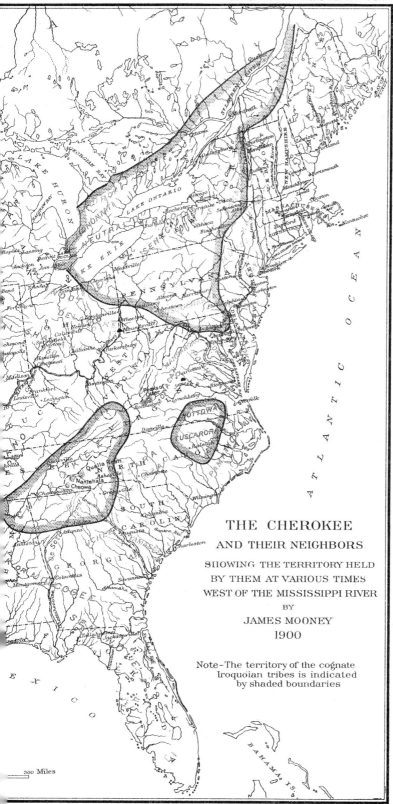

THE CHEROKEE

AND THEIR NEIGHBORS

SHOWING THE TERRITORY HELD
BY THEM AT VARIOUS TIMES
WEST OF THE MISSISSIPPI RIVER

BY

JAMES MOONEY

1900

Note–The territory of the cognate
Iroquoian tribes is indicated
by shaded boundaries

300 Miles

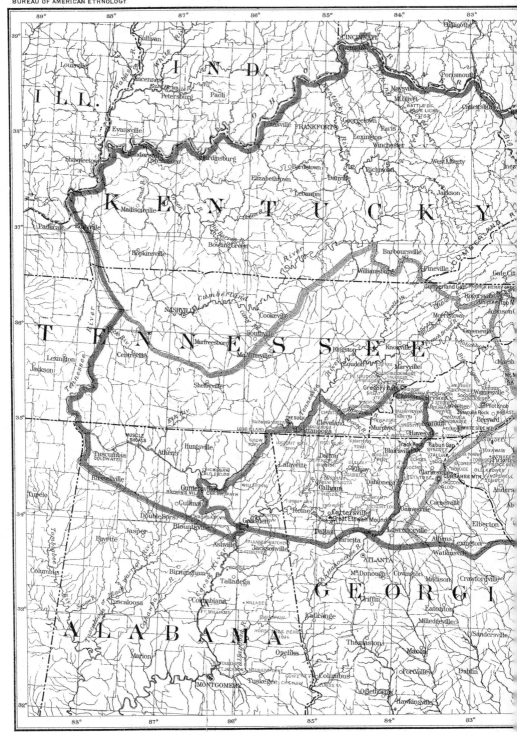

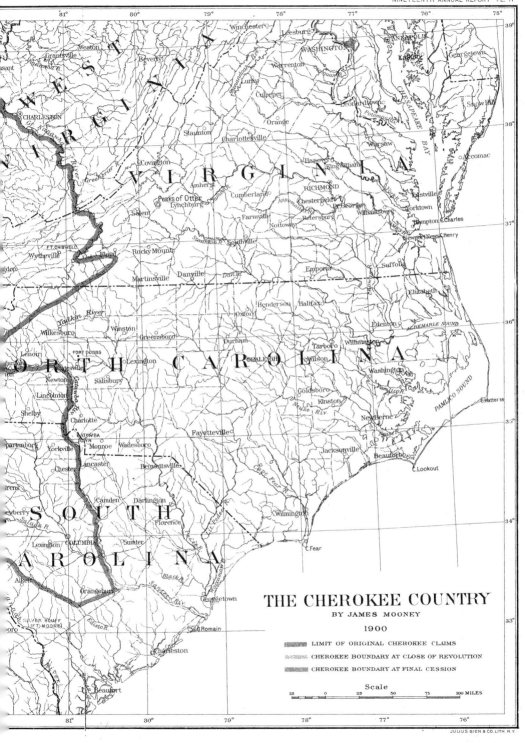

THE CHEROKEE COUNTRY

BY JAMES MOONEY

1900

LIMIT OF ORIGINAL CHEROKEE CLAIMS
CHEROKEE BOUNDARY AT CLOSE OF REVOLUTION
CHEROKEE BOUNDARY AT FINAL CESSION

Scale

25   0   25   50   75   100 MILES

IN THE CHEROKEE MOUNTAINS

PHOTOGRAPH BY AUTHOR, 1888

MYTHS OF THE CHEROKEE

By James Mooney

I—INTRODUCTION

The myths given in this paper are part of a large body of material collected among the Cherokee, chiefly in successive field seasons from 1887 to 1890, inclusive, and comprising more or less extensive notes, together with original Cherokee manuscripts, relating to the history, archeology, geographic nomenclature, personal names, botany, medicine, arts, home life, religion, songs, ceremonies, and language of the tribe. It is intended that this material shall appear from time to time in a series of papers which, when finally brought together, shall constitute a monograph upon the Cherokee Indians. This paper may be considered the first of the series, all that has hitherto appeared being a short paper upon the sacred formulas of the tribe, published in the Seventh Annual Report of the Bureau in 1891 and containing a synopsis of the Cherokee medico-religious theory, with twenty-eight specimens selected from a body of about six hundred ritual formulas written down in the Cherokee language and alphabet by former doctors of the tribe and constituting altogether the largest body of aboriginal American literature in existence.

Although the Cherokee are probably the largest and most important tribe in the United States, having their own national government and numbering at any time in their history from 20,000 to 25,000 persons, almost nothing has yet been written of their history or general ethnology, as compared with the literature of such northern tribes as the Delawares, the Iroquois, or the Ojibwa. The difference is due to historical reasons which need not be discussed here.

It might seem at first thought that the Cherokee, with their civilized code of laws, their national press, their schools and seminaries, are so far advanced along the white man's road as to offer but little inducement for ethnologic study. This is largely true of those in the Indian Territory, with whom the enforced deportation, two generations ago, from accustomed scenes and surroundings did more at a single stroke to obliterate Indian ideas than could have been accomplished

11

by fifty years of slow development. There remained behind, however, in the heart of the Carolina mountains, a considerable body, outnumbering today such well-known western tribes as the Omaha, Pawnee, Comanche, and Kiowa, and it is among these, the old conservative Kitu'hwa element, that the ancient things have been preserved. Mountaineers guard well the past, and in the secluded forests of Nantahala and Oconaluftee, far away from the main-traveled road of modern progress, the Cherokee priest still treasures the legends and repeats the mystic rituals handed down from his ancestors. There is change indeed in dress and outward seeming, but the heart of the Indian is still his own.

For this and other reasons much the greater portion of the material herein contained has been procured among the East Cherokee living upon the Qualla reservation in western North Carolina and in various detached settlements between the reservation and the Tennessee line. This has been supplemented with information obtained in the Cherokee Nation in Indian Territory, chiefly from old men and women who had emigrated from what is now Tennessee and Georgia, and who consequently had a better local knowledge of these sections, as well as of the history of the western Nation, than is possessed by their kindred in Carolina. The historical matter and the parallels are, of course, collated chiefly from printed sources, but the myths proper, with but few exceptions, are from original investigation.

The historical sketch must be understood as distinctly a sketch, not a detailed narrative, for which there is not space in the present paper. The Cherokee have made deep impress upon the history of the southern states, and no more has been attempted here than to give the leading facts in connected sequence. As the history of the Nation after the removal to the West and the reorganization in Indian Territory presents but few points of ethnologic interest, it has been but briefly treated. On the other hand the affairs of the eastern band have been discussed at some length, for the reason that so little concerning this remnant is to be found in print.

One of the chief purposes of ethnologic study is to trace the development of human thought under varying conditions of race and environment, the result showing always that primitive man is essentially the same in every part of the world. With this object in view a considerable space has been devoted to parallels drawn almost entirely from Indian tribes of the United States and British America. For the southern countries there is but little trustworthy material, and to extend the inquiry to the eastern continent and the islands of the sea would be to invite an endless task.

The author desires to return thanks for many favors from the Library of Congress, the Geological Survey, and the Smithsonian Institution, and for much courteous assistance and friendly suggestion from the officers and staff of the Bureau of American Ethnology; and to acknowledge his indebtedness to the late Chief N. J. Smith and family for services as interpreter and for kindly hospitality during successive field seasons; to Agent H. W. Spray and wife for unvarying kindness manifested in many helpful ways; to Mr William Harden, librarian, and the Georgia State Historical Society, for facilities in consulting documents at Savannah, Georgia; to the late Col. W. H. Thomas; Lieut. Col. W. W. Stringfield, of Waynesville; Capt. James W. Terrell, of Webster; Mrs A. C. Avery and Dr P. L. Murphy, of Morganton; Mr W. A. Fair, of Lincolnton; the late Maj. James Bryson, of Dillsboro; Mr H. G. Trotter, of Franklin; Mr Sibbald Smith, of Cherokee; Maj. R. C. Jackson, of Smithwood, Tennessee; Mr D. R. Dunn, of Conasauga, Tennessee; the late Col. Z. A. Zile, of Atlanta; Mr L. M. Greer, of Ellijay, Georgia; Mr Thomas Robinson, of Portland, Maine; Mr Allen Ross, Mr W. T. Canup, editor of the *Indian Arrow*, and the officers of the Cherokee Nation, Tahlequah, Indian Territory; Dr D. T. Day, United States Geological Survey, Washington, D. C., and Prof. G. M. Bowers, of the United States Fish Commission, for valuable oral information, letters, clippings, and photographs; to Maj. J. Adger Smyth, of Charleston, S. C., for documentary material; to Mr Stansbury Hagar and the late Robert Grant Haliburton, of Brooklyn, N. Y., for the use of valuable manuscript notes upon Cherokee stellar legends; to Miss A. M. Brooks for the use of valuable Spanish document copies and translations entrusted to the Bureau of American Ethnology; to Mr James Blythe, interpreter during a great part of the time spent by the author in the field; and to various Cherokee and other informants mentioned in the body of the work, from whom the material was obtained.

II—HISTORICAL SKETCH OF THE CHEROKEE

The Traditionary Period

The Cherokee were the mountaineers of the South, holding the entire Allegheny region from the interlocking head-streams of the Kanawha and the Tennessee southward almost to the site of Atlanta, and from the Blue ridge on the east to the Cumberland range on the west, a territory comprising an area of about 40,000 square miles, now included in the states of Virginia, Tennessee, North Carolina, South Carolina, Georgia, and Alabama. Their principal towns were upon the headwaters of the Savannah, Hiwassee, and Tuckasegee, and along the whole length of the Little Tennessee to its junction with the main stream. Itsâtï, or Echota, on the south bank of the Little Tennessee, a few miles above the mouth of Tellico river, in Tennessee, was commonly considered the capital of the Nation. As the advancing whites pressed upon them from the east and northeast the more exposed towns were destroyed or abandoned and new settlements were formed lower down the Tennessee and on the upper branches of the Chattahoochee and the Coosa.

As is always the case with tribal geography, there were no fixed boundaries, and on every side the Cherokee frontiers were contested by rival claimants. In Virginia, there is reason to believe, the tribe was held in check in early days by the Powhatan and the Monacan. On the east and southeast the Tuscarora and Catawba were their inveterate enemies, with hardly even a momentary truce within the historic period; and evidence goes to show that the Sara or Cheraw were fully as hostile. On the south there was hereditary war with the Creeks, who claimed nearly the whole of upper Georgia as theirs by original possession, but who were being gradually pressed down toward the Gulf until, through the mediation of the United States, a treaty was finally made fixing the boundary between the two tribes along a line running about due west from the mouth of Broad river on the Savannah. Toward the west, the Chickasaw on the lower Tennessee and the Shawano on the Cumberland repeatedly turned back the tide of Cherokee invasion from the rich central valleys, while the powerful Iroquois in the far north set up an almost unchallenged claim of paramount lordship from the Ottawa river of Canada southward at least to the Kentucky river.

14

On the other hand, by their defeat of the Creeks and expulsion of the Shawano, the Cherokee made good the claim which they asserted to all the lands from upper Georgia to the Ohio river, including the rich hunting grounds of Kentucky. Holding as they did the great mountain barrier between the English settlements on the coast and the French or Spanish garrisons along the Mississippi and the Ohio, their geographic position, no less than their superior number, would have given them the balance of power in the South but for a looseness of tribal organization in striking contrast to the compactness of the Iroquois league, by which for more than a century the French power was held in check in the north. The English, indeed, found it convenient to recognize certain chiefs as supreme in the tribe, but the only real attempt to weld the whole Cherokee Nation into a political unit was that made by the French agent, Priber, about 1736, which failed from its premature discovery by the English. We frequently find their kingdom divided against itself, their very number preventing unity of action, while still giving them an importance above that of neighboring tribes.

The proper name by which the Cherokee call themselves (1)[1] is Yûñ′wiyă′, or Ani′-Yûñ′wiyă′ in the third person, signifying "real people," or "principal people," a word closely related to Oñwe-hoñwe, the name by which the cognate Iroquois know themselves. The word properly denotes "Indians," as distinguished from people of other races, but in usage it is restricted to mean members of the Cherokee tribe, those of other tribes being designated as Creek, Catawba, etc., as the case may be. On ceremonial occasions they frequently speak of themselves as Ani′-Kitu′hwagĭ, or "people of Kĭtu′hwa," an ancient settlement on Tuckasegee river and apparently the original nucleus of the tribe. Among the western Cherokee this name has been adopted by a secret society recruited from the full-blood element and pledged to resist the advances of the white man's civilization. Under the various forms of Cuttawa, Gattochwa, Kittuwa, etc., as spelled by different authors, it was also used by several northern Algonquian tribes as a synonym for Cherokee.

Cherokee, the name by which they are commonly known, has no meaning in their own language, and seems to be of foreign origin. As used among themselves the form is Tsa′lăgĭ′ or Tsa′răgĭ′. It first appears as Chalaque in the Portuguese narrative of De Soto's expedition, published originally in 1557, while we find Cheraqui in a French document of 1699, and Cherokee as an English form as early, at least, as 1708. The name has thus an authentic history of 360 years. There is evidence that it is derived from the Choctaw word *choluk* or *chiluk*, signifying a pit or cave, and comes to us through the so-called Mobilian trade language, a corrupted Choctaw jargon formerly used as the

---

[1] See the notes to the historical sketch.

medium of communication among all the tribes of the Gulf states, as far north as the mouth of the Ohio (2). Within this area many of the tribes were commonly known under Choctaw names, even though of widely differing linguistic stocks, and if such a name existed for the Cherokee it must undoubtedly have been communicated to the first Spanish explorers by De Soto's interpreters. This theory is borne out by their Iroquois (Mohawk) name, Oyata'ge῾ronoñ', as given by Hewitt, signifying "inhabitants of the cave country," the Allegheny region being peculiarly a cave country, in which "rock shelters," containing numerous traces of Indian occupancy, are of frequent occurrence. Their Catawba name also, Mañterañ, as given by Gatschet, signifying "coming out of the ground," seems to contain the same reference. Adair's attempt to connect the name Cherokee with their word for fire, *atsila*, is an error founded upon imperfect knowledge of the language.

Among other synonyms for the tribe are Rickahockan, or Recnahecrian, the ancient Powhatan name, and Tallige', or Tallige'wi, the ancient name used in the Walam Olum chronicle of the Lenape'. Concerning both the application and the etymology of this last name there has been much dispute, but there seems no reasonable doubt as to the identity of the people.

Linguistically the Cherokee belong to the Iroquoian stock, the relationship having been suspected by Barton over a century ago, and by Gallatin and Hale at a later period, and definitely established by Hewitt in 1887.[1] While there can now be no question of the connection, the marked lexical and grammatical differences indicate that the separation must have occurred at a very early period. As is usually the case with a large tribe occupying an extensive territory, the language is spoken in several dialects, the principal of which may, for want of other names, be conveniently designated as the Eastern, Middle, and Western. Adair's classification into "Ayrate" (*é'ladĭ*), or low, and "Ottare" (*â'talĭ*), or mountainous, must be rejected as imperfect.

The Eastern dialect, formerly often called the Lower Cherokee dialect, was originally spoken in all the towns upon the waters of the Keowee and Tugaloo, head-streams of Savannah river, in South Carolina and the adjacent portion of Georgia. Its chief peculiarity is a rolling *r*, which takes the place of the *l* of the other dialects. In this dialect the tribal name is Tsa'răgĭ', which the English settlers of Carolina corrupted to Cherokee, while the Spaniards, advancing from the south, became better familiar with the other form, which they wrote as Chalaque. Owing to their exposed frontier position, adjoining the white settlements of Carolina, the Cherokee of this division

[1] Barton, Benj. S., New Views on the Origin of the Tribes and Nations of America, p. xlv, passim; Phila., 1797; Gallatin, Albert, Synopsis of Indian Tribes, Trans. American Antiquarian Society, II, p. 91; Cambridge, 1836; Hewitt, J. N. B., The Cherokee an Iroquoian Language, Washington, 1887 (MS in the archives of the Bureau of American Ethnology).

were the first to feel the shock of war in the campaigns of 1760 and 1776, with the result that before the close of the Revolution they had been completely extirpated from their original territory and scattered as refugees among the more western towns of the tribe. The consequence was that they lost their distinctive dialect, which is now practically extinct. In 1888 it was spoken by but one man on the reservation in North Carolina.

The Middle dialect, which might properly be designated the Kituhwa dialect, was originally spoken in the towns on the Tuckasegee and the headwaters of the Little Tennessee, in the very heart of the Cherokee country, and is still spoken by the great majority of those now living on the Qualla reservation. In some of its phonetic forms it agrees with the Eastern dialect, but resembles the Western in having the *l* sound.

The Western dialect was spoken in most of the towns of east Tennessee and upper Georgia and upon Hiwassee and Cheowa rivers in North Carolina. It is the softest and most musical of all the dialects of this musical language, having a frequent liquid *l* and eliding many of the harsher consonants found in the other forms. It is also the literary dialect, and is spoken by most of those now constituting the Cherokee Nation in the West.

Scattered among the other Cherokee are individuals whose pronunciation and occasional peculiar terms for familiar objects give indication of a fourth and perhaps a fifth dialect, which can not now be localized. It is possible that these differences may come from foreign admixture, as of Natchez, Taskigi, or Shawano blood. There is some reason for believing that the people living on Nantahala river differed dialectically from their neighbors on either side (3).

The Iroquoian stock, to which the Cherokee belong, had its chief home in the north, its tribes occupying a compact territory which comprised portions of Ontario, New York, Ohio, and Pennsylvania, and extended down the Susquehanna and Chesapeake bay almost to the latitude of Washington. Another body, including the Tuscarora, Nottoway, and perhaps also the Meherrin, occupied territory in northeastern North Carolina and the adjacent portion of Virginia. The Cherokee themselves constituted the third and southernmost body. It is evident that tribes of common stock must at one time have occupied contiguous territories, and such we find to be the case in this instance. The Tuscarora and Meherrin, and presumably also the Nottoway, are known to have come from the north, while traditional and historical evidence concur in assigning to the Cherokee as their early home the region about the headwaters of the Ohio, immediately to the southward of their kinsmen, but bitter enemies, the Iroquois. The theory which brings the Cherokee from northern Iowa and the Iroquois from Manitoba is unworthy of serious consideration. (4)

The most ancient tradition concerning the Cherokee appears to be the Delaware tradition of the expulsion of the Talligewi from the north, as first noted by the missionary Heckewelder in 1819, and published more fully by Brinton in the Walam Olum in 1885. According to the first account, the Delawares, advancing from the west, found their further progress opposed by a powerful people called Alligewi or Talligewi, occupying the country upon a river which Heckewelder thinks identical with the Mississippi, but which the sequel shows was more probably the upper Ohio. They were said to have regularly built earthen fortifications, in which they defended themselves so well that at last the Delawares were obliged to seek the assistance of the "Mengwe," or Iroquois, with the result that after a warfare extending over many years the Alligewi finally received a crushing defeat, the survivors fleeing down the river and abandoning the country to the invaders, who thereupon parceled it out amongst themselves, the "Mengwe" choosing the portion about the Great lakes while the Delawares took possession of that to the south and east. The missionary adds that the Allegheny (and Ohio) river was still called by the Delawares the Alligewi Sipu, or river of the Alligewi. This would seem to indicate it as the true river of the tradition. He speaks also of remarkable earthworks seen by him in 1789 in the neighborhood of Lake Erie, which were said by the Indians to have been built by the extirpated tribe as defensive fortifications in the course of this war. Near two of these, in the vicinity of Sandusky, he was shown mounds under which it was said some hundreds of the slain Talligewi were buried.[1] As is usual in such traditions, the Alligewi were said to have been of giant stature, far exceeding their conquerors in size.

In the Walam Olum, which is, it is asserted, a metrical translation of an ancient hieroglyphic bark record discovered in 1820, the main tradition is given in practically the same way, with an appendix which follows the fortunes of the defeated tribe up to the beginning of the historic period, thus completing the chain of evidence. (5)

In the Walam Olum also we find the Delawares advancing from the west or northwest until they come to "Fish river"—the same which Heckewelder makes the Mississippi (6). On the other side, we are told, "The Talligewi possessed the East." The Delaware chief "desired the eastern land," and some of his people go on, but are killed by the Talligewi. The Delawares decide upon war and call in the help of their northern friends, the "Talamatan," i. e., the Wyandot and other allied Iroquoian tribes. A war ensues which continues through the terms of four successive chiefs, when victory declares for the invaders, and "all the Talega go south." The country is then divided, the Talamatan taking the northern portion, while the Delawares "stay south of the lakes." The chronicle proceeds to tell how, after eleven more chiefs have ruled, the Nanticoke and Shawano separate from the

---

[1] Heckewelder, John, Indian Nations of Pennsylvania, pp. 47–49, ed. 1876.

parent tribe and remove to the south.   Six other chiefs follow in succession until we come to the seventh, who "went to the Talega mountains."   By this time the Delawares have reached the ocean.   Other
chiefs succeed, after whom "the Easterners and the Wolves"—probably the Mahican or Wappinger and the Munsee—move off to the
northeast.   At last, after six more chiefs, "the whites came on the
eastern sea," by which is probably meant the landing of the Dutch on
Manhattan in 1609 (7).   We may consider this a tally date, approximating the beginning of the seventeenth century.   Two more chiefs
rule, and of the second we are told that "He fought at the south; he
fought in the land of the Talega and Koweta," and again the fourth
chief after the coming of the whites "went to the Talega."   We have
thus a traditional record of a war of conquest carried on against the
Talligewi by four successive chiefs, and a succession of about twenty-
five chiefs between the final expulsion of that tribe and the appearance
of the whites, in which interval the Nanticoke, Shawano, Mahican,
and Munsee branched off from the parent tribe of the Delawares.
Without venturing to entangle ourselves in the devious maze of Indian
chronology, it is sufficient to note that all this implies a very long period
of time—so long, in fact, that during it several new tribes, each of
which in time developed a distinct dialect, branch off from the main
Lenape' stem.   It is distinctly stated that all the Talega went south
after their final defeat; and from later references we find that they took
refuge in the mountain country in the neighborhood of the Koweta
(the Creeks), and that Delaware war parties were still making raids
upon both these tribes long after the first appearance of the whites.

Although at first glance it might be thought that the name Tallige-wi
is but a corruption of Tsalagi, a closer study leads to the opinion that it
is a true Delaware word, in all probability connected with *waloh* or
walok, signifying a cave or hole (Zeisberger), whence we find in the
Walam Olum the word *oligonunk* rendered as "at the place of caves."
It would thus be an exact Delaware rendering of the same name,
"people of the cave country," by which, as we have seen, the Cherokee were commonly known among the tribes.   Whatever may be the
origin of the name itself, there can be no reasonable doubt as to its
application.   "Name, location, and legends combine to identify the
Cherokees or Tsalaki with the Tallike; and this is as much evidence as
we can expect to produce in such researches."[1]

The Wyandot confirm the Delaware story and fix the identification of
the expelled tribe.   According to their tradition, as narrated in 1802,
the ancient fortifications in the Ohio valley had been erected in the
course of a long war between themselves and the Cherokee, which
resulted finally in the defeat of the latter.[2]

The traditions of the Cherokee, so far as they have been preserved,

[1] Brinton, D. G., Walam Olum, p. 231; Phila., 1885.
[2] Schoolcraft, H. R., Notes on the Iroquois, p. 162; Albany, 1847.

supplement and corroborate those of the northern tribes, thus bringing the story down to their final settlement upon the headwaters of
the Tennessee in the rich valleys of the southern Alleghenies. Owing
to the Cherokee predilection for new gods, contrasting strongly with
the conservatism of the Iroquois, their ritual forms and national epics
had fallen into decay even before the Revolution, as we learn from
Adair. Some vestiges of their migration legend still existed in Haywood's time, but it is now completely forgotten both in the East and
in the West.

According to Haywood, who wrote in 1823 on information obtained
directly from leading members of the tribe long before the Removal,
the Cherokee formerly had a long migration legend, which was already
lost, but which, within the memory of the mother of one informant—
say about 1750—was still recited by chosen orators on the occasion of
the annual green-corn dance. This migration legend appears to have
resembled that of the Delawares and the Creeks in beginning with
genesis and the period of animal monsters, and thence following the
shifting fortune of the chosen band to the historic period. The tradition recited that they had originated in a land toward the rising sun,
where they had been placed by the command of "the four councils
sent from above." In this pristine home were great snakes and water
monsters, for which reason it was supposed to have been near the sea-
coast, although the assumption is not a necessary corollary, as these
are a feature of the mythology of all the eastern tribes. After this
genesis period there began a slow migration, during which "towns of
people in many nights' encampment removed," but no details are given.
From Heckewelder it appears that the expression, "a night's encampment," which occurs also in the Delaware migration legend, is an Indian
figure of speech for a halt of one year at a place.[1]

In another place Haywood says, although apparently confusing the
chronologic order of events: "One tradition which they have amongst
them says they came from the west and exterminated the former
inhabitants; and then says they came from the upper parts of the
Ohio, where they erected the mounds on Grave creek, and that they
removed thither from the country where Monticello (near Charlottesville, Virginia) is situated."[2] The first reference is to the celebrated
mounds on the Ohio near Moundsville, below Wheeling, West Virginia;
the other is doubtless to a noted burial mound described by Jefferson
in 1781 as then existing near his home, on the low grounds of Rivanna
river opposite the site of an ancient Indian town. He himself had
opened it and found it to contain perhaps a thousand disjointed
skeletons of both adults and children, the bones piled in successive
layers, those near the top being least decayed. They showed no signs

[1] Heckewelder, Indian Nations, p. 47, ed. 1876.
[2] Haywood, John, Natural and Aboriginal History of Tennessee, pp. 225–226; Nashville, 1823.

of violence, but were evidently the accumulation of long years from the neighboring Indian town. The distinguished writer adds: "But on whatever occasion they may have been made, they are of considerable notoriety among the Indians: for a party passing, about thirty years ago [i. e., about 1750], through the part of the country where this barrow is, went through the woods directly to it without any instructions or enquiry, and having staid about it some time, with expressions which were construed to be those of sorrow, they returned to the high road, which they had left about half a dozen miles to pay this visit, and pursued their journey."[1] Although the tribe is not named, the Indians were probably Cherokee, as no other southern Indians were then accustomed to range in that section. As serving to corroborate this opinion we have the statement of a prominent Cherokee chief, given to Schoolcraft in 1846, that acccording to their tradition his people had formerly lived at the Peaks of Otter, in Virginia, a noted landmark of the Blue ridge, near the point where Staunton river breaks through the mountains.[2]

From a careful sifting of the evidence Haywood concludes that the authors of the most ancient remains in Tennessee had spread over that region from the south and southwest at a very early period, but that the later occupants, the Cherokee, had entered it from the north and northeast in comparatively recent times, overrunning and exterminating the aborigines. He declares that the historical fact seems to be established that the Cherokee entered the country from Virginia, making temporary settlements upon New river and the upper Holston, until, under the continued hostile pressure from the north, they were again forced to remove farther to the south, fixing themselves upon the Little Tennessee, in what afterward became known as the middle towns. By a leading mixed blood of the tribe he was informed that they had made their first settlements within their modern home territory upon Nolichucky river, and that, having lived there for a long period, they could give no definite account of an earlier location. Echota, their capital and peace town, "claimed to be the eldest brother in the nation," and the claim was generally acknowledged.[3] In confirmation of the statement as to an early occupancy of the upper Holston region, it may be noted that "Watauga Old Fields," now Elizabethtown, were so called from the fact that when the first white settlement within the present state of Tennessee was begun there, so early as 1769, the bottom lands were found to contain graves and other numerous ancient remains of a former Indian town which tradition ascribed to the Cherokee, whose nearest settlements were then many miles to the southward.

While the Cherokee claimed to have built the mounds on the upper

[1] Jefferson, Thomas, Notes on Virginia, pp. 136–137; ed. Boston, 1802.
[2] Schoolcraft, Notes on the Iroquois, p. 163, 1847.
[3] Haywood, Natural and Aboriginal History of Tennessee, pp. 233, 236, 269, 1823.

Ohio, they yet, according to Haywood, expressly disclaimed the authorship of the very numerous mounds and petroglyphs in their later home
territory, asserting that these ancient works had exhibited the same
appearance when they themselves had first occupied the region.[1] This
accords with Bartram's statement that the Cherokee, although sometimes utilizing the mounds as sites for their own town houses, were as
ignorant as the whites of their origin or purpose, having only a general tradition that their forefathers had found them in much the same
condition on first coming into the country.[2]

Although, as has been noted, Haywood expresses the opinion that
the invading Cherokee had overrun and exterminated the earlier
inhabitants, he says in another place, on halfbreed authority, that
the newcomers found no Indians upon the waters of the Tennessee,
with the exception of some Creeks living upon that river, near the
mouth of the Hiwassee, the main body of that tribe being established
upon and claiming all the streams to the southward.[3] There is
considerable evidence that the Creeks preceded the Cherokee, and
within the last century they still claimed the Tennessee, or at least
the Tennessee watershed, for their northern boundary.

There is a dim but persistent tradition of a strange white race preceding the Cherokee, some of the stories even going so far as to locate
their former settlements and to identify them as the authors of the
ancient works found in the country. The earliest reference appears
to be that of Barton in 1797, on the statement of a gentleman whom
he quotes as a valuable authority upon the southern tribes. "The
Cheerake tell us, that when they first arrived in the country which
they inhabit, they found it possessed by certain 'moon-eyed people,'
who could not see in the day-time. These wretches they expelled."
He seems to consider them an albino race.[4] Haywood, twenty-six
years later, says that the invading Cherokee found "white people"
near the head of the Little Tennessee, with forts extending thence down
the Tennessee as far as Chickamauga creek. He gives the location of
three of these forts. The Cherokee made war against them and
drove them to the mouth of Big Chickamauga creek, where they
entered into a treaty and agreed to remove if permitted to depart in
peace. Permission being granted, they abandoned the country. Elsewhere he speaks of this extirpated white race as having extended into
Kentucky and probably also into western Tennessee, according to the
concurrent traditions of different tribes. He describes their houses,
on what authority is not stated, as having been small circular structures

[1] Haywood, Nat. and Aborig. Hist. Tennessee, pp. 226, 234, 1823.
[2] Bartram, Wm., Travels, p. 365; reprint, London, 1792.
[3] Haywood, op. cit., pp. 234–237.
[4] Barton, New Views, p. xliv, 1797.

of upright logs, covered with earth which had been dug out from the inside.[1]

Harry Smith, a halfbreed born about 1815, father of the late chief of the East Cherokee, informed the author that when a boy he had been told by an old woman a tradition of a race of very small people, perfectly white, who once came and lived for some time on the site of the ancient mound on the northern side of Hiwassee, at the mouth of Peachtree creek, a few miles above the present Murphy, North Carolina. They afterward removed to the West. Colonel Thomas, the white chief of the East Cherokee, born about the beginning of the century, had also heard a tradition of another race of people, who lived on Hiwassee, opposite the present Murphy, and warned the Cherokee that they must not attempt to cross over to the south side of the river or the great leech in the water would swallow them.[2] They finally went west, "long before the whites came." The two stories are plainly the same, although told independently and many miles apart.

THE PERIOD OF SPANISH EXPLORATION—1540–?

The definite history of the Cherokee begins with the year 1540, at which date we find them already established, where they were always afterward known, in the mountains of Carolina and Georgia. The earliest Spanish adventurers failed to penetrate so far into the interior, and the first entry into their country was made by De Soto, advancing up the Savannah on his fruitless quest for gold, in May of that year.

While at Cofitachiqui, an important Indian town on the lower Savannah governed by a "queen," the Spaniards had found hatchets and other objects of copper, some of which was of finer color and appeared to be mixed with gold, although they had no means of testing it.[3] On inquiry they were told that the metal had come from an interior mountain province called Chisca, but the country was represented as thinly peopled and the way as impassable for horses. Some time before, while advancing through eastern Georgia, they had heard also of a rich and plentiful province called Coça, toward the northwest, and by the people of Cofitachiqui they were now told that Chiaha, the nearest town of Coça province, was twelve days inland. As both men and animals were already nearly exhausted from hunger and hard travel, and the Indians either could not or would not furnish sufficient provision for their needs, De Soto determined not to attempt the passage of the mountains then, but to push on at once to Coça, there to rest and recuperate before undertaking further exploration. In the mean-

[1] Haywood, Nat. and Aborig. Hist. Tennessee, pp. 166, 234–235, 287–289, 1823.
[2] See story, "The Great Leech of Tlanusi'yĭ," p. 328.
[3] Garcilaso de la Vega, La Florida del Inca, pp. 129, 133–134; Madrid, 1723.

time he hoped also to obtain more definite information concerning the mines. As the chief purpose of the expedition was the discovery of the mines, many of the officers regarded this change of plan as a mistake, and favored staying where they were until the new crop should be ripened, then to go directly into the mountains, but as the general was "a stern man and of few words," none ventured to oppose his resolution.[1] The province of Coça was the territory of the Creek Indians, called Ani'-Kusa by the Cherokee, from Kusa, or Coosa, their ancient capital, while Chiaha was identical with Chehaw, one of the principal Creek towns on Chattahoochee river. Cofitachiqui may have been the capital of the Uchee Indians.

The outrageous conduct of the Spaniards had so angered the Indian queen that she now refused to furnish guides and carriers, whereupon De Soto made her a prisoner, with the design of compelling her to act as guide herself, and at the same time to use her as a hostage to command the obedience of her subjects. Instead, however, of conducting the Spaniards by the direct trail toward the west, she led them far out of their course until she finally managed to make her escape, leaving them to find their way out of the mountains as best they could.

Departing from Cofitachiqui, they turned first toward the north, passing through several towns subject to the queen, to whom, although a prisoner, the Indians everywhere showed great respect and obedience, furnishing whatever assistance the Spaniards compelled her to demand for their own purposes. In a few days they came to "a province called Chalaque," the territory of the Cherokee Indians, probably upon the waters of Keowee river, the eastern head-stream of the Savannah. It is described as the poorest country for corn that they had yet seen, the inhabitants subsisting on wild roots and herbs and on game which they killed with bows and arrows. They were naked, lean, and unwarlike. The country abounded in wild turkeys ("gallinas"), which the people gave very freely to the strangers, one town presenting them with seven hundred. A chief also gave De Soto two deerskins as a great present.[2] Garcilaso, writing on the authority of an old soldier nearly fifty years afterward, says that the "Chalaques" deserted their towns on the approach of the white men and fled to the mountains, leaving behind only old men and women and some who were nearly blind.[3] Although it was too early for the new crop, the poverty of the people may have been more apparent than real, due to their unwillingness to give any part of their stored-up provision to the unwelcome strangers. As the Spaniards were greatly in need of corn for themselves and their horses, they made no stay, but hurried on. In a few days they arrived

[1] Gentleman of Elvas, Publications of the Hakluyt Society, IX, pp. 52, 58, 64; London, 1851.
[2] Ibid., p. 60.
[3] Garcilaso, La Florida del Inca, p. 136, ed. 1723.

at Guaquili, which is mentioned only by Ranjel, who does not specify whether it was a town or a province—i. e., a tribal territory. It was probably a small town. Here they were welcomed in a friendly manner, the Indians giving them a little corn and many wild turkeys, together with some dogs of a peculiar small species, which were bred for eating purposes and did not bark.[1] They were also supplied with men to help carry the baggage. The name Guaquili has a Cherokee sound and may be connected with *wa'guli'*, "whippoorwill," *uwâ'gi'lĭ*, "foam," or *gi'lĭ*, "dog."

Traveling still toward the north, they arrived a day or two later in the province of Xuala, in which we recognize the territory of the Suwali, Sara, or Cheraw Indians, in the piedmont region about the head of Broad river in North Carolina. Garcilaso, who did not see it, represents it as a rich country, while the Elvas narrative and Biedma agree that it was a rough, broken country, thinly inhabited and poor in provision. According to Garcilaso, it was under the rule of the queen of Cofitachiqui, although a distinct province in itself.[2] The principal town was beside a small rapid stream, close under a mountain. The chief received them in friendly fashion, giving them corn, dogs of the small breed already mentioned, carrying baskets, and burden bearers. The country roundabout showed greater indications of gold mines than any they had yet seen.[1]

Here De Soto turned to the west, crossing a very high mountain range, which appears to have been the Blue ridge, and descending on the other side to a stream flowing in the opposite direction, which was probably one of the upper tributaries of the French Broad.[3] Although it was late in May, they found it very cold in the mountains.[4] After several days of such travel they arrived, about the end of the month, at the town of Guasili, or Guaxule. The chief and principal men came out some distance to welcome them, dressed in fine robes of skins, with feather head-dresses, after the fashion of the country. Before reaching this point the queen had managed to make her escape, together with three slaves of the Spaniards, and the last that was heard of her was that she was on her way back to her own country with one of the runaways as her husband. What grieved De Soto most in the matter was that she took with her a small box of pearls, which he had intended to take from her before releasing her, but had left with her for the present in order "not to discontent her altogether."[5]

Guaxule is described as a very large town surrounded by a number of small mountain streams which united to form the large river down which the Spaniards proceeded after leaving the place.[6] Here, as

---

[1] Ranjel, in Oviedo, Historia General y Natural de las Indias, I, p. 562; Madrid, 1851.
[2] Garcilaso, La Florida del Inca, p. 137, 1723.   [4] Ranjel, op. cit., I, p. 562.
[3] See note 8, De Soto's route.   [5] Elvas, Hakluyt Society, IX, p. 61, 1851.
[6] Garcilaso, op. cit., p. 139.

elsewhere, the Indians received the white men with kindness and hospitality—so much so that the name of Guaxule became to the army a
synonym for good fortune.[1]   Among other things they gave the Spaniards 300 dogs for food, although, according to the Elvas narrative,
the Indians themselves did not eat them.[2]   The principal officers of
the expedition were lodged in the "chief's house," by which we are to
understand the townhouse, which was upon a high hill with a roadway
to the top.[3]   From a close study of the narrative it appears that this
"hill" was no other than the great Nacoochee mound, in White
county, Georgia, a few miles northwest of the present Clarkesville.[4]
It was within the Cherokee territory, and the town was probably a
settlement of that tribe.   From here De Soto sent runners ahead to
notify the chief of Chiaha of his approach, in order that sufficient corn
might be ready on his arrival.

Leaving Guaxule, they proceeded down the river, which we identify
with the Chattahoochee, and in two days arrived at Canasoga, or Canasagua, a frontier town of the Cherokee.   As they neared the town
they were met by the Indians, bearing baskets of "mulberries,"[5] more
probably the delicious service-berry of the southern mountains, which
ripens in early summer, while the mulberry matures later.

From here they continued down the river, which grew constantly
larger, through an uninhabited country which formed the disputed
territory between the Cherokee and the Creeks.   About five days after
leaving Canasagua they were met by messengers, who escorted them
to Chiaha, the first town of the province of Coça.   De Soto had crossed
the state of Georgia, leaving the Cherokee country behind him, and
was now among the Lower Creeks, in the neighborhood of the present
Columbus, Georgia.[6]   With his subsequent wanderings after crossing
the Chattahoochee into Alabama and beyond we need not concern
ourselves (8).

While resting at Chiaha De Soto met with a chief who confirmed
what the Spaniards had heard before concerning mines in the province
of Chisca, saying that there was there "a melting of copper" and of
another metal of about the same color, but softer, and therefore not so
much used.[7]   The province was northward from Chiaha, somewhere in
upper Georgia or the adjacent part of Alabama or Tennessee, through
all of which mountain region native copper is found.   The other
mineral, which the Spaniards understood to be gold, may have been
iron pyrites, although there is some evidence that the Indians occasionally found and shaped gold nuggets.[6]

---

[1] Ranjel, in Oviedo, Historia, I, p. 563, 1851.
[2] Elvas, Biedma, and Ranjel all make special reference to the dogs given them at this place; they
seem to have been of the same small breed ("perrillos") which Ranjel says the Indians used for food.
[3] Garcilaso, La Florida del Inca, p. 139, 1723.   [4] See note 8, De Soto's route.
[5] See Elvas, Hakluyt Society, IX, p. 61, 1851; and Ranjel, op. cit., p. 563.
[6] See note 8, De Soto's route.   [7] Elvas, op. cit., p. 64.

Accordingly two soldiers were sent on foot with Indian guides to find Chisca and learn the truth of the stories. They rejoined the army some time after the march had been resumed, and reported, according to the Elvas chronicler, that their guides had taken them through a country so poor in corn, so rough, and over so high mountains that it would be impossible for the army to follow, wherefore, as the way grew long and lingering, they had turned back after reaching a little poor town where they saw nothing that was of any profit. They brought back with them a dressed buffalo skin which the Indians there had given them, the first ever obtained by white men, and described in the quaint old chronicle as "an ox hide as thin as a calf's skin, and the hair like a soft wool between the coarse and fine wool of sheep." [1]

Garcilaso's glowing narrative gives a somewhat different impression. According to this author the scouts returned full of enthusiasm for the fertility of the country, and reported that the mines were of a fine species of copper, and had indications also of gold and silver, while their progress from one town to another had been a continual series of feastings and Indian hospitalities. [2] However that may have been, De Soto made no further effort to reach the Cherokee mines, but continued his course westward through the Creek country, having spent altogether a month in the mountain region.

There is no record of any second attempt to penetrate the Cherokee country for twenty-six years (9). In 1561 the Spaniards took formal possession of the bay of Santa Elena, now Saint Helena, near Port Royal, on the coast of South Carolina. The next year the French made an unsuccessful attempt at settlement at the same place, and in 1566 Menendez made the Spanish occupancy sure by establishing there a fort which he called San Felipe. [3] In November of that year Captain Juan Pardo was sent with a party from the fort to explore the interior. Accompanied by the chief of "Juada" (which from Vandera's narrative we find should be "Joara," i. e., the Sara Indians already mentioned in the De Soto chronicle), he proceeded as far as the territory of that tribe, where he built a fort, but on account of the snow in the mountains did not think it advisable to go farther, and returned, leaving a sergeant with thirty soldiers to garrison the post. Soon after his return he received a letter from the sergeant stating that the chief of Chisca—the rich mining country of which De Soto had heard—was very hostile to the Spaniards, and that in a recent battle the latter had killed a thousand of his Indians and burned fifty houses with almost no damage to themselves. Either the sergeant or his chronicler must have been an unconscionable liar, as it was asserted that all this was done with only fifteen men. Immediately afterward, according to the same story, the sergeant marched with twenty men about a day's

[1] Elvas, Hakluyt Society, IX, p. 66, 1851.   [2] Garcilaso, La Florida del Inca, p. 141, ed. 1723.
[3] Shea, J. G., in Winsor, Justin, Narrative and Critical History of America, II, pp. 260, 278; Boston, 1886.

distance in the mountains against another hostile chief, whom he found in a strongly palisaded town, which, after a hard fight, he and his men stormed and burned, killing fifteen hundred Indians without losing a single man themselves. Under instructions from his superior officer, the sergeant with his small party then proceeded to explore what lay beyond, and, taking a road which they were told led to the territory of a great chief, after four days of hard marching they came to his town, called Chiaha (Chicha, by mistake in the manuscript translation), the same where De Soto had rested. It is described at this time as palisaded and strongly fortified, with a deep river on each side, and defended by over three thousand fighting men, there being no women or children among them. It is possible that in view of their former experience with the Spaniards, the Indians had sent their families away from the town, while at the same time they may have summoned warriors from the neighboring Creek towns in order to be prepared for any emergency. However, as before, they received the white men with the greatest kindness, and the Spaniards continued for twelve days through the territories of the same tribe until they arrived at the principal town (Kusa?), where, by the invitation of the chief, they built a small fort and awaited the coming of Pardo, who was expected to follow with a larger force from Santa Elena, as he did in the summer of 1567, being met on his arrival with every show of hospitality from the Creek chiefs. This second fort was said to be one hundred and forty leagues distant from that in the Sara country, which latter was called one hundred and twenty leagues from Santa Elena.[1]

In the summer of 1567, according to previous agreement, Captain Pardo left the fort at Santa Elena with a small detachment of troops, and after a week's travel, sleeping each night at a different Indian town, arrived at "Canos, which the Indians call Canosi, and by another name, Cofetaçque" (the Cofitachiqui of the De Soto chronicle), which is described as situated in a favorable location for a large city, fifty leagues from Santa Elena, to which the easiest road was by a river (the Savannah) which flowed by the town, or by another which they had passed ten leagues farther back. Proceeding, they passed Jagaya, Gueza, and Arauchi, and arrived at Otariyatiqui, or Otari, in which we have perhaps the Cherokee ä'tărĭ or ä'tălĭ, "mountain". It may have been a frontier Cherokee settlement, and, according to the old chronicler, its chief and language ruled much good country. From here a trail went northward to Guatari, Sauxpa, and Usi, i. e., the Wateree, Waxhaw (or Sissipahaw ?), and Ushery or Catawba.

Leaving Otariyatiqui, they went on to Quinahaqui, and then, turning to the left, to Issa, where they found mines of crystal (mica?). They came next to Aguaquiri (the Guaquili of the De Soto chronicle), and then to Joara, "near to the mountain, where Juan Pardo arrived

---

[1] Narrative of Pardo's expedition by Martinez, about 1568, Brooks manuscripts.

with his sergeant on his first trip." This, as has been noted, was the Xuala of the De Soto chronicle, the territory of the Sara Indians, in the foothills of the Blue ridge, southeast from the present Asheville, North Carolina. Vandera makes it one hundred leagues from Santa Elena, while Martinez, already quoted, makes the distance one hundred and twenty leagues. The difference is not important, as both statements were only estimates. From there they followed "along the mountains" to Tocax (Toxaway?), Cauchi (Nacoochee?), and Tanasqui—apparently Cherokee towns, although the forms can not be identified—and after resting three days at the last-named place went on "to Solameco, otherwise called Chiaha," where the sergeant met them. The combined forces afterward went on, through Cossa (Kusa), Tasquiqui (Taskigi), and other Creek towns, as far as Tascaluza, in the Alabama country, and returned thence to Santa Elena, having apparently met with a friendly reception everywhere along the route. From Cofitachiqui to Tascaluza they went over about the same road traversed by De Soto in 1540.[1]

We come now to a great gap of nearly a century. Shea has a notice of a Spanish mission founded among the Cherokee in 1643 and still flourishing when visited by an English traveler ten years later,[2] but as his information is derived entirely from the fraudulent work of Davies, and as no such mission is mentioned by Barcia in any of these years, we may regard the story as spurious (10). The first mission work in the tribe appears to have been that of Priber, almost a hundred years later. Long before the end of the sixteenth century, however, the existence of mines of gold and other metals in the Cherokee country was a matter of common knowledge among the Spaniards at St. Augustine and Santa Elena, and more than one expedition had been fitted out to explore the interior.[3] Numerous traces of ancient mining operations, with remains of old shafts and fortifications, evidently of European origin, show that these discoveries were followed up, although the policy of Spain concealed the fact from the outside world. How much permanent impression this early Spanish intercourse made on the Cherokee it is impossible to estimate, but it must have been considerable (11).

THE COLONIAL AND REVOLUTIONARY PERIOD—1654–1784

It was not until 1654 that the English first came into contact with the Cherokee, called in the records of the period Rechahecrians, a corruption of Rickahockan, apparently the name by which they were known to the Powhatan tribes. In that year the Virginia colony, which had only recently concluded a long and exterminating war with the Powhatan, was thrown into alarm by the news that a great body of

[1] Vandera narrative, 1569, in French, B. F., Hist. Colls. of La., new series, pp. 289–292; New York, 1875.
[2] Shea, J. G., Catholic Missions, p. 72; New York, 1855.
[3] See Brooks manuscripts, in the archives of the Bureau of American Ethnology.

six or seven hundred Rechahecrian Indians—by which is probably meant that number of warriors—from the mountains had invaded the lower country and established themselves at the falls of James river, where now is the city of Richmond. The assembly at once passed resolutions "that these new come Indians be in no sort suffered to seat themselves there, or any place near us, it having cost so much blood to expel and extirpate those perfidious and treacherous Indians which were there formerly." It was therefore ordered that a force of at least 100 white men be at once sent against them, to be joined by the warriors of all the neighboring subject tribes, according to treaty obligation. The Pamunkey chief, with a hundred of his men, responded to the summons, and the combined force marched against the invaders. The result was a bloody battle, with disastrous outcome to the Virginians, the Pamunkey chief with most of his men being killed, while the whites were forced to make such terms of peace with the Rechahecrians that the assembly cashiered the commander of the expedition and compelled him to pay the whole cost of the treaty from his own estate.[1] Owing to the imperfection of the Virginia records we have no means of knowing the causes of the sudden invasion or how long the invaders retained their position at the falls. In all probability it was only the last of a long series of otherwise unrecorded irruptions by the mountaineers on the more peaceful dwellers in the lowlands. From a remark in Lederer it is probable that the Cherokee were assisted also by some of the piedmont tribes hostile to the Powhatan. The Peaks of Otter, near which the Cherokee claim to have once lived, as has been already noted, are only about one hundred miles in a straight line from Richmond, while the burial mound and town site near Charlottesville, mentioned by Jefferson, are but half that distance.

In 1655 a Virginia expedition sent out from the falls of James river (Richmond) crossed over the mountains to the large streams flowing into the Mississippi. No details are given and the route is uncertain, but whether or not they met Indians, they must have passed through Cherokee territory.[2]

In 1670 the German traveler, John Lederer, went from the falls of James river to the Catawba country in South Carolina, following for most of the distance the path used by the Virginia traders, who already had regular dealings with the southern tribes, including probably the Cherokee. He speaks in several places of the Rickahockan, which seems to be a more correct form than Rechahecrian, and his narrative and the accompanying map put them in the mountains of North Carolina, back of the Catawba and the Sara and southward from the head of Roanoke river. They were apparently on hostile terms with the tribes to the eastward, and while the traveler was stopping at an Indian

[1] Burk, John, History of Virginia, II, pp. 104–107; Petersburg, 1805.
[2] Ramsey, J. G. M., Annals of Tennessee, p. 37; Charleston, 1853 (quoting Martin, North Carolina, I, p. 115, 1853).

village on Dan river, about the present Clarksville, Virginia, a delegation of Rickahockan, which had come on tribal business, was barbarously murdered at a dance prepared on the night of their arrival by their treacherous hosts. On reaching the Catawba country he heard of white men to the southward, and incidentally mentions that the neighboring mountains were called the Suala mountains by the Spaniards.[1] In the next year, 1671, a party from Virginia under Thomas Batts explored the northern branch of Roanoke river and crossed over the Blue ridge to the headwaters of New river, where they found traces of occupancy, but no Indians. By this time all the tribes of this section, east of the mountains, were in possession of firearms.[2]

The first permanent English settlement in South Carolina was established in 1670. In 1690 James Moore, secretary of the colony, made an exploring expedition into the mountains and reached a point at which, according to his Indian guides, he was within twenty miles of where the Spaniards were engaged in mining and smelting with bellows and furnaces, but on account of some misunderstanding he returned without visiting the place, although he procured specimens of ores, which he sent to England for assay.[3] It may have been in the neighborhood of the present Lincolnton, North Carolina, where a dam of cut stone and other remains of former civilized occupancy have recently been discovered (11). In this year, also, Cornelius Dougherty, an Irishman from Virginia, established himself as the first trader among the Cherokee, with whom he spent the rest of his life.[4] Some of his descendants still occupy honored positions in the tribe.

Among the manuscript archives of South Carolina there was said to be, some fifty years ago, a treaty or agreement made with the government of that colony by the Cherokee in 1684, and signed with the hieroglyphics of eight chiefs of the lower towns, viz, Corani, the Raven (Kâ'lanû); Sinnawa, the Hawk (Tlă'nuwă); Nellawgitehi, Gorhaleke, and Owasta, all of Toxawa; and Canacaught, the great Conjuror, Gohoma, and Caunasaita, of Keowa. If still in existence, this is probably the oldest Cherokee treaty on record.[5]

What seems to be the next mention of the Cherokee in the South Carolina records occurs in 1691, when we find an inquiry ordered in regard to a report that some of the colonists " have, without any proclamation of war, fallen upon and murdered" several of that tribe.[6]

In 1693 some Cherokee chiefs went to Charleston with presents for the governor and offers of friendship, to ask the protection of South Carolina against their enemies, the Esaw (Catawba), Savanna (Shawano),

[1] Lederer, John, Discoveries, pp. 15, 26, 27, 29, 33, and map; reprint, Charleston, 1891; Mooney, Siouan Tribes of the East (bulletin of Bureau of Ethnology), pp. 53–54, 1894.
[2] Mooney, op. cit., pp. 34–35.
[3] Document of 1699, quoted in South Carolina Hist. Soc. Colls., I, p. 209; Charleston, 1857.
[4] Haywood, Nat. and Aborig. Hist. Tennessee, p. 233, 1823.
[5] Noted in Cherokee Advocate, Tahlequah, Indian Territory, January 30, 1845.
[6] Document of 1691, South Carolina Hist. Soc. Colls., I, p. 126.

and Congaree, all of that colony, who had made war upon them and sold a number of their tribesmen into slavery. They were told that their kinsmen could not now be recovered, but that the English desired friendship with their tribe, and that the Government would see that there would be no future ground for such complaint.[1] The promise was apparently not kept, for in 1705 we find a bitter accusation brought against Governor Moore, of South Carolina, that he had granted commissions to a number of persons "to set upon, assault, kill, destroy, and take captive as many Indians as they possible [*sic*] could," the prisoners being sold into slavery for his and their private profit. By this course, it was asserted, he had "already almost utterly ruined the trade for skins and furs, whereby we held our chief correspondence with England, and turned it into a trade of Indians or slave making, whereby the Indians to the south and west of us are already involved in blood and confusion." The arraignment concludes with a warning that such conditions would in all probability draw down upon the colony an Indian war with all its dreadful consequences.[2] In view of what happened a few years later this reads like a prophecy.

About the year 1700 the first guns were introduced among the Cherokee, the event being fixed traditionally as having occurred in the girlhood of an old woman of the tribe who died about 1775.[3] In 1708 we find them described as a numerous people, living in the mountains northwest from the Charleston settlements and having sixty towns, but of small importance in the Indian trade, being "but ordinary hunters and less warriors."[4]

In the war with the Tuscarora in 1711–1713, which resulted in the expulsion of that tribe from North Carolina, more than a thousand southern Indians reenforced the South Carolina volunteers, among them being over two hundred Cherokee, hereditary enemies of the Tuscarora. Although these Indian allies did their work well in the actual encounters, their assistance was of doubtful advantage, as they helped themselves freely to whatever they wanted along the way, so that the settlers had reason to fear them almost as much as the hostile Tuscarora. After torturing a large number of their prisoners in the usual savage fashion, they returned with the remainder, whom they afterward sold as slaves to South Carolina.[5]

Having wiped out old scores with the Tuscarora, the late allies of the English proceeded to discuss their own grievances, which, as we have seen, were sufficiently galling. The result was a combination

---

[1] Hewat, South Carolina and Georgia, I, p. 127, 1778.

[2] Documents of 1705, in North Carolina Colonial Records, II, p. 904; Raleigh, 1886.

[3] Haywood, Nat. and Aborig. Tenn., p. 237, 1823; with the usual idea that Indians live to extreme old age, Haywood makes her 110 years old at her death, putting back the introduction of firearms to 1677.

[4] Letter of 1708, in Rivers, South Carolina, p. 238, 1856.

[5] Royce, Cherokee Nation, Fifth Ann. Rep. Bureau of Ethnology, p. 140, 1888; Hewat, op. cit., p. 216 et passim.

against the whites, embracing all the tribes from Cape Fear to the Chattahoochee, including the Cherokee, who thus for the first time raised their hand against the English. The war opened with a terrible massacre by the Yamassee in April, 1715, followed by assaults along the whole frontier, until for a time it was seriously feared that the colony of South Carolina would be wiped out of existence. In a contest between savagery and civilization, however, the final result is inevitable. The settlers at last rallied their whole force under Governor Craven and administered such a crushing blow to the Yamassee that the remnant abandoned their country and took refuge with the Spaniards in Florida or among the Lower Creeks. The English then made short work with the smaller tribes along the coast, while those in the interior were soon glad to sue for peace.[1]

A number of Cherokee chiefs having come down to Charleston in company with a trader to express their desire for peace, a force of several hundred white troops and a number of negroes under Colonel Maurice Moore went up the Savannah in the winter of 1715–16 and made headquarters among the Lower Cherokee, where they were met by the chiefs of the Lower and some of the western towns, who reaffirmed their desire for a lasting peace with the English, but refused to fight against the Yamassee, although willing to proceed against some other tribes. They laid the blame for most of the trouble upon the traders, who "had been very abuseful to them of late." A detachment under Colonel George Chicken, sent to the Upper Cherokee, penetrated to "Quoneashee" (Tlanusi'yǐ, on Hiwassee, about the present Murphy) where they found the chiefs more defiant, resolved to continue the war against the Creeks, with whom the English were then trying to make peace, and demanding large supplies of guns and ammunition, saying that if they made a peace with the other tribes they would have no means of getting slaves with which to buy ammunition for themselves. At this time they claimed 2,370 warriors, of whom half were believed to have guns. As the strength of the whole Nation was much greater, this estimate may have been for the Upper and Middle Cherokee only. After "abundance of persuading" by the officers, they finally "told us they would trust us once again," and an arrangement was made to furnish them two hundred guns with a supply of ammunition, together with fifty white soldiers, to assist them against the tribes with which the English were still at war. In March, 1716, this force was increased by one hundred men. The detachment under Colonel Chicken returned by way of the towns on the upper part of the Little Tennessee, thus penetrating the heart of the Cherokee country.[2]

[1] Hewat, South Carolina and Georgia, I, p. 216 et passim, 1778.
[2] See Journal of Colonel George Chicken, 1715–16, with notes, in Charleston Yearbook, pp. 313–354, 1894.

Steps were now taken to secure peace by inaugurating a satisfactory trade system, for which purpose a large quantity of suitable goods was purchased at the public expense of South Carolina, and a correspondingly large party was equipped for the initial trip.[1] In 1721, in order still more to systematize Indian affairs, Governor Nicholson of South Carolina invited the chiefs of the Cherokee to a conference, at which thirty-seven towns were represented. A treaty was made by which trading methods were regulated, a boundary line between their territory and the English settlements was agreed upon, and an agent was appointed to superintend their affairs. At the governor's suggestion, one chief, called Wrosetasatow (?)[2] was formally commissioned as supreme head of the Nation, with authority to punish all offenses, including murder, and to represent all Cherokee claims to the colonial government. Thus were the Cherokee reduced from their former condition of a free people, ranging where their pleasure led, to that of dependent vassals with bounds fixed by a colonial governor. The negotiations were accompanied by a cession of land, the first in the history of the tribe. In little more than a century thereafter they had signed away their whole original territory.[3]

The document of 1716 already quoted puts the strength of the Cherokee at that time at 2,370 warriors, but in this estimate the Lower Cherokee seem not to have been included. In 1715, according to a trade census compiled by Governor Johnson of South Carolina, the tribe had thirty towns, with 4,000 warriors and a total population of 11,210.[4] Another census in 1721 gives them fifty-three towns with 3,510 warriors and a total of 10,379,[5] while the report of the board of trade for the same year gives them 3,800 warriors,[6] equivalent, by the same proportion, to nearly 12,000 total. Adair, a good authority on such matters, estimates, about the year 1735, when the country was better known, that they had "sixty-four towns and villages, populous and full of children," with more than 6,000 fighting men,[7] equivalent on the same basis of computation to between 16,000 and 17,000 souls. From what we know of them in later times, it is probable that this last estimate is very nearly correct.

By this time the colonial government had become alarmed at the advance of the French, who had made their first permanent establishment in the Gulf states at Biloxi bay, Mississippi, in 1699, and in 1714 had built Fort Toulouse, known to the English as "the fort at

---

[1] Journal of South Carolina Assembly, in North Carolina Colonial Records, II, pp. 225–227, 1886.

[2] For notice, see the glossary.

[3] Hewat, South Carolina and Georgia, I, pp. 297–298, 1778; Royce, Cherokee Nation, in Fifth Ann. Rep. Bureau of Ethnology, p. 144 and map, 1888.

[4] Royce, op. cit., p. 142.

[5] Document of 1724, in Fernow, Berthold, Ohio Valley in Colonial Days, pp. 273–275; Albany, 1890.

[6] Report of Board of Trade, 1721, in North Carolina Colonial Records, II, p. 422, 1886.

[7] Adair, James, American Indians, p. 227; London, 1775.

the Alabamas," on Coosa river, a few miles above the present Montgomery, Alabama.   From this central vantage point they had rapidly extended their influence among all the neighboring tribes until in 1721 it was estimated that 3,400 warriors who had formerly traded with Carolina had been "entirely debauched to the French interest," while 2,000 more were wavering, and only the Cherokee could still be considered friendly to the English.[1]   From this time until the final withdrawal of the French in 1763 the explanation of our Indian wars is to be found in the struggle between the two nations for territorial and commercial supremacy, the Indian being simply the cat's-paw of one or the other.   For reasons of their own, the Chickasaw, whose territory lay within the recognized limits of Louisiana, soon became the uncompromising enemies of the French, and as their position enabled them in a measure to control the approach from the Mississippi, the Carolina government saw to it that they were kept well supplied with guns and ammunition.   British traders were in all their towns, and on one occasion a French force, advancing against a Chickasaw palisaded village, found it garrisoned by Englishmen flying the British flag.[2]   The Cherokee, although nominally allies of the English, were strongly disposed to favor the French, and it required every effort of the Carolina government to hold them to their allegiance.

In 1730, to further fix the Cherokee in the English interest, Sir Alexander Cuming was dispatched on a secret mission to that tribe, which was again smarting under grievances and almost ready to join with the Creeks in an alliance with the French.   Proceeding to the ancient town of Nequassee (Nĭkwăsĭ', at the present Franklin, North Carolina), he so impressed the chiefs by his bold bearing that they conceded without question all his demands, submitting themselves and their people for the second time to the English dominion and designating Moytoy,[3] of Tellico, to act as their "emperor" and to represent the Nation in all transactions with the whites.   Seven chiefs were selected to visit England, where, in the palace at Whitehall, they solemnly renewed the treaty, acknowledging the sovereignty of England and binding themselves to have no trade or alliance with any other nation, not to allow any other white people to settle among them, and to deliver up any fugitive slaves who might seek refuge with them.   To confirm their words they delivered a "crown", five eagle-tails, and four scalps, which they had brought with them.   In return they received the usual glittering promises of love and perpetual friendship, together with a substantial quantity of guns, ammunition, and red paint.   The treaty being concluded in September,

---

[1] Board of Trade report, 1721, North Carolina Colonial Records, II, p. 422, 1886.
[2] Pickett, H. A., History of Alabama, pp. 234, 280, 288; reprint, Sheffield, 1896.
[3] For notice, see the glossary.

they took ship for Carolina, where they arrived, as we are told by the governor, "in good health and mightily well satisfied with His Majesty's bounty to them."[1]

In the next year some action was taken to use the Cherokee and Catawba to subdue the refractory remnant of the Tuscarora in North Carolina, but when it was found that this was liable to bring down the wrath of the Iroquois upon the Carolina settlements, more peaceable methods were used instead.[2]

In 1738 or 1739 the smallpox, brought to Carolina by slave ships, broke out among the Cherokee with such terrible effect that, according to Adair, nearly half the tribe was swept away within a year. The awful mortality was due largely to the fact that as it was a new and strange disease to the Indians they had no proper remedies against it, and therefore resorted to the universal Indian panacea for "strong" sickness of almost any kind, viz, cold plunge baths in the running stream, the worst treatment that could possibly be devised. As the pestilence spread unchecked from town to town, despair fell upon the nation. The priests, believing the visitation a penalty for violation of the ancient ordinances, threw away their sacred paraphernalia as things which had lost their protecting power. Hundreds of the warriors committed suicide on beholding their frightful disfigurement. "Some shot themselves, others cut their throats, some stabbed themselves with knives and others with sharp-pointed canes; many threw themselves with sullen madness into the fire and there slowly expired, as if they had been utterly divested of the native power of feeling pain."[3] Another authority estimates their loss at a thousand warriors, partly from smallpox and partly from rum brought in by the traders.[4]

About the year 1740 a trading path for horsemen was marked out by the Cherokee from the new settlement of Augusta, in Georgia, to their towns on the headwaters of Savannah river and thence on to the west. This road, which went up the south side of the river, soon became much frequented.[4] Previous to this time most of the trading goods had been transported on the backs of Indians. In the same year a party of Cherokee under the war chief Kâ'lanû. "The Raven," took part in Oglethorpe's expedition against the Spaniards of Saint Augustine.[5]

In 1736 Christian Priber, said to be a Jesuit acting in the French interest, had come among the Cherokee, and, by the facility with which he learned the language and adapted himself to the native dress and

---

[1] Hewat, South Carolina and Georgia, II, pp. 3–11, 1779; treaty documents of 1730, North Carolina Colonial Records, III, pp. 128–133, 1886; Jenkinson, Collection of Treaties, II, pp. 315–318; Drake, S. G., Early History of Georgia: Cuming's Embassy; Boston, 1872; letter of Governor Johnson, December 27, 1730, noted in South Carolina Hist. Soc. Colls., I, p. 246, 1857.

[2] Documents of 1731 and 1732, North Carolina Colonial Records, III, pp. 153, 202, 345, 369, 393, 1886.

[3] Adair, American Indians, pp. 232–234, 1775.

[4] Meadows (?), State of the Province of Georgia, p. 7, 1742, in Force Tracts, I, 1836.

[5] Jones, C. C., History of Georgia, I, pp. 327, 328; Boston, 1883.

mode of life, had quickly acquired a leading influence among them.
He drew up for their adoption a scheme of government modeled after
the European plan, with the capital at Great Tellico, in Tennessee,
the principal medicine man as emperor, and himself as the emperor's
secretary.   Under this title he corresponded with the South Carolina
government until it began to be feared that he would ultimately win
over the whole tribe to the French side.   A commissioner was sent to
arrest him, but the Cherokee refused to give him up, and the deputy
was obliged to return under safe-conduct of an escort furnished by
Priber.   Five years after the inauguration of his work, however, he
was seized by some English traders while on his way to Fort Toulouse,
and brought as a prisoner to Frederica, in Georgia, where he soon
afterward died while under confinement.   Although his enemies had
represented him as a monster, inciting the Indians to the grossest
immoralities, he proved to be a gentleman of polished address, extensive learning, and rare courage, as was shown later on the occasion of
an explosion in the barracks magazine.   Besides Greek, Latin, French,
German, Spanish, and fluent English, he spoke also the Cherokee,
and among his papers which were seized was found a manuscript
dictionary of the language, which he had prepared for publication—
the first, and even yet, perhaps, the most important study of the language ever made.   Says Adair: "As he was learned and possessed
of a very sagacious penetrating judgment, and had every qualification
that was requisite for his bold and difficult enterprise, it was not to be
doubted that, as he wrote a Cheerake dictionary, designed to be
published at Paris, he likewise set down a great deal that would have
been very acceptable to the curious and serviceable to the representatives of South Carolina and Georgia, which may be readily found in
Frederica if the manuscripts have had the good fortune to escape the
despoiling hands of military power."   He claimed to be a Jesuit, acting
under orders of his superior, to introduce habits of steady industry,
civilized arts, and a regular form of government among the southern
tribes, with a view to the ultimate founding of an independent Indian
state.   From all that can be gathered of him, even though it comes
from his enemies, there can be little doubt that he was a worthy
member of that illustrious order whose name has been a synonym for
scholarship, devotion, and courage from the days of Jogues and Mar-
quette down to De Smet and Mengarini.[1]

Up to this time no civilizing or mission work had been undertaken
by either of the Carolina governments among any of the tribes within
their borders.   As one writer of the period quaintly puts it, "The
gospel spirit is not yet so gloriously arisen as to seek them more than
theirs," while another in stronger terms affirms, "To the shame of

---

[1] Adair, American Indians, pp. 240–243, 1775; Stevens, W. B., History of Georgia, I, pp. 104–107; Phila
1847.

the Christian name, no pains have ever been taken to convert them to Christianity; on the contrary, their morals are perverted and corrupted by the sad example they daily have of its depraved professors residing in their towns."[1] Readers of Lawson and other narratives of the period will feel the force of the rebuke.

Throughout the eighteenth century the Cherokee were engaged in chronic warfare with their Indian neighbors. As these quarrels concerned the whites but little, however momentous they may have been to the principals, we have but few details. The war with the Tuscarora continued until the outbreak of the latter tribe against Carolina in 1711 gave opportunity to the Cherokee to cooperate in striking the blow which drove the Tuscarora from their ancient homes to seek refuge in the north. The Cherokee then turned their attention to the Shawano on the Cumberland, and with the aid of the Chickasaw finally expelled them from that region about the year 1715. Inroads upon the Catawba were probably kept up until the latter had become so far reduced by war and disease as to be mere dependent pensioners upon the whites. The former friendship with the Chickasaw was at last broken through the overbearing conduct of the Cherokee, and a war followed of which we find incidental notice in 1757,[2] and which terminated in a decisive victory for the Chickasaw about 1768. The bitter war with the Iroquois of the far north continued, in spite of all the efforts of the colonial governments, until a formal treaty of peace was brought about by the efforts of Sir William Johnson (12) in the same year.

The hereditary war with the Creeks for possession of upper Georgia continued, with brief intervals of peace, or even alliance, until the United States finally interfered as mediator between the rival claimants. In 1718 we find notice of a large Cherokee war party moving against the Creek town of Coweta, on the lower Chattahoochee, but dispersing on learning of the presence there of some French and Spanish officers, as well as some English traders, all bent on arranging an alliance with the Creeks. The Creeks themselves had declared their willingness to be at peace with the English, while still determined to keep the bloody hatchet uplifted against the Cherokee.[3] The most important incident of the struggle between the two tribes was probably the battle of Tali'wa about the year 1755.[4]

By this time the weaker coast tribes had become practically extinct, and the more powerful tribes of the interior were beginning to take the alarm, as they saw the restless borderers pushing every year farther into the Indian country. As early as 1748 Dr Thomas Walker, with a company of hunters and woodsmen from Virginia, crossed the moun-

---

[1] Anonymous writer in Carroll, Hist. Colls. of South Carolina, II, pp. 97-98, 517, 1836.

[2] Buckle, Journal, 1757, in Rivers, South Carolina, p. 57, 1856.

[3] Barcia, A. G., Ensayo Chronologico para la Historia General de la Florida, pp. 335, 336, Madrid, 1723.

[4] For more in regard to these intertribal wars see the historical traditions.

tains to the southwest, discovering and naming the celebrated Cumberland gap and passing on to the headwaters of Cumberland river. Two years later he made a second exploration and penetrated to Kentucky river, but on account of the Indian troubles no permanent settlement was then attempted.[1] This invasion of their territory awakened a natural resentment of the native owners, and we find proof also in the Virginia records that the irresponsible borderers seldom let pass an opportunity to kill and plunder any stray Indian found in their neighborhood.

In 1755 the Cherokee were officially reported to number 2,590 warriors, as against probably twice that number previous to the great smallpox epidemic sixteen years before. Their neighbors and ancient enemies, the Catawba, had dwindled to 240 men.[2]

Although war was not formally declared by England until 1756, hostilities in the seven year's struggle between France and England, commonly known in America as the " French and Indian war," began in April, 1754, when the French seized a small post which the English had begun at the present site of Pittsburg, and which was afterward finished by the French under the name of Fort Du Quesne. Strenuous efforts were made by the English to secure the Cherokee to their interest against the French and their Indian allies, and treaties were negotiated by which they promised assistance.[3] As these treaties, however, carried the usual cessions of territory, and stipulated for the building of several forts in the heart of the Cherokee country, it is to be feared that the Indians were not duly impressed by the disinterested character of the proceeding. Their preference for the French was but thinly veiled, and only immediate policy prevented them from throwing their whole force into the scale on that side. The reasons for this preference are given by Timberlake, the young Virginian officer who visited the tribe on an embassy of conciliation a few years later:

I found the nation much attached to the French, who have the prudence, by familiar politeness—which costs but little and often does a great deal—and conforming themselves to their ways and temper, to conciliate the inclinations of almost all the Indians they are acquainted with, while the pride of our officers often disgusts them. Nay, they did not scruple to own to me that it was the trade alone that induced them to make peace with us, and not any preference to the French, whom they loved a great deal better. . . . The English are now so nigh, and encroached daily so far upon them, that they not only felt the bad effects of it in their hunting grounds, which were spoiled, but had all the reason in the world to apprehend being swallowed up by so potent neighbors or driven from the country inhabited by their fathers, in which they were born and brought up, in fine, their native soil, for which all men have a particular tenderness and affection.

[1] Walker, Thomas, Journal of an Exploration, etc., pp. 8, 35–37; Boston, 1888; Monette (Valley of the Miss. I, p. 317; New York, 1848) erroneously makes the second date 1758.

[2] Letter of Governor Dobbs, 1755, in North Carolina Colonial Records, v. pp. 320, 321, 1887.

[3] Ramsey, Tennessee, pp. 50–52, 1853; Royce, Cherokee Nation, in Fifth Ann. Rep. Bur. of Ethnology, p. 145, 1888.

He adds that only dire necessity had induced them to make peace with the English in 1761.[1]

In accordance with the treaty stipulations Fort Prince George was built in 1756 adjoining the important Cherokee town of Keowee, on the headwaters of the Savannah, and Fort Loudon near the junction of Tellico river with the Little Tennessee, in the center of the Cherokee towns beyond the mountains.[2] By special arrangement with the influential chief, Ata-kullakulla (Ătă'-gûl'kălû'),[3] Fort Dobbs was also built in the same year about 20 miles west of the present Salisbury, North Carolina.[4]

The Cherokee had agreed to furnish four hundred warriors to cooperate against the French in the north, but before Fort Loudon had been completed it was very evident that they had repented of their promise, as their great council at Echota ordered the work stopped and the garrison on the way to turn back, plainly telling the officer in charge that they did not want so many white people among them. Ata-kullakulla, hitherto supposed to be one of the stanchest friends of the English, was now one of the most determined in the opposition. It was in evidence also that they were in constant communication with the French. By much tact and argument their objections were at last overcome for a time, and they very unwillingly set about raising the promised force of warriors. Major Andrew Lewis, who superintended the building of the fort, became convinced that the Cherokee were really friendly to the French, and that all their professions of friendship and assistance were "only to put a gloss on their knavery." The fort was finally completed, and, on his suggestion, was garrisoned with a strong force of two hundred men under Captain Demeré.[5] There was strong ground for believing that some depredations committed about this time on the heads of Catawba and Broad rivers, in North Carolina, were the joint work of Cherokee and northern Indians.[6] Notwithstanding all this, a considerable body of Cherokee joined the British forces on the Virginia frontier.[7]

Fort Du Quesne was taken by the American provincials under Washington, November 25, 1758. Quebec was taken September 13, 1759, and by the final treaty of peace in 1763 the war ended with the transfer of Canada and the Ohio valley to the crown of England. Louisiana had already been ceded by France to Spain.

Although France was thus eliminated from the Indian problem, the

---

[1] Timberlake, Henry, Memoirs, pp. 73, 74; London, 1765.

[2] Ramsey, Tennessee, p. 51, 1853; Royce, Cherokee Nation, in Fifth Ann. Rept. Bur. of Ethnology, p. 145, 1888.

[3] For notice see Ătă'-gûl"kălû', in the glossary.

[4] Ramsey, op. cit., p. 50.

[5] Letters of Major Andrew Lewis and Governor Dinwiddie, 1756, in North Carolina Colonial Records v, pp. 585, 612–614, 635, 637, 1887; Ramsey, op. cit., pp. 51, 52.

[6] Letter of Governor Dobbs, 1756, in North Carolina Colonial Records, v, p. 604, 1887.

[7] Dinwiddie letter, 1757, ibid., p. 765.

Indians themselves were not ready to accept the settlement. In the north the confederated tribes under Pontiac continued to war on their own account until 1765. In the South the very Cherokee who had acted as allies of the British against Fort Du Quesne, and had voluntarily offered to guard the frontier south of the Potomac, returned to rouse their tribe to resistance.

The immediate exciting cause of the trouble was an unfortunate expedition undertaken against the hostile Shawano in February, 1756, by Major Andrew Lewis (the same who had built Fort Loudon) with some two hundred Virginia troops assisted by about one hundred Cherokee. After six weeks of fruitless tramping through the woods, with the ground covered with snow and the streams so swollen by rains that they lost their provisions and ammunition in crossing, they were obliged to return to the settlements in a starving condition, having killed their horses on the way. The Indian contingent had from the first been disgusted at the contempt and neglect experienced from those whom they had come to assist. The Tuscarora and others had already gone home, and the Cherokee now started to return on foot to their own country. Finding some horses running loose on the range, they appropriated them, on the theory that as they had lost their own animals, to say nothing of having risked their lives, in the service of the colonists, it was only a fair exchange. The frontiersmen took another view of the question however, attacked the returning Cherokee, and killed a number of them, variously stated at from twelve to forty, including several of their prominent men. According to Adair they also scalped and mutilated the bodies in the savage fashion to which they had become accustomed in the border wars, and brought the scalps into the settlements, where they were represented as those of French Indians and sold at the regular price then established by law. The young warriors at once prepared to take revenge, but were restrained by the chiefs until satisfaction could be demanded in the ordinary way, according to the treaties arranged with the colonial governments. Application was made in turn to Virginia, North Carolina, and South Carolina, but without success. While the women were still wailing night and morning for their slain kindred, and the Creeks were taunting the warriors for their cowardice in thus quietly submitting to the injury, some lawless officers of Fort Prince George committed an unpardonable outrage at the neighboring Indian town while most of the men were away hunting.[1] The warriors could no longer be restrained. Soon there was news of attacks upon the back settlements of Carolina, while on the other side of the mountains two soldiers of the Fort Loudon garrison were killed. War seemed at hand.

[1] Adair, American Indians, 245–246, 1775; North Carolina Colonial Records, v, p. xlviii, 1887; Hewat, quoted in Ramsey, Tennessee, p. 54, 1853.

At this juncture, in November, 1758, a party of influential chiefs, having first ordered back a war party just about to set out from the western towns against the Carolina settlements, came down to Charleston and succeeded in arranging the difficulty upon a friendly basis. The assembly had officially declared peace with the Cherokee, when, in May of 1759, Governor Lyttleton unexpectedly came forward with a demand for the surrender for execution of every Indian who had killed a white man in the recent skirmishes, among these being the chiefs of Citico and Tellico. At the same time the commander at Fort Loudon, forgetful of the fact that he had but a small garrison in the midst of several thousands of restless savages, made a demand for twenty-four other chiefs whom he suspected of unfriendly action. To compel their surrender orders were given to stop all trading supplies intended for the upper Cherokee.

This roused the whole Nation, and a delegation representing every town came down to Charleston, protesting the desire of the Indians for peace and friendship, but declaring their inability to surrender their own chiefs. The governor replied by declaring war in November, 1759, at once calling out troops and sending messengers to secure the aid of all the surrounding tribes against the Cherokee. In the meantime a second delegation of thirty-two of the most prominent men, led by the young war chief Oconostota (Ăgăn-stâta),[1] arrived to make a further effort for peace, but the governor, refusing to listen to them, seized the whole party and confined them as prisoners at Fort Prince George, in a room large enough for only six soldiers, while at the same time he set fourteen hundred troops in motion to invade the Cherokee country. On further representation by Ata-kullakulla (Ătă'-gûl'′kălû'), the civil chief of the Nation and well known as a friend of the English, the governor released Oconostota and two others after compelling some half dozen of the delegation to sign a paper by which they pretended to agree for their tribe to kill or seize any Frenchmen entering their country, and consented to the imprisonment of the party until all the warriors demanded had been surrendered for execution or otherwise. At this stage of affairs the smallpox broke out in the Cherokee towns, rendering a further stay in their neighborhood unsafe, and thinking the whole matter now settled on his own basis, Lyttleton returned to Charleston.

The event soon proved how little he knew of Indian temper. Oconostota at once laid siege to Fort Prince George, completely cutting off communication at a time when, as it was now winter, no help could well be expected from below. In February, 1760, after having kept the fort thus closely invested for some weeks, he sent word one day by an Indian woman that he wished to speak to the commander, Lieutenant Coytmore. As the lieutenant stepped out from the stockade

---

[1] For notices see the glossary.

to see what was wanted, Oconostota, standing on the opposite side of the river, swung a bridle above his head as a signal to his warriors concealed in the bushes, and the officer was at once shot down. The soldiers immediately broke into the room where the hostages were confined, every one being a chief of prominence in the tribe, and butchered them to the last man.

It was now war to the end. Led by Oconostota, the Cherokee descended upon the frontier settlements of Carolina, while the warriors across the mountains laid close siege to Fort Loudon. In June, 1760, a strong force of over 1,600 men, under Colonel Montgomery, started to reduce the Cherokee towns and relieve the beleaguered garrison. Crossing the Indian frontier, Montgomery quickly drove the enemy from about Fort Prince George and then, rapidly advancing, surprised Little Keowee, killing every man of the defenders, and destroyed in succession every one of the Lower Cherokee towns, burning them to the ground, cutting down the cornfields and orchards, killing and taking more than a hundred of their men, and driving the whole population into the mountains before him. His own loss was very slight. He then sent messengers to the Middle and Upper towns, summoning them to surrender on penalty of the like fate, but, receiving no reply, he led his men across the divide to the waters of the Little Tennessee and continued down that stream without opposition until he came in the vicinity of Echoee (Itse'yĭ), a few miles above the sacred town of Nĭkwăsĭ', the present Franklin, North Carolina. Here the Cherokee had collected their full force to resist his progress, and the result was a desperate engagement on June 27, 1760, by which Montgomery was compelled to retire to Fort Prince George, after losing nearly one hundred men in killed and wounded. The Indian loss is unknown.

His retreat sealed the fate of Fort Loudon. The garrison, though hard pressed and reduced to the necessity of eating horses and dogs, had been enabled to hold out through the kindness of the Indian women, many of whom, having found sweethearts among the soldiers, brought them supplies of food daily. When threatened by the chiefs the women boldly replied that the soldiers were their husbands and it was their duty to help them, and that if any harm came to themselves for their devotion their English relatives would avenge them.[1] The end was only delayed, however, and on August 8, 1760, the garrison of about two hundred men, under Captain Demeré, surrendered to Oconostota on promise that they should be allowed to retire unmolested with their arms and sufficient ammunition for the march, on condition of delivering up all the remaining warlike stores.

The troops marched out and proceeded far enough to camp for the night, while the Indians swarmed into the fort to see what plunder they might find. "By accident a discovery was made of ten bags of

---

[1] Timberlake, Memoirs, p. 65, 1765.

powder and a large quantity of ball that had been secretly buried in
the fort, to prevent their falling into the enemy's hands" (Hewat).
It is said also that cannon, small arms, and ammunition had been
thrown into the river with the same intention (Haywood). Enraged
at this breach of the capitulation the Cherokee attacked the soldiers
next morning at daylight, killing Demeré and twenty-nine others at
the first fire. The rest were taken and held as prisoners until ransomed some time after. The second officer, Captain Stuart (13), for
whom the Indians had a high regard, was claimed by Ata-kullakulla,
who soon after took him into the woods, ostensibly on a hunting
excursion, and conducted him for nine days through the wilderness
until he delivered him safely into the hands of friends in Virginia.
The chief's kindness was well rewarded, and it was largely through
his influence that peace was finally brought about.

It was now too late, and the settlements were too much exhausted,
for another expedition, so the fall and winter were employed by the
English in preparations for an active campaign the next year in force
to crush out all resistance. In June 1761, Colonel Grant with an
army of 2,600 men, including a number of Chickasaw and almost
every remaining warrior of the Catawba,[1] set out from Fort Prince
George. Refusing a request from Ata-kullakulla for a friendly accommodation, he crossed Rabun gap and advanced rapidly down the
Little Tennessee along the same trail taken by the expedition of the
previous year. On June 10, when within two miles of Montgomery's
battlefield, he encountered the Cherokee, whom he defeated, although
with considerable loss to himself, after a stubborn engagement lasting
several hours. Having repulsed the Indians, he proceeded on his
way, sending out detachments to the outlying settlements, until in
the course of a month he had destroyed every one of the Middle
towns, 15 in all, with all their granaries and cornfields, driven the
inhabitants into the mountains, and "pushed the frontier seventy
miles farther to the west."

The Cherokee were now reduced to the greatest extremity. With
some of their best towns in ashes, their fields and orchards wasted for
two successive years, their ammunition nearly exhausted, many of
their bravest warriors dead, their people fugitives in the mountains,
hiding in caves and living like beasts upon roots or killing their
horses for food, with the terrible scourge of smallpox adding to the
miseries of starvation, and withal torn by factional differences which
had existed from the very beginning of the war—it was impossible
for even brave men to resist longer. In September Ata-kullakulla,
who had all along done everything in his power to stay the disaffec-
tion, came down to Charleston, a treaty of peace was made, and the

---

[1] Catawba reference from Milligan, 1763, in Carroll, South Carolina Historical Collections, II, p.
519, 1836.

war was ended.   From an estimated population of at least 5,000 warriors some years before, the Cherokee had now been reduced to about 2,300 men.[1]

In the meantime a force of Virginians under Colonel Stephen had advanced as far as the Great island of the Holston—now Kingsport, Tennessee—where they were met by a large delegation of Cherokee, who sued for peace, which was concluded with them by Colonel Stephen on November 19, 1761, independently of what was being done in South Carolina.   On the urgent request of the chief that an officer might visit their people for a short time to cement the new friendship, Lieutenant Henry Timberlake, a young Virginian who had already distinguished himself in active service, volunteered to return with them to their towns, where he spent several months.   He afterward conducted a delegation of chiefs to England, where, as they had come without authority from the Government, they met such an unpleasant reception that they returned disgusted.[2]

On the conclusion of peace between England and France in 1763, by which the whole western territory was ceded to England, a great council was held at Augusta, which was attended by the chiefs and principal men of all the southern Indians, at which Captain John Stuart, superintendent for the southern tribes, together with the colonial governors of Virginia, North Carolina, South Carolina, and Georgia, explained fully to the Indians the new condition of affairs, and a treaty of mutual peace and friendship was concluded on November 10 of that year.[3]

Under several leaders, as Walker, Wallen, Smith, and Boon, the tide of emigration now surged across the mountains in spite of every effort to restrain it,[4] and the period between the end of the Cherokee war and the opening of the Revolution is principally notable for a number of treaty cessions by the Indians, each in fruitless endeavor to fix a permanent barrier between themselves and the advancing wave of white settlement.   Chief among these was the famous Henderson purchase in 1775, which included the whole tract between the Kentucky and Cumberland rivers, embracing the greater part of the present state of Kentucky.   By these treaties the Cherokee were shorn of practically all their ancient territorial claims north of the present Tennessee line and east of the Blue ridge and the Savannah, including much of their best hunting range; their home settlements were, however, left still in their possession.[5]

---

[1] Figures from Adair, American Indians, p. 227, 1775.   When not otherwise noted this sketch of the Cherokee war of 1760–61 is compiled chiefly from the contemporary dispatches in the Gentleman's Magazine, supplemented from Hewat's Historical account of South Carolina and Georgia, 1778; with additional details from Adair, American Indians; Ramsey, Tennessee; Royce, Cherokee Nation; North Carolina Colonial Records, v, documents and introduction; etc.

[2] Timberlake, Memoirs, p. 9 et passim, 1765.

[3] Stevens, Georgia, II, pp. 26–29, 1859.   [4] Ramsey, Tennessee, pp. 65–70, 1853.

[5] Royce, Cherokee Nation, in Fifth Ann. Rep. Bur. of Ethnology, pp. 146–149, 1888.

As one consequence of the late Cherokee war, a royal proclamation had been issued in 1763, with a view of checking future encroachments by the whites, which prohibited any private land purchases from the Indians, or any granting of warrants for lands west of the sources of the streams flowing into the Atlantic.[1] In 1768, on the appeal of the Indians themselves, the British superintendent for the southern tribes, Captain John Stuart, had negotiated a treaty at Hard Labor in South Carolina by which Kanawha and New rivers, along their whole course downward from the North Carolina line, were fixed as the boundary between the Cherokee and the whites in that direction. In two years, however, so many borderers had crossed into the Indian country, where they were evidently determined to remain, that it was found necessary to substitute another treaty, by which the line was made to run due south from the mouth of the Kanawha to the Holston, thus cutting off from the Cherokee almost the whole of their hunting grounds in Virginia and West Virginia. Two years later, in 1772, the Virginians demanded a further cession, by which everything east of Kentucky river was surrendered; and finally, on March 17, 1775, the great Henderson purchase was consummated, including the whole tract between the Kentucky and Cumberland rivers. By this last cession the Cherokee were at last cut off from Ohio river and all their rich Kentucky hunting grounds.[2]

While these transactions were called treaties, they were really forced upon the native proprietors, who resisted each in turn and finally signed only under protest and on most solemn assurances that no further demands would be made. Even before the purchases were made, intruders in large numbers had settled upon each of the tracts in question, and they refused to withdraw across the boundaries now established, but remained on one pretext or another to await a new adjustment. This was particularly the case on Watauga and upper Holston rivers in northeastern Tennessee, where the settlers, finding themselves still within the Indian boundary and being resolved to remain, effected a temporary lease from the Cherokee in 1772. As was expected and intended, the lease became a permanent occupancy, the nucleus settlement of the future State of Tennessee.[3]

Just before the outbreak of the Revolution, the botanist, William Bartram, made an extended tour of the Cherokee country, and has left us a pleasant account of the hospitable character and friendly disposition of the Indians at that time. He gives a list of forty-three towns then inhabited by the tribe.[4]

The opening of the great Revolutionary struggle in 1776 found the Indian tribes almost to a man ranged on the British side against the

[1] Royce, Cherokee Nation, op. cit., p. 149; Ramsey, Tennessee, p. 71, 1853.
[2] Ramsey, op. cit., pp. 93–122; Royce, op. cit. pp. 146–149.
[3] Ramsey, op. cit., pp. 109–122; Royce, op. cit. p. 146 et passim.
[4] Bartram, Travels, pp. 366–372, 1792.

Americans. There was good reason for this. Since the fall of the French power the British government had stood to them as the sole representative of authority, and the guardian and protector of their rights against constant encroachments by the American borderers. Licensed British traders were resident in every tribe and many had intermarried and raised families among them, while the border man looked upon the Indian only as a cumberer of the earth. The British superintendents, Sir William Johnson in the north and Captain John Stuart in the south, they knew as generous friends, while hardly a warrior of them all was without some old cause of resentment against their backwoods neighbors. They felt that the only barrier between themselves and national extinction was in the strength of the British government, and when the final severence came they threw their whole power into the British scale. They were encouraged in this resolution by presents of clothing and other goods, with promises of plunder from the settlements and hopes of recovering a portion of their lost territories. The British government having determined, as early as June, 1775, to call in the Indians against the Americans, supplies of hatchets, guns, and ammunition were issued to the warriors of all the tribes from the lakes to the gulf, and bounties were offered for American scalps brought in to the commanding officer at Detroit or Oswego.[1] Even the Six Nations, who had agreed in solemn treaty to remain neutral, were won over by these persuasions. In August, 1775, an Indian "talk" was intercepted in which the Cherokee assured Cameron, the resident agent, that their warriors, enlisted in the service of the king, were ready at a signal to fall upon the back settlements of Carolina and Georgia.[2] Circular letters were sent out to all those persons in the back country supposed to be of royalist sympathies, directing them to repair to Cameron's headquarters in the Cherokee country to join the Indians in the invasion of the settlements.[3]

In June, 1776, a British fleet under command of Sir Peter Parker, with a large naval and military force, attacked Charleston, South Carolina, both by land and sea, and simultaneously a body of Cherokee, led by Tories in Indian disguise, came down from the mountains and ravaged the exposed frontier of South Carolina, killing and burning as they went. After a gallant defense by the garrison at Charleston the British were repulsed, whereupon their Indian and Tory allies withdrew.[4]

About the same time the warning came from Nancy Ward (14), a noted friendly Indian woman of great authority in the Cherokee Nation, that seven hundred Cherokee warriors were advancing in two divisions against the Watauga and Holston settlements, with the design of

---

[1] Ramsey, Tennessee, pp. 143–150, 1853; Monette, Valley of the Mississippi, I, pp. 400, 401, 431, 432, and II, pp. 33, 34, 1846; Roosevelt, Winning of the West, I, pp. 276–281, and II, pp. 1–6, 1889.

[2] Ramsey, op. cit., p. 143.

[3] Quoted from Stedman, in Ramsey, op. cit., p. 162.

[4] Ramsey, op. cit., p. 162.

destroying everything as far up as New river. The Holston men
from both sides of the Virginia line hastily collected under Captain
Thompson and marched against the Indians, whom they met and
defeated with signal loss after a hard-fought battle near the Long
island in the Holston (Kingsport, Tennessee), on August 20. The
next day the second division of the Cherokee attacked the fort at
Watauga, garrisoned by only forty men under Captain James Robertson (15), but was repulsed without loss to the defenders, the Indians
withdrawing on news of the result at the Long island. A Mrs. Bean
and a boy named Moore were captured on this occasion and carried to
one of the Cherokee towns in the neighborhood of Tellico, where the
boy was burned, but the woman, after she had been condemned to
death and everything was in readiness for the tragedy, was rescued by
the interposition of Nancy Ward. Two other Cherokee detachments
moved against the upper settlements at the same time. One of these,
finding all the inhabitants securely shut up in forts, returned without
doing much damage. The other ravaged the country on Clinch river
almost to its head, and killed a man and wounded others at Black's
station, now Abingdon, Virginia.[1]

At the same time that one part of the Cherokee were raiding the
Tennessee settlements others came down upon the frontiers of Carolina and Georgia. On the upper Catawba they killed many people, but
the whites took refuge in the stockade stations, where they defended
themselves until General Rutherford (16) came to their relief. In
Georgia an attempt had been made by a small party of Americans to
seize Cameron, who lived in one of the Cherokee towns with his Indian
wife, but, as was to have been expected, the Indians interfered, killing
several of the party and capturing others, who were afterward tortured
to death. The Cherokee of the Upper and Middle towns, with some
Creeks and Tories of the vicinity, led by Cameron himself, at once
began ravaging the South Carolina border, burning houses, driving off
cattle, and killing men, women, and children without distinction, until
the whole country was in a wild panic, the people abandoning their
farms to seek safety in the garrisoned forts. On one occasion an
attack by two hundred of the enemy, half of them being Tories, stripped
and painted like Indians, was repulsed by the timely arrival of a body
of Americans, who succeeded in capturing thirteen of the Tories. The
invasion extended into Georgia, where also property was destroyed
and the inhabitants were driven from their homes.[2]

Realizing their common danger, the border states determined to
strike such a concerted blow at the Cherokee as should render them
passive while the struggle with England continued. In accord with
this plan of cooperation the frontier forces were quickly mobilized and

---

[1] Ramsey, Tennessee, pp. 150–159, 1853.
[2] Roosevelt, Winning of the West, I, pp. 293–297, 1889.

in the summer of 1776 four expeditions were equipped from Virginia, North Carolina, South Carolina, and Georgia, to enter the Cherokee territory simultaneously from as many different directions.

In August of that year the army of North Carolina, 2,400 strong, under General Griffith Rutherford, crossed the Blue ridge at Swannanoa gap, and following the main trail almost along the present line of the railroad, struck the first Indian town, Stikâ'yĭ, or Stecoee, on the Tuckasegee, near the present Whittier. The inhabitants having fled, the soldiers burned the town, together with an unfinished townhouse ready for the roof, cut down the standing corn, killed one or two straggling Indians, and then proceeded on their mission of destruction. Every town upon Oconaluftee, Tuckasegee, and the upper part of Little Tennessee, and on Hiwassee to below the junction of Valley river—thirty-six towns in all—was destroyed in turn, the corn cut down or trampled under the hoofs of the stock driven into the fields for that purpose, and the stock itself killed or carried off. Before such an overwhelming force, supplemented as it was by three others simultaneously advancing from other directions, the Cherokee made but poor resistance, and fled with their women and children into the fastnesses of the Great Smoky mountains, leaving their desolated fields and smoking towns behind them. As was usual in Indian wars, the actual number killed or taken was small, but the destruction of property was beyond calculation. At Sugartown (Kûlsetsi'yĭ, east of the present Franklin) one detachment, sent to destroy it, was surprised, and escaped only through the aid of another force sent to its rescue. Rutherford himself, while proceeding to the destruction of the Hiwassee towns, encountered the Indians drawn up to oppose his progress in the Waya gap of the Nantahala mountains, and one of the hardest fights of the campaign resulted, the soldiers losing over forty killed and wounded, although the Cherokee were finally repulsed (17). One of the Indians killed on this occasion was afterward discovered to be a woman, painted and armed like a warrior.[1]

On September 26 the South Carolina army, 1,860 strong, under Colonel Andrew Williamson, and including a number of Catawba Indians, effected a junction with Rutherford's forces on Hiwassee river, near the present Murphy, North Carolina. It had been expected that Williamson would join the northern army at Cowee, on the Little Tennessee, when they would proceed together against the western towns, but he had been delayed, and the work of destruction in that direction was already completed, so that after a short rest each army returned home along the route by which it had come.

The South Carolina men had centered by different detachments in

---

[1] See no. 110, "Incidents of Personal Heroism." For Rutherford's expedition, see Moore, Rutherford's Expedition, in North Carolina University Magazine, February, 1888; Swain, Sketch of the Indian War in 1776, ibid., May, 1852, reprinted in Historical Magazine, November, 1867; Ramsey, Tennessee, p. 164, 1853; Roosevelt, Winning of the West, I, pp. 294–302, 1889, etc

the lower Cherokee towns about the head of Savannah river, burning one town after another, cutting down the peach trees and ripened corn, and having an occasional brush with the Cherokee, who hung constantly upon their flanks. At the town of Seneca, near which they encountered Cameron with his Indians and Tories, they had destroyed six thousand bushels of corn, besides other food stores, after burning all the houses, the Indians having retreated after a stout resistance. The most serious encounter had taken place at Tomassee, where several whites and sixteen Cherokee were killed, the latter being all scalped afterward. Having completed the ruin of the Lower towns, Williamson had crossed over Rabun gap and descended into the valley of the Little Tennessee to cooperate with Rutherford in the destruction of the Middle and Valley towns. As the army advanced every house in every settlement met was burned—ninety houses in one settlement alone—and detachments were sent into the fields to destroy the corn, of which the smallest town was estimated to have two hundred acres, besides potatoes, beans, and orchards of peach trees. The stores of dressed deerskins and other valuables were carried off. Everything was swept clean, and the Indians who were not killed or taken were driven, homeless refugees, into the dark recesses of Nantahala or painfully made their way across to the Overhill towns in Tennessee, which were already menaced by another invasion from the north.[1]

In July, while Williamson was engaged on the the upper Savannah, a force of two hundred Georgians, under Colonel Samuel Jack, had marched in the same direction and succeeded in burning two towns on the heads of Chattahoochee and Tugaloo rivers, destroying the corn and driving off the cattle, without the loss of a man, the Cherokee having apparently fallen back to concentrate for resistance in the mountains.[2]

The Virginia army, about two thousand strong, under Colonel William Christian (18), rendezvoused in August at the Long island of the Holston, the regular gathering place on the Tennessee side of the mountains. Among them were several hundred men from North Carolina, with all who could be spared from the garrisons on the Tennessee side. Paying but little attention to small bodies of Indians, who tried to divert attention or to delay progress by flank attacks, they advanced steadily, but cautiously, along the great Indian warpath (19) toward the crossing of the French Broad, where a strong force of Cherokee was reported to be in waiting to dispute their passage. Just before reaching the river the Indians sent a Tory trader

---

[1] For Williamson's expedition, see Ross Journal, with Rockwell's notes, in Historical Magazine, October, 1876; Swain, Sketch of the Indian War in 1776, in North Carolina University Magazine for May, 1852, reprinted in Historical Magazine, November, 1867; Jones, Georgia, II, p. 246 et passim, 1883; Ramsey, Tennessee, 163–164, 1853; Roosevelt, Winning of the West, I, pp. 296-303, 1889.

[2] Jones, op. cit., p. 246; Ramsey, op. cit., p. 163; Roosevelt, op. cit., p. 295.

with a flag of truce to discuss terms. Knowing that his own strength was overwhelming, Christian allowed the envoy to go through the whole camp and then sent him back with the message that there could be no terms until the Cherokee towns had been destroyed. Arriving at the ford, he kindled fires and made all preparations as if intending to camp there for several days. As soon as night fell, however, he secretly drew off half his force and crossed the river lower down, to come upon the Indians in their rear. This was a work of great difficulty; as the water was so deep that it came up almost to the shoulders of the men, while the current was so rapid that they were obliged to support each other four abreast to prevent being swept off their feet. However, they kept their guns and powder dry. On reaching the other side they were surprised to find no enemy. Disheartened at the strength of the invasion, the Indians had fled without even a show of resistance. It is probable that nearly all their men and resources had been drawn off to oppose the Carolina forces on their eastern border, and the few who remained felt themselves unequal to the contest.

Advancing without opposition, Christian reached the towns on Little Tennessee early in November, and, finding them deserted, proceeded to destroy them, one after another, with their outlying fields. The few lingering warriors discovered were all killed. In the meantime messages had been sent out to the farther towns, in response to which several of their head men came into Christian's camp to treat for peace. On their agreement to surrender all the prisoners and captured stock in their hands and to cede to the whites all the disputed territory occupied by the Tennessee settlements, as soon as representatives of the whole tribe could be assembled in the spring, Christian consented to suspend hostilities and retire without doing further injury. An exception was made against Tuskegee and another town, which had been concerned in the burning of the boy taken from Watauga, already noted, and these two were reduced to ashes. The sacred "peace town," Echota (20), had not been molested. Most of the troops were disbanded on their return to the Long island, but a part remained and built Fort Patrick Henry, where they went into winter quarters.[1]

From incidental notices in narratives written by some of the participants, we obtain interesting side-lights on the merciless character of this old border warfare. In addition to the ordinary destruction of war—the burning of towns, the wasting of fruitful fields, and the killing of the defenders—we find that every Indian warrior killed was scalped, when opportunity permitted; women, as well as men, were shot down and afterward "helped to their end"; and prisoners taken were put up at auction as slaves when not killed on the spot. Near Tomassee a small

---

[1] For the Virginia-Tennessee expedition see Roosevelt, Winning of the West, I, pp. 303–305, 1889; Ramsey, Tennessee, pp. 165–170, 1853.

party of Indians was surrounded and entirely cut off. "Sixteen were found dead in the valley when the battle ended. These our men scalped." In a personal encounter "a stout Indian engaged a sturdy young white man, who was a good bruiser and expert at gouging. After breaking their guns on each other they laid hold of one another, when the cracker had his thumbs instantly in the fellow's eyes, who roared and cried '*canaly*'—enough, in English. 'Damn you,' says the white man, 'you can never have enough while you are alive.' He then threw him down, set his foot upon his head, and scalped him alive; then took up one of the broken guns and knocked out his brains. It would have been fun if he had let the latter action alone and sent him home without his nightcap, to tell his countrymen how he had been treated." Later on some of the same detachment (Williamson's) seeing a woman ahead, fired on her and brought her down with two serious wounds, but yet able to speak. After getting what information she could give them, through a half-breed interpreter, "the informer being unable to travel, some of our men favored her so far that they killed her there, to put her out of pain." A few days later "a party of Colonel Thomas's regiment, being on a hunt of plunder, or some such thing, found an Indian squaw and took her prisoner, she being lame, was unable to go with her friends. She was so sullen that she would, as an old saying is, neither lead nor drive, and by their account she died in their hands; but I suppose they helped her to her end." At this place—on the Hiwassee—they found a large town, having "upwards of ninety houses, and large quantities of corn," and "we encamped among the corn, where we had a great plenty of corn, peas, beans, potatoes, and hogs," and on the next day "we were ordered to assemble in companies to spread through the town to destroy, cut down, and burn all the vegetables belonging to our heathen enemies, which was no small undertaking, they being so plentifully supplied." Continuing to another town, "we engaged in our former labor, that is, cutting and destroying all things that might be of advantage to our enemies. Finding here curious buildings, great apple trees, and white-man-like improvements, these we destroyed."[1]

While crossing over the mountains Rutherford's men approached a house belonging to a trader, when one of his negro slaves ran out and "was shot by the Reverend James Hall, the chaplain, as he ran, mistaking him for an Indian."[2] Soon after they captured two women and a boy. It was proposed to auction them off at once to the highest bidder, and when one of the officers protested that the matter should be left to the disposition of Congress, "the greater part swore bloodily that if they were not sold for slaves upon the spot they would kill and

[1] Ross Journal, in Historical Magazine, October, 1867.
[2] Swain, Sketch of the Indian War of 1776, in Historical Magazine, November, 1867.

scalp them immediately." The prisoners were accordingly sold for about twelve hundred dollars.[1]

At the Wolf Hills settlement, now Abingdon, Virginia, a party sent out from the fort returned with the scalps of eleven warriors. Having recovered the books which their minister had left behind in his cabin, they held a service of prayer for their success, after which the fresh scalps were hung upon a pole above the gate of the fort. The barbarous custom of scalping to which the border men had become habituated in the earlier wars was practiced upon every occasion when opportunity presented, at least upon the bodies of warriors, and the South Carolina legislature offered a bounty of seventy-five pounds for every warrior's scalp, a higher reward, however, being offered for prisoners.[2] In spite of all the bitterness which the war aroused there seems to be no record of any scalping of Tories or other whites by the Americans (21).

The effect upon the Cherokee of this irruption of more than six thousand armed enemies into their territory was well nigh paralyzing. More than fifty of their towns had been burned, their orchards cut down, their fields wasted, their cattle and horses killed or driven off, their stores of buckskin and other personal property plundered. Hundreds of their people had been killed or had died of starvation and exposure, others were prisoners in the hands of the Americans, and some had been sold into slavery. Those who had escaped were fugitives in the mountains, living upon acorns, chestnuts, and wild game, or were refugees with the British.[3] From the Virginia line to the Chattahoochee the chain of destruction was complete. For the present at least any further resistance was hopeless, and they were compelled to sue for peace.

By a treaty concluded at DeWitts Corners in South Carolina on May 20, 1777, the first ever made with the new states, the Lower Cherokee surrendered to the conqueror all of their remaining territory in South Carolina, excepting a narrow strip along the western boundary. Just two months later, on July 20, by treaty at the Long island, as had been arranged by Christian in the preceding fall, the Middle and Upper Cherokee ceded everything east of the Blue ridge, together with all the disputed territory on the Watauga, Nolichucky, upper Holston, and New rivers. By this second treaty also Captain James Robertson was appointed agent for the Cherokee, to reside at Echota, to watch their movements, recover any captured property, and prevent their correspondence with persons unfriendly to the American cause. As the Federal government was not yet in perfect operation these treaties

---

[1] Moore's narrative, in North Carolina University Magazine, February, 1888.

[2] Roosevelt, Winning of the West, I, pp. 285, 290, 303, 1889.

[3] About five hundred sought refuge with Stuart, the British Indian superintendent in Florida, where they were fed for some time at the expense of the British government (Jones, Georgia, II, p. 246, 1883).

were negotiated by commissioners from the four states adjoining the Cherokee country, the territory thus acquired being parceled out to South Carolina, North Carolina, and Tennessee.[1]

While the Cherokee Nation had thus been compelled to a treaty of peace, a very considerable portion of the tribe was irreconcilably hostile to the Americans and refused to be a party to the late cessions, especially on the Tennessee side. Although Ata-kullakulla sent word that he was ready with five hundred young warriors to fight for the Americans against the English or Indian enemy whenever called upon, Dragging-canoe (Tsiyu-gûnsi'nĭ), who had led the opposition against the Watauga settlements, declared that he would hold fast to Cameron's talk and continue to make war upon those who had taken his hunting grounds. Under his leadership some hundreds of the most warlike and implacable warriors of the tribe, with their families, drew out from the Upper and Middle towns and moved far down upon Tennessee river, where they established new settlements on Chickamauga creek, in the neighborhood of the present Chattanooga. The locality appears to have been already a rendezvous for a sort of Indian banditti, who sometimes plundered boats disabled in the rapids at this point while descending the river. Under the name "Chickamaugas" they soon became noted for their uncompromising and never-ceasing hostility. In 1782, in consequence of the destruction of their towns by Sevier and Campbell, they abandoned this location and moved farther down the river, where they built what were afterwards known as the "five lower towns," viz, Running Water, Nickajack, Long Island, Crow town, and Lookout Mountain town. These were all on the extreme western Cherokee frontier, near where Tennessee river crosses the state line, the first three being within the present limits of Tennessee, while Lookout Mountain town and Crow town were respectively in the adjacent corners of Georgia and Alabama. Their population was recruited from Creeks, Shawano, and white Tories, until they were estimated at a thousand warriors. Here they remained, a constant thorn in the side of Tennessee, until their towns were destroyed in 1794.[2]

The expatriated Lower Cherokee also removed to the farthest western border of their tribal territory, where they might hope to be secure from encroachment for a time at least, and built new towns for themselves on the upper waters of the Coosa. Twenty years after-

[1] Royce, Cherokee Nation, in Fifth Ann. Rep. Bureau of Ethnology, p. 150 and map, 1888; Ramsey, Tennessee, pp. 172–174, 1853; Stevens, Georgia, II, p. 144, 1859; Roosevelt, Winning of the West, I, p. 306, 1889.

[2] Ramsey, op. cit., pp. 171–177, 185–186, 610 et passim; Royce, op. cit., p. 150; Campbell letter, 1782, and other documents in Virginia State Papers, III, pp. 271, 571, 599, 1883, and IV, pp. 118, 286, 1884; Blount letter, January 14, 1793, American State Papers: Indian Affairs, I, p. 431, 1832. Campbell says they abandoned their first location on account of the invasion from Tennessee. Governor Blount says they left on account of witches.

ward Hawkins found the population of Willstown, in extreme western Georgia, entirely made up of refugees from the Savannah, and the children so familiar from their parents with stories of Williamson's invasion that they ran screaming from the face of a white man (22).[1]

In April, 1777, the legislature of North Carolina, of which Tennessee was still a part, authorized bounties of land in the new territory to all able-bodied men who should volunteer against the remaining hostile Cherokee. Under this act companies of rangers were kept along the exposed border to cut off raiding parties of Indians and to protect the steady advance of the pioneers, with the result that the Tennessee settlements enjoyed a brief respite and were even able to send some assistance to their brethren in Kentucky, who were sorely pressed by the Shawano and other northern tribes.[2]

The war between England and the colonies still continued, however, and the British government was unremitting in its effort to secure the active assistance of the Indians. With the Creeks raiding the Georgia and South Carolina frontier, and with a British agent, Colonel Brown, and a number of Tory refugees regularly domiciled at Chickamauga,[3] it was impossible for the Cherokee long to remain quiet. In the spring of 1779 the warning came from Robertson, stationed at Echota, that three hundred warriors from Chickamauga had started against the back settlements of North Carolina. Without a day's delay the states of North Carolina (including Tennessee) and Virginia united to send a strong force of volunteers against them under command of Colonels Shelby and Montgomery. Descending the Holston in April in a fleet of canoes built for the occasion, they took the Chickamauga towns so completely by surprise that the few warriors remaining fled to the mountains without attempting to give battle. Several were killed, Chickamauga and the outlying villages were burned, twenty thousand bushels of corn were destroyed and large numbers of horses and cattle captured, together with a great quantity of goods sent by the British Governor Hamilton at Detroit for distribution to the Indians. The success of this expedition frustrated the execution of a project by Hamilton for uniting all the northern and southern Indians, to be assisted by British regulars, in a concerted attack along the whole American frontier. On learning, through runners, of the blow that had befallen them, the Chickamauga warriors gave up all idea of invading the settlements, and returned to their wasted villages.[4] They, as well as the Creeks, however, kept in constant communication with

---

[1] Hawkins, manuscript journal, 1796, with Georgia Historical Society.

[2] Ramsey, Tennessee, pp. 174–178, 1853.

[3] Campbell letter, 1782, Virginia State Papers, III, p. 271, 1883.

[4] Ramsey, op. cit, pp. 186–188; Roosevelt, Winning of the West, II, pp. 236–238, 1889. Ramsey's statements, chiefly on Haywood's authority, of the strength of the expedition, the number of warriors killed, etc., are so evidently overdrawn that they are here omitted.

the British commander in Savannah.   In this year also a delegation of
Cherokee visited the Ohio towns to offer condolences on the death of
the noted Delaware chief, White-eyes.[1]

In the early spring of 1780 a large company of emigrants under
Colonel John Donelson descended the Holston and the Tennessee to
the Ohio, whence they ascended the Cumberland, effected a junction
with another party under Captain James Robertson, which had just
arrived by a toilsome overland route, and made the first settlement on
the present site of Nashville.   In passing the Chickamauga towns they
had run the gauntlet of the hostile Cherokee, who pursued them for a
considerable distance beyond the whirlpool known as the Suck, where
the river breaks through the mountain.   The family of a man named
Stuart being infected with the smallpox, his boat dropped behind, and
all on board, twenty-eight in number, were killed or taken by the
Indians, their cries being distinctly heard by their friends ahead who
were unable to help them.   Another boat having run upon the rocks,
the three women in it, one of whom had become a mother the night
before, threw the cargo into the river, and then, jumping into the
water, succeeded in pushing the boat into the current while the husband of one of them kept the Indians at bay with his rifle.   The infant
was killed in the confusion.   Three cowards attempted to escape,
without thought of their companions.   One was drowned in the river;
the other two were captured and carried to Chickamauga, where one
was burned and the other was ransomed by a trader.   The rest went
on their way to found the capital of a new commonwealth.[2]   As if in
retributive justice, the smallpox broke out in the Chickamauga band in
consequence of the capture of Stuart's family, causing the death of
a great number.[3]

The British having reconquered Georgia and South Carolina and
destroyed all resistance in the south, early in 1780 Cornwallis, with his
subordinates, Ferguson and the merciless Tarleton, prepared to invade
North Carolina and sweep the country northward to Virginia.   The
Creeks under McGillivray (23), and a number of the Cherokee under
various local chiefs, together with the Tories, at once joined his
standard.

While the Tennessee backwoodsmen were gathered at a barbecue to
contest for a shooting prize, a paroled prisoner brought a demand
from Ferguson for their submission; with the threat, if they refused,
that he would cross the mountains, hang their leaders, kill every man
found in arms and burn every settlement.   Up to this time the mountain men had confined their effort to holding in check the Indian
enemy, but now, with the fate of the Revolution at stake, they felt

[1] Heckewelder, Indian Nations, p. 327, reprint of 1876.
[2] Donelson's Journal, etc., in Ramsey, Tennessee, pp. 197–203, 1853; Roosevelt, Winning of the West,
II, pp. 324–340, 1889.
[3] Ibid., II, p. 337.

that the time for wider action had come. They resolved not to await the attack, but to anticipate it. Without order or authority from Congress, without tents, commissary, or supplies, the Indian fighters of Virginia, North Carolina, and Tennessee quickly assembled at the Sycamore shoals of the Watauga to the number of about one thousand men under Campbell of Virginia, Sevier (24) and Shelby of Tennessee, and McDowell of North Carolina. Crossing the mountains, they met Ferguson at Kings mountain in South Carolina on October 7, 1780, and gained the decisive victory that turned the tide of the Revolution in the South.[1]

It is in place here to quote a description of these men in buckskin, white by blood and tradition, but half Indian in habit and instinct, who, in half a century of continuous conflict, drove back Creeks, Cherokee, and Shawano, and with one hand on the plow and the other on the rifle redeemed a wilderness and carried civilization and free government to the banks of the Mississippi.

"They were led by leaders they trusted, they were wonted to Indian warfare, they were skilled as horsemen and marksmen, they knew how to face every kind of danger, hardship, and privation. Their fringed and tasseled hunting shirts were girded by bead-worked belts, and the trappings of their horses were stained red and yellow. On their heads they wore caps of coon skin or mink skin, with the tails hanging down, or else felt hats, in each of which was thrust a buck tail or a sprig of evergreen. Every man carried a small-bore rifle, a tomahawk, and a scalping knife. A very few of the officers had swords, and there was not a bayonet nor a tent in the army."[2]

To strike the blow at Kings mountain the border men had been forced to leave their own homes unprotected. Even before they could cross the mountains on their return the news came that the Cherokee were again out in force for the destruction of the upper settlements, and their numerous small bands were killing, burning, and plundering in the usual Indian fashion. Without loss of time the Holston settlements of Virginia and Tennessee at once raised seven hundred mounted riflemen to march against the enemy, the command being assigned to Colonel Arthur Campbell of Virginia and Colonel John Sevier of Tennessee.

Sevier started first with nearly three hundred men, going south along the great Indian war trail and driving small parties of the Cherokee before him, until he crossed the French Broad and came upon seventy of them on Boyds creek, not far from the present Sevierville, on December 16, 1780. Ordering his men to spread out into a half circle, he sent ahead some scouts, who, by an attack and feigned retreat, managed to draw the Indians into the trap thus prepared,

---

[1] Roosevelt, Winning of the West, II, pp. 241–294, 1889; Ramsey, Tennessee, pp. 208–249, 1853.

[2] Roosevelt, op. cit., p. 256.

with the result that they left thirteen dead and all their plunder, while not one of the whites was even wounded.[1]

A few days later Sevier was joined by Campbell with the remainder of the force. Advancing to the Little Tennessee with but slight resistance, they crossed three miles below Echota while the Indians were watching for them at the ford above. Then dividing into two bodies, they proceeded to destroy the towns along the river. The chiefs sent peace talks through Nancy Ward, the Cherokee woman who had so befriended the whites in 1776, but to these overtures Campbell returned an evasive answer until he could first destroy the towns on lower Hiwassee, whose warriors had been particularly hostile. Continuing southward, the troops destroyed these towns, Hiwassee and Chestuee, with all their stores of provisions, finishing the work on the last day of the year. The Indians had fled before them, keeping spies out to watch their movements. One of these, while giving signals from a ridge by beating a drum, was shot by the whites. The soldiers lost only one man, who was buried in an Indian cabin which was then burned down to conceal the trace of the interment. The return march was begun on New Year's day. Ten principal towns, including Echota, the capital, had been destroyed, besides several smaller villages, containing in the aggregate over one thousand houses, and not less than fifty thousand bushels of corn and large stores of other provision. Everything not needed on the return march was committed to the flames or otherwise wasted. Of all the towns west of the mountains only Talassee, and one or two about Chickamauga or on the headwaters of the Coosa, escaped. The whites had lost only one man killed and two wounded. Before the return a proclamation was sent to the Cherokee chiefs, warning them to make peace on penalty of a worse visitation.[2]

Some Cherokee who met them at Echota, on the return march, to talk of peace, brought in and surrendered several white prisoners.[3] One reason for the slight resistance made by the Indians was probably the fact that at the very time of the invasion many of their warriors were away, raiding on the Upper Holston and in the neighborhood of Cumberland gap.[4]

Although the Upper or Overhill Cherokee were thus humbled, those of the middle towns, on the head waters of Little Tennessee, still continued to send out parties against the back settlements. Sevier

---

[1] Roosevelt, Winning of the West, II, pp. 298–300, 1889; Ramsey, Tennessee, pp. 261–264, 1853. There is great discrepancy in the various accounts of this fight, from the attempts of interested historians to magnify the size of the victory. One writer gives the Indians 1,000 warriors. Here, as elsewhere, Roosevelt is a more reliable guide, his statements being usually from official documents.

[2] Roosevelt, op. cit., pp. 300–304; Ramsey, op. cit., pp. 265–268; Campbell, report, January 15, 1781, in Virginia State Papers, I, p. 436. Haywood and others after him make the expedition go as far as Chickamauga and Coosa river, but Campbell's report expressly denies this.

[3] Ramsey, op. cit., p. 266.

[4] Roosevelt, op. cit., p. 302.

determined to make a sudden stroke upon them, and early in March of the same year, 1781, with 150 picked horsemen, he started to cross the Great Smoky mountains over trails never before attempted by white men, and so rough in places that it was hardly possible to lead horses. Falling unexpectedly upon Tuckasegee, near the present Webster, North Carolina, he took the town completely by surprise, killing several warriors and capturing a number of women and children. Two other principal towns and three smaller settlements were taken in the same way, with a quantity of provision and about 200 horses, the Indians being entirely off their guard and unprepared to make any effective resistance. Having spread destruction through the middle towns, with the loss to himself of only one man killed and another wounded, he was off again as suddenly as he had come, moving so rapidly that he was well on his homeward way before the Cherokee could gather for pursuit.[1] At the same time a smaller Tennessee expedition went out to disperse the Indians who had been making headquarters in the mountains about Cumberland gap and harassing travelers along the road to Kentucky.[2] Numerous indications of Indians were found, but none were met, although the country was scoured for a considerable distance.[3] In summer the Cherokee made another incursion, this time upon the new settlements on the French Broad, near the present Newport, Tennessee. With a hundred horsemen Sevier fell suddenly upon their camp on Indian creek, killed a dozen warriors, and scattered the rest.[4] By these successive blows the Cherokee were so worn out and dispirited that they were forced to sue for peace, and in midsummer of 1781 a treaty of peace—doubtful though it might be—was negotiated at the Long island of the Holston.[5] The respite came just in time to allow the Tennesseeans to send a detachment against Cornwallis.

Although there was truce in Tennessee, there was none in the South. In November of this year the Cherokee made a sudden inroad upon the Georgia settlements, destroying everything in their way. In retaliation a force under General Pickens marched into their country, destroying their towns as far as Valley river. Finding further progress blocked by heavy snows and learning through a prisoner that the Indians, who had retired before him, were collecting to oppose him in the mountains, he withdrew, as he says, "through absolute necessity," having accomplished very little of the result expected. Shortly afterward the Cherokee, together with some Creeks, again invaded Georgia,

[1] Campbell, letter, March 28, 1781, in Virginia State Papers, I, p. 602, 1875; Martin, letter, March 31, 1781, ibid., p. 613; Ramsey, Tennessee, p. 268, 1853; Roosevelt, Winning of the West, II, pp. 305–307, 1889.

[2] Campbell, letter, March 28, 1781, in Virginia State Papers, I, p. 602, 1875.

[3] Ramsey, op. cit., p. 269.

[4] Ibid.; Roosevelt, op. cit., p. 307.

[5] Ibid.; Ramsey, op. cit., pp. 267, 268. The latter authority seems to make it 1782, which is evidently a mistake.

but were met on Oconee river and driven back by a detachment of American troops.[1]

The Overhill Cherokee, on lower Little Tennessee, seem to have been trying in good faith to hold to the peace established at the Long island. Early in 1781 the government land office had been closed to further entries, not to be opened again until peace had been declared with England, but the borderers paid little attention to the law in such matters, and the rage for speculation in Tennessee lands grew stronger daily.[2] In the fall of 1782 the chief, Old Tassel of Echota, on behalf of all the friendly chiefs and towns, sent a pathetic talk to the governors of Virginia and North Carolina, complaining that in spite of all their efforts to remain quiet the settlers were constantly encroaching upon them, and had built houses within a day's walk of the Cherokee towns. They asked that all those whites who had settled beyond the boundary last established should be removed.[3] As was to have been expected, this was never done.

The Chickamauga band, however, and those farther to the south, were still bent on war, being actively encouraged in that disposition by the British agents and refugee loyalists living among them. They continued to raid both north and south, and in September, 1782, Sevier, with 200 mounted men, again made a descent upon their towns, destroying several of their settlements about Chickamauga creek, and penetrating as far as the important town of Ustana'li, on the headwaters of Coosa river, near the present Calhoun, Georgia. This also he destroyed. Every warrior found was killed, together with a white man found in one of the towns, whose papers showed that he had been active in inciting the Indians to war. On the return the expedition halted at Echota, where new assurances were received from the friendly element.[4] In the meantime a Georgia expedition of over 400 men, under General Pickens, had been ravaging the Cherokee towns in the same quarter, with such effect that the Cherokee were forced to purchase peace by a further surrender of territory on the head of Broad river in Georgia.[5] This cession was concluded at a treaty of peace held with the Georgia commissioners at Augusta in the next year, and was confirmed later by the Creeks, who claimed an interest in the same lands, but was never accepted by either as the voluntary act of their tribe as a whole.[6]

By the preliminary treaty of Paris, November 30, 1782, the long Revolutionary struggle for independence was brought to a close, and the Cherokee, as well as the other tribes, seeing the hopelessness of con-

[1] Stevens, Georgia, II, pp. 282–285, 1859; Jones, Georgia, II, p. 503, 1883.

[2] Roosevelt, Winning of the West, II, p. 311, 1889.

[3] Old Tassel's talk, in Ramsey, Tennessee, p. 271, 1853, and in Roosevelt, op. cit., p. 315.

[4] Ramsey, op. cit., p. 272; Roosevelt, op. cit., p. 317 et passim.

[5] Stevens, op. cit., pp. 411–415.

[6] Royce, Cherokee Nation, in Fifth Ann. Rep. Bureau of Ethnology, p. 151, 1888.

tinuing the contest alone, began to sue for peace. By seven years of constant warfare they had been reduced to the lowest depth of misery, almost indeed to the verge of extinction. Over and over again their towns had been laid in ashes and their fields wasted. Their best warriors had been killed and their women and children had sickened and starved in the mountains. Their great war chief, Oconostota, who had led them to victory in 1780, was now a broken old man, and in this year, at Echota, formally resigned his office in favor of his son, The Terrapin. To complete their brimming cup of misery the smallpox again broke out among them in 1783.[1] Deprived of the assistance of their former white allies they were left to their own cruel fate, the last feeble resistance of the mountain warriors to the advancing tide of settlement came to an end with the burning of Cowee town,[2] and the way was left open to an arrangement. In the same year the North Carolina legislature appointed an agent for the Cherokee and made regulations for the government of traders among them.[3]

RELATIONS WITH THE UNITED STATES

FROM THE FIRST TREATY TO THE REMOVAL—1785–1838

Passing over several unsatisfactory and generally abortive negotiations conducted by the various state governments in 1783–84, including the treaty of Augusta already noted,[4] we come to the turning point in the history of the Cherokee, their first treaty with the new government of the United States for peace and boundary delimitation, concluded at Hopewell (25) in South Carolina on November 28, 1785. Nearly one thousand Cherokee attended, the commissioners for the United States being Colonel Benjamin Hawkins (26), of North Carolina; General Andrew Pickens, of South Carolina; Cherokee Agent Joseph Martin, of Tennessee, and Colonel Lachlan McIntosh, of Georgia. The instrument was signed by thirty-seven chiefs and principal men, representing nearly as many different towns. The negotiations occupied ten days, being complicated by a protest on the part of North Carolina and Georgia against the action of the government commissioners in confirming to the Indians some lands which had already been appropriated as bounty lands for state troops without the consent of the Cherokee. On the other hand the Cherokee complained that 3,000 white settlers were at that moment in occupancy of unceded land between the Holston and the French Broad. In spite of their protest these intruders were allowed to remain, although the territory was not acquired by treaty until some years later. As finally arranged the treaty left the Middle and Upper towns, and those in the vicinity

---

[1] See documents in Virginia State Papers, III, pp. 234, 398, 527, 1883.
[2] Ramsey, Tennessee, p. 280, 1853.   [3] Ibid., p. 276.
[4] See Royce, Cherokee Nation, op. cit., pp. 151, 152; Ramsey, op. cit., p. 299 et passim.

of Coosa river, undisturbed, while the whole country east of the Blue ridge, with the Watauga and Cumberland settlements, was given over to the whites.   The general boundary followed the dividing ridge between Cumberland river and the more southern waters of the Tennessee eastward to the junction of the two forks of Holston, near the present Kingsport, Tennessee, thence southward to the Blue ridge and southwestward to a point not far from the present Atlanta, Georgia, thence westward to the Coosa river and northwestward to a creek running into Tennessee river at the western line of Alabama, thence northward with the Tennessee river to the beginning.   The lands south and west of these lines were recognized as belonging to the Creeks and Chickasaw.   Hostilities were to cease and the Cherokee were taken under the protection of the United States.   The proceedings ended with the distribution of a few presents.[1]

While the Hopewell treaty defined the relations of the Cherokee to the general government and furnished a safe basis for future negotiation, it yet failed to bring complete peace and security.   Thousands of intruders were still settled on Indian lands, and minor aggressions and reprisals were continually occurring.   The Creeks and the northern tribes were still hostile and remained so for some years later, and their warriors, cooperating with those of the implacable Chickamauga towns, continued to annoy the exposed settlements, particularly on the Cumberland., The British had withdrawn from the South, but the Spaniards and French, who claimed the lower Mississippi and the Gulf region and had their trading posts in west Tennessee, took every opportunity to encourage the spirit of hostility to the Americans.[2] But the spirit of the Cherokee nation was broken and the Holston settlements were now too surely established to be destroyed.

The Cumberland settlements founded by Robertson and Donelson in the winter of 1779–80 had had but short respite.   Early in spring the Indians—Cherokee, Creeks, Chickasaw, and northern Indians—had begun a series of attacks with the design of driving these intruders from their lands, and thenceforth for years no man's life was safe outside the stockade.   The long list of settlers shot down at work or while hunting in the woods, of stock stolen and property destroyed, while of sorrowful interest to those most nearly concerned, is too tedious for recital here, and only leading events need be chronicled.   Detailed notice may be found in the works of local historians.

On the night of January 15, 1781, a band of Indians stealthily approached Freeland's station and had even succeeded in unfastening

[1] Indian Treaties, p. 8 et passim, 1837.   For a full discussion of the Hopewell treaty, from official documents, see Royce, Cherokee Nation, in Fifth Ann. Rep. Bureau of Ethnology, pp. 152–158, 1888, with map; Treaty Journal, etc., American State Papers; Indian Affairs, I, pp. 38–44, 1832; also Stevens, Georgia, II, pp. 417–429, 1859; Ramsey, Tennessee, pp. 336, 337, 1853; see also the map accompanying this work.
[2] Ramsey, op. cit., pp. 459–461; Agent Martin and Hopewell commissioners, ibid., pp. 318–336; Bledsoe and Robertson letter, ibid., p. 465; Roosevelt, Winning of the West, II, p. 368, 1899.

the strongly barred gate when Robertson, being awake inside, heard the noise and sprang up just in time to rouse the garrison and beat off the assailants, who continued to fire through the loopholes after they had been driven out of the fort. Only two Americans were killed, although the escape was a narrow one.[1]

About three months later, on April 2, a large body of Cherokee approached the fort at Nashville (then called Nashborough, or simply "the Bluff"), and by sending a decoy ahead succeeded in drawing a large part of the garrison into an ambush. It seemed that they would be cut off, as the Indians were between them and the fort, when those inside loosed the dogs, which rushed so furiously upon the Indians that the latter found work enough to defend themselves, and were finally forced to retire, carrying with them, however, five American scalps.[2]

The attacks continued throughout this and the next year to such an extent that it seemed at one time as if the Cumberland settlements must be abandoned, but in June, 1783, commissioners from Virginia and North Carolina arranged a treaty near Nashville (Nashborough) with chiefs of the Chickasaw, Cherokee, and Creeks. This treaty, although it did not completely stop the Indian inroads, at least greatly diminished them. Thereafter the Chickasaw remained friendly, and only the Cherokee and Creeks continued to make trouble.[3]

The valley towns on Hiwassee, as well as those of Chickamauga, seem to have continued hostile. In 1786 a large body of their warriors, led by the mixed-blood chief, John Watts, raided the new settlements in the vicinity of the present Knoxville, Tennessee. In retaliation Sevier again marched his volunteers across the mountain to the valley towns and destroyed three of them, killing a number of warriors; but he retired on learning that the Indians were gathering to give him battle.[4] In the spring of this year Agent Martin, stationed at Echota, had made a tour of inspection of the Cherokee towns and reported that they were generally friendly and anxious for peace, with the exception of the Chickamauga band, under Dragging-canoe, who, acting with the hostile Creeks and encouraged by the French and Spaniards, were making preparations to destroy the Cumberland settlements. Notwithstanding the friendly professions of the others, a party sent out to obtain satisfaction for the murder of four Cherokee by the Tennesseeans had come back with fifteen white scalps, and sent word to Sevier that they wanted peace, but if the whites wanted war they would get it.[5] With lawless men on both sides it is evident that peace was in jeopardy. In August, in consequence of further killing and reprisals, commissioners of the new "state of Franklin," as Tennessee was now

[1] Roosevelt, Winning of the West, II, p. 353, 1889.
[2] Ibid., p. 355, 1889; Ramsey, Tennessee, pp. 452–454, 1853.
[3] Ibid., pp. 358–366, 1889.   [4] Ibid., p. 341, 1853.
[5] Martin letter of May 11, 1786, ibid., p. 342.

called, concluded a negotiation, locally known as the "treaty of Coyatee," with the chiefs of the Overhill towns. In spite of references to peace, love, and brotherly friendship, it is very doubtful if the era of good will was in any wise hastened by the so-called treaty, as the Tennesseeans, who had just burned another Indian town in reprisal for the killing of a white man, announced, without mincing words, that they had been given by North Carolina—against which state, by the way, they were then in organized rebellion—the whole country north of the Tennessee river as far west as the Cumberland mountain, and that they intended to take it "by the sword, which is the best right to all countries." As the whole of this country was within the limits of the territory solemnly guaranteed to the Cherokee by the Hopewell treaty only the year before, the chiefs simply replied that Congress had said nothing to them on the subject, and so the matter rested.[1] The theory of state's rights was too complicated for the Indian understanding.

While this conflict between state and federal authority continued, with the Cherokee lands as the prize, there could be no peace. In March, 1787, a letter from Echota, apparently written by Agent Martin, speaks of a recent expedition against the Cherokee towns, and the confusion and alarm among them in consequence of the daily encroachments of the "Franklinites" or Tennesseeans, who had proceeded to make good their promise by opening a land office for the sale of all the lands southward to Tennessee river, including even a part of the beloved town of Echota. At the same time messengers were coming to the Cherokee from traders in the foreign interest, telling them that England, France, and Spain had combined against the Americans and urging them with promises of guns and ammunition to join in the war.[2] As a result each further advance of the Tennessee settlements, in defiance as it was of any recognized treaty, was stubbornly contested by the Indian owners of the land. The record of these encounters, extending over a period of several years, is too tedious for recital. "Could a diagram be drawn, accurately designating every spot signalized by an Indian massacre, surprise, or depredation, or courageous attack, defense, pursuit, or victory by the whites, or station or fort or battlefield, or personal encounter, the whole of that section of country would be studded over with delineations of such incidents. Every spring, every ford, every path, every farm, every trail, every house nearly, in its first settlement, was once the scene of danger, exposure, attack, exploit, achievement, death."[3] The end was the winning of Tennessee.

In the meantime the inroads of the Creeks and their Chickamauga

---

[1] Reports of Tennessee commissioners and replies by Cherokee chiefs, etc., 1786, in Ramsey, Tennessee, pp. 343–346, 1853.
[2] Martin (?) letter of March 25, 1787, ibid., p. 359.
[3] Ibid., p. 370.

allies upon the Georgia frontier and the Cumberland settlements around Nashville became so threatening that measures were taken for a joint campaign by the combined forces of Georgia and Tennessee ("Franklin"). The enterprise came to naught through the interference of the federal authorities.[1] All through the year 1788 we hear of attacks and reprisals along the Tennessee border, although the agent for the Cherokee declared in his official report that, with the exception of the Chickamauga band, the Indians wished to be at peace if the whites would let them. In March two expeditions under Sevier and Kennedy set out against the towns in the direction of the French Broad. In May several persons of a family named Kirk were murdered a few miles south of Knoxville. In retaliation Sevier raised a large party and marching against a town on Hiwassee river— one of those which had been destroyed some years before and rebuilt— and burned it, killing a number of the inhabitants in the river while they were trying to escape. He then turned, and proceeding to the towns on Little Tennessee burned several of them also, killing a number of Indians. Here a small party of Indians, including Abraham and Tassel, two well-known friendly chiefs, was brutally massacred by one of the Kirks, no one interfering, after they had voluntarily come in on request of one of the officers. This occurred during the temporary absence of Sevier. Another expedition under Captain Fayne was drawn into an ambuscade at Citico town and lost several in killed and wounded. The Indians pursued the survivors almost to Knoxville, attacking a small station near the present Maryville by the way. They were driven off by Sevier and others, who in turn invaded the Indian settlements, crossing the mountains and penetrating as far as the valley towns on Hiwassee, hastily retiring as they found the Indians gathering in their front.[2] In the same summer another expedition was organized against the Chickamauga towns. The chief command was given to General Martin, who left White's fort, now Knoxville, with four hundred and fifty men and made a rapid march to the neighborhood of the present Chattanooga, where the main force encamped on the site of an old Indian settlement. A detachment sent ahead to surprise a town a few miles farther down the river was fired upon and driven back, and a general engagement took place in the narrow pass between the bluff and the river, with such disastrous results that three captains were killed and the men so badly demoralized that they refused to advance. Martin was compelled to turn back, after burying the dead officers in a large townhouse, which was then burned down to conceal the grave.[3]

In October a large party of Cherokee and Creeks attacked Gillespie's station, south of the present Knoxville. The small garrison was

---

[1] Ramsey, Tennessee, pp. 393–399, 1853.   [2] Ibid., pp. 417–423, 1853.
[3] Ibid., pp. 517–519, and Brown's narrative, ibid., p. 515.

overpowered after a short resistance, and twenty-eight persons, including several women and children, were killed. The Indians left behind a letter signed by four chiefs, including John Watts, expressing regret for what they called the accidental killing of the women and children, reminding the whites of their own treachery in killing Abraham and the Tassel, and defiantly concluding, "When you move off the land, then we will make peace." Other exposed stations were attacked, until at last Sevier again mustered a force, cleared the enemy from the frontier, and pursued the Indians as far as their towns on the head waters of Coosa river, in such vigorous fashion that they were compelled to ask for terms of peace and agree to a surrender of prisoners, which was accomplished at Coosawatee town, in upper Georgia, in the following April.[1]

Among the captives thus restored to their friends were Joseph Brown, a boy of sixteen, with his two younger sisters, who, with several others, had been taken at Nickajack town while descending the Tennessee in a flatboat nearly a year before. His father and the other men of the party, about ten in all, had been killed at the time, while the mother and several other children were carried to various Indian towns, some of them going to the Creeks, who had aided the Cherokee in the capture. Young Brown, whose short and simple narrative is of vivid interest, was at first condemned to death, but was rescued by a white man living in the town and was afterward adopted into the family of the chief, in spite of the warning of an old Indian woman that if allowed to live he would one day guide an army to destroy them. The warning was strangely prophetic, for it was Brown himself who guided the expedition that finally rooted out the Chickamauga towns a few years later. When rescued at Coosawatee he was in Indian costume, with shirt, breechcloth, scalp lock, and holes bored in his ears. His little sister, five years old, had become so attached to the Indian woman who had adopted her, that she refused to go to her own mother and had to be pulled along by force.[2] The mother and another of the daughters, who had been taken by the Creeks, were afterwards ransomed by McGillivray, head chief of the Creek Nation, who restored them to their friends, generously refusing any compensation for his kindness.

An arrangement had been made with the Chickasaw, in 1783, by which they surrendered to the Cumberland settlement their own claim to the lands from the Cumberland river south to the dividing ridge of Duck river.[3] It was not, however, until the treaty of Hopewell, two years later, that the Cherokee surrendered their claim to the same region, and even then the Chickamauga warriors, with their allies, the

[1] Ramsey, Tennessee, pp. 515, 519.
[2] Brown's narrative, etc., ibid., pp. 508–516.
[3] Ibid., pp. 459, 489.

hostile Creeks and Shawano, refused to acknowledge the cession and continued their attacks, with the avowed purpose of destroying the new settlements. Until the final running of the boundary line, in 1797, Spain claimed all the territory west of the mountains and south of Cumberland river, and her agents were accused of stirring up the indians against the Americans, even to the extent of offering rewards for American scalps.[1] One of these raiding parties, which had killed the brother of Captain Robertson, was tracked to Coldwater, a small mixed town of Cherokee and Creeks, on the south side of Tennessee river, about the present Tuscumbia, Alabama. Robertson determined to destroy it, and taking a force of volunteers, with a couple of Chickasaw guides, crossed the Tennessee without being discovered and surprised and burnt the town. The Indians, who numbered less than fifty men, attempted to escape to the river, but were surrounded and over twenty of them killed, with a loss of but one man to the Tennesseeans. In the town were found also several French traders. Three of these, who refused to surrender, were killed, together with a white woman who was accidentally shot in one of the boats. The others were afterward released, their large stock of trading goods having been taken and sold for the benefit of the troops. The affair took place about the end of June, 1787. Through this action, and an effort made by Robertson about the same time to come to an understanding with the Chickamauga band, there was a temporary cessation of hostile inroads upon the Cumberland, but long before the end of the year the attacks were renewed to such an extent that it was found necessary to keep out a force of rangers with orders to scour the country and kill every Indian found east of the Chickasaw boundary.[2]

The Creeks seeming now to be nearly as much concerned in these raids as the Cherokee, a remonstrance was addressed to McGillivray, their principal chief, who replied that, although the Creeks, like the other southern tribes, had adhered to the British interest during the Revolution, they had accepted proposals of friendship, but while negotiations were pending six of their people had been killed in the affair at Coldwater, which had led to a renewal of hostile feeling. He promised, however, to use his best efforts to bring about peace, and seems to have kept his word, although the raids continued through this and the next year, with the usual sequel of pursuit and reprisal. In one of these skirmishes a company under Captain Murray followed some Indian raiders from near Nashville to their camp on Tennessee river and succeeded in killing the whole party of eleven warriors.[3] A treaty of peace was signed with the Creeks in 1790, but, owing to the intrigues of the Spaniards, it had little practical effect,[4] and not

---

[1] Bledsoe and Robertson letter of June 12, 1787, in Ramsey, Tennessee, p. 465, 1853.
[2] Ibid., with Robertson letter, pp. 465–476.
[3] Ibid., pp. 479–486.
[4] Monette, Valley of the Mississippi, I, p. 505, 1846.

until Wayne's decisive victory over the confederated northern tribes
in 1794 and the final destruction of the Nickajack towns in the same
year did real peace came to the frontier.

By deed of cession of February 25, 1790, Tennessee ceased to be a
part of North Carolina and was organized under federal laws as "The
Territory of the United States south of the Ohio river," preliminary
to taking full rank as a state six years later.   William Blount (27)
was appointed first territorial governor and also superintendent for the
southern Indians, with a deputy resident with each of the four principal tribes.[1]   Pensacola, Mobile, St. Louis, and other southern posts
were still held by the Spaniards, who claimed the whole country south
of the Cumberland, while the British garrisons had not yet been withdrawn from the north.   The resentment of the Indians at the occupancy
of their reserved and guaranteed lands by the whites was sedulously
encouraged from both quarters, and raids along the Tennessee frontier were of common occurrence.   At this time, according to the
official report of President Washington, over five hundred families of
intruders were settled upon lands belonging rightly to the Cherokee,
in addition to those between the French Broad and the Holston.[2]
More than a year before the Secretary of War had stated that "the
disgraceful violation of the treaty of Hopewell with the Cherokee
requires the serious consideration of Congress.   If so direct and manifest contempt of the authority of the United States be suffered with
impunity, it will be in vain to attempt to extend the arm of government to the frontiers.   The Indian tribes can have no faith in such
imbecile promises, and the lawless whites will ridicule a government
which shall on paper only make Indian treaties and regulate Indian
boundaries."[3]   To prevent any increase of the dissatisfaction, the
general government issued a proclamation forbidding any further
encroachment upon the Indian lands on Tennessee river; notwithstanding which, early in 1791, a party of men descended the river in
boats, and, landing on an island at the Muscle shoals, near the present
Tuscumbia, Alabama, erected a blockhouse and other defensive works.
Immediately afterward the Cherokee chief, Glass, with about sixty
warriors, appeared and quietly informed them that if they did not at
once withdraw he would kill them.   After some parley the intruders
retired to their boats, when the Indians set fire to the buildings and
reduced them to ashes.[4]

To forestall more serious difficulty it was necessary to negotiate a
new treaty with a view to purchasing the disputed territory.   Accordingly, through the efforts of Governor Blount, a convention was held
with the principal men of the Cherokee at White's fort, now Knox-

1 Ramsey, Tennessee, pp. 522, 541, 561, 1853.
2 Washington to the Senate, August 11, 1790, American State Papers: Indian Affairs, I, p. 83, 1832.
3 Secretary Knox to President Washington, July 7, 1789, ibid., p. 53.
4 Ramsey, op. cit., pp. 550, 551.

ville, Tennessee, in the summer of 1791. With much difficulty the Cherokee were finally brought to consent to a cession of a triangular section in Tennessee and North Carolina extending from Clinch river almost to the Blue ridge, and including nearly the whole of the French Broad and the lower Holston, with the sites of the present Knoxville, Greenville, and Asheville. The whole of this area, with a considerable territory adjacent, was already fully occupied by the whites. Permission was also given for a road from the eastern settlements to those on the Cumberland, with the free navigation of Tennessee river. Prisoners on both sides were to be restored and perpetual peace was guaranteed. In consideration of the lands surrendered the Cherokee were to receive an annuity of one thousand dollars with some extra goods and some assistance on the road to civilization. A treaty was signed by forty-one principal men of the tribe and was concluded July 2, 1791. It is officially described as being held "on the bank of the Holston, near the mouth of the French Broad," and is commonly spoken of as the "treaty of Holston."

The Cherokee, however, were dissatisfied with the arrangement, and before the end of the year a delegation of six principal chiefs appeared at Philadelphia, then the seat of government, without any previous announcement of their coming, declaring that when they had been summoned by Governor Blount to a conference they were not aware that it was to persuade them to sell lands; that they had resisted the proposition for days, and only yielded when compelled by the persistent and threatening demands of the governor; that the consideration was entirely too small; and that they had no faith that the whites would respect the new boundary, as they were in fact already settling beyond it. Finally, as the treaty had been signed, they asked that these intruders be removed. As their presentation of the case seemed a just one and it was desirable that they should carry home with them a favorable impression of the government's attitude toward them, a supplementary article was added, increasing the annuity to eight thousand five hundred dollars. On account of renewed Indian hostilities in Ohio valley and the desire of the government to keep the good will of the Cherokee long enough to obtain their help against the northern tribes, the new line was not surveyed until 1797.[1]

As illustrating Indian custom it may be noted that one of the principal signers of the original treaty was among the protesting delegates, but having in the meantime changed his name, it appears on the supplementary paragraph as "Iskagua, or Clear Sky, formerly Nenetooyah, or Bloody Fellow."[2] As he had been one of the prin-

[1] Indian Treaties, pp. 34–38, 1837; Secretary of War, report, January 5, 1798, in American State Papers, I, pp. 628–631, 1832; Ramsey, Tennessee, pp. 554–560, 1853; Royce, Cherokee Nation, Fifth Ann. Rep. Bureau of Ethnology, pp. 158–170. with full discussion and map, 1888.
[2] Indian Treaties, pp. 37, 38, 1837.

cipal raiders on the Tennessee frontier, the new name may have been symbolic of his change of heart at the prospect of a return of peace.

The treaty seems to have had little effect in preventing Indian hostilities, probably because the intruders still remained upon the Indian lands, and raiding still continued. The Creeks were known to be responsible for some of the mischief, and the hostile Chickamaugas were supposed to be the chief authors of the rest.[1] Even while the Cherokee delegates were negotiating the treaty in Philadelphia a boat which had accidentally run aground on the Muscle shoals was attacked by a party of Indians under the pretense of offering assistance, one man being killed and another severely wounded with a hatchet.[2]

While these negotiations had been pending at Philadelphia a young man named Leonard D. Shaw, a student at Princeton college, had expressed to the Secretary of War an earnest desire for a commission which would enable him to accompany the returning Cherokee delegates to their southern home, there to study Indian life and characteristics. As the purpose seemed a useful one, and he appeared well qualified for such a work, he was accordingly commissioned as deputy agent to reside among the Cherokee to observe and report upon their movements, to aid in the annuity distributions, and to render other assistance to Governor Blount, superintendent for the southern tribes, to study their language and home life, and to collect materials for an Indian history. An extract from the official instructions under which this first United States ethnologist began his work will be of interest. After defining his executive duties in connection with the annuity distributions, the keeping of accounts and the compiling of official reports, Secretary Knox continues—

A due performance of your duty will probably require the exercise of all your patience and fortitude and all your knowledge of the human character. The school will be a severe but interesting one. If you should succeed in acquiring the affections and a knowledge of the characters of the southern Indians, you may be at once useful to the United States and advance your own interest.

You will endeavor to learn their languages; this is essential to your communications. You will collect materials for a history of all the southern tribes and all things thereunto belonging. You will endeavor to ascertain their respective limits, make a vocabulary of their respective languages, teach them agriculture and such useful arts as you may know or can acquire. You will correspond regularly with Governor Blount, who is superintendent for Indian affairs, and inform him of all occurrences. You will also cultivate a correspondence with Brigadier-General McGillivray [the Creek chief], and you will also keep a journal of your proceedings and transmit them to the War Office. . . . You are to exhibit to Governor Blount the Cherokee book and all the writings therein, the messages to the several tribes of Indians, and these instructions.

Your route will be hence to Reading; thence Harris's ferry [Harrisburg, Pennsylvania] to Carlisle; to ——— ferry on the Potomac; to Winchester; to Staunton; to

[1] Ramsey, Tennessee, p. 557, 1853.
[2] Abel deposition, April 16, 1792, American State Papers: Indian Affairs, I, p. 274, 1832.

———, and to Holston. I should hope that you would travel upwards of twenty miles each day, and that you would reach Holston in about thirty days.[1]

The journey, which seemed then so long, was to be made by wagons from Philadelphia to the head of navigation on Holston river, thence by boats to the Cherokee towns. Shaw seems to have taken up his residence at Ustanali, which had superseded Echota as the Cherokee capital. We hear of him as present at a council there in June of the same year, with no evidence of unfriendliness at his presence.[2] The friendly feeling was of short continuance, however, for a few months later we find him writing from Ustanali to Governor Blount that on account of the aggressive hostility of the Creeks, whose avowed intention was to kill every white man they met, he was not safe 50 yards from the house. Soon afterwards the Chickamauga towns again declared war, on which account, together with renewed threats by the Creeks, he was advised by the Cherokee to leave Ustanali, which he did early in September, 1792, proceeding to the home of General Pickens, near Seneca, South Carolina, escorted by a guard of friendly Cherokee. In the following winter he was dismissed from the service on serious charges, and his mission appears to have been a failure.[3]

To prevent an alliance of the Cherokee, Creeks, and other southern Indians with the confederated hostile northern tribes, the government had endeavored to persuade the former to furnish a contingent of warriors to act with the army against the northern Indians, and special instruction had been given to Shaw to use his efforts for this result. Nothing, however, came of the attempt. St Clair's defeat turned the scale against the United States, and in September, 1792, the Chickamauga towns formally declared war.[4]

In November of this year the governor of Georgia officially reported that a party of lawless Georgians had gone into the Cherokee Nation, and had there burned a town and barbarously killed three Indians, while about the same time two other Cherokee had been killed within the settlements. Fearing retaliation, he ordered out a patrol of troops to guard the frontier in that direction, and sent a conciliatory letter to the chiefs, expressing his regret for what had happened. No answer was returned to the message, but a few days later an entire family was found murdered—four women, three children, and a young man—all scalped and mangled and with arrows sticking in the bodies, while, according to old Indian war custom, two war clubs were left upon

---

[1] Henry Knox, Secretary of War, Instructions to Leonard Shaw, temporary agent to the Cherokee Nation of Indians, February 17, 1792, in American State Papers: Indian Affairs, I, 247, 1832; also Knox, letters to Governor Blount, January 31 and February 16, 1792, ibid., pp. 245, 246.

[2] Estanaula conference report, June 26, 1792, ibid., p. 271; Deraque, deposition, September 15, 1792, ibid., p. 292; Pickens, letter, September 12, 1792, ibid., p. 317.

[3] See letters of Shaw, Casey, Pickens, and Blount, 1792-93, ibid., pp. 277, 278, 317, 436, 437, 440.

[4] Knox, instructions to Shaw, February 17, 1792, ibid., p. 247; Blount, letter, March 20, 1792, ibid., p. 263; Knox, letters, October 9, 1792, ibid., pp. 261, 262.

the ground to show by whom the deed was done.   So swift was savage vengeance.[1]

Early in 1792 a messenger who had been sent on business for Governor Blount to the Chickamauga towns returned with the report that a party had just come in with prisoners and some fresh scalps, over which the chiefs and warriors of two towns were then dancing; that the Shawano were urging the Cherokee to join them against the Americans; that a strong body of Creeks was on its way against the Cumberland settlements, and that the Creek chief, McGillivray, was trying to form a general confederacy of all the Indian tribes against the whites.   To understand this properly it must be remembered that at this time all the tribes northwest of the Ohio and as far as the heads of the Mississippi were banded together in a grand alliance, headed by the warlike Shawano, for the purpose of holding the Ohio river as the Indian boundary against the advancing tide of white settlement. They had just cut to pieces one of the finest armies ever sent into the West, under the veteran General St Clair (28), and it seemed for the moment as if the American advance would be driven back behind the Alleghenies.

In the emergency the Secretary of War directed Governor Blount to hold a conference with the chiefs of the Chickasaw, Choctaw, and Cherokee at Nashville in June to enlist their warriors, if possible, in active service against the northern tribes.   The conference was held as proposed, in August, but nothing seems to have come of it, although the chiefs seemed to be sincere in their assurances of friendship. Very few of the Choctaw or Cherokee were in attendance.   At the annuity distribution of the Cherokee, shortly before, the chiefs had also been profuse in declarations of their desire for peace.[2]   Notwithstanding all this the attacks along the Tennessee frontier continued to such an extent that the blockhouses were again put in order and garrisoned.   Soon afterwards the governor reported to the Secretary of War that the five lower Cherokee towns on the Tennessee (the Chickamauga), headed by John Watts, had finally declared war against the United States, and that from three to six hundred warriors, including a hundred Creeks, had started against the settlements.   The militia was at once called out, both in eastern Tennessee and on the Cumberland.   On the Cumberland side it was directed that no pursuit should be continued beyond the Cherokee boundary, the ridge between the waters of Cumberland and Duck rivers.   The order issued by Colonel White, of Knox county, to each of his captains shows how great was the alarm:

---

[1] Governor Telfair's letters of November 14 and December 5, with inclosure, 1792, American State Papers: Indian Affairs, I, pp. 332, 336, 337, 1832.

[2] Ramsey, Tennessee, pp. 562–563, 598, 1853.

KNOXVILLE, *September 11, 1792.*

SIR: You are hereby commanded to repair with your company to Knoxville, equipped, to protect the frontiers; there is imminent danger. Bring with you two days' provisions, if possible; but you are not to delay an hour on that head.

I am, sir, yours,

JAMES WHITE.[1]

About midnight on the 30th of September, 1792, the Indian force, consisting of several hundred Chickamaugas and other Cherokee, Creeks, and Shawano, attacked Buchanan's station, a few miles south of Nashville. Although numbers of families had collected inside the stockade for safety, there were less than twenty able-bodied men among them. The approach of the enemy alarmed the cattle, by which the garrison had warning just in time to close the gate when the Indians were already within a few yards of the entrance. The assault was furious and determined, the Indians rushing up to the stockade, attempting to set fire to it, and aiming their guns through the port holes. One Indian succeeded in climbing upon the roof with a lighted torch, but was shot and fell to the ground, holding his torch against the logs as he drew his last breath. It was learned afterward that he was a half blood, the stepson of the old white trader who had once rescued the boy Joseph Brown at Nickajack. He was a desperate warrior and when only twenty-two years of age had already taken six white scalps. The attack was repulsed at every point, and the assailants finally drew off, with considerable loss, carrying their dead and wounded with them, and leaving a number of hatchets, pipes, and other spoils upon the ground. Among the wounded was the chief John Watts. Not one of those in the fort was injured. It has been well said that the defense of Buchanan's station by such a handful of men against an attacking force estimated all the way at from three to seven hundred Indians is a feat of bravery which has scarcely been surpassed in the annals of border warfare. The effect upon the Indians must have been thoroughly disheartening.[2]

In the same month arrangements were made for protecting the frontier along the French Broad by means of a series of garrisoned blockhouses, with scouts to patrol regularly from one to another, North Carolina cooperating on her side of the line. The hostile inroads still continued in this section, the Creeks acting with the hostile Cherokee. One raiding party of Creeks having been traced toward Chilhowee town on Little Tennessee, the whites were about to burn that and a neighboring Cherokee town when Sevier interposed and prevented.[3] There is no reason to suppose that the people of these towns were directly concerned in the depredations along the frontier at this period,

---

[1] Ramsey, Tennessee, pp. 562–565, 1853.

[2] Blount, letter, October 2, 1792, in American State Papers: Indian Affairs, I, p. 294, 1832; Blount, letter, etc., in Ramsey, op. cit., pp. 566, 567, 599–601; see also Brown's narrative, ibid., 511, 512; Royce, Cherokee Nation, Fifth Ann. Rep. Bureau of Ethnology, p. 170, 1888.

[3] Ramsey, op. cit., 569–571.

the mischief being done by those farther to the south, in conjunction with the Creeks.

Toward the close of this year, 1792, Captain Samuel Handley, while leading a small party of men to reenforce the Cumberland settlement, was attacked by a mixed force of Cherokee, Creeks, and Shawano, near the Crab Orchard, west of the present Kingston, Tennessee. Becoming separated from his men he encountered a warrior who had lifted his hatchet to strike when Handley seized the weapon, crying out "Canaly" (for *higina'lii*), "friend," to which the Cherokee responded with the same word, at once lowering his arm. Handley was carried to Willstown, in Alabama, where he was adopted into the Wolf clan (29) and remained until 'the next spring. After having made use of his services in writing a peace letter to Governor Blount the Cherokee finally sent him home in safety to his friends under a protecting escort of eight warriors, without any demand for ransom. He afterward resided near Tellico blockhouse, near Loudon, where, after the wars were over, his Indian friends frequently came to visit and stop with him.[1]

The year 1793 began with a series of attacks all along the Tennessee frontier. As before, most of the depredation was by Chickamaugas and Creeks, with some stray Shawano from the north. The Cherokee from the towns on Little Tennessee remained peaceable, but their temper was sorely tried by a regrettable circumstance which occurred in June. While a number of friendly chiefs were assembled for a conference at Echota, on the express request of the President, a party of men under command of a Captain John Beard suddenly attacked them, killing about fifteen Indians, including several chiefs and two women, one of them being the wife of Hanging-maw (Ushwâ'li-gûtă), principal chief of the Nation, who was himself wounded. The murderers then fled, leaving others to suffer the consequences. Two hundred warriors at once took up arms to revenge their loss, and only the most earnest appeal from the deputy governor could restrain them from swift retaliation. While the chief, whose wife was thus murdered and himself wounded, forebore to revenge himself, in order not to bring war upon his people, the Secretary of War was obliged to report, "to my great pain, I find to punish Beard by law just now is out of the question." Beard was in fact arrested, but the trial was a farce and he was acquitted.[2]

Believing that the Cherokee Nation, with the exception of the Chickamaugas, was honestly trying to preserve peace, the territorial government, while making provision for the safety of the exposed settlements, had strictly prohibited any invasion of the Indian country. The frontier people were of a different opinion, and in spite of the prohibition a company of nearly two hundred mounted men under

[1] Ramsey, Tennessee, pp. 571–573, 1853.   [2] Ibid., pp. 574–578, 1853.

Colonels Doherty and McFarland crossed over the mountains in the summer of this year and destroyed six of the middle towns, returning with fifteen scalps and as many prisoners.[1]

Late in September a strong force estimated at one thousand warriors—seven hundred Creeks and three hundred Cherokee—under John Watts and Doublehead, crossed the Tennessee and advanced in the direction of Knoxville, where the public stores were then deposited. In their eagerness to reach Knoxville they passed quietly by one or two smaller settlements until within a short distance of the town, when, at daybreak of the 25th, they heard the garrison fire the sunrise gun and imagined that they were discovered. Differences had already broken out among the leaders, and without venturing to advance farther they contented themselves with an attack upon a small blockhouse a few miles to the west, known as Cavitts station, in which at the time were only three men with thirteen women and children. After defending themselves bravely for some time these surrendered on promise that they should be held for exchange, but as soon as they came out Doublehead's warriors fell upon them and put them all to death with the exception of a boy, who was saved by John Watts. This bloody deed was entirely the work of Doublehead, the other chiefs having done their best to prevent it.[2]

A force of seven hundred men under General Sevier was at once put upon their track, with orders this time to push the pursuit into the heart of the Indian nation. Crossing Little Tennessee and Hiwassee they penetrated to Ustanali town, near the present Calhoun, Georgia. Finding it deserted, although well filled with provision, they rested there a few days, the Indians in the meantime attempting a night attack without success. After burning the town, Sevier continued down the river to Etowah town, near the present site of Rome. Here the Indians—Cherokee and Creeks—had dug intrenchments and prepared to make a stand, but, being, outflanked, were defeated with loss and compelled to retreat. This town, with several others in the neighborhood belonging to both Cherokee and Creeks, was destroyed, with all the provision of the Indians, including three hundred cattle, after which the army took up the homeward march. The Americans had lost but three men. This was the last military service of Sevier.[3]

During the absence of Sevier's force in the south the Indians made a sudden inroad on the French Broad, near the present Dandridge, killing and scalping a woman and a boy. While their friends were accompanying the remains to a neighboring burial ground for interment, two men who had incautiously gone ahead were fired upon. One

[1] Ramsey, Tennessee, p. 579.

[2] Ibid., pp. 580–583, 1853; Smith, letter, September 27, 1793, American State Papers: Indian Affairs, I, p. 468, 1832. Ramsey gives the Indian force 1,000 warriors; Smith says that in many places they marched in files of 28 abreast, each file being supposed to number 40 men.

[3] Ramsey, op. cit., pp. 584–588.

of them escaped, but the other one was found killed and scalped when the rest of the company came up, and was buried with the first victims. Sevier's success brought temporary respite to the Cumberland settlements. During the early part of the year the Indian attacks by small raiding parties had been so frequent and annoying that a force of men had been kept out on patrol service under officers who adopted with some success the policy of hunting the Indians in their camping places in the thickets, rather than waiting for them to come into the settlements.[1]

In February, 1794, the Territorial assembly of Tennessee met at Knoxville and, among other business transacted, addressed a strong memorial to Congress calling for more efficient protection for the frontier and demanding a declaration of war against the Creeks and Cherokee. The memorial states that since the treaty of Holston (July, 1791), these two tribes had killed in a most barbarous and inhuman manner more than two hundred citizens of Tennessee, of both sexes, had carried others into captivity, destroyed their stock, burned their houses, and laid waste their plantations, had robbed the citizens of their slaves and stolen at least two thousand horses. Special attention was directed to the two great invasions in September, 1792, and September, 1793, and the memorialists declare that there was scarcely a man of the assembly but could tell of "a dear wife or child, an aged parent or near relation, besides friends, massacred by the hands of these bloodthirsty nations in their house or fields."[2]

In the meantime the raids continued and every scattered cabin was a target for attack. In April a party of twenty warriors surrounded the house of a man named Casteel on the French Broad about nine miles above Knoxville and massacred father, mother, and four children in most brutal fashion. One child only was left alive, a girl of ten years, who was found scalped and bleeding from six tomahawk gashes, yet survived. The others were buried in one grave. The massacre roused such a storm of excitement that it required all the effort of the governor and the local officials to prevent an invasion in force of the Indian country. It was learned that Doublehead, of the Chickamauga towns, was trying to get the support of the valley towns, which, however, continued to maintain an attitude of peace. The friendly Cherokee also declared that the Spaniards were constantly instigating the lower towns to hostilities, although John Watts, one of their principal chiefs, advocated peace.[3]

In June a boat under command of William Scott, laden with pots, hardware, and other property, and containing six white men, three women, four children, and twenty negroes, left Knoxville to descend

---

[1] Ramsey, Tennessee, pp. 590, 602–605, 1853.

[2] Haywood, Civil and Political History of Tennessee, pp. 300–302; Knoxville, 1823.

[3] Ibid., pp. 303–308, 1823; Ramsey, op. cit., pp. 591–594. Haywood's history of this period is little more han a continuous record of killings and petty encounters.

Tennessee river to Natchez. As it passed the Chickamauga towns it was fired upon from Running Water and Long island without damage. The whites returned the fire, wounding two Indians. A large party of Cherokee, headed by White-man-killer (Une'ga-dihǐ'), then started in pursuit of the boat, which they overtook at Muscle shoals, where they killed all the white people in it, made prisoners of the negroes, and plundered the goods. Three Indians were killed and one was wounded in the action.[1] It is said that the Indian actors in this massacre fled across the Mississippi into Spanish territory and became the nucleus of the Cherokee Nation of the West, as will be noted elsewhere.

On June 26, 1794, another treaty, intended to be supplementary to that of Holston in 1791, was negotiated at Philadelphia, being signed by the Secretary of War and by thirteen principal men of the Cherokee. An arrangement was made for the proper marking of the boundary then established, and the annuity was increased to five thousand dollars, with a proviso that fifty dollars were to be deducted for every horse stolen by the Cherokee and not restored within three months.[2]

In July a man named John Ish was shot down while plowing in his field eighteen miles below Knoxville. By order of Hanging-maw, the friendly chief of Echota, a party of Cherokee took the trail and captured the murderer, who proved to be a Creek, whom they brought in to the agent at Tellico blockhouse, where he was formally tried and hanged. When asked the usual question he said that his people were at war with the whites, that he had left home to kill or be killed, that he had killed the white man and would have escaped but for the Cherokee, and that there were enough of his nation to avenge his death. A few days later a party of one hundred Creek warriors crossed Tennessee river against the settlements. The alarm was given by Hanging-maw, and fifty-three Cherokee with a few federal troops started in pursuit. On the 10th of August they came up with the Creeks, killing one and wounding another, one Cherokee being slightly wounded. The Creeks retreated and the victors returned to the Cherokee towns, where their return was announced by the death song and the firing of guns. "The night was spent in dancing the scalp dance, according to the custom of warriors after a victory over their enemies, in which the white and red people heartily joined. The Upper Cherokee had now stepped too far to go back, and their professions of friendship were now no longer to be questioned." In the same month there was an engagement between a detachment of about

---

[1] Haywood, Civil and Political History of Tennessee, p. 308, 1823; Ramsey, Tennessee, p. 594. 1853; see also memorial in Putnam, Middle Tennessee, p. 502, 1859. Haywood calls the leader Unacala, which should be Une'ga-dihǐ', "White-man-killer." Compare Haywood's statement with that of Washburn, on page 100.

[2] Indian Treaties, pp. 39, 40, 1837; Royce, Cherokee Nation, Fifth Ann. Rep. Bureau of Ethnology, pp. 171, 172, 1888; Documents of 1797–98, American State Papers: Indian Affairs, I, pp. 628–631, 1832. The treaty is not mentioned by the Tennessee historians.

forty soldiers and a large body of Creeks near Crab Orchard, in which several of each were killed.[1] It is evident that much of the damage on both sides of the Cumberland range was due to the Creeks.

In the meantime Governor Blount was trying to negotiate peace with the whole Cherokee Nation, but with little success. The Cherokee claimed to be anxious for permanent peace, but said that it was impossible to restore the property taken by them, as it had been taken in war, and they had themselves been equal losers from the whites. They said also that they could not prevent the hostile Creeks from passing through their territory. About the end of July it was learned that a strong body of Creeks had started north against the settlements. The militia was at once ordered out along the Tennessee frontier, and the friendly Cherokees offered their services, while measures were taken to protect their women and children from the enemy. The Creeks advanced as far as Willstown, when the news came of the complete defeat of the confederated northern tribes by General Wayne (30), and fearing the same fate for themselves, they turned back and scattered to their towns.[2]

The Tennesseeans, especially those on the Cumberland, had long ago come to the conclusion that peace could be brought about only through the destruction of the Chickamauga towns. Anticipating some action of this kind, which the general government did not think necessary or advisable, orders against any such attempt had been issued by the Secretary of War to Governor Blount. The frontier people went about their preparations, however, and it is evident from the result that the local military authorities were in connivance with the undertaking. General Robertson was the chief organizer of the volunteers about Nashville, who were reenforced by a company of Kentuckians under Colonel Whitley. Major Ore had been sent by Governor Blount with a detachment of troops to protect the Cumberland settlements, and on arriving at Nashville entered as heartily into the project as if no counter orders had ever been issued, and was given chief command of the expedition, which for this reason is commonly known as "Ore's expedition."

On September 7, 1794, the army of five hundred and fifty mounted men left Nashville, and five days later crossed the Tennessee near the mouth of the Sequatchee river, their guide being the same Joseph Brown of whom the old Indian woman had said that he would one day bring the soldiers to destroy them. Having left their horses on the other side of the river, they moved up along the south bank just after daybreak of the 13th and surprised the town of Nickajack, killing several warriors and taking a number of prisoners. Some who attempted to escape in canoes were shot in the water. The warriors

---

[1] Haywood, Civil and Political History of Tennessee, pp. 309-311, 1823; Ramsey, Tennessee, pp. 594, 595, 1853.

[2] Haywood, op. cit., pp. 314-316; Ramsey, op. cit., p. 596.

in Running Water town, four miles above, heard the firing and came at once to the assistance of their friends, but were driven back after attempting to hold their ground, and the second town shared the fate of the first.   More than fifty Indians had been killed, a number were prisoners, both towns and all their contents had been destroyed, with a loss to the assailants of only three men wounded.   The Breath, the chief of Running Water, was among those killed.   Two fresh scalps with a large quantity of plunder from the settlements were found in the towns, together with a supply of ammunition said to have been furnished by the Spaniards.[1]

Soon after the return of the expedition Robertson sent a message to John Watts, the principal leader of the hostile Cherokee, threatening a second visitation if the Indians did not very soon surrender their prisoners and give assurances of peace.[2]   The destruction of their towns on Tennessee and Coosa and the utter defeat of the northern confederates had now broken the courage of the Cherokee, and on their own request Governor Blount held a conference with them at Tellico blockhouse, November 7 and 8, 1794, at which Hanging-maw, head chief of the Nation, and Colonel John Watt, principal chief of the hostile towns, with about four hundred of their warriors, attended.   The result was satisfactory; all differences were arranged on a friendly basis and the long Cherokee war came to an end.[3]

Owing to the continued devastation of their towns during the Revolutionary struggle, a number of Cherokee, principally of the Chickamauga band, had removed across the Ohio about 1782 and settled on Paint creek, a branch of the Scioto river, in the vicinity of their friends and allies, the Shawano.   In 1787 they were reported to number about seventy warriors.   They took an active part in the hostilities along the Ohio frontier and were present in the great battle at the Maumee rapids, by which the power of the confederated northern tribes was effectually broken.   As they had failed to attend the treaty conference held at Greenville in August, 1795, General Wayne sent them a special message, through their chief Long-hair, that if they refused to come in and make terms as the others had done they would be considered outside the protection of the government.   Upon this a part of them came in and promised that as soon as they could gather their crops the whole band would leave Ohio forever and return to their people in the south.[4]

---

[1] Haywood, Political and Civil History of Tennessee, pp. 392–396, 1823; Ramsey, Tennessee (with Major Ore's report), pp. 608–618, 1853; Royce, Cherokee Nation, Fifth Ann. Rep. Bureau Ethnology, p. 171, 1888; Ore, Robertson, and Blount, reports, American State Papers: Indian Affairs, I, pp. 632–634, 1832.

[2] Ramsey, op. cit., p. 618.

[3] Tellico conference, November 7–8, 1794, American State Papers: Indian Affairs, I, pp. 536–538, 1832, Royce, op. cit., p. 173; Ramsey, op. cit., p. 596.

[4] Beaver's talk, 1784, Virginia State Papers, III, p. 571, 1883; McDowell, report, 1786, ibid., IV, p. 118, 1884; McDowell, report, 1787, ibid., p. 286; Todd, letter, 1787, ibid., p. 277; Tellico conference, November 7, 1794, American State Papers: Indian Affairs, I, p. 538, 1832; Greenville treaty conference, August, 1795, ibid., pp. 582–583.

The Creeks were still hostile and continued their inroads upon the western settlements. Early in January, 1795, Governor Blount held another conference with the Cherokee and endeavored to persuade them to organize a company of their young men to patrol the frontier against the Creeks, but to this proposal the chiefs refused to consent.[1]

In the next year it was discovered that a movement was on foot to take possession of certain Indian lands south of the Cumberland on pretense of authority formerly granted by North Carolina for the relief of Revolutionary soldiers. As such action would almost surely have resulted in another Indian war, Congress interposed, on the representation of President Washington, with an act for the regulation of intercourse between citizens of the United States and the various Indian tribes. Its main purpose was to prevent intrusion upon lands to which the Indian title had not been extinguished by treaty with the general government, and under its provisions a number of squatters were ejected from the Indian country and removed across the boundary. The pressure of border sentiment, however, was constantly for extending the area of white settlement and the result was an immediate agitation to procure another treaty cession.[2]

In consequence of urgent representations from the people of Tennessee, Congress took steps in 1797 for procuring a new treaty with the Cherokee by which the ejected settlers might be reinstated and the boundaries of the new state so extended as to bring about closer communication between the eastern settlements and those on the Cumberland. The Revolutionary warfare had forced the Cherokee west and south, and their capital and central gathering place was now Ustanali town, near the present Calhoun, Georgia, while Echota, their ancient capital and beloved peace town, was almost on the edge of the white settlements. The commissioners wished to have the proceedings conducted at Echota, while the Cherokee favored Ustanali. After some debate a choice was made of a convenient place near Tellico blockhouse, where the conference opened in July, but was brought to an abrupt close by the peremptory refusal of the Cherokee to sell any lands or to permit the return of the ejected settlers.

The rest of the summer was spent in negotiation along the lines already proposed, and on October 2, 1798, a treaty, commonly known as the "first treaty of Tellico," was concluded at the same place, and was signed by thirty-nine chiefs on behalf of the Cherokee. By this treaty the Indians ceded a tract between Clinch river and the Cumberland ridge, another along the northern bank of Little Tennessee extending up to Chilhowee mountain, and a third in North Carolina on the heads of French Broad and Pigeon rivers and including the sites

---

[1] Royce, Cherokee Nation, Fifth Ann. Rep. Bureau of Ethnology, p. 173, 1888.
[2] Ibid., pp. 174, 175; Ramsey, Tennessee, pp. 679–685, 1853.

of the present Waynesville and Hendersonville. These cessions included most or all of the lands from which settlers had been ejected. Permission was also given for laying out the "Cumberland road," to connect the east Tennessee settlements with those about Nashville. In consideration of the lands and rights surrendered, the United States agreed to deliver to the Cherokee five thousand dollars in goods, and to increase their existing annuity by one thousand dollars, and as usual, to "continue the guarantee of the remainder of their country forever."[1]

Wayne's victory over the northern tribes at the battle of the Maumee rapids completely broke their power and compelled them to accept the terms of peace dictated at the treaty of Greenville in the summer of 1795. The immediate result was the surrender of the Ohio river boundary by the Indians and the withdrawal of the British garrisons from the interior posts, which up to this time they had continued to hold in spite of the treaty made at the close of the Revolution. By the treaty made at Madrid in October, 1795, Spain gave up all claim on the east side of the Mississippi north of the thirty-first parallel, but on various pretexts the formal transfer of posts was delayed and a Spanish garrison continued to occupy San Fernando de Barrancas, at the present Memphis, Tennessee, until the fall of 1797, while that at Natchez, in Mississippi, was not surrendered until March, 1798. The Creeks, seeing the trend of affairs, had made peace at Colerain, Georgia, in June, 1796. With the hostile European influence thus eliminated, at least for the time, the warlike tribes on the north and on the south crushed and dispirited and the Chickamauga towns wiped out of existence, the Cherokee realized that they must accept the situation and, after nearly twenty years of continuous warfare, laid aside the tomahawk to cultivate the arts of peace and civilization.

The close of the century found them still a compact people (the westward movement having hardly yet begun) numbering probably about 20,000 souls. After repeated cessions of large tracts of land, to some of which they had but doubtful claim, they remained in recognized possession of nearly 43,000 square miles of territory, a country about equal in extent to Ohio, Virginia, or Tennessee. Of this territory about one-half was within the limits of Tennessee, the remainder being almost equally divided between Georgia and Alabama, with a small area in the extreme southwestern corner of North Carolina.[2] The old Lower towns on Savannah river had been broken up for twenty years, and the whites had so far encroached upon the Upper towns that the capital and council fire of the nation had been removed from the ancient peace town of Echota to Ustanali, in Georgia. The

---

[1] Indian Treaties, pp. 78–82, 1837; Ramsey, Tennessee, pp. 692–697, 1853; Royce, Cherokee Nation (with map and full discussion), Fifth Ann. Rep. Bureau of Ethnology, pp. 174–183, 1888.

[2] See table in Royce, op. cit., p. 378.

towns on Coosa river and in Alabama were almost all of recent establishment, peopled by refugees from the east and north. The Middle towns, in North Carolina, were still surrounded by Indian country.

Firearms had been introduced into the tribe about one hundred years before, and the Cherokee had learned well their use. Such civilized goods as hatchets, knives, clothes, and trinkets had become so common before the first Cherokee war that the Indians had declared that they could no longer live without the traders. Horses and other domestic animals had been introduced early in the century, and at the opening of the war of 1760, according to Adair, the Cherokee had "a prodigious number of excellent horses," and although hunger had compelled them to eat a great many of these during that period, they still had, in 1775, from two to a dozen each, and bid fair soon to have plenty of the best sort, as, according to the same authority, they were skilful jockeys and nice in their choice. Some of them had grown fond of cattle, and they had also an abundance of hógs and poultry, the Indian pork being esteemed better than that raised in the white settlements on account of the chestnut diet.[1] In Sevier's expedition against the towns on Coosa river, in 1793, the army killed three hundred beeves at Etowah and left their carcasses rotting on the ground. While crossing the Cherokee country in 1796 Hawkins met an Indian woman on horseback driving ten very fat cattle to the settlements for sale. Peach trees and potatoes, as well as the native corn and beans, were abundant in their fields, and some had bees and honey and did a considerable trade in beeswax. They seem to have quickly recovered from the repeated ravages of war, and there was a general air of prosperity throughout the nation. The native arts of pottery and basket-making were still the principal employment of the women, and the warriors hunted with such success that a party of traders brought down thirty wagon loads of skins on one trip.[2] In dress and house-building the Indian style was practically unchanged.

In pursuance of a civilizing policy, the government had agreed, by the treaty of 1791, to furnish the Cherokee gratuitously with farming tools and similar assistance. This policy was continued and broadened to such an extent that in 1801 Hawkins reports that "in the Cherokee agency, the wheel, the loom, and the plough is [sic] in pretty general use, farming, manufactures, and stock raising the topic of conversation among the men and women." At a conference held this year we find the chiefs of the mountain towns complaining that the people of the more western and southwestern settlements had received more than their share of spinning wheels and cards, and were consequently more advanced in making their own clothing as well as in farming, to which

---

[1] Adair, American Indians, pp. 230, 231, 1775.

[2] See Hawkins, MS journal from South Carolina to the Creeks, 1796, in library of Georgia Historical Society.

the others retorted that these things had been offered to all alike at the same time, but while the lowland people had been quick to accept, the mountaineers had hung back. "Those who complain came in late. We have got the start of them, which we are determined to keep." The progressives, under John Watts, Doublehead, and Will, threatened to secede from the rest and leave those east of Chilhowee mountain to shift for themselves.[1] We see here the germ of dissatisfaction which led ultimately to the emigration of the western band. Along with other things of civilization, negro slavery had been introduced and several of the leading men were now slaveholders (31).

Much of the advance in civilization had been due to the intermarriage among them of white men, chiefly traders of the ante-Revolutionary period, with a few Americans from the back settlements. The families that have made Cherokee history were nearly all of this mixed descent. The Doughertys, Galpins, and Adairs were from Ireland; the Rosses, Vanns, and McIntoshes, like the McGillivrays and Graysons among the Creeks, were of Scottish origin; the Waffords and others were Americans from Carolina or Georgia, and the father of Sequoya was a (Pennsylvania?) German. Most of this white blood was of good stock, very different from the "squaw man" element of the western tribes. Those of the mixed blood who could afford it usually sent their children away to be educated, while some built schoolhouses upon their own grounds and brought in private teachers from the outside. With the beginning of the present century we find influential mixed bloods in almost every town, and the civilized idea dominated even the national councils. The Middle towns, shut in from the outside world by high mountains, remained a stronghold of Cherokee conservatism.

With the exception of Priber, there seems to be no authentic record of any missionary worker among the Cherokee before 1800. There is, indeed, an incidental notice of a Presbyterian minister of North Carolina being on his way to the tribe in 1758, but nothing seems to have come of it, and we find him soon after in South Carolina and separated from his original jurisdiction.[2] The first permanent mission was established by the Moravians, those peaceful German immigrants whose teachings were so well exemplified in the lives of Zeisberger and Heckewelder. As early as 1734, while temporarily settled in Georgia, they had striven to bring some knowledge of the Christian religion to the Indians immediately about Savannah, including perhaps some stray Cherokee. Later on they established missions among the Delawares in Ohio, where their first Cherokee convert was received in 1773, being one who had been captured by the Delawares when a boy and had grown up and married in the tribe. In 1752 they had formed a settlement on the upper Yadkin, near the present Salem,

---

[1] Hawkins, Treaty Commission, 1801, manuscript No. 5, in library of Georgia Historical Society.
[2] Foote (?), in North Carolina Colonial Records, v, p. 1226, 1887.

North Carolina, where they made friendly acquaintance with the Cherokee.[1] In 1799, hearing that the Cherokee desired teachers—or perhaps by direct invitation of the chiefs—two missionaries visited the tribe to investigate the matter. Another visit was made in the next summer, and a council was held at Tellico agency, where, after a debate in which the Indians showed considerable difference of opinion, it was decided to open a mission. Permission having been obtained from the government, the work was begun in April, 1801, by Rev. Abraham Steiner and Rev. Gottlieb Byhan at the residence of David Vann, a prominent mixed-blood chief, who lodged them in his own house and gave them every assistance in building the mission, which they afterward called Spring place, where now is the village of the same name in Murray county, northwestern Georgia. They were also materially aided by the agent, Colonel Return J. Meigs (32). It was soon seen that the Cherokee wanted civilizers for their children, and not new theologies, and when they found that a school could not at once be opened the great council at Ustanali sent orders to the missionaries to organize a school within six months or leave the nation. Through Vann's help the matter was arranged and a school was opened, several sons of prominent chiefs being among the pupils. Another Moravian mission was established by Reverend J. Gambold at Oothcaloga, in the same county, in 1821. Both were in flourishing condition when broken up, with other Cherokee missions, by the State of Georgia in 1834. The work was afterward renewed beyond the Mississippi.[2]

In 1804 the Reverend Gideon Blackburn, a Presbyterian minister of Tennessee, opened a school among the Cherokee, which continued for several years until abandoned for lack of funds.[3]

Notwithstanding the promise to the Cherokee in the treaty of 1798 that the Government would "continue the guarantee of the remainder of their country forever," measures were begun almost immediately to procure another large cession of land and road privileges. In spite of the strenuous objection of the Cherokee, who sent a delegation of prominent chiefs to Washington to protest against any further sales, such pressure was brought to bear, chiefly through the efforts of the agent, Colonel Meigs, that the object of the Government was accomplished, and in 1804 and 1805 three treaties were negotiated at Tellico agency, by which the Cherokee were shorn of more than eight thousand square miles of their remaining territory.

By the first of these treaties—October 24, 1804—a purchase was made of a small tract in northeastern Georgia, known as the "Wafford

---

[1] North Carolina Colonial Records, V, p. x, 1887.

[2] Reichel, E. H., Historical Sketch of the Church and Missions of the United Brethren, pp. 65-81; Bethlehem, Pa., 1848; Holmes, John, Sketches of the Missions of the United Brethren, pp. 124, 125, 209-212; Dublin, 1818; Thompson, A. C., Moravian Missions, p. 341; New York, 1890; De Schweinitz, Edmund, Life of Zeisberger, pp. 394, 663, 696; Phila., 1870.

[3] Morse, American Geography, I, p. 577, 1819.

settlement," upon which a party led by Colonel Wafford had located some years before, under the impression that it was outside the boundary established by the Hopewell treaty. In compensation the Cherokee were to receive an immediate payment of five thousand dollars in goods or cash with an additional annuity of one thousand dollars. By the other treaties—October 25 and 27, 1805—a large tract was obtained in central Tennessee and Kentucky, extending between the Cumberland range and the western line of the Hopewell treaty, and from Cumberland river southwest to Duck river. One section was also secured at Southwest point (now Kingston, Tennessee) with the design of establishing there the state capital, which, however, was located at Nashville instead seven years later. Permission was also obtained for two mail roads through the Cherokee country into Georgia and Alabama. In consideration of the cessions by the two treaties the United States agreed to pay fifteen thousand six hundred dollars in working implements, goods, or cash, with an additional annuity of three thousand dollars. To secure the consent of some of the leading chiefs, the treaty commissioners resorted to the disgraceful precedent of secret articles, by which several valuable small tracts were reserved for Doublehead and Tollunteeskee, the agreement being recorded as a part of the treaty, but not embodied in the copy sent to the Senate for confirmation.[1] In consequence of continued abuse of his official position for selfish ends Doublehead was soon afterward killed in accordance with a decree of the chiefs of the Nation, Major Ridge being selected as executioner.[2]

By the treaty of October 25, 1805, the settlements in eastern Tennessee were brought into connection with those about Nashville on the Cumberland, and the state at last assumed compact form. The whole southern portion of the state, as defined in the charter, was still Indian country, and there was a strong and constant pressure for its opening, the prevailing sentiment being in favor of making Tennessee river the boundary between the two races. New immigrants were constantly crowding in from the east, and, as Royce says, "the desire to settle on Indian land was as potent and insatiable with the average border settler then as it is now." Almost within two months of the last treaties another one was concluded at Washington on January 7, 1806, by which the Cherokee ceded their claim to a large tract between Duck river and the Tennessee, embracing nearly seven thousand square miles in Tennessee and Alabama, together with the Long island (Great island) in Holston river, which up to this time they had claimed as theirs. They were promised in compensation ten thousand dollars in five cash installments, a grist mill and cotton gin, and a life annuity

---

[1] Indian treaties, pp. 108, 121, 125, 1837; Royce, Cherokee Nation, Fifth Ann. Rep. Bureau of Ethnology, pp. 183 193, 1888 (map and full discussion).

[2] McKenney and Hall, Indian Tribes, II, p. 92, 1858.

of one hundred dollars for Black-fox, the aged head chief of the nation. The signers of the instrument, including Doublehead and Tollunteeskee, were accompanied to Washington by the same commissioners who had procured the previous treaty. In consequence of some misunderstanding, the boundaries of the ceded tract were still further extended in a supplementary treaty concluded at the Chickasaw Old Fields on the Tennessee, on September 11, 1807. As the country between Duck river and the Tennessee was claimed also by the Chickasaw, their title was extinguished by separate treaties.[1] The ostensible compensation for this last Cherokee cession, as shown by the treaty, was two thousand dollars, but it was secretly agreed by Agent Meigs that what he calls a "silent consideration" of one thousand dollars and some rifles should be given to the chiefs who signed it.[2]

In 1807 Colonel Elias Earle, with the consent of the Government, obtained a concession from the Cherokee for the establishment of iron works at the mouth of Chickamauga creek, on the south side of Tennessee river, to be supplied from ores mined in the Cherokee country. It was hoped that this would be a considerable step toward the civilization of the Indians, besides enabling the Government to obtain its supplies of manufactured iron at a cheaper rate, but after prolonged effort the project was finally abandoned on account of the refusal of the state of Tennessee to sanction the grant.[3] In the same year, by arrangement with the general government, the legislature of Tennessee attempted to negotiate with the Cherokee for that part of their unceded lands lying within the state limits, but without success, owing to the unwillingness of the Indians to part with any more territory, and their special dislike for the people of Tennessee.[4]

In 1810 the Cherokee national council registered a further advance in civilization by formally abolishing the custom of clan revenge, hitherto universal among the tribes. The enactment bears the signatures of Black-fox (Ina'lǐ), principal chief, and seven others, and reads as follows:

In Council, Oostinaleh, *April 18, 1810.*

1. Be it known this day, That the various clans or tribes which compose the Cherokee nation have unanimously passed an act of oblivion for all lives for which they may have been indebted one to the other, and have mutually agreed that after this evening the aforesaid act shall become binding upon every clan or tribe thereof.

2. The aforesaid clans or tribes have also agreed that if, in future, any life should be lost without malice intended, the innocent aggressor shall not be accounted guilty;

[1] Indian Treaties, pp. 132–136, 1837; Royce, Cherokee Nation, Fifth Ann. Rep. Bureau of Ethnology, pp. 193–197, 1888.

[2] Meigs, letter, September 28, 1807, American State Papers: Indian Affairs, I, p. 754, 1832; Royce, op. cit., p. 197.

[3] See treaty, December 2, 1807, and Jefferson's message, with inclosures, March 10, 1808, American State Papers: Indian Affairs, I, pp. 752–754, 1832; Royce, op. cit., pp. 199–201.

[4] Ibid., pp. 201, 202.

and, should it so happen that a brother, forgetting his natural affections, should raise his hands in anger and kill his brother, he shall be accounted guilty of murder and suffer accordingly.

3. If a man have a horse stolen, and overtake the thief, and should his anger be so great as to cause him to shed his blood, let it remain on his own conscience, but no satisfaction shall be required for his life, from his relative or clan he may have belonged to.

By order of the seven clans.[1]

Under an agreement with the Cherokee in 1813 a company composed of representatives of Tennessee, Georgia, and the Cherokee nation was organized to lay out a free public road from Tennessee river to the head of navigation on the Tugaloo branch of Savannah river, with provision for convenient stopping places along the line. The road was completed within the next three years, and became the great highway from the coast to the Tennessee settlements. Beginning on the Tugaloo or Savannah a short distance below the entrance of Toccoa creek, it crossed the upper Chattahoochee, passing through Clarkesville, Nacoochee valley, the Unicoi gap, and Hiwassee in Georgia; then entering North Carolina it descended the Hiwassee, passing through Hayesville and Murphy and over the Great Smoky range into Tennessee, until it reached the terminus at the Cherokee capital, Echota, on Little Tennessee. It was officially styled the Unicoi turnpike,[2] but was commonly known in North Carolina as the Wachesa trail, from Watsi'sa or Wachesa, a prominent Indian who lived near the crossing-place on Beaverdam creek, below Murphy, this portion of the road being laid out along the old Indian trail which already bore that name.[3]

Passing over for the present some negotiations having for their purpose the removal of the Cherokee to the West, we arrive at the period of the Creek war.

Ever since the treaty of Greenville it had been the dream of Tecumtha, the great Shawano chief (33), to weld again the confederacy of the northern tribes as a barrier against the further aggressions of the white man. His own burning eloquence was ably seconded by the subtler persuasion of his brother, who assumed the role of a prophet with a new revelation, the burden of which was that the Indians must return to their old Indian life if they would preserve their national existence. The new doctrine spread among all the northern tribes and at last reached those of the south, where Tecumtha himself had gone to enlist the warriors in the great Indian confederacy. The prophets of the Upper Creeks eagerly accepted the doctrine and in a short time their warriors were dancing the "dance of the Indians of the lakes." In

[1] In American State Papers: Indian Affairs, II, p. 283, 1834.

[2] See contract appended to Washington treaty, 1819, Indian Treaties, pp. 269–271, 1837; Royce map, Fifth Ann. Rep. Bureau of Ethnology, 1888.

[3] Author's personal information.

anticipation of an expected war with the United States the British agents in Canada had been encouraging the hostile feeling toward the Americans by talks and presents of goods and ammunition, while the Spaniards also covertly fanned the flame of discontent.[1] At the height of the ferment war was declared between this country and England on June 28, 1812. Tecumtha, at the head of fifteen hundred warriors, at once entered the British service with a commission as general, while the Creeks began murdering and burning along the southern frontier. after having vainly attempted to secure the cooperation of the Cherokee.

From the Creeks the new revelation was brought to the Cherokee, whose priests at once began to dream dreams and to preach a return to the old life as the only hope of the Indian race. A great medicine dance was appointed at Ustanali, the national capital, where, after the dance was over, the doctrine was publicly announced and explained by a Cherokee prophet introduced by a delegation from Coosawatee. He began by saying that some of the mountain towns had abused him and refused to receive his message, but nevertheless he must continue to bear testimony of his mission whatever might happen. The Cherokee had broken the road which had been given to their fathers at the beginning of the world. They had taken the white man's clothes and trinkets, they had beds and tables and mills; some even had books and cats. All this was bad, and because of it their gods were angry and the game was leaving their country. If they would live and be happy as before they must put off the white man's dress, throw away his mills and looms, kill their cats, put on paint and buckskin, and be Indians again; otherwise swift destruction would come upon them.

His speech appealed strongly to the people, who cried out in great excitement that his talk was good. Of all those present only Major Ridge, a principal chief, had the courage to stand up and oppose it, warning his hearers that such talk would inevitably lead to war with the United States, which would end in their own destruction. The maddened followers of the prophet sprang upon Ridge and would have killed him but for the interposition of friends. As it was, he was thrown down and narrowly escaped with his life, while one of his defenders was stabbed by his side.

The prophet had threatened after a certain time to invoke a terrible storm, which should destroy all but the true believers, who were exhorted to gather for safety on one of the high peaks of the Great Smoky mountains. In full faith they abandoned their bees, their orchards, their slaves, and everything that had come to them from the white man, and took up their toilsome march for the high mountains. There they waited until the appointed day had come and passed, show-

---

[1] Mooney, Ghost-dance Religion, Fourteenth Ann. Rep. Bureau of Ethnology, p. 670 et passim, 1896; contemporary documents in American State Papers: Indian Affairs, I, pp. 798–801, 845–850, 1832.

ing their hopes and fears to be groundless, when they sadly returned to their homes and the great Indian revival among the Cherokee came to an end.[1]

Among the Creeks, where other hostile influences were at work, the excitement culminated in the Creek war. Several murders and outrages had already been committed, but it was not until the terrible massacre at Fort Mims (34), on August 30, 1813, that the whole American nation was aroused. Through the influence of Ridge and other prominent chiefs the Cherokee had refused to join the hostile Creeks, and on the contrary had promised to assist the whites and the friendly towns.[2] More than a year before the council had sent a friendly letter to the Creeks warning them against taking the British side in the approaching war, while several prominent chiefs had proposed to enlist a Cherokee force for the service of the United States.[3] Finding that no help was to be expected from the Cherokee, the Creeks took occasion to kill a Cherokee woman near the town of Etowah, in Georgia. With the help of a conjurer the murderers were trailed and overtaken and killed on the evening of the second day in a thicket where they had concealed themselves. After this there could be no alliance between the two tribes.[4]

At the time of the Fort Mims massacre McIntosh (35), the chief of the friendly Lower Creeks, was visiting the Cherokee, among whom he had relatives. By order of the Cherokee council he was escorted home by a delegation under the leadership of Ridge. On his return Ridge brought with him a request from the Lower Creeks that the Cherokee would join with them and the Americans in putting down the war. Ridge himself strongly urged the proposition, declaring that if the prophets were allowed to have their way the work of civilization would be destroyed. The council, however, decided not to interfere in the affairs of other tribes, whereupon Ridge called for volunteers, with the result that so many of the warriors responded that the council reversed its decision and declared war against the Creeks.[5] For a proper understanding of the situation it is necessary to state that the hostile feeling was confined almost entirely to the Upper Creek towns on the Tallapoosa, where the prophets of the new religion had their residence. The half-breed chief, Weatherford (36), was the leader of the war party. The Lower Creek towns on the Chattahoo-

---

[1] See Mooney, Ghost-dance Religion, Fourteenth Ann. Rep. Bureau of Ethnology, pp. 670–677, 1896; McKenney and Hall, Indian Tribes, II, pp. 93–95, 1858; see also contemporary letters (1813, etc.) by Hawkins, Cornells, and others in American State Papers: Indian Affairs, I, 1832.

[2] Letters of Hawkins, Pinckney, and Cussetah King, July, 1813, American State Papers: Indian Affairs, II, pp. 847–849, 1832.

[3] Meigs, letter, May 8, 1812, and Hawkins, letter, May 11, 1812, ibid., p. 809.

[4] Author's information from James D. Wafford.

[5] McKenney and Hall, Indian Tribes, II, pp. 96–97, 1858.

chee, under McIntosh, another half-breed chief, were friendly, and acted with the Cherokee and the Americans against their own brethren.

It is not our purpose to give a history of the Creek war, but only to note the part which the Cherokee had in it. The friendly Lower Creeks, under McIntosh, with a few refugees from the Upper towns, operated chiefly with the army under General Floyd which invaded the southern part of the Creek country from Georgia. Some friendly Choctaw and Chickasaw also lent their assistance in this direction. The Cherokee, with some friendly Creeks of the Upper towns, acted with the armies under Generals White and Jackson, which entered the Creek country from the Tennessee side. While some hundreds of their warriors were thus fighting in the field, the Cherokee at home were busily collecting provisions for the American troops.

As Jackson approached from the north, about the end of October, 1813, he was met by runners asking him to come to the aid of Path-killer, a Cherokee chief, who was in danger of being cut off by the hostiles, at his village of Turkeytown, on the upper Coosa, near the present Center, Alabama. A fresh detachment on its way from east Tennessee, under General White, was ordered by Jackson to relieve the town, and successfully performed this work. White's force consisted of one thousand men, including four hundred Cherokee under Colonel Gideon Morgan and John Lowrey.[1]

As the army advanced down the Coosa the Creeks retired to Tallasee-hatchee, on the creek of the same name, near the present Jacksonville, Calhoun county, Alabama. One thousand men under General Coffee, together with a company of Cherokee under Captain Richard Brown and some few Creeks, were sent against them. The Indian auxiliaries wore headdresses of white feathers and deertails. The attack was made at daybreak of November 3, 1813, and the town was taken after a desperate resistance, from which not one of the defenders escaped alive, the Creeks having been completely surrounded on all sides. Says Coffee in his official report:

They made all the resistance that an overpowered soldier could do—they fought as long as one existed, but their destruction was very soon completed. Our men rushed up to the doors of the houses and in a few minutes killed the last warrior of them. The enemy fought with savage fury and met death with all its horrors, without shrinking or complaining—not one asked to be spared, but fought as long as they could stand or sit.

Of such fighting stuff did the Creeks prove themselves, against overwhelming numbers, throughout the war. The bodies of nearly two hundred dead warriors were counted on the field, and the general reiterates that "not one of the warriors escaped." A number of women and children were taken prisoners. Nearly every man of the Creeks had a bow with a bundle of arrows, which he used after the

---

[1] Drake, Indians, pp. 395–396, 1880; Pickett, Alabama, p. 556, reprint of 1896.

first fire with his gun. The American loss was only five killed and forty-one wounded, which may not include the Indian contingent.[1]

White's advance guard, consisting chiefly of the four hundred other Cherokee under Morgan and Lowrey, reached Tallaseehatchee the same evening, only to find it already destroyed. They picked up twenty wounded Creeks, whom they brought with them to Turkeytown.[2]

The next great battle was at Talladega, on the site of the present town of the same name, in Talladega county, Alabama, on November 9, 1813. Jackson commanded in person with two thousand infantry and cavalry. Although the Cherokee are not specifically mentioned they were a part of the army and must have taken part in the engagement. The town itself was occupied by friendly Creeks, who were besieged by the hostiles, estimated at over one thousand warriors on the outside. Here again the battle was simply a slaughter, the odds being two to one, the Creeks being also without cover, although they fought so desperately that at one time the militia was driven back. They left two hundred and ninety-nine dead bodies on the field, which, according to their own statement afterwards, was only a part of their total loss. The Americans lost fifteen killed and eighty-five wounded.[3]

A day or two later the people of Hillabee town, about the site of the present village of that name in Clay county, Alabama, sent messengers to Jackson's camp to ask for peace, which that commander immediately granted. In the meantime, even while the peace messengers were on their way home with the good news, an army of one thousand men from east Tennessee under General White, who claimed to be independent of Jackson's authority, together with four hundred Cherokee under Colonel Gideon Morgan and John Lowrey, surrounded the town on November 18, 1813, taking it by surprise, the inhabitants having trusted so confidently to the success of their peace embassy that they had made no preparation for defense. Sixty warriors were killed and over two hundred and fifty prisoners taken, with no loss to the Americans, as there was practically no resistance. In White's official report of the affair he states that he had sent ahead a part of his force, together with the Cherokee under Morgan, to surround the town, and adds that "Colonel Morgan and the Cherokees under his command gave undeniable evidence that they merit the employ of their government."[4] Not knowing that the attack had been made without Jackson's sanction or knowledge, the Creeks naturally con-

---

[1] Coffee, report, etc., in Drake, Indians, p. 396, 1880; Lossing, Field Book of the War of 1812, pp. 762, 763 [n. d. (1869)]; Pickett, Alabama, p. 553, reprint of 1896.

[2] Ibid., p. 556.

[3] Drake, Indians, p. 396, 1880; Pickett, op. cit., pp. 554, 555.

[4] White's report, etc., in Fay and Davison, Sketches of the War, pp. 240, 241; Rutland, Vt., 1815; Low, John, Impartial History of the War, p. 199; New York, 1815; Drake, op. cit., p. 397; Pickett, op. cit., p. 557; Lossing, op. cit., p. 767. Low says White had about 1,100 mounted men, "including upward of 300 Cherokee Indians." Pickett gives White 400 Cherokee.

cluded that peace overtures were of no avail, and thenceforth until
the close of the war there was no talk of surrender.

On November 29, 1813, the Georgia army under General Floyd,
consisting of nine hundred and fifty American troops and four hundred friendly Indians, chiefly Lower Creeks under McIntosh, took
and destroyed Autossee town on the Tallapoosa, west of the present
Tuskegee, killing about two hundred warriors and burning four hundred well-built houses. On December 23 the Creeks were again
defeated by General Claiborne, assisted by some friendly Choctaws,
at Ecanachaca or the Holy Ground on Alabama river, near the present
Benton in Lowndes county. This town and another a few miles away
were also destroyed, with a great quantity of provisions and other
property.[1] It is doubtful if any Cherokee were concerned in either
action.

Before the close of the year Jackson's force in northern Alabama
had been so far reduced by mutinies and expiration of service terms
that he had but one hundred soldiers left and was obliged to employ
the Cherokee to garrison Fort Armstrong, on the upper Coosa, and to
protect his provision depot.[2] With the opening of the new year, 1814,
having received reinforcements from Tennessee, together with about
two hundred friendly Creeks and sixty-five more Cherokee, he left his
camp on the Coosa and advanced against the towns on the Tallapoosa.
Learning, on arriving near the river, that he was within a few miles
of the main body of the enemy, he halted for a reconnoissance and
camped in order of battle on Emukfaw creek, on the northern bank of
the Tallapoosa, only a short distance from the famous Horseshoe bend.
Here, on the morning of June 24, 1814, he was suddenly attacked by
the enemy with such fury that, although the troops charged with the
bayonet, the Creeks returned again to the fight and were at last broken
only by the help of the friendly Indians, who came upon them from
the rear. As it was, Jackson was so badly crippled that he retreated
to Fort Strother on the Coosa, carrying his wounded, among them General Coffee, on horse-hide litters. The Creeks pursued and attacked
him again as he was crossing Enotochopco creek on January 24, but
after a severe fight were driven back with discharges of grapeshot from
a six-pounder at close range. The army then continued its retreat to
Fort Strother. The American loss in these two battles was about one
hundred killed and wounded. The loss of the Creeks was much greater,
but they had compelled a superior force, armed with bayonet and
artillery, to retreat, and without the aid of the friendly Indians it is
doubtful if Jackson could have saved his army from demoralization.
The Creeks themselves claimed a victory and boasted afterward
that they had "whipped Jackson and run him to the Coosa river."

---

[1] Drake, Indians, pp. 391, 398, 1880; Pickett, Alabama, pp. 557-559, 572-576, reprint of 1896.
[2] Ibid., p. 579; Lossing, Field Book of the War of 1812, p. 773.

Pickett states, on what seems good authority, that the Creeks engaged did not number more than five hundred warriors. Jackson had probably at least one thousand two hundred men, including Indians.[1]

While these events were transpiring in the north, General Floyd again advanced from Georgia with a force of about one thousand three hundred Americans and four hundred friendly Indians, but was surprised on Caleebee creek, near the present Tuskegee, Alabama, on the morning of January 27, 1814, and compelled to retreat, leaving the enemy in possession of the field.[2]

We come now to the final event of the Creek war, the terrible battle of the Horseshoe bend. Having received large reenforcements from Tennessee, Jackson left a garrison at Fort Strother, and, about the middle of March, descended the Coosa river to the mouth of Cedar creek, southeast from the present Columbiana, where he built Fort Williams. Leaving his stores here with a garrison to protect them, he began his march for the Horseshoe bend of the Tallapoosa, where the hostiles were reported to have collected in great force. At this place, known to the Creeks as Tohopki or Tohopeka, the Tallapoosa made a bend so as to inclose some eighty or a hundred acres in a narrow peninsula opening to the north. On the lower side was an island in the river, and about a mile below was Emukfaw creek, entering from the north, where Jackson had been driven back two months before Both locations were in the present Tallapoosa county, Alabama, within two miles of the present post village of Tohopeka. Across the neck of the peninsula the Creeks had built a strong breastwork of logs, behind which were their houses, and behind these were a number of canoes moored to the bank for use if retreat became necessary. The fort was defended by a thousand warriors, with whom were also about three hundred women and children. Jackson's force numbered about two thousand men, including, according to his own statement, five hundred Cherokee. He had also two small cannon. The account of the battle, or rather massacre, which occurred on the morning of March 27, 1814, is best condensed from the official reports of the principal commanders.

Having arrived in the neighborhood of the fort, Jackson disposed his men for the attack by detailing General Coffee with the mounted men and nearly the whole of the Indian force to cross the river at a ford about three miles below and surround the bend in such manner that none could escape in that direction. He himself, with the rest of his force, advanced to the front of the breastwork and planted his can-

---

[1] Fay and Davison, Sketches of the War, pp. 247–250, 1815; Pickett, Alabama, pp. 579–584, reprint of 1896; Drake, Indians, pp. 398–400, 1880. Pickett says Jackson had "767 men, with 200 friendly Indians"; Drake says he started with 930 men and was joined at Talladega by 200 friendly Indians; Jackson himself, as quoted in Fay and Davison, says that he started with 930 men, *excluding Indians*, and was joined at Talladega "by between 200 and 300 friendly Indians," 65 being Cherokee, the rest Creeks. The inference is that he already had a number of Indians with him at the start—probably the Cherokee who had been doing garrison duty.

[2] Pickett, op. cit., pp. 584–586.

non upon a slight rise within eighty yards of the fortification.   He then directed a heavy cannonade upon the center of the breastwork, while the rifles and muskets kept up a galling fire upon the defenders whenever they showed themselves behind the logs.   The breastwork was very strongly and compactly built, from five to eight feet high, with a double row of portholes, and so planned that no enemy could approach without being exposed to a crossfire from those on the inside.   After about two hours of cannonading and rifle fire to no great purpose, "Captain Russell's company of spies and a party of the Cherokee force, headed by their gallant chieftain, Colonel Richard Brown, and conducted by the brave Colonel Morgan, crossed over to the peninsula in canoes and set fire to a few of their buildings there situated.   They then advanced with great gallantry toward the breastwork and commenced firing upon the enemy, who lay behind it.   Finding that this force, notwithstanding the determination they displayed, was wholly insufficient to dislodge the enemy, and that General Coffee had secured the opposite banks of the river, I now determined on taking possession of their works by storm." [1]

Coffee's official report to his commanding officer states that he had taken seven hundred mounted troops and about six hundred Indians, of whom five hundred were Cherokee and the rest friendly Creeks, and had come in behind, having directed the Indians to take position secretly along the bank of the river to prevent the enemy crossing, as already noted.   This was done, but with fighting going on so near at hand the Indians could not remain quiet.   Continuing, Coffee says:

The firing of your cannon and small arms in a short time became general and heavy, which animated our Indians, and seeing about one hundred of the warriors and all the squaws and children of the enemy running about among the huts of the village, which was open to our view, they could no longer remain silent spectators. While some kept up a fire across the river to prevent the enemy's approach to the bank, others plunged into the water and swam the river for canoes that lay at the other shore in considerable numbers and brought them over, in which crafts a number of them embarked and landed on the bend with the enemy.   Colonel Gideon Morgan, who commanded the Cherokees, Captain Kerr, and Captain William Russell, with a part of his company of spies, were among the first that crossed the river. They advanced into the village and very soon drove the enemy from the huts up the river bank to the fortified works from which they were fighting you.   They pursued and continued to annoy during your whole action.   This movement of my Indian forces left the river bank unguarded and made it necessary that I should send a part of my line to take possession of the river bank. [2]

According to the official report of Colonel Morgan, who commanded the Cherokee and who was himself severely wounded, the Cherokee took the places assigned them along the bank in such regular order

---

[1] Jackson's report to Governor Blount, March 31, 1814, in Fay and Davison, Sketches of the War, pp. 253, 254, 1815.

[2] General Coffee's report to General Jackson, April 1, 1814, ibid., p. 257.

that no part was left unoccupied, and the few fugitives who attempted to escape from the fort by water "fell an easy prey to their vengeance." Finally, seeing that the cannonade had no more effect upon the breastwork than to bore holes in the logs, some of the Cherokee plunged into the river, and swimming over to the town brought back a number of canoes. A part crossed in these, under cover of the guns of their companions, and sheltered themselves under the bank while the canoes were sent back for reenforcements. In this way they all crossed over and then advanced up the bank, where at once they were warmly assailed from every side except the rear, which they kept open only by hard fighting.[1]

The Creeks had been fighting the Americans in their front at such close quarters that their bullets flattened upon the bayonets thrust through the portholes. This attack from the rear by five hundred Cherokee diverted their attention and gave opportunity to the Tennesseeans, Sam Houston among them, cheering them on, to swarm over the breastwork. With death from the bullet, the bayonet and the hatchet all around them, and the smoke of their blazing homes in their eyes, not a warrior begged for his life. When more than half their number lay dead upon the ground, the rest turned and plunged into the river, only to find the banks on the opposite side lined with enemies and escape cut off in every direction. Says General Coffee:

Attempts to cross the river at all points of the bend were made by the enemy, but not one ever escaped. Very few ever reached the bank and that few was killed the instant they landed. From the report of my officers, as well as from my own observation, I feel warranted in saying that from two hundred and fifty to three hundred of the enemy was buried under water and was not numbered with the dead that were found.

Some swam for the island below the bend, but here too a detachment had been posted and "not one ever landed. They were sunk by Lieutenant Bean's command ere they reached the bank."[2]

Quoting again from Jackson—

The enemy, although many of them fought to the last with that kind of bravery which desperation inspires, were at last entirely routed and cut to pieces. The battle may be said to have continued with severity for about five hours, but the firing and slaughter continued until it was suspended by the darkness of night. The next morning it was resumed and sixteen of the enemy slain who had concealed themselves under the banks.[3]

It was supposed that the Creeks had about a thousand warriors, besides their women and children. The men sent out to count the dead found five hundred and fifty-seven warriors lying dead within the inclosure, and Coffee estimates that from two hundred and fifty to

---

[1] Colonel Morgan's report to Governor Blount, in Fay and Davison, Sketches of the War, pp. 258, 259 1815.

[2] Coffee's report to Jackson, ibid., pp. 257, 258.

[3] Jackson's report to Governor Blount, ibid., pp. 255, 256.

three hundred were shot in the water. How many more there may have been can not be known, but Jackson himself states that not more than twenty could have escaped. There is no mention of any wounded. About three hundred prisoners were taken, of whom only three were men. The defenders of the Horseshoe had been exterminated.[1]

On the other side the loss was 26 Americans killed and 107 wounded, 18 Cherokee killed and 36 wounded, 5 friendly Creeks killed and 11 wounded. It will be noted that the loss of the Cherokee was out of all proportion to their numbers, their fighting having been hand to hand work without protecting cover. In view of the fact that Jackson had only a few weeks before been compelled to retreat before this same enemy, and that two hours of artillery and rifle fire had produced no result until the Cherokee turned the rear of the enemy by their daring passage of the river, there is considerable truth in the boast of the Cherokee that they saved the day for Jackson at Horseshoe bend. In the number of men actually engaged and the immense proportion killed, this ranks as the greatest Indian battle in the history of the United States, with the possible exception of the battle of Mauvila, fought by the same Indians in De Soto's time. The result was decisive. Two weeks later Weatherford came in and surrendered, and the Creek war was at an end.

As is usual where Indians have acted as auxiliaries of white troops, it is difficult to get an accurate statement of the number of Cherokee engaged in this war or to apportion the credit among the various leaders. Coffee's official report states that five hundred Cherokee were engaged in the last great battle, and from incidental hints it seems probable that others were employed elsewhere, on garrison duty or otherwise, at the same time. McKenney and Hall state that Ridge recruited eight hundred warriors for Jackson,[2] and this may be near the truth, as the tribe had then at least six times as many fighting men. On account of the general looseness of Indian organization we commonly find the credit claimed for whichever chief may be best known to the chronicler. Thus, McKenney and Hall make Major Ridge the hero of the war, especially of the Horseshoe fight, although he is not mentioned in the official reports. Jackson speaks particularly of the Cherokee in that battle as being "headed by their gallant chieftain, Colonel Richard Brown, and conducted by the brave Colonel Morgan." Coffee says that Colonel Gideon Morgan "commanded the Cherokees," and it is Morgan who makes the official report of their part in the battle. In a Washington newspaper notice of the treaty

---

[1] Jackson's report and Colonel Morgan's report, in Fay and Davison, Sketches of the War, pp. 255, 256, 259, 1815. Pickett makes the loss of the white troops 32 killed and 99 wounded. The Houston reference is from Lossing. The battle is described also by Pickett, Alabama, pp. 588–591, reprint of 1896; Drake, Indians, pp. 391, 400, 1880; McKenney and Hall, Indian Tribes, II, pp. 98, 99, 1858.

[2] McKenney and Hall, op. cit., p. 98.

delegation of 1816 the six signers are mentioned as Colonel [John] Lowrey, Major [John] Walker, Major Ridge, Captain [Richard] Taylor, Adjutant [John] Ross, and Kunnesee (Tsi'yu-gûnsi'nĭ, Cheucunsene) and are described as men of cultivation, nearly all of whom had served as officers of the Cherokee forces with Jackson and distinguished themselves as well by their bravery as by their attachment to the United States.[1] Among the East Cherokee in Carolina the only name still remembered is that of their old chief, Junaluska (Tsunu'lahuñ'skĭ), who said afterward: "If I had known that Jackson would drive us from our homes I would have killed him that day at the Horseshoe."

The Cherokee returned to their homes to find them despoiled and ravaged in their absence by disorderly white troops. Two years afterward, by treaty at Washington, the Government agreed to reimburse them for the damage. Interested parties denied that they had suffered any damage or rendered any services, to which their agent indignantly replied: "It may be answered that thousands witnessed both; that in nearly all the battles with the Creeks the Cherokees rendered the most efficient service, and at the expense of the lives of many fine men, whose wives and children and brothers and sisters are mourning their fall."[2]

In the spring of 1816 a delegation of seven principal men, accompanied by Agent Meigs, visited Washington, and the result was the negotiation of two treaties at that place on the same date, March 22, 1816. By the first of these the Cherokee ceded for five thousand dollars their last remaining territory in South Carolina, a small strip in the extreme northwestern corner, adjoining Chattooga river. By the second treaty a boundary was established between the lands claimed by the Cherokee and Creeks in northern Alabama. This action was made necessary in order to determine the boundaries of the great tract which the Creeks had been compelled to surrender in punishment for their late uprising. The line was run from a point on Little Bear creek in northwestern Alabama direct to the Ten islands of the Coosa at old Fort Strother, southeast of the present Asheville. General Jackson protested strongly against this line, on the ground that all the territory south of Tennessee river and west of the Coosa belonged to the Creeks and was a part of their cession. The Chickasaw also protested against considering this tract as Cherokee territory. The treaty also granted free and unrestricted road privileges throughout the Cherokee country, this concession being the result of years of persistent effort on the part of the Government; and an appropriation of twenty-five thousand five hundred dollars was made

---

[1] Drake, Indians, p. 401, 1880.

[2] Indian Treaties, p. 187, 1837; Meigs' letter to Secretary of War, August 19, 1816, in American State Papers: Indian Affairs, II, pp. 113, 114, 1834.

for damages sustained by the Cherokee from the depredations of the troops passing through their country during the Creek war.[1]

At the last treaty the Cherokee had resisted every effort to induce them to cede more land on either side of the Tennessee, the Government being especially desirous to extinguish their claim north of that river within the limits of the state of Tennessee. Failing in this, pressure was at once begun to bring about a cession in Alabama, with the result that on September 14 of the same year a treaty was concluded at the Chickasaw council-house, and afterward ratified in general council at Turkeytown on the Coosa, by which the Cherokee ceded all their claims in that state south of Tennessee river and west of an irregular line running from Chickasaw island in that stream, below the entrance of Flint river, to the junction of Wills creek with the Coosa, at the present Gadsden. For this cession, embracing an area of nearly three thousand five hundred square miles, they were to receive sixty thousand dollars in ten annual payments, together with five thousand dollars for the improvements abandoned.[2]

We turn aside now for a time from the direct narrative to note the development of events which culminated in the forced expatriation of the Cherokee from their ancestral homes and their removal to the far western wilderness.

With a few notable exceptions the relations between the French and Spanish colonists and the native tribes, after the first occupation of the country, had been friendly and agreeable. Under the rule of France or Spain there was never any Indian boundary. Pioneer and Indian built their cabins and tilled their fields side by side, ranged the woods together, knelt before the same altar and frequently intermarried on terms of equality, so far as race was concerned. The result is seen to-day in the mixed-blood communities of Canada, and in Mexico, where a nation has been built upon an Indian foundation. Within the area of English colonization it was otherwise. From the first settlement to the recent inauguration of the allotment system it never occurred to the man of Teutonic blood that he could have for a neighbor anyone not of his own stock and color. While the English colonists recognized the native proprietorship so far as to make treaties with the Indians, it was chiefly for the purpose of fixing limits beyond which the Indian should never come after he had once parted with his title for a consideration of goods and trinkets. In an early Virginia treaty it was even stipulated that friendly Indians crossing the line should suffer death. The Indian was regarded as an incumbrance to be cleared off, like the trees and the wolves, before white men could live in the country. Intermarriages were practically

---

[1] Indian Treaties, pp. 185–187, 1837; Royce, Cherokee Nation, Fifth Ann. Rep. Bureau of Ethnology, pp. 197–209, 1888.

[2] Indian Treaties, pp. 199, 200, 1837; Royce, op. cit., pp. 209–211.

unknown, and the children of such union were usually compelled by race antipathy to cast their lot with the savage.

Under such circumstances the tribes viewed the advance of the English and their successors, the Americans, with keen distrust, and as early as the close of the French and Indian war we find some of them removing from the neighborhood of the English settlements to a safer shelter in the more remote territories still held by Spain. Soon after the French withdrew from Fort Toulouse, in 1763, a part of the Alabama, an incorporated tribe of the Creek confederacy, left their villages on the Coosa, and crossing the Mississippi, where they halted for a time on its western bank, settled on the Sabine river under Spanish protection.[1] They were followed some years later by a part of the Koasati, of the same confederacy,[2] the two tribes subsequently drifting into Texas, where they now reside. The Hichitee and others of the Lower Creeks moved down into Spanish Florida, where the Yamassee exiles from South Carolina had long before preceded them, the two combining to form the modern Seminole tribe. When the Revolution brought about a new line of division, the native tribes, almost without exception, joined sides with England as against the Americans, with the result that about one-half the Iroquois fled to Canada, where they still reside upon lands granted by the British government. A short time before Wayne's victory a part of the Shawano and Delawares, worn out by nearly twenty years of battle with the Americans, crossed the Mississippi and settled, by permission of the Spanish government, upon lands in the vicinity of Cape Girardeau, in what is now southeastern Missouri, for which they obtained a regular deed from that government in 1793.[3] Driven out by the Americans some twenty years later, they removed to Kansas and thence to Indian territory, where they are now incorporated with their old friends, the Cherokee.

When the first Cherokee crossed the Mississippi it is impossible to say, but there was probably never a time in the history of the tribe when their warriors and hunters were not accustomed to make excursions beyond the great river. According to an old tradition, the earliest emigration took place soon after the first treaty with Carolina, when a portion of the tribe, under the leadership of Yûñwĭ-usga'sĕ'tĭ, "Dangerous-man," forseeing the inevitable end of yielding to the demands of the colonists, refused to have any relations with the white man, and took up their long march for the unknown West. Communication was kept up with the home body until after crossing the Mississippi, when they were lost sight of and forgotten. Long years

[1] Claiborne, letter to Jefferson, November 5, 1808, American State Papers, I, p. 755, 1832; Gatschet, Creek Migration Legend, I, p. 88, 1884.

[2] Hawkins, 1799, quoted in Gatschet, op. cit., p. 89.

[3] See Treaty of St Louis, 1825, and of Castor hill, 1852, in Indian Treaties, pp. 388, 539, 1837.

afterward a rumor came from the west that they were still living near the base of the Rocky mountains.[1]   In 1782 the Cherokee, who had fought faithfully on the British side throughout the long Revolutionary struggle, applied to the Spanish governor at New Orleans for permission to settle on the west side of the Mississippi, within Spanish territory.   Permission was granted, and it is probable that some of them removed to the Arkansas country, although there seems to be no definite record of the matter.[2]   We learn incidentally, however, that about this period the hostile Cherokee, like the Shawano and other northern tribes, were in the habit of making friendly visits to the Spanish settlements in that quarter.

According to Reverend Cephas Washburn, the pioneer misssionary of the western Cherokee, the first permanent Cherokee settlement beyond the Mississippi was the direct result of the massacre, in 1794, of the Scott party at Muscle shoals, on Tennessee river, by the hostile warriors of the Chickamauga towns, in the summer.   As told by the missionary, the story differs considerably from that given by Haywood and other Tennessee historians, narrated in another place.[3]   According to Washburn, the whites were the aggressors, having first made the Indians drunk and then swindled them out of the annuity money with which they were just returning from the agency at Tellico.   When the Indians became sober enough to demand the return of their money the whites attacked and killed two of them, whereupon the others boarded the boat and killed every white man.   They spared the women and children, however, with their negro slaves and all their personal belongings, and permitted them to continue on their way, the chief and his party personally escorting them down Tennessee, Ohio, and Mississippi rivers as far as the mouth of the St. Francis, whence the emigrants descended in safety to New Orleans, while their captors, under their chief, The Bowl, went up St. Francis river—then a part of Spanish territory—to await the outcome of the event.   As soon as the news came to the Cherokee Nation the chiefs formally repudiated the action of the Bowl party and volunteered to assist in arresting those concerned.   Bowl and his men were finally exonerated, but had conceived such bitterness at the conduct of their former friends, and, moreover, had found the soil so rich and the game so abundant where they were, that they refused to return to their tribe and decided to remain permanently in the West.   Others joined them from time to time, attracted by the hunting prospect, until they were in sufficient number to obtain recognition from the Government.[4]

[1] See number 107, "The Lost Cherokee."
[2] See letter of Governor Estevan Miro to Robertson, April 20, 1783, in Roosevelt, Winning of the West, II, p. 407, 1889.
[3] See pp. 76–77.
[4] Washburn, Reminiscences, pp. 76–79, 1869; see also Royce, Cherokee Nation, Fifth Ann. Rep. Bureau of Ethnology, p. 204, 1888.

While the missionary may be pardoned for making the best show-ing possible for his friends, his statement contains several evident errors, and it is probable that Haywood's account is more correct in the main. As the Cherokee annuity at that time amounted to but fifteen hundred dollars for the whole tribe, or somewhat less than ten cents per head, they could hardly have had enough money from that source to pay such extravagant prices as sixteen dollars apiece for pocket mirrors, which it is alleged the boatmen obtained. Moreover, as the Chickamauga warriors had refused to sign any treaties and were notoriously hostile, they were not as yet entitled to receive payments. Haywood's statement that the emigrant party was first attacked while passing the Chickamauga towns and then pursued to the Muscle shoals and there massacred is probably near the truth, although it is quite possible that the whites may have provoked the attack in some such way as is indicated by the missionary. As Washburn got his account from one of the women of the party, living long afterward in New Orleans, it is certain that some at least were spared by the Indians, and it is probable that, as he states, only the men were killed.

The Bowl emigration may not have been the first, or even the most important removal to the western country, as the period was one of Indian unrest. Small bands were constantly crossing the Mississippi into Spanish territory to avoid the advancing Americans, only to find themselves again under American jurisdiction when the whole western country was ceded to the United States in 1803. The persistent land-hunger of the settler could not be restrained or satisfied, and early in the same year President Jefferson suggested to Congress the desira-bility of removing all the tribes to the west of the Mississippi. In the next year, 1804, an appropriation was made for taking prelimi-nary steps toward such a result.[1] There were probably but few Chero-kee on the Arkansas at this time, as they are not mentioned in Sibley's list of tribes south of that river in 1805.

In the summer of 1808, a Cherokee delegation being about to visit Washington, their agent, Colonel Meigs, was instructed by the Secre-tary of War to use every effort to obtain their consent to an exchange of their lands for a tract beyond the Mississippi. By this time the government's civilizing policy, as carried out in the annual distribution of farming tools, spinning wheels, and looms, had wrought a consider-able difference of habit and sentiment between the northern and southern Cherokee. Those on Little Tennessee and Hiwassee were generally farmers and stock raisers, producing also a limited quantity of cotton, which the women wove into cloth. Those farther down in Georgia and Alabama, the old hostile element, still preferred the hunting life and rejected all effort at innovation, although the game had now become so scarce that it was evident a change must soon

---

[1] Royce, Cherokee Nation, Fifth Ann. Rep. Bureau of Ethnology, pp. 202,203,1888.

come.   Jealousies had arisen in consequence, and the delegates representing the progressive element now proposed to the government that a line be run through the nation to separate the two parties, allowing those on the north to divide their lands in severalty and become citizens of the United States, while those on the south might continue to be hunters as long as the game should last.   Taking advantage of this condition of affairs, the government authorities instructed the agent to submit to the conservatives a proposition for a cession of their share of the tribal territory in return for a tract west of the Mississippi of sufficient area to enable them to continue the hunting life.   The plan was approved by President Jefferson, and a sum was appropriated to pay the expenses of a delegation to visit and inspect the lands on Arkansas and White rivers, with a view to removal.   The visit was made in the summer of 1809, and the delegates brought back such favorable report that a large number of Cherokee signified their intention to remove at once.   As no funds were then available for their removal, the matter was held in abeyance for several years, during which period families and individuals removed to the western country at their own expense until, before the year 1817, they numbered in all two or three thousand souls.[1] They became known as the Arkansas, or Western, Cherokee.

The emigrants soon became involved in difficulties with the native tribes, the Osage claiming all the lands north of Arkansas river, while the Quapaw claimed those on the south.   Upon complaining to the government the emigrant Cherokee were told that they had originally been permitted to remove only on condition of a cession of a portion of their eastern territory, and that nothing could be done to protect them in their new western home until such cession had been carried out.   The body of the Cherokee Nation, however, was strongly opposed to any such sale and proposed that the emigrants should be compelled to return.   After protracted negotiation a treaty was concluded at the Cherokee agency (now Calhoun, Tennessee) on July 8, 1817, by which the Cherokee Nation ceded two considerable tracts—the first in Georgia, lying east of the Chattahoochee, and the other in Tennessee, between Waldens ridge and the Little Sequatchee—as an equivalent for a tract to be assigned to those who had already removed, or intended to remove, to Arkansas.   Two smaller tracts on the north bank of the Tennessee, in the neighborhood of the Muscle shoals, were also ceded.   In return for these cessions the emigrant Cherokee were to receive a tract within the present limits of the state of Arkan-

---

[1] Royce, Cherokee Nation, Fifth Ann. Rep. Bureau of Ethnology, pp. 202–204, 1888; see also Indian Treaties, pp. 209–215, 1837.   The preamble to the treaty of 1817 says that the delegation of 1808 had desired a division of the tribal territory in order that the people of the Upper (northern) towns might "begin the establishment of fixed laws and a regular government," while those of the Lower (southern) towns desired to remove to the West.   Nothing is said of severalty allotments or citizenship.

sas, bounded on the north and south by White river and Arkansas river, respectively, on the east by a line running between those streams approximately from the present Batesville to Lewisburg, and on the west by a line to be determined later. As afterward established, this western line ran from the junction of the Little North Fork with White river to just beyond the point where the present western Arkansas boundary strikes Arkansas river. Provision was made for taking the census of the whole Cherokee nation east and west in order to apportion annuities and other payments properly in the future, and the two bands were still to be considered as forming one people. The United States agreed to pay for any substantial improvements abandoned by those removing from the ceded lands, and each emigrant warrior who left no such valuable property behind was to be given as full compensation for his abandoned field and cabin a rifle and ammunition, a blanket, and a kettle or a beaver trap. The government further agreed to furnish boats and provisions for the journey. Provision was also made that individuals residing upon the ceded lands might retain allotments and become citizens, if they so elected, the amount of the allotment to be deducted from the total cession.

The commissioners for the treaty were General Andrew Jackson, General David Meriwether, and Governor Joseph McMinn of Tennessee. On behalf of the Cherokee it was signed by thirty-one principal men of the eastern Nation and fifteen of the western band, who signed by proxy.[1]

The majority of the Cherokee were bitterly opposed to any cession or removal project, and before the treaty had been concluded a memorial signed by sixty-seven chiefs and headmen of the nation was presented to the commissioners, which stated that the delegates who had first broached the subject in Washington some years before had acted without any authority from the nation. They declared that the great body of the Cherokee desired to remain in the land of their birth, where they were rapidly advancing in civilization, instead of being compelled to revert to their original savage conditions and surroundings. They therefore prayed that the matter might not be pressed further, but that they might be allowed to remain in peaceable possession of the land of their fathers. No attention was paid to the memorial, and the treaty was carried through and ratified. Without waiting for the ratification, the authorities at once took steps for the removal of those who desired to go to the West. Boats were provided at points between Little Tennessee and Sequatchee rivers, and the emigrants were collected under the direction of Governor McMinn. Within the next year a large number had emigrated, and before the

---

[1] Indian Treaties, pp. 209–215, 1837; Royce, Cherokee Nation, Fifth Ann. Rep. Bureau of Ethnology, pp. 212–217, 1888; see also maps in Royce.

end of 1819 the number of emigrants was said to have increased to six thousand. The chiefs of the nation, however, claimed that the estimate was greatly in excess of the truth.[1]

"There can be no question that a very large portion, and probably a majority, of the Cherokee nation residing east of the Mississippi had been and still continued bitterly opposed to the terms of the treaty of 1817. They viewed with jealous and aching hearts all attempts to drive them from the homes of their ancestors, for they could not but consider the constant and urgent importunities of the federal authorities in the light of an imperative demand for the cession of more territory. They felt that they were, as a nation, being slowly but surely compressed within the contracting coils of the giant anaconda of civilization; yet they held to the vain hope that a spirit of justice and mercy would be born of their helpless condition which would finally prevail in their favor. Their traditions furnished them no guide by which to judge of the results certain to follow such a conflict as that in which they were engaged. This difference of sentiment in the nation upon a subject so vital to their welfare was productive of much bitterness and violent animosities. Those who had favored the emigration scheme and had been induced, either through personal preference or by the subsidizing influences of the government agents, to favor the conclusion of the treaty, became the object of scorn and hatred to the remainder of the nation. They were made the subjects of a persecution so relentless, while they remained in the eastern country, that it was never forgotten, and when, in the natural course of events, the remainder of the nation was forced to remove to the Arkansas country and join the earlier emigrants, the old hatreds and dissensions broke out afresh, and to this day they find lodgment in some degree in the breasts of their descendants."[2]

Two months after the signing of the treaty of July 8, 1817, and three months before its ratification, a council of the nation sent a delegation to Washington to recount in detail the improper methods and influences which had been used to consummate it, and to ask that it be set aside and another agreement substituted. The mission was without result.[3]

In 1817 the American Board of Commissioners for Foreign Missions established its first station among the Cherokee at Brainerd, in Tennessee, on the west side of Chickamauga creek, two miles from the Georgia line. The mission took its name from a distinguished pioneer worker among the northern tribes (37). The government aided in the erection of the buildings, which included a schoolhouse, gristmill, and workshops, in which, besides the ordinary branches, the boys were taught simple mechanic arts while the girls learned the use of the

[1] Royce, Cherokee Nation, Fifth Ann. Rep. Bureau of Ethnology, 217–218, 1888.
[2] Ibid., pp. 218–219.   [3] Ibid., p. 219.

needle and the spinningwheel. There was also a large work farm. The mission prospered and others were established at Willstown, Hightower, and elsewhere by the same board, in which two hundred pupils were receiving instruction in 1820.[1] Among the earliest and most noted workers at the Brainerd mission were Reverend D. S. Buttrick and Reverend S. A. Worcester (38), the latter especially having done much for the mental elevation of the Cherokee, and more than once having suffered imprisonment for his zeal in defending their cause. The missions flourished until broken up by the state of Georgia at the beginning of the Removal troubles, and they were afterwards renewed in the western country. Mission ridge preserves the memory of the Brainerd establishment.

Early in 1818 a delegation of emigrant Cherokee visited Washington for the purpose of securing a more satisfactory determination of the boundaries of their new lands on the Arkansas. Measures were soon afterward taken for that purpose. They also asked recognition in the future as a separate and distinct tribe, but nothing was done in the matter. In order to remove, if possible, the hostile feeling between the emigrants and the native Osage, who regarded the former as intruders, Governor William Clark, superintendent of Indian affairs for Missouri, arranged a conference of the chiefs of the two tribes at St. Louis in October of that year, at which, after protracted effort, he succeeded in establishing friendly relations between them. Efforts were made about the same time, both by the emigrant Cherokee and by the government, to persuade the Shawano and Delawares then residing in Missouri, and the Oneida in New York, to join the western Cherokee, but nothing came of the negotiations.[2] In 1825 a delegation of western Cherokee visited the Shawano in Ohio for the same purpose, but without success. Their object in thus inviting friendly Indians to join them was to strengthen themselves against the Osage and other native tribes.

In the meantime the government, through Governor McMinn, was bringing strong pressure to bear upon the eastern Cherokee to compel their removal to the West. At a council convened by him in November, 1818, the governor represented to the chiefs that it was now no longer possible to protect them from the encroachments of the surrounding white population; that, however the government might wish to help them, their lands would be taken, their stock stolen, their women corrupted, and their men made drunkards unless they removed to the western paradise. He ended by proposing to pay them one hundred thousand dollars for their whole territory, with the expense of removal, if they would go at once. Upon their prompt and indignant refusal he offered to double the amount, but with as little success.

[1] Morse, Geography, I, p. 577, 1819; and p. 185, 1822.
[2] Royce, Cherokee Nation, Fifth Ann. Rep. Bureau of Ethnology, pp. 221-222, 1888.

Every point of the negotiation having failed, another course was adopted, and a delegation was selected to visit Washington under the conduct of Agent Meigs. Here the effort was renewed until, wearied and discouraged at the persistent importunity, the chiefs consented to a large cession, which was represented as necessary in order to compensate in area for the tract assigned to the emigrant Cherokee in Arkansas in accordance with the previous treaty. This estimate was based on the figures given by Governor McMinn, who reported 5,291 Cherokee enrolled as emigrants, while the eastern Cherokee claimed that not more than 3,500 had removed and that those remaining numbered 12,544, or more than three-fourths of the whole nation. The governor, however, chose to consider one-half of the nation as in favor of removal and one-third as having already removed.[1]

The treaty, concluded at Washington on February 27, 1819, recites that the greater part of the Cherokee nation, having expressed an earnest desire to remain in the East, and being anxious to begin the necessary measures for the civilization and preservation of their nation, and to settle the differences arising out of the treaty of 1817, have offered to cede to the United States a tract of country "at least as extensive" as that to which the Government is entitled under the late treaty. The cession embraces (1) a tract in Alabama and Tennessee, between Tennessee and Flint rivers; (2) a tract in Tennessee, between Tennessee river and Waldens ridge; (3) a large irregular tract in Tennessee, North Carolina, and Georgia, embracing in Tennessee nearly all the remaining Cherokee lands north of Hiwassee river, and in North Carolina and Georgia nearly everything remaining to them east of the Nantahala mountains and the upper western branch of the Chattahoochee; (4) six small pieces reserved by previous treaties. The entire cession aggregated nearly six thousand square miles, or more than one-fourth of all then held by the nation. Individual reservations of one mile square each within the ceded area were allowed to a number of families which decided to remain among the whites and become citizens rather than abandon their homes. Payment was to be made for all substantial improvements abandoned, one-third of all tribal annuities were hereafter to be paid to the western band, and the treaty was declared to be a final adjustment of all claims and differences arising from the treaty of 1817.[2]

Civilization had now progressed so far among the Cherokee that in the fall of 1820 they adopted a regular republican form of government modeled after that of the United States. Under this arrangement the nation was divided into eight districts, each of which was entitled

---

[1] Royce, Cherokee Nation, Fifth Ann. Rep. Bureau of Ethnology, pp. 222–228, 1888.
[2] Indian Treaties, pp. 265–269, 1837; Royce, op. cit., pp. 219–221 and table, p. 378.

to send four representatives to the Cherokee national legislature, which met at Newtown, or New Echota, the capital, at the junction of Conasauga and Coosawatee rivers, a few miles above the present Calhoun, Georgia. The legislature consisted of an upper and a lower house, designated, respectively (in the Cherokee language), the national committee and national council, the members being elected for limited terms by the voters of each district. The principal officer was styled president of the national council; the distinguished John Ross was the first to hold this office. There was also a clerk of the committee and two principal members to express the will of the council or lower house. For each district there were appointed a council house for meetings twice a year, a judge, and a marshal. Companies of "light horse" were organized to assist in the execution of the laws, with a "ranger" for each district to look after stray stock. Each head of a family and each single man under the age of sixty was subject to a poll tax. Laws were passed for the collection of taxes and debts, for repairs on roads, for licenses to white persons engaged in farming or other business in the nation, for the support of schools, for the regulation of the liquor traffic and the conduct of negro slaves, to punish horse stealing and theft, to compel all marriages between white men and Indian women to be according to regular legal or church form, and to discourage polygamy. By special decree the right of blood revenge or capital punishment was taken from the seven clans and vested in the constituted authorities of the nation. It was made treason, punishable with death, for any individual to negotiate the sale of lands to the whites without the consent of the national council (39). White men were not allowed to vote or to hold office in the nation.[1] The system compared favorably with that of the Federal government or of any state government then existing.

At this time there were five principal missions, besides one or two small branch establishments in the nation, viz: Spring Place, the oldest, founded by the Moravians at Spring place, Georgia, in 1801; Oothcaloga, Georgia, founded by the same denomination in 1821 on the creek of that name, near the present Calhoun; Brainerd, Tennessee, founded by the American Board of Commissioners for Foreign Missions in 1817; "Valley-towns," North Carolina, founded by the Baptists in 1820, on the site of the old Natchez town on the north side of Hiwassee river, just above Peachtree creek; Coosawatee, Georgia ("Tensawattee," by error in the State Papers), founded also by the Baptists in 1821, near the mouth of the river of that name. All were in flourishing condition, the Brainerd establishment especially, with nearly one hundred pupils, being obliged to turn away applicants for

[1] Laws of the Cherokee Nation (several documents), 1820, American State Papers: Indian Affairs, II, pp. 279–283, 1834; letter quoted by McKenney, 1825, ibid., pp. 651, 652; Drake, Indians, pp. 437, 438, ed. 1880.

lack of accommodation.   The superintendent reported that the children
were apt to learn, willing to labor, and readily submissive to discipline,
adding that the Cherokee were fast advancing toward civilized life and
generally manifested an ardent desire for instruction.   The Valley-
towns mission, established at the instance of Currahee Dick, a prominent local mixed-blood chief, was in charge of the Reverend Evan
Jones, known as the translator of the New Testament into the Cherokee
language, his assistant being James D. Wafford, a mixed-blood pupil,
who compiled a spelling book in the same language.   Reverend S. A.
Worcester, a prolific translator and the compiler of the Cherokee
almanac and other works, was stationed at Brainerd, removing thence
to New Echota and afterward to the Cherokee Nation in the West.[1]
Since 1817 the American Board had also supported at Cornwall, Connecticut, an Indian school at which a number of young Cherokee were
being educated, among them being Elias Boudinot, afterward the
editor of the *Cherokee Phœnix*.

About this time occurred an event which at once placed the Cherokee
in the front rank among native tribes and was destined to have profound
influence on their whole future history, viz., the invention of the
alphabet.

The inventor, aptly called the Cadmus of his race, was a mixed-
blood known among his own people as Sikwâ'yĭ (Sequoya) and
among the whites as George Gist, or less correctly Guest or Guess.
As is usually the case in Indian biography much uncertainty exists in
regard to his parentage and early life.   Authorities generally agree
that his father was a white man, who drifted into the Cherokee Nation
some years before the Revolution and formed a temporary alliance
with a Cherokee girl of mixed blood, who thus became the mother of
the future teacher.   A writer in the *Cherokee Phœnix*, in 1828, says
that only his paternal grandfather was a white man.[2]   McKenney and
Hall say that his father was a white man named Gist.[3]   Phillips
asserts that his father was George Gist, an unlicensed German trader
from Georgia, who came into the Cherokee Nation in 1768.[4]   By a
Kentucky family it is claimed that Sequoya's father was Nathaniel Gist,
son of the scout who accompanied Washington on his memorable
excursion to the Ohio.   As the story goes, Nathaniel Gist was captured by the Cherokee at Braddock's defeat (1755) and remained a
prisoner with them for six years, during which time he became the
father of Sequoya.   On his return to civilization he married a white
woman in Virginia, by whom he had other children, and afterward

---

[1] List of missions and reports of missionaries, etc., American State Papers: Indian Affairs, II, pp.
277–279, 459, 1834; personal information from James D. Wafford concerning Valley-towns mission.
For notices of Worcester, Jones, and Wafford, see Pilling, Bibliography of the Iroquoian Languages,
1888.

[2] G. C., in Cherokee Phœnix; reprinted in Christian Advocate and Journal, New York, September 26,
1828.

[3] McKenney and Hall, Indian Tribes, I, p. 35, et passim, 1858.

[4] Phillips, Sequoyah, in Harper's Magazine, pp. 542–548, September, 1870.

SEQUOYA (SIKWÂYĬ)

(From McKenney and Hall's copy of the original painting of 1828)

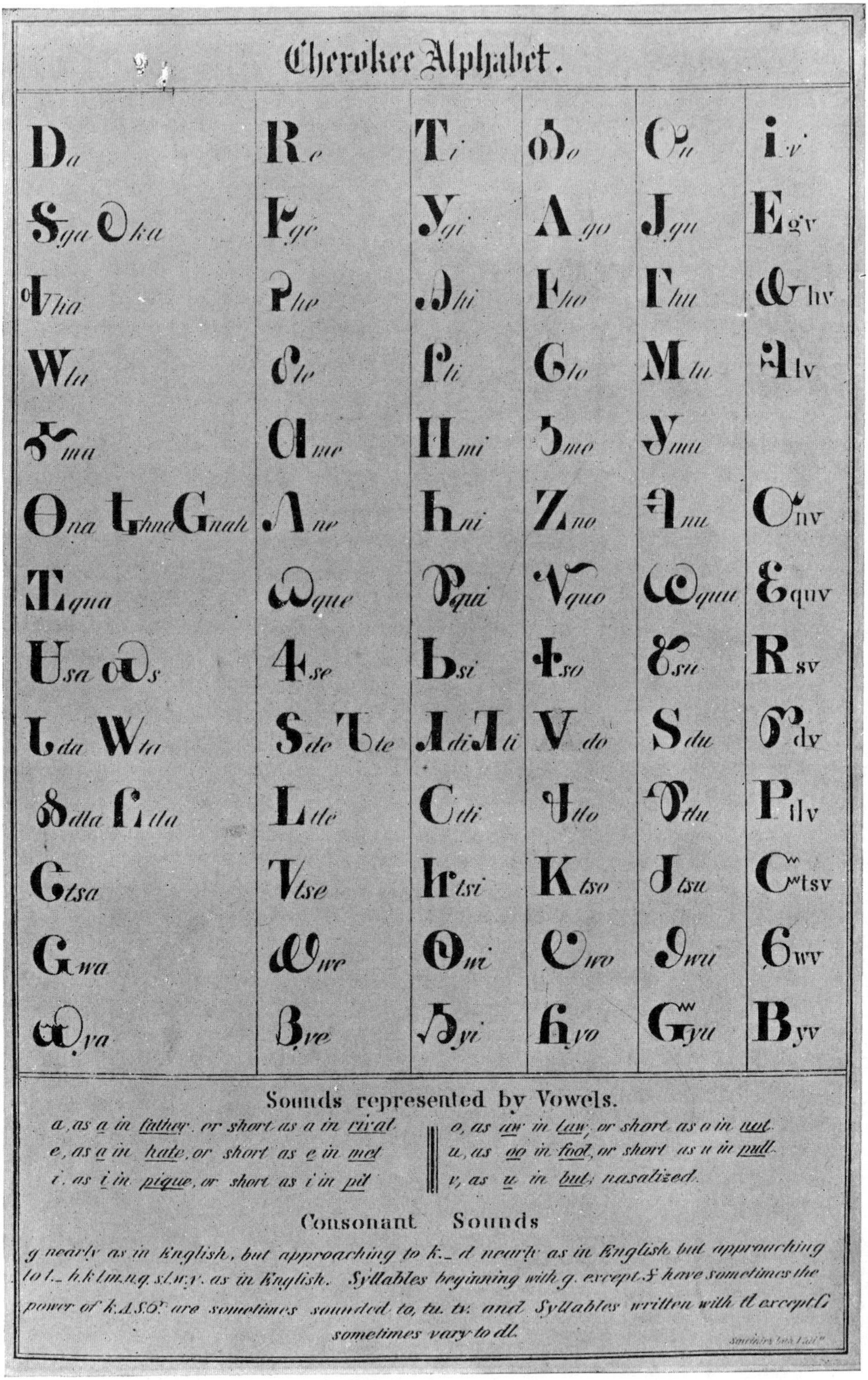

Cherokee Alphabet.

D a	R e	T i	ꭰ o	O u	i v
S ga O ka	F ge	Y gi	A go	J gu	E gv
O ha	P he	ꭿ hi	F ho	Γ hu	ꮵ hv
W la	ꮆ le	P li	G lo	M lu	ꭷ lv
ꮎ ma	O me	H mi	ꮒ mo	Y mu	
O na ꮧ hna G nah	Λ ne	h ni	Z no	ꮔ nu	O nv
T qua	ꮖ que	P qui	V quo	ꮖ quu	E quv
U sa ꭴ s	4 se	b si	ꮖ so	ꭿ su	R sv
L da W ta	S de ꮧ te	ꭰ di ꭿ ti	V do	S du	� dv
ꮪ dla ꮧ tla	L tle	C tli	ꮣ tlo	ꮧ tlu	P tlv
G tsa	V tse	h tsi	K tso	ꭰ tsu	C tsv
G wa	ꮺ we	O wi	ꮼ wo	ꮃ wu	6 wv
ꮎ ya	B ye	ꭶ yi	ꭶ yo	G yu	B yv

Sounds represented by Vowels.

a, as a in father, or short as a in rival

e, as a in hate, or short as e in met

i, as i in pique, or short as i in pit

o, as aw in law, or short as o in not.

u, as oo in fool, or short as u in pull.

v, as u in but, nasalized.

Consonant Sounds

g nearly as in English, but approaching to k.-- d nearly as in English but approaching to t.-- h.k.l.m.n.q. s.t.w.y. as in English. Syllables beginning with g. except ꮒ have sometimes the power of k.ꭰꮪ.ꮫ, are sometimes sounded to, tu, tv. and Syllables written with tl except ꮧ sometimes vary to dl.

THE CHEROKEE ALPHABET

removed to Kentucky, where Sequoya, then a Baptist preacher, frequently visited him and was always recognized by the family as his son.[1]

Aside from the fact that the Cherokee acted as allies of the English during the war in which Braddock's defeat occurred, and that Sequoya, so far from being a preacher, was not even a Christian, the story contains other elements of improbability and appears to be one of those genealogical myths built upon a chance similarity of name. On the other hand, it is certain that Sequoya was born before the date that Phillips allows. On his mother's side he was of good family in the tribe, his uncle being a chief in Echota.[2] According to personal information of James Wafford, who knew him well, being his second cousin, Sequoya was probably born about the year 1760, and lived as a boy with his mother at Tuskegee town in Tennessee, just outside of old Fort Loudon. It is quite possible that his white father may have been a soldier of the garrison, one of those lovers for whom the Cherokee women risked their lives during the siege.[3] What became of the father is not known, but the mother lived alone with her son.

The only incident of his boyhood that has come down to us is his presence at Echota during the visit of the Iroquois peace delegation, about the year 1770.[4] His early years were spent amid the stormy alarms of the Revolution, and as he grew to manhood he developed a considerable mechanical ingenuity, especially in silver working. Like most of his tribe he was also a hunter and fur trader. Having nearly reached middle age before the first mission was established in the Nation, he never attended school and in all his life never learned to speak, read, or write the English language. Neither did he ever abandon his native religion, although from frequent visits to the Moravian mission he became imbued with a friendly feeling toward the new civilization. Of an essentially contemplative disposition, he was led by a chance conversation in 1809 to reflect upon the ability of the white men to communicate thought by means of writing, with the result that he set about devising a similar system for his own people. By a hunting accident, which rendered him a cripple for life, he was fortunately afforded more leisure for study. The presence of his name, George Guess, appended to a treaty of 1816, indicates that he was already of some prominence in the Nation, even before the perfection of his great invention. After years of patient and unremitting labor in the face of ridicule, discouragement, and repeated failure, he finally evolved the Cherokee syllabary and in 1821 submitted it to a public test by the leading men of the Nation. By this time, in consequence of repeated cessions, the Cherokee had been dispossessed of the country about Echota, and Sequoya was now living at Willstown,

---

[1] Manuscript letters by John Mason Brown, January 17, 18, 22, and February 4, 1889, in archives of the Bureau of American Ethnology.

[2] McKenney and Hall, Indian Tribes, I, p. 45, 1858.

[3] See page 43.   [4] See number 89, "The Iroquois wars."

on an upper branch of Coosa river, in Alabama.   The syllabary was
soon recognized as an invaluable invention for the elevation of the
tribe, and within a few months thousands of hitherto illiterate Cherokee were able to read and write their own language, teaching each
other in the cabins and along the roadside.   The next year Sequoya
visited the West, to introduce the new science among those who had
emigrated to the Arkansas.   In the next year, 1823, he again visited
the Arkansas and took up his permanent abode with the western band,
never afterward returning to his eastern kinsmen.   In the autumn of
the same year the Cherokee national council made public acknowledgment of his merit by sending to him, through John Ross, then president of the national committee, a silver medal with a commemorative
inscription in both languages.[1]   In 1828 he visited Washington as one
of the delegates from the Arkansas band, attracting much attention,
and the treaty made on that occasion contains a provision for the payment to him of five hundred dollars, "for the great benefits he has
conferred upon the Cherokee people, in the beneficial results which
they are now experiencing from the use of the alphabet discovered by
him."[2]   His subsequent history belongs to the West and will be treated
in another place (40).[3]

The invention of the alphabet had an immediate and wonderful
effect on Cherokee development.   On account of the remarkable adaptation of the syllabary to the language, it was only necessary to learn
the characters to be able to read at once.   No schoolhouses were built
and no teachers hired, but the whole Nation became an academy for the
study of the system, until, "in the course of a few months, without
school or expense of time or money, the Cherokee were able to read
and write in their own language.[4]   An active correspondence began
to be carried on between the eastern and western divisions, and plans
were made for a national press, with a national library and museum to
be established at the capital, New Echota.[5]   The missionaries, who had
at first opposed the new alphabet on the ground of its Indian origin,
now saw the advisability of using it to further their own work.   In
the fall of 1824 Atsĭ or John Arch, a young native convert, made a
manuscript translation of a portion of St. John's gospel, in the syllabary, this being the first Bible translation ever given to the Cherokee.
It was copied hundreds of times and was widely disseminated through

---

[1] McKenney and Hall, Indian Tribes, I, p. 46, 1858; Phillips, in Harper's Magazine, p. 547, September, 1870.

[2] Indian Treaties, p. 425, 1837.

[3] For details concerning the life and invention of Sequoya, see McKenney and Hall, Indian Tribes, I, 1858; Phillips, Sequoyah, in Harper's Magazine, September 1870· Foster, Sequoyah, 1885, and Story of the Cherokee Bible, 1899, based largely on Phillips' article; G. C., Invention of the Cherokee Alphabet, in Cherokee Phœnix, republished in Christian Advocate and Journal, New York, September 26, 1828: Pilling, Bibliography of the Iroquoian Languages, 1888.

[4] G. C., Invention of the Cherokee Alphabet, op. cit.

[5] (Unsigned) letter of David Brown, September 2, 1825, quoted in American State Papers: Indian Affairs, II, p. 652, 1834.

the Nation.[1] In September, 1825, David Brown, a prominent half-breed preacher, who had already made some attempt at translation in the Roman alphabet, completed a translation of the New Testament in the new syllabary, the work being handed about in manuscript, as there were as yet no types cast in the Sequoya characters.[2] In the same month he forwarded to Thomas McKenney, chief of the Bureau of Indian Affairs at Washington, a manuscript table of the characters, with explanation, this being probably its first introduction to official notice.[3]

In 1827 the Cherokee council having formally resolved to establish a national paper in the Cherokee language and characters, types for that purpose were cast in Boston, under the supervision of the noted missionary, Worcester, of the American Board of Commissioners for Foreign Missions, who, in December of that year contributed to the *Missionary Herald* five verses of Genesis in the new syllabary, this seeming to be its first appearance in print. Early in the next year the press and types arrived at New Echota, and the first number of the new paper, *Tsa'lăgĭ Tsu'lehisanuñ'hĭ*, the *Cherokee Phœnix*, printed in both languages, appeared on February 21, 1828. The first printers were two white men, Isaac N. Harris and John F. Wheeler, with John Candy, a half-blood apprentice. Elias Boudinot (Gălagi'na, "The Buck"), an educated Cherokee, was the editor, and Reverend S. A. Worcester was the guiding spirit who brought order out of chaos and set the work in motion. The office was a log house. The hand press and types, after having been shipped by water from Boston, were transported two hundred miles by wagon from Augusta to their destination. The printing paper had been overlooked and had to be brought by the same tedious process from Knoxville. Cases and other equipments had to be devised and fashioned by the printers, neither of whom understood a word of Cherokee, but simply set up the characters, as handed to them in manuscript by Worcester and the editor. Such was the beginning of journalism in the Cherokee nation. After a precarious existence of about six years the *Phœnix* was suspended, owing to the hostile action of the Georgia authorities, who went so far as to throw Worcester and Wheeler into prison. Its successor, after the removal of the Cherokee to the West, was the *Cherokee Advocate*, of which the first number appeared at Tahlequah in 1844, with William P. Ross as editor. It is still continued under the auspices of the Nation, printed in both languages and distributed free at the expense of the Nation to those unable to read English—an example without parallel in any other government.

In addition to numerous Bible translations, hymn books, and other

---

[1] Foster, Sequoyah, pp. 120, 121, 1885.   [2] Pilling, Iroquoian Bibliography, p. 21, 1888.
[3] Brown letter (unsigned), in American State Papers: Indian Affairs, II, p. 652, 1834.

religious works, there have been printed in the Cherokee langua;e and
syllabary the *Cherokee Phœnix* (journal), *Cherokee Advocate* (journal),
Cherokee Messenger (periodical), *Cherokee Almanac* (annual), Cherokee
spelling books, arithmetics, and other schoolbooks for those unable to
read English, several editions of the laws of the Nation, and a large
body of tracts and minor publications. Space forbids even a mention
of the names of the devoted workers in this connection. Besides this
printed literature the syllabary is in constant and daily use among the
non-English-speaking element, both in Indian Territory and in North
Carolina, for letter writing, council records, personal memoranda, etc.
What is perhaps strangest of all in this literary evolution is the fact
that the same invention has been seized by the priests and conjurers
of the conservative party for the purpose of preserving to their successors the ancient rituals and secret knowledge of the tribe, whole
volumes of such occult literature in manuscript having been obtained
among them by the author.[1]

In 1819 the whole Cherokee population had been estimated at 15,000,
one-third of them being west of the Mississippi. In 1825 a census of
the eastern Nation showed: native Cherokee, 13,563; white men married into the Nation, 147; white women married into the Nation, 73;
negro slaves, 1,277. There were large herds of cattle, horses, hogs,
and sheep, with large crops of every staple, including cotton, tobacco,
and wheat, and some cotton was exported by boats as far as New Orleans. Apple and peach orchards were numerous, butter and cheese
were in use to some extent, and both cotton and woolen cloths, especially blankets, were manufactured. Nearly all the merchants were
native Cherokee. Mechanical industries flourished, the Nation was out
of debt, and the population was increasing.[2] Estimating one-third
beyond the Mississippi, the total number of Cherokee, exclusive of
adopted white citizens and negro slaves, must then have been about
20,000.

Simultaneously with the decrees establishing a national press, the
Cherokee Nation, in general convention of delegates held for the purpose at New Echota on July 26, 1827, adopted a national constitution,
based on the assumption of distinct and independent nationality. John
Ross, so celebrated in connection with the history of his tribe, was
president of the convention which framed the instrument. Charles R.
Hicks, a Moravian convert of mixed blood, and at that time the most
influential man in the Nation, was elected principal chief, with John

[1] For extended notice of Cherokee literature and authors see numerous references in Pilling, Bibliography of the Iroquoian Languages, 1888; also Foster, Sequoyah, 1885, and Story of the Cherokee
Bible, 1899. The largest body of original Cherokee manuscript material in existence, including
hundreds of ancient ritual formulas, was obtained by the writer among the East Cherokee, and is
now in possession of the Bureau of American Ethnology, to be translated at some future time.

[2] Brown letter (unsigned), September 2, 1825, American State Papers: Indian Affairs, II, pp. 651, 652,
1834.

Ross as assistant chief.[1] With a constitution and national press, a well-developed system of industries and home education, and a government administered by educated Christian men, the Cherokee were now justly entitled to be considered a civilized people.

The idea of a civilized Indian government was not a new one. The first treaty ever negotiated by the United States with an Indian tribe, in 1778, held out to the Delawares the hope that by a confederation of friendly tribes they might be able "to form a state, whereof the Delaware nation shall be the head and have a representation in Congress."[2] Priber, the Jesuit, had already familiarized the Cherokee with the forms of civilized government before the middle of the eighteenth century. As the gap between the conservative and progressive elements widened after the Revolution the idea grew, until in 1808 representatives of both parties visited Washington to propose an arrangement by which those who clung to the old life might be allowed to remove to the western hunting grounds, while the rest should remain to take up civilization and "begin the establishment of fixed laws and a regular government." The project received the warm encouragement of President Jefferson, and it was with this understanding that the western emigration was first officially recognized a few years later. Immediately upon the return of the delegates from Washington the Cherokee drew up their first brief written code of laws, modeled agreeably to the friendly suggestions of Jefferson.[3]

By this time the rapid strides of civilization and Christianity had alarmed the conservative element, who saw in the new order of things only the evidences of apostasy and swift national decay. In 1828 White-path (Nûñ'nâ-tsune'ga), an influential full-blood and councilor, living at Turniptown (Uʻlûñ'yĭ), near the present Ellijay, in Gilmer county, Georgia, headed a rebellion against the new code of laws, with all that it implied. He soon had a large band of followers, known to the whites as "Red-sticks," a title sometimes assumed by the more warlike element among the Creeks and other southern tribes. From the townhouse of Ellijay he preached the rejection of the new constitution, the discarding of Christianity and the white man's ways, and a return to the old tribal law and custom—the same doctrine that had more than once constituted the burden of Indian revelation in the past. It was now too late, however, to reverse the wheel of progress, and under the rule of such men as Hicks and Ross the conservative opposition gradually melted away. White-path was deposed from his seat

[1] See Royce, Cherokee Nation, Fifth Ann. Rep. Bureau of Ethnology, p. 241, 1888; Meredith, in The Five Civilized Tribes, Extra Census Bulletin, p. 41, 1894; Morse, American Geography, I, p. 577, 1819 (for Hicks).

[2] Fort Pitt treaty, September 17, 1778, Indian Treaties, p. 3, 1837.

[3] Cherokee Agency treaty, July 8, 1817, ibid., p. 209; Drake, Indians, p. 450, ed. 1880; Johnson in Senate Report on Territories; Cherokee Memorial, January 18, 1831; see laws of 1808, 1810, and later, in American State Papers: Indian Affairs, II, pp. 279–283, 1834. The volume of Cherokee laws, compiled in the Cherokee language by the Nation, in 1850, begins with the year 1808.

in council, but subsequently made submission and was reinstated. He was afterward one of the detachment commanders in the Removal, but died while on the march.[1]

In this year, also, John Ross became principal chief of the Nation, a position which he held until his death in 1866, thirty-eight years later.[2] In this long period, comprising the momentous episodes of the Removal and the War of the Rebellion, it may be truly said that his history is the history of the Nation.

And now, just when it seemed that civilization and enlightenment were about to accomplish their perfect work, the Cherokee began to hear the first low muttering of the coming storm that was soon to overturn their whole governmental structure and sweep them forever from the land of their birth.

By an agreement between the United States and the state of Georgia in 1802, the latter, for valuable consideration, had ceded to the general government her claims west of the present state boundary, the United States at the same time agreeing to extinguish, at its own expense, but for the benefit of the state, the Indian claims within the state limits, "as early as the same can be peaceably obtained on reasonable terms."[3] In accordance with this agreement several treaties had already been made with the Creeks and Cherokee, by which large tracts had been secured for Georgia at the expense of the general government. Notwithstanding this fact, and the terms of the proviso, Georgia accused the government of bad faith in not taking summary measures to compel the Indians at once to surrender all their remaining lands within the chartered state limits, coupling the complaint with a threat to take the matter into her own hands. In 1820 Agent Meigs had expressed the opinion that the Cherokee were now so far advanced that further government aid was unnecessary, and that their lands should be allotted and the surplus sold for their benefit, they themselves to be invested with full rights of citizenship in the several states within which they resided. This suggestion had been approved by President Monroe, but had met the most determined opposition from the states concerned. Tennessee absolutely refused to recognize individual reservations made by previous treaties, while North Carolina and Georgia bought in all such reservations with money appropriated by Congress.[4] No Indian was to be allowed to live within those states on any pretext whatsoever.

In the meantime, owing to persistent pressure from Georgia, repeated unsuccessful efforts had been made to procure from the Cherokee a cession of their lands within the chartered limits of the

---

[1] Personal information from James D. Wafford. So far as is known this rebellion of the conservatives has never hitherto been noted in print.

[2] See Resolutions of Honor, in Laws of the Cherokee Nation, pp. 137-140, 1868; Meredith, in The Five Civilized Tribes, Extra Census Bulletin, p. 41, 1894; Appleton, Cyclopedia of American Biography.

[3] See fourth article of "Articles of agreement and cession," April 24, 1802, in American State Papers: class VIII, Public Lands, I, quoted also by Greeley, American Conflict, I, p. 103, 1864.

[4] Royce, Cherokee Nation, Fifth Ann. Rep. Bureau of Ethnology, pp. 231-233, 1888.

state. Every effort met with a firm refusal, the Indians declaring that having already made cession after cession from a territory once extensive, their remaining lands were no more than were needed for themselves and their children, more especially as experience had shown that each concession would be followed by a further demand. They conclude: "It is the fixed and unalterable determination of this nation never again to cede one foot more of land." Soon afterward they addressed to the President a memorial of similar tenor, to which Calhoun, as Secretary of War, returned answer that as Georgia objected to their presence either as a tribe or as individual owners or citizens, they must prepare their minds for removal beyond the Mississippi.[1]

In reply, the Cherokee, by their delegates—John Ross, George Lowrey, Major Ridge, and Elijah Hicks—sent a strong letter calling attention to the fact that by the very wording of the 1802 agreement the compact was a conditional one which could not be carried out without their own voluntary consent, and suggesting that Georgia might be satisfied from the adjoining government lands in Florida. Continuing, they remind the Secretary that the Cherokee are not foreigners, but original inhabitants of America, inhabiting and standing now upon the soil of their own territory, with limits defined by treaties with the United States, and that, confiding in the good faith of the government to respect its treaty stipulations, they do not hesitate to say that their true interest, prosperity, and happiness demand their permanency where they are and the retention of their lands.[2]

A copy of this letter was sent by the Secretary to Governor Troup of Georgia, who returned a reply in which he blamed the missionaries for the refusal of the Indians, declared that the state would not permit them to become citizens, and that the Secretary must either assist the state in taking possession of the Cherokee lands, or, in resisting that occupancy, make war upon and shed the blood of brothers and friends. The Georgia delegation in Congress addressed a similar letter to President Monroe, in which the government was censured for having instructed the Indians in the arts of civilized life and having thereby imbued them with a desire to acquire property.[3]

For answer the President submitted a report by Secretary Calhoun showing that since the agreement had been made with Georgia in 1802 the government had, at its own expense, extinguished the Indian claim to 24,600 square miles within the limits of that state, or more than three-fifths of the whole Indian claim, and had paid on that and other accounts connected with the agreement nearly seven and a half million

[1] Cherokee correspondence, 1823 and 1824, American State Papers: Indian Affairs, II, pp. 468–473, 1834; Royce, Cherokee Nation, Fifth Ann. Rep. Bureau of Ethnology, pp. 236–237, 1888.

[2] Cherokee memorial, February 11, 1824, in American State Papers: Indian Affairs, II, pp. 473, 494, 1834; Royce, op. cit., p. 237.

[3] Letters of Governor Troup of Georgia, February 28, 1824, and of Georgia delegates, March 10, 1824, American State Papers: Indian Affairs, II, pp. 475, 477, 1834; Royce, op. cit., pp. 237, 238.

dollars, of which by far the greater part had gone to Georgia or her citizens. In regard to the other criticism the report states that the civilizing policy was as old as the government itself, and that in performing the high duties of humanity to the Indians, it had never been conceived that the stipulation of the convention was contravened. In handing in the report the President again called attention to the conditional nature of the agreement and declared it as his opinion that the title of the Indians was not in the slightest degree affected by it and that there was no obligation on the United States to remove them by force.[1]

Further efforts, even to the employment of secret methods, were made in 1827 and 1828 to induce a cession or emigration, but without avail. On July 26, 1827, as already noted, the Cherokee adopted a constitution as a distinct and sovereign Nation. Upon this the Georgia legislature passed resolutions affirming that that state "had the power and the right to possess herself, by any means she might choose, of the lands in dispute, and to extend over them her authority and laws," and recommending that this be done by the next legislature, if the lands were not already acquired by successful negotiation of the general government in the meantime. The government was warned that the lands belonged to Georgia, and she must and would have them. It was suggested, however, that the United States might be permitted to make a certain number of reservations to individual Indians.[2]

Passing over for the present some important negotiations with the western Cherokee, we come to the events leading to the final act in the drama. Up to this time the pressure had been for land only, but now a stronger motive was added. About the year 1815 a little Cherokee boy playing along Chestatee river, in upper Georgia, had brought in to his mother a shining yellow pebble hardly larger than the end of his thumb. On being washed it proved to be a nugget of gold, and on her next trip to the settlements the woman carried it with her and sold it to a white man. The news spread, and although she probably concealed the knowledge of the exact spot of its origin, it was soon known that the golden dreams of De Soto had been realized in the Cherokee country of Georgia. Within four years the whole territory east of the Chestatee had passed from the possession of the Cherokee. They still held the western bank, but the prospector was abroad in the mountains and it could not be for long.[3] About 1828 gold was found on Ward's creek, a western branch of Chestatee, near the present Dahlonega,[4] and the doom of the nation was sealed (41).

---

[1] Monroe, message to the Senate, with Calhoun's report, March 30, 1824, American State Papers: Indian Affairs, II, pp. 460, 462, 1834.

[2] Royce, Cherokee Nation, Fifth Ann. Rep. Bureau of Ethnology, pp. 241, 242, 1888.

[3] Personal information from J. D. Wafford.

[4] Nitze, H. B. C., in Twentieth Annual Report United States Geological Survey, part 6 (Mineral Resources), p. 112, 1899.

In November, 1828, Andrew Jackson was elected to succeed John Quincy Adams as President. He was a frontiersman and Indian hater, and the change boded no good to the Cherokee. His position was well understood, and there is good ground for believing that the action at once taken by Georgia was at his own suggestion.[1] On December 20, 1828, a month after his election, Georgia passed an act annexing that part of the Cherokee country within her chartered limits and extending over it her jurisdiction; all laws and customs established among the Cherokee were declared null and void, and no person of Indian blood or descent residing within the Indian country was henceforth to be allowed as a witness or party in any suit where a white man should be defendant. The act was to take effect June 1, 1830 (42). The whole territory was soon after mapped out into counties and surveyed by state surveyors into "land lots" of 160 acres each, and "gold lots" of 40 acres, which were put up and distributed among the white citizens of Georgia by public lottery, each white citizen receiving a ticket. Every Cherokee head of a family was, indeed, allowed a reservation of 160 acres, but no deed was given, and his continuance depended solely on the pleasure of the legislature. Provision was made for the settlement of contested lottery claims among the white citizens, but by the most stringent enactments, in addition to the sweeping law which forbade anyone of Indian blood to bring suit or to testify against a white man, it was made impossible for the Indian owner to defend his right in any court or to resist the seizure of his homestead, or even his own dwelling house, and anyone so resisting was made subject to imprisonment at the discretion of a Georgia court. Other laws directed to the same end quickly followed, one of which made invalid any contract between a white man and an Indian unless established by the testimony of two white witnesses—thus practically canceling all debts due from white men to Indians—while another obliged all white men residing in the Cherokee country to take a special oath of allegiance to the state of Georgia, on penalty of four years' imprisonment in the penitentiary, this act being intended to drive out all the missionaries, teachers, and other educators who refused to countenance the spoliation. About the same time the Cherokee were forbidden to hold councils, or to assemble for any public purpose,[2] or to dig for gold upon their own lands.

---

[1] See Butler letter, quoted in Royce, Cherokee Nation, Fifth Ann. Rep. Bureau of Ethnology, p. 297, 1888; see also Everett, speech in the House of Representatives on May 31, 1838, pp. 16–17, 32–33, 1839.

[2] For extracts and synopses of these acts see Royce, op. cit., pp. 259–264; Drake, Indians, pp. 438–456, 1880; Greeley, American Conflict, I, pp. 105, 106, 1864; Edward Everett, speech in the House of Representatives, February 14, 1831 (lottery law). The gold lottery is also noted incidentally by Lanman, Charles, Letters from the Alleghany Mountains, p. 10; New York, 1849, and by Nitze, in his report on the Georgia gold fields, in the Twentieth Annual Report of the United States Geological Survey, part 6 (Mineral Resources), p. 112, 1899. The author has himself seen in a mountain village in Georgia an old book titled "The Cherokee Land and Gold Lottery," containing maps and plats covering the whole Cherokee country of Georgia, with each lot numbered, and descriptions of the water courses, soil, and supposed mineral veins.

The purpose of this legislation was to render life in their own country intolerable to the Cherokee by depriving them of all legal protection and friendly counsel, and the effect was precisely as intended.   In an eloquent address upon the subject before the House of Representatives the distinguished Edward Everett clearly pointed out the encouragement which it gave to lawless men: " They have but to cross the Cherokee line; they have but to choose the time and the place where the eye of no white man can rest upon them, and they may burn the dwelling, waste the farm, plunder the property, assault the person, murder the children of the Cherokee subject of Georgia, and though hundreds of the tribe may be looking on, there is not one of them that can be permitted to bear witness against the spoiler."[1] Senator Sprague, of Maine, said of the law that it devoted the property of the Cherokee to the cupidity of their neighbors, leaving them exposed to every outrage which lawless persons could inflict, so that even robbery and murder might be committed with impunity at noonday, if not in the presence of whites who would testify against it.[2]

The prediction was fulfilled to the letter.   Bands of armed men invaded the Cherokee country, forcibly seizing horses and cattle, taking possession of houses from which they had ejected the occupants, and assaulting the owners who dared to make resistance.[3]   In one instance, near the present Dahlonega, two white men, who had been hospitably received and entertained at supper by an educated Cherokee citizen of nearly pure white blood, later in the evening, during the temporary absence of the parents, drove out the children and their nurse and deliberately set fire to the house, which was burned to the ground with all its contents.   They were pursued and brought to trial, but the case was dismissed by the judge on the ground that no Indian could testify against a white man.[4]   Cherokee miners upon their own ground were arrested, fined, and imprisoned, and their tools and machinery destroyed, while thousands of white intruders were allowed to dig in the same places unmolested.[5]   A Cherokee on trial in his own nation for killing another Indian was seized by the state authorities, tried and condemned to death, although, not understanding English, he was unable to speak in his own defense. A United States court forbade the execution, but the judge who had conducted the trial defied the writ, went to the place of execution, and stood beside the sheriff while the Indian was being hanged.[6]

[1] Speech of May 19, 1830, Washington; printed by Gales & Seaton, 1830.
[2] Speech in the Senate of the United States, April 16, 1830; Washington, Peter Force, printer, 1830.
[3] See Cherokee Memorial to Congress, January 18, 1831.
[4] Personal information from Prof. Clinton Duncan, of Tahlequah, Cherokee Nation, whose father's house was the one thus burned.
[5] Cherokee Memorial to Congress January 18, 1831.
[6] Ibid.; see also speech of Edward Everett in House of Representatives February 14, 1831; report of the select committee of the senate of Massachusetts upon the Georgia resolutions, Boston, 1831; Greeley, American Conflict, I, p. 106, 1864; Abbott, Cherokee Indians in Georgia; Atlanta Constitution, October 27, 1889.

Immediately on the passage of the first act the Cherokee appealed to President Jackson, but were told that no protection would be afforded them. Other efforts were then made—in 1829—to persuade them to removal, or to procure another cession—this time of all their lands in North Carolina—but the Cherokee remained firm. The Georgia law was declared in force on June 3, 1830, whereupon the President directed that the annuity payment due the Cherokee Nation under previous treaties should no longer be paid to their national treasurer, as hitherto, but distributed per capita by the agent. As a national fund it had been used for the maintenance of their schools and national press. As a per capita payment it amounted to forty-two cents to each individual. Several years afterward it still remained unpaid. Federal troops were also sent into the Cherokee country with orders to prevent all mining by either whites or Indians unless authorized by the state of Georgia. All these measures served only to render the Cherokee more bitter in their determination. In September, 1830, another proposition was made for the removal of the tribe, but the national council emphatically refused to consider the subject.[1]

In January, 1831, the Cherokee Nation, by John Ross as principal chief, brought a test suit of injunction against Georgia, in the United States Supreme Court. The majority of the court dismissed the suit on the ground that the Cherokee were not a foreign nation within the meaning of the Constitution, two justices dissenting from this opinion.[2]

Shortly afterward, under the law which forbade any white man to reside in the Cherokee Nation without taking an oath of allegiance to Georgia, a number of arrests were made, including Wheeler, the printer of the *Cherokee Phœnix*, and the missionaries, Worcester, Butler, Thompson, and Proctor, who, being there by permission of the agent and feeling that plain American citizenship should hold good in any part of the United States, refused to take the oath. Some of those arrested took the oath and were released, but Worcester and Butler, still refusing, were dressed in prison garb and put at hard labor among felons. Worcester had plead in his defense that he was a citizen of Vermont, and had entered the Cherokee country by permission of the President of the United States and approval of the Cherokee Nation; and that as the United States by several treaties had acknowledged the Cherokee to be a nation with a guaranteed and definite territory, the state had no right to interfere with him. He was sentenced to four years in the penitentiary. On March 3, 1832, the matter was appealed as a test case to the Supreme Court of the United States, which rendered a decision in favor of Worcester and the Cherokee Nation and ordered his release. Georgia, however, through her governor, had defied the summons with a threat of opposition, even to the

---

[1] Royce, Cherokee Nation, Fifth Ann. Rep. Bureau of Ethnology, pp. 261, 262, 1888.
[2] Ibid., p. 262.

annihilation of the Union, and now ignored the decision, refusing to release the missionary, who remained in prison until set free by the will of the governor nearly a year later. A remark attributed to President Jackson, on hearing of the result in the Supreme Court, may throw some light on the whole proceeding: "John Marshall has made his decision, now let him enforce it."[1]

On the 19th of July, 1832, a public fast was observed throughout the Cherokee Nation. In the proclamation recommending it, Chief Ross observes that "Whereas the crisis in the affairs of the Nation exhibits the day of tribulation and sorrow, and the time appears to be fast hastening when the destiny of this people must be sealed; whether it has been directed by the wonted depravity and wickedness of man, or by the unsearchable and mysterious will of an allwise Being, it equally becomes us, as a rational and Christian community, humbly to bow in humiliation," etc.[2]

Further attempts were made to induce the Cherokee to remove to the West, but met the same firm refusal as before. It was learned that in view of the harrassing conditions to which they were subjected the Cherokee were now seriously considering the project of emigrating to the Pacific Coast, at the mouth of the Columbia, a territory then claimed by England and held by the posts of the British Hudson Bay Company. The Secretary of War at once took steps to discourage the movement.[3] A suggestion from the Cherokee that the government satisfy those who had taken possession of Cherokee lands under the lottery drawing by giving them instead an equivalent from the unoccupied government lands was rejected by the President.

In the spring of 1834 the Cherokee submitted a memorial which, after asserting that they would never voluntarily consent to abandon their homes, proposed to satisfy Georgia by ceding to her a portion of their territory, they to be protected in possession of the remainder until the end of a definite period to be fixed by the United States, at the expiration of which, after disposing of their surplus lands, they should become citizens of the various states within which they resided. They were told that their difficulties could be remedied only by their removal to the west of the Mississippi. In the meantime a removal treaty was being negotiated with a self-styled committee of some fifteen or twenty Cherokee called together at the agency. It was carried through in spite of the protest of John Ross and the Cherokee Nation, as embodied in a paper said to contain the signatures of 13,000 Cherokee, but failed of ratification.[4]

Despairing of any help from the President, the Cherokee delega-

---

[1] Royce, Cherokee Nation, Fifth Ann. Rep. Bureau of Ethnology, pp. 264–266, 1888; Drake, Indians, pp. 454–457, 1880; Greeley, American Conflict, I, 106, 1864.

[2] Drake, Indians, p. 458, 1880.

[3] Royce, op. cit., pp. 262–264, 272, 273.

[4] Ibid., pp. 274, 275.

tion, headed by John Ross, addressed another earnest memorial to Congress on May 17, 1834. Royce quotes the document at length, with the remark, "Without affecting to pass judgment on the merits of the controversy, the writer thinks this memorial well deserving of reproduction here as evidencing the devoted and pathetic attachment with which the Cherokee clung to the land of their fathers, and, remembering the wrongs and humiliations of the past, refused to be convinced that justice, prosperity, and happiness awaited them beyond the Mississippi." [1]

In August of this year another council was held at Red Clay, southeastward from Chattanooga and just within the Georgia line, where the question of removal was again debated in what is officially described as a tumultuous and excited meeting. One of the principal advocates of the emigration scheme, a prominent mixed-blood named John Walker, jr., was assassinated from ambush while returning from the council to his home a few miles north of the present Cleveland, Tennessee. On account of his superior education and influential connections, his wife being a niece of former agent Return J. Meigs, the affair created intense excitement at the time. The assassination has been considered the first of the long series of political murders growing out of the removal agitation, but, according to the testimony of old Cherokee acquainted with the facts, the killing was due to a more personal motive. [2]

The Cherokee were now nearly worn out by constant battle against a fate from which they could see no escape. In February, 1835, two rival delegations arrived in Washington, One, the national party, headed by John Ross, came prepared still to fight to the end for home and national existence. The other, headed by Major John Ridge, a prominent subchief, despairing of further successful resistance, was prepared to negotiate for removal. Reverend J. F. Schermerhorn was appointed commissioner to arrange with the Ridge party a treaty to be confirmed later by the Cherokee people in general council. On this basis a treaty was negotiated with the Ridge party by which the Cherokee were to cede their whole eastern territory and remove to the West in consideration of the sum of $3,250,000 with some additional acreage in the West and a small sum for depredations committed upon them by the whites. Finding that these negotiations were proceeding, the Ross party filed a counter proposition for $20,000,000, which was rejected by the Senate as excessive. The Schermerhorn compact with the Ridge party, with the consideration changed to $4,500,000, was thereupon completed and signed on March 14, 1835, but with the express stipulation that it should receive the approval of

[1] Royce, Cherokee Nation, Fifth Ann. Report Bureau of Ethnology, p. 276, 1888.

[2] Commissioner Elbert Herring, November 25, Report of Indian Commissioner, p. 240, 1834; author's personal information from Major R. C. Jackson and J. D. Wafford.

the Cherokee nation in full council assembled before being considered of any binding force. This much accomplished, Mr. Schermerhorn departed for the Cherokee country, armed with an address from President Jackson in which the great benefits of removal were set forth to the Cherokee. Having exhausted the summer and fall in fruitless effort to secure favorable action, the reverend gentleman notified the President, proposing either to obtain the signatures of the leading Cherokee by promising them payment for their improvements at their own valuation, if in any degree reasonable, or to conclude a treaty with a part of the Nation and compel its acceptance by the rest. He was promptly informed by the Secretary of War, Lewis Cass, on behalf of the President, that the treaty, if concluded at all, must be procured upon fair and open terms, with no particular promise to any individual, high or low, to gain his aid or influence, and without sacrificing the interest of the whole to the cupidity of a few. He was also informed that, as it would probably be contrary to his wish, his letter would not be put on file.[1]

In October, 1835, the Ridge treaty was rejected by the Cherokee Nation in full council at Red Clay, even its main supporters, Ridge himself and Elias Boudinot, going over to the majority, most unexpectedly to Schermerhorn, who reports the result, piously adding, "but the Lord is able to overrule all things for good." During the session of this council notice was served on the Cherokee to meet commissioners at New Echota in December following for the purpose of negotiating a treaty. The notice was also printed in the Cherokee language and circulated throughout the Nation, with a statement that those who failed to attend would be counted as assenting to any treaty that might be made.[2]

The council had authorized the regular delegation, headed by John Ross, to conclude a treaty either there or at Washington, but, finding that Schermerhorn had no authority to treat on any other basis than the one rejected by the Nation, the delegates proceeded to Washington.[3] Before their departure John Ross, who had removed to Tennessee to escape persecution in his own state, was arrested at his home by the Georgia guard, all his private papers and the proceedings of the council being taken at the same time, and conveyed across the line into Georgia, where he was held for some time without charge against him, and at last released without apology or explanation. The poet, John Howard Payne, who was then stopping with Ross, engaged in the work of collecting historical and ethnologic material relating to the Cherokee, was seized at the same time, with all his letters and scien-

---

[1] Royce, Cherokee Nation, Fifth Ann. Rep. Bureau of Ethnology, pp. 278–280, 1888; Everett speech in House of Representatives, May 31, 1838, pp. 28, 29, 1839, in which the Secretary's reply is given in full.
[2] Royce, op. cit., pp. 280–281.   [3] Ibid., p. 281.

tific manuscripts. The national paper, the *Cherokee Phœnix*, had been suppressed and its office plant seized by the same guard a few days before.[1] Thus in their greatest need the Cherokee were deprived of the help and counsel of their teachers, their national press, and their chief.

Although for two months threats and inducements had been held out to secure a full attendance at the December conference at New Echota, there were present when the proceedings opened, according to the report of Schermerhorn himself, only from three hundred to five hundred men, women, and children, out of a population of over 17,000. Notwithstanding the paucity of attendance and the absence of the principal officers of the Nation, a committee was appointed to arrange the details of a treaty, which was finally drawn up and signed on December 29, 1835.[2]

Briefly stated, by this treaty of New Echota, Georgia, the Cherokee Nation ceded to the United States its whole remaining territory east of the Mississippi for the sum of five million dollars and a common joint interest in the territory already occupied by the western Cherokee, in what is now Indian Territory, with an additional smaller tract adjoining on the northeast, in what is now Kansas. Improvements were to be paid for, and the Indians were to be removed at the expense of the United States and subsisted at the expense of the Government for one year after their arrival in the new country. The removal was to take place within two years from the ratification of the treaty.

On the strong representations of the Cherokee signers, who would probably not have signed otherwise even then, it was agreed that a limited number of Cherokee who should desire to remain behind in North Carolina, Tennessee, and Alabama, and become citizens, having first been adjudged "qualified or calculated to become useful citizens," might so remain, together with a few holding individual reservations under former treaties. This provision was allowed by the commissioners, but was afterward struck out on the announcement by President Jackson of his determination "not to allow any preemptions or reservations, his desire being that the whole Cherokee people should remove together."

Provision was made also for the payment of debts due by the Indians out of any moneys coming to them under the treaty; for the reestablishment of the missions in the West; for pensions to Cherokee wounded in the service of the government in the war of 1812 and the Creek war; for permission to establish in the new country such military posts and roads for the use of the United States as should be deemed necessary; for satisfying Osage claims in the western territory and

[1] Royce, Cherokee Nation, op. cit. (Ross arrest), p. 281; Drake, Indians (Ross, Payne, Phœnix), p. 459, 1880; see also Everett speech of May 31, 1838, op. cit.

[2] Royce, op. cit., pp. 281, 282; see also Everett speech, 1838.

for bringing about a friendly understanding between the two tribes; and for the commutation of all annuities and other sums due from the United States into a permanent national fund, the interest to be placed at the disposal of the officers of the Cherokee Nation and by them disbursed, according to the will of their own people, for the care of schools and orphans, and for general national purposes.

The western territory assigned the Cherokee under this treaty was in two adjoining tracts, viz, (1) a tract of seven million acres, together with a "perpetual outlet west," already assigned to the western Cherokee under treaty of 1833, as will hereafter be noted,[1] being identical with the present area occupied by the Cherokee Nation in Indian Territory, together with the former "Cherokee strip," with the exception of a two-mile strip along the northern boundary, now included within the limits of Kansas; (2) a smaller additional tract of eight hundred thousand acres, running fifty miles north and south and twenty-five miles east and west, in what is now the southeastern corner of Kansas. For this second tract the Cherokee themselves were to pay the United States five hundred thousand dollars.

The treaty of 1833, assigning the first described tract to the western Cherokee, states that the United States agrees to "guaranty it to them forever, and that guarantee is hereby pledged." By the same treaty, "in addition to the seven millions of acres of land thus provided for and bounded, the United States further guaranty to the Cherokee nation a perpetual outlet west and a free and unmolested use of all the country lying west of the western boundary of said seven millions of acres, as far west as the sovereignty of the United States and their right of soil extend . . . and letters patent shall be issued by the United States as soon as practicable for the land hereby guaranteed." All this was reiterated by the present treaty, and made to include also the smaller (second) tract, in these words:

ART. 3. The United States also agree that the lands above ceded by the treaty of February 14, 1833, including the outlet, and those ceded by this treaty, shall all be included in one patent, executed to the Cherokee nation of Indians by the President of the United States, according to the provisions of the act of May 28, 1830. . . .

ART. 5. The United States hereby covenant and agree that the lands ceded to the Cherokee nation in the foregoing article shall in no future time, without their consent, be included within the territorial limits or jurisdiction of any state or territory. But they shall secure to the Cherokee nation the right of their national councils to make and carry into effect all such laws as they may deem necessary for the government and protection of the persons and property within their own country belonging to their people or such persons as have connected themselves with them: Provided always, that they shall not be inconsistent with the Constitution of the United States and such acts of Congress as have been or may be passed regulating trade and intercourse with the Indians; and also that they shall not be considered as extending to such citizens and army of the United States as may travel or reside in the Indian

[1] See Fort Gibson treaty, 1833, p. 142.

country by permission, according to the laws and regulations established by the government of the same. . . .

ART. 6. Perpetual peace and friendship shall exist between the citizens of the United States and the Cherokee Indians. The United States agree to protect the Cherokee nation from domestic strife and foreign enemies and against intestine wars between the several tribes. The Cherokees shall endeavor to preserve and maintain the peace of the country, and not make war upon their neighbors; they shall also be protected against interruption and intrusion from citizens of the United States who may attempt to settle in the country without their consent; and all such persons shall be removed from the same by order of the President of the United States. But this is not intended to prevent the residence among them of useful farmers, mechanics, and teachers for the instruction of the Indians according to treaty stipulations.

ARTICLE 7. The Cherokee nation having already made great progress in civilization, and deeming it important that every proper and laudable inducement should be offered to their people to improve their condition, as well as to guard and secure in the most effectual manner the rights guaranteed to them in this treaty, and with a view to illustrate the liberal and enlarged policy of the government of the United States toward the Indians in their removal beyond the territorial limits of the states, it is stipulated that they shall be entitled to a Delegate in the House of Representatives of the United States whenever Congress shall make provision for the same.

The instrument was signed by (Governor) William Carroll of Tennessee and (Reverend) J. F. Schermerhorn as commissioners—the former, however, having been unable to attend by reason of illness—and by twenty Cherokee, among whom the most prominent were Major Ridge and Elias Boudinot, former editor of the *Phœnix.* Neither John Ross nor any one of the officers of the Cherokee Nation was present or represented. After some changes by the Senate, it was ratified May 23, 1836.[1]

Upon the treaty of New Echota and the treaty previously made with the western Cherokee at Fort Gibson in 1833, the united Cherokee Nation based its claim to the present territory held by the tribe in Indian Territory and to the Cherokee outlet, and to national self-government, with protection from outside intrusion.

An official census taken in 1835 showed the whole number of Cherokee in Georgia, North Carolina, Alabama, and Tennessee to be 16,542, exclusive of 1,592 negro slaves and 201 whites intermarried with Cherokee. The Cherokee were distributed as follows: Georgia, 8,946; North Carolina, 3,644; Tennessee, 2,528; Alabama, 1,424.[2]

Despite the efforts of Ross and the national delegates, who presented protests with signatures representing nearly 16,000 Cherokee, the treaty

---

[1] See New Echota treaty, 1835, and Fort Gibson treaty, 1833, Indian Treaties, pp. 633–648 and 561–565, 1837; also, for full discussion of both treaties, Royce, Cherokee Nation, Fifth Ann. Rep. Bureau of Ethnology, pp. 249–298. For a summary of all the measures of pressure brought to bear upon the Cherokee up to the final removal see also Everett, speech in the House of Representatives, May 31, 1838; the chapters on "Expatriation of the Cherokees," Drake, Indians, 1880; and the chapter on "State Rights—Nullification," in Greeley, American Conflict, I, 1864. The Georgia side of the controversy is presented in E. J. Harden's Life of (Governor) George M. Troup, 1849.

[2] Royce, op. cit., p. 289. The Indian total is also given in the Report of the Indian Commissioner, p. 369, 1836.

had been ratified by a majority of one vote over the necessary number, and preliminary steps were at once taken to carry it into execution. Councils were held in opposition all over the Cherokee Nation, and resolutions denouncing the methods used and declaring the treaty absolutely null and void were drawn up and submitted to General Wool, in command of the troops in the Cherokee country, by whom they were forwarded to Washington. The President in reply expressed his surprise that an officer of the army should have received or transmitted a paper so disrespectful to the Executive, the Senate, and the American people; declared his settled determination that the treaty should be carried out without modification and with all consistent dispatch, and directed that after a copy of the letter had been delivered to Ross, no further communication, by mouth or writing, should be held with him concerning the treaty. It was further directed that no council should be permitted to assemble to discuss the treaty. Ross had already been informed that the President had ceased to recognize any existing government among the eastern Cherokee, and that any further effort by him to prevent the consummation of the treaty would be suppressed.[1]

Notwithstanding this suppression of opinion, the feeling of the Nation was soon made plain through other sources. Before the ratification of the treaty Major W. M. Davis had been appointed to enroll the Cherokee for removal and to appraise the value of their improvements. He soon learned the true condition of affairs, and, although holding his office by the good will of President Jackson, he addressed to the Secretary of War a strong letter upon the subject, from which the following extract is made:

I conceive that my duty to the President, to yourself, and to my country reluctantly compels me to make a statement of facts in relation to a meeting of a small number of Cherokees at New Echota last December, who were met by Mr. Schermerhorn and articles of a general treaty entered into between them for the whole Cherokee nation. . . . Sir, that paper, . . . called a treaty, is no treaty at all, because not sanctioned by the great body of the Cherokee and made without their participation or assent. I solemnly declare to you that upon its reference to the Cherokee people it would be instantly rejected by nine-tenths of them, and I believe by nineteen-twentieths of them. There were not present at the conclusion of the treaty more than one hundred Cherokee voters, and not more than three hundred, including women and children, although the weather was everything that could be desired. The Indians had long been notified of the meeting, and blankets were promised to all who would come and vote for the treaty. The most cunning and artful means were resorted to to conceal the paucity of numbers present at the treaty. No enumeration of them was made by Schermerhorn. The business of making the treaty was transacted with a committee appointed by the Indians present, so as not to expose their numbers. The power of attorney under which the committee acted was signed only by the president and secretary of the meeting, so as not to disclose their weakness. . . . Mr. Schermerhorn's apparent design was to conceal the real number present and to impose on the public and the government upon this point.

[1] Royce, Cherokee Nation, op. cit., pp. 283, 284; Report of Indian Commissioner, pp. 285, 286, 1836.

The delegation taken to Washington by Mr. Schermerhorn had no more authority to make a treaty than any other dozen Cherokee accidentally picked up for the purpose. I now warn you and the President that if this paper of Schermerhorn's called a treaty is sent to the Senate and ratified you will bring trouble upon the government and eventually destroy this [the Cherokee] Nation. The Cherokee are a peaceable, harmless people, but you may drive them to desperation, and this treaty can not be carried into effect except by the strong arm of force.[1]

General Wool, who had been placed in command of the troops concentrated in the Cherokee country to prevent opposition to the enforcement of the treaty, reported on February 18, 1837, that he had called them together and made them an address, but "it is, however, vain to talk to a people almost universally opposed to the treaty and who maintain that they never made such a treaty. So determined are they in their opposition that not one of all those who were present and voted at the council held but a day or two since, however poor or destitute, would receive either rations or clothing from the United States lest they might compromise themselves in regard to the treaty. These same people, as well as those in the mountains of North Carolina, during the summer past, preferred living upon the roots and sap of trees rather than receive provisions from the United States, and thousands, as I have been informed, had no other food for weeks. Many have said they will die before they will leave the country."[2]

Other letters from General Wool while engaged in the work of disarming and overawing the Cherokee show how very disagreeable that duty was to him and how strongly his sympathies were with the Indians, who were practically unanimous in repudiating the treaty. In one letter he says:

The whole scene since I have been in this country has been nothing but a heart-rending one, and such a one as I would be glad to get rid of as soon as circumstances will permit. Because I am firm and decided, do not believe I would be unjust. If I could, and I could not do them a greater kindness, I would remove every Indian to-morrow beyond the reach of the white men, who, like vultures, are watching, ready to pounce upon their prey and strip them of everything they have or expect from the government of the United States. Yes, sir, nineteen-twentieths, if not ninety-nine out of every hundred, will go penniless to the West.[3]

How it was to be brought about is explained in part by a letter addressed to the President by Major Ridge himself, the principal signer of the treaty:

We now come to address you on the subject of our griefs and afflictions from the acts of the white people. They have got our lands and now they are preparing to fleece us of the money accruing from the treaty. We found our plantations taken either in whole or in part by the Georgians—suits instituted against us for back rents for our own farms. These suits are commenced in the inferior courts, with the

---

[1] Quoted by Royce, Cherokee Nation, op. cit., pp. 284–285; quoted also, with some verbal differences, by Everett, speech in House of Representatives on May 31, 1838.

[2] Quoted in Royce, op. cit., p. 286.

[3] Letter of General Wool, September 10, 1836, in Everett, speech in House of Representatives, May 31, 1838.

evident design that, when we are ready to remove, to arrest our people, and on these vile claims to induce us to compromise for our own release, to travel with our families. Thus our funds will be filched from our people, and we shall be compelled to leave our country as beggars and in want.

Even the Georgia laws, which deny us our oaths, are thrown aside, and notwithstanding the cries of our people, and protestation of our innocence and peace, the lowest classes of the white people are flogging the Cherokees with cowhides, hickories, and clubs. We are not safe in our houses—our people are assailed by day and night by the rabble. Even justices of the peace and constables are concerned in this business. This barbarous treatment is not confined to men, but the women are stripped also and whipped without law or mercy. . . . Send regular troops to protect us from these lawless assaults, and to protect our people as they depart for the West. If it is not done, we shall carry off nothing but the scars of the lash on our backs, and our oppressors will get all the money. We talk plainly, as chiefs having property and life in danger, and we appeal to you for protection. . . .[1]

General Dunlap, in command of the Tennessee troops called out to prevent the alleged contemplated Cherokee uprising, having learned for himself the true situation, delivered an indignant address to his men in which he declared that he would never dishonor the Tennessee arms by aiding to carry into execution at the point of the bayonet a treaty made by a lean minority against the will and authority of the Cherokee people. He stated further that he had given the Cherokee all the protection in his power, the whites needing none.[2]

A confidential agent sent to report upon the situation wrote in September, 1837, that opposition to the treaty was unanimous and irreconcilable, the Cherokee declaring that it could not bind them because they did not make it, that it was the work of a few unauthorized individuals and that the Nation was not a party to it. They had retained the forms of their government, although no election had been held since 1830, having continued the officers then in charge until their government could again be reestablished regularly. Under this arrangement John Ross was principal chief, with influence unbounded and unquestioned. "The whole Nation of eighteen thousand persons is with him, the few—about three hundred—who made the treaty having left the country, with the exception of a small number of prominent individuals—as Ridge, Boudinot, and others—who remained to assist in carrying it into execution. It is evident, therefore, that Ross and his party are in fact the Cherokee Nation. . . . I believe that the mass of the Nation, particularly the mountain Indians, will stand or fall with Ross. . . ."[3]

So intense was public feeling on the subject of this treaty that it became to some extent a party question, the Democrats supporting President Jackson while the Whigs bitterly opposed him. Among

---

[1] Letter of June 30, 1836, to President Jackson, in Everett, speech in the House of Representatives, May 31, 1838.

[2] Quoted by Everett, ibid,; also by Royce, Cherokee Nation, op. cit., p. 286.

[3] Letter of J. M. Mason, jr., to Secretary of War, September 25, 1837, in Everett, speech in House of Representatives, May 31, 1838; also quoted in extract by Royce, op. cit., pp. 286–287.

notable leaders of the opposition were Henry Clay, Daniel Webster, Edward Everett, Wise of Virginia, and David Crockett. The speeches in Congress upon the subject "were characterized by a depth and bitterness of feeling such as had never been exceeded even on the slavery question."[1] It was considered not simply an Indian question, but an issue between state rights on the one hand and federal jurisdiction and the Constitution on the other.

In spite of threats of arrest and punishment, Ross still continued active effort in behalf of his people. Again, in the spring of 1838, two months before the time fixed for the removal, he presented to Congress another protest and memorial, which, like the others, was tabled by the Senate. Van Buren had now succeeded Jackson and was disposed to allow the Cherokee a longer time to prepare for emigration, but was met by the declaration from Governor Gilmer of Georgia that any delay would be a violation of the rights of that state and in opposition to the rights of *the owners of the soil*, and that if trouble came from any protection afforded by the government troops to the Cherokee a direct collision must ensue between the authorities of the state and general government.[2]

Up to the last moment the Cherokee still believed that the treaty would not be consummated, and with all the pressure brought to bear upon them only about 2,000 of the 17,000 in the eastern Nation had removed at the expiration of the time fixed for their departure, May 26, 1838. As it was evident that the removal could only be accomplished by force, General Winfield Scott was now appointed to that duty with instructions to start the Indians for the West at the earliest possible moment. For that purpose he was ordered to take command of the troops already in the Cherokee country, together with additional reenforcements of infantry, cavalry, and artillery, with authority to call upon the governors of the adjoining states for as many as 4,000 militia and volunteers. The whole force employed numbered about 7,000 men—regulars, militia, and volunteers.[3] The Indians had already been disarmed by General Wool.

On arriving in the Cherokee country Scott established headquarters at the capital, New Echota, whence, on May 10, he issued a proclamation to the Cherokee, warning them that the emigration must be commenced in haste and that before another moon had passed every Cherokee man, woman, and child must be in motion to join his brethren in the far West, according to the determination of the President, which he, the general, had come to enforce. The proclamation concludes: " My troops already occupy many positions . . . and

---

[1] Royce, Cherokee Nation, op. cit. pp. 287, 289.

[2] Ibid., pp. 289, 290.

[3] Ibid., p. 291. The statement of the total number of troops employed is from the speech of Everett in the House of Representatives, May 31, 1838, covering the whole question of the treaty.

thousands and thousands are approaching from every quarter to render resistance and escape alike hopeless. . . . Will you, then, by resistance compel us to resort to arms . . . or will you by flight seek to hide yourselves in mountains and forests and thus oblige us to hunt you down?"—reminding them that pursuit might result in conflict and bloodshed, ending in a general war.[1]

Even after this Ross endeavored, on behalf of his people, to secure some slight modification of the terms of the treaty, but without avail.[2]

THE REMOVAL—1838–39

The history of this Cherokee removal of 1838, as gleaned by the author from the lips of actors in the tragedy, may well exceed in weight of grief and pathos any other passage in American history. Even the much-sung exile of the Acadians falls far behind it in its sum of death and misery. Under Scott's orders the troops were disposed at various points throughout the Cherokee country, where stockade forts were erected for gathering in and holding the Indians preparatory to removal (43). From these, squads of troops were sent to search out with rifle and bayonet every small cabin hidden away in the coves or by the sides of mountain streams, to seize and bring in as prisoners all the occupants, however or wherever they might be found. Families at dinner were startled by the sudden gleam of bayonets in the doorway and rose up to be driven with blows and oaths along the weary miles of trail that led to the stockade. Men were seized in their fields or going along the road, women were taken from their wheels and children from their play. In many cases, on turning for one last look as they crossed the ridge, they saw their homes in flames, fired by the lawless rabble that followed on the heels of the soldiers to loot and pillage. So keen were these outlaws on the scent that in some instances they were driving off the cattle and other stock of the Indians almost before the soldiers had fairly started their owners in the other direction. Systematic hunts were made by the same men for Indian graves, to rob them of the silver pendants and other valuables deposited with the dead. A Georgia volunteer, afterward a colonel in the Confederate service, said: "I fought through the civil war and have seen men shot to pieces and slaughtered by thousands, but the Cherokee removal was the cruelest work I ever knew."

To prevent escape the soldiers had been ordered to approach and surround each house, so far as possible, so as to come upon the occupants without warning. One old patriarch, when thus surprised, calmly called his children and grandchildren around him, and, kneeling down, bid them pray with him in their own language, while the astonished soldiers looked on in silence. Then rising he led the way into

---

[1] Royce, Cherokee Nation, op. cit., p. 291,   [2] Ibid, p. 291.

exile.   A woman, on finding the house surrounded, went to the door and called up the chickens to be fed for the last time, after which, taking her infant on her back and her two other children by the hand, she followed her husband with the soldiers.

All were not thus submissive.   One old man named Tsalĭ, "Charley," was seized with his wife, his brother, his three sons and their families. Exasperated at the brutality accorded his wife, who, being unable to travel fast, was prodded with bayonets to hasten her steps, he urged the other men to join with him in a dash for liberty.   As he spoke in Cherokee the soldiers, although they heard, understood nothing until each warrior suddenly sprang upon the one nearest and endeavored to wrench his gun from him.   The attack was so sudden and unexpected that one soldier was killed and the rest fled, while the Indians escaped to the mountains.   Hundreds of others, some of them from the various stockades, managed also to escape to the mountains from time to time, where those who did not die of starvation subsisted on roots and wild berries until the hunt was over.   Finding it impracticable to secure these fugitives, General Scott finally tendered them a proposition, through (Colonel) W. H. Thomas, their most trusted friend, that if they would surrender Charley and his party for punishment, the rest would be allowed to remain until their case could be adjusted by the government.   On hearing of the proposition, Charley voluntarily came in with his sons, offering himself as a sacrifice for his people.   By command of General Scott, Charley, his brother, and the two elder sons were shot near the mouth of Tuckasegee, a detachment of Cherokee prisoners being compelled to do the shooting in order to impress upon the Indians the fact of their utter helplessness.   From those fugitives thus permitted to remain originated the present eastern band of Cherokee.[1]

When nearly seventeen thousand Cherokee had thus been gathered into the various stockades the work of removal began.   Early in June several parties, aggregating about five thousand persons, were brought down by the troops to the old agency, on Hiwassee, at the present Calhoun, Tennessee, and to Ross's landing (now Chattanooga), and Gunter's landing (now Guntersville, Alabama), lower down on the Tennessee, where they were put upon steamers and transported down the Tennessee and Ohio to the farther side of the Mississippi, when the journey was continued by land to Indian Territory.   This removal,

---

[1] The notes on the Cherokee round-up and Removal are almost entirely from author's information as furnished by actors in the events, both Cherokee and white, among whom may be named the late Colonel W. H. Thomas; the late Colonel Z. A. Zile, of Atlanta, of the Georgia volunteers; the late James Bryson, of Dillsboro, North Carolina, also a volunteer; James D. Wafford, of the western Cherokee Nation, who commanded one of the emigrant detachments; and old Indians, both east and west, who remembered the Removal and had heard the story from their parents.   Charley's story is a matter of common note among the East Cherokee, and was heard in full detail from Colonel Thomas and from Wasitûna ("Washington"), Charley's youngest son, who alone was spared by General Scott on account of his youth.   The incident is also noted, with some slight inaccuracies, in Lanman, Letters from the Alleghany Mountains.   See p. 157.

in the hottest part of the year, was attended with so great sickness and mortality that, by resolution of the Cherokee national council, Ross and the other chiefs submitted to General Scott a proposition that the Cherokee be allowed to remove themselves in the fall, after the sickly season had ended. This was granted on condition that all should have started by the 20th of October, excepting the sick and aged who might not be able to move so rapidly. Accordingly, officers were appointed by the Cherokee council to take charge of the emigration; the Indians being organized into detachments averaging one thousand each, with two leaders in charge of each detachment, and a sufficient number of wagons and horses for the purpose. In this way the remainder, enrolled at about 13,000 (including negro slaves), started on the long march overland late in the fall (44).

Those who thus emigrated under the management of their own officers assembled at Rattlesnake springs, about two miles south of Hiwassee river, near the present Charleston, Tennessee, where a final council was held, in which it was decided to continue their old constitution and laws in their new home. Then, in October, 1838, the long procession of exiles was set in motion. A very few went by the river route; the rest, nearly all of the 13,000, went overland. Crossing to the north side of the Hiwassee at a ferry above Gunstocker creek, they proceeded down along the river, the sick, the old people, and the smaller children, with the blankets, cooking pots, and other belongings in wagons, the rest on foot or on horses. The number of wagons was 645.

It was like the march of an army, regiment after regiment, the wagons in the center, the officers along the line and the horsemen on the flanks and at the rear. Tennessee river was crossed at Tuckers (?) ferry, a short distance above Jollys island, at the mouth of Hiwassee. Thence the route lay south of Pikeville, through McMinnville and on to Nashville, where the Cumberland was crossed. Then they went on to Hopkinsville, Kentucky, where the noted chief White-path, in charge of a detachment, sickened and died. His people buried him by the roadside, with a box over the grave and poles with streamers around it, that the others coming on behind might note the spot and remember him. Somewhere also along that march of death—for the exiles died by tens and twenties every day of the journey—the devoted wife of John Ross sank down, leaving him to go on with the bitter pain of bereavement added to heartbreak at the ruin of his nation. The Ohio was crossed at a ferry near the mouth of the Cumberland, and the army passed on through southern Illinois until the great Mississippi was reached opposite Cape Girardeau, Missouri. It was now the middle of winter, with the river running full of ice, so that several detachments were obliged to wait some time on the eastern bank for the channel to become clear. In talking with old men and women at Tahlequah the author found that the lapse of over half a century had not sufficed to wipe out the memory of the miseries of that halt beside the frozen river, with hundreds of sick and dying penned up in wagons or stretched upon the ground, with only a blanket overhead to keep out the January blast.   The crossing was made at last in two divisions, at Cape Girardeau and at Green's ferry, a short distance below, whence the march was on through Missouri to Indian Territory, the later detachments making a northerly circuit by Springfield, because those who had gone before had killed off all the game along the direct route.   At last their destination was reached.   They had started in October, 1838, and it was now March, 1839, the journey having occupied nearly six months of the hardest part of the year.[1]

It is difficult to arrive at any accurate statement of the number of Cherokee who died as the result of the Removal.   According to the official figures those who removed under the direction of Ross lost over 1,600 on the journey.[2]   The proportionate mortality among those previously removed under military supervision was probably greater, as it was their suffering that led to the proposition of the Cherokee national officers to take charge of the emigration.   Hundreds died in the stockades and the waiting camps, chiefly by reason of the rations furnished, which were of flour and other provisions to which they were unaccustomed and which they did not know how to prepare properly. Hundreds of others died soon after their arrival in Indian territory, from sickness and exposure on the journey.   Altogether it is asserted, probably with reason, that over 4,000 Cherokee died as the direct result of the removal.

On their arrival in Indian Territory the emigrants at once set about building houses and planting crops, the government having agreed under the treaty to furnish them with rations for one year after arrival. They were welcomed by their kindred, the "Arkansas Cherokee"— hereafter to be known for distinction as the "Old Settlers"—who held the country under previous treaties in 1828 and 1833.   These, however, being already regularly organized under a government and chiefs of their own, were by no means disposed to be swallowed by the governmental authority of the newcomers.   Jealousies developed in which the minority or treaty party of the emigrants, headed by Ridge, took sides with the Old Settlers against the Ross or national party, which outnumbered both the others nearly three to one.

While these differences were at their height the Nation was thrown into a fever of excitement by the news that Major Ridge, his son John Ridge, and Elias Boudinot—all leaders of the treaty party—had been killed by adherents of the national party, immediately after the close

---

[1] Author's personal information, as before cited.

[2] As quoted in Royce, Cherokee Nation, Fifth Ann. Rep. Bureau of Ethnology, p. 292, 1888, the disbursing agent makes the number unaccounted for 1,428; the receiving agent, who took charge of them on their arrival, makes it 1,645.

of a general council, which had adjourned after nearly two weeks of debate without having been able to bring about harmonious action. Major Ridge was waylaid and shot close to the Arkansas line, his son was taken from bed and cut to pieces with hatchets, while Boudinot was treacherously killed at his home at Park Hill, Indian territory, all three being killed upon the same day, June 22, 1839.

The agent's report to the Secretary of War, two days later, says of the affair:

The murder of Boudinot was treacherous and cruel. He was assisting some workmen in building a new house. Three men called upon him and asked for medicine. He went off with them in the direction of Wooster's, the missionary, who keeps medicine, about three hundred yards from Boudinot's. When they got about half way two of the men seized Boudinot and the other stabbed him, after which the three cut him to pieces with their knives and tomahawks. This murder taking place within two miles of the residence of John Ross, his friends were apprehensive it might be charged to his connivance; and at this moment I am writing there are six hundred armed Cherokee around the dwelling of Ross, assembled for his protection. The murderers of the two Ridges and Boudinot are certainly of the late Cherokee emigrants, and, of course, adherents of Ross, but I can not yet believe that Ross has encouraged the outrage. He is a man of too much good sense to embroil his nation at this critical time; and besides, his character, since I have known him, which is now twenty-five years, has been pacific. . . . Boudinot's wife is a white woman, a native of New Jersey, as I understand. He has six children. The wife of John Ridge, jr., is a white woman, but from whence, or what family left, I am not informed. Boudinot was in moderate circumstances. The Ridges, both father and son, were rich. . . .[1]

While all the evidence shows that Ross was in no way a party to the affair, there can be no question that the men were killed in accordance with the law of the Nation—three times formulated, and still in existence—which made it treason, punishable with death, to cede away lands except by act of the general council of the Nation. It was for violating a similar law among the Creeks that the chief, McIntosh, lost his life in 1825, and a party led by Major Ridge himself had killed Doublehead years before on suspicion of accepting a bribe for his part in a treaty.

On hearing of the death of the Ridges and Boudinot several other signers of the repudiated treaty, among whom were John Bell, Archilla Smith, and James Starr, fled for safety to the protection of the garrison at Fort Gibson. Boudinot's brother, Stand Watie, vowed vengeance against Ross, who was urged to flee, but refused, declaring his entire innocence. His friends rallied to his support, stationing a guard around his house until the first excitement had subsided. About three weeks afterward the national council passed decrees declaring that the men killed and their principal confederates

---

[1] Agent Stokes to Secretary of War, June 24, 1839, in Report Indian Commissioner, p. 355, 1839; Royce, Cherokee Nation, Fifth Ann. Rep. Bureau of Ethnology, p. 293, 1888; Drake, Indians, pp. 459-460, 1880; author's personal information. The agent's report incorrectly makes the killings occur on three different days.

had rendered themselves outlaws by their own conduct, extending amnesty on certain stringent conditions to their confederates, and declaring the slayers guiltless of murder and fully restored to the confidence and favor of the community. This was followed in August by another council decree declaring the New Echota treaty void and reasserting the title of the Cherokee to their old country, and three weeks later another decree summoned the signers of the treaty to appear and answer for their conduct under penalty of outlawry. At this point the United States interfered by threatening to arrest Ross as accessory to the killing of the Ridges.[1] In the meantime the national party and the Old Settlers had been coming together, and a few of the latter who had sided with the Ridge faction and endeavored to perpetuate a division in the Nation were denounced in a council of the Old Settlers, which declared that "in identifying themselves with those individuals known as the Ridge party, who by their conduct had rendered themselves odious to the Cherokee people, they have acted in opposition to the known sentiments and feelings of that portion of this Nation known as Old Settlers, frequently and variously and publicly expressed." The offending chiefs were at the same time deposed from all authority. Among the names of over two hundred signers attached that of "George Guess" (Sequoya) comes second as vice-president.[2]

On July 12, 1839, a general convention of the eastern and western Cherokee, held at the Illinois camp ground, Indian territory, passed an act of union, by which the two were declared "one body politic, under the style and title of the Cherokee Nation." On behalf of the eastern Cherokee the instrument bears the signature of John Ross, principal chief, George Lowrey, president of the council, and Goingsnake (I'nadû-na'ï), speaker of the council, with thirteen others. For the western Cherokee it was signed by John Looney, acting principal chief, George Guess (Sequoya), president of the council, and fifteen others. On September 6, 1839, a convention composed chiefly of eastern Cherokee assembled at Tahlequah, Indian territory—then first officially adopted as the national capital—adopted a new constitution, which was accepted by a convention of the Old Settlers at Fort Gibson, Indian Territory, on June 26, 1840, an act which completed the reunion of the Nation.[3]

THE ARKANSAS BAND—1817–1838

Having followed the fortunes of the main body of the Nation to their final destination in the West, we now turn to review briefly

---

[1] Royce, Cherokee Nation, op. cit., pp. 294, 295.

[2] Council resolutions, August 23, 1839, in Report Indian Commissioner, p. 387, 1839; Royce, op. cit., p. 294.

[3] See "Act of Union" and "Constitution" in Constitution and Laws of the Cherokee Nation, 1875; General Arbuckle's letter to the Secretary of War, June 28, 1840, in Report of Indian Commissioner, p. 46, 1840; also Royce, op. cit., pp. 294, 295.

the history of the earlier emigrants, the Arkansas or Old Settler Cherokee.

The events leading to the first westward migration and the subsequent negotiations which resulted in the assignment of a territory in Arkansas to the western Cherokee, by the treaty of 1817, have been already noted. The great majority of those thus voluntarily removing belonged to the conservative hunter element, who desired to reestablish in the western wilderness the old Indian life from which, through the influence of schools and intelligent leadership, the body of the Cherokee was rapidly drifting away. As the lands upon which the emigrants had settled belonged to the Osage, whose claim had not yet been extinguished by the United States, the latter objected to their presence, and the Cherokee were compelled to fight to maintain their own position, so that for the first twenty years or more the history of the western band is a mere petty chronicle of Osage raids and Cherokee retaliations, emphasized from time to time by a massacre on a larger scale. By the treaty of 1817 the western Cherokee acquired title to a definite territory and official standing under Government protection and supervision, the lands assigned them having been acquired by treaty from the Osage. The great body of the Cherokee in the East were strongly opposed to any recognition of the western band, seeing in such action only the beginning of an effort looking toward the ultimate removal of the whole tribe. The Government lent support to the scheme, however, and a steady emigration set in until, in 1819, the emigrants were said to number several thousands. Unsuccessful endeavors were made to increase the number by inducing the Shawano and Delawares of Missouri and the Oneida of New York to join them.[1]

In 1818 Tollunteeskee (Ata'lûñti'skǐ), principal chief of the Arkansas Cherokee, while on a visit to old friends in the East, had become acquainted with one of the officers of the American Board of Commissioners for Foreign Missions, and had asked for the establishment of a mission among his people in the West. In response to the invitation the Reverend Cephas Washburn and his assistant, Reverend Alfred Finney, with their families, set out the next year from the old Nation, and after a long and exhausting journey reached the Arkansas country, where, in the spring of 1820, they established Dwight mission, adjoining the agency at the mouth of Illinois creek, on the northern bank of the Arkansas, in what is now Pope county, Arkansas. The name was bestowed in remembrance of Timothy Dwight, a Yale president and pioneer organizer of the American Board. Tollunteeskee having died in the meantime was succeeded as principal chief by his brother, John Jolly,[2] the friend and adopted father of Samuel Houston. Jolly

---

[1] See ante, pp. 105–106; Nuttall, who was on the ground, gives them only 1,500.

[2] Washburn, Cephas, Reminiscences of the Indians, pp. 81,103; Richmond, 1869.

had removed from his old home at the mouth of Hiwassee, in Tennessee, in 1818.[1]

In the spring of 1819 Thomas Nuttall, the naturalist, ascended the Arkansas, and he gives an interesting account of the western Cherokee as he found them at the time. In going up the stream, " both banks of the river, as we proceeded, were lined with the houses and farms of the Cherokee, and though their dress was a mixture of indigenous and European taste, yet in their houses, which are decently furnished, and in their farms, which were well fenced and stocked with cattle, we perceive a happy approach toward civilization. Their numerous families, also, well fed and clothed, argue a propitious progress in their population. Their superior industry either as hunters or farmers proves the value of property among them, and they are no longer strangers to avarice and the distinctions created by wealth. Some of them are possessed of property to the amount of many thousands of dollars, have houses handsomely and conveniently furnished, and their tables spread with our dainties and luxuries." He mentions an engagement some time before between them and the Osage, in which the Cherokee had killed nearly one hundred of the Osage, besides taking a number of prisoners. He estimates them at about fifteen hundred, being about half the number estimated by the eastern Nation as having emigrated to the West, and only one-fourth of the official estimate. A few Delawares were living with them.[2]

The Osage troubles continued in spite of a treaty of peace between the two tribes made at a council held under the direction of Governor Clark at St. Louis, in October, 1818.[3] Warriors from the eastern Cherokee were accustomed to make the long journey to the Arkansas to assist their western brethren, and returned with scalps and captives.[4]

In the summer of 1820 a second effort for peace was made by Governor Miller of Arkansas territory. In reply to his talk the Osage complained that the Cherokee had failed to deliver their Osage captives as stipulated in the previous agreement at St. Louis. This, it appears, was due in part to the fact that some of these captives had been carried to the eastern Cherokee, and a messenger was accordingly dispatched to secure and bring them back. Another peace conference was held soon afterward at Fort Smith, but to very little purpose, as hostilities were soon resumed and continued until the United States actively interposed in the fall of 1822.[5]

In this year also Sequoya visited the western Cherokee to introduce

---

[1] Nuttall, Journal of Travels into the Arkansas Territory, etc., p. 129; Philadelphia, 1821.

[2] Ibid., pp. 123–136. The battle mentioned seems to be the same noted somewhat differently by Washburn, Reminiscences, p. 120, 1869.

[3] Royce, Cherokee Nation, op. cit., p. 222.

[4] Washburn, op. cit., p. 160, and personal information from J. D. Wafford.

[5] Royce, op. cit., pp. 242, 243; Washburn, op. cit., pp. 112–122 et passim; see also sketches of Tahchee and Tooantuh or Spring-frog, in McKenney and Hall, Indian Tribes, I and II, 1858.

to them the knowledge of his great invention, which was at once taken up through the influence of Takatoka (Degatâ'ga), a prominent chief who had hitherto opposed every effort of the missionaries to introduce their own schools and religion. In consequence perhaps of this encouragement Sequoya removed permanently to the West in the following year and became henceforth a member of the western Nation.[1]

Like other Indians, the western Cherokee held a firm belief in witchcraft, which led to frequent tragedies of punishment or retaliation. In 1824 a step forward was marked by the enactment of a law making it murder to kill any one for witchcraft, and an offense punishable with whipping to accuse another of witchcraft.[2] This law may have been the result of the silent working of missionary influence, supported by such enlightened men as Sequoya.

The treaty which assigned the Arkansas lands to the western Cherokee had stipulated that a census should be made of the eastern and western divisions of the Nation, separately, and an apportionment of the national annuity forthwith made on that basis. The western line of the Arkansas tract had also been left open, until according to another stipulation of the same treaty, the whole amount of land ceded through it to the United States by the Cherokee Nation in the East could be ascertained in order that an equal quantity might be included within the boundaries of the western tract.[3] These promises had not yet been fulfilled, partly because of the efforts of the Government to bring about a larger emigration or a further cession, partly on account of delay in the state surveys, and partly also because the Osage objected to the running of a line which should make the Cherokee their next door neighbors.[4] With their boundaries unadjusted and their annuities withheld, distress and dissatisfaction overcame the western Cherokee, many of whom, feeling themselves absolved from territorial restrictions, spread over the country on the southern side of Arkansas river,[5] while others, under the lead of a chief named The Bowl (Diwa''lĭ), crossed Red river into Texas—then a portion of Mexico—in a vain attempt to escape American jurisdiction.[6]

A provisional western boundary having been run, which proved unsatisfactory both to the western Cherokee and to the people of Arkansas, an effort was made to settle the difficulty by arranging an exchange of the Arkansas tract for a new country west of the Arkansas line. So strongly opposed, however, were the western Cherokee to this project that their council, in 1825, passed a law, as the eastern Cherokee and the Creeks had already done, fixing the death penalty

[1] Washburn, Reminiscences, p. 178, 1869; see also ante p. 206.
[2] Ibid, p. 138.
[3] See Treaty of 1817, Indian Treaties, 1837.
[4] Royce, Cherokee Nation, Fifth Report Bureau of Ethnology, pp. 243, 244, 1888.
[5] Ibid, p. 243.
[6] Author's personal information; see p. 143.

for anyone of the tribe who should undertake to cede or exchange land belonging to the Nation.[1]

After a long series of negotiations such pressure was brought to bear upon a delegation which visited Washington in 1828 that consent was at last obtained to an exchange of the Arkansas tract for another piece of seven million acres lying farther west, together with "a perpetual outlet west" of the tract thus assigned, as far west as the sovereignty of the United States might extend.[2] The boundaries given for this seven-million-acre tract and the adjoining western outlet were modified by treaty at Fort Gibson five years later so as to be practically equivalent to the present territory of the Cherokee Nation in Indian Territory, with the Cherokee strip recently ceded.

The preamble of the Washington treaty of May 6, 1828, recites that "Whereas, it being the anxious desire of the Government of the United States to secure to the Cherokee nation of Indians, as well those now living within the limits of the territory of Arkansas as those of their friends and brothers who reside in states east of the Mississippi, and who may wish to join their brothers of the West, *a permanent home*, and which shall, under the most solemn guarantee of the United States, be and remain theirs forever—a home that shall never, in all future time, be embarrassed by having extended around it the lines or placed over it the jurisdiction of a territory or state, nor be pressed upon by the extension in any way of any of the limits of any existing territory or state; and whereas the present location of the Cherokees in Arkansas being unfavorable to their present repose, and tending, as the past demonstrates, to their future degradation and misery, and the Cherokees being anxious to avoid such consequences," etc.—therefore, they cede everything confirmed to them in 1817.

Article 2 defines the boundaries of the new tract and the western outlet to be given in exchange, lying immediately west of the present Arkansas line, while the next article provides for the removal of all whites and others residing within the said boundaries, "so that no obstacles arising out of the presence of a white population, or any population of any other sort, shall exist to annoy the Cherokees, and also to keep all such from the west of said line in future."

Other articles provide for payment for improvements left behind; for a cash sum of $50,000 to pay for trouble and expense of removal and to compensate for the inferior quality of the lands in the new tract; for $6,000 to pay for recovering stock which may stray away "in quest of the pastures from which they may be driven;" $8,760 for spoliations committed by Osage and whites; $500 to George Guess (Sequoya)—who was himself one of the signers—in consideration of the beneficial results to his tribe from the alphabet invented by him; $20,000 in ten annual payments for education; $1,000 for a printing

---

[1] Royce, Cherokee Nation, op. cit., p. 245.   [2] Ibid., pp. 247, 248.

press and type to aid in the enlightenment of the people "in their own and our language"; a personal indemnity for false imprisonment; and for the removal and reestablishment of the Dwight mission.

In article 6 "it is moreover agreed by the United States, whenever the Cherokee may desire it, to give them a set of plain laws, suited to their condition; also, when they wish to lay off their lands and own them individually, a surveyor shall be sent to make the surveys at the cost of the United States." This article was annulled in 1833 by request of the Cherokee.

Article 9 provides for the Fort Gibson military reservation within the new tract, while article 7 binds the Cherokee to surrender and remove from all their lands in Arkansas within fourteen months.

Article 8 shows that all this was intended to be only preliminary to the removal of the whole Cherokee Nation from the east of the Mississippi, a consummation toward which the Jackson administration and the state of Georgia immediately began to bend every effort. It is as follows:

ARTICLE 8. The Cherokee nation, west of the Mississippi, having by this agreement freed themselves from the harassing and ruinous effects consequent upon a location amidst a white population, and secured to themselves and their posterity, under the solemn sanction of the guarantee of the United States as contained in this agreement, a large extent of unembarrassed country; and that their brothers yet remaining in the states may be induced to join them and enjoy the repose and blessings of such a state in the future, it is further agreed on the part of the United States that to each head of a Cherokee family now residing within the chartered limits of Georgia, or of either of the states east of the Mississippi, who may desire to remove west, shall be given, on enrolling himself for emigration, a good rifle, a blanket, a kettle, and five pounds of tobacco; (and to each member of his family one blanket), also a just compensation for the property he may abandon, to be assessed by persons to be appointed by the President of the United States. The cost of the emigration of all such shall also be borne by the United States, and good and suitable ways opened and procured for their comfort, accommodation, and support by the way, and provisions for twelve months after their arrival at the agency; and to each person, or head of a family, if he take along with him four persons, shall be paid immediately on his arriving at the agency and reporting himself and his family or followers as emigrants or permanent settlers, in addition to the above, *provided he and they shall have emigrated from within the chartered limits of the State of Georgia*, the sum of fifty dollars, and this sum in proportion to any greater or less number that may accompany him from within the aforesaid chartered limits of the State of Georgia.

A Senate amendment, defining the limits of the western outlet, was afterward found to be impracticable in its restrictions and was canceled by the treaty made at Fort Gibson in 1833.[1]

The Washington treaty was signed by several delegates, including Sequoya, four of them signing in Cherokee characters. As the laws

---

[1] Treaty of Washington, May 6, 1828, Indian Treaties, pp. 423–428, 1837; treaty of Fort Gibson, 1833, ibid., pp. 561–565; see also for synopsis, Royce, Cherokee Nation, Fifth Ann. Rep. Bureau of Ethnology, pp. 229, 230, 1888.

TAHCHEE (TATSĬ) OR DUTCH
(From Catlin's painting of 1834)

SPRING-FROG OR TOOANTUH (DU'TSU')
(From McKenney and Hall's copy of the original painting of about 1830)

of the western Cherokee made it a capital offense to negotiate any sale or exchange of land excepting by authority of council, and the delegates had acted without such authority, they were so doubtful as to what might happen on their return that the Secretary of War sent with them a letter of explanation assuring the Cherokee that their representatives had acted with integrity and earnest zeal for their people and had done the best that could be done with regard to the treaty. Notwithstanding this, they found the whole tribe so strongly opposed to the treaty that their own lives and property were unsafe. The national council pronounced them guilty of fraud and deception and declared the treaty null and void, as having been made without authority, and asked permission to send on a delegation authorized to arrange all differences.[1] In the meantime, however, the treaty had been ratified within three weeks of its conclusion, and thus, hardly ten years after they had cleared their fields on the Arkansas, the western Cherokee were forced to abandon their cabins and plantations and move once more into the wilderness.

·A considerable number, refusing to submit to the treaty or to trust longer to guarantees and promises, crossed Red river into Texas and joined the Cherokee colony already located there by The Bowl, under Mexican jurisdiction. Among those thus removing was the noted chief Tahchee (Tătsĭ′) or "Dutch," who had been one of the earliest emigrants to the Arkansas country. After several years in Texas, during which he led war parties against the wilder tribes, he recrossed Red river and soon made himself so conspicuous in raids upon the Osage that a reward of five hundred dollars was offered by General Arbuckle for his capture. To show his defiance of the proclamation, he deliberately journeyed to Fort Gibson, attacked a party of Osage at a trading post near by, and scalped one of them within hearing of the drums of the fort. With rifle in one hand and the bleeding scalp in the other, he leaped a precipice and made his escape, although a bullet grazed his cheek. On promise of amnesty and the withdrawal of the reward, he afterward returned and settled, with his followers, on the Canadian, southwest of Fort Gibson, establishing a reputation among army officers as a valuable scout and guide.[2]

By treaties made in 1826 and 1827 the Creeks had ceded all their remaining lands in Georgia and agreed to remove to Indian Territory. Some of these emigrants had settled along the northern bank of the Arkansas and on Verdigris river, on lands later found to be within the limits of the territory assigned to the western Cherokee by the treaty of 1828. This led to jealousies and collisions between

---

[1] Royce, Cherokee Nation, Fifth Ann. Rep. Bureau of Ethnology, p. 248, 1888.

[2] For a sketch of Tahchee, with portraits, see McKenney and Hall, I, pp. 251–260, 1858; Catlin, North American Indians, II, pp. 121, 122, 1844. Washburn also mentions the emigration to Texas consequent upon the treaty of 1828 (Reminiscences, p. 217, 1869).

the two tribes, and in order to settle the difficulty the United States convened a joint council of Creeks and Cherokee at Fort Gibson, with the result that separate treaties were concluded with each on February 14, 1833, defining their respective bounds to the satisfaction of all concerned. By this arrangement the upper Verdigris was confirmed to the Cherokee, and the Creeks who had settled along that portion of the stream agreed to remove to Creek territory immediately adjoining on the south.[1]

By the treaty made on this occasion with the Cherokee the boundaries of the tract of seven million acres granted by the treaty of 1828 are defined so as to correspond with the present boundaries of the Cherokee country in Indian territory, together with a strip two miles wide along the northern border, which was afterward annexed to the state of Kansas by the treaty of 1866. A tract in the northeastern corner, between Neosho or Grand river and the Missouri line, was set apart for the use of the Seneca and several other remnants of tribes removed from their original territories. The western outlet established by the treaty of 1828 was reestablished as a western extension from the seven-million-acre tract thus bounded, being what was afterward known as the Cherokee strip or outlet plus the two-mile strip extending westward along the south line of Kansas.

After describing the boundaries of the main residence tract, the first article continues:

> In addition to the seven millions of acres of land thus provided for and bounded the United States further guarantee to the Cherokee nation a perpetual outlet west and a free and unmolested use of all the country lying west of the western boundary of said seven millions of acres, as far west as the sovereignty of the United States and their right of soil extend—provided, however, that if the saline or salt plain on the great western prairie shall fall within said limits prescribed for said outlet the right is reserved to the United States to permit other tribes of red men to get salt on said plain in common with the Cherokees—and letters patent shall be issued by the United States as soon as practicable for the lands hereby guaranteed.

The third article cancels, at the particular request of the Cherokee, that article of the treaty of 1828 by which the government was to give to the Cherokee a set of laws and a surveyor to survey lands for individuals, when so desired by the Cherokee.[2]

Their differences with the Creeks having been thus adjusted, the Arkansas Cherokee proceeded to occupy the territory guaranteed to them, where they were joined a few years later by their expatriated kinsmen from the east. By tacit agreement some of the Creeks who had settled within the Cherokee bounds were permitted to remain. Among these were several families of Uchee—an incorporated tribe

---

[1] Treaties at Fort Gibson, February 14, 1833, with Creeks and Cherokee, in Indian Treaties, pp. 561–569, 1837.

[2] Treaty of 1833, Indian Treaties, pp. 561–565, 1837; Royce, Cherokee Nation, Fifth Ann. Rep. Bureau of Ethnology, pp. 249–253, 1888; see also Treaty of New Echota, 1835, ante, pp. 123–125.

of the Creek confederacy—who had fixed their residence at the spot where the town of Tahlequah was afterward established. They remained here until swept off by smallpox some sixty years ago.[1]

THE TEXAS BAND—1817–1900

As already stated, a band of western Cherokee under Chief Bowl, dissatisfied with the delay in fulfilling the terms of the treaty of 1817, had left Arkansas and crossed Red river into Texas, then under Mexican jurisdiction, where they were joined a few years later by Tahchee and others of the western band who were opposed to the treaty of 1828. Here they united with other refugee Indians from the United States, forming together a loose confederacy known afterward as "the Cherokee and their associated bands," consisting of Cherokee, Shawano, Delaware, Kickapoo, Quapaw, Choctaw, Biloxi, "Iawanie" (Heyowani, Yowani), "Unataqua" (Nada'ko or Anadarko, another Caddo subtribe), "Tahookatookie" (?), Alabama (a Creek subtribe), and "Cooshatta" (Koasa'ti, another Creek subtribe). The Cherokee being the largest and most important band, their chief, Bowl—known to the whites as Colonel Bowles—was regarded as the chief and principal man of them all.

The refugees settled chiefly along Angelina, Neches, and Trinity rivers in eastern Texas, where Bowl endeavored to obtain a grant of land for their use from the Mexican government. According to the Texan historians they were tacitly permitted to occupy the country and hopes were held out that a grant would be issued, but the papers had not been perfected when the Texas revolution began.[2] According to the Cherokee statement the grant was actually issued and the Spanish document inclosed in a tin box was on the person of Bowl when he was killed.[3] On complaint of some of the American colonists in Texas President Jackson issued a proclamation forbidding any Indians to cross the Sabine river from the United States.[4]

In 1826–27 a dissatisfied American colony in eastern Texas, under the leadership of Hayden Edwards, organized what was known as the "Fredonia rebellion" against the Mexican government. To secure the alliance of the Cherokee and their confederates the Americans entered into a treaty by which the Indians were guaranteed the lands

---

[1] Author's personal information. In 1891 the author opened two Uchee graves on the grounds of Cornelius Boudinot, at Tahlequah, finding with one body a number of French, Spanish, and American silver coins wrapped in cloth and deposited in two packages on each side of the head. They are now in the National Museum at Washington.

[2] Bonnell, Topographic Description of Texas, p. 141; Austin, 1840; Thrall, History of Texas, p. 58; New York, 1876.

[3] Author's personal information from J. D. Wafford and other old Cherokee residents and from recent Cherokee delegates. Bancroft agrees with Bonnell and Thrall that no grant was formally issued, but states that the Cherokee chief established his people in Texas " confiding in promises made to him, and a conditional agreement in 1822" with the Spanish governor (History of the North Mexican States and Texas, II, p. 103, 1889). It is probable that the paper carried by Bowl was the later Houston treaty. See next page.   [4] Thrall, op. cit.,s, p. 58.

occupied by them, but without specification as to boundaries. The Fredonia movement soon collapsed and nothing tangible seems to have come of the negotiations.[1]

In the fall of 1835 the Texan revolution began, resulting in the secession of Texas from Mexico and her establishment as an independent republic until annexed later to the United States. General Samuel Houston, a leading member of the revolutionary body, was an old friend of the Cherokee, and set forth so strongly the claims of them and their confederates that an act was passed by the convention pledging to these tribes all the lands which they had held under the Mexican government. In accordance with this act General Houston and John Forbes were appointed to hold a treaty with the Cherokee and their associated bands. They met the chiefs, including Bowl and Big-mush (Gatûñ'wa'lĭ, "Hard-mush"), of the Cherokee, at Bowl's village on February 23, 1836, and concluded a formal treaty by which the Cherokee and their allies received a fee simple title to all the land lying "west of the San Antonio road and beginning on the west at a point where the said road crosses the river Angelina, and running up said river until it reaches the mouth of the first large creek below the great Shawnee village, emptying into the said river from the northeast, thence running with said creek to its main source and from thence a due north line to the Sabine and with said river west. Then starting where the San Antonio road crosses the Angelina and with said road to where it crosses the Neches and thence running up the east side of said river in a northwest direction." The historian remarks that the description is somewhat vague, but is a literal transcription from the treaty.[2] The territory thus assigned was about equivalent to the present Cherokee county, Texas.

The treaty provoked such general dissatisfaction among the Texans that it was not presented to the convention for ratification. General Houston became President of Texas in November, 1836, but notwithstanding all his efforts in behalf of the Cherokee, the treaty was rejected by the Texas senate in secret session on December 16, 1837.[3] Texas having in the meantime achieved victorious independence was now in position to repudiate her engagements with the Indians, which she did, not only with the Cherokee, but with the Comanche and other wild tribes, which had been induced to remain neutral during the struggle on assurance of being secured in possession of their lands.

In the meantime President Houston was unremitting in his effort to secure the ratification of the Cherokee treaty, but without success. On the other hand the Cherokee were accused of various depredations, and it was asserted that they had entered into an agreement with

---

[1] Thrall, Texas, p. 46, 1879.   [3] Ibid., p. 143, 1840.
[2] Bonnell, Texas, pp. 142, 143, 1840.

Mexico by which they were to be secured in the territory in question on condition of assisting to drive out the Americans.[1] The charge came rather late in the day, and it was evident that President Houston put no faith in it, as he still continued his efforts in behalf of the Cherokee, even so far as to order the boundary line to be run, according to the terms of the treaty (45).[2]

In December, 1838, Houston was succeeded as President by Mirabeau B. Lamar, who at once announced his intention to expel every Indian tribe from Texas, declaring in his inaugural message that "the sword should mark the boundaries of the republic." At this time the Indians in eastern Texas, including the Cherokee and their twelve confederate bands and some others, were estimated at 1,800 warriors, or perhaps 8,000 persons.[3]

A small force of troops sent to take possession of the salt springs in the Indian country at the head of the Neches was notified by Bowl that such action would be resisted. The Indians were then informed that they must prepare to leave the country in the fall, but that they would be paid for the improvements abandoned. In the meantime the neighboring Mexicans made an effort to free themselves from Texan rule and sent overtures to the Indians to make common cause with them. This being discovered, the crisis was precipitated, and a commission consisting of General Albert Sidney Johnston (secretary of war of the republic), Vice-President Burnet, and some other officials, backed up by several regiments of troops, was sent to the Cherokee village on Angelina river to demand of the Indians that they remove at once across the border. The Indians refused and were attacked and defeated on July 15, 1839, by the Texan troops under command of General Douglas. They were pursued and a second engagement took place the next morning, resulting in the death of Bowl himself and his assistant chief Gatûñ'wa'lĭ, "Hard-mush," and the dispersion of the Indian forces, with a loss in the two engagements of about 55 killed and 80 wounded, the Texan loss being comparatively trifling. The first fight took place at a hill close to the main Cherokee village on the Angelina, where the Indians made a stand and defended their position well for some time. The second occurred at a ravine near Neches river, where they were intercepted in their retreat. Says Thrall, "After this fight the Indians abandoned Texas, leaving their fine lands in possession of the whites."[4]

By these two defeats the forces of the Cherokee and their confederates were completely broken up. A part of the Cherokee recrossed Red river and rejoined their kinsmen in Indian territory, bringing with them the blood-stained canister containing the patent for their

[1] Bonnell, Texas, pp. 143, 144.
[2] Ibid., pp. 144, 146.
[3] Thrall, Texas, pp. 116–168, 1876.
[4] Bonnell, op. cit., pp. 146–150; Thrall, op. cit., pp. 118–120.

Texas land, which Bowl had carried about with him since the treaty with Houston and which he had upon his person when shot. It is still kept in the Nation.[1] Others, with the Kickapoo, Delawares, and Caddo, scattered in small bands along the western Texas frontier, where they were occasionally heard from afterward. On Christmas day of the same year a fight occurred on Cherokee creek, San Saba county, in which several Indians were killed and a number of women and children captured, including the wife and family of the dead chief Bowl.[2] Those of the Cherokee who did not return to Indian territory gradually drifted down into Mexico, where some hundreds of them are now permanently and prosperously domiciled far south in the neighborhood of Guadalajara and Lake Chapala, communication being still kept up through occasional visits from their kinsmen in the territory.[3]

THE CHEROKEE NATION IN THE WEST—1840–1900

With the final removal of the Cherokee from their native country and their reunion and reorganization under new conditions in Indian Territory in 1840 their aboriginal period properly comes to a close and the rest may be dismissed in a few paragraphs as of concern rather to the local historian than to the ethnologist. Having traced for three full centuries their gradual evolution from a savage tribe to a civilized Christian nation, with a national constitution and national press printed in their own national alphabet, we can afford to leave the rest to others, the principal materials being readily accessible in the Cherokee national archives at Tahlequah, in the files of the *Cherokee Advocate* and other newspapers published in the Nation, and in the annual reports and other documents of the Indian office.

For many years the hunter and warrior had been giving place to the farmer and mechanic, and the forced expatriation made the change complete and final. Torn from their native streams and mountains, their council fires extinguished and their townhouses burned behind them, and transported bodily to a far distant country where everything was new and strange, they were obliged perforce to forego the old life and adjust themselves to changed surroundings. The ballplay was neglected and the green-corn dance proscribed, while the heroic tradition of former days became a fading memory or a tale to amuse a child. Instead of ceremonials and peace councils we hear now of railroad deals and contracts with cattle syndicates, and instead of the old warrior chiefs who had made the Cherokee name a terror—Oconostota, Hanging-maw, Doublehead, and Pathkiller—we find the destinies of the

---

[1] Author's personal information from J. D. Wafford and other old western Cherokee, and recent Cherokee delegates; by some this is said to have been a Mexican patent, but it is probably the one given by Texas. See ante, p. 143.

[2] Thrall, Texas, p. 120, 1876.

[3] Author's personal information from Mexican and Cherokee sources.

nation guided henceforth by shrewd mixed-blood politicians, bearing white men's names and speaking the white man's language, and frequently with hardly enough Indian blood to show itself in the features.

The change was not instantaneous, nor is it even yet complete, for although the tendency is constantly away from the old things, and although frequent intermarriages are rapidly bleaching out the brown of the Indian skin, there are still several thousand full-blood Cherokee—enough to constitute a large tribe if set off by themselves—who speak only their native language and in secret bow down to the nature-gods of their fathers.   Here, as in other lands, the conservative element has taken refuge in the mountain districts, while the mixed-bloods and the adopted whites are chiefly on the richer low grounds and in the railroad towns.

On the reorganization of the united Nation the council ground at Tahlequah was designated as the seat of government, and the present town was soon afterward laid out upon the spot, taking its name from the old Cherokee town of Tălikwă', or Tellico, in Tennessee.   The missions were reestablished, the *Advocate* was revived, and the work of civilization was again taken up, though under great difficulties, as continued removals and persecutions, with the awful suffering and mortality of the last great emigration, had impoverished and more than decimated the Nation and worn out the courage even of the bravest.   The bitterness engendered by the New Echota treaty led to a series of murders and assassinations and other acts of outlawry, amounting almost to civil war between the Ross and Ridge factions, until the Government was at last obliged to interfere.   The Old Settlers also had their grievances and complaints against the newcomers, so that the history of the Cherokee Nation for the next twenty years is largely a chronicle of factional quarrels, through which civilization and every good work actually retrograded behind the condition of a generation earlier.

Sequoya, who had occupied a prominent position in the affairs of the Old Settlers and assisted much in the reorganization of the Nation, had become seized with a desire to make linguistic investigations among the remote tribes, very probably with a view of devising a universal Indian alphabet.   His mind dwelt also on the old tradition of a lost band of Cherokee living somewhere toward the western mountains. In 1841 and 1842, with a few Cherokee companions and with his provisions and papers loaded in an ox cart, he made several journeys into the West, received everywhere with kindness by even the wildest tribes. Disappointed in his philologic results, he started out in 1843 in quest of the lost Cherokee, who were believed to be somewhere in northern Mexico, but, being now an old man and worn out by hardship, he sank under the effort and died—alone and unattended, it is said—near the village of San Fernando, Mexico, in August of that year. Rumors having come of his helpless condition, a party had been sent out from the Nation to bring him back, but arrived too late to find him alive. A pension of three hundred dollars, previously voted to him by the Nation, was continued to his widow—the only literary pension in the United States. Besides a wife he left two sons and a daughter.[1] Sequoyah district of the Cherokee Nation was named in his honor, and the great trees of California (*Sequoia gigantea*) also preserve his memory.

In 1846 a treaty was concluded at Washington by which the conflicting claims of the Old Settlers and later emigrants were adjusted, reimbursement was promised for sums unjustly deducted from the five-million-dollar payment guaranteed under the treaty of 1835, and a general amnesty was proclaimed for all past offenses within the Nation.[2] Final settlement of the treaty claims has not yet been made, and the matter is still a subject of litigation, including all the treaties and agreements up to the present date.

In 1859 the devoted missionary Samuel Worcester, author of numerous translations and first organizer of the *Advocate*, died at Park Hill mission, in the Cherokee Nation, after thirty-five years spent in the service of the Cherokee, having suffered chains, imprisonment, and exile for their sake.[3]

The breaking out of the civil war in 1861 found the Cherokee divided in sentiment. Being slave owners, like the other Indians removed from the southern states, and surrounded by southern influences, the agents in charge being themselves southern sympathizers, a considerable party in each of the tribes was disposed to take active part with the Confederacy. The old Ridge party, headed by Stand Watie and supported by the secret secession organization known as the Knights of the Golden Circle, declared for the Confederacy. The National party, headed by John Ross and supported by the patriotic organization known as the Kitoowah society—whose members were afterward known as Pin Indians—declared for strict neutrality. At last, however, the pressure became too strong to be resisted, and on October 7, 1861, a treaty was concluded at Tahlequah, with General Albert Pike, commissioner for the Confederate states, by which the Cherokee Nation cast its lot with the Confederacy, as the Creeks, Choctaw, Chickasaw, Seminole, Osage, Comanche, and several smaller tribes had already done.[4]

---

[1] W. A. Phillips, Sequoyah, in Harper's Magazine, September, 1870; Foster, Sequoyah, 1885; Royce, Cherokee Nation, Fifth Ann. Rep. Bureau of Ethnology, p. 302, 1888; letter of William P. Ross, former editor of Cherokee Advocate, March 11, 1889, in archives of Bureau of American Ethnology; Cherokee Advocate, October 19, 1844, November 2, 1844, and March 6, 1845; author's personal information. San Fernando seems to have been a small village in Chihuahua, but is not shown on the maps.

[2] For full discussion see Royce, op. cit., pp. 298–312.

[3] Pilling, Bibliography of the Iroquoian Languages (bulletin of the Bureau of Ethnology), p. 174, 1888.

[4] See treaties with Cherokee, October 7, 1861, and with other tribes, in Confederate States Statutes at Large, 1864; Royce, op. cit., pp. 324–328; Greeley, American Conflict, ii, pp. 30–34, 1866; Reports of Indian Commissioner for 1860 to 1862.

Two Cherokee regiments were raised for the Confederate service, under command of Stand Watie and Colonel Drew, respectively, the former being commissioned as brigadier-general. They participated in several engagements, chief among them being the battle of Pea Ridge, Arkansas, on March 7, 1862.[1] In the following summer the Union forces entered the Cherokee country and sent a proposition to Ross, urging him to repudiate the treaty with the Confederate states, but the offer was indignantly declined. Shortly afterward, however, the men of Drew's regiment, finding themselves unpaid and generally neglected by their allies, went over almost in a body to the Union side, thus compelling Ross to make an arrangement with the Union commander, Colonel Weir. Leaving the Cherokee country, Ross retired to Philadelphia, from which he did not return until the close of the war.[2] In the meantime Indian Territory was ravaged alternately by contending factions and armed bodies, and thousands of loyal fugitives were obliged to take refuge in Kansas, where they were cared for by the government. Among these, at the close of 1862, were two thousand Cherokee. In the following spring they were sent back to their homes under armed escort to give them an opportunity to put in a crop, seeds and tools being furnished for the purpose, but had hardly begun work when they were forced to retire by the approach of Stand Watie and his regiment of Confederate Cherokee, estimated at seven hundred men. Stand Watie and his men, with the Confederate Creeks and others, scoured the country at will, destroying or carrying off everything belonging to the loyal Cherokee, who had now, to the number of nearly seven thousand, taken refuge at Fort Gibson. Refusing to take sides against a government which was still unable to protect them, they were forced to see all the prosperous accumulations of twenty years of industry swept off in this guerrilla warfare. In stock alone their losses were estimated at more than 300,000 head.[3]

"The events of the war brought to them more of desolation and ruin than perhaps to any other community. Raided and sacked alternately, not only by the Confederate and Union forces, but by the vindictive ferocity and hate of their own factional divisions, their country became a blackened and desolate waste. Driven from comfortable homes, exposed to want, misery, and the elements, they perished like sheep in a snow storm. Their houses, fences, and other improvements were burned, their orchards destroyed, their flocks and herds slaughtered or driven off, their schools broken up, their schoolhouses given to the flames, and their churches and public buildings subjected to a similar fate; and that entire portion of their country which

---

[1] In this battle the Confederates were assisted by from 4,000 to 5,000 Indians of the southern tribes, including the Cherokee, under command of General Albert Pike.

[2] Royce, Cherokee Nation, Fifth Ann. Rep. Bureau of Ethnology, pp. 329, 330, 1888.

[3] Ibid, p. 331.

had been occupied by their settlements was distinguishable from the virgin prairie only by the scorched and blackened chimneys and the plowed but now neglected fields."[1]

After five years of desolation the Cherokee emerged from the war with their numbers reduced from 21,000 to 14,000,[2] and their whole country in ashes. On July 19, 1866, by a treaty concluded at Tahlequah, the nation was received back into the protection of the United States, a general amnesty was proclaimed, and all confiscations on account of the war prohibited; slavery was abolished without compensation to former owners, and all negroes residing within the Nation were admitted to full Cherokee citizenship. By articles 15 and 16 permission was given the United States to settle friendly Indians within the Cherokee home country or the Cherokee strip by consent and purchase from the Nation. By article 17 the Cherokee sold the 800,000-acre tract in Kansas secured by the treaty of 1835, together with a two-mile strip running along the southern border of Kansas, and thereafter to be included within the limits of that state, thus leaving the Cherokee country as it was before the recent cession of the Cherokee strip. Payment was promised for spoliations by United States troops during the war; and $3,000 were to be paid out of the Cherokee funds to the Reverend Evan Jones, then disabled and in poverty, as a reward for forty years of faithful missionary labors. By article 26 "the United States guarantee to the Cherokees the quiet and peaceable possession of their country and protection against domestic feuds and insurrection as well as hostilities of other tribes. They shall also be protected from intrusion by all unauthorized citizens of the United States attempting to settle on their lands or reside in their territory."[3]

The missionary, Reverend Evan Jones, who had followed the Cherokee into exile, and his son, John B. Jones, had been admitted to Cherokee citizenship the year before by vote of the Nation. The act conferring this recognition recites that "we do bear witness that they have done their work well."[4]

John Ross, now an old man, had been unable to attend this treaty, being present at the time in Washington on business for his people. Before its ratification he died in that city on August 1, 1866, at the age of seventy-seven years, fifty-seven of which had been given to the service of his Nation. No finer panegyric was ever pronounced than the memorial resolution passed by the Cherokee Nation on learning of his death.[5] Notwithstanding repeated attempts to subvert his authority, his people had remained steadfast in their fidelity to him,

---

[1] Royce, Cherokee Nation, op. cit., p. 376.
[2] Ibid., p. 376. A census of 1867 gives them 13,566 (ibid., p. 351).
[3] See synopsis and full discussion in Royce, op. cit., pp. 334–340.
[4] Act of Citizenship, November 7, 1865, Laws of the Cherokee Nation, p. 119; St. Louis, 1868.
[5] See Resolutions of Honor, ibid., pp. 137–140.

JOHN ROSS (GU'WISGUWĬ')

(From McKenney and Hall's copy of the original painting of about 1835)

COL. W. H. THOMAS (WIL-USDI')

(From photograph of 1858 kindly loaned by Capt. James W. Terrell)

and he died, as he had lived for nearly forty years, the officially recognized chief of the Nation. With repeated opportunities to enrich himself at the expense of his tribe, he died a poor man. His body was brought back and interred in the territory of the Nation. In remembrance of the great chief one of the nine districts of the Cherokee Nation has been called by his Indian name, Cooweescoowee (46).

Under the provisions of the late treaty the Delawares in Kansas, to the number of 985, removed to Indian territory in 1867 and became incorporated as citizens of the Cherokee Nation. They were followed in 1870 by the Shawano, chiefly also from Kansas, to the number of 770.[1] These immigrants settled chiefly along the Verdigris, in the northwestern part of the Nation. Under the same treaty the Osage, Kaw, Pawnee, Ponca, Oto and Missouri, and Tonkawa were afterward settled on the western extension known then as the Cherokee strip. The captive Nez Percés of Joseph's band were also temporarily located there, but have since been removed to the states of Washington and Idaho.

In 1870 the Missouri, Kansas and Texas railway, a branch of the Union Pacific system, was constructed through the lands of the Cherokee Nation under an agreement ratified by the Government, it being the first railroad to enter that country.[2] Several others have since been constructed or projected.

The same year saw a Cherokee literary revival. The publication of the *Advocate*, which had been suspended since some years before the war, was resumed, and by authority of the Nation John B. Jones began the preparation of a series of schoolbooks in the Cherokee language and alphabet for the benefit of those children who knew no English.[3]

In the spring of 1881 a delegation from the Cherokee Nation visited the East Cherokee still remaining in the mountains of North Carolina and extended to them a cordial and urgent invitation to remove and incorporate upon equal terms with the Cherokee Nation in the Indian territory. In consequence several parties of East Cherokee, numbering in all 161 persons, removed during the year to the western Nation, the expense being paid by the Federal government. Others afterwards applied for assistance to remove, but as no further appropriation was made for the purpose nothing more was done.[4] In 1883 the East Cherokee brought suit for a proportionate division of the Cherokee funds and other interests under previous treaties,[5] but their claim was

[1] Royce, Cherokee Nation, Fifth Ann. Rep. Bureau of Ethnology, pp. 356–358, 1888; Constitution and Laws of the Cherokee Nation, pp. 277–284; St. Louis, 1875.
[2] Royce, op. cit., p. 367.
[3] Foster, Sequoyah, pp. 147, 148, 1885; Pilling, Iroquoian Bibliography, 1888, articles "Cherokee Advocate" and "John B. Jones." The schoolbook series seems to have ended with the arithmetic—cause, as the Cherokee national superintendent of schools explained to the author, "too much white man."
[4] Commissioner H. Price, Report of Indian Commissioner, p. lxv, 1881, and p. lxx, 1882; see also p. 175.
[5] Report of Indian Commissioner, p. lxv, 1883.

finally decided adversely three years later on appeal to the Supreme Court.[1]

In 1889 the Cherokee female seminary was completed at Tahlequah at a cost of over $60,000, supplementing the work of the male seminary, built some years before at a cost of $90,000. The Cherokee Nation was now appropriating annually over $80,000 for school purposes, including the support of the two seminaries, an orphan asylum, and over one hundred primary schools, besides which there were a number of mission schools.[2]

For a number of years the pressure for the opening of lndian territory to white settlement had been growing in strength. Thousands of intruders had settled themselves upon the lands of each of the five civilized tribes, where they remained upon various pretexts in spite of urgent and repeated appeals to the government by the Indians for their removal. Under treaties with the five civilized tribes, the right to decide citizenship or residence claims belonged to the tribes concerned, but the intruders had at last become so numerous and strong that they had formed an organization among themselves to pass upon their own claims, and others that might be submitted to them, with attorneys and ample funds to defend each claim in outside courts against the decision of the tribe. At the same time the Government policy was steadily toward the reduction or complete breaking up of Indian reservations and the allotment of lands to the Indians in severalty, with a view to their final citizenship, and the opening of the surplus lands to white settlement. As a part of the same policy the jurisdiction of the United States courts was gradually being extended over the Indian country, taking cognizance of many things hitherto considered by the Indian courts under former treaties with the United States. Against all this the Cherokee and other civilized tribes protested, but without avail. To add to the irritation, companies of armed "boomers" were organized for the express purpose of invading and seizing the Cherokee outlet and other unoccupied portions of the Indian territory—reserved by treaty for future Indian settlement—in defiance of the civil and military power of the Government.

We come now to what seems the beginning of the end of Indian autonomy. In 1889 a commission, afterward known as the Cherokee Commission, was appointed, under act of Congress, to "negotiate with the Cherokee Indians, and with all other Indians owning or claiming lands lying west of the ninety-sixth degree of longitude in the Indian territory, for the cession to the United States of all their title, claim, or interest of every kind or character in and to said lands." In August of that year the commission made a proposition to

---

[1] Commissioner J. D. C. Atkins, Report of Indian Commissioner, p. xlv, 1886, and p. lxxvii, 1887.
[2] Agent L. E. Bennett, in Report of Indian Commissioner, p. 93, 1890.

Chief J. B. Mayes for the cession of all the Cherokee lands thus described, being that portion known as the Cherokee outlet or strip. The proposition was declined on the ground that the Cherokee constitution forbade its consideration.[1] Other tribes were approached for a similar purpose, and the commission was continued, with changing personnel from year to year, until agreements for cession and the taking of allotments had been made with nearly all the wilder tribes in what is now Oklahoma.

In the meantime the Attorney-General had rendered a decision denying the right of Indian tribes to lease their lands without permission of the Government. At this time the Cherokee were deriving an annual income of $150,000 from the lease of grazing privileges upon the strip, but by a proclamation of President Harrison on February 17, 1890, ordering the cattlemen to vacate before the end of the year, this income was cut off and the strip was rendered practically valueless to them.[2] The Cherokee were now forced to come to terms, and a second proposition for the cession of the Cherokee strip was finally accepted by the national council on January 4, 1892. "It was known to the Cherokees that for some time would-be settlers on the lands of the outlet had been encamped in the southern end of Kansas, and by every influence at their command had been urging the Government to open the country to settlement and to negotiate with the Cherokees afterwards, and that a bill for that purpose had been introduced in Congress." The consideration was nearly $8,600,000, or about $1.25 per acre, for something over 6,000,000 acres of land. One article of the agreement stipulates for "the reaffirmation to the Cherokee Nation of the right of local self-government."[3] The agreement having been ratified by Congress, the Cherokee strip was opened by Presidential proclamation on September 16, 1893.[4]

The movement for the abolition of the Indian governments and the allotment and opening of the Indian country had now gained such force that by act of Congress approved March 3, 1893, the President was authorized to appoint a commission of three—known later as the Dawes Commission, from its distinguished chairman, Senator Henry L. Dawes of Massachusetts—to negotiate with the five civilized tribes of Indian territory, viz, the Cherokee, Choctaw, Chickasaw, Creek, and Seminole, for "the extinguishment of tribal titles to any lands within that territory, now held by any and all of such nations and tribes, either by cession of the same or some part thereof to the United States, or by the allotment and division of the same in severalty among the Indians of such nations or tribes respectively as may be

---

[1] Report of Indian Commissioner, p. 22, 1889.
[2] See proclamation by President Harrison and order from Indian Commissioner in Report of Indian Commissioner, pp. lxxii–lxxiii, 421–422, 1890. The lease figures are from personal information.
[3] Commissioner T. J. Morgan, Report of Indian Commissioner, pp. 79–80, 1892.
[4] Commissioner D. M. Browning, Report of Indian Commissioner, pp. 33–34, 1893.

entitled to the same, or by such other method as may be agreed upon
. . . to enable the ultimate creation of a state or states of the
Union, which shall embrace the land within the said Indian territory."[1]
The commission appointed arrived in the Indian territory in January,
1894, and at once began negotiations.[2]

At this time the noncitizen element in Indian Territory was officially
reported to number at least 200,000 souls, while those having rights
as citizens of the five civilized tribes, including full-blood and mixed-
blood Indians, adopted whites, and negroes, numbered but 70,500.[3]
Not all of the noncitizens were intruders, many being there by permission of the Indian governments or on official or other legitimate
business, but the great body of them were illegal squatters or unrecognized claimants to Indian rights, against whose presence the Indians
themselves had never ceased to protest. A test case brought this year
in the Cherokee Nation was decided by the Interior Department against
the claimants and in favor of the Cherokee. Commenting upon threats
made in consequence by the rejected claimants, the agent for the five
tribes remarks: "It is not probable that Congress will establish a
court to nullify and vacate a formal decision of the Interior Department."[4] A year later he says of these intruders that "so long as they
have a foothold—a residence, legal or not—in the Indian country they
will be disturbers of peace and promoters of discord, and while they
cry aloud, and spare not, for allotment and statehood, they are but
stumbling blocks and obstacles to that mutual good will and fraternal
feeling which must be cultivated and secured before allotment is practicable and statehood desirable."[5] The removal of the intruders was
still delayed, and in 1896 the decision of citizenship claims was taken
from the Indian government and relegated to the Dawes Commission.[6]

In 1895 the commission was increased to five members, with enlarged
powers. In the meantime a survey of Indian Territory had been
ordered and begun. In September the agent wrote: "The Indians
now know that a survey of their lands is being made, and whether
with or without their consent, the survey is going on. The meaning
of such survey is too plain to be disregarded, and it is justly considered as the initial step, solemn and authoritative, toward the over-
throw of their present communal holdings. At this writing surveying
corps are at work in the Creek, Choctaw, and Chickasaw Nations, and
therefore each one of these tribes has an ocular demonstration of the
actual intent and ultimate purpose of the government of the United
States."[7]

---

[1] Quotation from act, etc., Report of Indian Commissioner for 1894, p. 27, 1895.
[2] Report of Agent D. M. Wisdom, ibid., p. 141.
[3] Ibid., and statistical table, p. 570.
[4] Report of Agent D. M. Wisdom, ibid., p. 145.
[5] Agent D. M. Wisdom, in Report Indian Commissioner for 1895, p. 155, 1896.
[6] Commissioner D. M. Browning, Report of Indian Commissioner, p. 81, 1896.
[7] Report of Agent D. M. Wisdom, Report of Indian Commissioner for 1895, pp. 159, 160, 1896.

The general prosperity and advancement of the Cherokee Nation at this time may be judged from the report of the secretary of the Cherokee national board of education to Agent Wisdom. He reports 4,800 children attending two seminaries, male and female, two high schools, and one hundred primary schools, teachers being paid from $35 to $100 per month for nine months in the year. Fourteen primary schools were for the use of the negro citizens of the Nation, besides which they had a fine high school, kept up, like all the others, at the expense of the Cherokee goverment. Besides the national schools there were twelve mission schools helping to do splendid work for children of both citizens and noncitizens. Children of noncitizens were not allowed to attend the Cherokee national schools, but had their own subscription schools. The orphan asylum ranked as a high school, in which 150 orphans were boarded and educated, with graduates every year. It was a large brick building of three stories, 80 by 240 feet. The male seminary, accommodating 200 pupils, and the female seminary, accommodating 225 pupils, were also large brick structures, three stories in height and 150 by 240 feet on the ground. Three members, all Cherokee by blood, constituted a board of education. The secretary adds that the Cherokee are proud of their schools and educational institutions, and that no other country under the sun is so blessed with educational advantages at large.[1]

At this time the Cherokee Nation numbered something over 25,000 Indian, white, and negro citizens; the total citizen population of the three races in the five civilized tribes numbered about 70,000, while the noncitizens had increased to 250,000 and their number was being rapidly augmented.[2] Realizing that the swift, inevitable end must be the destruction of their national governments, the Cherokee began once more to consider the question of removal from the United States. The scheme is outlined in a letter written by a brother of the principal chief of the Cherokee Nation under date of May 31, 1895, from which we quote.

After prefacing that the government of the United States seems determined to break up the tribal autonomy of the five civilized tribes and to divide their lands, thus bringing about conditions under which the Cherokee could not exist, he continues:

Then for a remedy that will lead us out of it, away from it, and one that promises our preservation as a distinct race of people in the enjoyment of customs, social and political, that have been handed down to us from remote generations of the past. My plan is for the Cherokees to sell their entire landed possessions to the United States, divide the proceeds thereof per capita, then such as desire to do so unite in the formation of an Indian colony, and with their funds jointly purchase in Mexico

---

[1] Letter of A. E. Ivy, Secretary of the Board of Education, in Report of Indian Commissioner for 1895, p. 161, 1896. The author can add personal testimony as to the completeness of the seminary establishment.

[2] Report of Agent Wisdom, ibid., p. 162.

or South America a body of land sufficient for all their purposes, to be forever their joint home. . . . I believe also that for such Indians as did not desire to join the colony and leave the country provision should be made for them to repurchase their old homes, or such other lands in the country here as they might desire, and they could remain here and meet such fate as awaits them. I believe this presents the most feasible and equitable solution of the questions that we must decide in the near future, and will prove absolutely just and fair to all classes and conditions of our citizens. I also believe that the same could be acted upon by any or all of the five civilized tribes. . . .[1]

The final chapter is nearly written. By successive enactments within the last ten years the jurisdiction of the Indian courts has been steadily narrowed and the authority of the Federal courts proportionately extended; the right to determine Indian citizenship has been taken from the Indians and vested in a Government commission; the lands of the five tribes have been surveyed and sectionized by Government surveyors; and by the sweeping provisions of the Curtis act of June 28, 1898, "for the protection of the people of the Indian Territory," the entire control of tribal revenues is taken from the five Indian tribes and vested with a resident supervising inspector, the tribal courts are abolished, allotments are made compulsory, and authority is given to incorporate white men's towns in the Indian tribes.[2] By this act the five civilized tribes are reduced to the condition of ordinary reservation tribes under government agents with white communities planted in their midst. In the meantime the Dawes commission, continued up to the present, has by unremitting effort broken down the opposition of the Choctaw and Chickasaw, who have consented to allotment, while the Creeks and the Seminole are now wavering.[3] The Cherokee still hold out, the Ketoowah secret society (47) especially being strong in its resistance, and when the end comes it is possible that the protest will take shape in a wholesale emigration to Mexico. Late in 1897 the agent for the five tribes reports that "there seems a determined purpose on the part of many fullbloods . . . to emigrate to either Mexico or South America and there purchase new homes for themselves and families. Such individual action may grow to the proportion of a colony, and it is understood that liberal grants of land can be secured from the countries mentioned.[4] Mexican agents are now (1901) among the Cherokee advocating the scheme, which may develop to include a large proportion of the five civilized tribes.[5]

By the census of 1898, the most recent taken, as reported by Agent

---

[1] Letter of Bird Harris, May 31, 1895, in Report of Indian Commissioner for 1895, p. 160, 1896.

[2] Synopsis of Curtis act, pp. 75–79, and Curtis act in full, p. 425 et seq., in Report of Indian Commissioner for 1898; noted also in Report of Indian Commissioner, p. 84 et seq., 1899.

[3] Commissioner W. A. Jones, ibid., pp. i, 84 et seq. (Curtis act and Dawes commission).

[4] Report of Agent D. M. Wisdom, Report of Indian Commissioner, pp. 141–144, 1897.

[5] Author's personal information; see also House bill No. 1165 " for the relief of certain Indians in Indian Territory," etc., Fifty-sixth Congress, first session; 1900.

Wisdom, the Cherokee Nation numbered 34,461 persons, as follows: Cherokee by blood (including all degrees of admixture), 26,500; inter-married whites, 2,300; negro freedmen, 4,000; Delaware, 871; Shaw-nee, 790. The total acreage of the Nation was 5,031,351 acres, which, if divided per capita under the provisions of the Curtis bill, after deducting 60,000 acres reserved for town-site and other purposes, would give to each Cherokee citizen 144 acres.[1] It must be noted that the official rolls include a large number of persons whose claims are disputed by the Cherokee authorities.

THE EASTERN BAND

It remains to speak of the eastern band of Cherokee—the remnant which still clings to the woods and waters of the old home country. As has been said, a considerable number had eluded the troops in the general round-up of 1838 and had fled to the fastnesses of the high mountains. Here they were joined by others who had managed to break through the guard at Calhoun and other collecting stations, until the whole number of fugitives in hiding amounted to a thousand or more, principally of the mountain Cherokee of North Carolina, the purest-blooded and most conservative of the Nation. About one-half the refugee warriors had put themselves under command of a noted leader named U'tsălă, " Lichen, " who made his headquarters amid the lofty peaks at the head of Oconaluftee, from which secure hiding place, although reduced to extremity of suffering from starvation and exposure, they defied every effort to effect their capture.

The work of running down these fugitives proved to be so difficult an undertaking and so well-nigh barren of result that when Charley and his sons made their bold stroke for freedom[2] General Scott eagerly seized the incident as an opportunity for compromise. To this end he engaged the services of William H. Thomas, a trader who for more than twenty years had been closely identified with the mountain Cher-okee and possessed their full confidence, and authorized him to submit to U'tsălă a proposition that if the latter would seize Charley and the others who had been concerned in the attack upon the soldiers and surrender them for punishment, the pursuit would be called off and the fugitives allowed to stay unmolested until an effort could be made to secure permission from the general government for them to remain.

Thomas accepted the commission, and taking with him one or two Indians made his way over secret paths to U'tsălă's hiding place. He presented Scott's proposition and represented to the chief that by aiding in bringing Charley's party to punishment according to the rules of war he could secure respite for his sorely pressed followers, with the ultimate hope that they might be allowed to remain in their

---

[1] Report of Agent D. M. Wisdom, Report of Indian Commissioner, p. 159, 1898.
[2] See page 131.

own country, whereas if he rejected the offer the whole force of the
seven thousand troops which had now completed the work of gathering up and deporting the rest of the tribe would be set loose upon his
own small band until the last refugee had been either taken or
killed.

U′tsălă turned the proposition in his mind long and seriously. His
heart was bitter, for his wife and little son had starved to death on the
mountain side, but he thought of the thousands who were already on
their long march into exile and then he looked round upon his little
band of followers. If only they might stay, even though a few must
be sacrificed, it was better than that all should die—for they had sworn
never to leave their country. He consented and Thomas returned to
report to General Scott.

Now occurred a remarkable incident which shows the character of
Thomas and the masterly influence which he already had over the
Indians, although as yet he was hardly more than thirty years old. It
was known that Charley and his party were in hiding in a cave of the
Great Smokies, at the head of Deep creek, but it was not thought
likely that he could be taken without bloodshed and a further delay
which might prejudice the whole undertaking. Thomas determined to
go to him and try to persuade him to come in and surrender. Declining Scott's offer of an escort, he went alone to the cave, and, getting
between the Indians and their guns as they were sitting around the
fire near the entrance, he walked up to Charley and announced his
message. The old man listened in silence and then said simply, "I
will come in. I don't want to be hunted down by my own people."
They came in voluntarily and were shot, as has been already narrated,
one only, a mere boy, being spared on account of his youth. This
boy, now an old man, is still living, Wasitû′na, better known to the
whites as Washington.[1]

A respite having thus been obtained for the fugitives, Thomas next
went to Washington to endeavor to make some arrangement for their
permanent settlement. Under the treaty of New Echota, in 1835, the
Cherokee were entitled, besides the lump sum of five million dollars
for the lands ceded, to an additional compensation for the improvements which they were forced to abandon and for spoliations by white
citizens, together with a per capita allowance to cover the cost of
removal and subsistence for one year in the new country. The twelfth
article had also provided that such Indians as chose to remain in the
East and become citizens there might do so under certain conditions,

---

[1] Charley's story as here given is from the author's personal information, derived chiefly from conversations with Colonel Thomas and with Wasitû′na and other old Indians. An ornate but somewhat inaccurate account is given also in Lanman's Letters from the Alleghany Mountains, written on
the ground ten years after the events described. The leading facts are noted in General Scott's official
dispatches.

each head of a family thus remaining to be confirmed in a preemption right to 160 acres. In consequence of the settled purpose of President Jackson to deport every Indian, this permission was canceled and supplementary articles substituted by which some additional compensation was allowed in lieu of the promised preemptions and all individual reservations granted under previous treaties.[1] Every Cherokee was thus made a landless alien in his original country.

The last party of emigrant Cherokee had started for the West in December, 1838. Nine months afterwards the refugees still scattered about in the mountains of North Carolina and Tennessee were reported to number 1,046.[2] By persistent effort at Washington from 1836 to 1842, including one continuous stay of three years at the capital city, Thomas finally obtained governmental permission for these to remain, and their share of the moneys due for improvements and reservations confiscated was placed at his disposal, as their agent and trustee, for the purpose of buying lands upon which they could be permanently settled. Under this authority he bought for them, at various times up to the year 1861, a number of contiguous tracts of land upon Oconaluftee river and Soco creek, within the present Swain and Jackson counties of North Carolina, together with several detached tracts in the more western counties of the same state. The main body, upon the waters of Oconaluftee, which was chiefly within the limits of the cession of 1819, came afterward to be known as the Qualla boundary, or Qualla reservation, taking the name from Thomas' principal trading store and agency headquarters. The detached western tracts were within the final cession of 1835, but all alike were bought by Thomas from white owners. As North Carolina refused to recognize Indians as landowners within the state, and persisted in this refusal until 1866,[3] Thomas, as their authorized agent under the Government, held the deeds in his own name. Before it was legally possible under the state laws to transfer the title to the Indians, his own affairs had become involved and his health impaired by age and the hardships of military service so that his mind gave way, thus leaving the whole question of the Indian title a subject of litigation until its adjudication by the United States in 1875, supplemented by further decisions in 1894.

To Colonel William Holland Thomas the East Cherokee of to-day owe their existence as a people, and for half a century he was as intimately connected with their history as was John Ross with that of the main Cherokee Nation. Singularly enough, their connection with Cherokee affairs extended over nearly the same period, but while Ross participated in their national matters Thomas gave his effort to

---

[1] See New Echota treaty, December 29, 1835, and supplementary articles, March 1, 1836, in Indian Treaties, pp. 633–648, 1837; also full discussion of same treaty in Royce, Cherokee Nation, Fifth Ann. Rep. Bureau of Ethnology, 1888.

[1] Royce, op. cit., p. 292.   [1] Ibid., p. 314.

a neglected band hardly known in the councils of the tribe. In his many-sided capacity he strikingly resembles another white man prominent in Cherokee history, General Sam Houston.

Thomas was born in the year 1805 on Raccoon creek, about two miles from Waynesville in North Carolina. His father, who was related to President Zachary Taylor, came of a Welsh family which had immigrated to Virginia at an early period, while on his mother's side he was descended from a Maryland family of Revolutionary stock. He was an only and posthumous child, his father having been accidentally drowned a short time before the boy was born. Being unusually bright for his age, he was engaged when only twelve years old to tend an Indian trading store on Soco creek, in the present Jackson county, owned by Felix Walker, son of the Congressman of the same name who made a national reputation by "talking for Buncombe." The store was on the south side of the creek, about a mile above the now abandoned Macedonia mission, within the present reservation, and was a branch of a larger establishment which Walker himself kept at Waynesville. The trade was chiefly in skins and ginseng, or "sang," the latter for shipment to China, where it was said to be worth its weight in silver. This trade was very profitable, as the price to the Indians was but ten cents per pound in merchandise for the green root, whereas it now brings seventy-five cents in cash upon the reservation, the supply steadily diminishing with every year. The contract was for three years' service for a total compensation of one hundred dollars and expenses, but Walker devoted so much of his attention to law studies that the Waynesville store was finally closed for debt, and at the end of his contract term young Thomas was obliged to accept a lot of second-hand law books in lieu of other payment. How well he made use of them is evident from his subsequent service in the state senate and in other official capacities.

Soon after entering upon his duties he attracted the notice of Yonaguska, or Drowning-bear (Yâ'na-gûñ'skǐ, "Bear-drowning-him"), the acknowledged chief of all the Cherokee then living on the waters of Tuckasegee and Oconaluftee—the old Kituhwa country. On learning that the boy had neither father nor brother, the old chief formally adopted him as his son, and as such he was thenceforth recognized in the tribe under the name of Wil-Usdi', or "Little Will," he being of small stature even in mature age. From his Indian friends, particularly a boy of the same age who was his companion in the store, he learned the language as well as a white man has ever learned it, so that in his declining years it dwelt in memory more strongly than his mother tongue. After the invention of the Cherokee alphabet, he learned also to read and write the language.

In 1819 the lands on Tuckasegee and its branches were sold by the

Indians, and Thomas's mother soon after removed from Waynesville to
a farm which she purchased on the west bank of Oconaluftee, opposite
the mouth of Soco, where her son went to live with her, having now
set up in business for himself at Qualla.   Yonaguska and his immediate connection continued to reside on a small reservation in the same
neighborhood, while the rest of the Cherokee retired to the west of
the Nantahala mountains, though still visiting and trading on Soco.
After several shiftings Thomas finally, soon after the removal in 1838,
bought a farm on the northern bank of Tuckasegee, just above the
present town of Whittier in Swain county, and built there a homestead which he called Stekoa, after an Indian town destroyed by
Rutherford which had occupied the same site.   At the time of the
removal he was the proprietor of five trading stores in or adjoining the
Cherokee country, viz, at Qualla town, near the mouth of Soco creek;
on Scott's creek, near Webster; on Cheowa, near the present Robbinsville; at the junction of Valley river and Hiwassee, now Murphy; and
at the Cherokee agency at Calhoun (now Charleston), Tennessee.
Besides carrying on a successful trading business he was also studying
law and taking an active interest in local politics.

In his capacity as agent for the eastern Cherokee he laid off the
lands purchased for them into five districts or "towns," which he
named Bird town, Paint town, Wolf town, Yellow hill, and Big cove,
the names which they still retain, the first three being those of Cherokee clans.[1]   He also drew up for them a simple form of government,
the execution of which was in his own and Yonaguska's hands until the
death of the latter, after which the band knew no other chief than
Thomas until his retirement from active life.   In 1848 he was elected
to the state senate and continued to serve in that capacity until the
outbreak of the civil war.   As state senator he inaugurated a system of
road improvements for western North Carolina and was also the father
of the Western North Carolina Railroad (now a part of the Southern
system), originally projected to develop the copper mines of Ducktown,
Tennessee.

With his colleagues in the state senate he voted for secession in 1861,
and at once resigned to recruit troops for the Confederacy, to which,
until the close of the war, he gave his whole time, thought, and effort.
In 1862 he organized the Thomas Legion, consisting of two regiments
of infantry, a battalion of cavalry, a company of engineers, and a field
battery, he himself commanding as colonel, although then nearly sixty
years of age.   Four companies were made up principally of his own
Cherokee.   The Thomas Legion operated chiefly as a frontier guard

---

[1] In the Cherokee language Tsiskwâ'hĭ, "Bird place," Ani'-Wâ'dihĭ, "Paint place," Wa'yâ'hĭ, "Wolf
place," E'lawâ'di, "Red earth" (now Cherokee post-office and agency), and Kâlănûñ'yĭ, "Raven
place."   There was also, for a time, a "Pretty-woman town" (Ani'-Gilâ'hĭ?).

for the Confederacy along the mountain region southward from Cumberland gap.

After the close of the conflict he returned to his home at Stekoa and again took charge, unofficially, of the affairs of the Cherokee, whom he attended during the smallpox epidemic of 1866 and assisted through the unsettled conditions of the reconstruction period. His own resources had been swept away by the war, and all his hopes had gone down with the lost cause. This, added to the effects of three years of hardship and anxiety in the field when already almost past the age limit, soon after brought about a physical and mental collapse, from which he never afterward rallied except at intervals, when for a short time the old spirit would flash out in all its brightness. He died in 1893 at the advanced age of nearly ninety, retaining to the last the courteous manner of a gentleman by nature and training, with an exact memory and the clear-cut statement of a lawyer and man of affairs. To his work in the state senate the people of western North Carolina owe more than to that of any other man, while among the older Cherokee the name of Wil-Usdi' is still revered as that of a father and a great chief.[1]

Yonaguska, properly Yâ'nû-gûñ'skĭ, the adopted father of Thomas, is the most prominent chief in the history of the East Cherokee, although, singularly enough, his name does not occur in connection with any of the early wars or treaties. This is due partly to the fact that he was a peace chief and counselor rather than a war leader, and in part to the fact that the isolated position of the mountain Cherokee kept them aloof in a great measure from the tribal councils of those living to the west and south. In person he was strikingly handsome, being six feet three inches in height and strongly built, with a faint tinge of red, due to a slight strain of white blood on his father's side, relieving the brown of his cheek. In power of oratory he is said to have surpassed any other chief of his day. When the Cherokee lands on Tuckasegee were sold by the treaty of 1819, Yonaguska continued to reside on a reservation of 640 acres in a bend of the river a short distance above the present Bryson City, on the site of the ancient Kituhwa. He afterward moved over to Oconaluftee, and finally, after the Removal, gathered his people about him and settled with them on Soco creek on lands purchased for them by Thomas.

---

[1] The facts concerning Colonel Thomas's career are derived chiefly from the author's conversations with Thomas himself, supplemented by information from his former assistant, Capt. James W. Terrell, and others who knew him, together with an admirable sketch in the North Carolina University Magazine for May 1899, by Mrs. A. C. Avery, his daughter. He is also frequently noticed, in connection with East Cherokee matters, in the annual reports of the Commissioner of Indian Affairs; in the North Carolina Confederate Roster; in Lanman's Letters from the Alleghany Mountains; and in Zeigler and Grosscup's Heart of the Alleghanies, etc. Some manuscript contributions to the library of the Georgia Historical Society in Savannah—now unfortunately mislaid—show his interest in Cherokee linguistics.

He was a prophet and reformer as well as a chief. When about
sixty years of age he had a severe sickness, terminating in a trance,
during which his people mourned him as dead. At the end of twenty-
four hours, however, he awoke to consciousness and announced that he
had been to the spirit world, where he had talked with friends who
had gone before, and with God, who had sent him back with a message
to the Indians, promising to call him again at a later time. From
that day until his death his words were listened to as those of one
inspired. He had been somewhat addicted to liquor, but now, on the
recommendation of Thomas, not only quit drinking himself, but organized his tribe into a temperance society. To accomplish this he called
his people together in council, and, after clearly pointing out to them
the serious effect of intemperance, in an eloquent speech that moved
some of his audience to tears, he declared that God had permitted him
to return to earth especially that he might thus warn his people and
banish whisky from among them. He then had Thomas write out a
pledge, which was signed first by the chief and then by each one of the
council, and from that time until after his death whisky was unknown
among the East Cherokee.

Although frequent pressure was brought to bear to induce him and
his people to remove to the West, he firmly resisted every persuasion,
declaring that the Indians were safer from aggression among their
rocks and mountains than they could ever be in a land which the white
man could find profitable, and that the Cherokee could be happy only
in the country where nature had planted him. While counseling peace
and friendship with the white man, he held always to his Indian faith
and was extremely suspicious of missionaries. On one occasion, after
the first Bible translation into the Cherokee language and alphabet,
some one brought a copy of Matthew from New Echota, but Yonaguska would not allow it to be read to his people until it had first been
read to himself. After listening to one or two chapters the old chief
dryly remarked: "Well, it seems to be a good book—strange that the
white people are not better, after having had it so long."

He died, aged about eighty, in April, 1839, within a year after the
Removal. Shortly before the end he had himself carried into the
townhouse on Soco, of which he had supervised the building, where,
extended on a couch, he made a last talk to his people, commend-
ing Thomas to them as their chief and again warning them earnestly
against ever leaving their own country. Then wrapping his blanket
around him, he quietly lay back and died. He was buried beside
Soco, about a mile below the old Macedonia mission, with a rude
mound of stones to mark the spot. He left two wives and considerable property, including an old negro slave named Cudjo, who was
devotedly attached to him. One of his daughters, Katâ′lsta, still sur-

vives, and is the last conservator of the potter's art among the East Cherokee.[1]

Yonaguska had succeeded in authority to Yane'gwa, "Big-bear," who appears to have been of considerable local prominence in his time, but whose name, even with the oldest of the band, is now but a memory. He was among the signers of the treaties of 1798 and 1805, and by the treaty of 1819 was confirmed in a reservation of 640 acres as one of those living within the ceded territory who were "believed to be persons of industry and capable of managing their property with discretion," and who had made considerable improvements on the tracts reserved. This reservation, still known as the Big-bear farm, was on the western bank of Oconaluftee, a few miles above its mouth, and appears to have been the same afterward occupied by Yonaguska.[2]

Another of the old notables among the East Cherokee was Tsunu'lă-hûñ'skĭ, corrupted by the whites to Junaluska, a great warrior, from whom the ridge west of Waynesville takes its name. In early life he was known as Gûl'kăla'skĭ.[3] On the outbreak of the Creek war in 1813 he raised a party of warriors to go down, as he boasted, "to exterminate the Creeks." Not meeting with complete success, he announced the result, according to the Cherokee custom, at the next dance after his return in a single word, *detsinu'lăhûñgû'*, "I tried, but could not," given out as a cue to the song leader, who at once took it as the burden of his song. Thenceforth the disappointed warrior was known as Tsunu'lăhûñ'skĭ, "One who tries, but fails." He distinguished himself at the Horseshoe bend, where the action of the Cherokee decided the battle in favor of Jackson's army, and was often heard to say after the removal: "If I had known that Jackson would drive us from our homes, I would have killed him that day at the Horseshoe." He accompanied the exiles of 1838, but afterward returned to his old home; he was allowed to remain, and in recognition of his services the state legislature, by special act, in 1847 conferred upon him the right of citizenship and granted to him a tract of land in fee simple, but without power of alienation.[4] This reservation was in the Cheowa Indian settlement, near the present Robbinsville, in Graham county, where he died about the year 1858. His grave is still to be seen just outside of Robbinsville.

---

[1] The facts concerning Yonaguska are based on the author's personal information obtained from Colonel Thomas, supplemented from conversations with old Indians. The date of his death and his approximate age are taken from the Terrell roll. He is also noticed at length in Lanman's Letters from the Alleghany Mountains, 1848, and in Zeigler and Grosscup's Heart of the Alleghanies, 1883. The trance which, according to Thomas and Lanman, lasted about one day, is stretched by the last-named authors to fifteen days, with the whole 1,200 Indians marching and countermarching around the sleeping body!

[2] The name in the treaties occurs as Yonahequah (1798), Yohanaqua (1805), and Yonah (1819).—Indian Treaties, pp. 82, 123, 268; Washington, 1837.

[3] The name refers to something habitually falling from a leaning position.

[4] Act quoted in Report of Indian Commissioner for 1895, p. 636, 1896.

As illustrative of his shrewdness it is told that he once tracked a little Indian girl to Charleston, South Carolina, where she had been carried by kidnappers and sold as a slave, and regained her freedom by proving, from expert microscopic examination, that her hair had none of the negro characteristics.[1]

Christianity was introduced among the Kituhwa Cherokee shortly before the Removal through Worcester and Boudinot's translation of Matthew, first published at New Echota in 1829. In the absence of missionaries the book was read by the Indians from house to house. After the Removal a Methodist minister, Reverend Ulrich Keener, began to make visits for preaching at irregular intervals, and was followed several years later by Baptist workers.[2]

In the fall of 1839 the Commissioner of Indian Affairs reported that the East Cherokee had recently expressed a desire to join their brethren in the West, but had been deterred from so doing by the unsettled condition of affairs in the Territory. He states that "they have a right to remain or to go," but that as the interests of others are involved in their decision they should decide without delay.[3]

In 1840 about one hundred Catawba, nearly all that were left of the tribe, being dissatisfied with their condition in South Carolina, moved up in a body and took up their residence with the Cherokee. Latent tribal jealousies broke out, however, and at their own request negotiations were begun in 1848, through Thomas and others, for their removal to Indian Territory. The effort being without result, they soon after began to drift back to their own homes, until, in 1852, there were only about a dozen remaining among the Cherokee. In 1890 only one was left, an old woman, the widow of a Cherokee husband. She and her daughter, both of whom spoke the language, were expert potters according to the Catawba method, which differs markedly from that of the Cherokee. There are now two Catawba women, both married to Cherokee husbands, living with the tribe, and practicing their native potter's art. While residing among the Cherokee, the Catawba acquired a reputation as doctors and leaders of the dance.[4]

On August 6, 1846, a treaty was concluded at Washington with the representatives of the Cherokee Nation west by which the rights of the East Cherokee to a participation in the benefits of the New Echota treaty of 1835 were distinctly recognized, and provision was made for a final adjustment of all unpaid and pending claims due under that treaty. The right claimed by the East Cherokee to participate in the

---

[1] The facts concerning Junaluska are from the author's information obtained from Colonel Thomas, Captain James Terrell, and Cherokee informants.

[2] Author's information from Colonel Thomas.

[3] Commissioner Crawford, November 25, Report of Indian Commissioner, p. 333, 1839.

[4] Author's information from Colonel Thomas, Captain Terrell, and Indian sources; Commissioner W. Medill, Report of Indian Commissioner, p. 399, 1848; Commissioner Orlando Brown, Report of Indian Commissioner for 1849, p. 14, 1850.

benefits of the New Echota treaty, although not denied by the government, had been held to be conditional upon their removal to the West.[1]

In the spring of 1848 the author, Lanman, visited the East Cherokee and has left an interesting account of their condition at the time, together with a description of their ballplays, dances, and customs generally, having been the guest of Colonel Thomas, of whom he speaks as the guide, counselor, and friend of the Indians, as well as their business agent and chief, so that the connection was like that existing between a father and his children. He puts the number of Indians at about 800 Cherokee and 100 Catawba on the " Qualla town " reservation—the name being in use thus early—with 200 more Indians residing in the more westerly portion of the state. Of their general condition he says:

About three-fourths of the entire population can read in their own language, and, though the majority of them understand English, a very few can speak the language. They practice, to a considerable extent, the science of agriculture, and have acquired such a knowledge of the mechanic arts as answers them for all ordinary purposes, for they manufacture their own clothing, their own ploughs, and other farming utensils, their own axes, and even their own guns. Their women are no longer treated as slaves, but as equals; the men labor in the fields and their wives are devoted entirely to household employments. They keep the same domestic animals that are kept by their white neighbors, and cultivate all the common grains of the country. They are probably as temperate as any other class of people on the face of the earth, honest in their business intercourse, moral in their thoughts, words, and deeds, and distinguished for their faithfulness in performing the duties of religion. They are chiefly Methodists and Baptists, and have regularly ordained ministers, who preach to them on every Sabbath, and they have also abandoned many of their mere senseless superstitions. They have their own court and try their criminals by a regular jury. Their judges and lawyers are chosen from among themselves. They keep in order the public roads leading through their settlement. By a law of the state they have a right to vote, but seldom exercise that right, as they do not like the idea of being identified with any of the political parties. Excepting on festive days, they dress after the manner of the white man, but far more picturesquely. They live in small log houses of their own construction, and have everything they need or desire in the way of food. They are, in fact, the happiest community that I have yet met with in this southern country.[2]

Among the other notables Lanman speaks thus of Salâ′lĭ, "Squirrel," a born mechanic of the band, who died only a few years since:

He is quite a young man and has a remarkably thoughtful face. He is the blacksmith of his nation, and with some assistance supplies the whole of Qualla town with all their axes and plows; but what is more, he has manufactured a number of very superior rifles and pistols, including stock, barrel, and lock, and he is also the builder of grist mills, which grind all the corn which his people eat. A specimen of his workmanship in the way of a rifle may be seen at the Patent Office in Washington, where it was deposited by Mr. Thomas; and I believe Salola is the first Indian who

[1] Synopsis of the treaty, etc., in Royce, Cherokee Nation, Fifth Ann. Rep. Bureau of Ethnology, pp. 300–313, 1888; see also ante, p. 148.
[2] Lanman, Letters from the Alleghany Mountains, pp. 94–95, 1849.

ever manufactured an entire gun.   But when it is remembered that he never received a particle of education in any of the mechanic arts but is entirely self-taught, his attainments must be considered truly remarkable.[1]

On July 29, 1848, Congress approved an act for taking a census of all those Cherokee who had remained in North Carolina after the Removal, and who still resided east of the Mississippi, in order that their share of the "removal and subsistence fund" under the New Echota treaty might be set aside for them.   A sum equivalent to $53.33⅓ was at the same time appropriated for each one, or his representative, to be available for defraying the expenses of his removal to the Cherokee Nation west and subsistence there for one year whenever he should elect so to remove.   Any surplus over such expense was to be paid to him in cash after his arrival in the west.   The whole amount thus expended was to be reimbursed to the Government from the general fund to the credit of the Cherokee Nation under the terms of the treaty of New Echota.   In the meantime it was ordered that to each individual thus entitled should be paid the accrued interest on this per capita sum from the date of the ratification of the New Echota treaty (May 23, 1836), payment of interest at the same rate to continue annually thereafter.[2]   In accordance with this act a census of the Cherokee then residing in North Carolina, Tennessee, and Georgia, was completed in the fall of 1848 by J. C. Mullay, making the whole number 2,133.   On the basis of this enrollment several payments were made to them by special agents within the next ten years, one being a per-capita payment by Alfred Chapman in 1851–52 of unpaid claims arising under the treaty of New Echota and amounting in the aggregate to $197,534.50, the others being payments of the annual interest upon the "removal and subsistence fund" set apart to their credit in 1848.   In the accomplishment of these payments two other enrollments were made by D. W. Siler in 1851 and by Chapman in 1852, the last being simply a corrected revision of the Siler roll, and neither varying greatly from the Mullay roll.[3]

Upon the appointment of Chapman to make the per capita payment above mentioned, the Cherokee Nation west had filed a protest against the payment, upon the double ground that the East Cherokee had forfeited their right to participation, and furthermore that their census was believed to be enormously exaggerated.   As a matter of fact the number first reported by Mullay was only 1,517, to which so many

[1] Lanman, Letters from the Alleghany Mountains, p. 111.

[2] See act quoted in "The United States of America v. William H, Thomas et al."; also Royce, Cherokee Nation, Fifth Ann. Rep. Bureau of Ethnology, p. 313, 1888.   In the earlier notices the terms "North Carolina Cherokee" and "Eastern Cherokee" are used synonymously, as the original fugitives were all in North Carolina.

[3] See Royce, op. cit., pp. 313–314; Commissioner H. Price, Report of Indian Commissioner, p. li, 1884; Report of Indian Commissioner, p. 495, 1898; also references by Commissioner W. Medill, Report of Indian Commissioner, p. 399, 1848; and Report of Indian Commissioner for 1855, p. 255, 1856.

were subsequently added as to increase the number by more than 600.[1]
A census taken by their agent, Colonel Thomas, in 1841, gave the
number of East Cherokee (possibly only those in North Carolina
intended) as 1,220,[2] while a year later the whole number residing in
North Carolina, Tennessee, Alabama, and Georgia was officially estimated at from 1,000 to 1,200.[3] It is not the only time a per capita
payment has resulted in a sudden increase of the census population.

In 1852 (Capt.) James W. Terrell was engaged by Thomas, then in
the state senate, to take charge of his store at Qualla, and remained
associated with him and in close contact with the Indians from then until
after the close of the war, assisting, as special United States agent, in
the disbursement of the interest payments, and afterward as a Confederate officer in the organization of the Indian companies, holding a
commission as captain of Company A, Sixty-ninth North Carolina
Confederate infantry. Being of an investigating bent, Captain Terrell
was led to give attention to the customs and mythology of the Cherokee, and to accumulate a fund of information on the subject seldom
possessed by a white man. He still resides at Webster, a few miles
from the reservation, and is now seventy-one years of age.

In 1855 Congress directed the per capita payment to the East Cherokee of the removal fund established for them in 1848, provided that
North Carolina should first give assurance that they would be allowed
to remain permanently in that state. This assurance, however, was
not given until 1866, and the money was therefore not distributed,
but remained in the treasury until 1875, when it was made applicable
to the purchase of lands and the quieting of titles for the benefit of
the Indians.[4]

From 1855 until after the civil war we find no official notice of the
East Cherokee, and our information must be obtained from other
sources. It was, however, a most momentous period in their history.
At the outbreak of the war Thomas was serving his seventh consecutive term in the state senate. Being an ardent Confederate sym-
pathizer, he was elected a delegate to the convention which passed the
secession ordinance, and immediately after voting in favor of that
measure resigned from the senate in order to work for the southern
cause. As he was already well advanced in years it is doubtful if his
effort would have gone beyond the raising of funds and other supplies
but for the fact that at this juncture an effort was made by the Confederate General Kirby Smith to enlist the East Cherokee for active
service.

The agent sent for this purpose was Washington Morgan, known to
the Indians as Â'ganstâ'ta, son of that Colonel Gideon Morgan who

---

[1] Royce, Cherokee Nation, op. cit., p. 313 and note.
[2] Report of the Indian Commissioner, pp. 459–460, 1845.
[3] Commissioner Crawford, Report of Indian Commissioner, p. 3, 1842.
[4] Royce, op. cit., p. 314.

had commanded the Cherokee at the Horseshoe bend. By virtue of his Indian blood and historic ancestry he was deemed the most fitting emissary for the purpose. Early in 1862 he arrived among the Cherokee, and by appealing to old-time memories so aroused the war spirit among them that a large number declared themselves ready to follow wherever he led. Conceiving the question at issue in the war to be one that did not concern the Indians, Thomas had discouraged their participation in it and advised them to remain at home in quiet neutrality. Now, however, knowing Morgan's reputation for reckless daring, he became alarmed at the possible result to them of such leadership. Forced either to see them go from his own protection or to lead them himself, he chose the latter alternative and proposed to them to enlist in the Confederate legion which he was about to organize. His object, as he himself has stated, was to keep them out of danger so far as possible by utilizing them as scouts and home guards through the mountains, away from the path of the large armies. Nothing of this was said to the Indians, who might not have been satisfied with such an arrangement. Morgan went back alone and the Cherokee enrolled under the command of their white chief. [1]

The "Thomas Legion," recruited in 1862 by William H. Thomas for the Confederate service and commanded by him as colonel, consisted originally of one infantry regiment of ten companies (Sixty-ninth North Carolina Infantry), one infantry battalion of six companies, one cavalry battalion of eight companies (First North Carolina Cavalry Battalion), one field battery (Light Battery) of 103 officers and men, and one company of engineers; in all about 2,800 men. The infantry battalion was recruited toward the close of the war to a full regiment of ten companies. Companies A and B of the Sixty-ninth regiment and two other companies of the infantry regiment recruited later were composed almost entirely of East Cherokee Indians, most of the commissioned officers being white men. The whole number of Cherokee thus enlisted was nearly four hundred, or about every able-bodied man in the tribe. [2]

In accordance with Thomas's plan the Indians were employed chiefly as scouts and home guards in the mountain region along the Tennessee-Carolina border, where, according to the testimony of Colonel String-

[1] The history of the events leading to the organization of the "Thomas Legion" is chiefly from the author's conversations with Colonel Thomas himself, corroborated and supplemented from other sources. In the words of Thomas, "If it had not been for the Indians I would not have been in the war."

[2] This is believed to be a correct statement of the strength and make-up of the Thomas Legion. Owing to the imperfection of the records and the absence of reliable memoranda among the surviving officers, no two accounts exactly coincide. The roll given in the North Carolina Confederate Roster, handed in by Captain Terrell, assistant quartermaster, was compiled early in the war and contains no notice of the engineer company or of the second infantry regiment, which included two other Indian companies. The information therein contained is supplemented from conversations and personal letters of Captain Terrell, and from letters and newspaper articles by Lieutenant-Colonel Stringfield of the Sixty-ninth. Another statement is given in Mrs Avery's sketch of Colonel Thomas in the North Carolina University Magazine for May, 1899.

field, "they did good work and service for the South." The most important engagement in which they were concerned occurred at Baptist gap, Tennessee, September 15, 1862, where Lieutenant Astu'-gatâ'ga, "a splendid specimen of Indian manhood," was killed in a charge. The Indians were furious at his death, and before they could be restrained they scalped one or two of the Federal dead. For this action ample apologies were afterward given by their superior officers. The war, in fact, brought out all the latent Indian in their nature. Before starting to the front every man consulted an oracle stone to learn whether or not he might hope to return in safety. The start was celebrated with a grand old-time war dance at the townhouse on Soco, and the same dance was repeated at frequent intervals thereafter, the Indians being "painted and feathered in good old style," Thomas himself frequently assisting as master of ceremonies. The ballplay, too, was not forgotten, and on one occasion a detachment of Cherokee, left to guard a bridge, became so engrossed in the excitement of the game as to narrowly escape capture by a sudden dash of the Federals. Owing to Thomas's care for their welfare, they suffered but slightly in actual battle, although a number died of hardship and disease. When the Confederates evacuated eastern Tennessee, in the winter of 1863–64, some of the white troops of the legion, with one or two of the Cherokee companies, were shifted to western Virginia, and by assignment to other regiments a few of the Cherokee were present at the final siege and surrender of Richmond. The main body of the Indians, with the rest of the Thomas Legion, crossed over into North Carolina and did service protecting the western border until the close of the war, when they surrendered on parole at Waynesville, North Carolina, in May, 1865, all those of the command being allowed to keep their guns. It is claimed by their officers that they were the last of the Confederate forces to surrender. About fifty of the Cherokee veterans still survive, nearly half of whom, under conduct of Colonel Stringfield, attended the Confederate reunion at Louisville, Kentucky, in 1900, where they attracted much attention.[1]

In 1863, by resolution of February 12, the Confederate House of Representatives called for information as to the number and condition of the East Cherokee, and their pending relations with the Federal government at the beginning of the war, with a view to continuing these relations under Confederate auspices. In response to this inquiry a report was submitted by the Confederate commissioner of Indian affairs, S. S. Scott, based on information furnished by Colonel Thomas and Captain James W. Terrell, their former disbursing agent, showing that interest upon the " removal and subsistence fund " estab-

[1] Personal Information from Colonel W. H. Thomas, Lieutenant-Colonel W. W. Stringfield, Captain James W. Terrell, Chief N. J. Smith (first sergeant Company B), and others, with other details from Moore's (Confederate) Roster of North Carolina Troops, IV; Raleigh, 1882; also list of survivors in 1890, by Carrington, in Eastern Band of Cherokees, Extra Bulletin of Eleventh Census, p. 21, 1892.

lished in 1848 had been paid annually up to and including the year 1859, at the rate of $3.20 per capita, or an aggregate, exclusive of disbursing agent's commission, of $4,838.40 annually, based upon the original Mullay enumeration of 1,517.

Upon receipt of this report it was enacted by the Confederate congress that the sum of $19,352.36 be paid the East Cherokee to cover the interest period of four years from May 23, 1860, to May 23, 1864. In this connection the Confederate commissioner suggested that the payment be made in provisions, of which the Indians were then greatly in need, and which, if the payment were made in cash, they would be unable to purchase, on account of the general scarcity. He adds that, according to his information, almost every Cherokee capable of bearing arms was then in the Confederate service. The roll furnished by Captain Terrell is the original Mullay roll corrected to May, 1860, no reference being made to the later Mullay enumeration (2,133), already alluded to. There is no record to show that the payment thus authorized was made, and as the Confederate government was then in hard straits it is probable that nothing further was done in the matter.

In submitting his statement of previous payments, Colonel Thomas, their former agent, adds:

As the North Carolina Cherokees have, like their brethren west, taken up arms against the Lincoln government, it is not probable that any further advances of interest will be made by that government to any portion of the Cherokee tribe. I also enclose a copy of the act of July 29, 1848, so far as relates to the North Carolina Cherokees, and a printed explanation of their rights, prepared by me in 1851, and submitted to the attorney-general, and his opinion thereon, which may not be altogether uninteresting to those who feel an interest in knowing something of the history of the Cherokee tribe of Indians, whose destiny is so closely identified with that of the Southern Confederacy.[1]

In a skirmish near Bryson City (then Charleston), Swain county, North Carolina, about a year after enlistment, a small party of Cherokee—perhaps a dozen in number—was captured by a detachment of Union troops and carried to Knoxville, where, having become dissatisfied with their experience in the Confederate service, they were easily persuaded to go over to the Union side. Through the influence of their principal man, Digăne'skĭ, several others were induced to desert to the Union army, making about thirty in all. As a part of the Third North Carolina Mounted Volunteer Infantry, they served with the Union forces in the same region until the close of the war, when they returned to their homes to find their tribesmen so bitterly incensed against them that for some time their lives were in danger. Eight of these are still alive in 1900.[2]

One of these Union Cherokee had brought back with him the small-

[1] Thomas-Terrell manuscript East Cherokee roll, with accompanying letters, 1864 (Bur. Am. Eth. archives).

[2] Personal information from Colonel W. H. Thomas, Captain J. W. Terrell, Chief N. J. Smith, and others; see also Carrington, Eastern Band of Cherokees, Extra Bulletin of Eleventh Census, p. 21, 1892.

pox from an infected camp near Knoxville. Shortly after his return he became sick and soon died. As the characteristic pustules had not appeared, the disease seeming to work inwardly, the nature of his sickness was not at first suspected—smallpox having been an unknown disease among the Cherokee for nearly a century—and his funeral was largely attended. A week later a number of those who had been present became sick, and the disease was recognized by Colonel Thomas as smallpox in all its virulence. It spread throughout the tribe, this being in the early spring of 1866, and in spite of all the efforts of Thomas, who brought a doctor from Tennessee to wait upon them, more than one hundred of the small community died in consequence. The fatal result was largely due to the ignorance of the Indians, who, finding their own remedies of no avail, used the heroic aboriginal treatment of the plunge bath in the river and the cold-water douche, which resulted in death in almost every case. Thus did the war bring its harvest of death, misery, and civil feud to the East Cherokee.[1]

Shortly after this event Colonel Thomas was compelled by physical and mental infirmity to retire from further active participation in the affairs of the East Cherokee, after more than half a century spent in intimate connection with them, during the greater portion of which time he had been their most trusted friend and adviser. Their affairs at once became the prey of confusion and factional strife, which continued until the United States stepped in as arbiter.

In 1868 Congress ordered another census of the East Cherokee, to serve as a guide in future payments, the roll to include only those persons whose names had appeared upon the Mullay roll of 1848 and their legal heirs and representatives. The work was completed in the following year by S. H. Sweatland, and a payment of interest then due under former enactment was made by him on this basis.[2] "In accordance with their earnestly expressed desire to be brought under the immediate charge of the government as its wards," the Congress which ordered this last census directed that the Commissioner of Indian Affairs should assume the same charge over the East Cherokee as over other tribes, but as no extra funds were made available for the purpose the matter was held in abeyance.[3] An unratified treaty made this year with the Cherokee Nation west contained a stipulation that any Cherokee east of the Mississippi who should remove to the Cherokee nation within three years should be entitled to full citizenship and privileges therein, but after that date could be admitted only by act of the Cherokee national council.[4]

After the retirement of Thomas, in the absence of any active

---

[1] Author's information from Colonel Thomas and others. Various informants have magnified the number of deaths to several hundred, but the estimate here given, obtained from Thomas, is probably more reliable.

[2] Royce, Cherokee Nation, Fifth Ann. Rep. Bureau of Ethnology, p. 314, 1888.

[3] Commissioner F. A. Walker, Report of Indian Commissioner, p. 25, 1872.

[4] Royce, op. cit., p. 353.

governmental supervision, need was felt of some central authority. On December 9, 1868, a general council of the East Cherokee assembled at Cheowa, in Graham county, North Carolina, took preliminary steps toward the adoption of a regular form of tribal government under a constitution. N. J. Smith, afterward principal chief, was clerk of the council. The new government was formally inaugurated on December 1, 1870. It provided for a first and a second chief to serve for a term of two years, minor officers to serve one year, and an annual council representing each Cherokee settlement within the state of North Carolina. Kâ'lahû', "All-bones," commonly known to the whites as Flying-squirrel or Sawnook (Sawănu'gĭ), was elected chief. A new constitution was adopted five years later, by which the chief's term of office was fixed at four years.[1]

The status of the lands held by the Indians had now become a matter of serious concern, As has been stated, the deeds had been made out by Thomas in his own name, as the state laws at that time forbade Indian ownership of real estate. In consequence of his losses during the war and his subsequent disability, the Thomas properties, of which the Cherokee lands were technically a part, had become involved, so that the entire estate had passed into the hands of creditors, the most important of whom, William Johnston, had obtained sheriff's deeds in 1869 for all of these Indian lands under three several judgments against Thomas, aggregating $33,887.11. To adjust the matter so as to secure title and possession to the Indians, Congress in 1870 authorized suit to be brought in their name for the recovery of their interest. This suit was begun in May, 1873, in the United States circuit court for western North Carolina. A year later the matters in dispute were submitted by agreement to a board of arbitrators, whose award was confirmed by the court in November, 1874.

The award finds that Thomas had purchased with Indian funds a tract estimated to contain 50,000 acres on Oconaluftee river and Soco creek, and known as the Qualla boundary, together with a number of individual tracts outside the boundary; that the Indians were still indebted to Thomas toward the purchase of the Qualla boundary lands for the sum of $18,250, from which should be deducted $6,500 paid by them to Johnston to release titles, with interest to date of award, making an aggregate of $8,486, together with a further sum of $2,478, which had been intrusted to Terrell, the business clerk and assistant of Thomas, and by him turned over to Thomas, as creditor of the Indians, under power of attorney, this latter sum, with interest to date of award, aggregating $2,697.89; thus leaving a balance due from the Indians to Thomas or his legal creditor, Johnston, of $7,066.11. The award declares that on account of the questionable manner in

---

[1] Constitution, etc., quoted in Carrington, Eastern Band of Cherokees, Extra Bulletin Eleventh Census, pp. 18–20, 1892; author's personal information.

which the disputed lands had been bought in by Johnston, he should be allowed to hold them only as security for the balance due him until paid, and that on the payment of the said balance of $7,066.11, with interest at 6 per cent from the date of the award, the Indians should be entitled to a clear conveyance from him of the legal title to all the lands embraced within the Qualla boundary.[1]

To enable the Indians to clear off this lien on their lands and for other purposes, Congress in 1875 directed that as much as remained of the " removal and subsistence fund" set apart for their benefit in 1848 should be used "in perfecting the titles to the lands awarded to them, and to pay the costs, expenses, and liabilities attending their recent litigations, also to purchase and extinguish the titles of any white persons to lands within the general boundaries allotted to them by the court, and for the education, improvement, and civilization of their people." In accordance with this authority the unpaid balance and interest due Johnston, amounting to $7,242.76, was paid him in the same year, and shortly afterward there was purchased on behalf of the Indians some fifteen thousand acres additional, the Commissioner of Indian Affairs being constituted trustee for the Indians. For the better protection of the Indians the lands were made inalienable except by assent of the council and upon approval of the President of the United States. The deeds for the Qualla boundary and the 15,000 acre purchase were executed respectively on October 9, 1876, and August 14, 1880.[2] As the boundaries of the different purchases were but vaguely defined, a new survey of the whole Qualla boundary and adjoining tracts was authorized. The work was intrusted to M. S. Temple, deputy United States surveyor, who completed it in 1876, his survey maps of the reservation being accepted as the official standard.[3]

The titles and boundaries having been adjusted, the Indian Office assumed regular supervision of East Cherokee affairs, and in June, 1875, the first agent since the retirement of Thomas was sent out in the person of W. C. McCarthy. He found the Indians, according to his report, destitute and discouraged, almost without stock or farming tools. There were no schools, and very few full-bloods could speak English, although to their credit nearly all could read and write their own language, the parents teaching the children. Under his authority a distribution was made of stock animals, seed wheat, and farming tools, and several schools were started. In the next year, however,

---

[1] See award of arbitrators, Rufus Barringer, John H. Dillard, and T. Ruffin, with full statement, in Eastern Band of Cherokee Indians against W. T. Thomas *et al.* H. R. Ex. Doc. 128, 53d Cong., 2d sess., 1894; summary in Royce, Cherokee Nation, Fifth Ann. Rep. Bureau of Ethnology, pp. 315–318, 1888.

[2] See Royce, op. cit., pp. 315–318; Commissioner T. J. Morgan, Report of Indian Commissioner, p. xxix, 1890. The final settlement, under the laws of North Carolina, was not completed until 1894.

[3] Royce, op. cit., pp. 315–318; Carrington, Eastern Band of Cherokees, with map of Temple survey, Extra Bulletin of Eleventh Census, 1892.

the agency was discontinued and the educational interests of the band turned over to the state school superintendent.[1]

In the meantime Kâ'lahû' had been succeeded as chief by Lloyd R. Welch (Da'si'giya'gĭ), an educated mixed-blood of Cheowa, who served about five years, dying shortly after his reelection to a second term (48). He made a good record by his work in reconciling the various factions which had sprung up after the withdrawal of the guiding influence of Thomas, and in defeating the intrigues of fraudulent white claimants and mischief makers. Shortly before his death the Government, through Special Agent John A. Sibbald, recognized his authority as principal chief, together with the constitution which had been adopted by the band under his auspices in 1875. N. J. Smith (Tsa'-lădihĭ'), who had previously served as clerk of the council, was elected to his unexpired term and continued to serve until the fall of 1890.[2]

We find no further official notice of the East Cherokee until 1881, when Commissioner Price reported that they were still without agent or superintendent, and that so far as the Indian Office was concerned their affairs were in an anomalous and unsatisfactory condition, while factional feuds were adding to the difficulties and retarding the progress of the band. In the spring of that year a visiting delegation from the Cherokee Nation west had extended to them an urgent invitation to remove to Indian Territory and the Indian Office had encouraged the project, with the result that 161 persons of the band removed during the year to Indian Territory, the expense being borne by the Government. Others were represented as being desirous to remove, and the Commissioner recommended an appropriation for the purpose, but as Congress failed to act the matter was dropped.[3]

The neglected condition of the East Cherokee having been brought to the attention of those old-time friends of the Indian, the Quakers, through an appeal made in their behalf by members of that society residing in North Carolina, the Western Yearly Meeting, of Indiana, volunteered to undertake the work of civilization and education. On May 31, 1881, representatives of the Friends entered into a contract with the Indians, subject to approval by the Government, to establish and continue among them for ten years an industrial school and other common schools, to be supported in part from the annual interest of the trust fund held by the Government to the credit of the East Cherokee and in part by funds furnished by the Friends themselves. Through the efforts of Barnabas C. Hobbs, of the Western Yearly Meeting, a yearly contract to the same effect was entered into with the Commis-

[1] Report of Agent W. C. McCarthy, Report of Indian Commissioner, pp. 343–344, 1875; and Report of Indian Commissione, pp. 118–119, 1876.

[2] Author's personal information; see also Carrington, Eastern Band of Cherokees; Zeigler and Grosscup, Heart of the Alleghanies, pp. 35–36, 1883.

[3] Commissioner H. Price, Report of Indian Commissioner, pp. lxiv–lxv, 1881, and Report of Indian Commissioner, pp. lxix–lxx, 1882; see also ante, p. 151.

sioner of Indian Affairs later in the same year, and was renewed by successive commissioners to cover the period of ten years ending June 30, 1892, when the contract system was terminated and the Government assumed direct control.   Under the joint arrangement, with some aid at the outset from the North Carolina Meeting, work was begun in 1881 by Thomas Brown with several teachers sent out by the Indiana Friends, who established a small training school at the agency head-quarters at Cherokee, and several day schools in the outlying settle-ments.   He was succeeded three years later by H. W. Spray, an expe-rienced educator, who, with a corps of efficient assistants and greatly enlarged facilities, continued to do good work for the elevation of the Indians until the close of the contract system eight years later.[1]   After an interregnum, during which the schools suffered from frequent changes, he was reappointed as government agent and superintendent in 1898, a position which he still holds in 1901.   To the work con-ducted under his auspices the East Cherokee owe much of what they have to-day of civilization and enlightenment.

From some travelers who visited the reservation about this time we have a pleasant account of a trip along Soco and a day with Chief Smith at Yellow Hill.   They describe the Indians as being so nearly like the whites in their manner of living that a stranger could rarely distinguish an Indian's cabin or little cove farm from that of a white man.   Their principal crop was corn, which they ground for them-selves, and they had also an abundance of apples, peaches, and plums, and a few small herds of ponies and cattle.   Their wants were so few that they had but little use for money.   Their primitive costume had long been obsolete, and their dress was like that of the whites, except-ing that moccasins took the place of shoes, and they manufactured their own clothing by the aid of spinning-wheels and looms.   Finely cut pipes and well-made baskets were also produced, and the good influence of the schools recently established was already manifest in the children.[2]

In 1882 the agency was reestablished and provision was made for taking a new census of all Cherokee east of the Mississippi, Joseph G. Hester being appointed to the work.[3]   The census was submitted as complete in June, 1884, and contained the names of 1,881 persons in North Carolina, 758 in Georgia, 213 in Tennessee, 71 in Alabama, and 33 scattering, a total of 2,956.[4]   Although this census received the approval and certificate of the East Cherokee council, a large portion of the band still refuse to recognize it as authoritative, claiming that a large number of persons therein enrolled have no Cherokee blood.

[1] See Commissioner T. J. Morgan, Report of Indian Commissioner, pp. 141–145, 1892; author's per-sonal information from B. C. Hobbs, Chief N. J. Smith, and others.   For further notice of school growth see also Report of Indian Commissioner, pp. 426–427, 1897.

[2] Zeigler and Grosscup, Heart of the Alleghanies, pp. 36–42, 1883.

[3] Commissioner H. Price, Report of Indian Commissioner, pp. lxix–lxx, 1882.

[4] Report of Indian Commissioner, pp. li–lii, 1884.

The East Cherokee had never ceased to contend for a participation in the rights and privileges accruing to the western Nation under treaties with the Government. In 1882 a special agent had been appointed to investigate their claims, and in the following year, under authority of Congress, the eastern band of Cherokee brought suit in the Court of Claims against the United States and the Cherokee Nation west to determine its rights in the permanent annuity fund and other trust funds held by the United States for the Cherokee Indians.[1] The case was decided adversely to the eastern band, first by the Court of Claims in 1885,[2] and finally, on appeal, by the Supreme Court on March 1, 1886, that court holding in its decision that the Cherokee in North Carolina had dissolved their connection with the Cherokee Nation and ceased to be a part of it when they refused to accompany the main body at the Removal, and that if Indians in North Carolina or in any state east of the Mississippi wished to enjoy the benefits of the common property of the Cherokee Nation in any form whatever they must be readmitted to citizenship in the Cherokee Nation and comply with its constitution and laws. In accordance with this decision the agent in the Indian territory was instructed to issue no more residence permits to claimants for Cherokee citizenship, and it was officially announced that all persons thereafter entering that country without consent of the Cherokee authorities would be treated as intruders.[3] This decision, cutting off the East Cherokee from all hope of sharing in any of the treaty benefits enjoyed by their western kinsmen, was a sore disappointment to them all, especially to Chief Smith, who had worked unceasingly in their behalf from the institution of the proceedings. In view of the result, Commissioner Atkins strongly recommended, as the best method of settling them in permanent homes, secure from white intrusion and from anxiety on account of their uncertain tenure and legal status in North Carolina, that negotiations be opened through government channels for their readmission to citizenship in the Cherokee Nation, to be followed, if successful, by the sale of their lands in North Carolina and their removal to Indian Territory.[4]

In order to acquire a more definite legal status, the Cherokee residing in North Carolina—being practically all those of the eastern band having genuine Indian interests—became a corporate body under the laws of the state in 1889. The act, ratified on March 11, declares in its first section "That the North Carolina or Eastern Cherokee Indians, resident or domiciled in the counties of Jackson, Swain, Graham, and Cherokee, be and at the same time are hereby

---

[1] Commissioner H. Price, Report of Indian Commissioner, pp. lxix-lxxi, 1882, also "Indian legislation," ibid., p. 214; Commissioner H. Price, Report of Indian Commissioner, pp. lxv-lxvi, 1883.

[2] Commissioner J. D. C. Atkins, Report of Indian Commissioner, p. lxx, 1885.

[3] Same commissioner, Report of the Indian Commissioner, p. xlv, 1886; decision quoted by same commissioner, Report of Indian Commissioner, p. lxxvii, 1887.

[4] Same commissioner, Report of the Indian Commissioner, p. li, 1886; reiterated by him in Report for 1887, p. lxxvii.

created and constituted a body politic and corporate under the name, style, and title of the Eastern Band of Cherokee Indians, with all the rights, franchises, privileges and powers incident and belonging to corporations under the laws of the state of North Carolina.[1]

On August 2, 1893, ex-Chief Smith died at Cherokee, in the fifty-seventh year of his life, more than twenty of which had been given to the service of his people. Nimrod Jarrett Smith, known to the Cherokee as Tsa'lădihï', was the son of a halfbreed father by an Indian mother, and was born near the present Murphy, Cherokee county, North Carolina, on January 3, 1837. His earliest recollections were thus of the miseries that attended the flight of the refugees to the mountains during the Removal period. His mother spoke very little English, but his father was a man of considerable intelligence, having acted as interpreter and translator for Reverend Evan Jones at the old Valleytown mission. As the boy grew to manhood he acquired a fair education, which, aided by a commanding presence, made him a person of influence among his fellows. At twenty-five years of age he enlisted in the Thomas Legion as first sergeant of Company B, Sixty-ninth North Carolina (Confederate) Infantry, and served in that capacity till the close of the war. He was clerk of the council that drafted the first East Cherokee constitution in 1868, and on the death of Principal Chief Lloyd Welch in 1880 was elected to fill the unexpired term, continuing in office by successive reelections until the close of 1891, a period of about twelve years, the longest term yet filled by an incumbent. As principal chief he signed the contract under which the school work was inaugurated in 1881. For several years thereafter his duties, particularly in connection with the suit against the western Cherokee, required his presence much of the time at Washington, while at home his time was almost as constantly occupied in attending to the wants of a dependent people. Although he was entitled under the constitution of the band to a salary of five hundred dollars per year, no part of this salary was ever paid, because of the limited resources of his people, and only partial reimbursement was made to him, shortly before his death, for expenses incurred in official visits to Washington. With frequent opportunities to enrich himself at the expense of his people, he maintained his honor and died a poor man.

In person Chief Smith was a splendid specimen of physical manhood, being six feet four inches in height and built in proportion, erect in figure, with flowing black hair curling down over his shoulders, a deep musical voice, and a kindly spirit and natural dignity that never failed to impress the stranger. His widow—a white woman—and several children survive him.[2]

---

[1] See act in full, Report of Indian Commissioner, vol. I, pp. 680–681, 1891.

[2] From author's personal acquaintance; see also Zeigler and Grosscup, Heart of the Alleghanies, pp. 38–39, 1883; Agent J. L. Holmes, in Report of Indian Commissioner, p. 160, 1885; Commissioner T. J. Morgan, Report of Indian Commissioner, p. 142, 1892; Moore, Roster of the North Carolina Troops, IV, 1882.

PHOTOGRAPH, 1886

CHIEF N. J. SMITH (TSALĂDIHĬ')

In 1894 the long-standing litigation between the East Cherokee and a number of creditors and claimants to Indian lands within and adjoining the Qualla boundary was finally settled by a compromise by which the several white tenants and claimants within the boundary agreed to execute a quitclaim and vacate on payment to them by the Indians of sums aggregating $24,552, while for another disputed adjoining tract of 33,000 acres the United States agreed to pay, for the Indians, at the rate of $1.25 per acre. The necessary Government approval having been obtained, Congress appropriated a sufficient amount for carrying into effect the agreement, thus at last completing a perfect and unincumbered title to all the lands claimed by the Indians, with the exception of a few outlying tracts of comparative unimportance.[1]

In 1895 the Cherokee residing in North Carolina upon the reservation and in the outlying settlements were officially reported to number 1,479.[2] A year later an epidemic of grippe spread through the band, with the result that the census of 1897 shows but 1,312,[3] among those who died at this time being Big-witch (Tskĭl-e′gwa), the oldest man of the band, who distinctly remembered the Creek war, and Wadi′yăhĭ, the last old woman who preserved the art of making double-walled baskets. In the next year the population had recovered to 1,351. The description of the mode of living then common to most of the Indians will apply nearly as well to-day:

While they are industrious, these people are not progressive farmers and have learned nothing of modern methods. The same crops are raised continuously until the soil will yield no more or is washed away, when new ground is cleared or broken. The value of rotation and fertilizing has not yet been discovered or taught. . . .

That these people can live at all upon the products of their small farms is due to the extreme simplicity of their food, dress, and manner of living. The typical house is of logs, is about fourteen by sixteen feet, of one room, just high enough for the occupants to stand erect, with perhaps a small loft for the storage of extras. The roof is of split shingles or shakes. There is no window, the open door furnishing what light is required. At one end of the house is the fireplace, with outside chimney of stones or sticks chinked with clay. The furniture is simple and cheap. An iron pot, a bake kettle, a coffeepot and mill, small table, and a few cups, knives, and spoons are all that is needed. These, with one or two bedsteads, homemade, a few pillows and quilts, with feather mattresses for winter covering, as well as for the usual purpose, constitute the principal house possessions. For outdoor work there is an ax, hoe, and shovel plow. A wagon or cart may be owned, but is not essential. The outfit is inexpensive and answers every purpose. The usual food is bean bread, with coffee. In the fall chestnut bread is also used. Beef is seldom eaten, but pork is highly esteemed, and a considerable number of hogs are kept, running wild and untended in summer.[4]

By the most recent official count, in 1900, the East Cherokee residing in North Carolina under direct charge of the agent and included

---

[1] Commissioner D. M. Browning, Report of Indian Commissioner for 1894, pp. 81–82, 1895; also Agent T. W. Potter, ibid., p. 398.

[2] Agent T. W. Potter, Report of Indian Commissioner for 1895, p. 387, 1896.

[3] Agent J. C. Hart, Report of Indian Commissioner, p. 208, 1897.

[4] Agent J. C. Hart, Report of Indian Commissioner, pp. 218–219, 1898.

within the act of incorporation number 1,376, of whom about 1,100 are on the reservation, the rest living farther to the west, on Nantahala, Cheowa, and Hiwassee rivers. This does not include mixed-bloods in adjoining states and some hundreds of unrecognized claimants. Those enumerated own approximately 100,000 acres of land, of which 83,000 are included within the Qualla reservation and a contiguous tract in Jackson and Swain counties. They receive no rations or annuities and are entirely self-supporting, the annual interest on their trust fund established in 1848, which has dwindled to about $23,000, being applied to the payment of taxes upon their unoccupied common lands. From time to time they have made leases of timber, gold-washing, and grazing privileges, but without any great profit to themselves. By special appropriation the government supports an industrial training school at Cherokee, the agency headquarters, in which 170 pupils are now being boarded, clothed, and educated in the practical duties of life. This school, which in its workings is a model of its kind, owes much of its usefulness and high standing to the efficient management of Prof. H. W. Spray (Wĭlsĭnĭ'), already mentioned, who combines the duties of superintendent and agent for the band. His chief clerk, Mr James Blythe (Diskwa'̓nĭ, "Chestnut-bread"), a Cherokee by blood, at one time filled the position of agent, being perhaps the only Indian who has ever served in such capacity.

The exact legal status of the East Cherokee is still a matter of dispute, they being at once wards of the government, citizens of the United States, and (in North Carolina) a corporate body under state laws. They pay real estate taxes and road service, exercise the voting privilege,[1] and are amenable to the local courts, but do not pay poll tax or receive any pauper assistance from the counties; neither can they make free contracts or alienate their lands (49). Under their tribal constitution they are governed by a principal and an assistant chief, elected for a term of four years, with an executive council appointed by the chief, and sixteen councilors elected by the various settlements for a term of two years. The annual council is held in October at Cherokee, on the reservation, the proceedings being in the Cherokee language and recorded by their clerk in the Cherokee alphabet, as well as in English. The present chief is Jesse Reid (Tsĕ'si-Ska'tsĭ, "Scotch Jesse"), an intelligent mixed-blood, who fills the office with dignity and ability. As a people they are peaceable and law-abiding, kind and hospitable, providing for their simple wants by their own industry without asking or expecting outside assistance. Their fields, orchards, and fish traps, with some few domestic animals and occasional hunting, supply them with food, while by the sale of

---

[1] At the recent election in November, 1900, they were debarred by the local polling officers from either registering or voting, and the matter is now being contested.

ginseng and other medicinal plants gathered in the mountains, with fruit and honey of their own raising, they procure what additional supplies they need from the traders. The majority are fairly comfortable, far above the condition of most Indian tribes, and but little, if any, behind their white neighbors. In literary ability they may even be said to surpass them, as in addition to the result of nearly twenty years of school work among the younger people, nearly all the men and some of the women can read and write their own language. All wear civilized costumes, though an occasional pair of moccasins is seen, while the women find means to gratify the racial love of color in the wearing of red bandanna kerchiefs in place of bonnets. The older people still cling to their ancient rites and sacred traditions, but the dance and the ballplay wither and the Indian day is nearly spent.

III—NOTES TO THE HISTORICAL SKETCH

(1) TRIBAL SYNONYMY (page 15): Very few Indian tribes are known to us under the names by which they call themselves. One reason for this is the fact that the whites have usually heard of a tribe from its neighbors, speaking other languages, before coming upon the tribe itself. Many of the popular tribal names were originally nicknames bestowed by neighboring tribes, frequently referring to some peculiar custom, and in a large number of cases would be strongly repudiated by the people designated by them. As a rule each tribe had a different name in every surrounding Indian language, besides those given by Spanish, French, Dutch, or English settlers.

Yûñ'wiyă'—This word is compounded from *yûñwĭ* (person) and *yă* (real or principal). The assumption of superiority is much in evidence in Indian tribal names; thus, the Iroquois, Delawares, and Pawnee call themselves, respectively, Oñwehoñwe, Leni-lenape', and Tsariksi-tsa'riks, all of which may be rendered "men of men," "men surpassing other men," or "real men."

Kĭtu'hwagĭ—This word, which can not be analyzed, is derived from Kĭtu'hwă, the name of an ancient Cherokee settlement formerly on Tuckasegee river, just above the present Bryson City, in Swain county, North Carolina. It is noted in 1730 as one of the "seven mother towns" of the tribe. Its inhabitants were called Ani'-Kĭtu'hwagĭ (people of Kituhwa), and seem to have exercised a controlling influence over those of all the towns on the waters of Tuckasegee and the upper part of Little Tennessee, the whole body being frequently classed together as Ani'-Kĭtu'hwagĭ. The dialect of these towns held a middle place linguistically between those spoken to the east, on the heads of Savannah, and to the west, on Hiwassee, Cheowah, and the lower course of Little Tennessee. In various forms the word was adopted by the Delawares, Shawano, and other northern Algonquian tribes as a synonym for Cherokee, probably from the fact that the Kituhwa people guarded the Cherokee northern frontier. In the form Cuttawa it appears on the French map of Vaugondy in 1755. From a similarity of spelling, Schoolcraft incorrectly makes it a synonym for Catawba, while Brinton incorrectly asserts that it is an Algonquian term, fancifully rendered, "inhabitants of the great wilderness." Among the western Cherokee it is now the name of a powerful secret society, which had its origin shortly before the War of the Rebellion.

Cherokee—This name occurs in fully fifty different spellings. In the standard recognized form, which dates back at least to 1708, it has given name to counties in North Carolina, South Carolina, Georgia, and Alabama, within the ancient territory of the tribe, and to as many as twenty other geographic locations within the United States. In the Eastern or Lower dialect, with which the English settlers first became familiar, the form is Tsa'răgĭ', whence we get Cherokee. In the other dialects the form is Tsa'lăgĭ'. It is evidently foreign to the tribe, as is frequently the case in tribal names, and in all probability is of Choctaw origin, having come up from the south through the medium of the Mobilian trade jargon. It will be noted that De Soto, whose chroniclers first use the word, in the form Chalaque, obtained his interpreters from the Gulf coast of Florida. Fontanedo, writing about the year 1575, mentions other inland tribes known to the natives of Florida under names which seem to be

182

of Choctaw origin; for instance, the Canogacole, interpreted "wicked people," the final part being apparently the Choctaw word *okla* or *ogula*, "people", which appears also in Pascagoula, Bayou Goula, and Pensacola. Shetimasha, Atakapa, and probably Biloxi, are also Choctaw names, although the tribes themselves are of other origins. As the Choctaw held much of the Gulf coast and were the principal traders of that region, it was natural that explorers landing among them should adopt their names for the more remote tribes.

The name seems to refer to the fact that the tribe occupied a cave country. In the "Choctaw Leksikon" of Allen Wright, 1880, page 87, we find *choluk*, a noun, signifying a hole, cavity, pit, chasm, etc., and as an adjective signifying hollow. In the manuscript Choctaw dictionary of Cyrus Byington, in the library of the Bureau of American Ethnology, we find *chiluk*, noun, a hole, cavity, hollow, pit, etc., with a statement that in its usual application it means a cavity or hollow, and not a hole through anything. As an adjective, the same form is given as signifying hollow, having a hole, as *iti chiluk*, a hollow tree; *aboha chiluk*, an empty house; *chiluk chukoa*, to enter a hole. Other noun forms given are *chuluk* and *achiluk* in the singular and *chilukoa* in the plural, all signifying hole, pit, or cavity. Verbal forms are *chilukikbi*, to make a hole, and *chilukba*, to open and form a fissure.

In agreement with the genius of the Cherokee language the root form of the tribal name takes nominal or verbal prefixes according to its connection with the rest of the sentence, and is declined, or rather conjugated, as follows: SINGULAR—first person, *tsi-Tsa'lăgĭ*, I (am) a Cherokee; second person, *hi-Tsa'lăgĭ*, thou art a Cherokee; third person, *a-Tsa'lăgĭ*, he is a Cherokee. DUAL—first person, *ăsti-Tsa'lăgĭ*, we two are Cherokee; second person, *sti-Tsa'lăgĭ*, you two are Cherokee; third person, *ani'-Tsa'lăgĭ*, they two are Cherokee. PLURAL—first person, *atsi-Tsa'lăgĭ*, we (several) are Cherokee; second person, *hitsi-Tsa'lăgĭ*, you (several) are Cherokee; third person, *ani'-Tsa'lăgĭ*, they (several) are Cherokee. It will be noticed that the third person dual and plural are alike.

Oyata'ge'ronoñ', etc.—The Iroquois (Mohawk) form is given by Hewitt as O-yata'-ge'ronoñ', of which the root is *yata'*, cave, *o* is the assertive prefix, *ge* is the locative at, and *ronoñ'* is the tribal suffix, equivalent to (English) *-ites* or people. The word, which has several dialectic forms, signifies "inhabitants of the cave country," or "cave-country people," rather than "people who dwell in caves," as rendered by Schoolcraft. The same radix *yata'* occurs also in the Iroquois name for the opossum, which is a burrowing animal. As is well known, the Allegheny region is peculiarly a cave country, the caves having been used by the Indians for burial and shelter purposes, as is proved by numerous remains found in them. It is probable that the Iroquois simply translated the name (Chalaque) current in the South, as we find is the case in the West, where the principal plains tribes are known under translations of the same names in all the different languages. The Wyandot name for the Cherokee, Wataiyo-ronoñ', and their Catawba name, Mañterañ', both seem to refer to coming out of the ground, and may have been originally intended to convey the same idea of cave people.

Rickahockan—This name is used by the German explorer, Lederer, in 1670, as the name of the people inhabiting the mountains to the southwest of the Virginia settlements. On his map he puts them in the mountains on the southern head streams of Roanoke river, in western North Carolina. He states that, according to his Indian informants, the Rickahockan lived beyond the mountains in a land of great waves, which he interpreted to mean the sea shore (!), but it is more likely that the Indians were trying to convey, by means of the sign language, the idea of a succession of mountain ridges. The name was probably of Powhatan origin, and is evidently identical with Rechahecrian of the Virginia chronicles of about the same period, the *r* in the latter form being perhaps a misprint. It may be connected with Righka-hauk, indicated on Smith's map of Virginia, in 1607, as the name of a town within the

Powhatan territory, and still preserved in Rockahock, the name of an estate on lower Pamunkey river. We have too little material of the Powhatan language to hazard an interpretation, but it may possibly contain the root of the word for sand, which appears as *lekawa, nikawa, negaw, rigawa, rekwa*, etc, in various eastern Algonquian dialects, whence Rockaway (sand), and Recgawawank (sandy place). The Powhatan form, as given by Strachey, is *racawh* (sand). He gives also *rocoyhook* (otter), *reihcahahcoik*, hidden under a cloud, overcast, *rickahone* or *reihcoan* (a comb), and *rickewh* (to divide in halves).

Talligewi—As Brinton well says: "No name in the Lenape' legends has given rise to more extensive discussion than this." On Colden's map in his "History of the Five Nations," 1727, we find the "Alleghens" indicated upon Allegheny river. Heckewelder, who recorded the Delaware tradition in 1819, says: "Those people, as I was told, called themselves Talligeu or Talligewi. Colonel John Gibson, however, a gentleman who has a thorough knowledge of the Indians, and speaks several of their languages, is of the opinion that they were not called Talligewi, but Alligewi; and it would seem that he is right from the traces of their name which still remain in the country, the Allegheny river and mountains having indubitably been named after them. The Delawares still call the former Alligewi Sipu (the river of the Alligewi)"—Indian Nations, p. 48, ed. 1876. Loskiel, writing on the authority of Zeisberger, says that the Delawares knew the whole country drained by the Ohio under the name of Alligewinengk, meaning "the land in which they arrived from distant places," basing his interpretation upon an etymology compounded from *talli* or *alli*, there, *icku*, to that place, and *ewak*, they go, with a locative final. Ettwein, another Moravian writer, says the Delawares called "the western country" Alligewenork, meaning a warpath, and called the river Alligewi Sipo. This definition would make the word come from *palliton* or *alliton*, to fight, to make war, *ewak*, they go, and a locative, i. e., "they go there to fight." Trumbull, an authority on Algonquian languages, derives the river name from *wulik*, good, best, *hanne*, rapid stream, and *sipu*, river, of which rendering its Iroquois name, *Ohio*, is nearly an equivalent. Rafinesque renders Talligewi as "there found," from *talli*, there, and some other root, not given (Brinton, Walam Olum, pp. 229–230, 1885).

It must be noted that the names Ohio and Alligewi (or Allegheny) were not applied by the Indians, as with us, to different parts of the same river, but to the whole stream, or at least the greater portion of it from its head downward. Although Brinton sees no necessary connection between the river name and the traditional tribal name, the statement of Heckewelder, generally a competent authority on Delaware matters, makes them identical.

In the traditional tribal name, Talligewi or Alligewi, *wi* is an assertive verbal suffix, so that the form properly means "he is a Tallige," or "they are Tallige." This comes very near to Tsa'lăgĭ', the name by which the Cherokee call themselves, and it may have been an early corruption of that name. In Zeisberger's Delaware dictionary, however, we find *waloh* or *walok*, signifying a cave or hole, while in the "Walam Olum" we have *oligonunk* rendered "at the place of caves," the region being further described as a buffalo land on a pleasant plain, where the Lenape', advancing seaward from a less abundant northern region, at last found food (Walam Olum, pp. 194–195). Unfortunately, like other aboriginal productions of its kind among the northern tribes, the Lenape chronicle is suggestive rather than complete and connected. With more light it may be that seeming discrepancies would disappear and we should find at last that the Cherokee, in ancient times as in the historic period, were always the southern vanguard of the Iroquoian race, always primarily a mountain people, but with their flank resting upon the Ohio and its great tributaries, following the trend of the Blue ridge and the Cumberland as they slowly gave way before the pressure from the north until they were finally cut off from the parent stock by the wedge of Algonquian invasion, but always, whether in the north or in the south, keeping their distinctive title among the tribes as the "people of the cave country."

As the Cherokee have occupied a prominent place in history for so long a period their name appears in many synonyms and diverse spellings. The following are among the principal of these:

SYNONYMS

Tsa'lăgĭ' (plural, Ani'-Tsa'lăgĭ'). Proper form in the Middle and Western Cherokee dialects.

Tsa'răgĭ'. Proper form in the Eastern or Lower Cherokee dialect.

Achalaque. Schoolcraft, Notes on Iroquois, 1847 (incorrectly quoting Garcilaso).

Chalakee. Nuttall, Travels, 124, 1821.

Chalaque. Gentleman of Elvas, 1557; Publications of Hakluyt Society, IX, 60, 1851.

Chalaquies. Barcia, Ensayo, 335, 1723.

Charakeys. Homann heirs' map, about 1730.

Charikees. Document of 1718, *fide* Rivers, South Carolina, 55, 1856.

Charokees. Governor Johnson, 1720, *fide* Rivers, Early History South Carolina, 93, 1874.

Cheelake. Barton, New Views, xliv, 1798.

Cheerake. Adair, American Indians, 226, 1775.

Cheerakee. Ibid., 137.

Cheeraque's. Moore, 1704, in Carroll, Hist. Colls. South Carolina, II, 576, 1836.

Cheerokee. Ross (?), 1776, in Historical Magazine, 2d series, II, 218, 1867.

Chel-a-ke. Long, Expedition to Rocky Mountains, II, lxx, 1823.

Chelakees. Gallatin, Trans. Am. Antiq. Soc., II, 90, 1836.

Chelaques. Nuttall, Travels, 247, 1821.

Chelekee. Keane, in Stanford's Compendium, 506, 1878.

Chellokee. Schoolcraft, Indian Tribes, II, 204, 1852.

Cheloculgee. White, Statistics of Georgia, 28, 1849 (given as plural form of Creek name).

Chelokees. Gallatin, Trans. Am. Antiq. Soc., II, 104, 1836.

Cheokees. Johnson, 1772, in New York Doc. Col. Hist., VIII, 314, 1857 (misprint for *Cherokees*).

Cheraguees. Coxe, Carolina, II, 1741.

Cherakees. Ibid., map, 1741.

Cherakis. Chauvignerie, 1736, *fide* Schoolcraft, Indian Tribes, III, 555, 1853.

Cheraquees. Coxe, Carolana, 13, 1741.

Cheraquis. Penicaut, 1699, in Margry, V, 404, 1883.

Cherickees. Clarke, 1739, in New York Doc. Col. Hist., VI, 148, 1855.

Cherikee. Albany conference, 1742, ibid., 218.

Cherokee. Governor Johnson, 1708, in Rivers, South Carolina, 238, 1856.

Cherookees. Croghan, 1760, in Mass. Hist. Soc. Colls., 4th series, IX, 372, 1871.

Cheroquees. Campbell, 1761, ibid., 416.

Cherrackees. Evans, 1755, in Gregg, Old Cheraws, 15, 1867.

Cherrokees. Treaty of 1722, *fide* Drake, Book of Indians, bk. 4, 32, 1848.

Cherrykees. Weiser, 1748, *fide* Kauffman, Western Pennsylvania, appendix, 18, 1851.

Chirakues. Randolph, 1699, in Rivers, South Carolina, 449, 1856.

Chirokys. Writer about 1825, Annales de la Prop. de la Foi, II, 384, 1841.

Chorakis. Document of 1748, New York Doc. Col. Hist., X, 143, 1858.

Chreokees. Pike, Travels, 173, 1811 (misprint, transposed).

Shanaki. Gatschet, Caddo MS, Bureau Am. Ethn., 1882 (Caddo name).

Shan-nack. Marcy, Red River, 273, 1854 (Wichita name).

Shannaki. Gatschet, Fox MS, Bureau Am. Ethn., 1882 (Fox name: plural form, *Shannakiak*).

Shayage. Gatschet, Kaw MS, Bur. Am. Ethn., 1878 (Kaw name).

Sulluggoes. Coxe, Carolana, 22, 1741.

Tcalke. Gatschet, Tonkawa MS, Bur. Am. Ethn., 1882 (Tonkawa name, *Chal-ke*).

Tcerokiec. Gatschet, Wichita MS, Bur. Am. Ethn., 1882 (Wichita name, *Cherokish*).

Tchatakes. La Salle, 1682, in Margry, ii, 197, 1877 (misprint).

Tsalakies. Gallatin, Trans. Am. Antiq. Soc., ii, 90, 1836.

Tsallakee. Schoolcraft, Notes on Iroquois, 310, 1847.

Tsä-ló-kee. Morgan, Ancient Society, 113, 1878.

Tschirokesen. Wrangell, Ethn. Nachrichten, xiii, 1839 (German form).

Tsŭlahkĭ. Grayson, Creek MS, Bur. Am. Ethn., 1885 (Creek name; plural form, *Tsălgăl'gi* or *Tsŭlgŭl'gi*—Mooney).

Tzerrickey. Urlsperger, *fide* Gatschet, Creek Migration Legend, i, 26, 1884.

Tzulukis. Rafinesque, Am. Nations, i, 123, 1836.

Zolucans.
Zulocans. } Rafinesque, in Marshall, Kentucky, i, 23, 1824.

TALLIGEU.
TALLIGEWI. } Heckewelder, 1819, Indian Nations, 48, reprint of 1876 (traditional Delaware name; singular, *Tallige'* or *Allige'* (see preceding explanation).
ALLIGEWI.

Alleg. Schoolcraft, Indian Tribes, v, 133, 1855.

Allegans. Colden, map, 1727, *fide* Schoolcraft, ibid., iii, 525, 1853.

Allegewi. Schoolcraft, ibid., v, 133, 1855.

Alleghans. Colden, 1727, quoted in Schoolcraft, Notes on Iroquois, 147, 1847.

Alleghanys. Rafinesque, in Marshall, Kentucky, i, 34, 1824.

Alleghens. Colden, map, 1727, *fide* Schoolcraft, Notes on Iroquois, 305, 1847.

Allegwi. Squier, in Beach, Indian Miscellany, 26, 1877.

Alli. Schoolcraft, Indian Tribes, v, 133, 1855.

Allighewis. Keane, in Stanford's Compendium, 500, 1878.

Talagans. Rafinesque, in Marshall, Kentucky, i, 28, 1824.

Talega. Brinton, Walam Olum, 201, 1885.

Tallagewy. Schoolcraft, Indian Tribes, ii, 36, 1852.

Tallegwi. Rafinesque, *fide* Mercer, Lenape Stone, 90, 1885.

Talligwee. Schoolcraft, Notes on Iroquois, 310, 1847.

Tallike. Brinton, Walam Olum, 230, 1885.

KĬTU'HWAGĬ (plural, *Anĭ'-Kĭtu'hwagĭ*. See preceding explanation).

Cuttawa. Vaugondy, map, Partie de l'Amérique, Septentrionale 1755.

Gatohua.
Gattochwa. } Gatschet, Creek Migration Legend, i, 28, 1884.
Katowa (plural, *Katowagi*).

Ketawaugas. Haywood, Natural and Aboriginal Tennessee, 233, 1823.

Kĭttuwa. Brinton, Walam Olum, 16, 1885 (Delaware name).

Kuttoowauw. Aupaumut, 1791, *fide* Brinton, ibid., 16 (Mahican name).

OYATA'GE'RONOÑ'. Hewitt, oral information (Iroquois (Mohawk) name. See preceding explanation).

Ojadagochroene. Livingston, 1720, in New York Doc. Col. Hist., v, 567, 1855.

Ondadeonwas. Bleeker, 1701, ibid., iv, 918, 1854.

Oyadackuchraono. Weiser, 1753, ibid., vi, 795, 1855.

Oyadagahroenes. Letter of 1713, ibid., v, 386, 1855 (incorrectly stated to be the Flatheads, i. e., either Catawbas or Choctaws).

Oyadage'ono. Gatschet, Seneca MS, 1882, Bur. Am. Ethn. (Seneca name).

O-ya-dä'-go-o-no. Morgan, League of Iroquois, 337, 1851.

Oyaudah. Schoolcraft, Notes on Iroquois, 448, 1847 (Seneca name).

Uwata'-yo-ro'-no. Gatschet, Creek Migration Legend, 28, 1884 (Wyandot name).

Uyada. Ibid. (Seneca name).

We-yau-dah. Schoolcraft, Notes on Iroquois, 253, 1847.

Wa-tai-yo-ro-noñ'. Hewitt, Wyandot MS, 1893, Bur. Am. Ethn. (Wyandot name).

RICKAHOCKANS. Lederer, 1672, Discoveries, 26, reprint of 1891 (see preceding explanation).

Rickohockans. Map, ibid.

Rechahecrians. Drake, Book of Indians, book 4, 22, 1848 (from old Virginia documents).

Rechehecrians. Rafinesque, in Marshall, Kentucky, I, 36, 1824.

MÂÑTEᴋÂÑ'. Gatschet, Catawba MS, 1881, Bur. Am. Ethn. (Catawba name. See preceding explanation).

ENTARIRONNON. ⎧ Potier, Racines Huronnes et Grammaire, MS, 1751 (Wyandot
OCHIE'TARIRONNON. ⎨ names. The first, according to Hewitt, is equivalent to
⎩ "ridge, or mountain, people").

T'ᴋwEⁿ-TAH-E-U-HA-NE. Beauchamp, in Journal Am. Folklore, V, 225, 1892 (given as the Onondaga name and rendered, "people of a beautiful red color").

C ᴜGACOLE(?). Fontanedo, about 1575, Memoir, translated in French Hist. Colls., II, 257, 1875 (rendered "wicked people").

(2) MOBILIAN TRADE LANGUAGE (page 16): This trade jargon, based upon Choctaw, but borrowing also from all the neighboring dialects and even from the more northern Algonquian languages, was spoken and understood among all the tribes of the Gulf states, probably as far west as Matagorda bay and northward along both banks of the Mississippi to the Algonquian frontier about the entrance of the Ohio. It was called Mobilienne by the French, from Mobile, the great trading center of the Gulf region. Along the Mississippi it was sometimes known also as the Chickasaw trade language, the Chickasaw being a dialect of the Choctaw language proper. Jeffreys, in 1761, compares this jargon in its uses to the lingua franca of the Levant, and it was evidently by the aid of this intertribal medium that De Soto's interpreter from Tampa bay could converse with all the tribes they met until they reached the Mississippi. Some of the names used by Fontanedo about 1575 for the tribes northward from Appalachee bay seem to be derived from this source, as in later times were the names of the other tribes of the Gulf region, without regard to·linguistic affinities, including among others the Taensa, Tunica, Atakapa, and Shetimasha, representing as many different linguistic stocks. In his report upon the southwestern tribes in 1805, Sibley says that the "Mobilian" was spoken in addition to their native languages by all the Indians who had come from the east side of the Mississippi. Among those so using it he names the Alabama, Apalachi, Biloxi, Chactoo, Pacana, Pascagula, Taensa, and Tunica. Woodward, writing from Louisiana more than fifty years later, says: "There is yet a language the Texas Indians call the Mobilian tongue, that has been the trading language of almost all the tribes that have inhabited the country. I know white men that now speak it. There is a man now living near me that is fifty years of age, raised in Texas, that speaks the language well. It is a mixture of Creek, Choctaw, Chickasay, Netches [Natchez], and Apelash [Apalachi]"—Reminiscences, 79. For further information see also Gatschet, Creek Migration Legend, and Sibley, Report.

The Mobilian trade jargon was not unique of its kind. In America, as in other parts of the world, the common necessities of intercommunication have resulted in the formation of several such mongrel dialects, prevailing sometimes over wide areas. In some cases, also, the language of a predominant tribe serves as the common medium for all the tribes of a particular region. In South America we find the lingoa geral, based upon the Tupi' language, understood for everyday purposes by all the tribes of the immense central region from Guiana to Paraguay, including almost the whole Amazon basin. On the northwest coast we find the well-known "Chinook jargon," which takes its name from a small tribe formerly residing at the mouth of the Columbia, in common use among all the tribes from California far up into Alaska, and eastward to the great divide of the Rocky mountains. In the southwest the Navaho-Apache language is understood by nearly all the Indians of Arizona and New Mexico, while on the plains the Sioux language in the north and the Comanche in the south hold almost the same position. In addition to these we have also the noted "sign language," a gesture system used and perfectly understood as a fluent means of communication among all the hunting tribes of the plains from the Saskatchewan to the Rio Grande.

(3) DIALECTS (page 17): The linguistic affinity of the Cherokee and northern Iroquoian dialects, although now well established, is not usually obvious on the surface, but requires a close analysis of words, with a knowledge of the laws of phonetic changes, to make it appear. The superficial agreement is perhaps most apparent between the Mohawk and the Eastern (Lower) Cherokee dialects, as both of these lack the labials entirely and use *r* instead of *l*. In the short table given below the Iroquois words are taken, with slight changes in the alphabet used, from Hewitt's manuscripts, the Cherokee from those of the author:

	Mohawk	Cherokee (Eastern)
person	oñgwe'	yûñwĭ
fire	otsi'ra'	atsi'ra (atsi'la)
water	awĕñ'	ăwä' (ămä')
stone	onĕñya'	nûñyû'
arrow	ka'noñ'	kûnĭ'
pipe	kanoñnăwĕñ'	kănûñ'năwû
hand (arm)	owe'ya'	uwä'yĭ
milk	unĕñ'ta'	unûñ'tĭ
five	wĭsk	hĭskĭ
tobacco	[tcărhû', Tuscarora]	tsârû (tsâlû)
fish	otcoñ'ta'	û'tsûtĭ'
ghost	o'skĕñna'	asgi'na
snake	ĕñnătûñ	i'nădû'

Comparison of Cherokee dialects

	Eastern (Lower)	Middle	Western (Upper)
fire	atsi'ra	atsi'la	atsi'la
water	ăwä'	ămä'	ămä'
dog	gi'rĭ'	gi'lĭ'	gi'lĭ'
hair	gitsû'	gitsû'	gitlû'
hawk	tsă'nuwă'	tsă'nuwă'	tlă'nuwă'
leech	tsanu'sĭ'	tsanu'sĭ'	tlanu'sĭ'
bat	tsa'wehă'	tsa'mehă'	tla'mehă'
panther	tsûñtû'tsĭ	tsûñtû'tsĭ	tlûñtû'tsĭ
jay	tsay'kû'	tsay'kû'	tlay'kû'
martin (bird)	tsutsû'	tsutsû'	tlutlû'
war-club	atăsû'	atăsû'	atăsĭ'
heart	unăhû'	unăhû'	unăhwĭ'
where?	ga'tsû	ga'tsû	ha'tlû
how much?	hûñgû'	hûñgû'	hila'gû
key	stugi'stĭ	stugi'stĭ	stui'stĭ
I pick it up (long)	tsĭnigi'û	tsĭnigi'û	tsĭne'û
my father	agidâ'tă	agidâ'tă	edâ'tă
my mother	a'gitsĭ'	a'gitsĭ'	etsĭ'
my father's father	agini'sĭ	agini'sĭ	eni'sĭ
my mother's father	agidu'tû	agidu'tû	edu'tû'

It will be noted that the Eastern and Middle dialects are about the same, excepting for the change of *l* to *r*, and the entire absence of the labial *m* from the Eastern dialect, while the Western differs considerably from the others, particularly in the greater frequency of the liquid *l* and the softening of the guttural *g*, the changes tending to render it the most musical of all the Cherokee dialects. It is also the standard literary dialect. In addition to these three principal dialects there are some peculiar forms and expressions in use by a few individuals which indicate the former existence of one or more other dialects now too far extinct to be reconstructed. As in most other tribes, the ceremonial forms used by the priesthood are so filled with archaic and figurative expressions as to be almost unintelligible to the laity.

(4) IROQUOIAN TRIBES AND MIGRATIONS (p. 17): The Iroquoian stock, taking its name from the celebrated Iroquois confederacy, consisted formerly of from fifteen to twenty tribes, speaking nearly as many different dialects, and including, among others, the following:

Wyandot, or Huron. ⎫
Tionontati, or Tobacco nation. ⎪
Attiwan'daron, or Neutral nation. ⎬ Ontario, Canada.
Tohotaenrat. ⎪
Wenrorono. ⎭

Mohawk. ⎫
Oneida. ⎪
Onondaga. ⎬ Iroquois, or Five Nations, New York.
Cayuga. ⎪
Seneca. ⎭

Erie. Northern Ohio, etc.

Conestoga, or Susquehanna. Southern Pennsylvania and Maryland.

Nottoway. ⎫
Meherrin?. ⎭ Southern Virginia.

Tuscarora. Eastern North Carolina.

Cherokee. Western Carolina, etc.

Tradition and history alike point to the St. Lawrence region as the early home of this stock. Upon this point all authorities concur. Says Hale, in his paper on Indian Migrations (p. 4): "The constant tradition of the Iroquois represents their ancestors as emigrants from the region north of the Great lakes, where they dwelt in early times with their Huron brethren. This tradition is recorded with much particularity by Cadwallader Colden, surveyor-general of New York, who in the early part of the last century composed his well known 'History of the Five Nations.' It is told in a somewhat different form by David Cusick, the Tuscarora historian, in his 'Sketches of Ancient History of the Six Nations,' and it is repeated by Mr. L. H. Morgan in his now classical work, 'The League of the Iroquois,' for which he procured his information chiefly among the Senecas. Finally, as we learn from the narrative of the Wyandot Indian, Peter Clarke, in his book entitled 'Origin and Traditional History of the Wyandotts,' the belief of the Hurons accords in this respect with that of the Iroquois. Both point alike to the country immediately north of the St. Lawrence, and especially to that portion of it lying east of Lake Ontario, as the early home of the Huron-Iroquois nations." Nothing is known of the traditions of the Conestoga or the Nottoway, but the tradition of the Tuscarora, as given by Cusick and other authorities, makes them a direct offshoot from the northern Iroquois, with whom they afterward reunited. The traditions of the Cherokee also, as we have seen, bring them from the north, thus completing the cycle. "The striking fact has become evident that the course of migration of the Huron-Cherokee family has been from the northeast to the southwest—that is, from eastern Canada, on the Lower St. Lawrence, to the mountains of northern Alabama."—Hale, Indian Migrations, p. 11.

The retirement of the northern Iroquoian tribes from the St. Lawrence region was due to the hostility of their Algonquian neighbors, by whom the Hurons and their allies were forced to take refuge about Georgian bay and the head of Lake Ontario, while the Iroquois proper retreated to central New York. In 1535 Cartier found the shores of the river from Quebec to Montreal occupied by an Iroquoian people, but on the settlement of the country seventy years later the same region was found in possession of Algonquian tribes. The confederation of the five Iroquois nations, probably about the year 1540, enabled them to check the Algonquian invasion and to assume the offensive. Linguistic and other evidence shows that the separation of the Cherokee from the parent stock must have far antedated this period.

(5) WALAM OLUM (p. 18): The name signifies "red score," from the Delaware *walam*, "painted," more particularly "painted red," and *olum*, "a score, tally-mark." The Walam Olum was first published in 1836 in a work entitled "The American Nations," by Constantine Samuel Rafinesque, a versatile and voluminous, but very erratic, French scholar, who spent the latter half of his life in this country, dying in Philadelphia in 1840. He asserted that it was a translation of a manuscript in the Delaware language, which was an interpretation of an ancient sacred metrical legend of the Delawares, recorded in pictographs cut upon wood, obtained in 1820 by a medical friend of his among the Delawares then living in central Indiana. He says himself: "These actual *olum* were first obtained in 1820 as a reward for a medical cure, deemed a curiosity, and were unexplicable. In 1822 were obtained from another individual the songs annexed thereto in the original language, but no one could be found by me able to translate them. I had therefore to learn the language since, by the help of Zeisberger, Heckewelder, and a manuscript dictionary, on purpose to translate them, which I only accomplished in 1833." On account of the unique character of the alleged Indian record and Rafinesque's own lack of standing among his scientific contemporaries, but little attention was paid to the discovery until Brinton took up the subject a few years ago. After a critical sifting of the evidence from every point of view he arrived at the conclusion that the work is a genuine native production, although the manuscript rendering is faulty, partly from the white scribe's ignorance of the language and partly from the Indian narrator's ignorance of the meaning of the archaic forms. Brinton's edition (q. v.), published from Rafinesque's manuscript, gives the legend in triplicate form—pictograph, Delaware, and English translation, with notes and glossary, and a valuable ethnologic introduction by Brinton himself.

It is not known that any of the original woodcut pictographs of the Walam Olum are now in existence, although a statement of Rafinesque implies that he had seen them. As evidence of the truth of his statement, however, we have the fact that precisely similar pictographic series cut upon birch bark, each pictograph representing a line or couplet of a sacred metrical recitation, are now known to be common among the Ojibwa, Menomini, and other northern tribes. In 1762 a Delaware prophet recorded his visions in hieroglyphics cut upon a wooden stick, and about the year 1827 a Kickapoo reformer adopted the same method to propagate a new religion among the tribes. One of these "prayer sticks" is now in the National Museum, being all that remains of a large basketful delivered to a missionary in Indiana by a party of Kickapoo Indians in 1830 (see plate and description, pp. 665, 697 et seq. in the author's Ghost-dance Religion, Fourteenth Annual Report of the Bureau of Ethnology).

(6) FISH RIVER (p. 18): Namæsi Sipu (Heckewelder, Indian Nations, 49), or Namassipi (Walam Olum, p. 198). Deceived by a slight similarity of sound, Heckewelder makes this river identical with the Mississippi, but as Schoolcraft shows (Notes on Iroquois, p. 316) the true name of the Mississippi is simply Misi-sipi, "great river," and "fish river" would be a most inappropriate name for such a turbulent current, where only the coarser species can live. The mere fact that there can be a question of identity among experts familiar with Indian nomenclature would indicate that it

was not one of the larger streams. Although Heckewelder makes the Alligewi, as ne
prefers to call them, flee down the Mississippi after their final defeat, the Walam
Olum chronicle says only "all the Talega go south." It was probably a gradual
withdrawal, rather than a sudden and concerted flight (see Hale, Indian Migrations, pp. 19–22).

(7) FIRST APPEARANCE OF WHITES (p. 19): It is possible that this may refer to one
of the earlier adventurers who coasted along the North Atlantic in the first decades
after the discovery of America, among whom were Sebastian Cabot, in 1498; Verra-
zano, in 1524; and Gomez, in 1525. As these voyages were not followed up by permanent occupation of the country it is doubtful if they made any lasting impression
upon Indian tradition. The author has chosen to assume, with Brinton and Rafinesque, that the Walam Olum reference is to the settlement of the Dutch at New
York and the English in Virginia soon after 1600.

(8) DE SOTO'S ROUTE (p. 26): On May 30, 1539, Hernando de Soto, of Spain, with
600 armed men and 213 horses, landed at Tampa bay, on the west coast of Florida, in
search of gold. After more than four years of hardship and disappointed wandering
from Florida to the great plains of the West and back again to the Mississippi, where
De Soto died and his body was consigned to the great river, 311 men, all that were
left of the expedition, arrived finally at Pánuco, in Mexico, on September 10, 1543.

For the history of this expedition, the most important ever undertaken by Spain
within eastern United States, we have four original authorities. First is the very
brief, but evidently truthful (Spanish) report of Biedma, an officer of the expedition, presented to the King in 1544, immediately after the return to Spain. Next
in order, but of first importance for detail and general appearance of reliability, is
the narrative of an anonymous Portuguese cavalier of the expedition, commonly
known as the Gentleman of Elvas, originally published in the Portuguese language
in 1557. Next comes the (Spanish) narrative of Garcilaso, written, but not published, in 1587.   Unlike the others, the author was not an eyewitness of what he
describes, but made up his account chiefly from the oral recollections of an old
soldier of the expedition more than forty years after the event, this information
being supplemented from papers written by two other soldiers of De Soto. As might
be expected, the Garcilaso narrative, although written in flowery style, abounds in
exaggeration and trivial incident, and compares unfavorably with the other accounts,
while probably giving more of the minor happenings. The fourth original account
is an unfinished (Spanish) report by Ranjel, secretary of the expedition, written
soon after reaching Mexico, and afterward incorporated with considerable change by
Oviedo, in his "Historia natural y general de las Indias." As this fourth narrative
remained unpublished until 1851 and has never been translated, it has hitherto been
entirely overlooked by the commentators, excepting Winsor, who notes it incidentally. In general it agrees well with the Elvas narrative and throws valuable light
upon the history of the expedition.

The principal authorities, while preserving a general unity of narrative, differ
greatly in detail, especially in estimates of numbers and distances, frequently to such
an extent that it is useless to attempt to reconcile their different statements. In general the Gentleman of Elvas is most moderate in his expression, while Biedma takes
a middle ground and Garcilaso exaggerates greatly. Thus the first named gives
De Soto 600 men, Biedma makes the number 620, while Garcilaso says 1,000. At a
certain stage of the journey the Portuguese Gentleman gives De Soto 700 Indians as
escort, Biedma says 800, while Garcilaso makes it 8,000. At the battle of Mavilla the
Elvas account gives 18 Spaniards and 2,500 Indians killed, Biedma says 20 Spaniards
killed, without giving an estimate of the Indians, while Garcilaso has 82 Spaniards
and over 11,000 Indians killed. In distances there is as great discrepancy. Thus
Biedma makes the distance from Guaxule to Chiaha four days, Garcilaso has it six
days, and Elvas seven days. As to the length of an average day's march we find it

estimated all the way from "four leagues, more or less" (Garcilaso) to "every day seven or eight leagues" (Elvas). In another place the Elvas chronicler states that they usually made five or six leagues a day through inhabited territories, but that in crossing uninhabited regions—as that between Canasagua and Chiaha, they marched every day as far as possible for fear of running out of provisions. One of the most glaring discrepancies appears in regard to the distance between Chiaha and Coste. Both the Portuguese writer and Garcilaso put Chiaha upon an island—a statement which in itself is at variance with any present conditions,—but while the former makes the island a fraction over a league in length the latter says that it was five leagues long. The next town was Coste, which Garcilaso puts immediately at the lower end of the same island while the Portuguese Gentleman represents it as seven days distant, although he himself has given the island the shorter length.

 Notwithstanding a deceptive appearance of exactness, especially in the Elvas and Ranjel narratives, which have the form of a daily journal, the conclusion is irresistible that much of the record was made after dates had been forgotten, and the sequence of events had become confused. Considering all the difficulties, dangers, and uncertainties that constantly beset the expedition, it would be too much to expect the regularity of a ledger, and it is more probable that the entries were made, not from day to day, but at irregular intervals as opportunity presented at the several resting places. The story must be interpreted in the light of our later knowledge of the geography and ethnology of the country traversed.

Each of the three principal narratives has passed through translations and later editions of more or less doubtful fidelity to the original, the English edition in some cases being itself a translation from an earlier French or Dutch translation. English speaking historians of the expedition have usually drawn their material from one or the other of these translations, without knowledge of the original language, of the etymologies of the Indian names or the relations of the various tribes mentioned, or of the general system of Indian geographic nomenclature. One of the greatest errors has been the attempt to give in every case a fixed local habitation to a name which in some instances is not a proper name at all, and in others is merely a descriptive term or a duplicate name occurring at several places in the same tribal territory. Thus Tali is simply the Creek word *talua*, town, and not a definite place name as represented by a mistake natural in dealing through interpreters with an unknown Indian language. Tallise and Tallimuchase are respectively "Old town" and "New town" in Creek, and there can be no certainty that the same names were applied to the same places a century later. Canasagua is a corruption of a Cherokee name which occurs in at least three other places in the old Cherokee country in addition to the one mentioned in the narrative, and almost every old Indian local name was thus repeated several times, as in the case of such common names as Short creek, Whitewater, Richmond, or Lexington among ourselves. The fact that only one name of the set has been retained on the map does not prove its identity with the town of the old chronicle. Again such loose terms as "a large river," "a beautiful valley," have been assumed to mean something more definitely localized than the wording warrants. The most common error in translation has been the rendering of the Spanish "despoblado" as "desert." There are no deserts in the Gulf states, and the word means simply an uninhabited region, usually the debatable strip between two tribes.

There have been many attempts to trace De Soto's route. As nearly every historian who has written of the southern states has given attention to this subject it is unnecessary to enumerate them all. Of some thirty works consulted by the author, in addition to the original narratives already mentioned, not more than two or three can be considered as speaking with any authority, the rest simply copying from these without investigation. The first attempt to locate the route definitely was made by Meek (Romantic Passages, etc.) in 1839 (reprinted in 1857), his conclusions being based upon his general knowledge of the geography of the region. In 1851 Pickett tried to locate the route, chiefly, he asserts, from Indian tradition as related by mixed-bloods. How much dependence can be placed upon Indian tradition as thus interpreted three centuries after the event it is unnecessary to say. Both these writers have brought De Soto down the Coosa river, in which they have been followed without investigation by Irving, Shea and others, but none of these was aware of the existence of a Suwali tribe or correctly acquainted with the Indian nomenclature of the upper country, or of the Creek country as so well summarized by Gatschet in his Creek Migration Legend. They are also mistaken in assuming that only De Soto passed through the country, whereas we now know that several Spanish explorers and numerous French adventurers traversed the same territory, the latest expeditions of course being freshest in Indian memory. Jones in his "De Soto's March Through Georgia" simply dresses up the earlier statements in more literary style, sometimes changing surmises to positive assertions, without mentioning his authorities. Maps of the supposed route, all bringing De Soto down the Coosa instead of the Chattahoochee, have been published in Irving's Conquest of Florida, the Hakluyt Society's edition of the Gentleman of Elva's account, and in Buckingham Smith's translation of the same narrative, as well as in several other works. For the eastern portion, with which we have to deal, all of these are practically duplicates of one another. On several old Spanish and French maps the names mentioned in the narrative seem to have been set down merely to fill space, without much reference to the text of the chronicle. For a list and notices of principal writers who have touched upon this subject see the appendix to Shea's chapter on "Ancient Florida" in Winsor's Narrative and Critical History of America, II; Boston, 1886. We shall speak only of that part of the route which lay near the Cherokee mountains.

The first location which concerns us in the narrative is Cofitachiqui, the town from which De Soto set out for the Cherokee country. The name appears variously as Cofitachequi (Ranjel), Cofitachique (Biedma), Cofachiqui (Garcilaso), Cutifa-Chiqui (by transposition, Elvas), Cofetaçque (Vandera), Catafachique (Williams) and Cosatachiqui (misprint, Brooks MSS), and the Spaniards first heard of the region as Yupaha from a tribe farther to the south. The correct form appears to be that first given, which Gatschet, from later information than that quoted in his Creek Migration Legend, makes a Hitchitee word about equivalent to "Dogwood town," from *cofi*, "dogwood," *cofita*, "dogwood thicket," and *chiki*, "house," or collectively "town." McCulloch puts the town upon the headwaters of the Ocmulgee; Williams locates it on the Chattahoochee; Gallatin on the Oconee or the Savannah; Meek and Monette, following him, probably in the fork of the Savannah and the Broad; Pickett, with Jones and others following him, at Silver bluff on the east (north) bank of the Savannah, in Barnwell county, South Carolina, about 25 miles by water below the present Augusta. It will thus be seen that at the very outset of our inquiry the commentators differ by a distance equal to more than half the width of the state of Georgia. It will suffice here to say, without going into the argument, that the author is inclined to believe that the Indian town was on or near Silver bluff, which was noted for its extensive ancient remains as far back as Bartram's time (Travels, 313), and where the noted George Galphin established a trading post in 1736. The original site has since been almost entirely worn away by the river. According to the Indians of Cofitachiqui, the town, which was on the farther (north) bank of the stream, was two day's journey from the sea, probably by canoe, and the sailors with the expedition believed the river to be the same one that entered at St. Helena, which was a very close guess. The Spaniards were shown here European articles which they were told had been obtained from white men who had entered the river's mouth many years before. These they conjectured to have been the men with Ayllon, who had landed on that coast in 1520 and again in 1524. The town was probably the ancient capital of the Uchee Indians, who, before their absorption by the Creeks, held or claimed most of the territory on both banks of Savannah river from the Cherokee border to within about forty miles of Savannah and westward to the Ogeechee and Cannouchee rivers (see Gatschet, Creek Migration Legend, I, 17–24). The country was already on the decline in 1540 from a recent fatal epidemic, but was yet populous and wealthy, and was ruled by a woman chief whose authority extended for a considerable distance. The town was visited also by Pardo in 1567 and again by Torres in 1628, when it was still a principal settlement, as rich in pearls as in De Soto's time (Brooks MSS, in the archives of the Bureau of American Ethnology).

Somewhere in southern Georgia De Soto had been told of a rich province called Coça (Coosa, the Creek country) toward the northwest. At Cofitachiqui he again heard of it and of one of its principal towns called Chiaha (Chehaw) as being twelve days inland. Although on first hearing of it he had kept on in the other direction in order to reach Cofitachiqui, he now determined to go there, and made the queen a prisoner to compel her to accompany him a part of the way as guide. Coça province was, though he did not know it, almost due west, and he was in haste to reach it in order to obtain corn, as his men and horses were almost worn out from hunger. It is apparent, however, that the unwilling queen, afraid of being carried beyond her own territories, led the Spaniards by a roundabout route in the hope of making her escape, as she finally did, or perhaps of leaving them to starve and die in the mountains, precisely the trick attempted by the Indians upon another Spanish adventurer, Coronado, entering the great plains from the Pacific coast in search of golden treasure in the same year.

Instead therefore of recrossing the river to the westward, the Spaniards, guided by the captive queen, took the direction of the north ("la vuelta del norte"— Biedma), and, after passing through several towns subject to the queen, came in seven days to "the province of Chalaque" (Elvas). Elvas, Garcilaso, and Ranjel agree upon the spelling, but the last named makes the distance only two days from Cofitachiqui. Biedma does not mention the country at all. The trifling difference in statement of five days in seven need not trouble us, as Biedma makes the whole distance from Cofitachiqui to Xuala eight days, and from Guaxule to Chiaha four days, where Elvas makes it, respectively, twelve and seven days. Chalaque is, of course, Cherokee, as all writers agree, and De Soto was now probably on the waters of Keowee river, the eastern head stream of Savannah river, where the Lower Cherokee had their towns. Finding the country bare of corn, he made no stay.

Proceeding six days farther they came next to Guaquili, where they were kindly received. This name occurs only in the Ranjel narrative, the other three being entirely silent in regard to such a halting place. The name has a Cherokee sound (Wakili), but if we allow for a dialectic substitution of *l* for *r* it may be connected with such Catawba names as Congaree, Wateree, and Sugeree. It was probably a village of minor importance.

They came next to the province of Xuala, or Xualla, as the Elvas narrative more often has it. In a French edition it appears as Chouala. Ranjel makes it three days from Guaquili or five from Chalaque. Elvas also makes it five days from Chalaque, while Biedma makes it eight days from Cofitachiqui, a total discrepancy of four days from the last-named place. Biedma describes it as a rough mountain country, thinly populated, but with a few Indian houses, and thinks that in these mountains the great river of Espiritu Santo (the Mississippi) had its birth. Ranjel describes the town as situated in a plain in the vicinity of rivers and in a country with greater appearance of gold mines than any they had yet seen. The Portuguese gentleman describes it as having very little corn, and says that they reached it from Cofitachiqui over a hilly country. In his final chapter he states that the course from Cofitachiqui to this place was from south to north, thus agreeing with Biedma. According to Garcilaso (pp. 136–137) it was fifty leagues by the road along which the Spaniards had come from Cofitachiqui to the first valley of the province of Xuala, with but few mountains on the way, and the town itself was situated close under a mountain ("a la falda de una sierra") beside a small but rapid stream which formed the boundary of the territory of Cofitachiqui in this direction. From Ranjel we learn that on the same day after leaving this place for the next "province" the Spaniards crossed a very high mountain ridge ("una sierra muy alta").

Without mentioning the name, Pickett (1851) refers to Xuala as "a town in the present Habersham county, Georgia," but gives no reason for this opinion. Rye and Irving, of the same date, arguing from a slight similarity of name, think it may have been on the site of a former Cherokee town, Qualatchee, on the head of Chattahoochee river in Georgia. The resemblance, however, is rather farfetched, and moreover this same name is found on Keowee river in South Carolina. Jones (De Soto in Georgia, 1880) interprets Garcilaso's description to refer to "Nacoochee valley, Habersham county"—which should be White county—and the neighboring Mount Yonah, overlooking the fact that the same description of mountain, valley, and swift flowing stream might apply equally well to any one of twenty other localities in this southern mountain country. With direct contradiction Garcilaso says that the Spaniards rested here fifteen days because they found provisions plentiful, while the Portuguese Gentleman says that they stopped but two days because they found so little corn! Ranjel makes them stop four days and says they found abundant provisions and assistance.

However that may have been, there can be no question of the identity of the name. As the province of Chalaque is the country of the Cherokee, so the province of Xuala is the territory of the Suwali or Sara Indians, better known later as Cheraw, who lived in early times in the piedmont country about the head of Broad river in North Carolina, adjoining the Cherokee, who still remember them under the name of Ani'-Suwa'li. A principal trail to their country from the west led up Swannanoa river and across the gap which, for this reason, was known to the Cherokee as Suwa'li-nuñnâ, "Suwali trail," corrupted by the whites to Swannanoa. Lederer, who found them in the same general region in 1670, calls this gap the "Suala pass" and the neighboring mountains the Sara mountains, "which," he says, "The Spaniards make Suala." They afterward shifted to the north and finally returned and were incorporated with the Catawba (see Mooney, Siouan Tribes of the East, bulletin of the Bureau of Ethnology, 1894).

Up to this point the Spaniards had followed a north course from Cofitachiqui (Biedma and Elvas), but they now turned to the west (Elvas, final chapter). On the same day on which they left Xuala they crossed "a very high mountain ridge," and descended the next day to a wide meadow bottom ("savana"), through which flowed a river which they concluded was a part of the Espiritu Santo, the Mississippi (Ranjel). Biedma speaks of crossing a mountain country and mentions the river, which he also says they thought to be a tributary of the Mississippi. Garcilaso says that this portion of their route was through a mountain country without inhabitants ("despoblado") and the Portuguese gentleman describes it as being over "very rough and high ridges." In five days of such travel—for here, for a wonder, all the narratives agree—they came to Guaxule. This is the form given by Garcilaso and the Gentleman of Elvas; Biedma has Guasula, and Ranjel Guasili or Guasuli. The translators and commentators have given us such forms as Guachoule, Quaxule, Quaxulla, and Quexale. According to the Spanish method of writing Indian words the name was pronounced Washulé or Wasuli, which has a Cherokee sound, although it can not be translated. Buckingham Smith (Narratives, p. 222) hints that the Spaniards may have changed Guasili to Guasule, because of the similarity of the latter form to a town name in southern Spain. Such corruptions of Indian names are of frequent occurrence. Garcilaso speaks of it as a "province and town," while Biedma and Ranjel call it simply a town ("pueblo"). Before reaching this place the Indian queen had managed to make her escape. All the chroniclers tell of the kind reception which the Spaniards met here, but the only description of the town itself is from Garcilaso, who says that it was situated in the midst of many small streams which came down from the mountains round about, that it consisted of three hundred houses, which is probably an exaggeration, though it goes to show that the village was of considerable size, and that the chief's house, in which the principal officers were lodged, was upon a high hill ("un cerro alto"), around which was a roadway ("paseadero") wide enough for six men to walk abreast. By the "chief's house" we are to understand the town-house, while from various similar references in other parts of the narrative there can be no doubt that the "hill" upon which it stood was an artificial mound. In modern Spanish writing such artificial elevations are more often called *lomas*, but these early adventurers may be excused for not noting the distinction. Issuing from the mountains round about the town were numerous small streams, which united to form the river which the Spaniards henceforth followed from here down to Chiaha, where it was as large as the Guadalquivir at Sevilla (Garcilaso).

Deceived by the occurrence, in the Portuguese narrative, of the name Canasagua, which they assumed could belong in but one place, earlier commentators have identified this river with the Coosa, Pickett putting Guaxule somewhere upon its upper waters, while Jones improves upon this by making the site "identical, or very nearly so, with Coosawattee Old town, in the southeastern corner of Murray county," Georgia. As we shall show, however, the name in question was duplicated in several states, and a careful study of the narratives, in the light of present knowledge of the country, makes it evident that the river was not the Coosa, but the Chattahoochee.

Turning our attention once more to Xuala, the most northern point reached by De Soto, we have seen that this was the territory of the Suwala or Sara Indians, in the eastern foothills of the Alleghenies, about the head waters of Broad and Catawba rivers, in North Carolina. As the Spaniards turned here to the west they probably did not penetrate far beyond the present South Carolina boundary. The "very high mountain ridge" which they crossed immediately after leaving the town was in all probability the main chain of the Blue ridge, while the river which they found after descending to the savanna on the other side, and which they guessed to be a branch of the Mississippi, was almost as certainly the upper part of the French Broad, the first stream flowing in an opposite direction from those which they had previously encountered. They may have struck it in the neighborhood of Hendersonville or Brevard, there being two gaps, passable for vehicles, in the main ridge eastward from the first-named town. The uninhabited mountains through which they struggled for several days on their way to Chiaha and Coça (the Creek country) in the southwest were the broken ridges in which the Savannah and the Little Tennessee have their sources, and if they followed an Indian trail they may have passed through the Rabun gap, near the present Clayton, Georgia. Guaxule, and not Xuala, as Jones supposes, was in Nacoochee valley, in the present White county, Georgia, and the small streams which united to form the river down which the Spaniards proceeded to Chiaha were the headwaters of the Chattahoochee. The hill upon which the townhouse was built must have been the great Nacoochee mound, the most prominent landmark in the valley, on the east bank of Sautee creek, in White county, about twelve miles northwest of Clarkesville. This is the largest mound in upper Georgia, with the exception of the noted Etowah mound near Cartersville, and is the only one which can fill the requirements of the case. There are but two considerable mounds in western North Carolina, that at Franklin and a smaller one on Oconaluftee river, on the present East Cherokee reservation, and as both of these are on streams flowing away from the Creek country, this fact alone would bar them from consideration. The only large mounds in upper Georgia are this one at Nacoochee and the group on the Etowah river, near Cartersville. The largest of the Etowah group is some fifty feet in height and is ascended on one side by means of a roadway about fifty feet wide at the base and narrowing gradually to the top.   Had this been the mound of the narrative it is hardly possible that the chronicler would have failed to notice also the two other mounds of the group or the other one on the opposite side of the river, each of these being from twenty to twenty-five feet in height, to say nothing of thè great ditch a quarter of a mile in length which encircles the group. Moreover, Cartersville is at some distance from the mountains, and the Etowah river at this point does not answer the description of a small rushing mountain stream. There is no considerable mound at Coosawatee or in any of the three counties adjoining.

The Nacoochee mound has been cleared and cultivated for many years and does not now show any appearance of a roadway up the side, but from its great height we may be reasonably sure that some such means of easy ascent existed in ancient times.   In other respects it is the only mound in the whole upper country which fills the conditions.   The valley is one of the most fertile spots in Georgia and numerous ancient remains give evidence that it was a favorite center of settlement in early days.   At the beginning of the modern historic period it was held by the Cherokee, who had there a town called Nacoochee, but their claim was disputed by the Creeks.   The Gentleman of Elvas states that Guaxule was subject to the queen of Cofitachiqui, but this may mean only that the people of the two towns or tribes were in friendly alliance.   The modern name is pronounced *Nagu'tsï'* by the Cherokee, who say, however, that it is not of their language.   The terminal may be the Creek *udshi*, "small," or it may have a connection with the name of the Uchee Indians.

From Guaxule the Spaniards advanced to Canasoga (Ranjel) or Canasagua (Elvas), one or two days' march from Guaxule, according to one·or the other authority. Garcilaso and Biedma do not mention the name.   As Garcilaso states that from Guaxule to Chiaha the march was down the bank of the same river, which we identify with the Chattahoochee, the town may have been in the neighborhood of the present Gainesville.   As we have seen, however, it is unsafe to trust the estimates of distance.   Arguing from the name, Meek infers that the town was about Conasauga river in Murray county, and that the river down which they marched to reach it was "no doubt the Etowah," although to reach the first named river from the Etowah it would be necessary to make another sharp turn to the north.   From the same coincidence Pickett puts it on the Conasauga, "in the modern county of Murray, Georgia," while Jones, on the same theory, locates it "at or near the junction of the Connasauga and Coosawattee rivers, in originally Cass, now Gordon county." Here his modern geography as well as his ancient is at fault, as the original Cass county is now Bartow, the name having been changed in consequence of a local dislike for General Cass.   The whole theory of a march down the Coosa river rests upon this coincidence of the name.   The same name however, pronounced *Gänsä'gï* by the Cherokee, was applied by them to at least three different locations within their old territory, while the one mentioned in the narrative would make the fourth. The others were (1) on Oostanaula river, opposite the mouth of the Conasauga, where afterward was New Echota, in Gordon county, Georgia; (2) on Canasauga creek, in McMinn county, Tennessee; (3) on Tuckasegee river, about two miles above Webster, in Jackson county, North Carolina.   At each of these places are remains of ancient settlement.   It is possible that the name of Kenesaw mountain, near Marietta, in Cobb county, Georgia, may be a corruption of Gänsâgï, and if so, the Canasagua of the narrative may have been somewhere in this vicinity on the Chattahoochee. The meaning of the name is lost.

On leaving Canasagua they continued down the same river which they had followed from Guaxule (Garcilaso), and after traveling several days through an uninhabited ("despoblado") country (Elvas) arrived at Chiaha, which was subject to the great chief of Coça (Elvas).   The name is spelled Chiaha by Ranjel and the Gentleman of Elvas, Chiha by Biedma in the Documentos, China by a misprint in an English rendering, and Ychiaha by Garcilaso. It appears as Chiha on an English map of 1762 reproduced in Winsor, Westward Movement, page 31, 1897. Gallatin spells it Ichiaha, while Williams and Fairbanks, by misprint, make it Chiapa. According to both Ranjel and Elvas the army entered it on the 5th of June, although the former makes it four days from Canasagua, while the other makes it five. Biedma says it was four days from Guaxule, and, finally, Garcilaso says it was six days and thirty leagues from Guaxule and on the same river, which was, here at Chiaha, as large as the Guadalquivir at Sevilla. As we have seen, there is a great discrepancy in the statements of the distance from Cofitachiqui to this point. All four authorities agree that the town was on an island in the river, along which they had been marching for some time (Garcilaso, Ranjel), but while the Elvas narrative makes the island "two crossbow shot" in length above the town and one league in length below it, Garcilaso calls it a "great island more than five leagues long." On both sides of the island the stream was very broad and easily waded (Elvas). Finding welcome and food for men and horses the Spaniards rested here nearly a month (June 5–28, Ranjel; twenty-six or twenty-seven days, Biedma; thirty days, Elvas). In spite of the danger from attack De Soto allowed his men to sleep under trees in the open air, "because it was very hot and the people should have suffered great extremity if it had not been so" (Elvas). This in itself is evidence that the place was pretty far to the south, as it was yet only the first week in June. The town was subject to the chief of the great province of Coça, farther to the west. From here onward they began to meet palisaded towns.

On the theory that the march was down Coosa river, every commentator hitherto has located Chiaha at some point upon this stream, either in Alabama or Georgia. Gallatin (1836) says that it "must have been on the Coosa, probably some distance below the site of New Echota." He notes a similarity of sound between Ichiaha and "Echoy" (Itseyĭ), a Cherokee town name. Williams (1837) says that it was on Mobile (i. e., the Alabama or lower Coosa river). Meek (1839) says "there can be little doubt that Chiaha was situated but a short distance above the junction of the Coosa and Chattooga rivers," i. e., not far within the Alabama line. He notes the occurrence of a "Chiaha" (Chehawhaw) creek near Talladega, Alabama. In regard to the island upon which the town was said to have been situated he says: "There is no such island now in the Coosa. It is probable that the Spaniards either mistook the peninsula formed by the junction of two rivers, the Coosa and Chattooga, for an island, or that those two rivers were originally united so as to form an island near their present confluence. We have heard this latter supposition asserted by persons well acquainted with the country."—Romantic Passages, p. 222, 1857. Monette (1846) puts it on Etowah branch of the Coosa, probably in Floyd county, Georgia. Pickett (1851), followed in turn by Irving, Jones, and Shea, locates it at "the site of the modern Rome." The "island" is interpreted to mean the space between the two streams above the confluence.

Pickett, as has been stated, bases his statements chiefly or entirely upon Indian traditions as obtained from halfbreeds or traders. How much information can be gathered from such sources in regard to events that transpired three centuries before may be estimated by considering how much an illiterate mountaineer of the same region might be able to tell concerning the founding of the Georgia colony. Pickett himself seems to have been entirely unaware of the later Spanish expeditions of Pardo and De Luna through the same country, as he makes no mention of them in his history of Alabama, but ascribes everything to De Soto. Concerning Chiaha he says:

"The most ancient Cherokee Indians, whose tradition has been handed down to us through old Indian traders, disagree as to the precise place [!] where De Soto crossed the Oostanaula to get over into the town of Chiaha—some asserting that he passed over that river seven miles above its junction with the Etowah, and that he marched from thence down to Chiaha, which, all contend, lay immediately at the confluence of the two rivers; while other ancient Indians asserted that he crossed, with his army, immediately opposite the town. But this is not very important. Coupling the Indian traditions with the account by Garcellasso and that by the Portuguese eyewitness, we are inclined to believe the latter tradition that the expedition continued to advance down the western side of the Oostanaula until they halted in view of the mouth of the Etowah. De Soto, having arrived immediately opposite the great town of Chiaha, now the site of Rome, crossed the Oostanaula," etc. (History of Alabama, p. 23, reprint, 1896). He overlooks the fact that Chiaha was not a Cherokee town, but belonged to the province of Coça—i. e., the territory of the Creek Indians.

A careful study of the four original narratives makes it plain that the expedition did not descend either the Oostanaula or the Etowah, and that consequently Chiaha could not have been at their junction, the present site of Rome. On the other hand the conclusion is irresistible that the march was down the Chattahoochee from its extreme head springs in the mountains, and that the Chiaha of the narrative was the Lower Creek town of the same name, more commonly known as Chehaw, formerly on this river in the neighborhood of the modern city of Columbus, Georgia, while Coste, in the narrative the next adjacent town, was Kasi'ta, or Cusseta, of the same group of villages. The falls at this point mark the geologic break line where the river changes from a clear, swift current to a broad, slow-moving stream of the lower country. Attracted by the fisheries and the fertile bottom lands the Lower Creeks established here their settlement nucleus, and here, up to the beginning of the present century, they had within easy distance of each other on both sides of the river some fifteen towns, among which were Chiaha (Chehaw), Chiahudshi (Little Chehaw), and Kasi'ta (Cusseta). Most of these settlements were within what are now Muscogee and Chattahoochee counties, Georgia, and Lee and Russell counties, Alabama (see town list and map in Gatschet, Creek Migration Legend). Large mounds and other earthworks on both sides of the river in the vicinity of Columbus attest the importance of the site in ancient days, while the general appearance indicates that at times the adjacent low grounds were submerged or cut off by overflows from the main stream. A principal trail crossed here from the Ocmulgee, passing by Tuskegee to the Upper Creek towns about the junction of the Coosa and Tallapoosa in Alabama. At the beginning of the present century this trail was known to the traders as "De Soto's trace" (Woodward, Reminiscences, p. 76). As the Indian towns frequently shift their position within a limited range on account of epidemics, freshets, or impoverishment of the soil, it is not necessary to assume that they occupied exactly the same sites in 1540 as in 1800, but only that as a group they were in the same general vicinity. Thus Kasi'ta itself was at one period above the falls and at a later period some eight miles below them. Both Kasi'ta and Chiaha were principal towns, with several branch villages.

The time given as occupied on the march from Canasagua to Chiaha would seem too little for the actual distance, but as we have seen, the chroniclers do not agree among themselves. We can easily believe that the Spaniards, buoyed up by the certainty of finding food and rest at their next halting place, made better progress along the smooth river trail than while blundering helplessly through the mountains at the direction of a most unwilling guide. If Canasagua was anywhere in the neighborhood of Kenesaw, in Cobb county, the time mentioned in the Elvas or Garcilaso narrative would probably have been sufficient for reaching Chiaha at the falls. The uninhabited country between the two towns was the neutral ground between the two hostile tribes, the Cherokee and the Creeks, and it is worth noting that Kenesaw mountain was made a point on the boundary line afterward established between the two tribes through the mediation of the United States government.

There is no large island in either the Coosa or the Chattahoochee, and we are forced to the conclusion that what the chronicle describes as an island was really a portion of the bottom land temporarily cut off by back water from a freshet. In a similar way "The Slue," east of Flint river in Mitchell county, may have been formed by a shifting of the river channel. Two months later, in Alabama, the Spaniards reached a river so swollen by rains that they were obliged to wait six days before they could cross (Elvas). Lederer, while crossing South Carolina in 1670, found his farther progress barred by a "great lake," which he puts on his map as "Ushery lake," although there is no such lake in the state; but the mystery is explained by Lawson, who, in going over the same ground thirty years later, found all the bottom lands under water from a great flood, the Santee in particular being 36 feet above its normal level. As Lawson was a surveyor his figures may be considered reliable. The "Ushery lake" of Lederer was simply an overflow of Catawba river. Flood water in the streams of upper Georgia and Alabama would quickly be carried off, but would be apt to remain for some time on the more level country below the falls.

According to information supplied by Mr Thomas Robinson, an expert engineering authority familiar with the lower Chattahoochee, there was formerly a large mound, now almost entirely washed away, on the eastern bank of the river, about nine miles below Columbus, while on the western or Alabama bank, a mile or two farther down, there is still to be seen another of nearly equal size. "At extreme freshets both of these mounds were partly submerged. To the east of the former, known as the Indian mound, the flood plain is a mile or two wide, and along the eastern side of the plain stretches a series of swamps or wooded sloughs, indicating an old river bed. All the plain between the present river and the sloughs is river-made land. The river bluff along by the mound on the Georgia side is from twenty to thirty feet above the present low-water surface of the stream. About a mile above the mound are the remains of what was known as Jennies island. At ordinary stages of the river no island is there. The eastern channel was blocked by government works some years ago, and the whole is filled up and now used as a cornfield. The island remains can be traced now, I think, for a length of half a mile, with a possible extreme width of 300 feet. . . . This whole country, on both sides of the river, is full of Indian lore. I have mentioned both mounds simply to indicate that this portion of the river was an Indian locality, and have also stated the facts about the remains of Jennies island in order to give a possible clew to a professional who might study the ground."—Letter, April 22, 1900.

Chiaha was the first town of the "province of Coça," the territory of the Coosa or Creek Indians. The next town mentioned, Coste (Elvas and Ranjel), Costehe (Biedma) or Acoste (Garcilaso), was Kasi'ta, or Cusseta, as it was afterward known to the whites. While Garcilaso puts it at the lower end of the same island upon which Chiaha was situated, the Elvas narrative makes it seven days distant! The modern towns of Chehaw and Cusseta were within a few miles of each other on the Chattahoochee, the former being on the western or Alabama side, while Cusseta, in 1799, was on the east or Georgia side about eight miles below the falls at Columbus, and in Chattahoochee county, which has given its capital the same name, Cusseta. From the general tone of the narrative it is evident that the two towns were near together in De Soto's time, and it may be that the Elvas chronicle confounded Kasi'ta with Koasati, a principal Upper Creek town, a short distance below the junction of the Coosa and Tallapoosa. At Coste they crossed the river and continued westward "through many towns subject to the cacique of Coça" (Elvas) until they came to the great town of Coça itself. This was Kusa or Coosa, the ancient capital of the Upper Creeks. There were two towns of this name at different periods. One, described by Adair in 1775 as "the great and old beloved town of refuge, Koosah," was on the east bank of Coosa river, a few miles southwest of the present Talladega, Alabama. The other, known as "Old Coosa," and probably of more ancient origin, was on the west side of Alabama river, near the present site of Montgomery (see Gatschet, Creek Migration Legend). It was probably the latter which was visited by De Soto, and later on by De Luna, in 1559. Beyond Coça they passed through another Creek town, apparently lower down on the Alabama, the name of which is variously spelled Ytaua (Elvas, Force translation), Ytava (Elvas, Hakluyt Society translation), or Itaba (Ranjel), and which may be connected with I'tăwă', Etowah or "Hightower," the name of a former Cherokee settlement near the head of Etowah river in Georgia. The Cherokee regard this as a foreign name, and its occurrence in upper Georgia, as well as in central Alabama, may help to support the tradition that the southern Cherokee border was formerly held by the Creeks.

De Soto's route beyond the Cherokee country does not concern us except as it throws light upon his previous progress. In the seventeenth chapter the Elvas narrative summarizes that portion from the landing at Tampa bay to a point in southern Alabama as follows: "From the Port de Spirito Santo to Apalache, which is about an hundred leagues, the governor went from east to west; and from Apalache to Cutifachiqui, which are 430 leagues, from the southwest to the northeast; and from Cutifachiqui to Xualla, which are about 250 leagues, from the south to the north; and from Xualla to Tascaluca, which are 250 leagues more, an hundred and ninety of them he traveled from east to west, to wit, to the province of Coça; and the other 60, from Coça to Tascaluca, from the north to the south."

Chisca (Elvas and Ranjel), the mountainous northern region in search of which men were sent from Chiaha to look for copper and gold, was somewhere in the Cherokee country of upper Georgia or Alabama. The precise location is not material, as it is now known that native copper, in such condition as to have been easily workable by the Indians, occurs throughout the whole southern Allegheny region from about Anniston, Alabama, into Virginia. Notable finds of native copper have been made on the upper Tallapoosa, in Cleburne county, Alabama; about Ducktown, in Polk county, Tennessee, and in southwestern Virginia, one nugget from Virginia weighing several pounds. From the appearance of ancient soapstone vessels which have been found in the same region there is even a possibility that the Indians had some knowledge of smelting, as the Spanish explorers surmised (oral information from Mr W. H. Weed, U. S. Geological Survey). We hear again of this "province" after De Soto had reached the Mississippi, and in one place Garcilaso seems to confound it with another province called Quizqui (Ranjel) or Quizquiz (Elvas and Biedma). The name has some resemblance to the Cherokee word *tsiskwa*, "bird."

(9) DE LUNA AND ROGEL (p. 27): Jones, in his De Soto's March through Georgia, incorrectly ascribes certain traces of ancient mining operations in the Cherokee country, particularly on Valley river in North Carolina, to the followers of De Luna, "who, in 1560 . . . came with 300 Spanish soldiers into this region, and spent the summer in eager and laborious search for gold." Don Tristan de Luna, with fifteen hundred men, landed somewhere about Mobile bay in 1559 with the design of establishing a permanent Spanish settlement in the interior, but owing to a succession of unfortunate happenings the attempt was abandoned the next year. In the course of his wanderings he traversed the country of the Choctaw, Chickasaw, and Upper Creeks, as is shown by the names and other data in the narrative, but returned without entering the mountains or doing any digging (see Barcia, Ensayo Cronologico, pp. 32–41, 1723; Winsor, Narrative and Critical History, II, pp. 257–259).

In 1569 the Jesuit Rogel—called Father John Roger by Shea—began mission work among the South Carolina tribes inland from Santa Elena (about Port Royal). The mission, which at first promised well, was abandoned next year, owing to the unwillingness of the Indians to give up their old habits and beliefs. Shea, in his "Catholic Missions," supposes that these Indians were probably a part of the

Cherokee, but a study of the Spanish record in Barcia (Ensayo, pp. 138–141) shows that Rogel penetrated only a short distance from the coast.

(10) DAVIES' HISTORY OF THE CARRIBBY ISLANDS (p. 29): The fraudulent character of this work, which is itself an altered translation of a fictitious history by Rochefort, is noted by Buckingham Smith (Letter of Hernando de Soto, p. 36, 1854), Winsor (Narrative and Critical History, II, p. 289), and Field (Indian Bibliography, p. 95). Says Field: "This book is an example of the most unblushing effrontery. The pseudo author assumes the credit of the performance, with but the faintest allusion to its previous existence. It is a nearly faithful translation of Rochefort's 'Histoire des Antilles.' There is, however, a gratifying retribution in Davies' treatment of Rochefort, for the work of the latter was fictitious in every part which was not purloined from authors whose knowledge furnished him with all in his treatise which was true."

(11) ANCIENT SPANISH MINES (pp. 29, 31): As the existence of the precious metals in the southern Alleghenies was known to the Spaniards from a very early period, it is probable that more thorough exploration of that region will bring to light many evidences of their mining operations. In his "Antiquities of the Southern Indians," Jones describes a sort of subterranean village discovered in 1834 on Dukes creek, White county, Georgia, consisting of a row of small log cabins extending along the creek, but imbedded several feet below the surface of the ground, upon which large trees were growing, the inference being that the houses had been thus covered by successive freshets. The logs had been notched and shaped apparently with sharp metallic tools. Shafts have been discovered on Valley river, North Carolina, at the bottom of one of which was found, in 1854, a well-preserved windlass of hewn oak timbers, showing traces of having once been banded with iron. Another shaft, passing through hard rock, showed the marks of sharp tools used in the boring. The casing and other timbers were still sound (Jones, pp. 48, 49). Similar ancient shafts have been found in other places in upper Georgia and western North Carolina, together with some remarkable stone-built fortifications or corrals, notably at Fort mountain, in Murray county, Georgia, and on Silver creek, a few miles from Rome, Georgia.

Very recently remains of an early white settlement, traditionally ascribed to the Spaniards, have been reported from Lincolnton, North Carolina, on the edge of the ancient country of the Sara, among whom the Spaniards built a fort in 1566. The works include a dam of cut stone, a series of low pillars of cut stone, arranged in squares as though intended for foundations, a stone-walled well, a quarry from which the stone had been procured, a fire pit, and a series of sinks, extending along the stream, in which were found remains of timbers suggesting the subterranean cabins on Dukes creek. All these antedated the first settlement of that region, about the year 1750. Ancient mining indications are also reported from Kings mountain, about twenty miles distant (Reinhardt MS, 1900, in Bureau of American Ethnology archives). The Spanish miners of whom Lederer heard in 1670 and Moore in 1690 were probably at work in this neighborhood.

(12) SIR WILLIAM JOHNSON (p. 38): This great soldier, whose history is so inseparably connected with that of the Six Nations, was born in the county Meath, Ireland, in 1715, and died at Johnstown, New York, in 1774. The younger son of an Irish gentleman, he left his native country in 1738 in consequence of a disappointment in love, and emigrated to America, where he undertook the settlement of a large tract of wild land belonging to his uncle, which lay along the south side of the Mohawk river in what was then the wilderness of New York. This brought him into close contact with the Six Nations, particularly the Mohawks, in whom he became so much interested as to learn their language and in some degree to accommodate himself to their customs, sometimes even to the wearing of the native costume. This interest, together with his natural kindness and dignity, completely won the hearts of the Six

Nations, over whom he acquired a greater influence than has ever been exercised by any other white man before or since. He was formally adopted as a chief by the Mohawk tribe. In 1744, being still a very young man, he was placed in charge of British affairs with the Six Nations, and in 1755 was regularly commissioned at their own urgent request as superintendent for the Six Nations and their dependent and allied tribes, a position which he held for the rest of his life. In 1748 he was also placed in command of the New York colonial forces, and two years later was appointed to the governor's council. At the beginning of the French and Indian war he was commissioned a major-general. He defeated Dieskau at the battle of Lake George, where he was severely wounded early in the action, but refused to leave the field. For this service he received the thanks of Parliament, a grant of £5,000, and a baronetcy. He also distinguished himself at Ticonderoga and Fort Niagara, taking the latter after routing the French army sent to its relief. At the head of his Indian and colonial forces he took part in other actions and expeditions, and was present at the surrender of Montreal. For his services throughout the war he received a grant of 100,000 acres of land north of the Mohawk river. Here he built "Johnson Hall," which still stands, near the village of Johnstown, which was laid out by him with stores, church, and other buildings, at his own expense. At Johnson Hall he lived in the style of an old country baron, dividing his attention between Indian affairs and the raising of blooded stock, and dispensing a princely hospitality to all comers. His influence alone prevented the Six Nations joining Pontiac's great confederacy against the English. In 1768 he concluded the treaty of Fort Stanwix, which fixed the Ohio as the boundary between the northern colonies and the western tribes, the boundary for which the Indians afterward contended against the Americans until 1795. In 1739 he married a German girl of the Mohawk valley, who died after bearing him three children. Later in life he formed a connection with the sister of Brant, the Mohawk chief. He died from over-exertion at an Indian council. His son, Sir John Johnson, succeeded to his title and estates, and on the breaking out of the Revolution espoused the British side, drawing with him the Mohawks and a great part of the other Six Nations, who abandoned their homes and fled with him to Canada (see W. L. Stone, Life of Sir William Johnson).

(13) CAPTAIN JOHN STUART (p. 44): This distinguished officer was contemporaneous with Sir William Johnson, and sprang from the same adventurous Keltic stock which has furnished so many men conspicuous in our early Indian history. Born in Scotland about the year 1700, he came to America in 1733, was appointed to a subordinate command in the British service, and soon became a favorite with the Indians. When Fort Loudon was taken by the Cherokee in 1760, he was second in command, and his rescue by Ata-kullakulla is one of the romantic episodes of that period. In 1763 he was appointed superintendent for the southern tribes, a position which he continued to hold until his death. In 1768 he negotiated with the Cherokee the treaty of Hard Labor by which the Kanawha was fixed as the western boundary of Virginia, Sir William Johnson at the same time concluding a treaty with the northern tribes by which the boundary was continued northward along the Ohio. At the outbreak of the Revolution he organized the Cherokee and other southern tribes, with the white loyalists, against the Americans, and was largely responsible for the Indian outrages along the southern border. He planned a general invasion by the southern tribes along the whole frontier, in cooperation with a British force to be landed in western Florida, while a British fleet should occupy the attention of the Americans on the coast side and the Tories should rise in the interior. On the discovery of the plot and the subsequent defeat of the Cherokee by the Americans, he fled to Florida and soon afterward sailed for England, where he died in 1779.

(14) NANCY WARD (p. 47): A noted halfbreed Cherokee woman, the date and place of whose birth and death are alike unknown. It is said that her father was a

British officer named Ward and her mother a sister of Ata-kullakulla, principal chief of the Nation at the time of the first Cherokee war. She was probably related to Brian Ward, an oldtime trader among the Cherokee, mentioned elsewhere in connection with the battle of Tali′wă. During the Revolutionary period she resided at Echota, the national capital, where she held the office of "Beloved Woman," or "Pretty Woman," by virtue of which she was entitled to speak in councils and to decide the fate of captives. She distinguished herself by her constant friendship for the Americans, always using her best effort to bring about peace between them and her own people, and frequently giving timely warning of projected Indian raids, notably on the occasion of the great invasion of the Watauga and Holston settlements in 1776. A Mrs Bean, captured during this incursion, was saved by her interposition after having been condemned to death and already bound to the stake. In 1780, on occasion of another Cherokee outbreak, she assisted a number of traders to escape, and the next year was sent by the chiefs to make peace with Sevier and Campbell, who were advancing against the Cherokee towns. Campbell speaks of her in his report as "the famous Indian woman, Nancy Ward." Although peace was not then granted, her relatives, when brought in later with other prisoners, were treated with the consideration due in return for her good offices. She is described by Robertson, who visited her about this time, as "queenly and commanding" in appearance and manner, and her house as furnished in accordance with her high dignity. When among the Arkansas Cherokee in 1819, Nuttall was told that she had introduced the first cows into the Nation, and that by her own and her children's influence the condition of the Cherokee had been greatly elevated. He was told also that her advice and counsel bordered on supreme, and that her interference was allowed to be decisive even in affairs of life and death. Although he speaks in the present tense, it is hardly probable that she was then still alive, and he does not claim to have met her. Her descendants are still found in the Nation. See Haywood, Natural and Aboriginal Tennessee; Ramsey, Tennessee; Nuttall, Travels, p. 130, 1821; Campbell letter, 1781, and Springstone deposition, 1781, in Virginia State Papers I, pp. 435, 436, 447, 1875; Appleton's Cyclopædia of American Biography.

(15) GENERAL JAMES ROBERTSON (p. 48): This distinguished pioneer and founder of Nashville was born in Brunswick county, Virginia, in 1742, and died at the Chickasaw agency in west Tennessee in 1814. Like most of the men prominent in the early history of Tennessee, he was of Scotch-Irish ancestry. His father having removed about 1750 to western North Carolina, the boy grew up without education, but with a strong love for adventure, which he gratified by making exploring expeditions across the mountains. After his marriage his wife taught him to read and write. In 1771 he led a colony to the Watauga river and established the settlement which became the nucleus of the future state of Tennessee. He took a leading part in the organization of the Watauga Association, the earliest organized government within the state, and afterward served in Dunmore's war, taking part in the bloody battle of Point Pleasant in 1774. He participated in the earlier Revolutionary campaigns against the Cherokee, and in 1777 was appointed agent to reside at their capital, Echota, and act as a medium in their correspondence with the state governments of North Carolina (including Tennessee) and Virginia. In this capacity he gave timely warning of a contemplated invasion by the hostile portion of the tribe early in 1779. Soon after in the same year he led a preliminary exploration from Watauga to the Cumberland. He brought out a larger party late in the fall, and in the spring of 1780 built the first stockades on the site which he named Nashborough, now Nashville. Only his force of character was able to hold the infant settlement together in the face of hardships and Indian hostilities, but by his tact and firmness he was finally able to make peace with the surrounding tribes, and established the Cumberland settlement upon a secure basis. The Spanish government at one time unsuccessfully attempted to engage him in a plot to cut off the western territory from the

United States, but met a patriotic refusal. Having been commissioned a brigadier-general in 1790, he continued to organize campaigns, resist invasions, and negotiate treaties until the final close of the Indian wars in Tennessee. He afterward held the appointment of Indian commissioner to the Chickasaw and Choctaw. See Ramsey, Tennessee; Roosevelt, Winning of the West; Appleton's Cyclopædia of American Biography.

(16) GENERAL GRIFFITH RUTHERFORD (p. 48): Although this Revolutionary officer commanded the greatest expedition ever sent against the Cherokee, with such distinguished success that both North Carolina and Tennessee have named counties in his honor, little appears to be definitely known of his history. He was born in Ireland about 1731, and, emigrating to America, settled near Salisbury, North Carolina. On the opening of the Revolutionary struggle he became a member of the Provincial Congress and Council of Safety. In June, 1776, he was commissioned a brigadier-general in the American army, and a few months later led his celebrated expedition against the Cherokee, as elsewhere narrated. He rendered other important service in the Revolution, in one battle being taken prisoner by the British and held by them nearly a year. He afterward served in the state senate of North Carolina, and, subsequently removing to Tennessee, was for some time a member of its territorial council. He died in Tennessee about 1800.

(17) RUTHERFORD'S ROUTE (p. 49): The various North Carolina detachments which combined to form Rutherford's expedition against the Cherokee in the autumn of 1776 organized at different points about the upper Catawba and probably concentrated at Davidson's fort, now Old fort, in McDowell county. Thence, advancing westward closely upon the line of the present Southern railroad and its Western North Carolina branch, the army crossed the Blue ridge over the Swannanoa gap and went down the Swannanoa to its junction with the French Broad, crossing the latter at the Warrior ford, below the present Asheville; thence up Hominy creek and across the ridge to Pigeon river, crossing it a few miles below the junction of the East and West forks; thence to Richland creek, crossing it just above the present Waynesville; and over the dividing ridge between the present Haywood and Jackson counties to the head of Scott's creek; thence down that creek by "a blind path through a very mountainous bad way," as Moore's old narrative has it, to its junction with the Tuckasegee river just below the present Webster; thence, crossing to the west (south) side of the river, the troops followed a main trail down the stream for a few miles until they came to the first Cherokee town, Stekoa, on the site of the farm formerly owned by Colonel William H. Thomas, just above the present railroad village of Whittier, Swain county, North Carolina. After destroying the town a detachment left the main body and pursued the fugitives northward on the other side of the river to Oconaluftee river and Soco creek, getting back afterward to the settlements by steering an easterly course across the mountains to Richland creek (Moore narrative). The main army, under Rutherford, crossed the dividing ridge to the southward of Whittier and descended Cowee creek to the waters of Little Tennessee, in the present Macon county. After destroying the towns in this vicinity the army ascended Cartoogaja creek, west from the present Franklin, and crossed the Nantahala mountains at Waya gap—where a fight took place—to Nantahala river, probably at the town of the same name, about the present Jarretts station. From here the march was west across the mountain into the present Cherokee county and down Valley river to its junction with the Hiwassee, at the present Murphy. *Authorities:* Moore narrative and Wilson letter in North Carolina University Magazine, February, 1888; Ramsey, Tennessee, p. 164; Roosevelt, Winning of the West, I, pp. 300–302; Royce, Cherokee map; personal information from Colonel William H. Thomas, Major James Bryson, whose grandfather was with Rutherford, and Cherokee informants.

(18) COLONEL WILLIAM CHRISTIAN (p. 50): Colonel William Christian, some-

times incorrectly called Christy, was born in Berkeley county, Virginia, in 1732. Accustomed to frontier warfare almost from boyhood, he served in the French and Indian war with the rank of captain, and was afterward in command of the Tennessee and North Carolina forces which participated in the great battle of Point Pleasant in 1774, although he himself arrived too late for the fight. He organized a regiment at the opening of the Revolutionary war, and in 1776 led an expedition from Virginia against the Upper Cherokee and compelled them to sue for peace. In 1782, while upon an expedition against the Ohio tribes, he was captured and burned at the stake.

(19) THE GREAT INDIAN WAR PATH (p. 50): This noted Indian thoroughfare from Virginia through Kentucky and Tennessee to the Creek country in Alabama and Georgia is frequently mentioned in the early narrative of that section, and is indicated on the maps accompanying Ramsey's Annals of Tennessee and Royce's Cherokee Nation, in the Fifth Annual Report of the Bureau of Ethnology. Royce's map shows it in more correct detail. It was the great trading and war path between the northern and southern tribes, and along the same path Christian, Sevier, and others of the old Indian fighters led their men to the destruction of the towns on Little Tennessee, Hiwassee, and southward.

According to Ramsey (p. 88), one branch of it ran nearly on the line of the later stage road from Harpers ferry to Knoxville, passing the Big lick in Botetourt county, Virginia, crossing New river near old Fort Chiswell (which stood on the south bank of Reed creek of New river, about nine miles east from Wytheville, Virginia) crossing Holston at the Seven-mile ford, thence to the left of the stage road near the river to the north fork of Holston, "crossing as at present"; thence to Big creek, and, crossing the Holston at Dodson's ford, to the Grassy springs near the former residence of Micajah Lea; thence down the Nolichucky to Long creek, up it to its head, and down Dumplin creek nearly to its mouth, where the path bent to the left and crossed French Broad near Buckinghams island. Here a branch left it and went up the West fork of Little Pigeon and across the mountains to the Middle towns on Tuckasegee and the upper Little Tennessee. The main trail continued up Boyd's creek to its head, and down Ellejoy creek to Little river, crossing near Henry's place; thence by the present Maryville to the mouth of Tellico, and, passing through the Cherokee towns of Tellico, Echota, and Hiwassee, down the Coosa, connecting with the great war path of the Creeks. Near the Wolf hills, now Abingdon, Virginia, another path came in from Kentucky, passing through the Cumberland gap. It was along this latter road that the early explorers entered Kentucky, and along it also the Shawano and other Ohio tribes often penetrated to raid upon the Holston and New river settlements.

On Royce's map the trail is indicated from Virginia southward. Starting from the junction of Moccasin creek with the North fork of Holston, just above the Tennessee state line, it crosses the latter river from the east side at its mouth or junction with the South fork, just below Kingsport or the Long island; then follows down along the west side of the Holston, crossing Big creek at its mouth, and crossing to the south (east) side of Holston at Dodson's creek; thence up along the east side of Dodson's creek and across Big Gap creek, following it for a short distance and continuing southwest, just touching Nolichucky, passing up the west side of Long creek of that stream and down the same side of Dumplin creek, and crossing French Broad just below the mouth of the creek; thence up along the west side of Boyd's creek to its head and down the west side of Ellejoy creek to and across Little river; thence through the present Maryville to cross Little Tennessee at the entrance of Tellico river, where old Fort Loudon was built; thence turning up along the south side of Little Tennessee river to Echota, the ancient capital, and then southwest across Tellico river along the ridge between Chestua and Canasauga creeks, and crossing the latter near its mouth to strike Hiwassee river at the town of the same name;

thence southwest, crossing Ocoee river near its mouth, passing south of Cleveland, through the present Ooltewah and across Chickamauga creek into Georgia and Alabama.

According to Timberlake (Memoirs, with map, 1765), the trail crossed Little Tennessee from Echota, northward, in two places, just above and below Four-mile creek, the first camping place being at the junction of Ellejoy creek and Little river, at the old town site. It crossed Holston within a mile of Fort Robinson.

According to Hutchins (Topographical Description of America, p. 24, 1778), the road which went through Cumberland gap was the one taken by the northern Indians in their incursions into the "Cuttawa" country, and went from Sandusky, on Lake Erie, by a direct path to the mouth of Scioto (where Portsmouth now is) and thence across Kentucky to the gap.

(20) PEACE TOWNS AND TOWNS OF REFUGE (p. 51): Towns of refuge existed among the Cherokee, the Creeks, and probably other Indian tribes, as well as among the ancient Hebrews, the institution being a merciful provision for softening the harshness of the primitive law, which required a life for a life. We learn from Deuteronomy that Moses appointed three cities on the east side of Jordan "that the slayer might flee thither which should kill his neighbor unawares and hated him not in times past, and that fleeing into one of these cities he might live." It was also ordained that as more territory was conquered from the heathen three additional cities should be thus set aside as havens of refuge for those who should accidentally take human life, and where they should be safe until the matter could be adjusted. The wilful murderer, however, was not to be sheltered, but delivered up to punishment without pity (Deut. IV, 41–43, and XIX, 1–11).

Echota, the ancient Cherokee capital near the mouth of Little Tennessee, was the Cherokee town of refuge, commonly designated as the "white town" or "peace town." According to Adair, the Cherokee in his time, although extremely degenerate in other things, still observed the law so strictly in this regard that even a wilful murderer who might succeed in making his escape to that town was safe so long as he remained there, although, unless the matter was compounded in the meantime, the friends of the slain person would seldom allow him to reach home alive after leaving it. He tells how a trader who had killed an Indian to protect his own property took refuge in Echota, and after having been there for some months prepared to return to his trading store, which was but a short distance away, but was assured by the chiefs that he would be killed if he ventured outside the town. He was accordingly obliged to stay a longer time until the tears of the bereaved relatives had been wiped away with presents. In another place the same author tells how a Cherokee, having killed a trader, was pursued and attempted to take refuge in the town, but was driven off into the river as soon as he came in sight by the inhabitants, who feared either to have their town polluted by the shedding of blood or to provoke the English by giving him sanctuary (Adair, American Indians, p. 158, 1775). In 1768 Oconostota, speaking on behalf of the Cherokee delegates who had come to Johnson Hall to make peace with the Iroquois, said: "We come from Chotte, where the wise [white?] house, the house of peace is erected" (treaty record, 1768, New York Colonial Documents, VIII, p. 42, 1857). In 1786 the friendly Cherokee made "Chota" the watchword by which the Americans might be able to distinguish them from the hostile Creeks (Ramsey, Tennessee, p. 343). From conversation with old Cherokee it seems probable that in cases where no satisfaction was made by the relatives of the man-slayer he continued to reside close within the limits of the town until the next recurrence of the annual Green-corn dance, when a general amnesty was proclaimed.

Among the Creeks the ancient town of Kusa or Coosa, on Coosa river in Alabama, was a town of refuge. In Adair's time, although then almost deserted and in ruins, it was still a place of safety for one who had taken human life without design. Certain towns were also known as peace towns, from their prominence in peace ceremonials and treaty making. Upon this Adair says: "In almost every Indian nation there are several *peaceable towns*, which are called 'old beloved, ancient, holy, or white towns.' They seem to have been formerly towns of refuge, for it is not in the memory of their oldest people that ever human blood was shed in them, although they often force persons from thence and put them to death elsewhere."—Adair, American Indians, 159. A closely parallel institution seems to have existed among the Seneca. "The Seneca nation, ever the largest, and guarding the western door of the 'long house,' which was threatened alike from the north, west, and south, had traditions peculiarly their own, besides those common to the other members of the confederacy. The stronghold or fort, Gau-stra-yea, on the mountain ridge, four miles east of Lewiston, had a peculiar character as the residence of a virgin queen known as the 'Peacemaker.' When the Iroquois confederacy was first formed the prime factors were mutual protection and domestic peace, and this fort was designed to afford comfort and relieve the distress incident to war. It was a true 'city of refuge,' to which fugitives from battle, whatever their nationality, might flee for safety and find generous entertainment. Curtains of deerskin separated pursuer and pursued while they were being lodged and fed. At parting, the curtains were withdrawn, and the hostile parties, having shared the hospitality of the queen, could neither renew hostility or pursuit without the queen's consent. According to tradition, no virgin had for many generations been counted worthy to fill the place or possessed the genius and gifts to honor the position. In 1878 the Tonawanda band proposed to revive the office and conferred upon Caroline Parker the title."—Carrington, in Six Nations of New York, Extra Bulletin Eleventh Census, p. 73, 1892.

(21) SCALPING BY WHITES (p. 53): To the student, aware how easily the civilized man reverts to his original savagery when brought in close contact with its conditions, it will be no surprise to learn that every barbarous practice of Indian warfare was quickly adopted by the white pioneer and soldier and frequently legalized and encouraged by local authority. Scalping, while the most common, was probably the least savage and cruel of them all, being usually performed after the victim was already dead, with the primary purpose of securing a trophy of the victory. The tortures, mutilations, and nameless deviltries inflicted upon Indians by their white conquerors in the early days could hardly be paralleled even in civilized Europe, when burning at the stake was the punishment for holding original opinions and sawing into two pieces the penalty for desertion. Actual torture of Indians by legal sanction was rare within the English colonies, but mutilation was common and scalping was the rule down to the end of the war of 1812, and has been practiced more or less in almost every Indian war down to the latest. Captain Church, who commanded in King Philip's war in 1676, states that his men received thirty shillings a head for every Indian killed or taken, and Philip's head, after it was cut off, "went at the same price." When the chief was killed one of his hands was cut off and given to his Indian slayer, " to show to such gentlemen as would bestow gratuities upon him, and accordingly he got many a penny by it." His other hand was chopped off and sent to Boston for exhibition, his head was sent to Plymouth and exposed upon a scaffold there for twenty years, while the rest of his body was quartered and the pieces left hanging upon four trees. Fifty years later Massachusetts offered a bounty of one hundred pounds for every Indian scalp, and scalp hunting thus became a regular and usually a profitable business. On one occasion a certain Lovewell, having recruited a company of forty men for this purpose, discovered ten Indians lying asleep by their fire and killed the whole party. After scalping them they stretched the scalps upon hoops and marched thus into Boston, where the scalps were paraded and the bounty of one thousand pounds paid for them. By a few other scalps sold from time to time at the regular market rate, Lovewell was gradually acquiring a competency when in May, 1725, his company

met disaster. He discovered and shot a solitary hunter, who was afterward scalped by the chaplain of the party, but the Indian managed to kill Lovewell before being overpowered, on which the whites withdrew, but were pursued by the tribesmen of the slain hunter, with the result that but sixteen of them got home alive. A famous old ballad of the time tells how

> "Our worthy Captain Lovewell among them there did die.
> They killed Lieutenant Robbins and wounded good young Frye,
> Who was our English chaplain; he many Indians slew,
> And some of them he scalped when bullets round him flew."

When the mission village of Norridgewock was attacked by the New England men about the same time, women and children were made to suffer the fate of the warriors. The scholarly missionary, Rasles, author of the Abnaki Dictionary, was shot down at the foot of the cross, where he was afterward found with his body riddled with balls, his skull crushed and scalped, his mouth and eyes filled with earth, his limbs broken, and all his members mutilated—and this by white men. The border men of the Revolutionary period and later invariably scalped slain Indians as often as opportunity permitted, and, as has already been shown, both British and American officials encouraged the practice by offers of bounties and rewards, even, in the case of the former, when the scalps were those of white people. Our difficulties with the Apache date from a treacherous massacre of them in 1836 by a party of American scalp hunters in the pay of the governor of Sonora. The bounty offered was one ounce of gold per scalp. In 1864 the Colorado militia under Colonel Chivington attacked a party of Cheyennes camped under the protection of the United States flag, and killed, mutilated, and scalped 170 men, women, and children, bringing the scalps into Denver, where they were paraded in a public hall. One Lieutenant Richmond killed and scalped three women and five children. Scalps were taken by American troops in the Modoc war of 1873, and there is now living in the Comanche tribe a woman who was scalped, though not mortally wounded, by white soldiers in one of the later Indian encounters in Texas. *Authorities:* Drake, Indians (for New England wars); Roosevelt, Virginia State Papers, etc. (Revolution, etc.); Bancroft, Pacific States (Apache); Official Report on the Condition of the Indian Tribes, 1867 (for Chivington episode); author's personal information.

(22) LOWER CHEROKEE REFUGEES (p. 55): "In every hut I have visited I find the children exceedingly alarmed at the sight of white men, and here [at Willstown] a little boy of eight years old was excessively alarmed and could not be kept from screaming out until he got out of the door, and then he ran and hid himself; but as soon as I can converse with them and they are informed who I am they execute any order I give them with eagerness. I inquired particularly of the mothers what could be the reason for this. They said, this town was the remains of several towns who [*sic*] formerly resided on Tugalo and Keowee, and had been much harassed by the whites; that the old people remembered their former situation and suffering, and frequently spoke of them; that these tales were listened to by the children, and made an impression which showed itself in the manner I had observed. The women told me, who I saw gathering nuts, that they had sensations upon my coming to the camp, in the highest degree alarming to them, and when I lit from my horse, took them by the hand, and spoke to them, they at first could not reply, although one of them understood and spoke English very well."—Hawkins, manuscript journal, 1796, in library of Georgia Historical Society.

(23) GENERAL ALEXANDER McGILLIVRAY (p. 56): This famous Creek chieftain, like so many distinguished men of the southern tribes, was of mixed blood, being the son of a Scotch trader, Lachlan McGillivray, by a halfbreed woman of influential family, whose father was a French officer of Fort Toulouse. The future chief was born in the Creek Nation about 1740, and died at Pensacola, Florida, in 1793. He

was educated at Charleston, studying Latin in addition to the ordinary branches, and after leaving school was placed by his father with a mercantile firm in Savannah. He remained but a short time, when he returned to the Creek country, where he soon began to attract attention, becoming a partner in the firm of Panton, Forbes & Leslie, of Pensacola, which had almost a monopoly of the Creek trade. He succeeded to the chieftainship on the death of his mother, who came of ruling stock, but refused to accept the position until called to it by a formal council, when he assumed the title of emperor of the Creek Nation. His paternal estates having been confiscated by Georgia at the outbreak of the Revolution, he joined the British side with all his warriors, and continued to be a leading instigator in the border hostilities until 1790, when he visited New York with a large retinue and made a treaty of peace with the United States on behalf of his people. President Washington's instructions to the treaty commissioners, in anticipation of this visit, state that he was said to possess great abilities and an unlimited influence over the Creeks and part of the Cherokee, and that it was an object worthy of considerable effort to attach him warmly to the United States. In pursuance of this policy the Creek chiefs were entertained by the Tammany society, all the members being in full Indian dress, at which the visitors were much delighted and responded with an Indian dance, while McGillivray was induced to resign his commission as colonel in the Spanish service for a commission of higher grade in the service of the United States. Soon afterward, on account of some opposition, excited by Bowles, a renegade white man, he absented himself from his tribe for a time, but was soon recalled, and continued to rule over the Nation until his death.

McGillivray appears to have had a curious mixture of Scotch shrewdness, French love of display, and Indian secretiveness. He fixed his residence at Little Talassee, on the Coosa, a few miles above the present Wetumpka, Alabama, where he lived in a handsome house with extensive quarters for his negro slaves, so that his place had the appearance of a small town. He entertained with magnificence and traveled always in state, as became one who styled himself emperor. Throughout the Indian wars he strove, so far as possible, to prevent unnecessary cruelties, being noted for his kindness to captives; and his last years were spent in an effort to bring teachers among his people. On the other hand, he conformed much to the Indian customs; and he managed his negotiations with England, Spain, and the United States with such adroitness that he was able to play off one against the other, holding commissions by turn in the service of all three. Woodward, who knew of him by later reputation, asserts positively that McGillivray's mother was of pure Indian blood and that he himself was without education, his letters having been written for him by Leslie, of the trading firm with which he was connected. The balance of testimony, however, seems to leave no doubt that he was an educated as well as an able man, whatever may have been his origin. *Authorities:* Drake, American Indians; documents in American State Papers, Indian Affairs, I, 1832; Pickett, Alabama, 1896; Appleton's Cyclopædia of American Biography; Woodward, Reminiscences, p. 59 et passim, 1859.

(24) GOVERNOR JOHN SEVIER (p. 57): This noted leader and statesman in the pioneer history of Tennessee was born in Rockingham county, Virginia, in 1745, and died at the Creek town of Tukabatchee, in Alabama, in 1815. His father was a French immigrant of good birth and education, the original name of the family being Xavier. The son received a good education, and being naturally remarkably handsome and of polished manner, fine courage, and generous temperament, soon acquired a remarkable influence over the rough border men with whom his lot was cast and among whom he was afterward affectionately known as "Chucky Jack." To the Cherokee he was known as Tsan-usdi', "Little John." After some service against the Indians on the Virginia frontier he removed to the new Watauga settlement in Tennessee, in 1772, and at once became prominently identified with its affairs. He took

part in Dunmore's war in 1774 and, afterward, from the opening of the Revolution in 1775 until the close of the Indian wars in Tennessee—a period extending over nearly twenty years—was the acknowledged leader or organizer in every important Indian campaign along the Tennessee border. His services in this connection have been already noted. He also commanded one wing of the American forces at the battle of King's mountain in 1780, and in 1783 led a body of mountain men to the assistance of the patriots under Marion. At one time during the Revolution a Tory plot to assassinate him was revealed by the wife of the principal conspirator. In 1779 he had been commissioned as commander of the militia of Washington county, North Carolina—the nucleus of the present state of Tennessee—a position which he had already held by common consent. Shortly after the close of the Revolution he held for a short time the office of governor of the seceding "state of Franklin," for which he was arrested and brought to trial by the government of North Carolina, but made his escape, when the matter was allowed to drop. The question of jurisdiction was finally settled in 1790, when North Carolina ceded the disputed territory to the general government. Before this Sevier had been commissioned as brigadier-general. When Tennessee was admitted as a state in 1796 he was elected its first (state) governor, serving three terms, or six years. In 1803 he was again reelected, serving three more terms. In 1811 he was elected to Congress, where he served two terms and was reelected to a third, but died before he could take his seat, having contracted a fever while on duty as a boundary commissioner among the Creeks, being then in his seventy-first year. For more than forty years he had been continuously in the service of his country, and no man of his state was ever more loved and respected. In the prime of his manhood he was reputed the handsomest man and the best Indian fighter in Tennessee.

(25) HOPEWELL, SOUTH CAROLINA (p. 61): This place, designated in early treaties and also in Hawkins's manuscript journal as "Hopewell on the Keowee," was the plantation seat of General Andrew Pickens, who resided there from the close of the Revolution until his death in 1817. It was situated on the northern edge of the present Anderson county, on the east side of Keowee river, opposite and a short distance below the entrance of Little river, and about three miles from the present Pendleton. In sight of it, on the opposite side of Keowee, was the old Cherokee town of Seneca, destroyed by the Americans in 1776. Important treaties were made here with the Cherokee in 1785, and with the Chickasaw in 1786.

(26) COLONEL BENJAMIN HAWKINS (p. 61): This distinguished soldier, statesman, and author, was born in Warren county, North Carolina, in 1754, and died at Hawkinsville, Georgia, in 1816. His father, Colonel Philemon Hawkins, organized and commanded a regiment in the Revolutionary war, and was a member of the convention that ratified the national constitution. At the outbreak of the Revolution young Hawkins was a student at Princeton, but offered his services to the American cause, and on account of his knowledge of French and other modern languages was appointed by Washington his staff interpreter for communicating with the French officers cooperating with the American army. He took part in several engagements and was afterward appointed commissioner for procuring war supplies abroad. After the close of the war he was elected to Congress, and in 1785 was appointed on the commission which negotiated at Hopewell the first federal treaty with the Cherokee. He served a second term in the House and another in the Senate, and in 1796 was appointed superintendent for all the Indians south of the Ohio. He thereupon removed to the Creek country and established himself in the wilderness at what is now Hawkinsville, Georgia, where he remained in the continuance of his office until his death. As Senator he signed the deed by which North Carolina ceded Tennessee to the United States in 1790, and as Indian superintendent helped to negotiate seven different treaties with the southern tribes. He had an extensive knowledge of the customs and language of the Creeks, and his "Sketch of the Creek

Country," written in 1799 and published by the Historical Society of Georgia in 1848, remains a standard. His journal and other manuscripts are in possession of the same society, while a manuscript Cherokee vocabulary is in possession of the American Philosophical Society in Philadelphia. *Authorities:* Hawkins's manuscripts, with Georgia Historical Society; Indian Treaties, 1837; American State Papers: Indian Affairs, I, 1832; II, 1834; Gatschet, Creek Migration Legend; Appleton, Cyclopædia of American Biography.

(27) GOVERNOR WILLIAM BLOUNT (p. 68): William Blount, territorial governor of Tennessee, was born in North Carolina in 1744 and died at Knoxville, Tennessee, in 1800. He held several important offices in his native state, including two terms in the assembly and two others as delegate to the old congress, in which latter capacity he was one of the signers of the Federal constitution in 1787. On the organization of a territorial government for Tennessee in 1790, he was appointed territorial governor and also superintendent for the southern tribes, fixing his headquarters at Knoxville. In 1791 he negotiated an important treaty with the Cherokee, and had much to do with directing the operations against the Indians until the close of the Indian war. He was president of the convention which organized the state of Tennessee in 1796, and was elected to the national senate, but was expelled on the charge of having entered into a treasonable conspiracy to assist the British in conquering Louisiana from Spain. A United States officer was sent to arrest him, but returned without executing his mission on being warned by Blount's friends that they would not allow him to be taken from the state. The impeachment proceedings against him were afterward dismissed on technical grounds. In the meantime the people of his own state had shown their confidence in him by electing him to the state senate, of which he was chosen president. He died at the early age of fifty-three, the most popular man in the state next to Sevier. His younger brother, Willie Blount, who had been his secretary, was afterward governor of Tennessee, 1809–1815.

(28) ST CLAIR'S DEFEAT, 1791 (p. 72): Early in 1791 Major-General Arthur St Clair, a veteran officer in two wars and governor of the Northwestern Territory, was appointed to the chief command of the army operating against the Ohio tribes. On November 4 of that year, while advancing upon the Miami villages with an army of 1,400 men, he was surprised by an Indian force of about the same number under Little-turtle, the Miami chief, in what is now southwestern Mercer county, Ohio, adjoining the Indiana line. Because of the cowardly conduct of the militia he was totally defeated, with the loss of 632 officers and men killed and missing, and 263 wounded, many of whom afterward died. The artillery was abandoned, not a horse being left alive to draw it off, and so great was the panic that the men threw away their arms and fled for miles, even after the pursuit had ceased. It was afterward learned that the Indians lost 150 killed, besides many wounded. Two years later General Wayne built Fort Recovery upon the same spot. The detachment sent to do the work found within a space of 350 yards 500 skulls, while for several miles along the line of pursuit the woods were strewn with skeletons and muskets. The two cannon lost were found in the adjacent stream. *Authorities:* St Clair's report and related documents, 1791; American State Papers, Indian Affairs, I, 1832; Drake, Indians 570, 571, 1880; Appleton's Cyclopædia of American Biography.

(29) CHEROKEE CLANS, (p. 74): The Cherokee have seven clans, viz: Ani'-Wa'ya, Wolf; Ani'-Kawi', Deer; Ani'-Tsi'skwa, Bird; Ani'-Wắ'dĭ, Paint; Ani'-Sahä'nĭ; Ani'-Ga'tâge'wĭ; Ani'-Gilä'hĭ. The names of the last three can not be translated with certainty. The Wolf clan is the largest and most important in the tribe. It is probable that, in accordance with the general system in other tribes, each clan had formerly certain hereditary duties and privileges, but no trace of these now remains. Children belong to the clan of the mother, and the law forbidding marriage between persons of the same clan is still enforced among the conservative

full-bloods. The "seven clans" are frequently mentioned in the sacred formulas, and even in some of the tribal laws promulgated within the century. There is evidence that originally there were fourteen, which by extinction or absorption have been reduced to seven; thus, the ancient Turtle-dove and Raven clans now constitute a single Bird clan. The subject will be discussed more fully in a future Cherokee paper.

(30) WAYNE'S VICTORY, 1794 (p. 78): After the successive failures of Harmar and St Clair in their efforts against the Ohio tribes the chief command was assigned, in 1793, to Major-General Anthony Wayne, who had already distinguished himself by his fighting qualities during the Revolution. Having built Fort Recovery on the site of St Clair's defeat, he made that post his headquarters through the winter of 1793–94. In the summer of 1794 he advanced down the Maumee with an army of 3,000 men, two-thirds of whom were regulars. On August 20 he encountered the confederated Indian forces near the head of the Maumee rapids at a point known as the Fallen Timbers and defeated them with great slaughter, the pursuit being followed up by the cavalry until the Indians took refuge under the guns of the British garrison at Fort Miami, just below the rapids. His own loss was only 33 killed and 100 wounded, of whom 11 afterward died of their wounds. The loss of the Indians and their white auxiliaries was believed to be more than double this. The Indian force was supposed to number 2,000, while, on account of the impetuosity of Wayne's charge, the number of his troops actually engaged did not exceed 900. On account of this defeat and the subsequent devastation of their towns and fields by the victorious army the Indians were compelled to sue for peace, which was granted by the treaty concluded at Greenville, Ohio, August 3, 1795, by which the tribes represented ceded away nearly their whole territory in Ohio. *Authorities:* Wayne's report and related documents, 1794, American State Papers: Indian Affairs, I, 1832; Drake, Indians, 571–577, 1880; Greenville treaty, in Indian Treaties, 1837; Appleton's Cyclopædia of American Biography.

(31) FIRST THINGS OF CIVILIZATION (p. 83): We usually find that the first things adopted by the Indian from his white neighbor are improved weapons and cutting tools, with trinkets and articles of personal adornment. After a regular trade has been established certain traders marry Indian wives, and, taking up their permanent residence in the Indian country, engage in farming and stock raising according to civilized methods, thus, even without intention, constituting themselves industrial teachers for the tribe.

From data furnished by Haywood, guns appear to have been first introduced among the Cherokee about the year 1700 or 1710, although he himself puts the date much earlier. Horses were probably not owned in any great number before the marking out of the horse-path for traders from Augusta about 1740. The Cherokee, however, took kindly to the animal, and before the beginning of the war of 1760 had a "prodigious number." In spite of their great losses at that time they had so far recovered in 1775 that almost every man then had from two to a dozen (Adair, p. 231). In the border wars following the Revolution companies of hundreds of mounted Cherokee and Creeks sometimes invaded the settlements. The cow is called *wa'ka* by the Cherokee and *waga* by the Creeks, indicating that their first knowledge of it came through the Spaniards. Nuttall states that it was first introduced among the Cherokee by the celebrated Nancy Ward (Travels, p. 130). It was not in such favor as the horse, being valuable chiefly for food, of which at that time there was an abundant supply from the wild game. A potent reason for its avoidance was the Indian belief that the eating of the flesh of a slow-moving animal breeds a corresponding sluggishness in the eater. The same argument applied even more strongly to the hog, and to this day a few of the old conservatives among the East Cherokee will have nothing to do with beef, pork, milk, or butter. Nevertheless, Bartram tells of a trader in the Cherokee country as early as 1775 who had a stock of cattle, and whose Indian wife had learned to make butter and cheese (Travels, p. 347). In 1796 Hawkins mentions meeting two Cherokee women driving ten very fat cattle to market in the white settlements (manuscript journal, 1796). Bees, if not native, as the Indians claim, were introduced at so early a period that the Indians have forgotten their foreign origin. The De Soto narrative mentions the finding of a pot of honey in an Indian village in Georgia in 1540. The peach was cultivated in orchards a century before the Revolution, and one variety, known as early as 1700 as the Indian peach, the Indians claimed as their own, asserting that they had had it before the whites came to America (Lawson, Carolina, p. 182, ed. 1860). Potatoes were introduced early and were so much esteemed that, according to one old informant, the Indians in Georgia, before the Removal, "lived on them." Coffee came later, and the same informant remembered when the full-bloods still considered it poison, in spite of the efforts of the chief, Charles Hicks, to introduce it among them.

Spinning wheels and looms were introduced shortly before the Revolution. According to the Wahnenauhi manuscript the first among the Cherokee were brought over from England by an Englishman named Edward Graves, who taught his Cherokee wife to spin and weave. The anonymous writer may have confounded this early civilizer with a young Englishman who was employed by Agent Hawkins in 1801 to make wheels and looms for the Creeks (Hawkins, 1801, in American State Papers: Indian Affairs, I, p. 647). Wafford, in his boyhood, say about 1815, knew an old man named Tsĭ′nawĭ on Young-cane creek of Nottely river, in upper Georgia, who was known as a wheelwright and was reputed to have made the first spinning wheel and loom ever made among the mountain Cherokee, or perhaps in the Nation, long before Wafford's time, or "about the time the Cherokee began to drop their silver ornaments and go to work." In 1785 the commissioners for the Hopewell treaty reported that some of the Cherokee women had lately learned to spin, and many were very desirous of instruction in the raising, spinning, and weaving of flax, cotton, and wool (Hopewell Commissioners' Report, 1785, American State Papers: Indian Affairs, I, p. 39). In accordance with their recommendation the next treaty made with the tribe, in 1791, contained a provision for supplying the Cherokee with farming tools (Holston treaty, 1791, Indian Treaties, p. 36, 1837), and this civilizing policy was continued and broadened until, in 1801, their agent reported that at the Cherokee agency the wheel, the loom, and the plow were in pretty general use, and farming, manufacturing, and stock raising were the principal topics of conversation among men and women (Hawkins manuscripts, Treaty Commission of 1801).

(32) COLONEL RETURN J. MEIGS (p. 84): Return Jonathan Meigs was born in Middletown, Connecticut, December 17, 1734, and died at the Cherokee agency in Tennessee, January 28, 1823. He was the first-born son of his parents, who gave him the somewhat peculiar name of Return Jonathan to commemorate a romantic incident in their own courtship, when his mother, a young Quakeress, called back her lover as he was mounting his horse to leave the house forever after what he had supposed was a final refusal. The name has been handed down through five generations, every one of which has produced some man distinguished in the public service. The subject of this sketch volunteered immediately after the opening engagement of the Revolution at Lexington, and was assigned to duty under Arnold, with rank of major. He accompanied Arnold in the disastrous march through the wilderness against Quebec, and was captured in the assault upon the citadel and held until exchanged the next year. In 1777 he raised a regiment and was promoted to the rank of colonel. For a gallant and successful attack upon the enemy at Sag harbor, Long island, he received a sword and a vote of thanks from Congress, and by his conduct at the head of his regiment at Stony point won the favorable notice of Washington. After the close of the Revolution he removed to Ohio, where, as a member of the territorial legislature, he drew up the earliest code of regula-

tions for the pioneer settlers.   In 1801 he was appointed agent for the Cherokee and took up his residence at the agency at Tellico blockhouse, opposite the mouth of Tellico river, in Tennessee, continuing to serve in that capacity until his death.   He was succeeded as agent by Governor McMinn, of Tennessee.   In the course of twenty-two years he negotiated several treaties with the Cherokee and did much to further the work of civilization among them and to defend them against unjust aggression.   He also wrote a journal of the expedition to Quebec.   His grandson of the same name was special agent for the Cherokee and Creeks in 1834, afterward achieving a reputation in the legal profession both in Tennessee and in the District of Columbia. *Authorities:* Appleton, Cyclopædia of American Biography, 1894; Royce, Cherokee Nation, in Fifth Annual Report Bureau of Ethnology, 1888; documents in American State Papers, Indian Affairs, I and II.

(33) TECUMTHA (p. 87): This great chief of the Shawano and commander of the allied northern tribes in the British service was born near the present Chillicothe, in western Ohio, about 1770, and fell in the battle of the Thames, in Ontario, October 5, 1813.   His name signifies a "flying panther"—i. e., a meteor.   He came of fighting stock good even in a tribe distinguished for its warlike qualities, his father and elder brother having been killed in battle with the whites.   His mother is said to have died among the Cherokee.   Tecumtha is first heard of as taking part in an engagement with the Kentuckians when about twenty years old, and in a few years he had secured recognition as the ablest leader among the allied tribes.   It is said that he took part in every important engagement with the Americans from the time of Harmar's defeat in 1790 until the battle in which he lost his life.   When about thirty years of age he conceived the idea of uniting the tribes northwest of the Ohio, as Pontiac had united them before, in a great confederacy to resist the further advance of the Americans, taking the stand that the whole territory between the Ohio and the Mississippi belonged to all these tribes in common and that no one tribe had the right to sell any portion of it without the consent of the others.   The refusal of the government to admit this principle led him to take active steps to unite the tribes upon that basis, in which he was seconded by his brother, the Prophet, who supplemented Tecumtha's eloquence with his own claims to supernatural revelation.   In the summer of 1810 Tecumtha held a conference with Governor Harrison at Vincennes to protest against a recent treaty cession, and finding after exhausting his arguments that the effort was fruitless, he closed the debate with the words: "The President is far off and may sit in his town and drink his wine, but you and I will have to fight it out."   Both sides at once prepared for war, Tecumtha going south to enlist the aid of the Creek, Choctaw, and other southern tribes, while Harrison took advantage of his absence to force the issue by marching against the Prophet's town on the Tippecanoe river, where the hostile warriors from a dozen tribes had gathered.   A battle fought before daybreak of November 6, 1811, resulted in the defeat of the Indians and the scattering of their forces.   Tecumtha returned to find his plans brought to naught for the time, but the opening of the war between the United States and England a few months later enabled him to rally the confederated tribes once more to the support of the British against the Americans.   As a commissioned brigadier-general in the British service he commanded 2,000 warriors in the war of 1812, distinguishing himself no less by his bravery than by his humanity in preventing outrages and protecting prisoners from massacre, at one time saving the lives of four hundred American prisoners who had been taken in ambush near Fort Meigs and were unable to make longer resistance.   He was wounded at Maguagua, where nearly four hundred were killed and wounded on both sides.   He covered the British retreat after the battle of Lake Erie, and, refusing to retreat farther, compelled the British General Proctor to make a stand at the Thames river.   Almost the whole force of the American attack fell on Tecumtha's division.   Early in the

engagement he was shot through the arm, but continued to fight desperately until he received a bullet in the head and fell dead, surrounded by the bodies of 120 of his slain warriors. The services of Tecumtha and his Indians to the British cause have been recognized by an English historian, who says, "but for them it is probable we should not now have a Canada." *Authorities:* Drake, Indians, ed. 1880; Appleton's Cyclopædia of American Biography, 1894; Eggleston, Tecumseh and the Shawnee Prophet.

(34) FORT MIMS MASSACRE, 1813 (p. 89): Fort Mims, so called from an old Indian trader on whose lands it was built, was a stockade fort erected in the summer of 1813 for the protection of the settlers in what was known as the Tensaw district, and was situated on Tensaw lake, Alabama, one mile east of Alabama river and about forty miles above Mobile. It was garrisoned by about 200 volunteer troops under Major Daniel Beasley, with refugees from the neighboring settlement, making a total at the time of its destruction of 553 men, women, and children. Being carelessly guarded, it was surprised on the morning of August 30 by about 1,000 Creek warriors led by the mixed-blood chief, William Weatherford, who rushed in at the open gate, and, after a stout but hopeless resistance by the garrison, massacred all within, with the exception of the few negroes and halfbreeds, whom they spared, and about a dozen whites who made their escape. The Indian loss is unknown, but was very heavy, as the fight continued at close quarters until the buildings were fired over the heads of the defenders. The unfortunate tragedy was due entirely to the carelessness of the commanding officer, who had been repeatedly warned that the Indians were about, and at the very moment of the attack a negro was tied up waiting to be flogged for reporting that he had the day before seen a number of painted warriors lurking a short distance outside the stockade. *Authorities:* Pickett, Alabama, ed. 1896; Hamilton and Owen, note, p. 170, in Transactions Alabama Historical Society, II, 1898; Agent Hawkins's report, 1813, American State Papers: Indian Affairs, I, p. 853; Drake, Indians, ed. 1880. The figures given are those of Pickett, which in this instance seem most correct, while Drake's are evidently exaggerated.

(35) GENERAL WILLIAM MCINTOSH (p. 98): This noted halfbreed chief of the Lower Creeks was the son of a Scotch officer in the British army by an Indian mother, and was born at the Creek town of Coweta in Alabama, on the lower Chattahoochee, nearly opposite the present city of Columbus, Georgia, and killed at the same place by order of the Creek national council on April 30, 1825. Having sufficient education to keep up an official correspondence, he brought himself to public notice and came to be regarded as the principal chief of the Lower Creeks. In the Creek war of 1813–14 he led his warriors to the support of the Americans against his brethren of the Upper towns, and acted a leading part in the terrible slaughters at Autossee and the Horseshoe bend. In 1817 he again headed his warriors on the government side against the Seminole and was commissioned as major. His common title of general belonged to him only by courtesy. In 1821 he was the principal supporter of the treaty of Indian springs, by which a large tract between the Flint and Chattahoochee rivers was ceded. The treaty was repudiated by the Creek Nation as being the act of a small faction. Two other attempts were made to carry through the treaty, in which the interested motives of McIntosh became so apparent that he was branded as a traitor to his Nation and condemned to death, together with his principal underlings, in accordance with a Creek law making death the penalty for undertaking to sell lands without the consent of the national council. About the same time he was publicly exposed and denounced in the Cherokee council for an attempt to bribe John Ross and other chiefs of the Cherokee in the same fashion. At daylight of April 30, 1825, a hundred or more warriors sent by the Creek national council surrounded his house and, after allowing the women and children to come out, set fire to it and shot McIntosh and another chief

as they tried to escape. He left three wives, one of whom was a Cherokee. *Authorities:* Drake, Indians, ed. 1880; Letters from McIntosh's son and widows, 1825, in American State Papers: Indian Affairs, II, pp. 764 and 768.

(36) WILLIAM WEATHERFORD (p. 89): This leader of the hostiles in the Creek war was the son of a white father and a halfbreed woman of Tuskegee town whose father had been a Scotchman. Weatherford was born in the Creek Nation about 1780 and died on Little river, in Monroe county, Alabama, in 1826. He came first into prominence by leading the attack upon Fort Mims, August 30, 1813, which resulted in the destruction of the fort and the massacre of over five hundred inmates. It is maintained, with apparent truth, that he did his best to prevent the excesses which followed the victory, and left the scene rather than witness the atrocities when he found that he could not restrain his followers. The fact that Jackson allowed him to go home unmolested after the final surrender is evidence that he believed Weatherford guiltless. At the battle of the Holy Ground, in the following December, he was defeated and narrowly escaped capture by the troops under General Claiborne. When the last hope of the Creeks had been destroyed and their power of resistance broken by the bloody battle of the Horseshoe bend, March 27, 1814, Weatherford voluntarily walked into General Jackson's headquarters and surrendered, creating such an impression by his straightforward and fearless manner that the general, after a friendly interview, allowed him to go back alone to gather up his people preliminary to arranging terms of peace. After the treaty he retired to a plantation in Monroe county, where he lived in comfort and was greatly respected by his white neighbors until his death. As an illustration of his courage it is told how he once, single-handed, arrested two murderers immediately after the crime, when the local justice and a large crowd of bystanders were afraid to approach them. Jackson declared him to be as high toned and fearless as any man he had ever met. In person he was tall, straight, and well proportioned, with features indicating intelligence, bravery, and enterprise. *Authorities:* Pickett, Alabama, ed. 1896; Drake, Indians, ed. 1880; Woodward, Reminiscences, 1859.

(37) REVEREND DAVID BRAINERD (p. 104): The pioneer American missionary from whom the noted Cherokee mission took its name was born at Haddam, Connecticut, April 20, 1718, and died at Northampton, Massachusetts, October 9, 1747. He entered Yale college in 1739, but was expelled on account of his religious opinions. In 1742 he was licensed as a preacher and the next year began work as missionary to the Mahican Indians of the village of Kaunameek, twenty miles from Stockbridge, Massachusetts. He persuaded them to remove to Stockbridge, where he put them in charge of a resident minister, after which he took up work with good result among the Delaware and other tribes on the Delaware and Susquehanna rivers. In 1747 his health failed and he was forced to retire to Northampton, where he died a few months later. He wrote a journal and an account of his missionary labors at Kaunameek. His later mission work was taken up and continued by his brother. *Authority:* Appleton's Cyclopædia of American Biography, 1894.

(38) REVEREND SAMUEL AUSTIN WORCESTER (p. 105): This noted missionary and philologist, the son of a Congregational minister who was also a printer, was born at Worcester, Massachusetts, January 19, 1798, and died at Park Hill, in the Cherokee Nation west, April 20, 1859. Having removed to Vermont with his father while still a child, he graduated with the honors of his class at the state university at Burlington in 1819, and after finishing a course at the theological seminary at Andover was ordained to the ministry in 1825. A week later, with his newly wedded bride, he left Boston to begin mission work among the Cherokee, and arrived in October at the mission of the American board, at Brainerd, Tennessee, where he remained until the end of 1827. He then, with his wife, removed to New Echota, in Georgia, the capital of the Cherokee Nation, where he was the principal worker in the establishment of the *Cherokee Phœnix*, the first newspaper printed in the Cherokee

language and alphabet. In this labor his inherited printer's instinct came into play, for he himself supervised the casting of the new types and the systematic arrangement of them in the case. In March, 1831, he was arrested by the Georgia authorities for refusing to take a special oath of allegiance to the state. He was released, but was rearrested soon afterward, confined in the state penitentiary, and forced to wear prison garb, until January, 1833, notwithstanding a decision by the Supreme Court of the United States, nearly a year before, that his imprisonment was a violation of the law of the land. The *Cherokee Phœnix* having been suspended and the Cherokee Nation brought into disorder by the extension over it of the state laws, he then returned to Brainerd, which was beyond the limits of Georgia. In 1835 he removed to the Indian Territory, whither the Arkansas Cherokee had already gone, and after short sojourns at Dwight and Union missions took up his final residence at Park Hill in December, 1836. He had already set up his mission press at Union, printing both in the Cherokee and the Creek languages, and on establishing himself at Park Hill he began a regular series of publications in the Cherokee language. In 1843 he states that "at Park Hill, besides the preaching of the gospel, a leading object of attention is the preparation and publication of books in the Cherokee language" (Letter in Report of Indian Commissioner, p. 356, 1843). The list of his Cherokee publications (first editions) under his own name in Pilling's Bibliography comprises about twenty titles, including the Bible, hymn books, tracts, and almanacs in addition to the *Phœnix* and large number of anonymous works. Says Pilling: "It is very probable that he was the translator of a number of books for which he is not given credit here, especially those portions of the Scripture which are herein not assigned to any name. Indeed it is safe to say that during the thirty-four years of his connection with the Cherokee but little was done in the way of translating in which he had not a share." He also began a Cherokee geography and had both a grammar and a dictionary of the language under way when his work was interrupted by his arrest. The manuscripts, with all his personal effects, afterward went down with a sinking steamer on the Arkansas. His daughter, Mrs A. E. W. Robertson, became a missionary among the Creeks and has published a number of works in their language. *Authorities:* Pilling, Bibliography of the Iroquoian languages (articles Worcester, Cherokee Phœnix, etc.), 1888; Drake, Indians, ed. 1880: Report of Indian Commissioner, 1843 (Worcester letter).

(39) DEATH PENALTY FOR SELLING LANDS (p. 107): In 1820 the Cherokee Nation enacted a law making it treason punishable with death to enter into any negotiation for the sale of tribal lands without the consent of the national council. A similar law was enacted by the Creeks at about the same time. It was for violating these laws that McIntosh and Ridge suffered death in their respective tribes. The principal parts of the Cherokee law, as reenacted by the united Nation in the West in 1842, appear as follows in the compilation authorized in 1866:

"AN ACT AGAINST SALE OF LAND, ETC.: *Whereas*, The peace and prosperity of Indian nations are frequently sacrificed or placed in jeopardy by the unrestrained cupidity of their own individual citizens; *and whereas*, we ourselves are liable to suffer from the same cause, and be subjected to future removal and disturbances: Therefore, . . .

"*Be it further enacted*, That any person or persons who shall, contrary to the will and consent of the legislative council of this nation, in general council convened, enter into a treaty with any commissioner or commissioners of the United States, or any officer or officers instructed for the purpose, and agree to cede, exchange, or dispose in any way any part or portion of the lands belonging to or claimed by the Cherokees, west of the Mississippi, he or they so offending, upon conviction before any judge of the circuit or supreme courts, *shall suffer death*, and any of the aforesaid judges are authorized to call a court for the trial of any person or persons so transgressing.

" *Be it further enacted,* That any person or persons who shall violate the provisions of the second section of this act, and shall resist or refuse to appear at the place designated for trial, or abscond, are hereby declared to be outlaws; and any person or persons, citizens of this nation, may kill him or them so offending at any time and in any manner most convenient, within the limits of this nation, and shall not be held accountable to the laws for the same. . . .

" *Be it further enacted,* That no treaty shall be binding upon this nation which shall not be ratified by the general council, and approved by the principal chief of the nation. December 2, 1842."—Laws of the Cherokee Nation, 1868.

(40) THE CHEROKEE SYLLABARY (p. 110): In the various schemes of symbolic thought representation, from the simple pictograph of the primitive man to the finished alphabet of the civilized nations, our own system, although not yet perfect, stands at the head of the list, the result of three thousand years of development by Egyptian, Phœnician, and Greek. Sequoya's syllabary, the unaided work of an uneducated Indian reared amid semisavage surroundings, stands second.

Twelve years of his life are said to have been given to his great work. Being entirely without instruction and having no knowledge of the philosophy of language, being not even acquainted with English, his first attempts were naturally enough in the direction of the crude Indian pictograph. He set out to devise a symbol for each word of the language, and after several years of experiment, finding this an utterly hopeless task, he threw aside the thousands of characters which he had carved or scratched upon pieces of bark, and started in anew to study the construction of the language itself. By attentive observation for another long period he finally discovered that the sounds in the words used by the Cherokee in their daily conversation and their public speeches could be analyzed and classified, and that the thousands of possible words were all formed from varying combinations of hardly more than a hundred distinct syllables. Having thoroughly tested his discovery until satisfied of its correctness, he next proceeded to formulate a symbol for each syllable. For this purpose he made use of a number of characters which he found in an old English spelling book, picking out capitals, lower-case, italics, and figures, and placing them right side up or upside down, without any idea of their sound or significance as used in English (see plate v). Having thus utilized some thirty-five ready-made characters, to which must be added a dozen or more produced by modification of the same originals, he designed from his own imagination as many more as were necessary to his purpose, making eighty-five in all. The complete syllabary, as first elaborated, would have required some one hundred and fifteen characters, but after much hard study over the hissing sound in its various combinations, he hit upon the expedient of representing the sound by means of a distinct character—the exact equivalent of our letter *s*—whenever it formed the initial of a syllable. Says Gallatin, " It wanted but one step more, and to have also given a distinct character to each consonant, to reduce the whole number to sixteen, and to have had an alphabet similar to ours. In practice, however, and as applied to his own language, the superiority of Guess's alphabet is manifest, and has been fully proved by experience. You must indeed learn and remember eighty-five characters instead of twenty-five [*sic*]. But this once accomplished, the education of the pupil is completed; he can read and he is perfect in his orthography without making it the subject of a distinct study. The boy learns in a few weeks that which occupies two years of the time of ours." Says Phillips: " In my own observation Indian children will take one or two, at times several, years to master the English printed and written language, but in a few days can read and write in Cherokee. They do the latter, in fact, as soon as they learn to shape letters. As soon as they master the alphabet they have got rid of all the perplexing questions in orthography that puzzle the brains of our children. It is not too much to say that a child will learn in a month, by the same effort, as thoroughly in the language of Sequoyah, that which in ours consumes the time of our children for at least two years."

Although in theory the written Cherokee word has one letter for each syllable, the rule does not always hold good in practice, owing to the frequent elision of vowel sounds. Thus the word for "soul" is written with four letters as *a-da-nûñ-ta*, but pronounced in three syllables, *adanta*. In the same way *tsâ-lûñ-i-yu-sti* ("like tobacco," the cardinal flower) is pronounced *tsâliyustî*. There are also, as in other languages, a number of minute sound variations not indicated in the written word, so that it is necessary to have heard the language spoken in order to read with correct pronunciation. The old Upper dialect is the standard to which the alphabet has been adapted. There is no provision for the *r* of the Lower or the *sh* of the Middle dialect, each speaker usually making his own dialectic change in the reading. The letters of a word are not connected, and there is no difference between the written and the printed character. *Authorities:* Gallatin, Synopsis of the Indian Tribes, in Trans. Am. Antiq. Soc., II, 1836; Phillips, Sequoyah, in Harper's Magazine, September, 1870; Pilling, Bibliography of Iroquoian Languages (article on Guess and plate of syllabary), 1888; author's personal information.

(41) SOUTHERN GOLD FIELDS (p. 116): Almost every valuable mineral and crystal known to the manufacturer or the lapidary is found in the southern Alleghenies, although, so far as present knowledge goes, but few of these occur in paying quantities. It is probable, however, that this estimate may change with improved methods and enlarged railroad facilities. Leaving out of account the earlier operations by the Spanish, French, and English adventurers, of which mention has already been made, the first authentic account of gold finding in any of the states south of Mason and Dixon's line within what may be called the American period appears to be that given by Jefferson, writing in 1781, of a lump of ore found in Virginia, which yielded seventeen pennyweights of gold. This was probably not the earliest, however, as we find doubtful references to gold discoveries in both Carolinas before the Revolution. The first mint returns of gold were made from North Carolina in 1793, and from South Carolina in 1829, although gold is certainly known to have been found in the latter state some years earlier. The earliest gold records for the other southern states are, approximately, Georgia (near Dahlonega), 1815–1820; Alabama, 1830; Tennessee (Coco creek, Monroe county), 1831; Maryland (Montgomery county), 1849. Systematic tracing of gold belts southward from North Carolina began in 1829, and speedily resulted in the forcible eviction of the Cherokee from the gold-bearing region. Most of the precious metal was procured from placers or alluvial deposits by a simple process of digging and washing. Very little quartz mining has yet been attempted, and that usually by the crudest methods. In fact, for a long period gold working was followed as a sort of side issue to farming between crop seasons. In North Carolina prospectors obtained permission from the owners of the land to wash or dig on shares, varying from one-fourth to one-half, and the proprietor was accustomed to put his slaves to work in the same way along the creek bottoms after the crops had been safely gathered. "The dust became a considerable medium of circulation, and miners were accustomed to carry about with them quills filled with gold, and a pair of small hand scales, on which they weighed out gold at regular rates; for instance, $3\frac{1}{2}$ grains of gold was the customary equivalent of a pint of whisky." For a number of years, about 1830 and later, a man named Bechtler coined gold on his own account in North Carolina, and these coins, with Mexican silver, are said to have constituted the chief currency over a large region. A regular mint was established at Dahlonega in 1838 and maintained for some years. From 1804 to 1827 all the gold produced in the United States came from North Carolina, although the total amounted to but $110,000. The discovery of the rich deposits in California checked mining operations in the south, and the civil war brought about an almost complete suspen-

sion, from which there is hardly yet a revival. According to the best official estimates the gold production of the southern Allegheny region for the century from 1799
to 1898, inclusive, has been something over $46,000,000, distributed as follows:

North Carolina	$21,926,376
Georgia	16,658,630
South Carolina	3,961,863
Virginia, slightly in excess of	3,216,343
Alabama, slightly in excess of	437,927
Tennessee, slightly in excess of	167,405
Maryland	47,068
Total, slightly in excess of	46,415,612

Authorities: Becker, Gold Fields of the Southern Appalachians, in the Sixteenth
Annual Report United States Geological Survey, 1895; Day, Mineral Resources of
the United States, Seventeenth Annual Report United States Geological Survey,
part 3, 1896; Nitze, Gold Mining and Metallurgy in the Southern States, in North
Carolina Geological Survey Report, republished in Mineral Resources of the United
States, Twentieth Annual Report United States Geological Survey, part 6, 1899;
Lanman, Letters from the Alleghany Mountains, 1849.

(42) EXTENSION OF GEORGIA LAWS, 1830 (p. 117): "It is hereby ordained that all
the laws of Georgia are extended over the Cherokee country; that after the first day of
June, 1830, all Indians then and at that time residing in said territory, shall be liable
and subject to such laws and regulations as the legislature may hereafter prescribe;
that all laws, usages, and customs made and established and enforced in the said territory, by the said Cherokee Indians, be, and the same are hereby, on and after the
1st day of June, 1830, declared null and void; and no Indian, or descendant of an
Indian, residing within the Creek or Cherokee nations of Indians, shall be deemed
a competent witness or party to any suit in any court where a white man is a defendant."—Extract from the act passed by the Georgia legislature on December 20, 1828,
"to add the territory within this state and occupied by the Cherokee Indians to
the counties of DeKalb et al., and to extend the laws of this state over the same."
Authorities: Drake, Indians, p. 439, ed. 1880; Royce, Cherokee Nation of Indians, in
Fifth Ann. Rep. Bureau of Ethnology, p. 260, 1888.

(43) REMOVAL FORTS, 1838 (p. 130): For collecting the Cherokee preparatory to
the Removal, the following stockade forts were built: In North Carolina, Fort Lind-
say, on the south side of the Tennessee river at the junction of Nantahala, in Swain
county; Fort Scott, at Aquone, farther up Nantahala river, in Macon county; Fort
Montgomery, at Robbinsville, in Graham county; Fort Hembrie, at Hayesville, in
Clay county; Fort Delaney, at Valleytown, in Cherokee county; Fort Butler, at
Murphy, in the same county. In Georgia, Fort Scudder, on Frogtown creek, north
of Dahlonega, in Lumpkin county; Fort Gilmer, near Ellijay, in Gilmer county;
Fort Coosawatee, in Murray county; Fort Talking-rock, near Jasper, in Pickens
county; Fort Buffington, near Canton, in Cherokee county. In Tennessee, Fort
Cass, at Calhoun, on Hiwassee river, in McMinn county. In Alabama, Fort Turkeytown, on Coosa river, at Center, in Cherokee county. *Authority:* Author's personal
information.

(44) McNAIR'S GRAVE, (p. 132): Just inside the Tennessee line, where the Conasauga river bends again into Georgia, is a stone-walled grave, with a slab, on which
is an epitaph which tells its own story of the Removal heartbreak. McNair was a
white man, prominent in the Cherokee Nation, whose wife was a daughter of the
chief, Vann, who welcomed the Moravian missionaries and gave his own house for
their use. The date shows that she died while the Removal was in progress, possibly

while waiting in the stockade camp. The inscription, with details, is given from information kindly furnished by Mr D. K. Dunn of Conasauga, Tennessee, in a letter dated August 16, 1890:

"Sacred to the memory of David and Delilah A. McNair, who departed this life, the former on the 15th of August, 1836, and the latter on the 30th of November, 1838. Their children, being members of the Cherokee Nation and having to go with their people to the West, do leave this monument, not only to show their regard for their parents, but to guard their sacred ashes against the unhallowed intrusion of the white man."

(45) PRESIDENT SAMUEL HOUSTON, (p. 145): This remarkable man was born in Rockbridge county, Virginia, March 2, 1793, and died at Huntsville, Texas, July 25, 1863. Of strangely versatile, but forceful, character, he occupies a unique position in American history, combining in a wonderful degree the rough manhood of the pioneer, the eccentric vanity of the Indian, the stern dignity of the soldier, the genius of the statesman, and withal the high chivalry of a knight of the olden time. His erratic career has been the subject of much cheap romancing, but the simple facts are of sufficient interest in themselves without the aid of fictitious embellishment. To the Cherokee, whom he loved so well, he was known as Kâ'lanû, "The Raven," an old war title in the tribe.

His father having died when the boy was nine years old, his widowed mother removed with him to Tennessee, opposite the territory of the Cherokee, whose boundary was then the Tennessee river. Here he worked on the farm, attending school at intervals; but, being of adventurous disposition, he left home when sixteen years old, and, crossing over the river, joined the Cherokee, among whom he soon became a great favorite, being adopted into the family of Chief Jolly, from whom the island at the mouth of Hiwassee takes its name. After three years of this life, during which time he wore the Indian dress and learned the Indian language, he returned to civilization and enlisted as a private soldier under Jackson in the Creek war. He soon attracted favorable notice and was promoted to the rank of ensign. By striking bravery at the bloody battle of Horseshoe bend, where he scaled the breastworks with an arrow in his thigh and led his men into the thick of the enemy, he won the lasting friendship of Jackson, who made him a lieutenant, although he was then barely twenty-one. He continued in the army after the war, serving for a time as subagent for the Cherokee at Jackson's request, until the summer of 1818, when he resigned on account of some criticism by Calhoun, then Secretary of War. An official investigation, held at his demand, resulted in his exoneration.

Removing to Nashville, he began the study of law, and, being shortly afterward admitted to the bar, set up in practice at Lebanon. Within five years he was successively district attorney and adjutant-general and major-general of state troops. In 1823 he was elected to Congress, serving two terms, at the end of which, in 1827, he was elected governor of Tennessee by an overwhelming majority, being then thirty-four years of age. Shortly before this time he had fought and wounded General White in a duel. In January, 1829, he married a young lady residing near Nashville, but two months later, without a word of explanation to any outsider, he left her, resigned his governorship and other official dignities, and left the state forever, to rejoin his old friends, the Cherokee, in the West. For years the reason for this strange conduct was a secret, and Houston himself always refused to talk of it, but it is now understood to have been due to the fact that his wife admitted to him that she loved another and had only been induced to marry him by the over-persuasions of her parents.

From Tennessee he went to Indian Territory, whither a large part of the Cherokee had already removed, and once more took up his residence near Chief Jolly, who was now the principal chief of the western Cherokee. The great disappointment which seemed to have blighted his life at its brightest was heavy at his heart, and he sought forgetfulness in drink to such an extent that for a time his manhood seemed to have departed, notwithstanding which, such was his force of character and his past reputation, he retained his hold upon the affections of the Cherokee and his standing with the officers and their families at the neighboring posts of Fort Smith, Fort Gibson, and Fort Coffee. In the meantime his former wife in Tennessee had obtained a divorce, and Houston being thus free once more soon after married Talihina, the youngest daughter of a prominent mixed-blood Cherokee named Rogers, who resided near Fort Gibson. She was the niece of Houston's adopted father, Chief Jolly, and he had known her when a boy in the old Nation. Being a beautiful girl, and educated above her surroundings, she became a welcome guest wherever her husband was received. He started a trading store near Webbers Falls, but continued in his dissipated habits until recalled to his senses by the outcome of a drunken affray in which he assaulted his adopted father, the old chief, and was himself felled to the ground unconscious. Upon recovery from his injuries he made a public apology for his conduct and thenceforward led a sober life.

In 1832 he visited Washington in the interest of the western Cherokee, calling in Indian costume upon President Jackson, who received him with old-time friendship. Being accused while there of connection with a fraudulent Indian contract, he administered a severe beating to his accuser, a member of Congress. For this he was fined $500 and reprimanded by the bar of the House, but Jackson remitted the fine. Soon after his return to the West he removed to Texas to take part in the agitation just started against Mexican rule. He was a member of the convention which adopted a separate constitution for Texas in 1833, and two years later aided in forming a provisional government, and was elected commander-in-chief to organize the new militia. In 1836 he was a member of the convention which declared the independence of Texas. At the battle of San Jacinto in April of that year he defeated with 750 men Santa Ana's army of 1,800, inflicting upon the Mexicans the terrible loss of 630 killed and 730 prisoners, among whom was Santa Ana himself. Houston received a severe wound in the engagement. In the autumn of the same year he was elected first president of the republic of Texas, receiving more than four-fifths of the votes cast. He served two years and retired at the end of his term, leaving the country on good terms with both Mexico and the Indian tribes, and with its notes at par. He was immediately elected to the Texas congress and served in that capacity until 1841, when he was reelected president. It was during these years that he made his steadfast fight in behalf of the Texas Cherokee, as is narrated elsewhere, supporting their cause without wavering, at the risk of his own popularity and position. He frequently declared that no treaty made and carried out in good faith had ever been violated by Indians. His Cherokee wife having died some time before, he was again married in 1840, this time to a lady from Alabama, who exercised over him a restraining and ennobling influence through the stormy vicissitudes of his eventful life. In June, 1842, he vetoed a bill making him dictator for the purpose of resisting a threatened invasion from Mexico.

On December 29, 1845, Texas was admitted to the Union, and in the following March Houston was elected to the Senate, where he served continuously until 1859, when he resigned to take his seat as governor, to which position he had just been elected. From 1852 to 1860 his name was three times presented before national presidential nominating conventions, the last time receiving 57 votes. He had taken issue with the Democratic majority throughout his term in the Senate, and when Texas passed the secession ordinance in February, 1861, being an uncompromising Union man, he refused to take the oath of allegiance to the Confederacy and was accordingly deposed from the office of governor, declining the proffered aid of federal troops to keep him in his seat. Unwilling either to fight against the Union or to take sides against his friends, he held aloof from the great struggle, and remained in silent retirement until his death, two years later. No other man in American history has left such a record of continuous election to high office while steadily holding to his own convictions in the face of strong popular opposition. *Authorities:* Appleton's Cyclopædia of American Biography, 1894; Bonnell, Texas, 1840; Thrall, Texas, 1876; Lossing, Field Book of the War of 1812, 1869; author's personal information; various periodical and newspaper articles.

(46) CHIEF JOHN ROSS (p. 151): This great chief of the Cherokee, whose name is inseparable from their history, was himself but one-eighth of Indian blood and showed little of the Indian features, his father, Daniel Ross, having emigrated from Scotland before the Revolution and married a quarter-blood Cherokee woman whose father, John McDonald, was also from Scotland. He was born at or near the family residence at Rossville, Georgia just across the line from Chattanooga, Tennessee. As a boy, he was known among the Cherokee as Tsan-usdi′, "Little John," but after arriving at manhood was called Guwi′sguwĭ′, the name of a rare migratory bird, of large size and white or grayish plumage, said to have appeared formerly at long intervals in the old Cherokee country. It may have been the egret or the swan. He was educated at Kingston, Tennessee, and began his public career when barely nineteen years of age. His first wife, a full-blood Cherokee woman, died in consequence of the hardships of the Removal while on the western march and was buried at Little Rock, Arkansas. Some years later he married again, this time to a Miss Stapler of Wilmington, Delaware, the marriage taking place in Philadelphia (author's personal information from Mr Allen Ross, son of John Ross; see also Meredith, "The Cherokees," in the Five Civilized Tribes, Extra Bulletin Eleventh Census, 1894.) Cooweescoowee district of the Cherokee Nation west has been named in his honor. The following biographic facts are taken from the panegyric in his honor, passed by the national council of the Cherokee, on hearing of his death, "as feebly expressive of the loss they have sustained."

John Ross was born October 3, 1790, and died in the city of Washington, August 1, 1866, in the seventy-sixth year of his age. His official career began in 1809, when he was intrusted by Agent Return Meigs with an important mission to the Arkansas Cherokee. From that time until the close of his life, with the exception of two or three years in the earlier part, he was in the constant service of his people, "furnishing an instance of confidence on their part and fidelity on his which has never been surpassed in the annals of history." In the war of 1813–14 against the Creeks he was adjutant of the Cherokee regiment which cooperated with General Jackson, and was present at the battle of the Horseshoe, where the Cherokee, under Colonel Morgan, of Tennessee, rendered distinguished service. In 1817 he was elected a member of the national committee of the Cherokee council. The first duty assigned him was to prepare a reply to the United States commissioners who were present for the purpose of negotiating with the Cherokee for their lands east of the Mississippi, in firm resistance to which he was destined, a few years later, to test the power of truth and to attain a reputation of no ordinary character. In 1819, October 26, his name first appears on the statute book of the Cherokee Nation as president of the national committee, and is attached to an ordinance which looked to the improvement of the Cherokee people, providing for the introduction into the Nation of school-masters, blacksmiths, mechanics, and others. He continued to occupy that position till 1826. In 1827 he was associate chief with William Hicks, and president of the convention which adopted the constitution of that year. That constitution, it is believed, is the first effort at a regular government, with distinct branches and powers defined, ever made and carried into effect by any of the Indians of North America. From 1828 until the removal west, he was principal chief of the eastern Cherokee, and from 1839 to the time of his death, principal chief of the united Cherokee Nation.

In regard to the long contest which culminated in the Removal, the resolutions declare that "The Cherokees, with John Ross at their head, alone with their treaties, achieved a recognition of their rights, but they were powerless to enforce them. They were compelled to yield, but not until the struggle had developed the highest qualities of patience, fortitude, and tenacity of right and purpose on their part, as well as that of their chief. The same may be said of their course after their removal to this country, and which resulted in the reunion of the eastern and western Cherokees as one people and in the adoption of the present constitution."

Concerning the events of the civil war and the official attempt to depose Ross from his authority, they state that these occurrences, with many others in their trying history as a people, are confidently committed to the future page of the historian. "It is enough to know that the treaty negotiated at Washington in 1866 bore the full and just recognition of John Ross' name as principal chief of the Cherokee nation."

The summing up of the panegyric is a splendid tribute to a splendid manhood:

"Blessed with a fine constitution and a vigorous mind, John Ross had the physical ability to follow the path of duty wherever it led. No danger appalled him. He never faltered in supporting what he believed to be right, but clung to it with a steadiness of purpose which alone could have sprung from the clearest convictions of rectitude. He never sacrificed the interests of his nation to expediency. He never lost sight of the welfare of the people. For them he labored daily for a long life, and upon them he bestowed his last expressed thoughts. A friend of law, he obeyed it; a friend of education, he faithfully encouraged schools throughout the country, and spent liberally his means in conferring it upon others. Given to hospitality, none ever hungered around his door. A professor of the Christian religion, he practiced its precepts. His works are inseparable from the history of the Cherokee people for nearly half a century, while his example in the daily walks of life will linger in the future and whisper words of hope, temperance, and charity in the years of posterity."

Resolutions were also passed for bringing his body from Washington at the expense of the Cherokee Nation and providing for suitable obsequies, in order "that his remains should rest among those he so long served" (Resolutions in honor of John Ross, in Laws of the Cherokee Nation, 1869).

(47) THE KETOOWAH SOCIETY (p. 156): This Cherokee secret society, which has recently achieved some newspaper prominence by its championship of Cherokee autonomy, derives its name—properly Kĭtu′hwă, but commonly spelled Ketoowah in English print—from the ancient town in the old Nation which formed the nucleus of the most conservative element of the tribe and sometimes gave a name to the Nation itself (see Kĭtu′hwagĭ, under Tribal Synonyms). A strong band of comradeship, if not a regular society organization, appears to have existed among the warriors and leading men of the various settlements of the Kituhwa district from a remote period, so that the name is even now used in councils as indicative of genuine Cherokee feeling in its highest patriotic form. When, some years ago, delegates from the western Nation visited the East Cherokee to invite them to join their more prosperous brethren beyond the Mississippi, the speaker for the delegates expressed their fraternal feeling for their separated kinsmen by saying in his opening speech, "We are all Kituhwa people" (Ani′-Kĭtu′hwagĭ). The Ketoowah society in the Cherokee Nation west was organized shortly before the civil war by John B. Jones, son of the missionary, Evan Jones, and an adopted citizen of the Nation, as a secret society for the ostensible purpose of cultivating a national feeling among the fullbloods, in opposition to the innovating tendencies of the mixed-blood element. The real purpose was to counteract the influence of the "Blue Lodge" and other secret secessionist organizations among the wealthier slave-holding classes, made up chiefly of mixed-bloods and whites. It extended to the Creeks, and its members in both tribes rendered good service to the Union cause throughout the war. They were frequently known as "Pin Indians," for a reason explained below. Since the close of the great struggle the society has distinguished itself by its determined opposition

to every scheme looking to the curtailment or destruction of Cherokee national self-government.

The following account of the society was written shortly after the close of the civil war:

"Those Cherokees who were loyal to the Union combined in a secret organization for self-protection, assuming the designation of the Ketoowha society, which name was soon merged in that of "Pins." The Pins were so styled because of a peculiar manner they adopted of wearing a pin. The symbol was discovered by their enemies, who applied the term in derision; but it was accepted by this loyal league, and has almost superseded the designation which its members first assumed. The Pin organization originated among the members of the Baptist congregation at Peavine, Going-snake district, in the Cherokee nation. In a short time the society counted nearly three thousand members, and had commenced proselytizing the Creeks, when the rebellion, against which it was arming, preventing its further extension, the poor Creeks having been driven into Kansas by the rebels of the Golden Circle. During the war the Pins rendered services to the Union cause in many bloody encounters, as has been acknowledged by our generals. It was distinctly an anti-slavery organization. The slave-holding Cherokees, who constituted the wealthy and more intelligent class, naturally allied themselves with the South, while loyal Cherokees became more and more opposed to slavery. This was shown very clearly when the loyalists first met in convention, in February, 1863. They not only abolished slavery unconditionally and forever, before any slave state made a movement toward emancipation, but made any attempts at enslaving a grave misdemeanor.

The secret signs of the Pins were a peculiar way of touching the hat as a salutation, particularly when they were too far apart for recognition in other ways. They had a peculiar mode of taking hold of the lapel of the coat, first drawing it away from the body, and then giving it a motion as though wrapping it around the heart. During the war a portion of them were forced into the rebellion, but quickly rebelled against General Cooper, who was placed over them, and when they fought against that general, at Bird Creek, they wore a bit of corn-husk, split into strips, tied in their hair. In the night when two Pins met, and one asked the other, 'Who are you?' the reply or pass was, 'Tahlequah—who are you?' The response was, 'I am Ketoowha's son.'"—Dr D. J. MacGowan, Indian Secret Societies, in Historical Magazine, x, 1866.

(48) FAREWELL ADDRESS OF LLOYD WELCH (p. 175): In the sad and eventful history of the Cherokee their gifted leaders, frequently of white ancestry, have oftentimes spoken to the world with eloquent words of appeal, of protest, or of acknowledgment, but never more eloquently than in the last, farewell of Chief Lloyd Welch to the eastern band, as he felt the end draw near (leaflet, MacGowan, Chattanooga [n. d., 1880]):

"*To the Chairman and Council of the Eastern Band of Cherokees:*

"My Brothers: It becomes my imperative duty to bid you an affectionate farewell, and resign into your hands the trust you so generously confided to my keeping, principal chief of the Eastern Band. It is with great solicitude and anxiety for your welfare that I am constrained to take this course. But the inexorable laws of nature, and the rapid decline of my health, admonish me that soon, very soon, I will have passed from earth, my body consigned to the tomb, my spirit to God who gave it, in that happy home in the beyond, where there is no sickness, no sorrow, no pain, no death, but one eternal joy and happiness forever more.

"The only regret that I feel for thus being so soon called from among you, at the meridian of manhood, when hope is sweet, is the great anxiety I have to serve and benefit my race. For this I have studied and labored for the past ten years of my life, to secure to my brothers equal justice from their brothers of the west and the United States, and that you would no longer be hewers of wood and drawers of water, but assume that proud position among the civilized nations of the earth intended by the Creator that we should occupy, and which in the near future you will take or be exterminated. When you become educated, as a natural consequence you will become more intelligent, sober, industrious, and prosperous.

"It has been the aim of my life, the chief object, to serve my race faithfully, honestly, and to the best of my ability. How well I have succeeded I will leave to history and your magnanimity to decide, trusting an all-wise and just God to guide and protect you in the future, as He will do all things well. We may fail when on earth to see the goodness and wisdom of God in removing from us our best and most useful men, but when we have crossed over on the other shore to our happy and eternal home in the far beyond then our eyes will be opened and we will be enabled to see and realize the goodness and mercy of God in thus afflicting us while here on earth, and will be enabled more fully to praise God, from whom all blessings come.

"I hope that when you come to select one from among you to take the responsible position of principal chief of your band you will lay aside all personal considerations and select one in every respect competent, without stain on his fair fame, a pure, noble, honest, man—one who loves God and all that is pure—with intellect sufficient to know your rights, independence and nerve to defend them. Should you be thus fortunate in making your choice, all will be well. It has been truthfully said that 'when the righteous rule the people rejoice, but when the wicked rule the people mourn.'

"I am satisfied that you have among you many who are fully competent of the task. If I was satisfied it was your wish and for the good of my brothers I might mention some of them, but think it best to leave you in the hands of an all-wise God, who does all things right, to guide and direct you aright.

"And now, my brothers, in taking perhaps my last farewell on earth I do pray God that you may so conduct yourselves while here on earth that when the last sad rite is performed by loved friends we may compose one unbroken family above in that celestial city from whose bourne no traveler has ever returned to describe the beauty, grandeur, and happiness of the heaven prepared for the faithful by God himself beyond the sky. And again, my brothers, permit me to bid you a fond, but perhaps a last, farewell on earth, until we meet again where parting is never known and friends meet to part no more forever.

"L. R. WELCH,
"*Principal Chief Eastern Band Cherokee Indians.*

"Witness:
"SAMUEL W. DAVIDSON.
"B. B. MERONY."

(49) STATUS OF EASTERN BAND (p. 180): For some reason all authorities who have hitherto discussed the status of the eastern band of Cherokee seem to have been entirely unaware of the enactment of the supplementary articles to the treaty of New Echota, by which all preemption and reservation rights granted under the twelfth article were canceled. Thus, in the Cherokee case of "The United States *et al* against D. T. Boyd *et al*," we find the United States circuit judge quoting the twelfth article in its original form as a basis for argument, while his associate judge says: "Their forefathers availed themselves of a provision in the treaty of New Echota and remained in the state of North Carolina," etc. (Report of Indian Commissioner for 1895, pp. 633–635, 1896). The truth is that the treaty as ratified with its supplementary articles canceled the residence right of every Cherokee east of the Mississippi, and it was not until thirty years afterwards that North Carolina finally gave assurance that the eastern band would be permitted to remain within her borders.

The twelfth article of the new Echota treaty of December 29, 1835, provides for a pro rata apportionment to such Cherokee as desire to remain in the East, and continues: "Such heads of Cherokee families as are desirous to reside within the states of North Carolina, Tennessee, and Alabama, subject to the laws of the same, and who are qualified or calculated to become useful citizens, shall be entitled, on the certificate of the commissioners, to a preemption right to one hundred and sixty acres of land, or one quarter section, at the minimum Congress price, so as to include the present buildings or improvements of those who now reside there; and such as do not live there at present shall be permitted to locate within two years any lands not already occupied by persons entitled to preemption privilege under this treaty," etc.   Article 13 defines terms with reference to individual reservations granted under former treaties.   The preamble to the supplementary articles agreed upon on March 1, 1836, recites that, "Whereas the President of the United States has expressed his determination not to allow any preemptions or reservations, his desire being that the whole Cherokee people should remove together and establish themselves in the country provided for them west of the Mississippi river (article 1): It is therefore agreed that all preemption rights and reservations provided for in articles 12 and 13 shall be, and are hereby, relinquished and declared void."   The treaty, in this shape, was ratified on May 23, 1836 (see Indian Treaties, pp. 633-648, 1837).

SWIMMER (A'YÛṄ'INĬ)

JOHN AX (ITAGÛ′NÛHĬ)

III—STORIES AND STORY TELLERS

Cherokee myths may be roughly classified as sacred myths, animal stories, local legends, and historical traditions. To the first class belong the genesis stories, dealing with the creation of the world, the nature of the heavenly bodies and elemental forces, the origin of life and death, the spirit world and the invisible beings, the ancient monsters, and the hero-gods. It is almost certain that most of the myths of this class are but disjointed fragments of an original complete genesis and migration legend, which is now lost. With nearly every tribe that has been studied we find such a sacred legend, preserved by the priests of the tradition, who alone are privileged to recite and explain it, and dealing with the origin and wanderings of the people from the beginning of the world to the final settlement of the tribe in its home territory. Among the best examples of such genesis traditions are those recorded in the Walam Olum of the Delawares and Matthews' Navaho Origin Legend. Others may be found in Cusick's History of the Six Nations, Gatschet's Creek Migration Legend, and the author's Jicarilla Genesis.[1] The Cheyenne, Arapaho, and other plains tribes are known to have similar genesis myths.

The former existence of such a national legend among the Cherokee is confirmed by Haywood, writing in 1823, who states on information obtained from a principal man in the tribe that they had once a long oration, then nearly forgotten, which recounted the history of their wanderings from the time when they had been first placed upon the earth by some superior power from above. Up to about the middle of the last century this tradition was still recited at the annual Greencorn dance.[2] Unlike most Indians the Cherokee are not conservative, and even before the Revolution had so far lost their primitive customs from contact with the whites that Adair, in 1775, calls them a nest of apostate hornets who for more than thirty years had been fast degenerating.[3] Whatever it may have been, their national legend is now lost forever. The secret organizations that must have existed formerly among the priesthood have also disappeared, and each man now works independently according to his individual gifts and knowledge.

The sacred myths were not for every one, but only those might hear who observed the proper form and ceremony. When John Ax and

---

[1] American Anthropologist, vol. xi, July, 1898. [3] Adair, American Indians, p. 81, 1775.
[2] See page 20.

other old men were boys, now some eighty years ago, the myth-keepers and priests were accustomed to meet together at night in the âsĭ, or low-built log sleeping house, to recite the traditions and discuss their secret knowledge.   At times those who desired instruction from an adept in the sacred lore of the tribe met him by appointment in the âsĭ, where they sat up all night talking, with only the light of a small fire burning in the middle of the floor.   At daybreak the whole party went down to the running stream, where the pupils or hearers of the myths stripped themselves, and were scratched upon their naked skin with a bone-tooth comb in the hands of the priest, after which they waded out, facing the rising sun, and dipped seven times under the water, while the priest recited prayers upon the bank.   This purifica-tory rite, observed more than a century ago by Adair, is also a part of the ceremonial of the ballplay, the Green-corn dance, and, in fact, every important ritual performance.   Before beginning one of the stories of the sacred class the informant would sometimes suggest jokingly that the author first submit to being scratched and "go to water."

As a special privilege a boy was sometimes admitted to the âsĭ on such occasions, to tend the fire, and thus had the opportunity to listen to the stories and learn something of the secret rites.   In this way John Ax gained much of his knowledge, although he does not claim to be an adept.   As he describes it, the fire intended to heat the room—for the nights are cold in the Cherokee mountains—was built upon the ground in the center of the small house, which was not high enough to permit a standing position, while the occupants sat in a circle around it.   In front of the fire was placed a large flat rock, and near it a pile of pine knots or splints.   When the fire had burned down to a bed of coals, the boy lighted one or two of the pine knots and laid them upon the rock, where they blazed with a bright light until nearly consumed, when others were laid upon them, and so on until daybreak.

Sometimes the pine splints were set up crosswise, thus, ✕✕✕✕, in a circle around the fire, with a break at the eastern side.   They were then lighted from one end and burned gradually around the circle, fresh splints being set up behind as those in front were consumed. Lawson describes this identical custom as witnessed at a dance among the Waxhaw, on Catawba river, in 1701:

Now, to return to our state house, whither we were invited by the grandees.   As soon as we came into it, they placed our Englishmen near the king, it being my for-tune to sit next him, having his great general or war captain on my other hand. The house is as dark as a dungeon, and as hot as one of the Dutch stoves in Holland. They had made a circular fire of split canes in the middle of the house, it was one man's employment to add more split reeds to the one end as it consumed at the other, there being a small vacancy left to supply it with fuel.[1]

---

[1] Lawson, Carolina, 67–68, reprint 1860.

To the second class belong the shorter animal myths, which have lost whatever sacred character they may once have had, and are told now merely as humorous explanations of certain animal peculiarities. While the sacred myths have a constant bearing upon formulistic prayers and observances, it is only in rare instances that any rite or custom is based upon an animal myth. Moreover, the sacred myths are known as a rule only to the professional priests or conjurers, while the shorter animal stories are more or less familiar to nearly every-one and are found in almost identical form among Cherokee, Creeks, and other southern tribes.

The animals of the Cherokee myths, like the traditional hero-gods, were larger and of more perfect type than their present representa-tives. They had chiefs, councils, and townhouses, mingled with human kind upon terms of perfect equality and spoke the same language. In some unexplained manner they finally left this lower world and ascended to Galûñ'lătĭ, the world above, where they still exist. The removal was not simultaneous, but each animal chose his own time. The animals that we know, small in size and poor in intel-lect, came upon the earth later, and are not the descendants of the mythic animals, but only weak imitations. In one or two special cases, however, the present creature is the descendant of a former monster. Trees and plants also were alive and could talk in the old days, and had their place in council, but do not figure prominently in the myths.

Each animal had his appointed station and duty. Thus, the Walâ'sĭ frog was the marshal and leader in the council, while the Rabbit was the messenger to carry all public announcements, and usually led the dance besides. He was also the great trickster and mischief maker, a character which he bears in eastern and southern Indian myth gener-ally, as well as in the southern negro stories. The bear figures as having been originally a man, with human form and nature.

As with other tribes and countries, almost every prominent rock and mountain, every deep bend in the river, in the old Cherokee country has its accompanying legend. It may be a little story that can be told in a paragraph, to account for some natural feature, or it may be one chapter of a myth that has its sequel in a mountain a hundred miles away. As is usual when a people has lived for a long time in the same country, nearly every important myth is localized, thus assuming more definite character.

There is the usual number of anecdotes and stories of personal adventure, some of them irredeemably vulgar, but historical traditions are strangely wanting. The authentic records of unlettered peoples are short at best, seldom going back much farther than the memories of their oldest men; and although the Cherokee have been the most important of the southern tribes, making wars and treaties for three centuries with Spanish, English, French, and Americans, Iroquois,

Shawano, Catawba, and Creeks, there is little evidence of the fact in their traditions. This condition may be due in part to the temper of the Cherokee mind, which, as has been already stated, is accustomed to look forward to new things rather than to dwell upon the past. The first Cherokee war, with its stories of Âganstâ′ta and Ătă-gûl′kălû′, is absolutely forgotten. Of the long Revolutionary struggle they have hardly a recollection, although they were constantly fighting throughout the whole period and for several years after, and at one time were brought to the verge of ruin by four concerted expeditions, which ravaged their country simultaneously from different directions and destroyed almost every one of their towns. Even the Creek war, in which many of their warriors took a prominent part, was already nearly forgotten some years ago. Beyond a few stories of encounters with the Shawano and Iroquois there is hardly anything that can be called history until well within the present century.

With some tribes the winter season and the night are the time for telling stories, but to the Cherokee all times are alike. As our grandmothers begin, "Once upon a time," so the Cherokee story-teller introduces his narrative by saying: "This is what the old men told me when I was a boy."

Not all tell the same stories, for in tribal lore, as in all other sorts of knowledge, we find specialists. Some common minds take note only of common things—little stories of the rabbit, the terrapin, and the others, told to point a joke or amuse a child. Others dwell upon the wonderful and supernatural—Tsul′kălû′, Tsuwe′năhĭ, and the Thunderers—and those sacred things to be told only with prayer and purification. Then, again, there are still a few old warriors who live in the memory of heroic days when there were wars with the Seneca and the Shawano, and these men are the historians of the tribe and the conservators of its antiquities.

The question of the origin of myths is one which affords abundant opportunity for ingenious theories in the absence of any possibility of proof. Those of the Cherokee are too far broken down ever to be woven together again into any long-connected origin legend, such as we find with some tribes, although a few still exhibit a certain sequence which indicates that they once formed component parts of a cycle. From the prominence of the rabbit in the animal stories, as well as in those found among the southern negroes, an effort has been made to establish for them a negro origin, regardless of the fact that the rabbit—the Great White Rabbit—is the hero-god, trickster, and wonderworker of all the tribes east of the Mississippi from Hudson bay to the Gulf. In European folklore also the rabbit is regarded as something uncanny and half-supernatural, and even in far-off Korea he is the central figure in the animal myths. Just why this should be so is a question that may be left to the theorist to decide. Among the

Algonquian tribes the name, *wabos,* seems to have been confounded with that of the dawn, *waban,* so that the Great White Rabbit is really the incarnation of the eastern dawn that brings light and life and drives away the dark shadows which have held the world in chains. The animal itself seems to be regarded by the Indians as the fitting type of defenseless weakness protected and made safe by constantly alert vigilance, and with a disposition, moreover, for turning up at unexpected moments. The same characteristics would appeal as strongly to the primitive mind of the negro. The very expression which Harris puts into the mouth of Uncle Remus, "In dem days Brer Rabbit en his fambly wuz at the head er de gang w'en enny racket wus en hand,"[1] was paraphrased in the Cherokee language by Suyeta in introducing his first rabbit story: " *Tsi'stu wuliga'nătûtûñ' une'gutsătû' gese'ĭ*—the Rabbit was the leader of them all in mischief." The expression struck the author so forcibly that the words were recorded as spoken.

In regard to the contact between the two races, by which such stories could be borrowed from one by the other, it is not commonly known that in all the southern colonies Indian slaves were bought and sold and kept in servitude and worked in the fields side by side with negroes up to the time of the Revolution. Not to go back to the Spanish period, when such things were the order of the day, we find the Cherokee as early as 1693 complaining that their people were being kidnaped by slave hunters. Hundreds of captured Tuscarora and nearly the whole tribe of the Appalachee were distributed as slaves among the Carolina colonists in the early part of the eighteenth century, while the Natchez and others shared a similar fate in Louisiana, and as late at least as 1776 Cherokee prisoners of war were still sold to the highest bidder for the same purpose. At one time it was charged against the governor of South Carolina that he was provoking a general Indian war by his encouragement of slave hunts. Furthermore, as the coast tribes dwindled they were compelled to associate and intermarry with the negroes until they finally lost their identity and were classed with that race, so that a considerable proportion of the blood of the southern negroes is unquestionably Indian.

The negro, with his genius for imitation and his love for stories, especially of the comic variety, must undoubtedly have absorbed much from the Indian in this way, while on the other hand the Indian, with his pride of conservatism and his contempt for a subject race, would have taken but little from the negro, and that little could not easily have found its way back to the free tribes. Some of these animal stories are common to widely separated tribes among whom there can be no suspicion of negro influences. Thus the famous "tar baby" story has variants, not only among the Cherokee, but also in New

---

[1] Harris, J. C., Uncle Remus, His Songs and his Sayings, p. 29; New York, 1886.

Mexico, Washington, and southern Alaska—wherever, in fact, the piñon or the pine supplies enough gum to be molded into a ball for Indian uses—while the incident of the Rabbit dining the Bear is found with nearly every tribe from Nova Scotia to the Pacific. The idea that such stories are necessarily of negro origin is due largely to the common but mistaken notion that the Indian has no sense of humor.

In many cases it is not necessary to assume borrowing from either side, the myths being such as would naturally spring up in any part of the world among primitive people accustomed to observe the characteristics of animals, which their religious system regarded as differing in no essential from human kind, save only in outward form. Thus in Europe and America the terrapin has been accepted as the type of plodding slowness, while the rabbit, with his sudden dash, or the deer with his bounding stride, is the type of speed. What more natural than that the story-teller should set one to race against the other, with the victory in favor of the patient striver against the self-confident boaster? The idea of a hungry wolf or other beast of prey luring his victims by the promise of a new song or dance, during which they must close their eyes, is also one that would easily occur among any primitive people whose chief pastime is dancing.[1]

On the other hand, such a conception as that of Flint and the Rabbit could only be the outgrowth of a special cosmogonic theology, though now indeed broken and degraded, and it is probable that many myths told now only for amusement are really worn down fragments of ancient sacred traditions. Thus the story just noted appears in a different dress among the Iroquois as a part of their great creation myth. The Cherokee being a detached tribe of the Iroquois, we may expect to find among the latter, if it be not already too late, the explanation and more perfect statement of some things which are obscure in the Cherokee myths. It must not be forgotten, however, that the Indian, like other men, does some things for simple amusement, and it is useless to look for occult meanings where none exist.

Except as to the local traditions and a few others which are obviously the direct outgrowth of Cherokee conditions, it is impossible to fix a definite starting point for the myths. It would be unwise to assert that even the majority of them originated within the tribe. The Cherokee have strains of Creek, Catawba, Uchee, Natchez, Iroquois, Osage, and Shawano blood, and such admixture implies contact more or less intimate and continued. Indians are great wanderers, and a

---

[1] For a presentation of the African and European argument see Harris, Nights with Uncle Remus, introduction, 1883; and Uncle Remus, His Songs and His Sayings, introduction, 1886; Gerber, Uncle Remus Traced to the Old World, in Journal of American Folklore, VI, p. 23, October, 1893. In regard to tribal dissemination of myths see Boas, Dissemination of Tales among the Natives of North America, in Journal of American Folklore, IV, p. 12, January, 1891; The Growth of Indian Mythologies, in the same journal, IX, p. 32, January 1896; Northern Elements in the Mythology of the Navaho, in American Anthropologist, X, p. 11, November, 1897; introduction to Teit's Traditions of the Thompson River Indians, 1898. Dr Boas has probably devoted more study to the subject than any other anthropologist, and his personal observations include tribes from the Arctic regions to the Columbia.

myth can travel as far as a redstone pipe or a string of wampum. It was customary, as it still is to a limited extent in the West, for large parties, sometimes even a whole band or village, to make long visits to other tribes, dancing, feasting, trading, and exchanging stories with their friends for weeks or months at a time, with the expectation that their hosts would return the visit within the next summer. Regular trade routes crossed the continent from east to west and from north to south, and when the subject has been fully investigated it will be found that this intertribal commerce was as constant and well recognized a part of Indian life as is our own railroad traffic today. The very existence of a trade jargon or a sign language is proof of intertribal relations over wide areas. Their political alliances also were often far-reaching, for Pontiac welded into a warlike confederacy all the tribes from the Atlantic border to the head of the Mississippi, while the emissaries of the Shawano prophet carried the story of his revelations throughout the whole region from the Florida coast to the Saskatchewan.

In view of these facts it is as useless to attempt to trace the origin of every myth as to claim a Cherokee authorship for them all. From what we know of the character of the Shawano, their tendency toward the ceremonial and the mystic, and their close relations with the Cherokee, it may be inferred that some of the myths originated with that tribe. We should naturally expect also to find close correspondence with the myths of the Creeks and other southern tribes within the former area of the Mobilian trade language. The localization at home of all the more important myths indicates a long residence in the country. As the majority of those here given belong to the half dozen counties still familiar to the East Cherokee, we may guess how many attached to the ancient territory of the tribe are now irrecoverably lost.

Contact with the white race seems to have produced very little impression on the tribal mythology, and not more than three or four stories current among the Cherokee can be assigned to a Caucasian source. These have not been reproduced here, for the reason that they are plainly European, and the author has chosen not to follow the example of some collectors who have assumed that every tale told in an Indina language is necessarily an Indian story. Scores recorded in collections from the North and West are nothing more than variants from the celebrated Hausmärchen, as told by French trappers and voyageurs to their Indian campmates and halfbreed children. It might perhaps be thought that missionary influence would be evident in the genesis tradition, but such is not the case. The Bible story kills the Indian tradition, and there is no amalgamation. It is hardly necessary to say that stories of a great fish which swallows a man and of a great flood

which destroys a people are found the world over. The supposed
Cherokee hero-god, Wâsi, described by one writer as so remarkably
resembling the great Hebrew lawgiver is in fact that great teacher
himself, Wâsi being the Cherokee approximate for Moses, and the
good missionary who first recorded the story was simply listening to
a chapter taken by his convert from the Cherokee testament. The
whole primitive pantheon of the Cherokee is still preserved in their
sacred formulas.

As compared with those from some other tribes the Cherokee myths
are clean. For picturesque imagination and wealth of detail they
rank high, and some of the wonder stories may challenge those of
Europe and India. The numerous parallels furnished will serve to
indicate their relation to the general Indian system. Unless otherwise
noted, every myth here given has been obtained directly from the
Indians, and in nearly every case has been verified from several
sources.

> "I know not how the truth may be,
> I tell the tale as 'twas told to me."

First and chief in the list of story tellers comes Aʻyûñ'inĭ, "Swimmer," from whom nearly three-fourths of the whole number were
originally obtained, together with nearly as large a proportion of the
whole body of Cherokee material now in possession of the author.
The collection could not have been made without his help, and now
that he is gone it can never be duplicated. Born about 1835, shortly
before the Removal, he grew up under the instruction of masters to be
a priest, doctor, and keeper of tradition, so that he was recognized as
an authority throughout the band and by such a competent outside
judge as Colonel Thomas. He served through the war as second
sergeant of the Cherokee Company A, Sixty-ninth North Carolina
Confederate Infantry, Thomas Legion. He was prominent in the
local affairs of the band, and no Green-corn dance, ballplay, or other
tribal function was ever considered complete without his presence and
active assistance. A genuine aboriginal antiquarian and patriot,
proud of his people and their ancient system, he took delight in
recording in his native alphabet the songs and sacred formulas of
priests and dancers and the names of medicinal plants and the pre-
scriptions with which they were compounded, while his mind was a
storehouse of Indian tradition. To a happy descriptive style he added
a musical voice for the songs and a peculiar faculty for imitating
the characteristic cry of bird or beast, so that to listen to one of his
recitals was often a pleasure in itself, even to one who understood not a
word of the language. He spoke no English, and to the day of his death
clung to the moccasin and turban, together with the rattle, his badge
of authority. He died in March, 1899, aged about sixty-five, and was

buried like a true Cherokee on the slope of a forest-clad mountain. Peace to his ashes and sorrow for his going, for with him perished half the tradition of a people.

Next in order comes the name of Ităgû'năhĭ, better known as John Ax, born about 1800 and now consequently just touching the century mark, being the oldest man of the band. He has a distinct recollection of the Creek war, at which time he was about twelve years of age, and was already married and a father when the lands east of Nantahala were sold by the treaty of 1819. Although not a professional priest or doctor, he was recognized, before age had dulled his faculties, as an authority upon all relating to tribal custom, and was an expert in the making of rattles, wands, and other ceremonial paraphernalia. Of a poetic and imaginative temperament, he cared most for the wonder stories, of the giant Tsul'kălû', of the great Uktena or of the invisible spirit people, but he had also a keen appreciation of the humorous animal stories. He speaks no English, and with his erect spare figure and piercing eye is a fine specimen of the old-time Indian. Notwithstanding his great age he walked without other assistance than his stick to the last ball game, where he watched every run with the closest interest, and would have attended the dance the night before but for the interposition of friends.

Suyeta, "The Chosen One," who preaches regularly as a Baptist minister to an Indian congregation, does not deal much with the Indian supernatural, perhaps through deference to his clerical obligations, but has a good memory and liking for rabbit stories and others of the same class. He served in the Confederate army during the war as fourth sergeant in Company A, of the Sixty-ninth North Carolina, and is now a well-preserved man of about sixty-two. He speaks no English, but by an ingenious system of his own has learned to use a concordance for verifying references in his Cherokee bible. He is also a first-class carpenter and mason.

Another principal informant was Ta'gwădihĭ', "Catawba-killer," of Cheowa, who died a few years ago, aged about seventy. He was a doctor and made no claim to special knowledge of myths or ceremonials, but was able to furnish several valuable stories, besides confirmatory evidence for a large number obtained from other sources.

Besides these may be named, among the East Cherokee, the late Chief N. J. Smith; Salâ'lĭ, mentioned elsewhere, who died about 1895; Tsĕsa'nĭ or Jessan, who also served in the war; Ayâ'sta, one of the principal conservatives among the women; and James and David Blythe, younger men of mixed blood, with an English education, but inheritors of a large share of Indian lore from their father, who was a recognized leader of ceremony.

Among informants in the western Cherokee Nation the principal was James D. Wafford, known to the Indians as Tsuskwănûñ'năwa'tă,

"Worn-out-blanket," a mixed-blood speaking and writing both languages, born in the old Cherokee Nation near the site of the present Clarkesville, Georgia, in 1806, and dying when about ninety years of age at his home in the eastern part of the Cherokee Nation, adjoining the Seneca reservation. The name figures prominently in the early history of North Carolina and Georgia. His grandfather, Colonel Wafford, was an officer in the American Revolutionary army, and shortly after the treaty of Hopewell, in 1785, established a colony known as "Wafford's settlement," in upper Georgia, on territory which was afterward found to be within the Indian boundary and was acquired by special treaty purchase in 1804. His name is appended, as witness for the state of Georgia, to the treaty of Holston, in 1794.[1] On his mother's side Mr Wafford was of mixed Cherokee, Natchez, and white blood, she being a cousin of Sequoya. He was also remotely connected with Cornelius Dougherty, the first trader established among the Cherokee. In the course of his long life he filled many positions of trust and honor among his people. In his youth he attended the mission school at Valleytown under Reverend Evan Jones, and just before the adoption of the Cherokee alphabet he finished the translation into phonetic Cherokee spelling of a Sunday school speller noted in Pilling's Iroquoin Bibliography. In 1824 he was the census enumerator for that district of the Cherokee Nation embracing upper Hiwassee river, in North Carolina, with Nottely and Toccoa in the adjoining portion of Georgia. His fund of Cherokee geographic information thus acquired was found to be invaluable. He was one of the two commanders of the largest detachment of emigrants at the time of the removal, and his name appears as a councilor for the western Nation in the Cherokee Almanac for 1846. When employed by the author at Tahlequah in 1891 his mind was still clear and his memory keen. Being of practical bent, he was concerned chiefly with tribal history, geography, linguistics, and every-day life and custom, on all of which subjects his knowledge was exact and detailed, but there were few myths for which he was not able to furnish confirmatory testimony. Despite his education he was a firm believer in the Nûñnĕ'hĭ, and several of the best legends connected with them were obtained from him. His death takes from the Cherokee one of the last connecting links between the present and the past.

---

[1] See contemporary notice in the Historical Sketch.

IV—THE MYTHS

Cosmogonic Myths

1. HOW THE WORLD WAS MADE

The earth is a great island floating in a sea of water, and suspended at each of the four cardinal points by a cord hanging down from the sky vault, which is of solid rock. When the world grows old and worn out, the people will die and the cords will break and let the earth sink down into the ocean, and all will be water again. The Indians are afraid of this.

When all was water, the animals were above in Gălûñ'lătĭ, beyond the arch; but it was very much crowded, and they were wanting more room. They wondered what was below the water, and at last Dâyuni'sĭ, "Beaver's Grandchild," the little Water-beetle, offered to go and see if it could learn. It darted in every direction over the surface of the water, but could find no firm place to rest. Then it dived to the bottom and came up with some soft mud, which began to grow and spread on every side until it became the island which we call the earth. It was afterward fastened to the sky with four cords, but no one remembers who did this.

At first the earth was flat and very soft and wet. The animals were anxious to get down, and sent out different birds to see if it was yet dry, but they found no place to alight and came back again to Gălûñ'-lătĭ. At last it seemed to be time, and they sent out the Buzzard and told him to go and make ready for them. This was the Great Buzzard, the father of all the buzzards we see now. He flew all over the earth, low down near the ground, and it was still soft. When he reached the Cherokee country, he was very tired, and his wings began to flap and strike the ground, and wherever they struck the earth there was a valley, and where they turned up again there was a mountain. When the animals above saw this, they were afraid that the whole world would be mountains, so they called him back, but the Cherokee country remains full of mountains to this day.

When the earth was dry and the animals came down, it was still dark, so they got the sun and set it in a track to go every day across the island from east to west, just overhead. It was too hot this way, and Tsiska'gĭlĭ', the Red Crawfish, had his shell scorched a bright red, so that his meat was spoiled; and the Cherokee do not eat it. The conjurers put the sun another hand-breadth higher in the air, but it was still too hot. They raised it another time, and another, until it was seven handbreadths high and just under the sky arch. Then it was right, and they left it so. This is why the conjurers call the highest place Gûlkwâ′gine Di′gălûñ′lătiyûñ′, "the seventh height," because it is seven hand-breadths above the earth. Every day the sun goes along under this arch, and returns at night on the upper side to the starting place.

There is another world under this, and it is like ours in everything—animals, plants, and people—save that the seasons are different. The streams that come down from the mountains are the trails by which we reach this underworld, and the springs at their heads are the doorways by which we enter it, but to do this one must fast and go to water and have one of the underground people for a guide. We know that the seasons in the underworld are different from ours, because the water in the springs is always warmer in winter and cooler in summer than the outer air.

When the animals and plants were first made—we do not know by whom—they were told to watch and keep awake for seven nights, just as young men now fast and keep awake when they pray to their medicine. They tried to do this, and nearly all were awake through the first night, but the next night several dropped off to sleep, and the third night others were asleep, and then others, until, on the seventh night, of all the animals only the owl, the panther, and one or two more were still awake. To these were given the power to see and to go about in the dark, and to make prey of the birds and animals which must sleep at night. Of the trees only the cedar, the pine, the spruce, the holly, and the laurel were awake to the end, and to them it was given to be always green and to be greatest for medicine, but to the others it was said: "Because you have not endured to the end you shall lose your hair every winter."

Men came after the animals and plants. At first there were only a brother and sister until he struck her with a fish and told her to multiply, and so it was. In seven days a child was born to her, and thereafter every seven days another, and they increased very fast until there was danger that the world could not keep them. Then it was made that a woman should have only one child in a year, and it has been so ever since.

2. THE FIRST FIRE

In the beginning there was no fire, and the world was cold, until the Thunders (Ani′-Hyûñ′tĭkwălâ′skĭ), who lived up in Gălûñ′lătĭ, sent their 'lightning and put fire into the bottom of a hollow sycamore tree which grew on an island. The animals knew it was there, because they could see the smoke coming out at the top, but they could not get to it on account of the water, so they held a council to decide what to do. This was a long time ago.

Every animal that could fly or swim was anxious to go after the fire. The Raven offered, and because he was so large and strong they thought he could surely do the work, so he was sent first. He flew high and far across the water and alighted on the sycamore tree, but while he was wondering what to do next, the heat had scorched all his feathers black, and he was frightened and came back without the fire. The little Screech-owl (*Wa'huhu'*) volunteered to go, and reached the place safely, but while he was looking down into the hollow tree a blast of hot air came up and nearly burned out his eyes. He managed to fly home as best he could, but it was a long time before he could see well, and his eyes are red to this day. Then the Hooting Owl (*U'guku'*) and the Horned Owl (*Tskĭlĭ'*) went, but by the time they got to the hollow tree the fire was burning so fiercely that the smoke nearly blinded them, and the ashes carried up by the wind made white rings about their eyes. They had to come home again without the fire, but with all their rubbing they were never able to get rid of the white rings.

Now no more of the birds would venture, and so the little Uksu'hĭ snake, the black racer, said he would go through the water and bring back some fire. He swam across to the island and crawled through the grass to the tree, and went in by a small hole at the bottom. The heat and smoke were too much for him, too, and after dodging about blindly over the hot ashes until he was almost on fire himself he managed by good luck to get out again at the same hole, but his body had been scorched black, and he has ever since had the habit of darting and doubling on his track as if trying to escape from close quarters. He came back, and the great blacksnake, Gûle'gĭ, "The Climber," offered to go for fire. He swam over to the island and climbed up the tree on the outside, as the blacksnake always does, but when he put his head down into the hole the smoke choked him so that he fell into the burning stump, and before he could climb out again he was as black as the Uksu'hĭ.

Now they held another council, for still there was no fire, and the world was cold, but birds, snakes, and four-footed animals, all had some excuse for not going, because they were all afraid to venture near the burning sycamore, until at last Kănăne'skĭ Amai'yĕhĭ (the Water Spider) said she would go. This is not the water spider that looks like a mosquito, but the other one, with black downy hair and red stripes on her body. She can run on top of the water or dive to the bottom, so there would be no trouble to get over to the island, but the question was, How could she bring back the fire? "I'll manage that," said the Water Spider; so she spun a thread from her body and wove it into a *tusti* bowl, which she fastened on her back. Then she crossed over to the island and through the grass to where the fire was still burning. She put one little coal of fire into her bowl, and came back with it, and ever since we have had fire, and the Water Spider still keeps her tusti bowl.

3. KANA′TĬ AND SELU: THE ORIGIN OF GAME AND CORN

When I was a boy this is what the old men told me they had heard when they were boys.

Long years ago, soon after the world was made, a hunter and his wife lived at Pilot knob with their only child, a little boy. The father's name was Kana′tĭ (The Lucky Hunter), and his wife was called Selu (Corn). No matter when Kana′tĭ went into the wood, he never failed to bring back a load of game, which his wife would cut up and prepare, washing off the blood from the meat in the river near the house. The little boy used to play down by the river every day, and one morning the old people thought they heard laughing and talking in the bushes as though there were two children there. When the boy came home at night his parents asked him who had been playing with him all day. "He comes out of the water," said the boy, "and he calls himself my elder brother. He says his mother was cruel to him and threw him into the river." Then they knew that the strange boy had sprung from the blood of the game which Selu had washed off at the river's edge.

Every day when the little boy went out to play the other would join him, but as he always went back again into the water the old people never had a chance to see him. At last one evening Kana′tĭ said to his son, "Tomorrow, when the other boy comes to play, get him to wrestle with you, and when you have your arms around him hold on to him and call for us." The boy promised to do as he was told, so the next day as soon as his playmate appeared he challenged him to a wrestling match. The other agreed at once, but as soon as they had their arms around each other, Kana′tĭ's boy began to scream for his father. The old folks at once came running down, and as soon as the Wild Boy saw them he struggled to free himself and cried out, "Let me go; you threw me away!" but his brother held on until the parents reached the spot, when they seized the Wild Boy and took him home with them. They kept him in the house until they had tamed him, but he was always wild and artful in his disposition, and was the leader of his brother in every mischief. It was not long until the old people discovered that he had magic powers, and they called him I′năge-utăsûñ′hĭ (He-who-grew-up-wild).

Whenever Kana′tĭ went into the mountains he always brought back a fat buck or doe, or maybe a couple of turkeys. One day the Wild Boy said to his brother, "I wonder where our father gets all that game; let's follow him next time and find out." A few days afterward Kana′tĭ took a bow and some feathers in his hand and started off toward the west.   The boys waited a little while and then went after him, keeping out of sight until they saw him go into a swamp where there were a great many of the small reeds that hunters use to make arrowshafts.   Then the Wild Boy changed himself into a puff of bird's down, which the wind took up and carried until it alighted upon Kana'tĭ's shoulder just as he entered the swamp, but Kana'tĭ knew nothing about it.   The old man cut reeds, fitted the feathers to them and made some arrows, and the Wild Boy—in his other shape—thought, "I wonder what those things are for?"   When Kana'tĭ had his arrows finished he came out of the swamp and went on again.   The wind blew the down from his shoulder, and it fell in the woods, when the Wild Boy took his right shape again and went back and told his brother what he had seen.   Keeping out of sight of their father, they followed him up the mountain until he stopped at a certain place and lifted a large rock.   At once there ran out a buck, which Kana'tĭ shot, and then lifting it upon his back he started for home again.   "Oho!" exclaimed the boys, "he keeps all the deer shut up in that hole, and whenever he wants meat he just lets one out and kills it with those things he made in the swamp."   They hurried and reached home before their father, who had the heavy deer to carry, and he never knew that they had followed.

A few days later the boys went back to the swamp, cut some reeds, and made seven arrows, and then started up the mountain to where their father kept the game.   When they got to the place, they raised the rock and a deer came running out.   Just as they drew back to shoot it, another came out, and then another and another, until the boys got confused and forgot what they were about.   In those days all the deer had their tails hanging down like other animals, but as a buck was running past the Wild Boy struck its tail with his arrow so that it pointed upward.   The boys thought this good sport, and when the next one ran past the Wild Boy struck its tail so that it stood straight up, and his brother struck the next one so hard with his arrow that the deer's tail was almost curled over his back.   The deer carries his tail this way ever since.   The deer came running past until the last one had come out of the hole and escaped into the forest.   Then came droves of raccoons, rabbits, and all the other four-footed animals—all but the bear, because there was no bear then.   Last came great flocks of turkeys, pigeons, and partridges that darkened the air like a cloud and made such a noise with their wings that Kana'tĭ, sitting at home, heard the sound like distant thunder on the mountains and said to himself, " My bad boys have got into trouble; I must go and see what they are doing."

So he went up the mountain, and when he came to the place where he kept the game he found the two boys standing by the rock, and all the birds and animals were gone.   Kana'tĭ was furious, but without saying a word he went down into the cave and kicked the covers off four jars in one corner, when out swarmed bedbugs, fleas, lice, and gnats, and got all over the boys. They screamed with pain and fright and tried to beat off the insects, but the thousands of vermin crawled over them and bit and stung them until both dropped down nearly dead. Kana′tĭ stood looking on until he thought they had been punished enough, when he knocked off the vermin and made the boys a talk. "Now, you rascals," said he, "you have always had plenty to eat and never had to work for it. Whenever you were hungry all I had to do was to come up here and get a deer or a turkey and bring it home for your mother to cook; but now you have let out all the animals, and after this when you want a deer to eat you will have to hunt all over the woods for it, and then maybe not find one. Go home now to your mother, while I see if I can find something to eat for supper."

When the boys got home again they were very tired and hungry and asked their mother for something to eat. "There is no meat," said Selu, "but wait a little while and I'll get you something." So she took a basket and started out to the storehouse. This storehouse was built upon poles high up from the ground, to keep it out of the reach of animals, and there was a ladder to climb up by, and one door, but no other opening. Every day when Selu got ready to cook the dinner she would go out to the storehouse with a basket and bring it back full of corn and beans. The boys had never been inside the storehouse, so wondered where all the corn and beans could come from, as the house was not a very large one; so as soon as Selu went out of the door the Wild Boy said to his brother, "Let's go and see what she does." They ran around and climbed up at the back of the storehouse and pulled out a piece of clay from between the logs, so that they could look in. There they saw Selu standing in the middle of the room with the basket in front of her on the floor. Leaning over the basket, she rubbed her stomach—so—and the basket was half full of corn. Then she rubbed under her armpits—so—and the basket was full to the top with beans. The boys looked at each other and said, "This will never do; our mother is a witch. If we eat any of that it will poison us. We must kill her."

When the boys came back into the house, she knew their thoughts before they spoke. "So you are going to kill me?" said Selu. "Yes," said the boys, "you are a witch." "Well," said their mother, "when you have killed me, clear a large piece of ground in front of the house and drag my body seven times around the circle. Then drag me seven times over the ground inside the circle, and stay up all night and watch, and in the morning you will have plenty of corn." The boys killed her with their clubs, and cut off her head and put it up on the roof of the house with her face turned to the west, and told her to look for her husband. Then they set to work to clear the ground in front of the house, but instead of clearing the whole piece they cleared only seven little spots. This is why corn now grows only in a few places instead of over the whole world. They dragged the body of Selu around the circle, and wherever her blood fell on the ground the corn sprang up. But instead of dragging her body seven times across the ground they dragged it over only twice, which is the reason the Indians still work their crop but twice. The two brothers sat up and watched their corn all night, and in the morning it was full grown and ripe.

When Kana'tĭ came home at last, he looked around, but could not see Selu anywhere, and asked the boys where was their mother. "She was a witch, and we killed her," said the boys; "there is her head up there on top of the house." When he saw his wife's head on the roof, he was very angry, and said, "I won't stay with you any longer; I am going to the Wolf people." So he started off, but before he had gone far the Wild Boy changed himself again to a tuft of down, which fell on Kana'tĭ's shoulder. When Kana'tĭ reached the settlement of the Wolf people, they were holding a council in the townhouse. He went in and sat down with the tuft of bird's down on his shoulder, but he never noticed it. When the Wolf chief asked him his business, he said: "I have two bad boys at home, and I want you to go in seven days from now and play ball against them." Although Kana'tĭ spoke as though he wanted them to play a game of ball, the Wolves knew that he meant for them to go and kill the two boys. They promised to go. Then the bird's down blew off from Kana'tĭ's shoulder, and the smoke carried it up through the hole in the roof of the townhouse. When it came down on the ground outside, the Wild Boy took his right shape again and went home and told his brother all that he had heard in the townhouse. But when Kana'tĭ left the Wolf people, he did not return home, but went on farther.

The boys then began to get ready for the Wolves, and the Wild Boy—the magician—told his brother what to do. They ran around the house in a wide circle until they had made a trail all around it excepting on the side from which the Wolves would come, where they left a small open space. Then they made four large bundles of arrows and placed them at four different points on the outside of the circle, after which they hid themselves in the woods and waited for the Wolves. In a day or two a whole party of Wolves came and surrounded the house to kill the boys. The Wolves did not notice the trail around the house, because they came in where the boys had left the opening, but the moment they went inside the circle the trail changed to a high brush fence and shut them in. Then the boys on the outside took their arrows and began shooting them down, and as the Wolves could not jump over the fence they were all killed, excepting a few that escaped through the opening into a great swamp close by. The boys ran around the swamp, and a circle of fire sprang up in their tracks and set fire to the grass and bushes and burned up nearly all the other Wolves. Only two or three got away, and from these have come all the wolves that are now in the world.

Soon afterward some strangers from a distance, who had heard that the brothers had a wonderful grain from which they made bread, came to ask for some, for none but Selu and her family had ever known corn before. The boys gave them seven grains of corn, which they told them to plant the next night on their way home, sitting up all night to watch the corn, which would have seven ripe ears in the morning. These they were to plant the next night and watch in the same way, and so on every night until they reached home, when they would have corn enough to supply the whole people. The strangers lived seven days' journey away. They took the seven grains and watched all through the darkness until morning, when they saw seven tall stalks, each stalk bearing a ripened ear. They gathered the ears and went on their way. The next night they planted all their corn, and guarded it as before until daybreak, when they found an abundant increase. But the way was long and the sun was hot, and the people grew tired. On the last night before reaching home they fell asleep, and in the morning the corn they had planted had not even sprouted. They brought with them to their settlement what corn they had left and planted it, and with care and attention were able to raise a crop. But ever since the corn must be watched and tended through half the year, which before would grow and ripen in a night.

As Kana'tĭ did not return, the boys at last concluded to go and find him. The Wild Boy took a gaming wheel and rolled it toward the Darkening land. In a little while the wheel came rolling back, and the boys knew their father was not there. He rolled it to the south and to the north, and each time the wheel came back to him, and they knew their father was not there. Then he rolled it toward the Sun-land, and it did not return. "Our father is there," said the Wild Boy, "let us go and find him." So the two brothers set off toward the east, and after traveling a long time they came upon Kana'tĭ walking along with a little dog by his side. "You bad boys," said their father, "have you come here?" "Yes," they answered, "we always accomplish what we start out to do—we are men." "This dog overtook me four days ago," then said Kana'tĭ, but the boys knew that the dog was the wheel which they had sent after him to find him. "Well," said Kana'tĭ, "as you have found me, we may as well travel together, but I shall take the lead."

Soon they came to a swamp, and Kana'tĭ told them there was something dangerous there and they must keep away from it. He went on ahead, but as soon as he was out of sight the Wild Boy said to his brother, "Come and let us see what is in the swamp." They went in together, and in the middle of the swamp they found a large panther asleep. The Wild Boy got out an arrow and shot the panther in the side of the head. The panther turned his head and the other boy shot him on that side. He turned his head away again and the two brothers shot together—*tust, tust, tust!* But the panther was not hurt by the arrows and paid no more attention to the boys. They came out of the swamp and soon overtook Kana'tĭ, waiting for them. "Did you find it?" asked Kana'tĭ. "Yes," said the boys, "we found it, but it never hurt us. We are men." Kana'tĭ was surprised, but said nothing, and they went on again.

After a while he turned to them and said, "Now you must be careful. We are coming to a tribe called the Anăda'dûñtăskĭ ("Roasters," i. e., cannibals), and if they get you they will put you into a pot and feast on you." Then he went on ahead. Soon the boys came to a tree which had been struck by lightning, and the Wild Boy directed his brother to gather some of the splinters from the tree and told him what to do with them. In a little while they came to the settlement of the can-nibals, who, as soon as they saw the boys, came running out, crying, "Good, here are two nice fat strangers. Now we'll have a grand feast!" They caught the boys and dragged them into the townhouse, and sent word to all the people of the settlement to come to the feast. They made up a great fire, put water into a large pot and set it to boiling, and then seized the Wild Boy and put him down into it. His brother was not in the least frightened and made no attempt to escape, but quietly knelt down and began putting the splinters into the fire, as if to make it burn better. When the cannibals thought the meat was about ready they lifted the pot from the fire, and that instant a blinding light filled the townhouse, and the lightning began to dart from one side to the other, striking down the cannibals until not one of them was left alive. Then the lightning went up through the smoke-hole, and the next moment there were the two boys standing outside the townhouse as though nothing had happened. They went on and soon met Kana'tĭ, who seemed much surprised to see them, and said, "What! are you here again?" "O, yes, we never give up. We are great men!" "What did the cannibals do to you?" "We met them and they brought us to their townhouse, but they never hurt us." Kana'tĭ said nothing more, and they went on.

    *   *   *   *   *   *   *

He soon got out of sight of the boys, but they kept on until they came to the end of the world, where the sun comes out. The sky was just coming down when they got there, but they waited until it went up again, and then they went through and climbed up on the other side. There they found Kana'tĭ and Selu sitting together. The old folk received them kindly and were glad to see them, telling them they might stay there a while, but then they must go to live where the sun goes down. The boys stayed with their parents seven days and then went on toward the Darkening land, where they are now. We call them Anisga'ya Tsunsdi' (The Little Men), and when they talk to each other we hear low rolling thunder in the west.

*   *   *   *   *   *   *

After Kana'tï's boys had let the deer out from the cave where their father used to keep them, the hunters tramped about in the woods for a long time without finding any game, so that the people were very hungry. At last they heard that the Thunder Boys were now living in the far west, beyond the sun door, and that if they were sent for they could bring back the game. So they sent messengers for them, and the boys came and sat down in the middle of the townhouse and began to sing.

At the first song there was a roaring sound like a strong wind in the northwest, and it grew louder and nearer as the boys sang on, until at the seventh song a whole herd of deer, led by a large buck, came out from the woods. The boys had told the people to be ready with their bows and arrows, and when the song was ended and all the deer were close around the townhouse, the hunters shot into them and killed as many as they needed before the herd could get back into the timber.

Then the Thunder Boys went back to the Darkening land, but before they left they taught the people the seven songs with which to call up the deer. It all happened so long ago that the songs are now forgotten—all but two, which the hunters still sing whenever they go after deer.

WAHNENAUHI VERSION

After the world had been brought up from under the water, "They then made a man and a woman and led them around the edge of the island. On arriving at the starting place they planted some corn, and then told the man and woman to go around the way they had been led. This they did, and on returning they found the corn up and growing nicely. They were then told to continue the circuit. Each trip consumed more time. At last the corn was ripe and ready for use."

*   *   *   *   *   *   *

Another story is told of how sin came into the world. A man and a woman reared a large family of children in comfort and plenty, with very little trouble about providing food for them. Every morning the father went forth and very soon returned bringing with him a deer, or a turkey, or some other animal or fowl. At the same time the mother went out and soon returned with a large basket filled with ears of corn which she shelled and pounded in a mortar, thus making meal for bread.

When the children grew up, seeing with what apparent ease food was provided for them, they talked to each other about it, wondering that they never saw such things as their parents brought in. At last one proposed to watch when their parents went out and to follow them.

Accordingly next morning the plan was carried out. Those who followed the father saw him stop at a short distance from the cabin and turn over a large stone that appeared to be carelessly leaned against another. On looking closely they saw an entrance to a large cave, and in it were many different kinds of animals and birds, such as their father had sometimes brought in for food. The man standing at the entrance called a deer, which was lying at some distance and back of some other animals. It rose immediately as it heard the call and came close up to him. He picked it up, closed the mouth of the cave, and returned, not once seeming to suspect what his sons had done.

When the old man was fairly out of sight, his sons, rejoicing how they had outwitted him, left their hiding place and went to the cave, saying they would show the old folks that they, too, could bring in something. They moved the stone away, though it was very heavy and they were obliged to use all their united strength. When the cave was opened, the animals, instead of waiting to be picked up, all made a rush for the entrance, and leaping past the frightened and bewildered boys, scattered in all directions and disappeared in the wilderness, while the guilty offenders could do nothing but gaze in stupified amazement as they saw them escape. There were animals of all kinds, large and small—buffalo, deer, elk, antelope, raccoons, and squirrels; even catamounts and panthers, wolves and foxes, and many others, all fleeing together. At the same time birds of every kind were seen emerging from the opening, all in the same wild confusion as the quadrupeds—turkeys, geese, swans, ducks, quails, eagles, hawks, and owls.

Those who followed the mother saw her enter a small cabin, which they had never seen before, and close the door. The culprits found a small crack through which they could peer. They saw the woman place a basket on the ground and standing over it shake herself vigorously, jumping up and down, when lo and behold! large ears of corn began to fall into the basket. When it was well filled she took it up and, placing it on her head, came out, fastened the door, and prepared their breakfast as usual. When the meal had been finished in silence the man spoke to his children, telling them that he was aware of what they had done; that now he must die and they would be obliged to provide for themselves. He made bows and arrows for them, then sent them to hunt for the animals which they had turned loose.

Then the mother told them that as they had found out her secret she could do nothing more for them; that she would die, and they must drag her body around over the ground; that wherever her body was dragged corn would come up. Of this they were to make their bread. She told them that they must always save some for seed and plant every year.

4. ORIGIN OF DISEASE AND MEDICINE

In the old days the beasts, birds, fishes, insects, and plants could all talk, and they and the people lived together in peace and friendship. But as time went on the people increased so rapidly that their settlements spread over the whole earth, and the poor animals found themselves beginning to be cramped for room. This was bad enough, but to make it worse Man invented bows, knives, blowguns, spears, and hooks, and began to slaughter the larger animals, birds, and fishes for their flesh or their skins, while the smaller creatures, such as the frogs and worms, were crushed and trodden upon without thought, out of pure carelessness or contempt. So the animals resolved to consult upon measures for their common safety.

The Bears were the first to meet in council in their townhouse under Kuwâ'hĭ mountain, the "Mulberry place," and the old White Bear chief presided. After each in turn had complained of the way in which Man killed their friends, ate their flesh, and used their skins for his own purposes, it was decided to begin war at once against him. Some one asked what weapons Man used to destroy them. "Bows and arrows, of course," cried all the Bears in chorus. "And what are they made of?" was the next question. "The bow of wood, and the string of our entrails," replied one of the Bears. It was then proposed that they make a bow and some arrows and see if they could not use the same weapons against Man himself. So one Bear got a nice piece of locust wood and another sacrificed himself for the good of the rest in order to furnish a piece of his entrails for the string. But when everything was ready and the first Bear stepped up to make the trial, it was found that in letting the arrow fly after drawing back the bow, his long claws caught the string and spoiled the shot. This was annoying, but some one suggested that they might trim his claws, which was accordingly done, and on a second trial it was found that the arrow went straight to the mark. But here the chief, the old White Bear, objected, saying it was necessary that they should have long claws in order to be able to climb trees. "One of us has already died to furnish the bowstring, and if we now cut off our claws we must all starve together. It is better to trust to the teeth and claws that nature gave us, for it is plain that man's weapons were not intended for us."

No one could think of any better plan, so the old chief dismissed the council and the Bears dispersed to the woods and thickets without having concerted any way to prevent the increase of the human race. Had the result of the council been otherwise, we should now be at war with the Bears, but as it is, the hunter does not even ask the Bear's pardon when he kills one.

The Deer next held a council under their chief, the Little Deer, and after some talk decided to send rheumatism to every hunter who should kill one of them unless he took care to ask their pardon for the offense. They sent notice of their decision to the nearest settlement of Indians and told them at the same time what to do when necessity forced them to kill one of the Deer tribe. Now, whenever the hunter shoots a Deer, the Little Deer, who is swift as the wind and can not be wounded, runs quickly up to the spot and, bending over the blood-stains, asks the spirit of the Deer if it has heard the prayer of the hunter for pardon. If the reply be " Yes," all is well, and the Little Deer goes on his way; but if the reply be " No," he follows on the trail of the hunter, guided by the drops of blood on the ground, until he arrives at his cabin in the settlement, when the Little Deer enters invisibly and strikes the hunter with rheumatism, so that he becomes at once a helpless cripple. No hunter who has regard for his health ever fails to ask pardon of the Deer for killing it, although some hunters who have not learned the prayer may try to turn aside the Little Deer from his pursuit by building a fire behind them in the trail.

Next came the Fishes and Reptiles, who had their own complaints against Man. They held their council together and determined to make their victims dream of snakes twining about them in slimy folds and blowing foul breath in their faces, or to make them dream of eating raw or decaying fish, so that they would lose appetite, sicken, and die. This is why people dream about snakes and fish.

Finally the Birds, Insects, and smaller animals came together for the same purpose, and the Grubworm was chief of the council. It was decided that each in turn should give an opinion, and then they would vote on the question as to whether or not Man was guilty. Seven votes should be enough to condemn him. One after another denounced Man's cruelty and injustice toward the other animals and voted in favor of his death. The Frog spoke first, saying: " We must do something to check the increase of the race, or people will become so numerous that we shall be crowded from off the earth. See how they have kicked me about because I'm ugly, as they say, until my back is covered with sores;" and here he showed the spots on his skin. Next came the Bird—no one remembers now which one it was—who condemned Man "because he burns my feet off," meaning the way in which the hunter barbecues birds by impaling them on a stick set over the fire, so that their feathers and tender feet are singed off. Others followed in the same strain. The Ground-squirrel alone ventured to say a good word for Man, who seldom hurt him because he was so small, but this made the others so angry that they fell upon the Ground-squirrel and tore him with their claws, and the stripes are on his back to this day.

They began then to devise and name so many new diseases, one after another, that had not their invention at last failed them, no one of the human race would have been able to survive. The Grubworm grew constantly more pleased as the name of each disease was called off, until at last they reached the end of the list, when some one proposed to make menstruation sometimes fatal to women. On this he rose-up in his place and cried: "*Wadâñ′!* [Thanks!] I'm glad some more of them will die, for they are getting so thick that they tread on me." The thought fairly made him shake with joy, so that he fell over backward and could not get on his feet again, but had to wriggle off on his back, as the Grubworm has done ever since.

When the Plants, who were friendly to Man, heard what had been done by the animals, they determined to defeat the latters' evil designs. Each Tree, Shrub, and Herb, down even to the Grasses and Mosses, agreed to furnish a cure for some one of the diseases named, and each said: "I shall appear to help Man when he calls upon me in his need." Thus came medicine; and the plants, every one of which has its use if we only knew it, furnish the remedy to counteract the evil wrought by the revengeful animals. Even weeds were made for some good purpose, which we must find out for ourselves. When the doctor does not know what medicine to use for a sick man the spirit of the plant tells him.

5. THE DAUGHTER OF THE SUN

The Sun lived on the other side of the sky vault, but her daughter lived in the middle of the sky, directly above the earth, and every day as the Sun was climbing along the sky arch to the west she used to stop at her daughter's house for dinner.

Now, the Sun hated the people on the earth, because they could never look straight at her without screwing up their faces. She said to her brother, the Moon, "My grandchildren are ugly; they grin all over their faces when they look at me." But the Moon said, "I like my younger brothers; I think they are very handsome"—because they always smiled pleasantly when they saw him in the sky at night, for his rays were milder.

The Sun was jealous and planned to kill all the people, so every day when she got near her daughter's house she sent down such sultry rays that there was a great fever and the people died by hundreds, until everyone had lost some friend and there was fear that no one would be left. They went for help to the Little Men, who said the only way to save themselves was to kill the Sun.

The Little Men made medicine and changed two men to snakes, the Spreading-adder and the Copperhead, and sent them to watch near the door of the daughter of the Sun to bite the old Sun when she came next day. They went together and hid near the house until the Sun came, but when the Spreading-adder was about to spring, the bright light blinded him and he could only spit out yellow slime, as he does to this day when he tries to bite. She called him a nasty thing and went by into the house, and the Copperhead crawled off without trying to do anything.

So the people still died from the heat, and they went to the Little Men a second time for help. The Little Men made medicine again and changed one man into the great Uktena and another into the Rattlesnake and sent them to watch near the house and kill the old Sun when she came for dinner. They made the Uktena very large, with horns on his head, and everyone thought he would be sure to do the work, but the Rattlesnake was so quick and eager that he got ahead and coiled up just outside the house, and when the Sun's daughter opened the door to look out for her mother, he sprang up and bit her and she fell dead in the doorway. He forgot to wait for the old Sun, but went back to the people, and the Uktena was so very angry that he went back, too. Since then we pray to the rattlesnake and do not kill him, because he is kind and never tries to bite if we do not disturb him. The Uktena grew angrier all the time and very dangerous, so that if he even looked at a man, that man's family would die. After a long time the people held a council and decided that he was too dangerous to be with them, so they sent him up to Gălûñ'lătĭ, and he is there now. The Spreading-adder, the Copperhead, the Rattlesnake, and the Uktena were all men.

When the Sun found her daughter dead, she went into the house and grieved, and the people did not die any more, but now the world was dark all the time, because the Sun would not come out. They went again to the Little Men, and these told them that if they wanted the Sun to come out again they must bring back her daughter from Tsûsginâ'ĭ, the Ghost country, in Usûñhi'yĭ, the Darkening land in the west. They chose seven men to go, and gave each a sourwood rod a hand-breadth long. The Little Men told them they must take a box with them, and when they got to Tsûsginâ'ĭ they would find all the ghosts at a dance. They must stand outside the circle, and when the young woman passed in the dance they must strike her with the rods and she would fall to the ground. Then they must put her into the box and bring her back to her mother, but they must be very sure not to open the box, even a little way, until they were home again.

They took the rods and a box and traveled seven days to the west until they came to the Darkening land. There were a great many people there, and they were having a dance just as if they were at home in the settlements. The young woman was in the outside circle, and as she swung around to where the seven men were standing, one struck her with his rod and she turned her head and saw him. As she came around the second time another touched her with his rod, and then another and another, until at the seventh round she fell out of the ring, and they put her into the box and closed the lid fast. The other ghosts seemed never to notice what had happened.

They took up the box and started home toward the east. In a little while the girl came to life again and begged to be let out of the box, but they made no answer and went on. Soon she called again and said she was hungry, but still they made no answer and went on. After another while she spoke again and called for a drink and pleaded so that it was very hard to listen to her, but the men who carried the box said nothing and still went on. When at last they were very near home, she called again and begged them to raise the lid just a little, because she was smothering. They were afraid she was really dying now, so they lifted the lid a little to give her air, but as they did so there was a fluttering sound inside and something flew past them into the thicket and they heard a redbird cry, "*kwish! kwish! kwish!*" in the bushes. They shut down the lid and went on again to the settlements, but when they got there and opened the box it was empty.

So we know the Redbird is the daughter of the Sun, and if the men had kept the box closed, as the Little Men told them to do, they would have brought her home safely, and we could bring back our other friends also from the Ghost country, but now when they die we can never bring them back.

The Sun had been glad when they started to the Ghost country, but when they came back without her daughter she grieved and cried, "My daughter, my daughter," and wept until her tears made a flood upon the earth, and the people were afraid the world would be drowned. They held another council, and sent their handsomest young men and women to amuse her so that she would stop crying. They danced before the Sun and sang their best songs, but for a long time she kept her face covered and paid no attention, until at last the drummer suddenly changed the song, when she lifted up her face, and was so pleased at the sight that she forgot her grief and smiled.

6. HOW THEY BROUGHT BACK THE TOBACCO

In the beginning of the world, when people and animals were all the same, there was only one tobacco plant, to which they all came for their tobacco until the Dagûl'kû geese stole it and carried it far away to the south. The people were suffering without it, and there was one old woman who grew so thin and weak that everybody said she would soon die unless she could get tobacco to keep her alive.

Different animals offered to go for it, one after another, the larger ones first and then the smaller ones, but the Dagûl'kû saw and killed every one before he could get to the plant. After the others the little Mole tried to reach it by going under the ground, but the Dagûl'kû saw his track and killed him as he came out.

At last the Hummingbird offered, but the others said he was entirely too small and might as well stay at home. He begged them to let him try, so they showed him a plant in a field and told him to let them see how he would go about it.   The next moment he was gone and they saw him sitting on the plant, and then in a moment he was back again, but no one had seen him going or coming, because he was so swift. "This is the way I'll do," said the Hummingbird, so they let him try.

He flew off to the east, and when he came in sight of the tobacco the Dagûl'kû were watching all about it, but they could not see him because he was so small and flew so swiftly.   He darted down on the plant—*tsa!*—and snatched off the top with the leaves and seeds, and was off again before the Dagûl'kû knew what had happened.   Before he got home with the tobacco the old woman had fainted and they thought she was dead, but he blew the smoke into her nostrils, and with a cry of " *Tsâ'lû!* [Tobacco!]" she opened her eyes and was alive again.

SECOND VERSION

The people had tobacco in the beginning, but they had used it all, and there was great suffering for want of it.   There was one old man so old that he had to be kept alive by smoking, and as his son did not want to see him die he decided to go himself to try and get some more.   The tobacco country was far in the south, with high mountains all around it, and the passes were guarded, so that it was very hard to get into it, but the young man was a conjurer and was not afraid.   He traveled southward until he came to the mountains on the border of the tobacco country.   Then he opened his medicine bag and took out a hummingbird skin and put it over himself like a dress. Now he was a hummingbird and flew over the mountains to the tobacco field and pulled some of the leaves and seed and put them into his medicine bag.   He was so small and swift that the guards, whoever they were, did not see him, and when he had taken as much as he could carry he flew back over the mountains in the same way.   Then he took off the hummingbird skin and put it into his medicine bag, and was a man again.   He started home, and on his way came to a tree that had a hole in the trunk, like a door, near the first branches, and a very pretty woman was looking out from it.   He stopped and tried to climb the tree, but although he was a good climber he found that he always slipped back.   He put on a pair of medicine moccasins from his pouch, and then he could climb the tree, but when he reached the first branches he looked up and the hole was still as far away as before.   He climbed higher and higher, but every time he looked up the hole seemed to be farther than before, until at last he was tired and came down again. When he reached home he found his father very weak, but still alive, and one draw at the pipe made him strong again.   The people planted the seed and have had tobacco ever since.

7. THE JOURNEY TO THE SUNRISE

A long time ago several young men made up their minds to find the place where the Sun lives and see what the Sun is like.   They got ready their bows and arrows, their parched corn and extra moccasins, and started out toward the east.   At first they met tribes they knew, then they came to tribes they had only heard about, and at last to others of which they had never heard.

There was a tribe of root eaters and another of acorn eaters, with great piles of acorn shells near their houses.   In one tribe they found a sick man dying, and were told it was the custom there when a man died to bury his wife in the same grave with him.   They waited until he was dead, when they saw his friends lower the body into a great pit, so deep and dark that from the top they could not see the bottom. Then a rope was tied around the woman's body, together with a bundle of pine knots, a lighted pine knot was put into her hand, and she was lowered into the pit to die there in the darkness after the last pine knot was burned.

The young men traveled on until they came at last to the sunrise place where the sky reaches down to the ground.   They found that the sky was an arch or vault of solid rock hung above the earth and was always swinging up and down, so that when it went up there was an open place like a door between the sky and ground, and when it swung back the door was shut.   The Sun came out of this door from the east and climbed along on the inside of the arch.   It had a human figure, but was too bright for them to see clearly and too hot to come very near. They waited until the Sun had come out and then tried to get through while the door was still open, but just as the first one was in the doorway the rock came down and crushed him.   The other six were afraid to try it, and as they were now at the end of the world they turned around and started back again, but they had traveled so far that they were old men when they reached home.

8. THE MOON AND THE THUNDERS.

The Sun was a young woman and lived in the East, while her brother, the Moon, lived in the West.   The girl had a lover who used to come every month in the dark of the moon to court her.   He would come at night, and leave before daylight, and although she talked with him she could not see his face in the dark, and he would not tell her his name, until she was wondering all the time who it could be.   At last she hit upon a plan to find out, so the next time he came, as they were sitting together in the dark of the âsĭ, she slyly dipped her hand into the cinders and ashes of the fireplace and rubbed it over his face, saying, "Your face is cold; you must have suffered from the wind," and pretending to be very sorry for him, but he did not know that she had ashes on her hand.   After a while he left her and went away again.

The next night when the Moon came up in the sky his face was covered with spots, and then his sister knew he was the one who had been

TAGWĂDIHĬ'

PHOTOGRAPH BY AUTHOR, 1888

AYÂSTA

coming to see her. He was so much ashamed to have her know it that he kept as far away as he could at the other end of the sky all the night. Ever since he tries to keep a long way behind the Sun, and when he does sometimes have to come near her in the west he makes himself as thin as a ribbon so that he can hardly be seen.

Some old people say that the moon is a ball which was thrown up against the sky in a game a long time ago. They say that two towns were playing against each other, but one of them had the best runners and had almost won the game, when the leader of the other side picked up the ball with his hand—a thing that is not allowed in the game— and tried to throw it to the goal, but it struck against the solid sky vault and was fastened there, to remind players never to cheat. When the moon looks small and pale it is because some one has handled the ball unfairly, and for this reason they formerly played only at the time of a full moon.

When the sun or moon is eclipsed it is because a great frog up in the sky is trying to swallow it. Everybody knows this, even the Creeks and the other tribes, and in the olden times, eighty or a hundred years ago, before the great medicine men were all dead, whenever they saw the sun grow dark the people would come together and fire guns and beat the drum, and in a little while this would frighten off the great frog and the sun would be all right again.

The common people call both Sun and Moon *Nûñdă*, one being "Nûñdă that dwells in the day" and the other "Nûñdă that dwells in the night," but the priests call the Sun *Su'tălidihĭ'*, "Six-killer," and the Moon *Ge'ʻyăguʻga*, though nobody knows now what this word means, or why they use these names. Sometimes people ask the Moon not to let it rain or snow.

The great Thunder and his sons, the two Thunder boys, live far in the west above the sky vault. The lightning and the rainbow are their beautiful dress. The priests pray to the Thunder and call him the Red Man, because that is the brightest color of his dress. There are other Thunders that live lower down, in the cliffs and mountains, and under waterfalls, and travel on invisible bridges from one high peak to another where they have their town houses. The great Thunders above the sky are kind and helpful when we pray to them, but these others are always plotting mischief. One must not point at the rainbow, or one's finger will swell at the lower joint.

9. WHAT THE STARS ARE LIKE

There are different opinions about the stars. Some say they are balls of light, others say they are human, but most people say they are living creatures covered with luminous fur or feathers.

One night a hunting party camping in the mountains noticed two lights like large stars moving along the top of a distant ridge. They wondered and watched until the light disappeared on the other side. The next night, and the next, they saw the lights again moving along the ridge, and after talking over the matter decided to go on the morrow and try to learn the cause. In the morning they started out and went until they came to the ridge, where, after searching some time, they found two strange creatures about *so* large (making a circle with outstretched arms), with round bodies covered with fine fur or downy feathers, from which small heads stuck out like the heads of terrapins. As the breeze played upon these feathers showers of sparks flew out.

The hunters carried the strange creatures back to the camp, intending to take them home to the settlements on their return. They kept them several days and noticed that every night they would grow bright and shine like great stars, although by day they were only balls of gray fur, except when the wind stirred and made the sparks fly out. They kept very quiet, and no one thought of their trying to escape, when, on the seventh night, they suddenly rose from the ground like balls of fire and were soon above the tops of the trees. Higher and higher they went, while the wondering hunters watched, until at last they were only two bright points of light in the dark sky, and then the hunters knew that they were stars.

10. ORIGIN OF THE PLEIADES AND THE PINE

Long ago, when the world was new, there were seven boys who used to spend all their time down by the townhouse playing the gatayû'stĭ game, rolling a stone wheel along the ground and sliding a curved stick after it to strike it. Their mothers scolded, but it did no good, so one day they collected some gatayû'stĭ stones and boiled them in the pot with the corn for dinner. When the boys came home hungry their mothers dipped out the stones and said, "Since you like the gatayû'stĭ better than the cornfield, take the stones now for your dinner."

The boys were very angry, and went down to the townhouse, saying, "As our mothers treat us this way, let us go where we shall never trouble them any more." They began a dance—some say it was the Feather dance—and went round and round the townhouse, praying to the spirits to help them. At last their mothers were afraid something was wrong and went out to look for them. They saw the boys still dancing around the townhouse, and as they watched they noticed that their feet were off the earth, and that with every round they rose higher and higher in the air. They ran to get their children, but it was too late, for they were already above the roof of the townhouse—all but one, whose mother managed to pull him down with the gatayû'stĭ pole, but he struck the ground with such force that he sank into it and the earth closed over him.

The other six circled higher and higher until they went up to the sky, where we see them now as the Pleiades, which the Cherokee still call Ani'tsutsă (The Boys). The people grieved long after them, but the mother whose boy had gone into the ground came every morning and every evening to cry over the spot until the earth was damp with her tears. At last a little green shoot sprouted up and grew day by day until it became the tall tree that we call now the pine, and the pine is of the same nature as the stars and holds in itself the same bright light.

11. THE MILKY WAY

Some people in the south had a corn mill, in which they pounded the corn into meal, and several mornings when they came to fill it they noticed that some of the meal had been stolen during the night. They examined the ground and found the tracks of a dog, so the next night they watched, and when the dog came from the north and began to eat the meal out of the bowl they sprang out and whipped him. He ran off howling to his home in the north, with the meal dropping from his mouth as he ran, and leaving behind a white trail where now we see the Milky Way, which the Cherokee call to this day Gi‘lĭ'-utsûñ'stănûñ'yĭ, "Where the dog ran."

12. ORIGIN OF STRAWBERRIES

When the first man was created and a mate was given to him, they lived together very happily for a time, but then began to quarrel, until at last the woman left her husband and started off toward Nûñdâgûñ'yĭ, the Sun land, in the east. The man followed alone and grieving, but the woman kept on steadily ahead and never looked behind, until Une‘'lănûñ'hĭ, the great Apportioner (the Sun), took pity on him and asked him if he was still angry with his wife. He said he was not, and Une‘'lănûñ'hĭ then asked him if he would like to have her back again, to which he eagerly answered yes.

So Une‘'lănûñ'hĭ caused a patch of the finest ripe huckleberries to spring up along the path in front of the woman, but she passed by without paying any attention to them. Farther on he put a clump of blackberries, but these also she refused to notice. Other fruits, one, two, and three, and then some trees covered with beautiful red service berries, were placed beside the path to tempt her, but she still went on until suddenly she saw in front a patch of large ripe strawberries, the first ever known. She stooped to gather a few to eat, and as she picked them she chanced to turn her face to the west, and at once the memory of her husband came back to her and she found herself unable to go on. She sat down, but the longer she waited the stronger became her desire for her husband, and at last she gathered a bunch of the finest berries and started back along the path to give them to him. He met her kindly and they went home together.

13. THE GREAT YELLOW-JACKET: ORIGIN OF FISH AND FROGS

A long time ago the people of the old town of Kanu′ga ̔lâ′yĭ (" Brier place," or Briertown), on Nantahala river, in the present Macon county, North Carolina, were much annoyed by a great insect called U′la ̔gû′, as large as a house, which used to come from some secret hiding place, and darting swiftly through the air, would snap up children from their play and carry them away. It was unlike any other insect ever known, and the people tried many times to track it to its home, but it was too swift to be followed.

They killed a squirrel and tied a white string to it, so that its course could be followed with the eye, as bee hunters follow the flight of a bee to its tree. The U′la ̔gû′ came and carried off the squirrel with the string hanging to it, but darted away so swiftly through the air that it was out of sight in a moment. They killed a turkey and put a longer white string to it, and the U′la ̔gû′ came and took the turkey, but was gone again before they could see in what direction it flew. They took a deer ham and tied a white string to it, and again the U′la ̔gû′ swooped down and bore it off so swiftly that it could not be followed. At last they killed a yearling deer and tied a very long white string to it. The U′la ̔gû′ came again and seized the deer, but this time the load was so heavy that it had to fly slowly and so low down that the string could be plainly seen.

The hunters got together for the pursuit. They followed it along a ridge to the east until they came near where Franklin now is, when, on looking across the valley to the other side, they saw the nest of the U′la ̔gû′ in a large cave in the rocks. On this they raised a great shout and made their way rapidly down the mountain and across to the cave. The nest had the entrance below with tiers of cells built up one above another to the roof of the cave. The great U′la ̔gû′ was there, with thousands of smaller ones, that we now call yellow-jackets. The hunters built fires around the hole, so that the smoke filled the cave and smothered the great insect and multitudes of the smaller ones, but others which were outside the cave were not killed, and these escaped and increased until now the yellow-jackets, which before were unknown, are all over the world. The people called the cave Tsgâgûñ′yĭ, "Where the yellow-jacket was," and the place from which they first saw the nest they called A ̔tahi′ta, "Where they shouted," and these are their names today.

They say also that all the fish and frogs came from a great monster fish and frog which did much damage until at last they were killed by the people, who cut them up into little pieces which were thrown into the water and afterward took shape as the smaller fishes and frogs.

14. THE DELUGE

A long time ago a man had a dog, which began to go down to the river every day and look at the water and howl. At last the man was angry and scolded the dog, which then spoke to him and said: "Very soon there is going to be a great freshet and the water will come so high that everybody will be drowned; but if you will make a raft to get upon when the rain comes you can be saved, but you must first throw me into the water." The man did not believe it, and the dog said, "If you want a sign that I speak the truth, look at the back of my neck." He looked and saw that the dog's neck had the skin worn off so that the bones stuck out.

Then he believed the dog, and began to build a raft. Soon the rain came and he took his family, with plenty of provisions, and they all got upon it. It rained for a long time, and the water rose until the mountains were covered and all the people in the world were drowned. Then the rain stopped and the waters went down again, until at last it was safe to come off the raft. Now there was no one alive but the man and his family, but one day they heard a sound of dancing and shouting on the other side of the ridge. The man climbed to the top and looked over; everything was still, but all along the valley he saw great piles of bones of the people who had been drowned, and then he knew that the ghosts had been dancing.

QUADRUPED MYTHS

15. THE FOURFOOTED TRIBES

In Cherokee mythology, as in that of Indian tribes generally, there is no essential difference between men and animals. In the primal genesis period they seem to be completely undifferentiated, and we find all creatures alike living and working together in harmony and mutual helpfulness until man, by his aggressiveness and disregard for the rights of the others, provokes their hostility, when insects, birds, fishes, reptiles, and fourfooted beasts join forces against him (see story, "Origin of Disease and Medicine"). Henceforth their lives are apart, but the difference is always one of degree only. The animals, like the people, are organized into tribes and have like them their chiefs and townhouses, their councils and ballplays, and the same hereafter in the Darkening land of Usûñhi'yĭ. Man is still the paramount power, and hunts and slaughters the others as his own necessities compel, but is obliged to satisfy the animal tribes in every instance, very much as a murder is compounded for, according to the Indian system, by "covering the bones of the dead" with presents for the bereaved relatives.

This pardon to the hunter is made the easier through a peculiar doctrine of reincarnation, according to which, as explained by the shamans, there is assigned to every animal a definite life term which can not be curtailed by violent means.   If it is killed before the expiration of the allotted time the death is only temporary and the body is immediately resurrected in its proper shape from the blood drops, and the animal continues its existence until the end of the predestined period, when the body is finally dissolved and the liberated spirit goes to join its kindred shades in the Darkening land.   This idea appears in the story of the bear man and in the belief concerning the Little Deer.   Death is thus but a temporary accident and the killing a mere minor crime.   By some priests it is held that there are seven successive reanimations before the final end.

Certain supernatural personages, Kana'tĭ and Tsul'kălû' (see the myths), have dominion over the animals, and are therefore regarded as the distinctive gods of the hunter.   Kana'tĭ at one time kept the game animals, as well as the pestiferous insects, shut up in a cave under ground, from which they were released by his undutiful sons. The primeval animals—the actors in the animal myths and the predecessors of the existing species—are believed to have been much larger, stronger, and cleverer than their successors of the present day.   In these myths we find the Indian explanation of certain peculiarities of form, color, or habit, and the various animals are always consistently represented as acting in accordance with their well-known characteristics.

First and most prominent in the animal myths is the Rabbit (*Tsistu*), who figures always as a trickster and deceiver, generally malicious, but often beaten at his own game by those whom he had intended to victimize.   The connection of the rabbit with the dawn god and the relation of the Indian myths to the stories current among the southern negroes are discussed in another place.   Ball players while in training are forbidden to eat the flesh of the rabbit, because this animal so easily becomes confused in running.   On the other hand, their spies seek opportunity to strew along the path which must be taken by their rivals a soup made of rabbit hamstrings, with the purpose of rendering them timorous in action.

In a ball game between the birds and the fourfooted animals (see story) the Bat, which took sides with the birds, is said to have won the victory for his party by his superior dodging abilities.   For this reason the wings or sometimes the stuffed skin of the bat are tied to the implements used in the game to insure success for the players.   According to the same myth the Flying Squirrel (*Tewa*) also aided in securing the victory, and hence both these animals are still invoked by the ball player.   The meat of the common gray squirrel (*sălâ'lĭ*) is forbidden to rheumatic patients, on account of the squirrel's habit of assuming a cramped position when eating.   The stripes upon the back of the ground squirrel (*kiyu'ga*) are the mark of scratches made by the angry animals at a memorable council in which he took it upon himself to say a good word for the archenemy, Man (see "Origin of Disease and Medicine"). The peculiarities of the mink (*sûñgĭ*) are accounted for by another story.

The buffalo, the largest game animal of America, was hunted in the southern Allegheny region until almost the close of the last century, the particular species being probably that known in the West as the wood or mountain buffalo. The name in use among the principal gulf tribes was practically the same, and can not be analyzed, viz, Cherokee, *yûñsû'*; Hichitee, *ya'nasi*; Creek, *yĕna'sa*; Choctaw, *yanash*. Although the flesh of the buffalo was eaten, its skin dressed for blankets and bed coverings, its long hair woven into belts, and its horns carved into spoons, it is yet strangely absent from Cherokee folklore. So far as is known it is mentioned in but a single one of the sacred formulas, in which a person under treatment for rheumatism is forbidden to eat the meat, touch the skin, or use a spoon made from the horn of the buffalo, upon the ground of an occult connection between the habitual cramped attitude of a rheumatic and the natural "hump" of that animal.

The elk is known, probably by report, under the name of *a'wĭ' e'gwa*, "great deer", but there is no myth or folklore in connection with it.

The deer, *a'wĭ'*, which is still common in the mountains, was the principal dependence of the Cherokee hunter, and is consequently prominent in myth, folklore, and ceremonial. One of the seven gentes of the tribe is named from it (Ani'-Kawĭ', "Deer People"). According to a myth given elsewhere, the deer won his horns in a successful race with the rabbit. Rheumatism is usually ascribed to the work of revengeful deer ghosts, which the hunter has neglected to placate, while on the other hand the aid of the deer is invoked against frostbite, as its feet are believed to be immune from injury by frost. The wolf, the fox, and the opossum are also invoked for this purpose, and for the same reason. When the redroot (*Ceanothus americanus*) puts forth its leaves the people say the young fawns are then in the mountains. On killing a deer the hunter always cuts out the hamstring from the hind quarter and throws it away, for fear that if he ate it he would thereafter tire easily in traveling.

The powerful chief of the deer tribe is the A'wĭ' Usdi', or "Little Deer," who is invisible to all except the greatest masters of the hunting secrets, and can be wounded only by the hunter who has supplemented years of occult study with frequent fasts and lonely vigils. The Little Deer keeps constant protecting watch over his subjects, and sees well to it that not one is ever killed in wantonness. When a deer is shot by the hunter the Little Deer knows it at once and is instantly at the spot. Bending low his head he asks of the blood stains upon the ground if they have heard—i. e., if the hunter has asked pardon for the life that he has taken. If the formulistic prayer has been made, all is well, because the necessary sacrifice has been atoned for; but if otherwise, the Little Deer tracks the hunter to his house by the blood drops along the trail, and, unseen and unsuspected, puts into his body the spirit of rheumatism that shall rack him with aches and pains from that time henceforth. As seen at rare intervals—perhaps once in a long lifetime—the Little Deer is pure white and about the size of a small dog, has branching antlers, and is always in company with a large herd of deer. Even though shot by the master hunter, he comes to life again, being immortal, but the fortunate huntsman who can thus make prize of his antlers has in them an unfailing talisman that brings him success in the chase forever after. The smallest portion of one of those horns of the Little Deer, when properly consecrated, attracts the deer to the hunter, and when exposed from the wrapping dazes them so that they forget to run and thus become an easy prey. Like the Ulûñsû'tĭ stone (see number 50), it is a dangerous prize when not treated with proper respect, and is—or was—kept always in a secret place away from the house to guard against sacrilegious handling.

Somewhat similar talismanic power attached to the down from the young antler of the deer when properly consecrated. So firm was the belief that it had influence over "anything about a deer" that eighty and a hundred years ago even white traders used to bargain with the Indians for such charms in order to increase their store of deerskins by drawing the trade to themselves. The faith in the existence of the miraculous Little Deer is almost as strong and universal to-day among the older Cherokee as is the belief in a future life.

The bears (yânû) are transformed Cherokee of the old clan of the Ani'-Tsâ'gŭhĭ (see story, "Origin of the Bear"). Their chief is the White Bear, who lives at Kuwâ'hĭ, "Mulberry place," one of the high peaks of the Great Smoky mountains, near to the enchanted lake of Atagâ'hĭ (see number 69), to which the wounded bears go to be cured of their hurts. Under Kuwâ'hĭ and each of three other peaks in the same mountain region the bears have townhouses, where they congregate and hold dances every fall before retiring to their dens for the winter. Being really human, they can talk if they only would, and once a mother bear was heard singing to her cub in words which the hunter understood. There is one variety known as kalâs'-gŭnăhi'ta, "long hams," described as a large black bear with long legs and small feet, which is always lean, and which the hunter does not care to shoot, possibly on account of its leanness. It is believed that new-born cubs are hairless, like mice.

The wolf (wa'ya) is revered as the hunter and watchdog of Kana'tĭ, and the largest gens in the tribe bears the name of Ani'-wa'ya, "Wolf people." The ordinary Cherokee will never kill one if he can possibly avoid it, but will let the animal go by unharmed, believing that the kindred of a slain wolf will surely revenge his death, and that the weapon with which the deed is done will be rendered worthless for further shooting until cleaned and exorcised by a medicine man. Certain persons, however, having knowledge of the proper atonement rites, may kill wolves with impunity, and are hired for this purpose by others who have suffered from raids upon their fish traps or their stock. Like the eagle killer (see "The Bird Tribes"), the professional wolf killer, after killing one of these animals, addresses to it a prayer in which he seeks to turn aside the vengeance of the tribe by laying the burden of blame upon the people of some other settlement. He then unscrews the barrel of his gun and inserts into it seven small sourwood rods heated over the fire, and allows it to remain thus overnight in the running stream; in the morning the rods are taken out and the barrel is thoroughly dried and cleaned.

The dog (gĭʻlĭ'), although as much a part of Indian life among the Cherokee as in other tribes, hardly appears in folklore. One myth makes him responsible for the milky way; another represents him as driving the wolf from the comfortable house fire and taking the place for himself. He figures also in connection with the deluge. There is no tradition of the introduction of the horse (sâ'gwălĭ, from asâ'gwălihûʻ, "a pack or burden") or of the cow (waʻka, from the Spanish, vaca). The hog is called sĭkwă, this being originally the name of the opossum, which somewhat resembles it in expression, and which is now distinguished as sĭkwă utse'tstĭ, "grinning sĭkwă." In the same way the sheep, another introduced animal, is called aʻwĭ' unăde'na, "woolly deer"; the goat, aʻwĭ' ahănu'lăhĭ, "bearded deer," and the mule, "sâ'gwălĭ digû'lanăhi'ta, "long-eared horse." The cat, also obtained from the whites, is called wesă, an attempt at the English "pussy." When it purrs by the fireside, the children say it is counting in Cherokee, "ta'ladu', nûñ'gĭ, ta'ladu', nûñ'gĭ," "sixteen, four, sixteen, four." The elephant, which a few of the Cherokee have seen in shows, is called by them kăma'mă u'tănû, "great butterfly," from the supposed resemblance of its long trunk and flapping ears to the proboscis and wings of that insect. The anatomical peculiarities of the opossum, of both sexes, are the subject of much curious speculation among the Indians, many of whom believe that its young are produced without any help from the male. It occurs in one or two of the minor myths.

The fox (tsuʻlă) is mentioned in one of the formulas, but does no appear in the tribal folklore. The black fox is known by a different name (inâ'lĭ). The odor of the skunk (dĭlă') is believed to keep off contagious diseases, and the scent bag is therefore taken out and hung over the doorway, a small hole being pierced in it in order that the contents may ooze out upon the timbers. At times, as in the

266 MYTHS OF THE CHEROKEE [ETH. ANN. 19

smallpox epidemic of 1866, the entire body of the animal was thus hung up, and in some cases, as an additional safeguard, the meat was cooked and eaten and the oil rubbed over the skin of the person. The underlying idea is that the fetid smell repels the disease spirit, and upon the same principle the buzzard, which is so evidently superior to carrion smells, is held to be powerful against the same diseases.

The beaver (*dâ'yĭ*), by reason of its well-known gnawing ability, against which even the hardest wood is not proof, is invoked on behalf of young children just getting their permanent teeth. According to the little formula which is familiar to nearly every mother in the tribe, when the loosened milk tooth is pulled out or drops out of itself, the child runs with it around the house, repeating four times, "*Dâ'yĭ, skĭntă'* (Beaver, put a new tooth into my jaw)" after which he throws the tooth upon the roof of the house.

In a characteristic song formula to prevent frostbite the traveler, before starting out on a cold winter morning, rubs his feet in the ashes of the fire and sings a song of four verses, by means of which, according to the Indian idea, he acquires in turn the cold-defying powers of the wolf, deer, fox, and opossum, four animals whose feet, it is held, are never frostbitten. After each verse he imitates the cry and the action of the animal. The words used are archaic in form and may be rendered "I become a real wolf," etc. The song runs:

Tsûñ'wa''ya-ya' (repeated four times), *wa + a!* (prolonged howl). (Imitates a wolf pawing the ground with his feet.)

Tsûñ'-ka'wi-ye' (repeated four times), *sauh! sauh! sauh! sauh!* (Imitates call and jumping of a deer.)

Tsûñ'-tsu''la-ya' (repeated four times), *gaih! gaih! gaih! gaih!* (Imitates barking and scratching of a fox.)

Tsûñ'-sĭ'kwa-ya' (repeated four times), *kĭ +.* (Imitates the cry of an opossum when cornered, and throws his head back as that animal does when feigning death.)

16. THE RABBIT GOES DUCK HUNTING

The Rabbit was so boastful that he would claim to do whatever he saw anyone else do, and so tricky that he could usually make the other animals believe it all. Once he pretended that he could swim in the water and eat fish just as the Otter did, and when the others told him to prove it he fixed up a plan so that the Otter himself was deceived.

Soon afterward they met again and the Otter said, "I eat ducks sometimes." Said the Rabbit, "Well, I eat ducks too." The Otter challenged him to try it; so they went up along the river until they saw several ducks in the water and managed to get near without being seen. The Rabbit told the Otter to go first. The Otter never hesitated, but dived from the bank and swam under water until he reached the ducks, when he pulled one down without being noticed by the others, and came back in the same way.

While the Otter had been under the water the Rabbit had peeled some bark from a sapling and made himself a noose. "Now," he said, "Just watch me;" and he dived in and swam a little way under the water until he was nearly choking and had to come up to the top to breathe. He went under again and came up again a little nearer to the ducks. He took another breath and dived under, and this time he came up among the ducks and threw the noose over the head of one and caught it. The duck struggled hard and finally spread its wings and flew up from the water with the Rabbit hanging on to the noose.

It flew on and on until at last the Rabbit could not hold on any longer, but had to let go and drop. As it happened, he fell into a tall, hollow sycamore stump without any hole at the bottom to get out from, and there he stayed until he was so hungry that he had to eat his own fur, as the rabbit does ever since when he is starving. After several days, when he was very weak with hunger, he heard children playing outside around the trees. He began to sing:

> Cut a door and look at me;
> I'm the prettiest thing you ever did see.

The children ran home and told their father, who came and began to cut a hole in the tree. As he chopped away the Rabbit inside kept singing, "Cut it larger, so you can see me better; I'm so pretty." They made the hole larger, and then the Rabbit told them to stand back so that they could take a good look as he came out. They stood away back, and the Rabbit watched his chance and jumped out and got away.

17. HOW THE RABBIT STOLE THE OTTER'S COAT

The animals were of different sizes and wore coats of various colors and patterns. Some wore long fur and others wore short. Some had rings on their tails, and some had no tails at all. Some had coats of brown, others of black or yellow. They were always disputing about their good looks, so at last they agreed to hold a council to decide who had the finest coat.

They had heard a great deal about the Otter, who lived so far up the creek that he seldom came down to visit the other animals. It was said that he had the finest coat of all, but no one knew just what it was like, because it was a long time since anyone had seen him. They did not even know exactly where he lived—only the general direction; but they knew he would come to the council when the word got out.

Now the Rabbit wanted the verdict for himself, so when it began to look as if it might go to the Otter he studied up a plan to cheat him out of it. He asked a few sly questions until he learned what trail the Otter would take to get to the council place. Then, without saying anything, he went on ahead and after four days' travel he met the Otter and knew him at once by his beautiful coat of soft dark-brown fur. The Otter was glad to see him and asked him where he was going.

"O," said the Rabbit, "the animals sent me to bring you to the council; because you live so far away they were afraid you mightn't know the road." The Otter thanked him, and they went on together.

They traveled all day toward the council ground, and at night the Rabbit selected the camping place, because the Otter was a stranger in that part of the country, and cut down bushes for beds and fixed everything in good shape. The next morning they started on again. In the afternoon the Rabbit began to pick up wood and bark as they went along and to load it on his back. When the Otter asked what this was for the Rabbit said it was that they might be warm and comfortable at night. After a while, when it was near sunset, they stopped and made their camp.

When supper was over the Rabbit got a stick and shaved it down to a paddle. The Otter wondered and asked again what that was for.

"I have good dreams when I sleep with a paddle under my head," said the Rabbit.

When the paddle was finished the Rabbit began to cut away the bushes so as to make a clean trail down to the river. The Otter wondered more and more and wanted to know what this meant.

Said the Rabbit, "This place is called Di'tatlâski'yĭ [The Place Where it Rains Fire]. Sometimes it rains fire here, and the sky looks a little that way to-night. You go to sleep and I'll sit up and watch, and if the fire does come, as soon as you hear me shout, you run and jump into the river. Better hang your coat on a limb over there, so it won't get burnt."

The Otter did as he was told, and they both doubled up to go to sleep, but the Rabbit kept awake. After a while the fire burned down to red coals. The Rabbit called, but the Otter was fast asleep and made no answer. In a little while he called again, but the Otter never stirred. Then the Rabbit filled the paddle with hot coals and threw them up into the air and shouted, "It's raining fire! It's raining fire!"

The hot coals fell all around the Otter and he jumped up. "To the water!" cried the Rabbit, and the Otter ran and jumped into the river, and he has lived in the water ever since.

The Rabbit took the Otter's coat and put it on, leaving his own instead, and went on to the council. All the animals were there, every one looking out for the Otter. At last they saw him in the distance, and they said one to the other, "The Otter is coming!" and sent one of the small animals to show him the best seat. They were all glad to see him and went up in turn to welcome him, but the Otter kept his head down, with one paw over his face. They wondered that he was so bashful, until the Bear came up and pulled the paw away, and there was the Rabbit with his split nose. He sprang up and started to run, when the Bear struck at him and pulled his tail off, but the Rabbit was too quick for them and got away.

18. WHY THE POSSUM'S TAIL IS BARE

The Possum used to have a long, bushy tail, and was so proud of it that he combed it out every morning and sang about it at the dance, until the Rabbit, who had had no tail since the Bear pulled it out, became very jealous and made up his mind to play the Possum a trick.

There was to be a great council and a dance at which all the animals were to be present. It was the Rabbit's business to send out the news, so as he was passing the Possum's place he stopped to ask him if he intended to be there. The Possum said he would come if he could have a special seat, "because I have such a handsome tail that I ought to sit where everybody can see me." The Rabbit promised to attend to it and to send some one besides to comb and dress the Possum's tail for the dance, so the Possum was very much pleased and agreed to come.

Then the Rabbit went over to the Cricket, who is such an expert hair cutter that the Indians call him the barber, and told him to go next morning and dress the Possum's tail for the dance that night. He told the Cricket just what to do and then went on about some other mischief.

In the morning the Cricket went to the Possum's house and said he had come to get him ready for the dance. So the Possum stretched himself out and shut his eyes while the Cricket combed out his tail and wrapped a red string around it to keep it smooth until night. But all this time, as he wound the string around, he was clipping off the hair close to the roots, and the Possum never knew it.

When it was night the Possum went to the townhouse where the dance was to be and found the best seat ready for him, just as the Rabbit had promised. When his turn came in the dance he loosened the string from his tail and stepped into the middle of the floor. The drummers began to drum and the Possum began to sing, "See my beautiful tail." Everybody shouted and he danced around the circle and sang again, "See what a fine color it has." They shouted again and he danced around another time, singing, "See how it sweeps the ground." The animals shouted more loudly than ever, and the Possum was delighted. He danced around again and sang, "See how fine the fur is." Then everybody laughed so long that the Possum wondered what they meant. He looked around the circle of animals and they were all laughing at him. Then he looked down at his beautiful tail and saw that there was not a hair left upon it, but that it was as bare as the tail of a lizard. He was so much astonished and ashamed that he could not say a word, but rolled over helpless on the ground and grinned, as the Possum does to this day when taken by surprise.

19. HOW THE WILDCAT CAUGHT THE GOBBLER

The Wildcat once caught the Rabbit and was about to kill him, when the Rabbit begged for his life, saying: "I'm so small I would make only a mouthful for you, but if you let me go I'll show you where you can get a whole drove of Turkeys." So the Wildcat let him up and went with him to where the Turkeys were.

When they came near the place the Rabbit said to the Wildcat, "Now, you must do just as I say. Lie down as if you were dead and don't move, even if I kick you, but when I give the word jump up and catch the largest one there." The Wildcat agreed and stretched out as if dead, while the Rabbit gathered some rotten wood and crumbled it over his eyes and nose to make them look flyblown, so that the Turkeys would think he had been dead some time.

Then the Rabbit went over to the Turkeys and said, in a sociable way, "Here, I've found our old enemy, the Wildcat, lying dead in the trail. Let's have a dance over him." The Turkeys were very doubtful, but finally went with him to where the Wildcat was lying in the road as if dead. Now, the Rabbit had a good voice and was a great dance leader, so he said, "I'll lead the song and you dance around him." The Turkeys thought that fine, so the Rabbit took a stick to beat time and began to sing: " *Gălăgi'na hasuyak'*, *Gălăgi'na hasuyak'* (pick out the Gobbler, pick out the Gobbler)."

"Why do you say that?" said the old Turkey. "O, that's all right," said the Rabbit, "that's just the way he does, and we sing about it." He started the song again and the Turkeys began to dance around the Wildcat. When they had gone around several times the Rabbit said, "Now go up and hit him, as we do in the war dance." So the Turkeys, thinking the Wildcat surely dead, crowded in close around him and the old gobbler kicked him. Then the Rabbit drummed hard and sang his loudest, "Pick out the Gobbler, pick out the Gobbler," and the Wildcat jumped up and caught the Gobbler.

20. HOW THE TERRAPIN BEAT THE RABBIT

The Rabbit was a great runner, and everybody knew it. No one thought the Terrapin anything but a slow traveler, but he was a great warrior and very boastful, and the two were always disputing about their speed. At last they agreed to decide the matter by a race. They fixed the day and the starting place and arranged to run across four mountain ridges, and the one who came in first at the end was to be the winner.

The Rabbit felt so sure of it that he said to the Terrapin, "You know you can't run. You can never win the race, so I'll give you the first ridge and then you'll have only three to cross while I go over four."

The Terrapin said that would be all right, but that night when he went home to his family he sent for his Terrapin friends and told them he wanted their help. He said he knew he could not outrun the Rabbit, but he wanted to stop the Rabbit's boasting. He explained his plan to his friends and they agreed to help him.

When the day came all the animals were there to see the race. The Rabbit was with them, but the Terrapin was gone ahead toward the first ridge, as they had arranged, and they could hardly see him on account of the long grass. The word was given and the Rabbit started off with long jumps up the mountain, expecting to win the race before the Terrapin could get down the other side. But before he got up the mountain he saw the Terrapin go over the ridge ahead of him. He ran on, and when he reached the top he looked all around, but could not see the Terrapin on account of the long grass. He kept on down the mountain and began to climb the second ridge, but when he looked up again there was the Terrapin just going over the top. Now he was surprised and made his longest jumps to catch up, but when he got to the top there was the Terrapin away in front going over the third ridge. The Rabbit was getting tired now and nearly out of breath, but he kept on down the mountain and up the other ridge until he got to the top just in time to see the Terrapin cross the fourth ridge and thus win the race.

The Rabbit could not make another jump, but fell over on the ground, crying *mĭ, mĭ, mĭ, mĭ*, as the Rabbit does ever since when he is too tired to run any more. The race was given to the Terrapin and all the animals wondered how he could win against the Rabbit, but he kept still and never told. It was easy enough, however, because all the Terrapin's friends looked just alike, and he had simply posted one near the top of each ridge to wait until the Rabbit came in sight and then climb over and hide in the long grass. When the Rabbit came on he could not find the Terrapin and so thought the Terrapin was ahead, and if he had met one of the other terrapins he would have thought it the same one because they looked so much alike. The real Terrapin had posted himself on the fourth ridge, so as to come in at the end of the race and be ready to answer questions if the animals suspected anything.

Because the Rabbit had to lie down and lose the race the conjurer now, when preparing his young men for the ball play, boils a lot of rabbit hamstrings into a soup, and sends some one at night to pour it across the path along which the other players are to come in the morning, so that they may become tired in the same way and lose the game. It is not always easy to do this, because the other party is expecting it and has watchers ahead to prevent it.

21. THE RABBIT AND THE TAR WOLF

Once there was such a long spell of dry weather that there was no more water in the creeks and springs, and the animals held a council to see what to do about it. They decided to dig a well, and all agreed to help except the Rabbit, who was a lazy fellow, and said, "I don't need to dig for water. The dew on the grass is enough for me." The others did not like this, but they went to work together and dug their well.

They noticed that the Rabbit kept sleek and lively, although it was still dry weather and the water was getting low in the well. They said, "That tricky Rabbit steals our water at night," so they made a wolf of pine gum and tar and set it up by the well to scare the thief. That night the Rabbit came, as he had been coming every night, to drink enough to last him all next day. He saw the queer black thing by the well and said, "Who's there?" but the tar wolf said nothing. He came nearer, but the wolf never moved, so he grew braver and said, "Get out of my way or I'll strike you." Still the wolf never moved and the Rabbit came up and struck it with his paw, but the gum held his foot and it stuck fast. Now he was angry and said, "Let me go or I'll kick you." Still the wolf said nothing. Then the Rabbit struck again with his hind foot, so hard that it was caught in the gum and he could not move, and there he stuck until the animals came for water in the morning. When they found who the thief was they had great sport over him for a while and then got ready to kill him, but as soon as he was unfastened from the tar wolf he managed to get away.—Wafford.

SECOND VERSION

" Once upon a time there was such a severe drought that all streams of water and all lakes were dried up. In this emergency the beasts assembled together to devise means to procure water. It was proposed by one to dig a well. All agreed to do so except the hare. She refused because it would soil her tiny paws. The rest, however, dug their well and were fortunate enough to find water. The hare beginning to suffer and thirst, and having no right to the well, was thrown upon her wits to procure water. She determined, as the easiest way, to steal from the public well. The rest of the animals, surprised to find that the hare was so well supplied with water, asked her where she got it. She replied that she arose betimes in the morning and gathered the dewdrops. However the wolf and the fox suspected her of theft and hit on the following plan to detect her:

They made a wolf of tar and placed it near the well. On the following night the hare came as usual after her supply of water. On seeing the tar wolf she demanded who was there. Receiving no answer she repeated the demand, threatening to kick the wolf if he did not reply. She receiving no reply kicked the wolf, and by this means adhered to the tar and was caught. When the fox and wolf got hold of her they consulted what it was best to do with her. One proposed cutting her head off. This the hare protested would be useless, as it had often been tried without hurting her. Other methods were proposed for dispatching her, all of which she said would be useless. At last it was proposed to let her loose to perish in a thicket. Upon this the hare affected great uneasiness and pleaded hard for life. Her enemies, however, refused to listen and she was accordingly let loose. As soon, however, as she was out of reach of her enemies she gave a whoop, and bounding away she exclaimed: 'This is where I live.' "— Cherokee Advocate, December 18, 1845.

22. THE RABBIT AND THE POSSUM AFTER A WIFE

The Rabbit and the Possum each wanted a wife, but no one would marry either of them. They talked over the matter and the Rabbit said, "We can't get wives here; let's go to the next settlement. I'm the messenger for the council, and I'll tell the people that I bring an order that everybody must take a mate at once, and then we'll be sure to get our wives."

The Possum thought this a fine plan, so they started off together to the next town. As the Rabbit traveled faster he got there first and waited outside until the people noticed him and took him into the townhouse. When the chief came to ask his business the Rabbit said he brought an important order from the council that everybody must get married without delay. So the chief called the people together and told them the message from the council. Every animal took a mate at once, and the Rabbit got a wife.

The Possum traveled so slowly that he got there after all the animals had mated, leaving him still without a wife. The Rabbit pretended to feel sorry for him and said, "Never mind, I'll carry the message to the people in the next settlement, and you hurry on as fast as you can, and this time you will get your wife."

So he went on to the next town, and the Possum followed close after him. But when the Rabbit got to the townhouse he sent out the word that, as there had been peace so long that everybody was getting lazy the council had ordered that there must be war at once and they must begin right in the townhouse. So they all began fighting, but the Rabbit made four great leaps and got away just as the Possum came in. Everybody jumped on the Possum, who had not thought of bringing his weapons on a wedding trip, and so could not defend himself. They had nearly beaten the life out of him when he fell over and pretended to be dead until he saw a good chance to jump up and get away. The Possum never got a wife, but he remembers the lesson, and ever since he shuts his eyes and pretends to be dead when the hunter has him in a close corner.

23. THE RABBIT DINES THE BEAR

The Bear invited the Rabbit to dine with him. They had beans in the pot, but there was no grease for them, so the Bear cut a slit in his side and let the oil run out until they had enough to cook the dinner. The Rabbit looked surprised, and thought to himself, " That's a handy way. I think I'll try that." When he started home he invited the Bear to come and take dinner with him four days later.

When the Bear came the Rabbit said, "I have beans for dinner, too. Now I'll get the grease for them." So he took a knife and drove it into his side, but instead of oil, a stream of blood gushed out and he fell over nearly dead. The Bear picked him up and had hard work to tie up the wound and stop the bleeding. Then he scolded him, "You little fool, I'm large and strong and lined with fat all over; the knife don't hurt me; but you're small and lean, and you can't do such things."

24. THE RABBIT ESCAPES FROM THE WOLVES

Some Wolves once caught the Rabbit and were going to eat him when he asked leave to show them a new dance he was practicing. They knew that the Rabbit was a great song leader, and they wanted to learn the latest dance, so they agreed and made a ring about him while he got ready. He patted his feet and began to dance around in a circle, singing:

> Tlâge'sitûñ' găli'sgi'sidâ'hă—
> Ha'nia lĭl! lĭl! Ha'nia lĭl! lĭl!
>
> On the edge of the field I dance about—
> Ha'nia lĭl! lĭl! Ha'nia lĭl! lĭl!

"Now," said the Rabbit, "when I sing 'on the edge of the field,' I dance that way"—and he danced over in that direction—"and when I sing 'lĭl! lĭl!' you must all stamp your feet hard." The Wolves thought it fine. He began another round singing the same song, and danced a little nearer to the field, while the Wolves all stamped their feet. He sang louder and louder and danced nearer and nearer to the field until at the fourth song, when the Wolves were stamping as hard as they could and thinking only of the song, he made one jump and was off through the long grass. They were after him at once, but he ran for a hollow stump and climbed up on the inside. When the the Wolves got there one of them put his head inside to look up, but the Rabbit spit into his eye, so that he had to pull his head out again. The others were afraid to try, and they went away, with the Rabbit still in the stump.

25. FLINT VISITS THE RABBIT

In the old days Tăwi'skălă (Flint) lived up in the mountains, and all the animals hated him because he had helped to kill so many of them. They used to get together to talk over means to put him out of the way, but everybody was afraid to venture near his house until the Rabbit, who was the boldest leader among them, offered to go after Flint and try to kill him. They told him where to find him, and the Rabbit set out and at last came to Flint's house.

Flint was standing at his door when the Rabbit came up and said, sneeringly, "*Siyu'!* Hello! Are you the fellow they call Flint?" "Yes; that's what they call me," answered Flint. "Is this where you live?" "Yes; this is where I live." All this time the Rabbit was looking about the place trying to study out some plan to take Flint off his guard. He had expected Flint to invite him into the house, so he waited a little while, but when Flint made no move, he said, "Well, my name is Rabbit; I've heard a good deal about you, so I came to invite you to come and see me."

Flint wanted to know where the Rabbit's house was, and he told him it was down in the broom-grass field near the river. So Flint promised to make him a visit in a few days. "Why not come now and have supper with me?" said the Rabbit, and after a little coaxing Flint agreed and the two started down the mountain together.

When they came near the Rabbit's hole the Rabbit said, "There is my house, but in summer I generally stay outside here where it is cooler." So he made a fire, and they had their supper on the grass. When it was over, Flint stretched out to rest and the Rabbit got some heavy sticks and his knife and cut out a mallet and wedge. Flint looked up and asked what that was for. "Oh," said the Rabbit, "I like to be doing something, and they may come handy." So Flint lay down again, and pretty soon he was sound asleep. The Rabbit spoke to him once or twice to make sure, but there was no answer. Then he came over to Flint and with one good blow of the mallet he drove the sharp stake into his body and ran with all his might for his own hole; but before he reached it there was a loud explosion, and pieces of flint flew all about. That is why we find flint in so many places now. One piece struck the Rabbit from behind and cut him just as he dived into his hole. He sat listening until everything seemed quiet again. Then he put his head out to look around, but just at that moment another piece fell and struck him on the lip and split it, as we still see it.

26. HOW THE DEER GOT HIS HORNS

In the beginning the Deer had no horns, but his head was smooth just like a doe's. He was a great runner and the Rabbit was a great jumper, and the animals were all curious to know which could go farther in the same time. They talked about it a good deal, and at last arranged a match between the two, and made a nice large pair of antlers for a prize to the winner. They were to start together from one side of a thicket and go through it, then turn and come back, and the one who came out first was to get the horns.

On the day fixed all the animals were there, with the antlers put down on the ground at the edge of the thicket to mark the starting point. While everybody was admiring the horns the Rabbit said: "I don't know this part of the country; I want to take a look through the bushes where I am to run." They thought that all right, so the Rabbit went into the thicket, but he was gone so long that at last the animals suspected he must be up to one of his tricks. They sent a messenger to look for him, and away in the middle of the thicket he found the Rabbit gnawing down the bushes and pulling them away until he had a road cleared nearly to the other side.

The messenger turned around quietly and came back and told the other animals. When the Rabbit came out at last they accused him of cheating, but he denied it until they went into the thicket and found the cleared road. They agreed that such a trickster had no right to enter the race at all, so they gave the horns to the Deer, who was admitted to be the best runner, and he has worn them ever since. They told the Rabbit that as he was so fond of cutting down bushes he might do that for a living hereafter, and so he does to this day.

27. WHY THE DEER'S TEETH ARE BLUNT

The Rabbit felt sore because the Deer had won the horns (see the last story), and resolved to get even. One day soon after the race he stretched a large grapevine across the trail and gnawed it nearly in two in the middle. Then he went back a piece, took a good run, and jumped up at the vine. He kept on running and jumping up at the vine until the Deer came along and asked him what he was doing?

"Don't you see?" says the Rabbit. "I'm so strong that I can bite through that grapevine at one jump."

The Deer could hardly believe this, and wanted to see it done. So the Rabbit ran back, made a tremendous spring, and bit through the vine where he had gnawed it before. The Deer, when he saw that, said, "Well, I can do it if you can." So the Rabbit stretched a larger grapevine across the trail, but without gnawing it in the middle. The Deer ran back as he had seen the Rabbit do, made a spring, and struck the grapevine right in the center, but it only flew back and threw him over on his head. He tried again and again, until he was all bruised and bleeding.

"Let me see your teeth," at last said the Rabbit. So the Deer showed him his teeth, which were long like a wolf's teeth, but not very sharp.

"No wonder you can't do it," says the Rabbit; "your teeth are too blunt to bite anything. Let me sharpen them for you like mine. My teeth are so sharp that I can cut through a stick just like a knife." And he showed him a black locust twig, of which rabbits gnaw the young shoots, which he had shaved off as well as a knife could do it, in regular rabbit fashion. The Deer thought that just the thing. So the Rabbit got a hard stone with rough edges and filed and filed away at the Deer's teeth until they were worn down almost to the gums.

"It hurts," said the Deer; but the Rabbit said it always hurt a little when they began to get sharp; so the Deer kept quiet.

"Now try it," at last said the Rabbit. So the Deer tried again, but this time he could not bite at all.

"Now you've paid for your horns," said the Rabbit, as he jumped away through the bushes. Ever since then the Deer's teeth are so blunt that he can not chew anything but grass and leaves.

28. WHAT BECAME OF THE RABBIT

The Deer was very angry at the Rabbit for filing his teeth and determined to be revenged, but he kept still and pretended to be friendly until the Rabbit was off his guard. Then one day, as they were going along together talking, he challenged the Rabbit to jump against him. Now the Rabbit is a great jumper, as every one knows, so he agreed at once. There was a small stream beside the path, as there generally is in that country, and the Deer said:

"Let's see if you can jump across this branch. We'll go back a piece, and then when I say *Kû!* then both run and jump."

"All right," said the Rabbit. So they went back to get a good start, and when the Deer gave the word *Kû!* they ran for the stream, and the Rabbit made one jump and landed on the other side. But the Deer had stopped on the bank, and when the Rabbit looked back the Deer had conjured the stream so that it was a large river. The Rabbit was never able to get back again and is still on the other side. The rabbit that we know is only a little thing that came afterwards.

29. WHY THE MINK SMELLS

The Mink was such a great thief that at last the animals held a council about the matter. It was decided to burn him, so they caught the Mink, built a great fire, and threw him into it. As the blaze went up and they smelt the roasted flesh, they began to think he was punished enough and would probably do better in the future, so they took him out of the fire. But the Mink was already burned black and is black ever since, and whenever he is attacked or excited he smells again like roasted meat. The lesson did no good, however, and he is still as great a thief as ever.

30. WHY THE MOLE LIVES UNDERGROUND

A man was in love with a woman who disliked him and would have nothing to do with him. He tried every way to win her favor, but to no purpose, until at last he grew discouraged and made himself sick thinking over it. The Mole came along, and finding him in such low condition asked what was the trouble. The man told him the whole story, and when he had finished the Mole said: "I can help you, so that she will not only like you, but will come to you of her own will."

So that night the Mole burrowed his way underground to where the girl was in bed asleep and took out her heart. He came back by the same way and gave the heart to the man, who could not see it even when it was put into his hand. "There," said the Mole, "swallow it, and she will be drawn to come to you and can not keep away." The man swallowed the heart, and when the girl woke up she somehow thought at once of him, and felt a strange desire to be with him, as though she must go to him at once. She wondered and could not understand it, because she had always disliked him before, but at last the feeling grew so strong that she was compelled to go herself to the man and tell him she loved him and wanted to be his wife. And so they were married, but all the magicians who had known them both were surprised and wondered how it had come about. When they found that it was the work of the Mole, whom they had always before thought too insignificant for their notice, they were very jealous and threatened to kill him, so that he hid himself under the ground and has never since dared to come up to the surface.

31. THE TERRAPIN'S ESCAPE FROM THE WOLVES

The Possum and the Terrapin went out together to hunt persimmons, and found a tree full of ripe fruit. The Possum climbed it and was throwing down the persimmons to the Terrapin when a wolf came up and began to snap at the persimmons as they fell, before the Terrapin could reach them. The Possum waited his chance, and at last managed to throw down a large one (some say a bone which he carried with him), so that it lodged in the wolf's throat as he jumped up at it and choked him to death. "I'll take his ears for hominy spoons," said the Terrapin, and cut off the wolf's ears and started home with them, leaving the Possum still eating persimmons up in the tree. After a while he came to a house and was invited to have some *kanahe'na* gruel from the jar that is set always outside the door. He sat down beside the jar and dipped up the gruel with one of the wolf's ears for a spoon. The people noticed and wondered. When he was satisfied he went on, but soon came to another house and was asked to have some more kanahe'na. He dipped it up again with the wolf's ear and went on when he had enough. Soon the news went around that the Terrapin had killed the Wolf and was using his ears for spoons. All the Wolves got together and followed the Terrapin's trail until they came up with him and made him prisoner. Then they held a council to decide what to do with him, and agreed to boil him in a clay pot. They brought in a pot, but the Terrapin only laughed at it and said that if they put him into that thing he would kick it all to pieces. They said they would burn him in the fire, but the Terrapin laughed again and said he would put it out. Then they decided to throw him into the deepest hole in the river and drown him. The Terrapin begged and prayed them not to do that, but they paid no attention, and dragged him over to the river and threw him in. That was just what the Terrapin had been waiting for all the time, and he dived under the water and came up on the other side and got away.

Some say that when he was thrown into the river he struck against a rock, which broke his back in a dozen places. He sang a medicine song:

> Gû′daye′wû, Gû′daye′wû,
> I have sewed myself together, I have sewed myself together,

and the pieces came together, but the scars remain on his shell to this day.

32. ORIGIN OF THE GROUNDHOG DANCE: THE GROUNDHOG'S HEAD

Seven wolves once caught a Groundhog and said, "Now we'll kill you and have something good to eat." But the Groundhog said, "When we find good food we must rejoice over it, as people do in the Green-corn dance. I know you mean to kill me and I can't help myself, but if you want to dance I'll sing for you. This is a new dance entirely. I'll lean up against seven trees in turn and you will dance out and then turn and come back, as I give the signal, and at the last turn you may kill me."

The wolves were very hungry, but they wanted to learn the new dance, so they told him to go ahead. The Groundhog leaned up against a tree and began the song, *Ha′wiye′ĕhĭ′*, and all the wolves danced out in front, until he gave the signal, *Yu!* and began with *Hĭ′yagu′wĕ*, when they turned and danced back in line. "That's fine," said the Groundhog, and went over to the next tree and started the second song. The wolves danced out and then turned at the signal and danced back again. "That's very fine," said the Groundhog, and went over to another tree and started the third song. The wolves danced their best and the Groundhog encouraged them, but at each song he took another tree, and each tree was a little nearer to his hole under a stump. At the seventh song he said, "Now, this is the last dance, and when I say *Yu!* you will all turn and come after me, and the one who gets me may have me." So he began the seventh song and kept it up until the wolves were away out in front. Then he gave the signal, *Yu!* and made a jump for his hole. The wolves turned and were after him, but he reached the hole first and dived in. Just as he got inside, the foremost wolf caught him by the tail and gave it such a pull that it broke off, and the Groundhog's tail has been short ever since.

*   *   *   *   *   *   *

The unpleasant smell of the Groundhog's head was given it by the other animals to punish an insulting remark made by him in council. The story is a vulgar one, without wit enough to make it worth recording.

33. THE MIGRATION OF THE ANIMALS

In the old times when the animals used to talk and hold councils, and the Grubworm and Woodchuck used to marry people, there was once a great famine of mast in the mountains, and all the animals and birds which lived upon it met together and sent the Pigeon out to the low country to see if any food could be found there. After a time she came back and reported that she had found a country where the mast was "up to our ankles" on the ground. So they got together and moved down into the low country in a great army.

34. THE WOLF'S REVENGE—THE WOLF AND THE DOG

Kana'tĭ had wolves to hunt for him, because they are good hunters and never fail. He once sent out two wolves at once. One went to the east and did not return. The other went to the north, and when he returned at night and did not find his fellow he knew he must be in trouble and started after him. After traveling on some time he found his brother lying nearly dead beside a great greensnake (sălikwâ'yĭ) which had attacked him. The snake itself was too badly wounded to crawl away, and the angry wolf, who had magic powers, taking out several hairs from his own whiskers, shot them into the body of the snake and killed it. He then hurried back to Kana'tĭ, who sent the Terrapin after a great doctor who lived in the west to save the wounded wolf. The wolf went back to help his brother and by his magic powers he had him cured long before the doctor came from the west, because the Terrapin was such a slow traveler and the doctor had to prepare his roots before he started.

*   *   *   *   *   *   *

In the beginning, the people say, the Dog was put on the mountain and the Wolf beside the fire. When the winter came the Dog could not stand the cold, so he came down to the settlement and drove the Wolf from the fire. The Wolf ran to the mountains, where it suited him so well that he prospered and increased, until after a while he ventured down again and killed some animals in the settlements. The people got together and followed and killed him, but his brothers came from the mountains and took such revenge that ever since the people have been afraid to hurt a wolf.

Bird Myths

35. THE BIRD TRIBES

Winged creatures of all kinds are classed under the generic term of aninâ'hilidâ'hĭ (flyers). Birds are called, alike in the singular and plural, tsi'skwa, the term being generally held to exclude the domestic fowls introduced by the whites. When it is necessary to make the distinction they are mentioned, respectively, as inăgĕhĭ (living in the woods), and *uluñni'ta* (tame). The robin is called *tsiskwa'gwă*, a name which can not be analyzed, while the little sparrow is called *tsiskwâ'yă* (the real or principal bird), perhaps, in accord with a principle in Indian nomenclature, on account of its wide distribution. As in other languages, many of the bird names are onomatopes, as *wa'huhu'* (the screech owl), *u'guku'* (the hooting owl), *waguli'* (the whippoorwill), *kâgû* (the crow), *gŭgwĕ'* (the quail), *huhu* (the yellow mocking-bird), *tsĭ'kĭlĭlĭ'* (the chickadee), *sa'sa'* (the goose). The turtledove is called *gulĕ'-diska'nihĭ'* (it cries for acorns), on account of the resemblance of its cry to the sound of the word for acorn (*gulĕ'*). The meadow lark is called *năkwĭsĭ'* (star), on account of the appearance of its tail when spread out as it soars. The nuthatch (*Sitta carolinensis*) is called *tsulie'na* (deaf), and is supposed to be without hearing, possibly on account of its fearless disregard for man's presence. Certain diseases are diagnosed by the doctors as due to birds, either revengeful bird ghosts, bird feathers about the house, or bird shadows falling upon the patient from overhead.

The eagle (*awâ'hĭlĭ*) is the great sacred bird of the Cherokee, as of nearly all our native tribes, and figures prominently in their ceremonial ritual, especially in all things relating to war. The particular species prized was the golden or war eagle (*Aquila chrysætus*), called by the Cherokee the "pretty-feathered eagle," on account of its beautiful tail feathers, white, tipped with black, which were in such great demand for decorative and ceremonial purposes that among the western tribes a single tail was often rated as equal in value to a horse. Among the Cherokee in the old times the killing of an eagle was an event which concerned the whole settlement, and could be undertaken only by the professional eagle killer, regularly chosen for the purpose on account of his knowledge of the prescribed forms and the prayers to be said afterwards in order to obtain pardon for the necessary sacrilege, and thus ward off vengeance from the tribe. It is told of one man upon the reservation that having deliberately killed an eagle in defiance of the ordinances he was constantly haunted by dreams of fierce eagles swooping down upon him, until the nightmare was finally exorcised after a long course of priestly treatment. In 1890 there was but one eagle killer remaining among the East Cherokee. It does not appear that the eagle was ever captured alive as among the plains tribes.

The eagle must be killed only in the winter or late fall after the crops were gathered and the snakes had retired to their dens. If killed in the summertime a frost would come to destroy the corn, while the songs of the Eagle dance, when the feathers were brought home, would so anger the snakes that they would become doubly dangerous. Consequently the Eagle songs were never sung until after the snakes had gone to sleep for the winter.

When the people of a town had decided upon an Eagle dance the eagle killer was called in, frequently from a distant settlement, to procure the feathers for the occasion.   He was paid for his services from offerings made later at the dance, and as the few professionals guarded their secrets carefully from outsiders their business was a quite profitable one.   After some preliminary preparation the eagle killer sets out alone for the mountains, taking with him his gun or bow and arrows.   Having reached the mountains, he goes through a vigil of prayer and fasting, possibly lasting four days, after which he hunts until he succeeds in killing a deer.   Then, placing the body in a con-

FIG. 1—Feather wand of Eagle dance (made by John Ax).

venient exposed situation upon one of the highest cliffs, he conceals himself near by and begins to sing in a low undertone the songs to call down the eagles from the sky.   When the eagle alights upon the carcass, which will be almost immediately if the singer understands his business, he shoots it, and then standing over the dead bird, he addresses to it a prayer in which he begs it not to seek vengeance upon his tribe, because it is not a Cherokee, but a Spaniard (*Askwa'nĭ*) that has done the deed.   The selection of such a vicarious victim of revenge is evidence at once of the antiquity of the prayer in its present form and of the enduring impression which the cruelties of the early Spanish adventurers made upon the natives.

The prayer ended, he leaves the dead eagle where it fell and makes all haste to the settlement, where the people are anxiously expecting his return. On meeting the first warriors he says simply, "A snowbird has died," and passes on at once to his own quarters, his work being now finished. The announcement is made in this form in order to insure against the vengeance of any eagles that might overhear, the little snowbird being considered too insignificant a creature to be dreaded.

Having waited four days to allow time for the insect parasites to leave the body, the hunters delegated for the purpose go out to bring in the feathers. On arriving at the place they strip the body of the large tail and wing feathers, which they wrap in a fresh deerskin brought with them, and then return to the settlement, leaving the body of the dead eagle upon the ground, together with that of the slain deer, the latter being intended as a sacrifice to the eagle spirits. On reaching the settlement, the feathers, still wrapped in the deerskin, are hung up in a small, round hut built for this special purpose near the edge of the dance ground (*detsănûñ'lĭ*) and known as the place "where the feathers are kept," or feather house. Some settlements had two such feather houses, one at each end of the dance ground. The Eagle dance was held on the night of the same day on which the feathers were brought in, all the necessary arrangements having been made beforehand. In the meantime, as the feathers were supposed to be hungry after their journey, a dish of venison and corn was set upon the ground below them and they were invited to eat. The body of a flaxbird or scarlet tanager (*Piranga rubra*) was also hung up with the feathers for the same purpose. The food thus given to the feathers was disposed of after the dance, as described in another place.

The eagle being regarded as a great ada'wehĭ, only the greatest warriors and those versed in the sacred ordinances would dare to wear the feathers or to carry them in the dance. Should any person in the settlement dream of eagles or eagle feathers he must arrange for an Eagle dance, with the usual vigil and fasting, at the first opportunity; otherwise some one of his family will die. Should the insect parasites which infest the feathers of the bird in life get upon a man they will breed a skin disease which is sure to develop, even though it may be latent for years. It is for this reason that the body of the eagle is allowed to remain four days upon the ground before being brought into the settlement.

The raven (*kâ'lănû*) is occasionally seen in the mountains, but is not prominent in folk belief, excepting in connection with the grewsome tales of the Raven Mocker (q. v.). In former times its name was sometimes assumed as a war title. The crow, so prominent in other tribal mythologies, does not seem to appear in that of the Cherokee. Three varieties of owls are recognized, each under a different name, viz: *tskĭlĭ'*, the dusky horned owl (*Bubo virginianus saturatus*); *u'guku'*, the barred or hooting owl (*Syrnium nebulosum*), and *wa'huhu'*, the screech owl (*Megascops asio*). The first of these names signifies a witch, the others being onomatopes. Owls and other night-crying birds are believed to be embodied ghosts or disguised witches, and their cry is dreaded as a sound of evil omen. If the eyes of a child be bathed with water in which one of the long wing or tail feathers of an owl has been soaked, the child will be able to keep awake all night. The feather must be found by chance, and not procured intentionally for the purpose. On the other hand, an application of water in which the feather of a blue jay, procured in the same way, has been soaked will make the child an early riser.

The buzzard (*sulĭ'*) is said to have had a part in shaping the earth, as was narrated in the genesis myth. It is reputed to be a doctor among birds, and is respected accordingly, although its feathers are never worn by ball players, for fear of becoming bald. Its own baldness is accounted for by a vulgar story. As it thrives upon carrion and decay, it is held to be immune from sickness, especially of a contagious character, and a small quantity of its flesh eaten, or of the soup used as a wash, is believed to be a sure preventive of smallpox, and was used for this purpose during the smallpox epidemic among the East Cherokee in 1866. According to the Wahnenauhi manuscript, it is said also that a buzzard feather placed over the cabin door will keep out witches. In treating gunshot wounds, the medicine is blown into the wound through a tube cut from a buzzard quill and some of the buzzard's down is afterwards laid over the spot.

There is very little concerning hawks, excepting as regards the great mythic hawk, the *Tlă'nuwă'*. The *tlă'nuwă' usdi'*, or "little tlă'nuwă," is described as a bird about as large as a turkey and of a grayish blue color, which used to follow the flocks of wild pigeons, flying overhead and darting down occasionally upon a victim, which it struck and killed with its sharp breast and ate upon the wing, without alighting. It is probably the goshawk (*Astur atricapillus*).

The common swamp gallinule, locally known as mudhen or didapper (*Gallinula galeata*), is called *diga'gwanĭ'* (lame or crippled), on account of its habit of flying only for a very short distance at a time. In the Diga'gwanĭ dance the performers sing the name of the bird and endeavor to imitate its halting movements. The *dagûl'kû*, or white-fronted goose (*Anser albifrons*), appears in connection with the myth of the origin of tobacco. The feathers of the *tskwâyĭ*, the great white heron or American egret (*Herodias egretta*), are worn by ball players, and this bird probably the "swan" whose white wing was used as a peace emblem in ancient times.

A rare bird said to have been seen occasionally upon the reservation

PHOTOGRAPH BY AUTHOR, 1888

SAWĂNU'GÎ, A CHEROKEE BALL-PLAYER

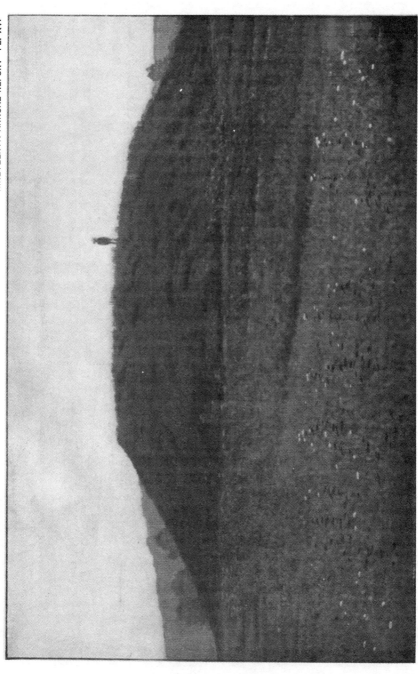

NĬKWĂSĬ MOUND AT FRANKLIN, NORTH CAROLINA.

(From photograph of 1890 furnished by Mr H. G. Trotter, owner of the mound)

many years ago was called by the curious name of *nûñdă-dikani'*, "it looks at the sun," "sun-gazer." It is described as resembling a blue crane, and may possibly have been the *Floridus cerulea*, or little blue heron. Another infrequent visitor, which sometimes passed over the mountain country in company with flocks of wild geese, was the *gu'wisguwĭ'*, so called from its cry. It is described as resembling a large snipe, with yellow legs and feet unwebbed, and is thought to visit Indian Territory at intervals. It is chiefly notable from the fact that the celebrated chief John Ross derives his Indian name, Gu'wisguwĭ', from this bird, the name being perpetuated in Coowee-scoowee district of the Cherokee Nation in the West.

Another chance visitant, concerning which there is much curious speculation among the older men of the East Cherokee, was called *tsun'digwûntsu'ˈgĭ* or *tsun'digwûn'tskĭ*, "forked," referring to the tail. It appeared but once, for a short season, about forty years ago, and has not been seen since. It is said to have been pale blue, with red in places, and nearly the size of a crow, and to have had a long forked tail like that of a fish. It preyed upon hornets, which it took upon the wing, and also feasted upon the larvæ in the nests. Appearing unexpectedly and as suddenly disappearing, it was believed to be not a bird but a transformed red-horse fish (*Moxostoma*, Cherokee *âligă'*), a theory borne out by the red spots and the long, forked tail. It is even maintained that about the time those birds first appeared some hunters on Oconaluftee saw seven of them sitting on the limb of a tree and they were still shaped like a red-horse, although they already had wings and feathers. It was undoubtedly the scissor-tail or swallow-tailed flycatcher (*Milvulus forficatus*), which belongs properly in Texas and the adjacent region, but strays occasionally into the eastern states.

On account of the red throat appendage of the turkey, somewhat resembling the goitrous growth known in the South as "kernels" (Cherokee, *dule'tsĭ*), the feathers of this bird are not worn by ball players, neither is the neck allowed to be eaten by children or sick persons, under the fear that a growth of "kernels" would be the result. The meat of the ruffed grouse, locally known as the pheasant (*Bonasa umbellus*), is tabued to a pregnant woman, because this bird hatches a large brood, but loses most of them before maturity. Under a stricter construction of the theory this meat is forbidden to a woman until she is past child bearing.

The redbird, *tatsu'hwă*, is believed to have been originally the daughter of the Sun (see the story). The *huhu*, or yellow mocking-bird, occurs in several stories. It is regarded as something supernatural, possibly on account of its imitative powers, and its heart is given to children to make them quick to learn.

The chickadee (*Parus carolinensis*), *tsĭkĭlilĭ'*, and the tufted tit-mouse, (*Parus bicolor*), *utsu'ˈgĭ*, or *u'stûtĭ*, are both regarded as news bringers, but the one is venerated as a truth teller while the other is scoffed at as a lying messenger, for reasons which appear in the story of Nûñyunu′wĭ (q. v.). When the tsĭkĭlilĭ′ perches on a branch near the house and chirps its song it is taken as an omen that an absent friend will soon be heard from or that a secret enemy is plotting mischief. Many stories are told in confirmation of this belief, among which may be instanced that of Tom Starr, a former noted outlaw of the Cherokee Nation of the West, who, on one occasion, was about to walk unwittingly into an ambush prepared for him along a narrow trail, when he heard the warning note of the tsĭkĭlilĭ′, and, turning abruptly, ran up the side of the ridge and succeeded in escaping with his life, although hotly pursued by his enemies.

36. THE BALL GAME OF THE BIRDS AND ANIMALS

Once the animals challenged the birds to a great ballplay, and the birds accepted. The leaders made the arrangements and fixed the day, and when the time came both parties met at the place for the ball dance, the animals on a smooth grassy bottom near the river and the birds in the treetops over by the ridge. The captain of the animals was the Bear, who was so strong and heavy that he could pull down anyone who got in his way. All along the road to the ball ground he was tossing up great logs to show his strength and boasting of what he would do to the birds when the game began. The Terrapin, too—not the little one we have now, but the great original Terrapin— was with the animals. His shell was so hard that the heaviest blows could not hurt him, and he kept rising up on his hind legs and dropping heavily again to the ground, bragging that this was the way he would crush any bird that tried to take the ball from him. Then there was the Deer, who could outrun every other animal. Altogether it was a fine company.

The birds had the Eagle for their captain, with the Hawk and the great Tlă′nuwă, all swift and strong of flight, but still they were a little afraid of the animals. The dance was over and they were all pruning their feathers up in the trees and waiting for the captain to give the word when here came two little things hardly larger than field mice climbing up the tree in which sat perched the bird captain. At last they reached the top, and creeping along the limb to where the Eagle captain sat they asked to be allowed to join in the game. The captain looked at them, and seeing that they were four-footed, he asked why they did not go to the animals, where they belonged. The little things said that they had, but the animals had made fun of them and driven them off because they were so small. Then the bird captain pitied them and wanted to take them.

But how could they join the birds when they had no wings? The Eagle, the Hawk, and the others consulted, and at last it was decided

to make some wings for the little fellows. They tried for a long time
to think of something that might do, until someone happened to
remember the drum they had used in the dance. The head was of
ground-hog skin and maybe they could cut off a corner and make
wings of it. So they took two pieces of leather from the drumhead
and cut them into shape for wings, and stretched them with cane
splints and fastened them on to the forelegs of one of the small animals, and in this way came *Tla'mehă*, the Bat. They threw the ball
to him and told him to catch it, and by the way he dodged and circled
about, keeping the ball always in the air and never letting it fall to the
ground, the birds soon saw that he would be one of their best men.

Now they wanted to fix the other little animal, but they had used
up all their leather to make wings for the Bat, and there was no time
to send for more. Somebody said that they might do it by stretching
his skin, so two large birds took hold from opposite sides with their
strong bills, and by pulling at his fur for several minutes they managed to stretch the skin on each side between the fore and hind
feet, until they had *Tewa*, the Flying Squirrel. To try him the bird
captain threw up the ball, when the Flying Squirrel sprang off the
limb after it, caught it in his teeth and carried it through the air to
another tree nearly across the bottom.

When they were all ready the signal was given and the game began,
but almost at the first toss the Flying Squirrel caught the ball and
carried it up a tree, from which he threw it to the birds, who kept it
in the air for some time until it dropped. The Bear rushed to get it,
but the Martin darted after it and threw it to the Bat, who was flying
near the ground, and by his dodging and doubling kept it out of the
way of even the Deer, until he finally threw it in between the posts and
won the game for the birds.

The Bear and the Terrapin, who had boasted so of what they would
do, never got a chance even to touch the ball. For saving the ball
when it dropped, the birds afterwards gave the Martin a gourd in
which to build his nest, and he still has it.

37. HOW THE TURKEY GOT HIS BEARD

When the Terrapin won the race from the Rabbit (see the story) all
the animals wondered and talked about it a great deal, because they
had always thought the Terrapin slow, although they knew that he
was a warrior and had many conjuring secrets beside. But the Turkey
was not satisfied and told the others there must be some trick about it.
Said he, "I know the Terrapin can't run—he can hardly crawl—and
I'm going to try him."

So one day the Turkey met the Terrapin coming home from war
with a fresh scalp hanging from his neck and dragging on the ground
as he traveled. The Turkey laughed at the sight and said: "That

scalp don't look right on you. Your neck is too short and low down to wear it that way. Let me show you."

The Terrapin agreed and gave the scalp to the Turkey, who fastened it around his neck. "Now," said the Turkey, "I'll walk a little way and you can see how it looks." So he walked ahead a short distance and then turned and asked the Terrapin how he liked it. Said the Terrapin, "It looks very nice; it becomes you."

"Now I'll fix it in a different way and let you see how it looks," said the Turkey. So he gave the string another pull and walked ahead again. "O, that looks very nice," said the Terrapin. But the Turkey kept on walking, and when the Terrapin called to him to bring back the scalp he only walked faster and broke into a run. Then the Terrapin got out his bow and by his conjuring art shot a number of cane splints into the Turkey's leg to cripple him so that he could not run, which accounts for all the many small bones in the Turkey's leg, that are of no use whatever; but the Terrapin never caught the Turkey, who still wears the scalp from his neck.

38. WHY THE TURKEY GOBBLES

The Grouse used to have a fine voice and a good halloo in the ball-play. All the animals and birds used to play ball in those days and were just as proud of a loud halloo as the ball players of to-day. The Turkey had not a good voice, so he asked the Grouse to give him lessons. The Grouse agreed to teach him, but wanted pay for his trouble, and the Turkey promised to give him some feathers to make himself a collar. That is how the Grouse got his collar of turkey feathers. They began the lessons and the Turkey learned very fast until the Grouse thought it was time to try his voice. "Now," said the Grouse, "I'll stand on this hollow log, and when I give the signal by tapping on it, you must halloo as loudly as you can." So he got upon the log ready to tap on it, as a Grouse does, but when he gave the signal the Turkey was so eager and excited that he could not raise his voice for a shout, but only gobbled, and ever since then he gobbles whenever he hears a noise.

39. HOW THE KINGFISHER GOT HIS BILL

Some old men say that the Kingfisher was meant in the beginning to be a water bird, but as he had not been given either web feet or a good bill he could not make a living. The animals held a council over it and decided to make him a bill like a long sharp awl for a fish-gig (fish-spear). So they made him a fish-gig and fastened it on in front of his mouth. He flew to the top of a tree, sailed out and darted down into the water, and came up with a fish on his gig. And he has been the best gigger ever since.

Some others say it was this way: A Blacksnake found a Yellowhammer's nest in a hollow tree, and after swallowing the young birds, coiled up to sleep in the nest, where the mother bird found him when she came home. She went for help to the Little People, who sent her to the Kingfisher. He came, and after flying back and forth past the hole a few times, made one dart at the snake and pulled him out dead. When they looked they found a hole in the snake's head where the Kingfisher had pierced it with a slender *tugălû'nă* fish, which he carried in his bill like a lance. From this the Little People concluded that he would make a first-class gigger if he only had the right spear, so they gave him his long bill as a reward.

40. HOW THE PARTRIDGE GOT HIS WHISTLE

In the old days the Terrapin had a fine whistle, but the Partridge had none. The Terrapin was constantly going about whistling and showing his whistle to the other animals until the Partridge became jealous, so one day when they met the Partridge asked leave to try it. The Terrapin was afraid to risk it at first, suspecting some trick, but the Partridge said, "I'll give it back right away, and if you are afraid you can stay with me while I practice." So the Terrapin let him have the whistle and the Partridge walked around blowing on it in fine fashion. "How does it sound with me?" asked the Partridge. "O, you do very well," said the Terrapin, walking alongside. "Now, how do you like it," said the Partridge, running ahead and whistling a little faster. "That's fine," answered the Terrapin, hurrying to keep up, "but don't run so fast." "And now, how do you like this?" called the Partridge, and with that he spread his wings, gave one long whistle, and flew to the top of a tree, leaving the poor Terrapin to look after him from the ground. The Terrapin never recovered his whistle, and from that, and the loss of his scalp, which the Turkey stole from him, he grew ashamed to be seen, and ever since he shuts himself up in his box when anyone comes near him.

41. HOW THE REDBIRD GOT HIS COLOR

A Raccoon passing a Wolf one day made several insulting remarks, until at last the Wolf became angry and turned and chased him. The Raccoon ran his best and managed to reach a tree by the river side before the Wolf came up. He climbed the tree and stretched out on a limb overhanging the water. When the Wolf arrived he saw the reflection in the water, and thinking it was the Raccoon he jumped at it and was nearly drowned before he could scramble out again, all wet and dripping. He lay down on the bank to dry and fell asleep, and while he was sleeping the Raccoon came down the tree and plastered his eyes with dung. When the Wolf awoke he found he could not open his eyes, and began to whine. Along came a little brown bird through the bushes and heard the Wolf crying and asked what was the matter. The Wolf told his story and said, "If you will get my eyes open, I will show you where to find some nice red paint to paint yourself." "All right," said the brown bird; so he pecked at the Wolf's eyes until he got off all the plaster. Then the Wolf took him to a rock that had streaks of bright red paint running through it, and the little bird painted himself with it, and has ever since been a Redbird.

42. THE PHEASANT BEATING CORN; ORIGIN OF THE PHEASANT DANCE

The Pheasant once saw a woman beating corn in a wooden mortar in front of the house. "I can do that, too," said he, but the woman would not believe it, so the Pheasant went into the woods and got upon a hollow log and "drummed" with his wings as a pheasant does, until the people in the house heard him and thought he was really beating corn.

     *   *   *   *   *   *   *

In the Pheasant dance, a part of the Green-corn dance, the instrument used is the drum, and the dancers beat the ground with their feet in imitation of the drumming sound made by the pheasant. They form two concentric circles, the men being on the inside, facing the women in the outer circle, each in turn advancing and retreating at the signal of the drummer, who sits at one side and sings the Pheasant songs. According to the story, there was once a winter famine among the birds and animals. No mast (fallen nuts) could be found in the woods, and they were near starvation when a Pheasant discovered a holly tree, loaded with red berries, of which the Pheasant is said to be particularly fond. He called his companion birds, and they formed a circle about the tree, singing, dancing, and drumming with their wings in token of their joy, and thus originated the Pheasant dance.

43. THE RACE BETWEEN THE CRANE AND THE HUMMINGBIRD

The Hummingbird and the Crane were both in love with a pretty woman. She preferred the Hummingbird, who was as handsome as the Crane was awkward, but the Crane was so persistent that in order to get rid of him she finally told him he must challenge the other to a race and she would marry the winner. The Hummingbird was so swift—almost like a flash of lightning—and the Crane so slow and heavy, that she felt sure the Hummingbird would win. She did not know the Crane could fly all night.

They agreed to start from her house and fly around the circle of the world to the beginning, and the one who came in first would marry the woman. At the word the Hummingbird darted off like an arrow and was out of sight in a moment, leaving his rival to follow heavily behind. He flew all day, and when evening came and he stopped to

roost for the night he was far ahead. But the Crane flew steadily all
night long, passing the Hummingbird soon after midnight and going
on until he came to a creek and stopped to rest about daylight. The
Hummingbird woke up in the morning and flew on again, thinking
how easily he would win the race, until he reached the creek and
there found the Crane spearing tadpoles, with his long bill, for breakfast. He was very much surprised and wondered how this could have
happened, but he flew swiftly by and soon left the Crane out of sight
again.

The Crane finished his breakfast and started on, and when evening
came he kept on as before. This time it was hardly midnight when
he passed the Hummingbird asleep on a limb, and in the morning he
had finished his breakfast before the other came up. The next day
he gained a little more, and on the fourth day he was spearing tadpoles
for dinner when the Hummingbird passed him. On the fifth and
sixth days it was late in the afternoon before the Hummingbird came
up, and on the morning of the seventh day the Crane was a whole
night's travel ahead. He took his time at breakfast and then fixed
himself up as nicely as he could at the creek and came in at the starting place where the woman lived, early in the morning. When the
Hummingbird arrived in the afternoon he found he had lost the race,
but the woman declared she would never have such an ugly fellow as
the Crane for a husband, so she stayed single.

44. THE OWL GETS MARRIED

A widow with one daughter was always warning the girl that she
must be sure to get a good hunter for a husband when she married.
The young woman listened and promised to do as her mother advised.
At last a suitor came to ask the mother for the girl, but the widow
told him that only a good hunter could have her daughter. "I'm just
that kind," said the lover, and again asked her to speak for him to the
young woman. So the mother went to the girl and told her a young
man had come a-courting, and as he said he was a good hunter she
advised her daughter to take him. "Just as you say," said the girl.
So when he came again the matter was all arranged, and he went to
live with the girl.

The next morning he got ready and said he would go out hunting,
but before starting he changed his mind and said he would go fishing.
He was gone all day and came home late at night, bringing only three
small fish, saying that he had had no luck, but would have better success to-morrow. The next morning he started off again to fish and
was gone all day, but came home at night with only two worthless
spring lizards (*duwĕ'gă*) and the same excuse. Next day he said he
would go hunting this time. He was gone again until night, and

returned at last with only a handful of scraps that he had found where some hunters had cut up a deer.

By this time the old woman was suspicious. So next morning when he started off again, as he said, to fish, she told her daughter to follow him secretly and see how he set to work. The girl followed through the woods and kept him in sight until he came down to the river, where she saw her husband change to a hooting owl (*uguku'*) and fly over to a pile of driftwood in the water and cry, "*U-gu-ku! hu! hu! u! u!*" She was surprised and very angry and said to herself, "I thought I had married a man, but my husband is only an owl." She watched and saw the owl look into the water for a long time and at last swoop down and bring up in his claws a handful of sand, from which he picked out a crawfish. Then he flew across to the bank, took the form of a man again, and started home with the crawfish. His wife hurried on ahead through the woods and got there before him. When he came in with the crawfish in his hand, she asked him where were all the fish he had caught. He said he had none, because an owl had frightened them all away. "I think you are the owl," said his wife, and drove him out of the house. The owl went into the woods and there he pined away with grief and love until there was no flesh left on any part of his body except his head.

45. THE HUHU GETS MARRIED

A widow who had an only daughter, but no son, found it very hard to make a living and was constantly urging upon the young woman that they ought to have a man in the family, who would be a good hunter and able to help in the field. One evening a stranger lover came courting to the house, and when the girl told him that she could marry only one who was a good worker, he declared that he was exactly that sort of man; so the girl talked to her mother, and on her advice they were married.

The next morning the widow gave her new son-in-law a hoe and sent him out to the cornfield. When breakfast was ready she went to call him, following a sound as of some one hoeing on stony soil, but when she came to the spot she found only a small circle of hoed ground and no sign of her son-in-law. Away over in the thicket she heard a huhu calling.

He did not come in for dinner, either, and when he returned home in the evening the old woman asked him where he had been all day. "Hard at work," said he. "But I didn't see you when I came to call you to breakfast." "I was down in the thicket cutting sticks to mark off the field," said he. "But why didn't you come in to dinner?" "I was too busy working," said he. So the old woman was satisfied, and they had their supper together.

Early next morning he started off with his hoe over his shoulder. When breakfast was ready the old woman went again to call him, but found no sign of him, only the hoe lying there and no work done. And away over in the thicket a huhu was calling, "*Sau-h! sau-h! sau-h! hu! hu! hu! hu! hu! hu! chi! chi! chi!—whew!*"

She went back to the house, and when at last he came home in the evening she asked him again what he had been doing all day. "Working hard," said he. "But you were not there when I came after you." "O, I just went over in the thicket a while to see some of my kinsfolk," said he. Then the old woman said, "I have lived here a long time and there is nothing living in the swamp but huhus. My daughter wants a husband that can work and not a lazy huhu; so you may go." And she drove him from the house.

46. WHY THE BUZZARD'S HEAD IS BARE

The buzzard used to have a fine topknot, of which he was so proud that he refused to eat carrion, and while the other birds were pecking at the body of a deer or other animal which they had found he would strut around and say: "You may have it all, it is not good enough for me." They resolved to punish him, and with the help of the buffalo carried out a plot by which the buzzard lost not his topknot alone, but nearly all the other feathers on his head. He lost his pride at the same time, so that he is willing enough now to eat carrion for a living.

47. THE EAGLE'S REVENGE

Once a hunter in the mountains heard a noise at night like a rushing wind outside the cabin, and on going out he found that an eagle had just alighted on the drying pole and was tearing at the body of a deer hanging there. Without thinking of the danger, he shot the eagle. In the morning he took the deer and started back to the settlement, where he told what he had done, and the chief sent out some men to bring in the eagle and arrange for an Eagle dance. They brought back the dead eagle, everything was made ready, and that night they started the dance in the townhouse.

About midnight there was a whoop outside and a strange warrior came into the circle and began to recite his exploits. No one knew him, but they thought he had come from one of the farther Cherokee towns. He told how he had killed a man, and at the end of the story he gave a hoarse yell, *Hi!* that startled the whole company, and one of the seven men with the rattles fell over dead. He sang of another deed, and at the end straightened up with another loud yell. A second rattler fell dead, and the people were so full of fear that they could not stir from their places. Still he kept on, and at every pause there came again that terrible scream, until the last of the seven rattlers fell dead, and then the stranger went out into the darkness. Long afterward they learned from the eagle killer that it was the brother of the eagle shot by the hunter.

48. THE HUNTER AND THE BUZZARD

A hunter had been all day looking for deer in the mountains without success until he was completely tired out and sat down on a log to rest and wonder what he should do, when a buzzard—a bird which always has magic powers—came flying overhead and spoke to him, asking him what was his trouble. When the hunter had told his story the buzzard said there were plenty of deer on the ridges beyond if only the hunter were high up in the air where he could see them, and proposed that they exchange forms for a while, when the buzzard would go home to the hunter's wife while the hunter would go to look for deer. The hunter agreed, and the buzzard became a man and went home to the hunter's wife, who received him as her husband, while the hunter became a buzzard and flew off over the mountain to locate the deer. After staying some time with the woman, who thought always it was her real husband, the buzzard excused himself, saying he must go again to look for game or they would have nothing to eat. He came to the place where he had first met the hunter, and found him already there, still in buzzard form, awaiting him. He asked the hunter what success he had had, and the hunter replied that he had found several deer over the ridge, as the buzzard had said. Then the buzzard restored the hunter to human shape, and became himself a buzzard again and flew away. The hunter went where he had seen the deer and killed several, and from that time he never returned empty-handed from the woods.

Snake, Fish, and Insect Myths

49. THE SNAKE TRIBE

The generic name for snakes is *inădû'*. They are all regarded as *anida'wehĭ*, "supernaturals," having an intimate connection with the rain and thunder gods, and possessing a certain influence over the other animal and plant tribes. It is said that the snakes, the deer, and the ginseng act as allies, so that an injury to one is avenged by all. The feeling toward snakes is one of mingled fear and reverence, and every precaution is taken to avoid killing or offending one, especially the rattlesnake. He who kills a snake will soon see others; and should he kill a second one, so many will come around him whichever way he may turn that he will become dazed at the sight of their glistening eyes and darting tongues and will go wandering about like a crazy man, unable to find his way out of the woods. To guard against this misfortune there are certain prayers which the initiated say in order that a snake may not cross their path, and on meeting the first one of the season the hunter humbly begs of him, "Let us not see each other this summer." Certain smells, as that of the wild parsnip, and certain songs, as those of the *Unika'wĭ* or Townhouse dance, are offensive to the snakes and make them angry. For this reason the Unika'wĭ dance is held only late in the fall, after they have retired to their dens for the winter.

When one dreams of being bitten by a snake he must be treated the same as for an actual bite, because it is a snake ghost that has bitten him; otherwise the place will swell and ulcerate in the same way, even though it be years afterwards. For fear of offending them, even in speaking, it is never said that a man has been bitten by a snake, but only that he has been "scratched by a brier." Most of the beliefs and customs in this connection have more special reference to the rattlesnake.

The rattlesnake is called *utsa'nătĭ*, which may be rendered, "he has a bell," alluding to the rattle. According to a myth given elsewhere, he was once a man, and was transformed to his present shape that he might save the human race from extermination by the Sun, a mission which he accomplished successfully after others had failed. By the old men he is also spoken of as "the Thunder's necklace" (see the story of Ûñtsaiyĭ'), and to kill one is to destroy one of the most prized ornaments of the thunder god. In one of the formulas addressed to the Little Men, the sons of the Thunder, they are implored to take the disease snake to themselves, because "it is just what you adorn yourselves with."

For obvious reasons the rattlesnake is regarded as the chief of the snake tribe and is feared and respected accordingly. Few Cherokee will venture to kill one except under absolute necessity, and even then the crime must be atoned for by asking pardon of the snake ghost, either in person or through the mediation of a priest, according to a set formula. Otherwise the relatives of the dead snake will send one of their number to track up the offender and bite him so that he will die (see story, "The Rattlesnake's Vengeance"). The only thing of which the rattlesnake is afraid is said to be the plant known as campion, or "rattlesnake's master" (*Silene stellata*), which is used by the doctors to counteract the effect of the bite, and it is believed that a snake will flee in terror from the hunter who carries a small piece of the root about his person. Chewed linn bark is also applied to the bite, perhaps from the supposed occult connection between the snake and the thunder, as this tree is said to be immune from the lightning stroke.

Notwithstanding the fear of the rattlesnake, his rattles, teeth, flesh, and oil are greatly prized for occult or medical uses, the snakes being killed for this purpose by certain priests who know the necessary rites and formulas for obtaining pardon. This device for whipping the devil around the stump, and incidentally increasing their own revenues, is a common trick of Indian medicine men.   Outsiders desiring to acquire this secret knowledge are discouraged by being told that it is a dangerous thing to learn, for the reason that the new initiate is almost certain to be bitten, in order that the snakes may "try" him to know if he has correctly learned the formula.   When a rattlesnake is killed the head must be cut off and buried an arm's length deep in the ground and the body carefully hidden away in a hollow log.   If it is left exposed to the weather, the angry snakes will send such torrents of rain that all the streams will overflow their banks.   Moreover, they will tell their friends, the deer, and the ginseng in the mountains, so that these will hide themselves and the hunters will seek them in vain.

The tooth of a rattlesnake which has been killed by the priest with the proper ceremonies while the snake was lying stretched out from east to west is used to scarify patients preliminary to applying the medicine in certain ailments.   Before using it the doctor holds it between the thumb and finger of his right hand and addresses it in a prayer, at the end of which the tooth "becomes alive," when it is ready for the operation.   The explanation is that the tense, nervous grasp of the doctor causes his hand to twitch and the tooth to move slightly between his fingers.   The rattles are worn on the head, and sometimes a portion of the flesh is eaten by ball players to make them more terrible to their opponents, but it is said to have the bad effect of making them cross to their wives.   From the lower half of the body, thought to be the fattest portion, the oil is extracted and is in as great repute among the Indians for rheumatism and sore joints as among the white mountaineers.   The doctor who prepares the oil must also eat the flesh of the snake.   In certain seasons of epidemic a roasted (barbecued) rattlesnake was kept hanging up in the house, and every morning the father of the family bit off a small piece and chewed it, mixing it then with water, which he spit upon the bodies of the others to preserve them from the contagion.   It was said to be a sure cure, but apt to make the patients hot tempered.

The copperhead, *wâ'dige-askâ'lĭ*, "brown-head," although feared on account of its poisonous bite, is hated, instead of being regarded with veneration, as is the rattlesnake.   It is believed to be a descendant of a great mythic serpent (see number 5) and is said to have "eyes of fire," on account of their intense brightness.   The blacksnake is called *gûlĕ'gĭ*, "the climber."   Biting its body is said to be a preventive of toothache, and there is also a belief, perhaps derived from the whites, that if the body of one be hung upon a tree it will bring rain within three (four?) days.   The small greensnake is called *sălikwâ'yĭ*, the same name being also applied to a certain plant, the *Eryngium virginianum*, or bear grass, whose long, slender leaves bear some resemblance to a greensnake.   As with the blacksnake, it is believed that toothache may be prevented and sound teeth insured as long as life lasts by

biting the greensnake along its body. It must be held by the head
and tail, and all the teeth at once pressed down four times along the
middle of its body, but without biting into the flesh or injuring the
snake. Some informants say that the operation must be repeated
four times upon as many snakes and that a certain food tabu must
also be observed. The water moccasin, *kanegwâ'tĭ*, is not specially
regarded, but a very rare wood snake, said to resemble it except that
it has blue eyes, is considered to have great supernatural powers,
in what way is not specified. The repulsive but harmless spreading
adder (*Heterodon*) is called *dalĭkstă'*, "vomiter," on account of its
habit of spitting, and sometimes *kwandăya'hû*, a word of uncertain
etymology. It was formerly a man, but was transformed into a snake
in order to accomplish the destruction of the Daughter of the Sun
(see the story). For its failure on this occasion it is generally
despised.

The Wahnenauhi manuscript mentions a legend of a great serpent
called on account of its color the "ground snake." To see it was an
omen of death to the one who saw it, and if it was seen by several persons some great tribal calamity was expected. For traditions and
beliefs in regard to the Uktena, the Uksuhĭ, and other mythic serpents, see under those headings.

50. THE UKTENA AND THE ULŬÑSŬ'TĬ

Long ago—*hĭlahi'yu*—when the Sun became angry at the people
on earth and sent a sickness to destroy them, the Little Men changed
a man into a monster snake, which they called Uktena, "The Keen-
eyed," and sent him to kill her. He failed to do the work, and the
Rattlesnake had to be sent instead, which made the Uktena so jealous
and angry that the people were afraid of him and had him taken up
to Gălûñ'lătĭ, to stay with the other dangerous things.[1] He left others
behind him, though, nearly as large and dangerous as himself, and
they hide now in deep pools in the river and about lonely passes in
the high mountains, the places which the Cherokee call "Where the
Uktena stays."

Those who know say that the Uktena is a great snake, as large around
as a tree trunk, with horns on its head, and a bright, blazing crest like
a diamond upon its forehead, and scales glittering like sparks of fire.
It has rings or spots of color along its whole length, and can not be
wounded except by shooting in the seventh spot from the head, because
under this spot are its heart and its life. The blazing diamond is
called *Ulŭñsŭ'tĭ*, "Transparent," and he who can win it may become
the greatest wonder worker of the tribe, but it is worth a man's life
to attempt it, for whoever is seen by the Uktena is so dazed by the
bright light that he runs toward the snake instead of trying to escape.

---

[1] See "The Daughter of the Sun."

Even to see the Uktena asleep is death, not to the hunter himself, but to *his family*.

Of all the daring warriors who have started out in search of the Ulûñsû′tĭ only Âgän-uni′tsĭ ever came back successful.[1] The East Cherokee still keep the one which he brought. It is like a large transparent crystal, nearly the shape of a cartridge bullet, with a blood-red streak running through the center from top to bottom. The owner keeps it wrapped in a whole deerskin, inside an earthen jar hidden away in a secret cave in the mountains. Every seven days he feeds it with the blood of small game, rubbing the blood all over the crystal as soon as the animal has been killed. Twice a year it must have the blood of a deer or some other large animal. Should he forget to feed it at the proper time it would come out from its cave at night in a shape of fire and fly through the air to slake its thirst with the lifeblood of the conjurer or some one of his people. He may save himself from this danger by telling it, when he puts it away, that he will not need it again for a long time. It will then go quietly to sleep and feel no hunger until it is again brought out to be consulted. Then it must be fed again with blood before it is used.

No white man must ever see it and no person but the owner will venture near it for fear of sudden death. Even the conjurer who keeps it is afraid of it, and changes its hiding place every once in a while so that it can not learn the way out. When he dies it will be buried with him. Otherwise it will come out of its cave, like a blazing star, to search for his grave, night after night for seven years, when, if still not able to find him, it will go back to sleep forever where he has placed it.

Whoever owns the Ulûñsû′tĭ is sure of success in hunting, love, rain-making, and every other business, but its great use is in life prophecy. When it is consulted for this purpose the future is seen mirrored in the clear crystal as a tree is reflected in the quiet stream below, and the conjurer knows whether the sick man will recover, whether the warrior will return from battle, or whether the youth will live to be old.

51. ÂGÄN-UNI′TSĬ'S SEARCH FOR THE UKTENA

In one of their battles with the Shawano, who are all magicians, the Cherokee captured a great medicine-man whose name was Âgän-uni′tsĭ, "The Ground-hogs' Mother." They had tied him ready for the torture when he begged for his life and engaged, if spared, to find for them the great wonder worker, the Ulûñsû′tĭ. Now, the Ulûñsû′tĭ is like a blazing star set in the forehead of the great Uktena serpent, and the medicine-man who could possess it might do marvelous things, but everyone knew this could not be, because it was certain death to

---

[1] See the next story.

meet the Uktena. They warned him of all this, but he only answered that his medicine was strong and he was not afraid. So they gave him his life on that condition and he began the search.

The Uktena used to lie in wait in lonely places to surprise its victims, and especially haunted the dark passes of the Great Smoky mountains. Knowing this, the magician went first to a gap in the range on the far northern border of the Cherokee country. He searched and found there a monster blacksnake, larger than had ever been known before, but it was not what he was looking for, and he laughed at it as something too small for notice. Coming southward to the next gap he found there a great moccasin snake, the largest ever seen, but when the people wondered he said it was nothing. In the next gap he found a greensnake and called the people to see "the pretty sălikwâ′yĭ," but when they found an immense greensnake coiled up in the path they ran away in fear. Coming on to U′tăwa-gûn′ta, the Bald mountain, he found there a great diya′hălĭ (lizard) basking, but, although it was large and terrible to look at, it was not what he wanted and he paid no attention to it. Going still south to Walâsi′yĭ, the Frog place, he found a great frog squatting in the gap, but when the people who came to see it were frightened like the others and ran away from the monster he mocked at them for being afraid of a frog and went on to the next gap. He went on to Duni-skwa′lgûñ′yĭ, the Gap of the Forked Antler, and to the enchanted lake of Atagâ′hĭ, and at each he found monstrous reptiles, but he said they were nothing. He thought the Uktena might be hiding in the deep water at Tlanusi′yĭ, the Leech place, on Hiwassee, where other strange things had been seen before, and going there he dived far down under the surface. He saw turtles and water snakes, and two immense sun-perches rushed at him and retreated again, but that was all. Other places he tried, going always southward, and at last on Gahû′tĭ mountain he found the Uktena asleep.

Turning without noise, he ran swiftly down the mountain side as far as he could go with one long breath, nearly to the bottom of the slope. There he stopped and piled up a great circle of pine cones, and inside of it he dug a deep trench. Then he set fire to the cones and came back again up the mountain.

The Uktena was still asleep, and, putting an arrow to his bow, Âgăn-uni′tsĭ shot and sent the arrow through its heart, which was under the seventh spot from the serpent's head. The great snake raised his head, with the diamond in front flashing fire, and came straight at his enemy, but the magician, turning quickly, ran at full speed down the mountain, cleared the circle of fire and the trench at one bound, and lay down on the ground inside.

The Uktena tried to follow, but the arrow was through his heart. and in another moment he rolled over in his death struggle, spitting poison over all the mountain side. But the poison drops could not pass the circle of fire, but only hissed and sputtered in the blaze, and the magician on the inside was untouched except by one small drop which struck upon his head as he lay close to the ground; but he did not know it. The blood, too, as poisonous as the froth, poured from the Uktena's wound and down the slope in a dark stream, but it ran into the trench and left him 'unharmed. The dying monster rolled over and over down the mountain, breaking down large trees in its path until it reached the bottom. Then Âgän-uni′tsĭ called every bird in all the woods to come to the feast, and so many came that when they were done not even the bones were left.

After seven days he went by night to the spot. The body and the bones of the snake were gone, all eaten by the birds, but he saw a bright light shining in the darkness, and going over to it he found, resting on a low-hanging branch, where a raven had dropped it, the diamond from the head of the Uktena. He wrapped it up carefully and took it with him, and from that time he became the greatest medicine-man in the whole tribe.

When Âgän-uni′tsĭ came down again to the settlement the people noticed a small snake hanging from his head where the single drop of poison from the Uktena had struck; but so long as he lived he himself never knew that it was there.

Where the blood of the Uktena had filled the trench a lake formed afterwards, and the water was black and in this water the women used to dye the cane splits for their baskets.

52. THE RED MAN AND THE UKTENA

Two brothers went hunting together, and when they came to a good camping place in the mountains they made a fire, and while one gathered bark to put up a shelter the other started up the creek to look for a deer. Soon he heard a noise on the top of the ridge as if two animals were fighting. He hurried through the bushes to see what it might be, and when he came to the spot he found a great uktena coiled around a man and choking him to death. The man was fighting for his life, and called out to the hunter: "Help me, nephew; he is your enemy as well as mine." The hunter took good aim, and, drawing the arrow to the head, sent it through the body of the uktena, so that the blood spouted from the hole. The snake loosed its coils with a snapping noise, and went tumbling down the ridge into the valley, tearing up the earth like a water spout as it rolled.

The stranger stood up, and it was the Asga′ya Gi′găgeĭ, the Red Man of the Lightning. He said to the hunter: "You have helped me, and now I will reward you, and give you a medicine so that you can always find game." They waited until it was dark, and then went down the ridge to where the dead uktena had rolled, but by this time the birds and insects had eaten the body and only the bones were left. In one place were flashes of light coming up from the ground, and on digging here, just under the surface, the Red Man found a scale of the uktena. Next he went over to a tree that had been struck by lightning, and gathering a handful of splinters he made a fire and burned the uktena scale to a coal. He wrapped this in a piece of deerskin and gave it to the hunter, saying: "As long as you keep this you can always kill game." Then he told the hunter that when he went back to camp he must hang up the medicine on a tree outside, because it was very strong and dangerous. He told him also that when he went into the cabin he would find his brother lying inside nearly dead on account of the presence of the uktena's scale, but he must take a small piece of cane, which the Red Man gave him, and scrape a little of it into water and give it to his brother to drink and he would be well again. Then the Red Man was gone, and the hunter could not see where he went. He returned to camp alone, and found his brother very sick, but soon cured him with the medicine from the cane, and that day and the next, and every day after, he found game whenever he went for it.

53. THE HUNTER AND THE UKSU′HĬ

A man living down in Georgia came to visit some relatives at Hickory-log. He was a great hunter, and after resting in the house a day or two got ready to go into the mountains. His friends warned him not to go toward the north, as in that direction, near a certain large uprooted tree, there lived a dangerous monster uksu′hĭ snake. It kept constant watch, and whenever it could spring upon an unwary hunter it would coil about him and crush out his life in its folds and then drag the dead body down the mountain side into a deep hole in Hiwassee.

He listened quietly to the warning, but all they said only made him the more anxious to see such a monster, so, without saying anything of his intention, he left the settlement and took his way directly up the mountain toward the north. Soon he came to the fallen tree and climbed upon the trunk, and there, sure enough, on the other side was the great uksu′hĭ stretched out in the grass, with its head raised, but looking the other way. It was about so large [making a circle of a foot in diameter with his hands]. The frightened hunter got down again at once and started to run; but the snake had heard the noise and turned quickly and was after him. Up the ridge the hunter ran, the snake close behind him, then down the other side toward the river. With all his running the uksu′hĭ gained rapidly, and just as he reached the low ground it caught up with him and wrapped around him, pinning one arm down by his side, but leaving the other free.

Now it gave him a terrible squeeze that almost broke his ribs, and then began to drag him along toward the water. With his free hand the hunter clutched at the bushes as they passed, but the snake turned its head and blew its sickening breath into his face until he had to let go his hold. Again and again this happened, and all the time they were getting nearer to a deep hole in the river, when, almost at the last moment, a lucky thought came into the hunter's mind.

He was sweating all over from his hard run across the mountain, and suddenly remembered to have heard that snakes can not bear the smell of perspiration. Putting his free hand into his bosom he worked it around under his armpit until it was covered with perspiration. Then withdrawing it he grasped at a bush until the snake turned its head, when he quickly slapped his sweaty hand on its nose. The uksu′hĭ gave one gasp almost as if it had been wounded, loosened its coil, and glided swiftly away through the bushes, leaving the hunter, bruised but not disabled, to make his way home to Hickory-log.

54. THE USTÛ′TLĬ

There was once a great serpent called the Ustû′tlĭ that made its haunt upon Cohutta mountain. It was called the Ustû′tlĭ or "foot" snake, because it did not glide like other snakes, but had feet at each end of its body, and moved by strides or jerks, like a great measuring worm. These feet were three-cornered and flat and could hold on to the ground like suckers. It had no legs, but would raise itself up on its hind feet, with its snaky head waving high in the air until it found a good place to take a fresh hold; then it would bend down and grip its front feet to the ground while it drew its body up from behind. It could cross rivers and deep ravines by throwing its head across and getting a grip with its front feet and then swinging its body over. Wherever its footprints were found there was danger. It used to bleat like a young fawn, and when the hunter heard a fawn bleat in the woods he never looked for it, but hurried away in the other direction. Up the mountain or down, nothing could escape the Ustû′tlĭ's pursuit, but along the side of the ridge it could not go, because the great weight of its swinging head broke its hold on the ground when it moved sideways.

It came to pass after a while that not a hunter about Cohutta would venture near the mountain for dread of the Ustû′tlĭ. At last a man from one of the northern settlements came down to visit some relatives in that neighborhood. When he arrived they made a feast for him, but had only corn and beans, and excused themselves for having no meat because the hunters were afraid to go into the mountains. He asked the reason, and when they told him he said he would go himself to-morrow and either bring in a deer or find the Ustû′tlĭ. They tried to dissuade him from it, but as he insisted upon going they warned him that if he heard a fawn bleat in the thicket he must run at once and if the snake came after him he must not try to run down the mountain, but along the side of the ridge.

In the morning he started out and went directly toward the mountain. Working his way through the bushes at the base, he suddenly heard a fawn bleat in front. He guessed at once that it was the Ustû'tlĭ, but he had made up his mind to see it, so he did not turn back, but went straight forward, and there, sure enough, was the monster, with its great head in the air, as high as the pine branches, looking in every direction to discover a deer, or maybe a man, for breakfast. It saw him and came at him at once, moving in jerky strides, every one the length of a tree trunk, holding its scaly head high above the bushes and bleating as it came.

The hunter was so badly frightened that he lost his wits entirely and started to run directly up the mountain. The great snake came after him, gaining half its length on him every time it took a fresh grip with its fore feet, and would have caught the hunter before he reached the top of the ridge, but that he suddenly remembered the warning and changed his course to run along the sides of the mountain. At once the snake began to lose ground, for every time it raised itself up the weight of its body threw it out of a straight line and made it fall a little lower down the side of the ridge. It tried to recover itself, but now the hunter gained and kept on until he turned the end of the ridge and left the snake out of sight. Then he cautiously climbed to the top and looked over and saw the Ustû'tlĭ still slowly working its way toward the summit.

He went down to the base of the mountain, opened his fire pouch, and set fire to the grass and leaves. Soon the fire ran all around the mountain and began to climb upward. When the great snake smelled the smoke and saw the flames coming it forgot all about the hunter and turned to make all speed for a high cliff near the summit. It reached the rock and got upon it, but the fire followed and caught the dead pines about the base of the cliff until the heat made the Ustû'tlĭ's scales crack. Taking a close grip of the rock with its hind feet it raised its body and put forth all its strength in an effort to spring across the wall of fire that surrounded it, but the smoke choked it and its hold loosened and it fell among the blazing pine trunks and lay there until it was burned to ashes.

55. THE UW'TSÛÑ'TA

At Nûñ'dăye''lĭ, the wildest spot on Nantahala river, in what is now Macon county, North Carolina, where the overhanging cliff is highest and the river far below, there lived in the old time a great snake called the Uw'tsûñ'ta or "bouncer," because it moved by jerks like a measuring worm, with only one part of its body on the ground at a time. It stayed generally on the east side, where the sun came first in the morning, and used to cross by reaching over from the highest point of the cliff until it could get a grip on the other side, when it would pull over the rest of its body. It was so immense that when it was thus stretched across its shadow darkened the whole valley below. For a long time the people did not know it was there, but when at last they found out about it they were afraid to live in the valley, so that it was deserted even while still Indian country.

56. THE SNAKE BOY

There was a boy who used to go bird hunting every day, and all the birds he brought home he gave to his grandmother, who was very fond of him. This made the rest of the family jealous, and they treated him in such fashion that at last one day he told his grandmother he would leave them all, but that she must not grieve for him. Next morning he refused to eat any breakfast, but went off hungry to the woods and was gone all day. In the evening he returned, bringing with him a pair of deer horns, and went directly to the hothouse (âsĭ), where his grandmother was waiting for him. He told the old woman he must be alone that night, so she got up and went into the house where the others were.

At early daybreak she came again to the hothouse and looked in, and there she saw an immense uktena that filled the âsĭ, with horns on its head, but still with two human legs instead of a snake tail. It was all that was left of her boy. He spoke to her and told her to leave him, and she went away again from the door. When the sun was well up, the uktena began slowly to crawl out, but it was full noon before it was all out of the âsĭ. It made a terrible hissing noise as it came out, and all the people ran from it. It crawled on through the settlement, leaving a broad trail in the ground behind it, until it came to a deep bend in the river, where it plunged in and went under the water.

The grandmother grieved much for her boy, until the others of the family got angry and told her that as she thought so much of him she ought to go and stay with him. So she left them and went along the trail made by the uktena to the river and walked directly into the water and disappeared. Once after that a man fishing near the place saw her sitting on a large rock in the river, looking just as she had always looked, but as soon as she caught sight of him she jumped into the water and was gone.

57. THE SNAKE MAN

Two hunters, both for some reason under a tabu against the meat of a squirrel or turkey, had gone into the woods together. When evening came they found a good camping place and lighted a fire to prepare their supper. One of them had killed several squirrels during the day, and now got ready to broil them over the fire. His companion warned him that if he broke the tabu and ate squirrel meat he would

become a snake, but the other laughed and said that was only a conjurer's story. He went on with his preparation, and when the squirrels
were roasted made his supper of them and then lay down beside the
fire to sleep.

Late that night his companion was aroused by groaning, and on
looking around he found the other lying on the ground rolling and
twisting in agony, and with the lower part of his body already changed
to the body and tail of a large water snake. The man was still able to
speak and called loudly for help, but his companion could do nothing,
but only sit by and try to comfort him while he watched the arms sink
into the body and the skin take on a scaly change that mounted gradually toward the neck, until at last even the head was a serpent's head
and the great snake crawled away from the fire and down the bank
into the river.

58. THE RATTLESNAKE'S VENGEANCE

One day in the old times when we could still talk with other creatures, while some children were playing about the house, their mother
inside heard them scream. Running out she found that a rattlesnake
had crawled from the grass, and taking up a stick she killed it. The
father was out hunting in the mountains, and that evening when coming home after dark through the gap he heard a strange wailing sound.
Looking about he found that he had come into the midst of a whole
company of rattlesnakes, which all had their mouths open and seemed
to be crying. He asked them the reason of their trouble, and they
told him that his own wife had that day killed their chief, the Yellow
Rattlesnake, and they were just now about to send the Black Rattlesnake to take revenge.

The hunter said he was very sorry, but they told him that if he
spoke the truth he must be ready to make satisfaction and give his
wife as a sacrifice for the life of their chief. Not knowing what might
happen otherwise, he consented. They then told him that the Black
Rattlesnake would go home with him and coil up just outside the
door in the dark. He must go inside, where he would find his wife
awaiting him, and ask her to get him a drink of fresh water from the
spring. That was all.

He went home and knew that the Black Rattlesnake was following.
It was night when he arrived and very dark, but he found his wife
waiting with his supper ready. He sat down and asked for a drink of
water. She handed him a gourd full from the jar, but he said he
wanted it fresh from the spring, so she took a bowl and went out of the
door. The next moment he heard a cry, and going out he found that
the Black Rattlesnake had bitten her and that she was already dying.
He stayed with her until she was dead, when the Black Rattlesnake
came out from the grass again and said his tribe was now satisfied.

He then taught the hunter a prayer song, and said, "When you meet any of us hereafter sing this song and we will not hurt you; but if by accident one of us should bite one of your people then sing this song over him and he will recover." And the Cherokee have kept the song to this day.

59. THE SMALLER REPTILES—FISHES AND INSECTS

There are several varieties of frogs and toads, each with a different name, but there is very little folklore in connection with them. The common green frog is called *walâ'sĭ*, and among the Cherokee, as among uneducated whites, the handling of it is thought to cause warts, which for this reason are called by the same name, *walâ'sĭ*. A solar eclipse is believed to be caused by the attempt of a great frog to swallow the sun, and in former times it was customary on such occasions to fire guns and make other loud noises to frighten away the frog. The smaller varieties are sometimes eaten, and on rare occasions the bull-frog also, but the meat is tabued to ball players while in training, for fear that the brittleness of the frog's bones would be imparted to those of the player.

The land tortoise (*tûksĭ'*) is prominent in the animal myths, and is reputed to have been a great warrior in the old times. On account of the stoutness of its legs ball players rub their limbs with them before going into the contest. The common water turtle (*săligu'gĭ*), which occupies so important a place in the mythology of the northern tribes, is not mentioned in Cherokee myth or folklore, and the same is true of the soft-shelled turtle (*u'lănă'wă*), perhaps for the reason that both are rare in the cold mountain streams of the Cherokee country.

There are perhaps half a dozen varieties of lizard, each with a different name. The gray road lizard, or *diyâ'hălĭ* (alligator lizard, *Sceloporus undulatus*), is the most common. On account of its habit of alternately puffing out and drawing in its throat as though sucking, when basking in the sun, it is invoked in the formulas for drawing out the poison from snake bites. If one catches the first diyâ'hălĭ seen in the spring, and, holding it between his fingers, scratches his legs downward with its claws, he will see no dangerous snakes all summer. Also, if one be caught alive at any time and rubbed over the head and throat of an infant, scratching the skin very slightly at the same time with the claws, the child will never be fretful, but will sleep quietly without complaining, even when sick or exposed to the rain. This is a somewhat risky experiment, however, as the child is liable thereafter to go to sleep wherever it may be laid down for a moment, so that the mother is in constant danger of losing it. According to some authorities this sleep lizard is not the diyâ'hălĭ, but a larger variety akin to the next described.

The *gigă-tsuha'lĭ* ("bloody mouth," *Pleistodon*?) is described as a very large lizard, nearly as large as a water dog, with the throat and corners of the mouth red, as though from drinking blood. It is believed to be not a true lizard but a transformed *ugûñste′lǐ* fish (described below) on account of the similarity of coloring and the fact that the fish disappears about the time the gigă-tsuha′′lǐ begins to come out. It is ferocious and a hard biter, and pursues other lizards. In dry weather it cries or makes a noise like a cicada, raising itself up as it cries. It has a habit of approaching near to where some person is sitting or standing, then halting and looking fixedly at him, and constantly puffing out its throat until its head assumes a bright red color. It is thought then to be sucking the blood of its victim, and is dreaded and shunned accordingly. The small scorpion lizard (*tsâne′nǐ*) is sometimes called also *gigă-danegi′skǐ*, "blood taker." It is a striped lizard which frequents sandy beaches and resemble the diyâ′hălǐ, but is of a brown color. It is believed also to be sucking blood in some mysterious way whenever it nods its head, and if its heart be eaten by a dog that animal will be able to extract all the nutrient properties from food by simply looking at those who are eating.

The small spring lizard (*duwĕ′′gă*), which lives in springs, is supposed to cause rain whenever it crawls out of the spring. It is frequently invoked in the formulas. Another spring (?) lizard, red, with black spots, is called *dăgan′′tû′* or *aniganti′′skǐ* "the rain maker," because its cry is said to bring rain. The water dog (*tsuwă′*, mud puppy, *Menopoma* or *Protonopsis*) is a very large lizard, or rather salamander, frequenting muddy water. It is rarely eaten, from an unexplained belief that if one who has eaten its meat goes into the field immediately afterward the crop will be ruined. There are names for one or two other varieties of lizard as well as for the alligator (*tsula′skǐ*), but no folklore in connection with them.

Although the Cherokee country abounds in swift-flowing streams well stocked with fish, of which the Indians make free use, there is but little fish lore. A number of "dream" diseases, really due to indigestion, are ascribed to revengeful fish ghosts, and the doctor usually tries to effect the cure by invoking some larger fish or fish-eating bird to drive out the ghost.

Toco creek, in Monroe county, Tennessee, derives its name from a mythic monster fish, the Dăkwă′, considered the father of all the fish tribe, which is said to have lived formerly in Little Tennessee river at that point (see story, "The Hunter and the Dăkwă′"). A fish called *ugûñste′lǐ*, "having horns," which appears only in spring, is believed to be transformed later into the giga-tsuha′′lǐ lizard, already mentioned. The fish is described as having horns or projections upon its nose and beautiful red spots upon its head, and as being attended or accompanied by many smaller red fish, all of which, including the ugûñste′lǐ, are accustomed to pile up small stones in the water. As the season advances it disappears and is believed then to have turned into a giga-tsuha'lĭ lizard, the change beginning at the head and finishing with the tail. It is probably the *Campostoma* or stone roller, which is conspicuous for its bright coloring in early spring, but loses its tints after spawning. The meat of the sluggish hog-sucker is tabued to the ball player, who must necessarily be active in movement. The fresh-water mussel is called *dăgŭ'nă*, and the same name is applied to certain pimples upon the face, on account of a fancied resemblance. The ball player rubs himself with an eel skin to make himself slippery and hard to hold, and, according to the Wahnenauhi manuscript, women formerly tied up their hair with the dried skin of an eel to make it grow long. A large red crawfish called *tsiska'gĭlĭ*, much resembling a lobster, is used to scratch young children in order to give them a strong grip, each hand of the child being lightly scratched once with the pincer of the living animal. A mother whose grown son had been thus treated when an infant claimed that he could hold anything with his thumb and finger. It is said, however, to render the child quarrelsome and disposed to bite.

Of insects there is more to be said. The generic name for all sorts of small insects and worms is *tsgâya*, and according to the doctors, who had anticipated the microbe theory by several centuries, these tsgâya are to blame for nearly every human ailment not directly traceable to the *asgina* of the larger animals or to witchcraft. The reason is plain. There are such myriads of them everywhere on the earth and in the air that mankind is constantly destroying them by wholesale, without mercy and almost without knowledge, and this is their method of taking revenge.

Beetles are classed together under a name which signifies "insects with shells." The little water-beetle or mellow-bug (*Dineutes discolor*) is called *dâyuni'sĭ*, "beaver's grandmother," and according to the genesis tradition it brought up the first earth from under the water. A certain green-headed beetle with horns (*Phanæus carnifex*) is spoken of as the dog of the Thunder boys, and the metallic-green luster upon its forehead is said to have been caused by striking at the celebrated mythic gambler, Ûñtsaiyĭ', "Brass" (see the story). The June-bug (*Allorhina nitida*), another green beetle, is *tagû*, but is frequently called by the curious name of *tu'ya-dĭ'skalaw'stĭ'skĭ*, "one who keeps fire under the beans." Its larva is the grubworm which presided at the meeting held by the insects to compass the destruction of the human race (see the story, "Origin of Disease and Medicine"). The large horned beetle (*Dynastes tityus?*) is called *tsistû'na*, "crawfish," *a'wĭ'*, "deer," or *gălăgi'na*, "buck," on account of its branching horns. The snapping beetle (*Alaus oculatus?*) is called *tûlsku'wa*, "one that snaps with his head."

When the *lâlû* or jar-fly (*Cicada auletes*) begins to sing in midsummer they say: "The jar-fly has brought the beans," his song being taken as the signal that beans are ripe and that green corn is not far behind. When the katydid (*tsĭkĭkĭ'*) is heard a little later they say, "Katydid has brought the roasting-ear bread." The cricket (*tăla'tŭ'*) is often called "the barber" (*ditastaye'skĭ*), on account of its habit of gnawing hair from furs, and when the Cherokee meet a man with his hair clipped unevenly they sometimes ask playfully, "Did the cricket cut your hair?" (see story, "Why the Possum's Tail is Bare"). Certain persons are said to drink tea made of crickets in order to become good singers.

The mole cricket (*Gryllotalpa*), so called because it tunnels in the earth and has hand-like claws fitted for digging, is known to the Cherokee as *gûl'kwâgĭ*, a word which literally means "seven," but is probably an onomatope. It is reputed among them to be alert, hard to catch, and an excellent singer, who "never makes mistakes." Like the crawfish and the cricket, it plays an important part in preparing people for the duties of life. Infants slow in learning to speak have their tongues scratched with the claw of a *gûl'kwâgĭ*, the living insect being held in the hand during the operation, in order that they may soon learn to speak distinctly and be eloquent, wise, and shrewd of speech as they grow older, and of such quick intelligence as to remember without effort anything once heard. The same desirable result may be accomplished with a grown person, but with much more difficulty, as in that case it is necessary to scratch the inside of the throat for four successive mornings, the insect being pushed down with the fingers and again withdrawn, while the regular tabus must be strictly observed for the same period, or the operation will be without effect. In some cases the insect is put into a small bowl of water overnight, and if still alive in the morning it is taken out and the water given to the patient to drink, after which the *gûl'kwâgĭ* is set at liberty.

Bees are kept by many of the Cherokee, in addition to the wild bees which are hunted in the woods. Although they are said to have come originally from the whites, the Cherokee have no tradition of a time when they did not know them; there seems, however, to be no folklore connected with them. The cow-ant (*Myrmica?*), a large, red, stinging ant, is called properly *dasûñ'tălĭ atatsûñ'skĭ*, "stinging ant," but, on account of its hard body-case, is frequently called *nûñ'yunu'wĭ*, "stone-dress," after a celebrated mythic monster. Strange as it may seem, there appears to be no folklore connected with either the firefly or the glowworm, while the spider, so prominent in other tribal mythologies, appears in but a single Cherokee myth, where it brings back the fire from across the water. In the formulas it is frequently invoked to entangle in its threads the soul of a victim whom the conjurer desires to bring under his evil spells. From a fancied resemblance in appearance the name for spider, *kǎ'nǎnĕ'skĭ*, is applied also to a watch or clock. A small yellowish moth which flies about the fire at night is called *tûñ'tăwû*, a name implying that it goes into and out of the fire, and when at last it flits too near and falls into the blaze the Cherokee say, "Tûñ'tăwû is going to bed." On account of its affinity for the fire it is invoked by the doctor in all "fire diseases," including sore eyes and frostbite.

60. WHY THE BULLFROG'S HEAD IS STRIPED

According to one version the Bullfrog was always ridiculing the great gambler Ûñtsai'yĭ, "Brass," (see the story) until the latter at last got angry and dared the Bullfrog to play the *gatayû'stĭ* (wheel-and-stick) game with him, whichever lost to be scratched on his forehead. Brass won, as he always did, and the yellow stripes on the Bullfrog's head show where the gambler's fingers scratched him.

Another story is that the Bullfrog had a conjurer to paint his head with yellow stripes (brass) to make him appear more handsome to a pretty woman he was courting.

61. THE BULLFROG LOVER

A young man courted a girl, who liked him well enough, but her mother was so much opposed to him that she would not let him come near the house. At last he made a trumpet from the handle of a gourd and hid himself after night near the spring until the old woman came down for water. While she was dipping up the water he put the trumpet to his lips and grumbled out in a deep voice like a bullfrog's:

> Yañdaska'gă hûñyahu'skă,
> Yañdaska'gă hûñyahu'skă.
> The faultfinder will die,
> The faultfinder will die.

The woman thought it a witch bullfrog, and was so frightened that she dropped her dipper and ran back to the house to tell the people They all agreed that it was a warning to her to stop interfering with her daughter's affairs, so she gave her consent, and thus the young man won his wife.

There is another story of a girl who, every day when she went down to the spring for water, heard a voice singing, *Kûnu'nŭ tû'tsahyesĭ', Kûnu'nŭ tû'tsahyesĭ'*, "A bullfrog will marry you, A bullfrog will marry you." She wondered much until one day when she came down she saw sitting on a stone by the spring a bullfrog, which suddenly took the form of a young man and asked her to marry him. She consented and took him back with her to the house. But although he had the shape of a man there was a queer bullfrog look about his face, so that the girl's family hated him and at last persuaded her to send him away. She told him and he went away, but when they next went down to the spring they heard a voice: *Stĕ'tsĭ tûya'husĭ, Stĕ'tsĭ tû'ya-husĭ'*, "Your daughter will die, Your daughter will die," and so it happened soon after.

As some tell it, the lover was a tadpole, who took on human shape, retaining only his tadpole mouth. To conceal it he constantly refused to eat with the family, but stood with his back to the fire and his face screwed up, pretending that he had a toothache. At last his wife grew suspicious and turning him suddenly around to the firelight, exposed the tadpole mouth, at which they all ridiculed him so much that he left the house forever.

62. THE KATYDID'S WARNING

Two hunters camping in the woods were preparing supper one night when a Katydid began singing near them. One of them said sneeringly, "*Kû!* It sings and don't know that it will die before the season ends." The Katydid answered: "*Kû! niwĭ* (onomatope); O, so you say; but you need not boast. You will die before to-morrow night." The next day they were surprised by the enemy and the hunter who had sneered at the Katydid was killed.

WONDER STORIES

63. ÛÑTSAIYĬ', THE GAMBLER

Thunder lives in the west, or a little to the south of west, near the place where the sun goes down behind the water. In the old times he sometimes made a journey to the east, and once after he had come back from one of these journeys a child was born in the east who, the people said, was his son. As the boy grew up it was found that he had scrofula sores all over his body, so one day his mother said to him, "Your father, Thunder, is a great doctor. He lives far in the west, but if you can find him he can cure you."

So the boy set out to find his father and be cured. He traveled long toward the west, asking of every one he met where Thunder lived, until at last they began to tell him that it was only a little way ahead. He went on and came to Ûñtiguhĭ', on Tennessee, where lived Ûñtsaiyĭ' "Brass." Now Ûñtsaiyĭ' was a great gambler, and made his living that way. It was he who invented the *gatayûstĭ* game that we play with a stone wheel and a stick. He lived on the south side of the river, and everybody who came that way he challenged to play against him. The large flat rock, with the lines and grooves where they used to roll the wheel, is still there, with the wheels themselves and the stick turned to stone. He won almost every time, because he was so tricky, so that he had his house filled with all kinds of fine things. Sometimes he would lose, and then he would bet all that he had, even to his own life, but the winner got nothing for his trouble, for Ûñtsaiyĭ' knew how to take on different shapes, so that he always got away.

As soon as Ûñtsaiyĭ' saw him he asked him to stop and play a while, but the boy said he was looking for his father, Thunder, and had no time to wait. "Well," said Ûñtsaiyĭ', "he lives in the next house; you can hear him grumbling over there all the time"—he meant the Thunder—"so we may as well have a game or two before you go on." The boy said he had nothing to bet. "That's all right," said the gambler, "we'll play for your pretty spots." He said this to make the boy angry so that he would play, but still the boy said he must go first and find his father, and would come back afterwards.

He went on, and soon the news came to Thunder that a boy was looking for him who claimed to be his son. Said Thunder, "I have traveled in many lands and have many children. Bring him here and we shall soon know." So they brought in the boy, and Thunder showed him a seat and told him to sit down. Under the blanket on the seat were long, sharp thorns of the honey locust, with the points all sticking up, but when the boy sat down they did not hurt him, and then Thunder knew that it was his son. He asked the boy why he had come. "I have sores all over my body, and my mother told me you were my father and a great doctor, and if I came here you would cure me." "Yes," said his father, "I am a great doctor, and I'll soon fix you."

There was a large pot in the corner and he told his wife to fill it with water and put it over the fire. When it was boiling, he put in some roots, then took the boy and put him in with them. He let it boil a long time until one would have thought that the flesh was boiled from the poor boy's bones, and then told his wife to take the pot and throw it into the river, boy and all. She did as she was told, and threw it into the water, and ever since there is an eddy there that we call Ûñ'tiguhĭ', "Pot-in-the-water." A service tree and a calico bush grew on the bank above. A great cloud of steam came up and made streaks and blotches on their bark, and it has been so to this day. When the steam cleared away she looked over and saw the boy clinging to the roots of the service tree where they hung down into the water, but now his skin was all clean. She helped him up the bank, and they went back to the house. On the way she told him, "When we go in, your father will put a new dress on you, but when he opens his box and tells you to pick out your ornaments be sure to take them from the bottom. Then he will send for his other sons to play ball against you. There is a honey-locust tree in front of the house, and as soon as you begin to get tired strike at that and your father will stop the play, because he does not want to lose the tree."

When they went into the house, the old man was pleased to see the boy looking so clean, and said, "I knew I could soon cure those spots. Now we must dress you." He brought out a fine suit of buckskin, with belt and headdress, and had the boy put them on. Then he opened a box and said, "Now pick out your necklace and bracelets."

The boy looked, and the box was full of all kinds of snakes gliding over each other with their heads up. He was not afraid, but remembered what the woman had told him, and plunged his hand to the bottom and drew out a great rattlesnake and put it around his neck for a necklace. He put down his hand again four times and drew up four copperheads and twisted them around his wrists and ankles. Then his father gave him a war club and said, "Now you must play a ball game with your two elder brothers. They live beyond here in the Darkening land, and I have sent for them." He said a ball game, but he meant that the boy must fight for his life. The young men came, and they were both older and stronger than the boy, but he was not afraid and fought against them. The thunder rolled and the lightning flashed at every stroke, for they were the young Thunders, and the boy himself was Lightning. At last he was tired from defending himself alone against two, and pretended to aim a blow at the honey-locust tree. Then his father stopped the fight, because he was afraid the lightning would split the tree, and he saw that the boy was brave and strong.

The boy told his father how Ûñtsaiyĭ′ had dared him to play, and had even offered to play for the spots on his skin. "Yes," said Thunder, "he is a great gambler and makes his living that way, but I will see that you win." He brought a small cymling gourd with a hole bored through the neck, and tied it on the boy's wrist. Inside the gourd there was a string of beads, and one end hung out from a hole in the top, but there was no end to the string inside. "Now," said his father, "go back the way you came, and as soon as he sees you he will want to play for the beads. He is very hard to beat, but this time he will lose every game. When he cries out for a drink, you will know he is getting discouraged, and then strike the rock with your war club and water will come, so that you can play on without stopping. At last he will bet his life, and lose. Then send at once for your brothers to kill him, or he will get away, he is so tricky."

The boy took the gourd and his war club and started east along the road by which he had come. As soon as Ûñtsaiyĭ′ saw him he called to him, and when he saw the gourd with the bead string hanging out he wanted to play for it. The boy drew out the string, but there seemed to be no end to it, and he kept on pulling until enough had come out to make a circle all around the playground. "I will play one game for this much against your stake," said the boy, "and when that is over we can have another game."

They began the game with the wheel and stick and the boy won. Ûñtsaiyĭ′ did not know what to think of it, but he put up another stake and called for a second game. The boy won again, and so they played on until noon, when Ûñtsaiyĭ′ had lost nearly everything he had and was about discouraged. It was very hot, and he said, "I am thirsty," and wanted to stop long enough to get a drink. "No," said the boy, and struck the rock with his club so that water came out, and they had a drink. They played on until Ûñtsaiyĭ' had lost all his buckskins and beaded work, his eagle feathers and ornaments, and at last offered to bet his wife. They played and the boy won her. Then Ûñtsaiyĭ' was desperate and offered to stake his life. "If I win I kill you, but if you win you may kill me." They played and the boy won.

"Let me go and tell my wife," said Ûñtsaiyĭ', "so that she will receive her new husband, and then you may kill me." He went into the house, but it had two doors, and although the boy waited long Ûñtsaiyĭ' did not come back. When at last he went to look for him he found that the gambler had gone out the back way and was nearly out of sight going east.

The boy ran to his father's house and got his brothers to help him. They brought their dog—the Horned Green Beetle—and hurried after the gambler. He ran fast and was soon out of sight, and they followed as fast as they could. After a while they met an old woman making pottery and asked her if she had seen Ûñtsaiyĭ' and she said she had not. . "He came this way," said the brothers. "Then he must have passed in the night," said the old woman, "for I have been here all day." They were about to take another road when the Beetle, which had been circling about in the air above the old woman, made a dart at her and struck her on the forehead, and it rang like brass— *ûñtsaiyĭ'!* Then they knew it was Brass and sprang at him, but he jumped up in his right shape and was off, running so fast that he was soon out of sight again. The Beetle had struck so hard that some of the brass rubbed off, and we can see it on the beetle's forehead yet.

They followed and came to an old man sitting by the trail, carving a stone pipe. They asked him if he had seen Brass pass that way and he said no, but again the Beetle—which could know Brass under any shape—struck him on the forehead so that it rang like metal, and the gambler jumped up in his right form and was off again before they could hold him. He ran east until he came to the great water; then he ran north until he came to the edge of the world, and had to turn again to the west. He took every shape to throw them off the track, but the Green Beetle always knew him, and the brothers pressed him so hard that at last he could go no more and they caught him just as he reached the edge of the great water where the sun goes down.

They tied his hands and feet with a grapevine and drove a long stake through his breast, and planted it far out in the deep water. They set two crows on the end of the pole to guard it and called the place *Kâgûñ'yĭ*, "Crow place." But Brass never died, and can not die until the end of the world, but lies there always with his face up. Sometimes he struggles under the water to get free, and sometimes the beavers, who are his friends, come and gnaw at the grapevine to

release him.   Then the pole shakes and the crows at the top cry *Ka!*
Ka! Ka! and scare the beavers away.

64. THE NEST OF THE TLĂ′NUWĂ

On the north bank of Little Tennessee river, in a bend below the
mouth of Citico creek, in Blount county, Tennessee, is a high cliff hanging over the water, and about halfway up the face of the rock is a cave
with two openings.   The rock projects outward above the cave, so that
the mouth can not be seen from above, and it seems impossible to
reach the cave either from above or below.   There are white streaks
in the rock from the cave down to the water.   The Cherokee call it
Tlă′nuwâ′ĭ, "the place of the Tlă′nuwă," or great mythic hawk.

In the old time, away back soon after the creation, a pair of Tlă′nuwăs
had their nest in this cave.   The streaks in the rock were made by the
droppings from the nest.   They were immense birds, larger than any
that live now, and very strong and savage.   They were forever flying
up and down the river, and used to come into the settlements and carry
off dogs and even young children playing near the houses.   No one
could reach the nest to kill them, and when the people tried to shoot
them the arrows only glanced off and were seized and carried away in
the talons of the Tlă′nuwăs.

At last the people went to a great medicine man, who promised to
help them.   Some were afraid that if he failed to kill the Tlă′nuwăs
they would take revenge on the people, but the medicine man said he
could fix that.   He made a long rope of linn bark, just as the Cherokee
still do, with loops in it for his feet, and had the people let him down
from the top of the cliff at a time when he knew that the old birds were
away.   When he came opposite the mouth of the cave he still could
not reach it, because the rock above hung over, so he swung himself
backward and forward several times until the rope swung near enough
for him to pull himself into the cave with a hooked stick that he carried, which he managed to fasten in some bushes growing at the
entrance.   In the nest he found four young ones, and on the floor of
the cave were the bones of all sorts of animals that had been carried
there by the hawks.   He pulled the young ones out of the nest and
threw them over the cliff into the deep water below, where a great
Uktena serpent that lived there finished them.   Just then he saw the
two old ones coming, and had hardly time to climb up again to the top
of the rock before they reached the nest.

When they found the nest empty they were furious, and circled
round and round in the air until they saw the snake put up its head
from the water.   Then they darted straight downward, and while one
seized the snake in his talons and flew far up in the sky with it, his
mate struck at it and bit off piece after piece until nothing was left.
They were so high up that when the pieces fell they made holes in the

rock, which are still to be seen there, at the place which we call "Where the Tlă'nuwă cut it up," opposite the mouth of Citico. Then the two Tlă'nuwăs circled up and up until they went out of sight, and they have never been seen since.

65. THE HUNTER AND THE TLĂ'NUWĂ

A hunter out in the woods one day saw a Tlă'nuwa overhead and tried to hide from it, but the great bird had already seen him, and sweep-ing down struck its claws into his hunting pack and carried him far up into the air. As it flew, the Tlă'nuwă, which was a mother bird, spoke and told the hunter that he need not be afraid, as she would not hurt him, but only wanted him to stay for a while with her young ones to guard them until they were old enough to leave the nest. At last they alighted at the mouth of a cave in the face of a steep cliff. Inside the water was dripping from the roof, and at the farther end was a nest of sticks in which were two young birds. The old Tlă'nuwă set the hunter down and then flew away, returning soon with a fresh-killed deer, which it tore in pieces, giving the first piece to the hunter and then feeding the two young hawks.

The hunter stayed in the cave many days until the young birds were nearly grown, and every day the old mother hawk would fly away from the nest and return in the evening with a deer or a bear, of which she always gave the first piece to the hunter. He grew very anxious to see his home again, but the Tlă'nuwă kept telling him not to be uneasy, but to wait a little while longer. At last he made up his mind to escape from the cave and finally studied out a plan. The next morn-ing, after the old bird had gone, he dragged one of the young birds to the mouth of the cave and tied himself to one of its legs with a strap from his hunting pack. Then with the flat side of his tomahawk he struck it several times in the head until it was dazed and helpless, and pushed the bird and himself together off the shelf of rock into the air.

They fell far, far down toward the earth, but the air from below held up the bird's wings, so that it was almost as if they were flying. As the Tlă'nuwă revived it tried to fly upward toward the nest, but the hunter struck it again with his hatchet until it was dazed and dropped again. At last they came down in the top of a poplar tree, when the hunter untied the strap from the leg of the young bird and let it fly away, first pulling out a feather from its wing. He climbed down from the tree and went to his home in the settlement, but when he looked in his pack for the feather he found a stone instead.

66. U'TLÛÑ'TĂ, THE SPEAR-FINGER

Long, long ago—*hĭlahi'yu*—there dwelt in the mountains a terrible ogress, a woman monster, whose food was human livers. She could take on any shape or appearance to suit her purpose, but in her right form she looked very much like an old woman, excepting that her whole body was covered with a skin as hard as a rock that no weapon could wound or penetrate, and that on her right hand she had a long, stony forefinger of bone, like an awl or spearhead, with which she stabbed everyone to whom she could get near enough. On account of this fact she was called *U'tlũñ'tă*, "Spear-finger," and on account of her stony skin she was sometimes called *Nũñ'yunu'wĭ*, "Stone-dress." There was another stone-clothed monster that killed people, but that is a different story.

Spear-finger had such powers over stone that she could easily lift and carry immense rocks, and could cement them together by merely striking one against another. To get over the rough country more easily she undertook to build a great rock bridge through the air from Nũñyû'-tlu'gûñ'yĭ, the "Tree rock," on Hiwassee, over to Sanigilâ'gĭ (Whiteside mountain), on the Blue ridge, and had it well started from the top of the "Tree rock" when the lightning struck it and scattered the fragments along the whole ridge, where the pieces can still be seen by those who go there. She used to range all over the mountains about the heads of the streams and in the dark passes of Nantahala, always hungry and looking for victims. Her favorite haunt on the Tennessee side was about the gap on the trail where Chilhowee mountain comes down to the river.

Sometimes an old woman would approach along the trail where the children were picking strawberries or playing near the village, and would say to them coaxingly, "Come, my grandchildren, come to your granny and let granny dress your hair." When some little girl ran up and laid her head in the old woman's lap to be petted and combed the old witch would gently run her fingers through the child's hair until it went to sleep, when she would stab the little one through the heart or back of the neck with the long awl finger, which she had kept hidden under her robe. Then she would take out the liver and eat it.

She would enter a house by taking the appearance of one of the family who happened to have gone out for a short time, and would watch her chance to stab some one with her long finger and take out his liver. She could stab him without being noticed, and often the victim did not even know it himself at the time—for it left no wound and caused no pain—but went on about his own affairs, until all at once he felt weak and began gradually to pine away, and was always sure to die, because Spear-finger had taken his liver.

When the Cherokee went out in the fall, according to their custom, to burn the leaves off from the mountains in order to get the chestnuts on the ground, they were never safe, for the old witch was always on the lookout, and as soon as she saw the smoke rise she knew there were Indians there and sneaked up to try to surprise one alone. So as well as they could they tried to keep together, and were very cautious of allowing any stranger to approach the camp. But if one went down to the spring for a drink they never knew but it might be the liver eater that came back and sat with them.

Sometimes she took her proper form, and once or twice, when far out from the settlements, a solitary hunter had seen an old woman, with a queer-looking hand, going through the woods singing low to herself:

> Uwe'la na'tsĭkŭ'.   Su' sŭ' sai'.
> Liver, I eat it.   Su' sa' sai'.

It was rather a pretty song, but it chilled his blood, for he knew it was the liver eater, and he hurried away, silently, before she might see him.

At last a great council was held to devise some means to get rid of U'tlûñ'tă before she should destroy everybody. The people came from all around, and after much talk it was decided that the best way would be to trap her in a pitfall where all the warriors could attack her at once. So they dug a deep pitfall across the trail and covered it over with earth and grass as if the ground had never been disturbed. Then they kindled a large fire of brush near the trail and hid themselves in the laurels, because they knew she would come as soon as she saw the smoke.

Sure enough they soon saw an old woman coming along the trail. She looked like an old woman whom they knew well in the village, and although several of the wiser men wanted to shoot at her, the others interfered, because they did not want to hurt one of their own people. The old woman came slowly along the trail, with one hand under her blanket, until she stepped upon the pitfall and tumbled through the brush top into the deep hole below. Then, at once, she showed her true nature, and instead of the feeble old woman there was the terrible U'tlûñ'tă with her stony skin, and her sharp awl finger reaching out in every direction for some one to stab.

The hunters rushed out from the thicket and surrounded the pit, but shoot as true and as often as they could, their arrows struck the stony mail of the witch only to be broken and fall useless at her feet, while she taunted them and tried to climb out of the pit to get at them. They kept out of her way, but were only wasting their arrows when a small bird, Utsu'gĭ, the titmouse, perched on a tree overhead and began to sing "un, un, un." They thought it was saying u'nahŭ', heart, meaning that they should aim at the heart of the stone witch. They directed their arrows where the heart should be, but the arrows only glanced off with the flint heads broken.

Then they caught the Utsŭ'gĭ and cut off its tongue, so that ever since its tongue is short and everybody knows it is a liar. When the hunters let it go it flew straight up into the sky until it was out of sight and never came back again. The titmouse that we know now is only an image of the other.

They kept up the fight without result until another bird, little Tsĭ´-kĭlilĭ´, the chickadee, flew down from a tree and alighted upon the witch's right hand. The warriors took this as a sign that they must aim there, and they were right, for her heart was on the inside of her hand, which she kept doubled into a fist, this same awl hand with which she had stabbed so many people. Now she was frightened in earnest, and began to rush furiously at them with her long awl finger and to jump about in the pit to dodge the arrows, until at last a lucky arrow struck just where the awl joined her wrist and she fell down dead.

Ever since the tsĭ´kĭlilĭ´ is known as a truth teller, and when a man is away on a journey, if this bird comes and perches near the house and chirps its song, his friends know he will soon be safe home.

67. NÛÑ´YUNU´WĬ, THE STONE MAN

This is what the old men told me when I was a boy.

Once when all the people of the settlement were out in the mountains on a great hunt one man who had gone on ahead climbed to the top of a high ridge and found a large river on the other side. While he was looking across he saw an old man walking about on the opposite ridge, with a cane that seemed to be made of some bright, shining rock. The hunter watched and saw that every little while the old man would point his cane in a certain direction, then draw it back and smell the end of it. At last he pointed it in the direction of the hunting camp on the other side of the mountain, and this time when he drew back the staff he sniffed it several times as if it smelled very good, and then started along the ridge straight for the camp. He moved very slowly, with the help of the cane, until he reached the end of the ridge, when he threw the cane out into the air and it became a bridge of shining rock stretching across the river. After he had crossed over upon the bridge it became a cane again, and the old man picked it up and started over the mountain toward the camp.

The hunter was frightened, and felt sure that it meant mischief, so he hurried on down the mountain and took the shortest trail back to the camp to get there before the old man. When he got there and told his story the medicine-man said the old man was a wicked cannibal monster called Nûñ´yunu´wĭ, "Dressed in Stone," who lived in that part of the country, and was always going about the mountains looking for some hunter to kill and eat. It was very hard to escape from him, because his stick guided him like a dog, and it was nearly as hard to kill him, because his whole body was covered with a skin of solid rock. If he came he would kill and eat them all, and there was only one way to save themselves. He could not bear to look upon a menstrual woman, and if they could find seven menstrual women to stand in the path as he came along the sight would kill him.

So they asked among all the women, and found seven who were sick in that way, and with one of them it had just begun. By the order of the medicine-man they stripped themselves and stood along the path where the old man would come. Soon they heard Nûñ'yunu'wĭ coming through the woods, feeling his way with his stone cane. He came along the trail to where the first woman was standing, and as soon as he saw her he started and cried out: "*Yu!* my grandchild; you are in a very bad state!" He hurried past her, but in a moment he met the next woman, and cried out again: "*Yu!* my child; you are in a terrible way," and hurried past her, but now he was vomiting blood. He hurried on and met the third and the fourth and the fifth woman, but with each one that he saw his step grew weaker until when he came to the last one, with whom the sickness had just begun, the blood poured from his mouth and he fell down on the trail.

Then the medicine-man drove seven sourwood stakes through his body and pinned him to the ground, and when night came they piled great logs over him and set fire to them, and all the people gathered around to see. Nûñ'yunu'wĭ was a great ada'wehĭ and knew many secrets, and now as the fire came close to him he began to talk, and told them the medicine for all kinds of sickness. At midnight he began to sing, and sang the hunting songs for calling up the bear and the deer and all the animals of the woods and mountains. As the blaze grew hotter his voice sank low and lower, until at last when daylight came, the logs were a heap of white ashes and the voice was still.

Then the medicine-man told them to rake off the ashes, and where the body had lain they found only a large lump of red wâ'dĭ paint and a magic u'lûñsû'ti stone. He kept the stone for himself, and calling the people around him he painted them, on face and breast, with the red wâ'dĭ, and whatever each person prayed for while the painting was being done—whether for hunting success, for working skill, or for a long life—that gift was his.

68. THE HUNTER IN THE DĂKWĂ'

In the old days there was a great fish called the Dăkwă', which lived in Tennessee river where Toco creek comes in at Dăkwâ'ĭ, the "Dăkwă' place," above the mouth of Tellico, and which was so large that it could easily swallow a man. Once a canoe filled with warriors was crossing over from the town to the other side of the river, when the Dăkwă' suddenly rose up under the boat and threw them all into the air. As they came down it swallowed one with a single snap of its jaws and dived with him to the bottom of the river. As soon as the hunter came to his senses he found that he had not been hurt, but it was so hot and close inside the Dăkwă' that he was nearly smothered. As he groped around in the dark his hand struck a lot of mussel shells which the fish had swallowed, and taking one of these for a knife he began to cut his way out, until soon the fish grew uneasy at the scraping inside his stomach and came up to the top of the water for air. He kept on cutting until the fish was in such pain that it swam this way and that across the stream and thrashed the water into foam with its tail. Finally the hole was so large that he could look out and saw that the Dăkwă′ was now resting in shallow water near the shore. Reaching up he climbed out from the side of the fish, moving very carefully so that the Dăkwă′ would not know it, and then waded to shore and got back to the settlement, but the juices in the stomach of the great fish had scalded all the hair from his head and he was bald ever after.

A boy was sent on an errand by his father, and not wishing to go ne ran away to the river. After playing in the sand for a short time some boys of his acquaintance came by in a canoe and invited him to join them. Glad of the opportunity to get away he went with them, but had no sooner got in than the canoe began to tip and rock most unaccountably. The boys became very much frightened, and in the confusion the bad boy fell into the water and was immediately swallowed by a large fish. After lying in its stomach for some time he became very hungry, and on looking around he saw the fish's liver hanging over his head. Thinking it dried meat, he tried to cut off a piece with a mussel shell he had been playing with and still held in his hand. The operation sickened the fish and it vomited the boy.

69. ATAGÂ′HĬ, THE ENCHANTED LAKE

Westward from the headwaters of Oconaluftee river, in the wildest depths of the Great Smoky mountains, which form the line between North Carolina and Tennessee, is the enchanted lake of Atagâ′hĭ, "Gall place." Although all the Cherokee know that it is there, no one has ever seen it, for the way is so difficult that only the animals know how to reach it. Should a stray hunter come near the place he would know of it by the whirring sound of the thousands of wild ducks flying about the lake, but on reaching the spot he would find only a dry flat, without bird or animal or blade of grass, unless he had first sharpened his spiritual vision by prayer and fasting and an all-night vigil.

Because it is not seen, some people think the lake has dried up long ago, but this is not true. To one who had kept watch and fast through the night it would appear at daybreak as a wide-extending but shallow sheet of purple water, fed by springs spouting from the high cliffs around. In the water are all kinds of fish and reptiles, and swimming upon the surface or flying overhead are great flocks of ducks and pigeons, while all about the shores are bear tracks crossing in every direction. It is the medicine lake of the birds and animals, and whenever a bear is wounded by the hunters he makes his way through the woods to this lake and plunges into the water, and when he comes out upon the other side his wounds are healed. For this reason the animals keep the lake invisible to the hunter.

70. THE BRIDE FROM THE SOUTH

The North went traveling, and after going far and meeting many different tribes he finally fell in love with the daughter of the South and wanted to marry her. The girl was willing, but her parents objected and said, "Ever since you came the weather has been cold, and if you stay here we may all freeze to death." The North pleaded hard, and said that if they would let him have their daughter he would take her back to his own country, so at last they consented. They were married and he took his bride to his own country, and when she arrived there she found the people all living in ice houses.

The next day, when the sun rose, the houses began to leak, and as it climbed higher they began to melt, and it grew warmer and warmer, until finally the people came to the young husband and told him he must send his wife home again, or the weather would get so warm that the whole settlement would be melted. He loved his wife and so held out as long as he could, but as the sun grew hotter the people were more urgent, and at last he had to send her home to her parents.

, The people said that as she had been born in the South, and nourished all her life upon food that grew in the same climate, her whole nature was warm and unfit for the North.

71. THE ICE MAN

Once when the people were burning the woods in the fall the blaze set fire to a poplar tree, which continued to burn until the fire went down into the roots and burned a great hole in the ground. It burned and burned, and the hole grew constantly larger, until the people became frightened and were afraid it would burn the whole world. They tried to put out the fire, but it had gone too deep, and they did not know what to do.

At last some one said there was a man living in a house of ice far in the north who could put out the fire, so messengers were sent, and after traveling a long distance they came to the ice house and found the Ice Man at home. He was a little fellow with long hair hanging down to the ground in two plaits. The messengers told him their errand and he at once said, "O yes, I can help you," and began to unplait his hair. When it was all unbraided he took it up in one hand and struck it once across his other hand, and the messengers felt a wind blow against their cheeks. A second time he struck his hair across his hand, and a light rain began to fall. The third time he struck his hair across his open hand there was sleet mixed with the raindrops, and when he struck the fourth time great hailstones fell upon the ground, as if they had come out from the ends of his hair. "Go back now," said the Ice Man, "and I shall be there to-morrow." So the messengers returned to their people, whom they found still gathered helplessly about the great burning pit.

The next day while they were all watching about the fire there came a wind from the north, and they were afraid, for they knew that it came from the Ice Man. But the wind only made the fire blaze up higher. Then a light rain began to fall, but the drops seemed only to make the fire hotter. Then the shower turned to a heavy rain, with sleet and hail that killed the blaze and made clouds of smoke and steam rise from the red coals. The people fled to their homes for shelter, and the storm rose to a whirlwind that drove the rain into every burning crevice and piled great hailstones over the embers, until the fire was dead and even the smoke ceased. When at last it was all over and the people returned they found a lake where the burning pit had been, and from below the water came a sound as of embers still crackling.

72. THE HUNTER AND SELU

A hunter had been tramping over the mountains all day long without finding any game and when the sun went down, he built a fire in a hollow stump, swallowed a few mouthfuls of corn gruel and lay down to sleep, tired out and completely discouraged. About the middle of the night he dreamed and seemed to hear the sound of beautiful singing, which continued until near daybreak and then appeared to die away into the upper air.

All next day he hunted with the same poor success, and at night made his lonely camp again in the woods. He slept and the strange dream came to him again, but so vividly that it seemed to him like an actual happening. Rousing himself before daylight, he still heard the song, and feeling sure now that it was real, he went in the direction of the sound and found that it came from a single green stalk of corn (selu). The plant spoke to him, and told him to cut off some of its roots and take them to his home in the settlement, and the next morning to chew them and "go to water" before anyone else was awake, and then to go out again into the woods, and he would kill many deer and from that time on would always be successful in the hunt. The corn plant continued to talk, teaching him hunting secrets and telling him always to be generous with the game he took, until it was noon and the sun was high, when it suddenly took the form of a woman and rose gracefully into the air and was gone from sight, leaving the hunter alone in the woods.

He returned home and told his story, and all the people knew that he had seen Selu, the wife of Kana'tĭ.　He did as the spirit had directed, and from that time was noted as the most successful of all the hunters in the settlement.

73. THE UNDERGROUND PANTHERS

A hunter was in the woods one day in winter when suddenly he saw a panther coming toward him and at once prepared to defend himself. The panther continued to approach, and the hunter was just about to shoot when the animal spoke, and at once it seemed to the man as if there was no difference between them, and they were both of the same nature.　The panther asked him where he was going, and the man said that he was looking for a deer.　"Well," said the panther, "we are getting ready for a Green-corn dance, and there are seven of us out after a buck, so we may as well hunt together."

The hunter agreed and they went on together.　They started up one deer and another, but the panther made no sign, and said only "Those are too small; we want something better."　So the hunter did not shoot, and they went on.　They started up another deer, a larger one, and the panther sprang upon it and tore its throat, and finally killed it after a hard struggle.　The hunter got out his knife to skin it, but the panther said the skin was too much torn to be used and they must try again.　They started up another large deer, and this the panther killed without trouble, and then, wrapping his tail around it, threw it across his back.　"Now, come to our townhouse," he said to the hunter.

The panther led the way, carrying the captured deer upon his back, up a little stream branch until they came to the head spring, when it seemed as if a door opened in the side of the hill and they went in. Now the hunter found himself in front of a large townhouse, with the finest detsănûñ'lĭ he had ever seen, and the trees around were green, and the air was warm, as in summer.　There was a great company there getting ready for the dance, and they were all panthers, but somehow it all seemed natural to the hunter.　After a while the others who had been out came in with the deer they had taken, and the dance began.　The hunter danced several rounds, and then said it was growing late and he must be getting home.　So the panthers opened the door and he went out, and at once found himself alone in the woods again, and it was winter and very cold, with snow on the ground and on all the trees.　When he reached the settlement he found a party just starting out to search for him.　They asked him where he had been so long, and he told them the story, and then he found that he had been in the panther townhouse several days instead of only a very short time, as he had thought.

He died within seven days after his return, because he had already begun to take on the panther nature, and so could not live again with men.　If he had stayed with the panthers he would have lived.

74. THE TSUNDIGE′WĬ

Once some young men of the Cherokee set out to see what was in the world and traveled south until they came to a tribe of little people called *Tsundige′wĭ*, with very queer shaped bodies, hardly tall enough to reach up to a man's knee, who had no houses, but lived in nests scooped in the sand and covered over with dried grass. The little fellows were so weak and puny that they could not fight at all, and were in constant terror from the wild geese and other birds that used to come in great flocks from the south to make war upon them.

Just at the time that the travelers got there they found the little men in great fear, because there was a strong wind blowing from the south and it blew white feathers and down along the sand, so that the Tsundige′wĭ knew their enemies were coming not far behind. The Cherokee asked them why they did not defend themselves, but they said they could not, because they did not know how. There was no time to make bows and arrows, but the travelers told them to take sticks for clubs, and showed them where to strike the birds on the necks to kill them.

The wind blew for several days, and at last the birds came, so many that they were like a great cloud in the air, and alighted on the sands. The little men ran to their nests, and the birds followed and stuck in their long bills to pull them out and eat them. This time, though, the Tsundige′wĭ had their clubs, and they struck the birds on the neck, as the Cherokee had shown them, and killed so many that at last the others were glad to spread their wings and fly away again to the south.

The little men thanked the Cherokee for their help and gave them the best they had until the travelers went on to see the other tribes. They heard afterwards that the birds came again several times, but that the Tsundige′wĭ always drove them off with their clubs, until a flock of sandhill cranes came. They were so tall that the little men could not reach up to strike them on the neck, and so at last the cranes killed them all.

75. ORIGIN OF THE BEAR: THE BEAR SONGS

Long ago there was a Cherokee clan called the Ani′-Tsâ′gûhĭ, and in one family of this clan was a boy who used to leave home and be gone all day in the mountains. After a while he went oftener and stayed longer, until at last he would not eat in the house at all, but started off at daybreak and did not come back until night. His parents scolded, but that did no good, and the boy still went every day until they noticed that long brown hair was beginning to grow out all over his body. Then they wondered and asked him why it was that he wanted to be so much in the woods that he would not even eat at home. Said the boy, "I find plenty to eat there, and it is better than the corn and beans we have in the settlements, and pretty soon I am going into the woods to stay all the time." His parents were worried and begged him not to leave them, but he said, "It is better there than here, and you see I am beginning to be different already, so that I can not live here any longer. If you will come with me, there is plenty for all of us and you will never have to work for it; but if you want to come you must first fast seven days."

The father and mother talked it over and then told the headmen of the clan. They held a council about the matter and after everything had been said they decided: "Here we must work hard and have not always enough. There he says there is always plenty without work. We will go with him." So they fasted seven days, and on the seventh morning all the Anı́-Tsấgŭhĭ left the settlement and started for the mountains as the boy led the way.

When the people of the other towns heard of it they were very sorry and sent their headmen to persuade the Ani'-Tsấgŭhĭ to stay at home and not go into the woods to live. The messengers found them already on the way, and were surprised to notice that their bodies were beginning to be covered with hair like that of animals, because for seven days they had not taken human food and their nature was changing. The Ani'-Tsấgŭhĭ would not come back, but said, "We are going where there is always plenty to eat. Hereafter we shall be called *yânû* (bears), and when you yourselves are hungry come into the woods and call us and we shall come to give you our own flesh. You need not be afraid to kill us, for we shall live always." Then they taught the messengers the songs with which to call them, and the bear hunters have these songs still. When they had finished the songs the Ani'-Tsấgŭhĭ started on again and the messengers turned back to the settlements, but after going a little way they looked back and saw a drove of bears going into the woods.

First Bear Song

He-e! Ani'-Tsấgŭhi, Ani'-Tsấgŭhi, akwandu'li e'lanti' ginŭn'ti,
Ani'-Tsấgŭhi, Ani'-Tsấgŭhi, akwandu'li e'lanti' ginŭn'ti—Yû!

He-e! The Ani'-Tsấgŭhi, the Ani'-Tsấgŭhi, I want to lay them low on the ground,
The Ani'-Tsấgŭhi, the Ani'-Tsấgŭhi, I want to lay them low on the ground—Yû!

The bear hunter starts out each morning fasting and does not eat until near evening. He sings this song as he leaves camp, and again the next morning, but never twice the same day.

* * * * * * *

Second Bear Song

This song also is sung by the bear hunter, in order to attract the bears, while on his way from the camp to the place where he expects to hunt during the day.   The melody is simple and plaintive.

He-e! Hayuya′haniwă′, hayuya′haniwă′, hayuya′haniwă′, hayuya′haniwă′,
Tsistuyi′ nehandu′yanú, Tsistuyi′ nehandu′yanú—Yoho-o!
He-e! Hayuya′haniwă′, hayuya′haniwă′, hayuya′haniwă′, hayuya′haniwă′,
Kuwáhi′ nehandu′yanú, Kuwáhi′ nehandu′yanú—Yoho-o!
He-e! Hayuya′haniwă′, hayuya′haniwă′, hayuya′haniwă′, hayuya′haniwă′,
Uyáhye′ nehandu′yanú, Uyáhye′ nehandu′yanú—Yoho-o!
He-e! Hayuya′haniwă′, hayuya′haniwă′, hayuya′haniwă′, hayuya′haniwă′,
Gátegwá′ nehandu′yanú, Gátegwá′ nehandu′yanú—Yoho-o!
(Recited) *Ûlĕ-′nú′ asĕhĭ′ tadeyá′statakûhĭ′ gûñ′năge astú′ tsĭkĭ′.*

He! Hayuya′haniwă′ (four times),
   In Tsistu′yĭ you were conceived (two times)—Yoho!
He! Hayuya′haniwă′ (four times),
   In Kuwâ′hĭ you were conceived (two times)—Yoho!
He! Hayuya′haniwă′ (four times),
   In Uyâ′hye you were conceived (two times)—Yoho!
He! Hayuya′haniwă′ (four times),
   In Gâte′gwâ you were conceived (two times)—Yoho!
And now surely we and the good black things, the best of all, shall see each other.

76. THE BEAR MAN

A man went hunting in the mountains and came across a black bear, which he wounded with an arrow.   The bear turned and started to run the other way, and the hunter followed, shooting one arrow after another into it without bringing it down.   Now, this was a medicine bear, and could talk or read the thoughts of people without their saying a word.   At last he stopped and pulled the arrows out of his side and gave them to the man, saying, "It is of no use for you to shoot at me, for you can not kill me.   Come to my house and let us live together."   The hunter thought to himself, "He may kill me;" but the bear read his thoughts and said, "No, I won't hurt you."   The man thought again, "How can I get anything to eat?" but the bear knew his thoughts, and said, "There shall be plenty."   So the hunter went with the bear.

They went on together until they came to a hole in the side of the mountain, and the bear said, "This is not where I live, but there is going to be a council here and we will see what they do."   They went in, and the hole widened as they went, until they came to a large cave like a townhouse.   It was full of bears—old bears, young bears, and cubs, white bears, black bears, and brown bears—and a large white bear was the chief.   They sat down in a corner, but soon the bears scented the hunter and began to ask, "What is it that smells

bad?" The chief said, "Don't talk so; it is only a stranger come to
see us. Let him alone." Food was getting scarce in the mountains,
and the council was to decide what to do about it. They had sent out
messengers all over, and while they were talking two bears came in
and reported that they had found a country in the low grounds where
there were so many chestnuts and acorns that mast was knee deep.
Then they were all pleased, and got ready for a dance, and the dance
leader was the one the Indians call Kalâs'-gûnăhi'ta, "Long Hams," a
great black bear that is always lean. After the dance the bears noticed
the hunter's bow and arrows, and one said, "This is what men use to
kill us. Let us see if we can manage them, and may be we can fight
man with his own weapons." So they took the bow and arrows from
the hunter to try them. They fitted the arrow and drew back the
string, but when they let go it caught in their long claws and the
arrows dropped to the ground. They saw that they could not use
the bow and arrows and gave them back to the man. When the dance
and the council were over, they began to go home, excepting the White
Bear chief, who lived there, and at last the hunter and the bear went
out together.

They went on until they came to another hole in the side of the
mountain, when the bear said, "This is where I live," and they went
in. By this time the hunter was very hungry and was wondering how
he could get something to eat. The other knew his thoughts, and sitting up on his hind legs he rubbed his stomach with his forepaws—so—
and at once he had both paws full of chestnuts and gave them to the
man. He rubbed his stomach again—so—and had his paws full of
huckleberries, and gave them to the man. He rubbed again—so—and
gave the man both paws full of blackberries. He rubbed again—so—
and had his paws full of acorns, but the man said that he could not
eat them, and that he had enough already.

The hunter lived in the cave with the bear all winter, until long
hair like that of a bear began to grow all over his body and he began
to act like a bear; but he still walked like a man. One day in early
spring the bear said to him, "Your people down in the settlement are
getting ready for a grand hunt in these mountains, and they will come
to this cave and kill me and take these clothes from me"—he meant
his skin—"but they will not hurt you and will take you home with
them." The bear knew what the people were doing down in the settlement just as he always knew what the man was thinking about.
Some days passed and the bear said again, "This is the day when the
Topknots will come to kill me, but the Split-noses will come first and
find us. When they have killed me they will drag me outside the
cave and take off my clothes and cut me in pieces. You must cover
the blood with leaves, and when they are taking you away look back
after you have gone a piece and you will see something."

Soon they heard the hunters coming up the mountain, and then the dogs found the cave and began to bark. The hunters came and looked inside and saw the bear and killed him with their arrows. Then they dragged him outside the cave and skinned the body and cut it in quarters to carry home. The dogs kept on barking until the hunters thought there must be another bear in the cave. They looked in again and saw the man away at the farther end. At first they thought it was another bear on account of his long hair, but they soon saw it was the hunter who had been lost the year before, so they went in and brought him out. Then each hunter took a load of the bear meat and they started home again, bringing the man and the skin with them. Before they left the man piled leaves over the spot where they had cut up the bear, and when they had gone a little way he looked behind and saw the bear rise up out of the leaves, shake himself, and go back into the woods.

When they came near the settlement the man told the hunters that he must be shut up where no one could see him, without anything to eat or drink for seven days and nights, until the bear nature had left him and he became like a man again. So they shut him up alone in a house and tried to keep very still about it, but the news got out and his wife heard of it. She came for her husband, but the people would not let her near him; but she came every day and begged so hard that at last after four or five days they let her have him. She took him home with her, but in a short time he died, because he still had a bear's nature and could not live like a man. If they had kept him shut up and fasting until the end of the seven days he would have become a man again and would have lived.

77. THE GREAT LEECH OF TLANUSI′YĬ

The spot where Valley river joins Hiwassee, at Murphy, in North Carolina, is known among the Cherokees as Tlanusi′yĭ, "The Leech place," and this is the story they tell of it:

Just above the junction is a deep hole in Valley river, and above it is a ledge of rock running across the stream, over which people used to go as on a bridge. On the south side the trail ascended a high bank, from which they could look down into the water. One day some men going along the trail saw a great red object, full as large as a house, lying on the rock ledge in the middle of the stream below them. As they stood wondering what it could be they saw it unroll—and then they knew it was alive—and stretch itself out along the rock until it looked like a great leech with red and white stripes along its body. It rolled up into a ball and again stretched out at full length, and at last crawled down the rock and was out of sight in the deep water. The water began to boil and foam, and a great column of white spray was thrown high in the air and came down like a waterspout upon the very spot where the men had been standing, and would have swept them all into the water but that they saw it in time and ran from the place.

More than one person was carried down in this way, and their friends would find the body afterwards lying upon the bank with the ears and nose eaten off, until at last the people were afraid to go across the ledge any more, on account of the great leech, or even to go along that part of the trail. But there was one young fellow who laughed at the whole story, and said that he was not afraid of anything in Valley river, as he would show them. So one day he painted his face and put on his finest buckskin and started off toward the river, while all the people followed at a distance to see what might happen. Down the trail he went and out upon the ledge of rock, singing in high spirits:

> *Tlanu'sĭ găne'ga digi'găge*
> *Dakwa'nitlaste'stĭ.*
> I'll tie red leech skins
> On my legs for garters.

But before he was half way across the water began to boil into white foam and a great wave rose and swept over the rock and carried him down, and he was never seen again.

Just before the Removal, sixty years ago, two women went out upon the ledge to fish. Their friends warned them of the danger, but one woman who had her baby on her back said, "There are fish there and I'm going to have some; I'm tired of this fat meat." She laid the child down on the rock and was preparing the line when the water suddenly rose and swept over the ledge, and would have carried off the child but that the mother ran in time to save it. The great leech is still there in the deep hole, because when people look down they see something alive moving about on the bottom, and although they can not distinguish its shape on account of the ripples on the water, yet they know it is the leech. Some say there is an underground waterway across to Nottely river, not far above the mouth, where the river bends over toward Murphy, and sometimes the leech goes over there and makes the water boil as it used to at the rock ledge. They call this spot on Nottely "The Leech place" also.

78. THE NŬÑNĔ'HĬ AND OTHER SPIRIT FOLK

The *Nŭñnĕ'hĭ* or immortals, the "people who live anywhere," were a race of spirit people who lived in the highlands of the old Cherokee country and had a great many townhouses, especially in the bald mountains, the high peaks on which no timber ever grows. They had large townhouses in Pilot knob and under the old Nĭkwăsĭ' mound in North Carolina, and another under Blood mountain, at the head of Nottely river, in Georgia. They were invisible excepting when they wanted to be seen, and then they looked and spoke just like other Indians. They were very fond of music and dancing, and hunters in the mountains would often hear the dance songs and the drum beating in some invisible townhouse, but when they went toward the sound it would shift about and they would hear it behind them or away in some other direction, so that they could never find the place where the dance was. They were a friendly people, too, and often brought lost wanderers to their townhouses under the mountains and cared for them there until they were rested and then guided them back to their homes. More than once, also, when the Cherokee were hard pressed by the enemy, the Nŭñnĕ'hĭ warriors have come out, as they did at old Nĭkwăsĭ', and have saved them from defeat. Some people have thought that they are the same as the Yŭñwĭ Tsunsdi', the "Little People"; but these are fairies, no larger in size than children.

There was a man in Nottely town who had been with the Nŭñnĕ'hĭ when he was a boy, and he told Wafford all about it. He was a truthful, hard-headed man, and Wafford had heard the story so often from other people that he asked this man to tell it. It was in this way:

When he was about 10 or 12 years old he was playing one day near the river, shooting at a mark with his bow and arrows, until he became tired, and started to build a fish trap in the water. While he was piling up the stones in two long walls a man came and stood on the bank and asked him what he was doing. The boy told him, and the man said, "Well, that's pretty hard work and you ought to rest a while. Come and take a walk up the river." The boy said, "No"; that he was going home to dinner soon. "Come right up to my house," said the stranger, "and I'll give you a good dinner there and bring you home again in the morning." So the boy went with him up the river until they came to a house, when they went in, and the man's wife and the other people there were very glad to see him, and gave him a fine dinner, and were very kind to him. While they were eating a man that the boy knew very well came in and spoke to him, so that he felt quite at home.

After dinner he played with the other children and slept there that night, and in the morning, after breakfast, the man got ready to take him home. They went down a path that had a cornfield on one side and a peach orchard fenced in on the other, until they came to another trail, and the man said, "Go along this trail across that ridge and you will come to the river road that will bring you straight to your home, and now I'll go back to the house." So the man went back to the house and the boy went on along the trail, but when he had gone a little way he looked back, and there was no cornfield or orchard or fence or house; nothing but trees on the mountain side.

He thought it very queer, but somehow he was not frightened, and went on until he came to the river trail in sight of his home. There were a great many people standing about talking, and when they saw him they ran toward him shouting, "Here he is! He is not drowned or killed in the mountains!" They told him they had been hunting him ever since yesterday noon, and asked him where he had been. "A man took me over to his house just across the ridge, and I had a fine dinner and a good time with the children," said the boy, "I thought Udsi′skală here"—that was the name of the man he had seen at dinner—"would tell you where I was." But Udsi′skală said, "I haven't seen you. I was out all day in my canoe hunting you. It was one of the Nûñně′hĭ that made himself look like me." Then his mother said, "You say you had dinner there? "Yes, and I had plenty, too," said the boy; but his mother answered, "There is no house there—only trees and rocks—but we hear a drum sometimes in the big bald above. The people you saw were the Nûñně′hĭ."

Once four Nûñně′hĭ women came to a dance at Nottely town, and danced half the night with the young men there, and nobody knew that they were Nûñně′hĭ, but thought them visitors from another settlement. About midnight they left to go home, and some men who had come out from the townhouse to cool off watched to see which way they went. They saw the women go down the trail to the river ford, but just as they came to the water they disappeared, although it was a plain trail, with no place where they could hide. Then the watchers knew they were Nûñně′hĭ women. Several men saw this happen, and one of them was Wafford's father-in-law, who was known for an honest man. At another time a man named Burnt-tobacco was crossing over the ridge from Nottely to Hemptown in Georgia and heard a drum and the songs of dancers in the hills on one side of the trail. He rode over to see who could be dancing in such a place, but when he reached the spot the drum and the songs were behind him, and he was so frightened that he hurried back to the trail and rode all the way to Hemptown as hard as he could to tell the story. He was a truthful man, and they believed what he said.

There must have been a good many of the Nûñně′hĭ living in that neighborhood, because the drumming was often heard in the high balds almost up to the time of the Removal.

On a small upper branch of Nottely, running nearly due north from Blood mountain, there was also a hole, like a small well or chimney, in in the ground, from which there came up a warm vapor that heated all the air around. People said that this was because the Nûñně′hĭ had a townhouse and a fire under the mountain. Sometimes in cold weather hunters would stop there to warm themselves, but they were afraid to stay long. This was more than sixty years ago, but the hole is probably there yet.

Close to the old trading path from South Carolina up to the Cherokee Nation, somewhere near the head of Tugaloo, there was formerly a noted circular depression about the size of a townhouse, and waist deep. Inside it was always clean as though swept by unknown hands. Passing traders would throw logs and rocks into it, but would always, on their return, find them thrown far out from the hole. The Indians said it was a Nûñnĕ'hĭ townhouse, and never liked to go near the place or even to talk about it, until at last some logs thrown in by the traders were allowed to remain there, and then they concluded that the Nûñnĕ'hĭ, annoyed by the persecution of the white men, had abandoned their townhouse forever.

There is another race of spirits, the *Yûñwĭ Tsunsdĭ'*, or "Little People," who live in rock caves on the mountain side. They are little fellows, hardly reaching up to a man's knee, but well shaped and handsome, with long hair falling almost to the ground. They are great wonder workers and are very fond of music, spending half their time drumming and dancing. They are helpful and kind-hearted, and often when people have been lost in the mountains, especially children who have strayed away from their parents, the Yûñwĭ Tsunsdi' have found them and taken care of them and brought them back to their homes. Sometimes their drum is heard in lonely places in the mountains, but it is not safe to follow it, because the Little People do not like to be disturbed at home, and they throw a spell over the stranger so that he is bewildered and loses his way, and even if he does at last get back to the settlement he is like one dazed ever after. Sometimes, also, they come near a house at night and the people inside hear them talking, but they must not go out, and in the morning they find the corn gathered or the field cleared as if a whole force of men had been at work. If anyone should go out to watch, he would die. When a hunter finds anything in the woods, such as a knife or a trinket, he must say, "Little People, I want to take this," because it may belong to them, and if he does not ask their permission they will throw stones at him as he goes home.

Once a hunter in winter found tracks in the snow like the tracks of little children. He wondered how they could have come there and followed them until they led him to a cave, which was full of Little People, young and old, men, women, and children. They brought him in and were kind to him, and he was with them some time; but when he left they warned him that he must not tell or he would die. He went back to the settlement and his friends were all anxious to know where he had been. For a long time he refused to say, until at last he could not hold out any longer, but told the story, and in a few days he died. Only a few years ago two hunters from Raventown, going behind the high fall near the head of Oconaluftee on the East Cherokee reservation, found there a cave with fresh footprints of the Little People all over the floor.

During the smallpox among the East Cherokee just after the war one sick man wandered off, and his friends searched, but could not find him. After several weeks he came back and said that the Little

People had found him and taken him to one of their caves and tended him until he was cured.

About twenty-five years ago a man named Tsantăwû′ was lost in the mountains on the head of Oconaluftee. It was winter time and very cold and his friends thought he must be dead, but after sixteen days he came back and said that the Little People had found him and taken him to their cave, where he had been well treated, and given plenty of everything to eat except bread. This was in large loaves, but when he took them in his hand to eat they seemed to shrink into small cakes so light and crumbly that though he might eat all day he would not be satisfied. After he was well rested they had brought him a part of the way home until they came to a small creek, about knee deep, when they told him to wade across to reach the main trail on the other side. He waded across and turned to look back, but the Little People were gone and the creek was a deep river. When he reached home his legs were frozen to the knees and he lived only a few days.

Once the Yûñwĭ Tsunsdi′ had been very kind to the people of a certain settlement, helping them at night with their work and taking good care of any lost children, until something happened to offend them and they made up their minds to leave the neighborhood. Those who were watching at the time saw the whole company of Little People come down to the ford of the river and cross over and disappear into the mouth of a large cave on the other side. They were never heard of near the settlement again.

There are other fairies, the *Yûñwĭ Amai′yĭnĕ′hĭ*, or Water-dwellers, who live in the water, and fishermen pray to them for help. Other friendly spirits live in people's houses, although no one can see them, and so long as they are there to protect the house no witch can come near to do mischief.

Tsăwa′sĭ and *Tsăga′sĭ* are the names of two small fairies, who are mischievous enough, but yet often help the hunter who prays to them. Tsăwa′sĭ, or Tsăwa′sĭ Usdi′ga (Little Tsăwa′sĭ), is a tiny fellow, very handsome, with long hair falling down to his feet, who lives in grassy patches on the hillsides and has great power over the game. To the deer hunter who prays to him he gives skill to slip up on the deer through the long grass without being seen. Tsăga′sĭ is another of the spirits invoked by the hunter and is very helpful, but when some-one trips and falls, we know that it is Tsăga′sĭ who has caused it. There are several other of these fairies with names, all good-natured, but more or less tricky. ·

Then there is *Dĕ′tsătă*. Dĕ′tsătă was once a boy who ran away to the woods to avoid a scratching and tries to keep himself invisible ever since. He is a handsome little fellow and spends his whole time hunting birds with blowgun and arrow. He has a great many children who are all just like him and have the same name. When a flock of birds flies up suddenly as if frightened it is because De'tsătă is chasing them. He is mischievous and sometimes hides an arrow from the bird hunter, who may have shot it off into a perfectly clear space, but looks and looks without finding it. Then the hunter says, "De'tsătă, you have my arrow, and if you don't give it up I'll scratch you," and when he looks again he finds it.

There is one spirit that goes about at night with a light. The Cherokee call it *Atsil'-dihye'gĭ*, "The Fire-carrier," and they are all afraid of it, because they think it dangerous, although they do not know much about it. They do not even know exactly what it looks like, because they are afraid to stop when they see it. It may be a witch instead of a spirit. Wafford's mother saw the "Fire-carrier" once when she was a young woman, as she was coming home at night from a trading post in South Carolina. It seemed to be following her from behind, and she was frightened and whipped up her horse until she got away from it and never saw it again.

79. THE REMOVED TOWNHOUSES

Long ago, long before the Cherokee were driven from their homes in 1838, the people on Valley river and Hiwassee heard voices of invisible spirits in the air calling and warning them of wars and misfortunes which the future held in store, and inviting them to come and live with the Nûñnĕ'hĭ, the Immortals, in their homes under the mountains and under the waters. For days the voices hung in the air, and the people listened until they heard the spirits say, "If you would live with us, gather everyone in your townhouses and fast there for seven days, and no one must raise a shout or a warwhoop in all that time. Do this and we shall come and you will see us and we shall take you to live with us."

The people were afraid of the evils that were to come, and they knew that the Immortals of the mountains and the waters were happy forever, so they counciled in their townhouses and decided to go with them. Those of Anisgayâ'yĭ town came all together into their townhouse and prayed and fasted for six days. On the seventh day there was a sound from the distant mountains, and it came nearer and grew louder until a roar of thunder was all about the townhouse and they felt the ground shake under them. Now they were frightened, and despite the warning some of them screamed out. The Nûñnĕ'hĭ, who had already lifted up the townhouse with its mound to carry it away, were startled by the cry and let a part of it fall to the earth, where now we see the mound of Sĕ'tsĭ. They steadied themselves again and bore the rest of the townhouse, with all the people in it, to the top of Tsuda'ye'lûñ'yĭ (Lone peak), near the head of Cheowa, where we can still see it, changed long ago to solid rock, but the people are invisible and immortal.

The people of another town, on Hiwassee, at the place which we call now Du'stiya'lŭñ'yĭ, where Shooting creek comes in, also prayed and fasted, and at the end of seven days the Nŭñně'hĭ came and took them away down under the water. They are there now, and on a warm summer day, when the wind ripples the surface, those who listen well can hear them talking below. When the Cherokee drag the river for fish the fish-drag always stops and catches there, although the water is deep, and the people know it is being held by their lost kinsmen, who do not want to be forgotten.

When the Cherokee were forcibly removed to the West one of the greatest regrets of those along Hiwassee and Valley rivers was that they were compelled to leave behind forever their relatives who had gone to the Nŭñně'hĭ.

In Tennessee river, near Kingston, 18 miles below Loudon, Tennessee, is a place which the Cherokee call Gustĭ', where there once was a settlement long ago, but one night while the people were gathered in the townhouse for a dance the bank caved in and carried them all down into the river. Boatmen passing the spot in their canoes see the round dome of the townhouse—now turned to stone—in the water below them and sometimes hear the sound of the drum and dance coming up, and they never fail to throw food into the water in return for being allowed to cross in safety.

80. THE SPIRIT DEFENDERS OF NĬKWĂSĬ'

Long ago a powerful unknown tribe invaded the country from the southeast, killing people and destroying settlements wherever they went. No leader could stand against them, and in a little while they had wasted all the lower settlements and advanced into the mountains. The warriors of the old town of Nĭkwăsĭ', on the head of Little Tennessee, gathered their wives and children into the townhouse and kept scouts constantly on the lookout for the presence of danger. One morning just before daybreak the spies saw the enemy approaching and at once gave the alarm. The Nĭkwăsĭ' men seized their arms and rushed out to meet the attack, but after a long, hard fight they found themselves overpowered and began to retreat, when suddenly a stranger stood among them and shouted to the chief to call off his men and he himself would drive back the enemy. From the dress and language of the stranger the Nĭkwăsĭ' people thought him a chief who had come with reinforcements from the Overhill settlements in Tennessee. They fell back along the trail, and as they came near the townhouse they saw a great company of warriors coming out from the side of the mound as through an open doorway. Then they knew that their friends were the Nŭñně'hĭ, the Immortals, although no one had ever heard before that they lived under Nĭkwăsĭ' mound.

The Nŭñně'hĭ poured out by hundreds, armed and painted for the fight, and the most curious thing about it all was that they became invisible as soon as they were fairly outside of the settlement, so that although the enemy saw the glancing arrow or the rushing tomahawk, and felt the stroke, he could not see who sent it. Before such invisible foes the invaders soon had to retreat, going first south along the ridge to where joins the main ridge which separates the French Broad from the Tuckasegee, and then turning with it to the northeast. As they retreated they tried to shield themselves behind rocks and trees, but the Nûñnĕ'hĭ arrows went around the rocks and killed them from the other side, and they could find no hiding place. All along the ridge they fell, until when they reached the head of Tuckasegee not more than half a dozen were left alive, and in despair they sat down and cried out for mercy. Ever since then the Cherokee have called the place Dayûlsûñ'yĭ, "Where they cried." Then the Nûñnĕ'hĭ chief told them they had deserved their punishment for attacking a peaceful tribe, and he spared their lives and told them to go home and take the news to their people. This was the Indian custom, always to spare a few to carry back the news of defeat. They went home toward the north and the Nûñnĕ'hĭ went back to the mound.

And they are still there, because, in the last war, when a strong party of Federal troops came to surprise a handful of Confederates posted there they saw so many soldiers guarding the town that they were afraid and went away without making an attack.

* * * * * * *

There is another story, that once while all the warriors of a certain town were off on a hunt, or at a dance in another settlement, one old man was chopping wood on the side of the ridge when suddenly a party of the enemy came upon him—Shawano, Seneca, or some other tribe. Throwing his hatchet at the nearest one, he turned and ran for the house to get his gun and make the best defense that he might. On coming out at once with the gun he was surprised to find a large body of strange warriors driving back the enemy. It was no time for questions, and taking his place with the others, they fought hard until the enemy was pressed back up the creek and finally broke and retreated across the mountain. When it was over and there was time to breathe again, the old man turned to thank his new friends, but found that he was alone—they had disappeared as though the mountain had swallowed them. Then he knew that they were the Nûñnĕ'hĭ, who had come to help their friends, the Cherokee.

81. TSUL'KĂLÛ', THE SLANT-EYED GIANT

A long time ago a widow lived with her one daughter at the old, town of Kănuga on Pigeon river. The girl was of age to marry, and her mother used to talk with her a good deal, and tell her she must be sure to take no one but a good hunter for a husband, so that they would have some one to take care of them and would always have plenty of meat in the house. The girl said such a man was hard to find, but her mother advised her not to be in a hurry, and to wait until the right one came.

Now the mother slept in the house while the girl slept outside in the âsĭ. One dark night a stranger came to the âsĭ wanting to court the girl, but she told him her mother would let her marry no one but a good hunter. "Well," said the stranger, "I am a great hunter," so she let him come in, and he stayed all night. Just before day he said he must go back now to his own place, but that he had brought some meat for her mother, and she would find it outside. Then he went away and the girl had not seen him. When day came she went out and found there a deer, which she brought into the house to her mother, and told her it was a present from her new sweetheart. Her mother was pleased, and they had deersteaks for breakfast.

He came again the next night, but again went away before daylight, and this time he left two deer outside. The mother was more pleased this time, but said to her daughter, "I wish your sweetheart would bring us some wood." Now wherever he might be, the stranger knew their thoughts, so when he came the next time he said to the girl, "Tell your mother I have brought the wood"; and when she looked out in the morning there were several great trees lying in front of the door, roots and branches and all. The old woman was angry, and said, "He might have brought us some wood that we could use instead of whole trees that we can't split, to litter up the road with brush." The hunter knew what she said, and the next time he came he brought nothing, and when they looked out in the morning the trees were gone and there was no wood at all, so the old woman had to go after some herself.

Almost every night he came to see the girl, and each time he brought a deer or some other game, but still he always left before daylight. At last her mother said to her, "Your husband always leaves before daylight. Why don't he wait? I want to see what kind of a son-in-law I have." When the girl told this to her husband he said he could not let the old woman see him, because the sight would frighten her. "She wants to see you, anyhow," said the girl, and began to cry, until at last he had to consent, but warned her that her mother must not say that he looked frightful (*usga'sě̆ ti'yu*).

The next morning he did not leave so early, but stayed in the âsĭ, and when it was daylight the girl went out and told her mother. The old woman came and looked in, and there she saw a great giant, with long slanting eyes (*tsul kălû'*), lying doubled up on the floor, with his head against the rafters in the left-hand corner at the back, and his toes scraping the roof in the right-hand corner by the door. She gave only one look and ran back to the house, crying, *Usga'sĕ᷉ti'yu!* *Usga'sĕ᷉ti'yu!*

Tsul'kălû' was terribly angry. He untwisted himself and came out of the âsï, and said good-bye to the girl, telling her that he would never let her mother see him again, but would go back to his own country. Then he went off in the direction of Tsunegûñ'yï.

Soon after he left the girl had her monthly period. There was a very great flow of blood, and the mother threw it all into the river. One night after the girl had gone to bed in the âsï her husband came again to the door and said to her, "It seems you are alone," and asked where was the child. She said there had been none. Then he asked where was the blood, and she said that her mother had thrown it into the river. She told just where the place was, and he went there and found a small worm in the water. He took it up and carried it back to the âsï, and as he walked it took form and began to grow, until, when he reached the âsï, it was a baby girl that he was carrying. He gave it to his wife and said, "Your mother does not like me and abuses our child, so come and let us go to my home." The girl wanted to be with her husband, so, after telling her mother good-bye, she took up the child and they went off together to Tsunegûñ'yï.

Now, the girl had an older brother, who lived with his own wife in another settlement, and when he heard that his sister was married he came to pay a visit to her and her new husband, but when he arrived at Kănuga his mother told him his sister had taken her child and gone away with her husband, nobody knew where. He was sorry to see his mother so lonely, so he said he would go after his sister and try to find her and bring her back. It was easy to follow the footprints of the giant, and the young man went along the trail until he came to a place where they had rested, and there were tracks on the ground where a child had been lying and other marks as if a baby had been born there. He went on along the trail and came to another place where they had rested, and there were tracks of a baby crawling about and another lying on the ground. He went on and came to where they had rested again, and there were tracks of a child walking and another crawling about. He went on until he came where they had rested again, and there were tracks of one child running and another walking. Still he followed the trail along the stream into the mountains, and came to the place where they had rested again, and this time there were footprints of two children running all about, and the footprints can still be seen in the rock at that place.

Twice again he found where they had rested, and then the trail led up the slope of Tsunegûñ'yï, and he heard the sound of a drum and voices, as if people were dancing inside the mountain. Soon he came to a cave like a doorway in the side of the mountain, but the rock was so steep and smooth that he could not climb up to it, but could only just look over the edge and see the heads and shoulders of a great many people dancing inside. He saw his sister dancing among them and called to her to come out. She turned when she heard his voice, and as soon as the drumming stopped for a while she came out to him, finding no trouble to climb down the rock, and leading her two little children by the hand. She was very glad to meet her brother and talked with him a long time, but did not ask him to come inside, and at last he went away without having seen her husband.

Several other times her brother came to the mountain, but always his sister met him outside, and he could never see her husband. After four years had passed she came one day to her mother's house and said her husband had been hunting in the woods near by, and they were getting ready to start home to-morrow, and if her mother and brother would come early in the morning they could see her husband. If they came too late for that, she said, they would find plenty of meat to take home. She went back into the woods, and the mother ran to tell her son. They came to the place early the next morning, but Tsul'-kǎlû' and his family were already gone. On the drying poles they found the bodies of freshly killed deer hanging, as the girl had promised, and there were so many that they went back and told all their friends to come for them, and there were enough for the whole settlement.

Still the brother wanted to see his sister and her husband, so he went again to the mountain, and she came out to meet him. He asked to see her husband, and this time she told him to come inside with her. They went in as through a doorway, and inside he found it like a great townhouse. They seemed to be alone, but his sister called aloud, "He wants to see you," and from the air came a voice, "You can not see me until you put on a new dress, and then you can see me." "I am willing," said the young man, speaking to the unseen spirit, and from the air came the voice again, "Go back, then, and tell your people that to see me they must go into the townhouse and fast seven days, and in all that time they must not come out from the townhouse or raise the war whoop, and on the seventh day I shall come with new dresses for you to put on so that you can all see me."

The young man went back to Kǎnuga and told the people. They all wanted to see Tsul'kǎlû', who owned all the game in the mountains, so they went into the townhouse and began the fast. They fasted the first day and the second and every day until the seventh—all but one man from another settlement, who slipped out every night when it was dark to get something to eat and slipped in again when no one was watching. On the morning of the seventh day the sun was just coming up in the east when they heard a great noise like the thunder of rocks rolling down the side of Tsunegûñ'yĭ. They were frightened and drew near together in the townhouse, and no one whispered.

Nearer and louder came the sound until it grew into an awful roar, and every one trembled and held his breath—all but one man, the stranger from the other settlement, who lost his senses from fear and ran out of the townhouse and shouted the war cry.

At once the roar stopped and for some time there was silence. Then they heard it again, but as if it were going farther away, and then farther and farther, until at last it died away in the direction of Tsunegûñ′yĭ, and then all was still again. The people came out from the townhouse, but there was silence, and they could see nothing but what had been seven days before.

Still the brother was not disheartened, but came again to see his sister, and she brought him into the mountain. He asked why Tsul‘kâlû′ had not brought the new dresses, as he had promised, and the voice from the air said, "I came with them, but you did not obey my word, but broke the fast and raised the war cry." The young man answered, "It was not done by our people, but by a stranger. If you will come again, we will surely do as you say." But the voice answered, "Now you can never see me." Then the young man could not say any more, and he went back to Kănuga.

82. KĂNA′STA, THE LOST SETTLEMENT

Long ago, while people still lived in the old town of Kăna′sta, on the French Broad, two strangers, who looked in no way different from other Cherokee, came into the settlement one day and made their way into the chief's house. After the first greetings were over the chief asked them from what town they had come, thinking them from one of the western settlements, but they said, "We are of your people and our town is close at hand, but you have never seen it. Here you have wars and sickness, with enemies on every side, and after a while a stronger enemy will come to take your country from you. We are always happy, and we have come to invite you to live with us in our town over there," and they pointed toward Tsuwa‘tel′da (Pilot knob). "We do not live forever, and do not always find game when we go for it, for the game belongs to Tsul‘kălû′, who lives in Tsunegûñ′yĭ, but we have peace always and need not think of danger. We go now, but if your people will live with us let them fast seven days, and we shall come then to take them." Then they went away toward the west.

The chief called his people together into the townhouse and they held a council over the matter and decided at last to go with the strangers. They got all their property ready for moving, and then went again into the townhouse and began their fast. They fasted six days, and on the morning of the seventh, before yet the sun was high, they saw a great company coming along the trail from the west, led by the two men who had stopped with the chief. They seemed just like Cherokee from another settlement, and after a friendly meeting they took up a part of the goods to be carried, and the two parties started back together for Tsuwa'tel'da. There was one man from another town visiting at Kăna'sta, and he went along with the rest.

When they came to the mountain, the two guides led the way into a cave, which opened out like a great door in the side of the rock. Inside they found an open country and a town, with houses ranged in two long rows from east to west. The mountain people lived in the houses on the south side, and they had made ready the other houses for the new comers, but even after all the people of Kăna'sta, with their children and belongings, had moved in, there were still a large number of houses waiting ready for the next who might come. The mountain people told them that there was another town, of a different people, above them in the same mountain, and still farther above, at the very top, lived the Ani'-Hyûñtĭkwălâ'skĭ (the Thunders).

Now all the people of Kăna'sta were settled in their new homes, but the man who had only been visiting with them wanted to go back to his own friends. Some of the mountain people wanted to prevent this, but the chief said, "No; let him go if he will, and when he tells his friends they may want to come, too. There is plenty of room for all." Then he said to the man, "Go back and tell your friends that if they want to come and live with us and be always happy, there is a place here ready and waiting for them. Others of us live in Datsu'-naiâsgûñ'yĭ and in the high mountains all around, and if they would rather go to any of them it is all the same. We see you wherever you go and are with you in all your dances, but you can not see us unless you fast. If you want to see us, fast four days, and we will come and talk with you; and then if you want to live with us, fast again seven days, and we will come and take you." Then the chief led the man through the cave to the outside of the mountain and left him there, but when the man looked back he saw no cave, but only the solid rock.

*   *   *   *   *   *   *

The people of the lost settlement were never seen again, and they are still living in Tsuwa'tel'da. Strange things happen there, so that the Cherokee know the mountain is haunted and do not like to go near it. Only a few years ago a party of hunters camped there, and as they sat around their fire at supper time they talked of the story and made rough jokes about the people of old Kăna'sta. That night they were aroused from sleep by a noise as of stones thrown at them from among the trees, but when they searched they could find nobody, and were so frightened that they gathered up their guns and pouches and left the place.

83. TSUWE′NĂHĬ: A LEGEND OF PILOT KNOB

In the old town of Kănuga, on Pigeon river, there was a lazy fellow named Tsuwe′năhĭ, who lived from house to house among his relatives and never brought home any game, although he used to spend nearly all his time in the woods. At last his friends got very tired of keeping him, so he told them to get some parched corn ready for him and he would go and bring back a deer or else would never trouble them again. They filled his pouch with parched corn, enough for a long trip, and he started off for the mountains. Day after day passed until they thought they had really seen the last of him, but before the month was half gone he was back again at Kănuga, with no deer, but with a wonderful story to tell.

He said that he had hardly turned away from the trail to go up the ridge when he met a stranger, who asked him where he was going. Tsuwe′năhĭ answered that his friends in the settlement had driven him out because he was no good hunter, and that if he did not find a deer this time he would never go back again. "Why not come with me?" said the stranger, "my town is not far from here, and you have relatives there." Tsuwe′năhĭ was very glad of the chance, because he was ashamed to go back to his own town; so he went with the stranger, who took him to Tsuwa'tel′da (Pilot knob). They came to a cave, and the other said, "Let us go in here;" but the cave ran clear to the heart of the mountain, and when they were inside the hunter found there an open country like a wide bottom land, with a great settlement and hundreds of people. They were all glad to see him, and brought him to their chief, who took him into his own house and showed him a seat near the fire. Tsuwe′năhĭ sat down, but he felt it move under him, and when he looked again he saw that it was a turtle, with its head sticking out from the shell. He jumped up, but the chief said, "It won't hurt you; it only wants to see who you are." So he sat down very carefully, and the turtle drew in its head again. They brought food, of the same kind that he had been accustomed to at home, and when he had eaten the chief took him through the settlement until he had seen all the houses and talked with most of the people. When he had seen everything and had rested some days, he was anxious to get back to his home, so the chief himself brought him to the mouth of the cave and showed him the trail that led down to the river. Then he said, "You are going back to the settlement, but you will never be satisfied there any more. Whenever you want to come to us, you know the way." The chief left him, and Tsuwe′năhĭ went down the mountain and along the river until he came to Kănuga.

He told his story, but no one believed it and the people only laughed at him. After that he would go away very often and be gone for several days at a time, and when he came back to the settlement he would

say he had been with the mountain people. At last one man said he
believed the story and would go with him to see. They went off
together to the woods, where they made a camp, and then Tsuwe′năhĭ
went on ahead, saying he would be back soon. The other waited for
him, doing a little hunting near the camp, and two nights afterwards
Tsuwe′năhĭ was back again. He seemed to be alone, but was talking
as he came, and the other hunter heard girls' voices, although he could
see no one. When he came up to the fire he said, "I have two friends
with me, and they say there is to be a dance in their town in two
nights, and if you want to go they will come for you." The hunter
agreed at once, and Tsuwe′năhĭ called out, as if to some one close by,
"He says he will go." Then he said, "Our sisters have come for some
venison." The hunter had killed a deer and had the meat drying over
the fire, so he said, "What kind do they want?" The voices answered,
"Our mother told us to ask for some of the ribs," but still he could
see nothing. He took down some rib pieces and gave them to Tsu-
we′năhĭ, who took them and said, "In two days we shall come again
for you." Then he started off, and the other heard the voices going
through the woods until all was still again.

In two days Tsuwe′năhĭ came, and this time he had two girls with
him. As they stood near the fire the hunter noticed that their feet
were short and round, almost like dogs' paws, but as soon as they saw
him looking they sat down so that he could not see their feet. After
supper the whole party left the camp and went up along the creek to
Tsuwa′tel′da. They went in through the cave door until they got to
the farther end and could see houses beyond, when all at once the
hunter's legs felt as if they were dead and he staggered and fell to
the ground. The others lifted him up, but still he could not stand,
until the medicine-man brought some "old tobacco" and rubbed it
on his legs and made him smell it until he sneezed. Then he was
able to stand again and went in with the others. He could not stand at
first, because he had not prepared himself by fasting before he started.

The dance had not yet begun and Tsuwe′năhĭ took the hunter into the
townhouse and showed him a seat near the fire, but it had long thorns
of honey locust sticking out from it and he was afraid to sit down.
Tsuwe′năhĭ told him not to be afraid, so he sat down and found that
the thorns were as soft as down feathers. Now the drummer came in
and the dancers, and the dance began. One man followed at the end
of the line, crying *Kû! Kû!* all the time, but not dancing. The
hunter wondered, and they told him, "This man was lost in the mountains and had been calling all through the woods for his friends until
his voice failed and he was only able to pant *Kû! Kû!* and then we
found him and took him in."

When it was over Tsuwe′năhĭ and the hunter went back to the settlement. At the next dance in Kănuga they told all they had seen at

Tsuwa'tel'da, what a large town was there and how kind everybody was, and this time—because there were two of them—the people believed it. Now others wanted to go, but Tsuwe'năhĭ told them they must first fast seven days, while he went ahead to prepare everything, and then he would come and bring them. He went away and the others fasted, until at the end of seven days he came for them and they went with him to Tsuwa'tel'da, and their friends in the settlement never saw them again.

84. THE MAN WHO MARRIED THE THUNDER'S SISTER

In the old times the people used to dance often and all night. Once there was a dance at the old town of Sâkwi'yĭ, on the head of Chattahoochee, and after it was well started two young women with beautiful long hair came in, but no one knew who they were or whence they had come. They danced with one partner and another, and in the morning slipped away before anyone knew that they were gone; but a young warrior had fallen in love with one of the sisters on account of her beautiful hair, and after the manner of the Cherokee had already asked her through an old man if she would marry him and let him live with her. To this the young woman had replied that her brother at home must first be consulted, and they promised to return for the next dance seven days later with an answer, but in the meantime if the young man really loved her he must prove his constancy by a rigid fast until then. The eager lover readily agreed and impatiently counted the days.

In seven nights there was another dance. The young warrior was on hand early, and later in the evening the two sisters appeared as suddenly as before. They told him their brother was willing, and after the dance they would conduct the young man to their home, but warned him that if he told anyone where he went or what he saw he would surely die.

He danced with them again and about daylight the three came away just before the dance closed, so as to avoid being followed, and started off together. The women led the way along a trail through the woods, which the young man had never noticed before, until they came to a small creek, where, without hesitating, they stepped into the water. The young man paused in surprise on the bank and thought to himself, "They are walking in the water; I don't want to do that." The women knew his thoughts just as though he had spoken and turned and said to him, "This is not water; this is the road to our house." He still hesitated, but they urged him on until he stepped into the water and found it was only soft grass that made a fine level trail.

They went on until the trail came to a large stream which he knew for Tallulah river. The women plunged boldly in, but again the warrior hesitated on the bank, thinking to himself, "That water is very deep and will drown me; I can't go on." They knew his thoughts and turned and said, "This is no water, but the main trail that goes past our house, which is now close by." He stepped in, and instead of water there was tall waving grass that closed above his head as he followed them.

They went only a short distance and came to a rock cave close under Ugûñ'yĭ (Tallulah falls). The women· entered, while the warrior stopped at the mouth; but they said, "This is our house; come in and our brother will soon be home; he is coming now." They heard low thunder in the distance. He went inside and stood up close to the entrance. Then the women took off their long hair and hung it up on a rock, and both their heads were as smooth as a pumpkin. The man thought, "It is not hair at all," and he was more frightened than ever.

The younger woman, the one he was about to marry, then sat down and told him to take a seat beside her. He looked, and it was a large turtle, which raised itself up and stretched out its claws as if angry at being disturbed. The young man said it was a turtle, and refused to sit down, but the woman insisted that it was a seat. Then there was a louder roll of thunder and the woman said, "Now our brother is nearly home." While they urged and he still refused to come nearer or sit down, suddenly there was a great thunder clap just behind him, and turning quickly he saw a man standing in the doorway of the cave.

"This is my brother," said the woman, and he came in and sat down upon the turtle, which again rose up and stretched out its claws. The young warrior still refused to come in. The brother then said that he was just about to start to a council, and invited the young man to go with him. The hunter said he was willing to go if only he had a horse; so the young woman was told to bring one. She went out and soon came back leading a great uktena snake, that curled and twisted along the whole length of the cave. Some people say this was a white uktena and that the brother himself rode a red one. The hunter was terribly frightened, and said "That is a snake; I can't ride that." The others insisted that it was no snake, but their riding horse. The brother grew impatient and said to the woman, "He may like it better if you bring him a saddle, and some bracelets for his wrists and arms." So they went out again and brought in a saddle and some arm bands, and the saddle was another turtle, which they fastened on the uktena's back, and the bracelets were living slimy snakes, which they got ready to twist around the hunter's wrists.

He was almost dead with fear, and said, "What kind of horrible place is this? I can never stay here to live with snakes and creeping things." The brother got very angry and called him a coward, and then it was as if lightening flashed from his eyes and struck the young man, and a terrible crash of thunder stretched him senseless.

When at last he came to himself again he was standing with his feet in the water and both hands grasping a laurel bush that grew out from the bank, and there was no trace of the cave or the Thunder People, but he was alone in the forest. He made his way out and finally reached his own settlement, but found then that he had been gone so very long that all the people had thought him dead, although to him it seemed only the day after the dance. His friends questioned him closely, and, forgetting the warning, he told the story; but in seven days he died, for no one can come back from the underworld and tell it and live.

<h3>85. THE HAUNTED WHIRLPOOL</h3>

At the mouth of Suck creek, on the Tennessee, about 8 miles below Chattanooga, is a series of dangerous whirlpools, known as "The Suck," and noted among the Cherokee as the place where Ûñtsaiyĭ′, the gambler, lived long ago (see the story). They call it Ûñ′tiguhĭ′, "Pot-in-the-water," on account of the appearance of the surging, tumbling water, suggesting a boiling pot. They assert that in the old times the whirlpools were intermittent in character, and the canoemen attempt-ing to pass the spot used to hug the bank, keeping constantly on the alert for signs of a coming eruption, and when they saw the water begin to revolve more rapidly would stop and wait until it became quiet again before attempting to proceed.

It happened once that two men, going down the river in a canoe, as they came near this place saw the water circling rapidly ahead of them. They pulled up to the bank to wait until it became smooth again, but the whirlpool seemed to approach with wider and wider circles, until they were drawn into the vortex. They were thrown out of the canoe and carried down under the water, where one man was seized by a great fish and was never seen again. The other was taken round and round down to the very lowest center of the whirlpool, when another circle caught him and bore him outward and upward until he was finally thrown up again to the surface and floated out into the shallow water, whence he made his escape to shore. He told afterwards that when he reached the narrowest circle of the maelstrom the water seemed to open below him and he could look down as through the roof beams of a house, and there on the bottom of the river he had seen a great company of people, who looked up and beckoned to him to join them, but as they put up their hands to seize him the swift current caught him and took him out of their reach.

<h3>86. YAHULA</h3>

Yahoola creek, which flows by Dahlonega, in Lumpkin county, Georgia, is called Yahulâ′ĭ (Yahula place) by the Cherokees, and this is the story of the name:

Years ago, long before the Revolution, Yahula was a prosperous stock trader among the Cherokee, and the tinkling of the bells hung around the necks of his ponies could be heard on every mountain trail. Once there was a great hunt and all the warriors were out, but when it was over and they were ready to return to the settlement Yahula was not with them. They waited and searched, but he could not be found, and at last they went back without him, and his friends grieved for him as for one dead. Some time after his people were surprised and delighted to have him walk in among them and sit down as they were at supper in the evening. To their questions he told them that he had been lost in the mountains, and that the Nûñně'hĭ, the Immortals, had found him and brought him to their town, where he had been kept ever since, with the kindest care and treatment, until the longing to see his old friends had brought him back. To the invitation of his friends to join them at supper he said that it was now too late—he had tasted the fairy food and could never again eat with human kind, and for the same reason he could not stay with his family, but must go back to the Nûñně'hĭ. His wife and children and brother begged him to stay, but he said that he could not; it was either life with the Immortals or death with his own people—and after some further talk he rose to go. They saw him as he sat talking to them and as he stood up, but the moment he stepped out the doorway he vanished as if he had never been.

After that he came back often to visit his people. They would see him first as he entered the house, and while he sat and talked he was his old self in every way, but the instant he stepped across the threshold he was gone, though a hundred eyes might be watching. He came often, but at last their entreaties grew so urgent that the Nûñně'hĭ must have been offended, and he came no more. On the mountain at the head of the creek, about 10 miles above the present Dahlonega, is a small square inclosure of uncut stone, without roof or entrance. Here it was said that he lived, so the Cherokee called it Yahulâ'ĭ and called the stream by the same name. Often at night a belated traveler coming along the trail by the creek would hear the voice of Yahula singing certain favorite old songs that he used to like to sing as he drove his pack of horses across the mountain, the sound of a voice urging them on, and the crack of a whip and the tinkling of bells went with the song, but neither driver nor horses could be seen, although the sounds passed close by. The songs and the bells were heard only at night.

There was one man who had been his friend, who sang the same songs for a time after Yahula had disappeared, but he died suddenly, and then the Cherokee were afraid to sing these songs any more until it was so long since anyone had heard the sounds on the mountain that they thought Yahula must be gone away, perhaps to the West, where others of the tribe had already gone. It is so long ago now that even the stone house may have been destroyed by this time, but more than one old man's father saw it and heard the songs and the bells a hundred years ago. When the Cherokee went from Georgia to Indian Territory in 1838 some of them said, "Maybe Yahula has gone there and we shall hear him," but they have never heard him again.

87. THE WATER CANNIBALS

Besides the friendly Nûñnĕ'hĭ of the streams and mountains there is a race of cannibal spirits, who stay at the bottom of the deep rivers and live upon human flesh, especially that of little children. They come out just after daybreak and go about unseen from house to house until they find some one still asleep, when they shoot him with their invisible arrows and carry the dead body down under the water to feast upon it. That no one may know what has happened they leave in place of the body a shade or image of the dead man or little child, that wakes up and talks and goes about just as he did, but there is no life in it, and in seven days it withers and dies, and the people bury it and think they are burying their dead friend. It was a long time before the people found out about this, but now they always try to be awake at daylight and wake up the children, telling them "The hunters are among you."

This is the way they first knew about the water cannibals: There was a man in Tĭkwăli'tsĭ town who became sick and grew worse until the doctors said he could not live, and then his friends went away from the house and left him alone to die. They were not so kind to each other in the old times as they are now, because they were afraid of the witches that came to torment dying people.

He was alone several days, not able to rise from his bed, when one morning an old woman came in at the door. She looked just like the other women of the settlement, but he did not know her. She came over to the bed and said, "You are very sick and your friends seem to have left you. Come with me and I will make you well." The man was so near death that he could not move, but now her words made him feel stronger at once, and he asked her where she wanted him to go. "We live close by; come with me and I will show you," said the woman, so he got up from his bed and she led the way down to the water. When she came to the water she stepped in and he followed, and there was a road under the water, and another country there just like that above.

They went on until they came to a settlement with a great many houses, and women going about their work and children playing. They met a party of hunters coming in from a hunt, but instead of deer or bear quarters hanging from their shoulders they carried the bodies of dead men and children, and several of the bodies the man knew for those of his own friends in Tĭkwăli'tsĭ. They came to a house and the woman said "This is where I live," and took him in and fixed a bed for him and made him comfortable.

By this time he was very hungry, but the woman knew his thoughts and said, "We must get him something to eat." She took one of the bodies that the hunters had just brought in and cut off a slice to roast. The man was terribly frightened, but she read his thoughts again and said, "I see you can not eat our food." Then she turned away from him and held her hands before her stomach—*so*—and when she turned around again she had them full of bread and beans such as he used to have at home.

So it was every day, until soon he was well and strong again. Then she told him he might go home now, but he must be sure not to speak to anyone for seven days, and if any of his friends should question him he must make signs as if his throat were sore and keep silent. She went with him along the same trail to the water's edge, and the water closed over her and he went back alone to Tĭkwăli′tsĭ. When he came there his friends were surprised, because they thought he had wandered off and died in the woods. They asked him where he had been, but he only pointed to his throat and said nothing, so they thought he was not yet well and let him alone until the seven days were past, when he began to talk again and told the whole story.

Historical Traditions

88. FIRST CONTACT WITH WHITES

There are a few stories concerning the first contact of the Cherokee with whites and negroes. They are very modern and have little value as myths, but throw some light upon the Indian estimate of the different races.

One story relates how the first whites came from the east and tried to enter into friendly relations, but the Indians would have nothing to do with them for a long time. At last the whites left a jug of whisky and a dipper near a spring frequented by the Indians. The Indians came along, tasted the liquor, which they had never known before, and liked it so well that they ended by all getting comfortably drunk. While they were in this happy frame of mind some white men came up, and this time the Indians shook hands with them and they have been friends after a fashion ever since. This may possibly be a Cherokee adaptation of the story of Hudson's first landing on the island of Manhattan.

   *   *   *   *   *   *   *

At the creation an ulûñsû′tĭ was given to the white man, and a piece of silver to the Indian. But the white man despised the stone and threw it away, while the Indian did the same with the silver. In going about the white man afterward found the silver piece and put it into his pocket and has prized it ever since. The Indian, in like manner, found the ulûñsû′tĭ where the white man had thrown it. He picked it up and has kept it since as his talisman, as money is the talismanic power of the white man. This story is quite general and is probably older than others of its class.

*   *   *   *   *   *   *

When Sequoya, the inventor of the Cherokee alphabet, was trying to introduce it among his people, about 1822, some of them opposed it upon the ground that Indians had no business with reading. They said that when the Indian and the white man were created, the Indian, being the elder, was given a book, while the white man received a bow and arrows. Each was instructed to take good care of his gift and make the best use of it, but the Indian was so neglectful of his book that the white man soon stole it from him, leaving the bow in its place, so that books and reading now belong of right to the white man, while the Indian ought to be satisfied to hunt for a living.—*Cherokee Advocate*, October 26, 1844.

*   *   *   *   *   *   *

The negro made the first locomotive for a toy and put it on a wooden track and was having great fun with it when a white man came along, watched until he saw how to run. it, and then killed the negro and took the locomotive for himself. This, also, although plainly of very recent origin, was heard from several informants.

89. THE IROQUOIS WARS

Long wars were waged between the Cherokee and their remote northern relatives, the Iroquois, with both of whom the recollection, now nearly faded, was a vivid tradition fifty years ago. The (Seneca) Iroquois know the Cherokee as Oyada'ge'oñnoñ, a name rather freely rendered "cave people." The latter call the Iroquois, or rather their largest and most aggressive tribe, the Seneca, Nûndăwe′gĭ, Ani′-Nûn-dăwe′gĭ, or Ani′-Sĕ′nikă, the first forms being derived from Nûndawa′ga or Nûndawa′-ono, "people of the great hills," the name by which the Seneca know themselves. According to authorities quoted by School-craft, the Seneca claim to have at one time had a settlement, from which they were afterward driven, at Seneca, South Carolina, known in history as one of the principal towns of the Lower Cherokee.

The league of the Iroquois was probably founded about the middle of the sixteenth century. Before 1680 they had conquered or exter-minated all the tribes upon their immediate borders and had turned their arms against the more distant Illinois, Catawba, and Cherokee. According to Iroquois tradition, the Cherokee were the aggressors, having attacked and plundered a Seneca hunting party somewhere in the west, while in another story they are represented as having violated a peace treaty by the murder of the Iroquois delegates.

Whatever the cause, the war was taken up by all the tribes of the league.

From the Iroquois country to the Cherokee frontier was considered a five days' journey for a rapidly traveling war party. As the distance was too great for large expeditions, the war consisted chiefly of a series of individual exploits, a single Cherokee often going hundreds of miles to strike a blow, which was sure to be promptly retaliated by the warriors from the north, the great object of every Iroquois boy being to go against the Cherokee as soon as he was old enough to take the war path. Captives were made on both sides, and probably in about equal numbers, the two parties being too evenly matched for either to gain any permanent advantage, and a compromise was finally made by which the Tennessee river came to be regarded as the boundary between their rival claims, all south of that stream being claimed by the Cherokee, and being acknowledged by the Iroquois, as the limit of their own conquests in that direction. This Indian boundary was recognized by the British government up to the time of the Revolution.

Morgan states that a curious agreement was once made between the two tribes, by which this river was also made the limit of pursuit. If a returning war party of the Cherokee could recross the Tennessee before they were overtaken by the pursuing Iroquois they were as safe from attack as though entrenched behind a stockade. The pursuers, if they chose, might still invade the territory of the enemy, but they passed by the camp of the retreating Cherokee without offering to attack them. A similar agreement existed for a time between the Seneca and the Erie.

The Buffalo dance of the Iroquois is traditionally said to have had its origin in an expedition against the Cherokee. When the warriors on their way to the south reached the Kentucky salt lick they found there a herd of buffalo, and heard them, for the first time, "singing their favorite songs," i. e., bellowing and snorting. From the bellowing and the movements of the animals were derived the music and action of the dance.

According to Cherokee tradition, as given by the chief Stand Watie, the war was finally brought to an end by the Iroquois, who sent a delegation to the Cherokee to propose a general alliance of the southern and western tribes. The Cherokee accepted the proposition, and in turn sent out invitations to the other tribes, all of which entered into the peace excepting the Osage, of whom it was therefore said that they should be henceforth like a wild fruit on the prairie, at which every bird should pick, and so the Osage have remained ever a predatory tribe without friends or allies. This may be the same treaty described in the story of "The Seneca Peacemakers." A formal and final peace between the two tribes was arranged through the efforts of the British agent, Sir William Johnson, in 1768.

In 1847 there were still living among the Seneca the grandchildren of Cherokee captives taken in these wars. In 1794 the Seneca pointed out to Colonel Pickering a chief who was a native Cherokee, having been taken when a boy and adopted among the Seneca, who afterward made him chief. This was probably the same man of whom they told Schoolcraft fifty years later. He was a full-blood Cherokee, but had been captured when too young to have any memory of the event. Years afterward, when he had grown to manhood and had become a chief in the tribe, he learned of his foreign origin, and was filled at once with an overpowering longing to go back to the south to find his people and live and die among them. He journeyed to the Cherokee country, but on arriving there found to his great disappointment that the story of his capture had been forgotten in the tribe, and that his relatives, if any were left, failed to recognize him. Being unable to find his kindred, he made only a short visit and returned again to the Seneca.

From James Wafford, of Indian Territory, the author obtained a detailed account of the Iroquois peace embassy referred to by Stand Watie, and of the wampum belt that accompanied it. Wafford's information concerning the proceedings at Echota was obtained directly from two eyewitnesses—Sequoya, the inventor of the alphabet, and Gatûñ'wa'lĭ, "Hard-mush," who afterward explained the belt at the great council near Tahlequah seventy years later. Sequoya, at the time of the Echota conference, was a boy living with his mother at Taskigi town a few miles away, while Gatûñ'wa'lĭ was already a young man.

The treaty of peace between the Cherokee and Iroquois, made at Johnson Hall in New York in 1768, appears from the record to have been brought about by the Cherokee, who sent for the purpose a delegation of chiefs, headed by Âgănstâ'ta, "Groundhog-sausage," of Echota, their great leader in the war of 1760–61 against the English. After the treaty had been concluded the Cherokee delegates invited some of the Iroquois chiefs to go home with them for a visit, but the latter declined on the ground that it was not yet safe, and in fact some of their warriors were at that very time out against the Cherokee, not yet being aware of the peace negotiations. It is probable, therefore, that the Iroquois delegates did not arrive at Echota until some considerable time, perhaps three years, after the formal preliminaries had been concluded in the north.

According to Sequoya's account, as given to Wafford, there had been a long war between the Cherokee and the northern Indians, who were never able to conquer the Cherokee or break their spirit, until at last the Iroquois were tired of fighting and sent a delegation to make peace. The messengers set out for the south with their wampum belts and peace emblems, but lost their way after passing Tennessee river, perhaps from the necessity of avoiding the main trail, and instead of arriving at Itsâ'tĭ or Echota, the ancient peace town and capital of the Cherokee Nation—situated on Little Tennessee river below Citico creek, in the present Monroe county, Tennessee—they

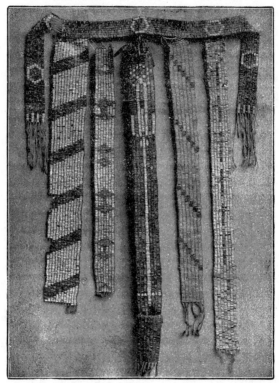

FIG. 2—Ancient Iroquois wampum belts.[1]

found themselves on the outskirts of Tă'likwă' or Tellico, on Tellico river, some 10 or 15 miles to the southward.

Concealing themselves in the neighborhood, they sent one of their number into the town to announce their coming.   As it happened the

[1] "The Onondagas retain the custody of the wampums of the Five Nations, and the keeper of the wampums, Thomas Webster, of the Snipe tribe, a consistent, thorough pagan, is their interpreter. Notwithstanding the claims made that the wampums can be read as a governing code of law, it is evident that they are simply monumental reminders of preserved traditions, without any literal details whatever.

"The first [of this] group from left to right, represents a convention of the Six Nations at the adoption of the Tuscaroras into the league; the second, the Five Nations, upon seven strands, illustrates a treaty with seven Canadian tribes before the year 1600; the third signifies the guarded approach of strangers to the councils of the Five Nations (a guarded gate, with a long, white path leading to the inner gate, where the Five Nations are grouped, with the Onondagas in the center and a safe council house behind all); the fourth represents a treaty when but four of the Six Nations were represented, and the fifth embodies the pledge of seven Canadian christianized nations to abandon their crooked ways and keep an honest peace (having a cross for each tribe, and with a zigzag line below, to indicate that their ways had been crooked but would ever after be as sacred as the cross).   Above this group is another, claiming to bear date about 1608, when Champlain joined the Algonquins against the Iroquois."—Carrington, in Six Nations of New York, Extra Bulletin, Eleventh Census, pp. 33–34, 1892.

chief and his family were at work in their cornfield, and his daughter had just gone up to the house for some reason when the Iroquois entered and asked for something to eat. Seeing that he was a stranger, she set out food for him according to the old custom of hospitality. While he was eating her father, the chief, came in to see what was delaying her, and was surprised to find there one of the hereditary enemies of his tribe. By this time the word had gone out that an Iroquois was in the chief's house, and the men of the town had left their work and seized their guns to kill him, but the chief heard them coming and standing in the doorway kept them off, saying: "This man has come here on a peace mission, and before you kill him you must first kill me." They finally listened to him, and allowed the messenger to go out and bring his companions to the chief's house, where they were all taken care of.

When they were well rested after their long journey the chief of Tä′likwǎ himself went with them to Itsâ′tĭ, the capital, where lived the great chief Âgănstâ′ta, who was now the civil ruler of the Nation. The chiefs of the various towns were summoned and a council was held, at which the speaker for the Iroquois delegation delivered his message and produced the wampum belts and pipes, which they brought as proofs of their mission and had carried all the way in packs upon their backs.

He said that for three years his people had been wanting to make peace. There was a spring of dark, cloudy water in their country, and they had covered it over for one year and then looked, but the water was still cloudy. Again they had covered it over, but when they looked at the end of another year it was still dark and troubled. For another year they had covered the spring, and this time when they looked the water was clear and sparkling. Then they knew the time had come, and they left home with their wampum belts to make peace with their enemies.

The friendly message was accepted by the Cherokee, and the belts and other symbolic peace tokens were delivered over to their keeping. Other belts in turn were probably given to the Iroquois, and after the usual round of feasting and dancing the messengers returned to their people in the north and the long war was at an end.

For nearly a century these symbolic records of the peace with the Iroquois were preserved by the Cherokee, and were carried with them to the western territory when the tribe was finally driven from its old home in 1838. They were then in the keeping of John Ross, principal chief at the time of the removal, and were solemnly produced at a great intertribal council held near Tahlequah, in the Indian Territory, in June, 1843, when they were interpreted by the Cherokee speaker, Gatûñ′wa‘lĭ, "Hard-mush," who had seen them delivered to the chiefs of his tribe at old Itsâ′tĭ seventy years before. Wafford was present on this occasion and describes it.

Holding the belts over his arm while speaking, Hard-mush told of the original treaty with the Iroquois, and explained the meaning of each belt in turn. According to the best of Wafford's recollection, there was one large belt, to which the smaller belts were fitted. The beads did not seem to be of shell, and may have been of porcelain. There were also red pipes for the warriors, grayish-white pipes for the chiefs who were foremost in making the peace, and some fans or other ornaments of feathers. There were several of the red pipes, resembling the red-stone pipes of the Sioux, but only one, or perhaps two, of the white peace pipes, which may have been only painted, and were much larger than the others. The pipes were passed around the circle at the council, so that each delegate might take a whiff. The objects altogether made a considerable package, which was carefully guarded by the Cherokee keeper. It is thought that they were destroyed in the War of the Rebellion when the house of John Ross, a few miles south of Tahlequah, was burned by the Confederate Cherokee under their general, Stand Watie.

90. HIADEONI, THE SENECA

"Hiadeoni was the father of the late chief Young-king. He was a Seneca warrior, a man of great prowess, dexterity, and swiftness of foot, and had established his reputation for courage and skill on many occasions. He resolved while the Seneca were still living on the Genesee river to make an incursion alone into the country of the Cherokee. He plumed himself with the idea that he could distinguish himself in this daring adventure, and he prepared for it, according to the custom of warriors. They never encumber themselves with baggage. He took nothing but his arms and the meal of a little parched and pounded corn. The forest gave him his meat.

Hiadeoni reached the confines of the Cherokee country in safety and alone. He waited for evening before he entered the precincts of a village. He found the people engaged in a dance. He watched his opportunity, and when one of the dancers went out from the ring into the bushes he dispatched him with his hatchet. In this way he killed two men that night in the skirts of the woods without exciting alarm, and took their scalps and retreated. It was late when he came to a lodge, standing remote from the rest, on his course homeward. Watching here, he saw a young man come out, and killed him as he had done the others, and took his scalp. Looking into the lodge cautiously he saw it empty, and ventured in with the hope of finding some tobacco and ammunition to serve him on his way home.

While thus busied in searching the lodge he heard footsteps at the door, and immediately threw himself on the bed from which the young man had risen, and covered his face, feigning sleep. They proved to be the footsteps of his last victim's mother. She, supposing him to be her son, whom she had a short time before left lying there, said,

"My son, I am going to such a place, and will not be back till morning." He made a suitable response, and the old woman went out. Insensibly he fell asleep, and knew nothing till morning, when the first thing he heard was the mother's voice. She, careful for her son, was at the fireplace very early, pulling some roasted squashes out of the ashes, and after putting them out, and telling him she left them for him to eat, she went away. He sprang up instantly and fled; but the early dawn had revealed his inroad, and he was hotly pursued. Light of foot, and having the start, he succeeded in reaching and concealing himself in a remote piece of woods, where he laid till night, and then pursued his way toward the Genesee, which, in due time he reached, bringing his three Cherokee scalps as trophies of his victory and prowess."—Schoolcraft, Notes on Iroquois, p. 253, 1847.

91. THE TWO MOHAWKS

"In the year 1747 a couple of the Mohawk Indians came against the lower towns of the Cheerake, and so cunningly ambuscaded them through most part of the spring and summer, as to kill above twenty in different attacks before they were discovered by any party of the enraged and dejected people. They had a thorough knowledge of the most convenient ground for their purpose, and were extremely swift and long-winded. Whenever they killed any and got the scalp they made off to the neighboring mountains, and ran over the broad ledges of rocks in contrary courses, as occasion offered, so as the pursuers could by no means trace them. Once, when a large company was in chase of them, they ran round a steep hill at the head of the main eastern branch of Savana river, intercepted, killed, and scalped the hindmost of the party, and then made off between them and Keeowhee. As this was the town to which the company belonged, they hastened home in a close body, as the proper place of security from such enemy wizards. In this manner did those two sprightly, gallant savages perplex and intimidate their foes for the space of four moons in the greatest security, though they often were forced to kill and barbecue what they chiefly lived upon, in the midst of their watchful enemies. Having sufficiently revenged their relations' blood and gratified their own ambition with an uncommon number of scalps, they resolved to captivate one and run home with him as a proof of their having killed none but the enemies of their country. Accordingly, they approached very near to Keeowhee, about half a mile below the late Fort Prince George. Advancing with the usual caution on such an occasion, one crawled along under the best cover of the place about the distance of a hundred yards ahead, while the other shifted from tree to tree, looking sharply every way. In the evening, however, an old, beloved man discovered them from the top of an adjoining hill, and knew them to be enemies by the cut of their hair, light trim for running, and their postures. He returned to the town and called first at the house of one of our traders and informed him of the affair, enjoining him not to mention it to any, lest the people should set off against them without success before their tracks were to be discovered and he be charged with having deceived them. But, contrary to the true policy of traders among unforgiving savages, that thoughtless member of the Choktah Sphynx Company busied himself, as usual, out of his proper sphere, sent for the headmen, and told them the story. As the Mohawks were allies and not known to molest any of the traders in the paths and woods, he ought to have observed a strict neutrality. The youth of the town, by order of their headmen, carried on their noisy public diversions in their usual manner to prevent their foes from having any suspicion of their danger, while runners were sent from the town to their neighbors to come silently and assist them to secure the prey in its state of security. They came like silent ghosts, concerted their plan of operation, passed over the river at the old trading ford opposite to the late fort, which lay between two contiguous commanding hills, and, proceeding downward over a broad creek, formed a large semicircle from the river bank, while the town seemed to be taking its usual rest. They then closed into a narrower compass, and at last discovered the two brave, unfortunate men lying close under the tops of some fallen young pine trees. The company gave the war signal, and the Mohawks, bounding up, bravely repeated it; but, by their sudden spring from under thick cover, their arms were useless. They made desperate efforts, however, to kill or be killed, as their situation required. One of the Cheerake, the noted half-breed of Istanare [Ustăna′lĭ] town, which lay 2 miles from thence, was at the first onset knocked down and almost killed with his own cutlass, which was wrested from him, though he was the strongest of the whole nation. But they were overpowered by numbers, captivated, and put to the most exquisite tortures of fire, amidst a prodigious crowd of exulting foes.

One of the present Choktah traders, who was on the spot, told me that when they were tied to the stake the younger of the two discovered our traders on a hill near, addressed them in English, and entreated them to redeem their lives. The elder immediately spoke to him, in his own language, to desist. On this, he recollected himself, and became composed like a stoic, manifesting an indifference to life or death, pleasure or pain, according to their standard of martial virtue, and their dying behaviour did not reflect the least dishonor on their former gallant actions. All the pangs of fiery torture served only to refine their manly spirits, and as it was out of the power of the traders to redeem them they, according to our usual custom, retired as soon as the Indians began the diabolical tragedy."—Adair, American Indians, p. 383, 1775.

PHOTOGRAPH BY AUTHOR, 1888

ANNIE AX (SADAYĬ)

PHOTOGRAPH BY AUTHOR, 1888

WALINÍ, A CHEROKEE WOMAN

92. ESCAPE OF THE SENECA BOYS

Some Seneca warriors were hunting in the woods, and one morning, on starting out for the day, they left two boys behind to take care of the camp. Soon after they had 'gone, a war party of Cherokee came up, and finding the boys alone took them both and started back to the south, traveling at such a rate that when the hunters returned in the evening they decided that it was of no use to follow them. When the Cherokee reached their own country they gave the boys to an old man, whose sons had been killed by the Seneca. He took the boys and adopted them for his own, and they grew up with him until they were large and strong enough to go hunting for themselves.

But all the time they remembered their own home, and one day the older one said to his brother, "Let's kill the old man and run away." "No," said the other, "we might get lost if we ran away, we are so far from home." "I remember the way," said his brother, so they made a plan to escape. A few days later the old man took the boys with him and the three set out together for a hunt in the mountains. When they were well away from the settlement the boys killed the old man, took all the meat and parched corn meal they could easily carry, and started to make their way back to the north, keeping away from the main trail and following the ridge of the mountains. After many days they came to the end of the mountains and found a trail which the older brother knew as the one along which they had been taken when they were first captured. They went on bravely now until they came to a wide clearing with houses at the farther end, and the older brother said, "I believe there is where we used to live." It was so long ago that they were not quite sure, and besides they were dressed now like Cherokee, so they thought it safer to wait until dark. They saw a river ahead and went down to it and sat behind a large tree to wait. Soon several women came down for water and passed close to the tree without noticing the boys. Said the older brother, "I know those women. One of them is our mother." They waited until the women had filled their buckets and started to the village, when both ran out to meet them with the Seneca hailing-shout, " *Gowĕ´! Gowĕ´!* " At first the women were frightened and thought it a party of Cherokee, but when they heard their own language they came nearer. Then the mother recognized her two sons, and said, "Let us go back and dance for the dead come to life," and they were all very glad and went into the village together.—Arranged from Curtin, Seneca manuscript.

93. THE UNSEEN HELPERS

Ganogwioeoñ, a war chief of the Seneca, led a party against the Cherokee. When they came near the first town he left his men outside and went in alone.   At the first house he found an old woman and her granddaughter.   They did not see him, and he went into the âsĭ and hid himself under some wood.   When darkness came on he heard the old woman say, "Maybe Ganogwioeoñ is near; I'll close the door." After a while he heard them going to bed.   When he thought they were asleep he went into the house.   The fire had burned down low, but the girl was still awake and saw him.   She was about to scream, when he said, "I am Ganogwioeoñ.   If you scream I'll kill you.   If you keep quiet I'll not hurt you."   They talked together, and he told her that in the morning she must bring the chief's daughter to him. She promised to do it, and told him where he should wait.   Just before daylight he left the house.

In the morning the girl went to the chief's house and said to his daughter, "Let's go out together for wood."   The chief's daughter got ready and went with her, and when they came to the place where Ganogwioeoñ was hiding he sprang out and killed her, but did not hurt the other girl.   He pulled off the scalp and gave such a loud scalp yell that all the warriors in the town heard it and came running out after him.   He shook the scalp at them and then turned and ran. He killed the first one that came up, but when he tried to shoot the next one the bow broke and the Cherokee got him.

They tied him and carried him to the two women of the tribe who had the power to decide what should be done with him.   Each of these women had two snakes tattooed on her lips, with their heads opposite each other, in such a way that when she opened her mouth the two snakes opened their mouths also.   They decided to burn the soles of his feet until they were blistered, then to put grains of corn under the skin and to chase him with clubs until they had beaten him to death.

They stripped him and burnt his feet.   Then they tied a bark rope around his waist, with an old man to hold the other end, and made him run between two lines of people, and with clubs in their hands.   When they gave the word to start Ganogwioeoñ pulled the rope away from the old man and broke through the line and ran until he had left them all out of sight.   When night came he crawled into a hollow log.   He was naked and unarmed, with his feet in a pitiful condition, and thought he could never get away.

He heard footsteps on the leaves outside and thought his enemies were upon him.   The footsteps came up to the log and some one said to another, "This is our friend."   Then the stranger said to Ganogwioeoñ, "You think you are the same as dead, but it is not so.   We will take care of you.   Stick out your feet."   He put out his feet from the log and felt something licking them.   After a while the voice said, "I think we have licked his feet enough.   Now we must crawl inside the log and lie on each side of him to keep him warm."   They crawled in beside him. In the morning they crawled out and told him to stick out his feet again. They licked them again and then said to him, "Now we have done all we can do this time. Go on until you come to the place where you made a bark shelter a long time ago, and under the bark you will find something to help you." Ganogwioeoñ crawled out of the log, but they were gone. His feet were better now and he could walk comfortably. He went on until about noon, when he came to the bark shelter, and under it he found a knife, an awl, and a flint, that his men had hidden there two years before. He took them and started on again.

Toward evening he looked around until he found another hollow tree and crawled into it to sleep. At night he heard the footsteps and voices again. When he put out his feet again, as the strangers told him to do, they licked his feet as before and then crawled in and lay down on each side of him to keep him warm. Still he could not see them. In the morning after they went out they licked his feet again and said to him, "At noon you will find food." Then they went away.

Ganogwioeoñ crawled out of the tree and went on. At noon he came to a burning log, and near it was a dead bear, which was still warm, as if it had been killed only a short time before. He skinned the bear and found it very fat. He cut up the meat and roasted as much as he could eat or carry. While it was roasting he scraped the skin and rubbed rotten wood dust on it to clean it until he was tired. When night came he lay down to sleep. He heard the steps and the voices again and one said, "Well, our friend is lying down. He has plenty to eat, and it does not seem as if he is going to die. Let us lick his feet again." When they had finished they said to him, "You need not worry any more now. You will get home all right." Before it was day they left him.

When morning came he put the bearskin around him like a shirt, with the hair outside, and started on again, taking as much of the meat as he could carry. That night his friends came to him again. They said, "Your feet are well, but you will be cold," so they lay again on each side of him. Before daylight they left, saying, "About noon you will find something to wear." He went on and about midday he came to two young bears just killed. He skinned them and dressed the skins, then roasted as much meat as he wanted and lay down to sleep. In the morning he made leggings of the skins, took some of the meat, and started on.

His friends came again the next night and told him that in the morning he would come upon something else to wear. As they said, about noon he found two fawns just killed. He turned the skins and made himself a pair of moccasins, then cut some of the meat, and traveled on until evening, when he made a fire and had supper.

That night again he heard the steps and voices, and one said, "My friend, very soon now you will reach home safely and find your friends all well. Now we will tell you why we have helped you. Whenever you went hunting you always gave the best part of the meat to us and kept only the smallest part for yourself. For that we are thankful and help you. In the morning you will see us and know who we are."

In the morning when he woke up they were still there—two men as he thought—but after he had said the last words to them and started on, he turned again to look, and one was a white wolf and the other a black wolf. That day he reached home.—Arranged from Curtin, Seneca manuscript.

94. HATCINOÑDOÑ'S ESCAPE FROM THE CHEROKEE

Hatcinoñdoñ was a great warrior, the greatest among the Seneca. Once he led a company against the Cherokee. They traveled until they came to the great ridge on the border of the Cherokee country, and then they knew their enemies were on the lookout on the other side. Hatcinoñdoñ told his men to halt where they were while he went ahead to see what was in front. The enemy discovered and chased him, and he ran into a canebrake, where the canes were in two great patches with a narrow strip of open ground between. They saw him go into the canes, so they set fire to the patch and watched at the open place for him to come out, but before they got around to it he had run across into the second patch and escaped. When the canes had burned down the Cherokee looked for his body in the ashes, but could not find any trace of it, so they went home.

When Hatcinoñdoñ got into the second canebrake he was tired out, so he lay down and fell asleep. At night while he was asleep two men came and took him by the arm, saying: "We have come for you. Somebody has sent for you." They took him a long way, above the sky vault, until they came to a house. Then they said: "This is where the man lives who sent for you." He looked, but could see no door. Then a voice from the inside said "Come in," and something like a door opened of itself. He went in and there sat Hawĕñni'o, the Thunder-god.

Hawĕñni'o said, "I have sent for you and you are here. Are you hungry?" Hatcinoñdoñ thought: "That's a strange way to talk; that's not the way I do—I give food." The Thunder knew his thoughts, so he laughed and said, "I said that only in fun." He rose and brought half a cake of bread, half of a wild apple, and half a pigeon. Hatcinoñdoñ said, "This is very little to fill me," but the Thunder replied, "If you eat that, there is more." He began eating, but, as he ate, everything became whole again, so that he was not able to finish it.

While he was sitting he heard some one running outside, and directly the door was thrown open and the Sun came in, so bright that Hatci-noñdoñ had to hold his head down. The two beings talked together, but the Seneca could not understand a word, and soon the visitor went out again. Then the Thunder said: "That is the one you call the Sun, who watches in the world below. It is night down there now, and he is hurrying to the east. He says there has just been a battle. I love both the Seneca and the Cherokee, and when you get back to your warriors you must tell them to stop fighting and go home." Again he brought food, half of each kind, and when Hatcinoñdoñ had eaten, the Thunder said, "Now my messengers will take you to your place."

The door opened again of itself, and Hatcinoñdoñ followed the two Sky People until they brought him to the place where he had slept, and there left him. He found his party and told the warriors what he had seen. They held a council over it and decided to strike the enemy once before going home. Hatcinoñdoñ led them. They met the Cherokee and went home with scalps.

He led another party against the Cherokee, but this time he was taken and carried to the Cherokee town. It was the custom among the Cherokee to let two women say what should be done with captives. They decided that he should be tortured with fire, so he was tied to a tree, and the wood was piled around him. Hatcinoñdoñ gave himself up for lost, when a rain storm came up and the people concluded to wait until it was over. They went away and left him tied to the tree.

Pretty soon an old woman came up to him, and said, "My grandson, you think you are going to die, but you are not. Try to stir your limbs." He struggled and finally got his limbs free. Then she said, "Now you are free. I have come to repay your kindness. You remember that you once found a frog in the middle of a circle of fire and that you picked it up and put it into the water. I was that frog, and now I help you. I sent the rain storm, and now you must go down to the creek and follow the current."

When the rain was over the people came back, but Hatcinoñdoñ was gone. They trailed him down to the creek, but he had found a hollow tree lying in the water, with a hole on the upper side through which he could breathe, so he crawled into it and they could not find him. Once two of the Cherokee came and sat on the log and he could hear them talking about him, but they did not know that he was inside. When they were all gone, he came out and kept on down the stream. After dark he came to a place where three hunters had made a fire and gone to sleep for the night. Their hatchets and arms were hung up on a tree. Hatcinoñdoñ was naked. He listened until he was sure the men were asleep, then he took one of their hatchets and killed all three, one after another. He dressed himself in the clothes of one, and put on his belt, with the knife and hatchet. Then he washed himself at the creek and sat down by the fire and cooked his supper.

After that he stretched and painted the three scalps and lay down by the fire to sleep. In the morning he took what provision he could carry and traveled in a great circle until he found the road by which he and his warriors had come. He found fresh tracks and followed them until he saw smoke ahead. He listened until he heard men speaking Seneca, and knew that it was his party. Then he gave the Seneca shout—*Gowĕ'!*—three times and his friends ran out to meet him. They had been afraid that he was killed, but were glad now that they had waited for him. They went home together. This is their story.—Arranged from Curtin, Seneca manuscript.

95. HEMP-CARRIER

On the southern slope of the ridge, along the trail from Robbinsville to Valley river, in Cherokee county, North Carolina, are the remains of a number of stone cairns. The piles are leveled now, but thirty years ago the stones were still heaped up into pyramids, to which every Cherokee who passed added a stone. According to the tradition these piles marked the graves of a number of women and children of the tribe who were surprised and killed on the spot by a raiding party of the Iroquois shortly before the final peace between the two Nations. As soon as the news was brought to the settlements on Hiwassee and Cheowa a party was made under Tâle'tanigi'skĭ, "Hemp-carrier," to follow and take vengeance on the enemy. Among others of the party was the father of the noted chief Tsunu'lăhûñ'skĭ, or Junaluska, who (Junaluska) died on Cheowa about 1855.

For days they followed the trail of the Iroquois across the Great Smoky mountains, through forests and over rivers, until they finally tracked them to their very town in the far northern Seneca country. On the way they met another war party headed for the south, and the Cherokee killed them all and took their scalps. When they came near the Seneca town it was almost night, and they heard shouts in the townhouse, where the women were dancing over the fresh Cherokee scalps. The avengers hid themselves near the spring, and as the dancers came down to drink the Cherokee silently killed one and another until they had counted as many scalps as had been taken on Cheowa, and still the dancers in the townhouse never thought that enemies were near. Then said the Cherokee leader, "We have covered the scalps of our women and children. Shall we go home now like cowards, or shall we raise the war whoop and let the Seneca know that we are men?" "Let them come, if they will," said his men; and they raised the scalp yell of the Cherokee. At once there was an answering shout from the townhouse, and the dance came to a sudden stop. The Seneca warriors swarmed out with ready gun and hatchet, but the nimble Cherokee were off and away. There was a hot pursuit in the darkness, but the Cherokee knew the trails and were light and active runners, and managed to get away with the loss of only a single man. The rest got home safely, and the people were so well pleased with Hemp-carrier's bravery and success that they gave him seven wives.

96. THE SENECA PEACEMAKERS

In the course of the long war with the Cherokee it happened once that eight Seneca determined to undertake a journey to the south to see if they could make a peace with their enemies. On coming near the border of the Cherokee country they met some hunters of that tribe to whom they told their purpose. The latter at once hurried ahead with the news, and when the peacemakers arrived they found themselves well received by the Cherokee chiefs, who called a council to consider the proposition. All but one of the chiefs favored the peace, but he demanded that the eight delegates should first join them in a war party which was just preparing to go against a tribe farther south, probably the Creeks. The Seneca agreed, and set out with the war party for the south; but in the fight which resulted, the Seneca leader, The Owl, was captured. The other seven escaped with the Cherokee.

A council was held in the enemy's camp, and it was decided that The Owl should be burned at the stake. The wood was gathered and everything made ready, but as they were about to tie him he claimed the warrior's privilege to sing his death song and strike the post as he recited his warlike deeds. The request pleased his enemies, who put a tomahawk into his hands and told him to begin.

He told first his exploits in the north, and then in the west, giving times and places and the number of scalps taken, until his enemies were so pleased and interested that they forgot the prisoner in the warrior. It was a long story, but at last he came to the battle in which he was taken. He told how many relatives he had killed of the very men around him, and then, striking the post with his tomahawk, "So many of your people have I killed, and so many will I yet kill;" and with that he struck down two men, sprang through the circle of warriors, and was away. It was all so sudden that it was some moments before his enemies could recover from their surprise. Then they seized their weapons and were after him through the woods, but he had had a good start and was running for his life, so that he outran the chase and finally reached the Cherokee camp in safety and rejoined his seven companions.

On this proof of good will the Cherokee then concluded the treaty, and the peacemakers returned to their own country.—Arranged from Schoolcraft, Notes on Iroquois, p. 258.

97. ORIGIN OF THE YONTOÑWISAS DANCE

Two Seneca women who were sisters, with the baby boy of the older one, were in a sugar grove near their home when a war party of

Cherokee came upon them and carried them off. When the people of the town learned what had happened, they decided not to go after the enemy for fear they would kill the women, so they made no pursuit.

The Cherokee carried the women with them until they were within one day of the Cherokee towns. The elder sister learned this and made up her mind to try to escape. She had a knife without a handle hidden under her belt, and that night when all lay down to sleep by the fire she kept awake. When they were sleeping soundly, she looked around. She and her sister were tied together, and on each side of them was a Cherokee with the end of the rope under his body on the ground. Taking out her knife, she cut the rope without waking the men, and then rousing her sister quietly she whispered to her to come. They were going to leave the little boy, but he started to cry, so she said, "Let us die together," and took him up on her back, and the two women hurried away. In a little while they heard an alarm behind them, and knew that their escape was discovered, and then they saw the blazing pine knots waving through the trees where the Cherokee were coming on looking for them. The women knew the Cherokee would hunt for them toward the north, along the trail to the Seneca country, so they made a circuit and went around to the south until they came in sight of a fire and saw a man sitting by a tree, shaking a rattle and singing in a low voice. They found they had come directly back to the enemy's camp, so the older sister said, "This will never do; we must try again. Let us go straight ahead to that big tree in front, and from that straight on to the next, and the next." In this way they kept on a straight course until morning. When the sun came up, they took another direction toward home, and at night they rested in the woods.

They traveled all the next day, and at night rested again. In the night a voice spoke to the younger woman, "Is that where you are resting?" and she answered, "Yes." The voice said again, "Keep on, and you will come out at the spot where you were captured. No harm will come to you. To-morrow you will find food." She roused her sister and told her what the voice had said.

In the morning they went on and at noon found a buck freshly killed. Near by they found a log on fire, so they roasted some of the meat, had a good meal, and carried away afterwards as much of the meat as they could. They kept on, camping every night, and when the meat was nearly gone they saved the rest for the little boy.

At last one night the voice spoke again to the younger sister and said, "You are on the right road, and to-morrow you will be on the border of the Seneca country. You will find food. That is all."

In the morning she told her older sister. They started on again and walked until about noon, when they came to a patch of wild potatoes. They dug and found plenty, and as they looked around they saw smoke where there had been a camp fire.   They gathered wood, made up the fire, and roasted the potatoes.   Then they ate as many as they wanted and carried the rest with them.

They traveled on until the potatoes were almost gone.   Then at night the voice came again to the younger woman, saying: "At noon tomorrow you will reach your home, and the first person you will meet will be your uncle.   When you get to the town, you must call the people together and tell them all that has happened.   You must go to the long house and take off your skirt and carry it on your shoulder. Then you must go inside and go around once, singing, 'We have come home; we are here.'   This is the *Yontoñwisas* song, and it shall be for women only.   Know now that we are the *Hadionyageonoñ*, the Sky People, who have watched over you all this time."

When the girl awoke, she told her sister, and they said, "We must do all this," and they began to sing as they went along.   About noon they heard the sound of chopping, and when they went to the place they found it was their uncle cutting blocks to make spoons.   He did not see them until they spoke, and at first could hardly believe that they were living women, because he knew that they had been taken by the Cherokee.   He was very glad to see them, and as they walked on to the town they told him all they had been commanded to do by the Sky People.   When they arrived at the town, he called all the people together, and they went to the long house.   There the two women sang their song and did everything exactly as they had been told to do, and when it was over they said, "This is all," and sat down.   This is the same Yontoñwisas song that is still sung by the women.—Arranged from Curtin, Seneca manuscript.

98. GA'NA'S ADVENTURES AMONG THE CHEROKEE

Ga'na' was a Seneca war chief.   He called a council and said, "We must go to the Cherokee and see if we can't agree to be friendly together and live in peace hereafter."   The people consented, and the chief said, "We must go to water first before we start."   So they went, a great party of warriors, far away into the deep forest by the river side.   There were no women with them.   For ten days they drank medicine every morning to make them vomit and washed and bathed in the river each day.

Then the chief said, "Now we must get the eagle feathers."   They went to the top of a high hill and dug a trench there the length of a man's body, and put a man into it, with boughs over the top so that he could not be seen, and above that they put the whole body of a deer.   Then the people went off out of sight, and said the words to invite Shada'ge'a, the great eagle that lives in the clouds, to come down.

The man under the brushwood heard a noise, and a common eagle came and ate a little and flew away again.   Soon it came back, ate a little more, and flew off in another direction. It told the other birds and they came, but the man scared them away, because he did not want common birds to eat the meat. After a while he heard a great noise coming through the air, and he knew it was Shada'ge'a, the bird he wanted. Shada'ge'a is very cautious, and looked around in every direction for some time before be began to eat the meat. As soon as he was eating the man put his hand up cautiously and caught hold of the bird's tail and held on to it. Shada'ge'a rose up and flew away, and the man had pulled out one feather. They had to trap a good many eagles in this way, and it was two years before they could get enough feathers to make a full tail, and were ready to start for the Cherokee country.

They were many days on the road, and when they got to the first Cherokee town they found there was a stockade around it so that no enemy could enter. They waited until the gate was open, and then two Seneca dancers went forward, carrying the eagle feathers and shouting the signal yell. When the Cherokee heard the noise they came out and saw the two men singing and dancing, and the chief said, "These men must have come upon some errand." The Seneca messengers came up and said, "Call a council; we have come to talk on important business." All turned and went toward the townhouse, the rest of the Seneca following the two who were dancing. The townhouse was crowded, and the Seneca sang and danced until they were tired before they stopped. The Cherokee did not dance.

After the dance the Seneca chief said, "Now I will tell you why we have come so far through the forest to see you. We have thought among ourselves that it is time to stop fighting. Your people and ours are always on the lookout to kill each other, and we think it is time for this to stop. Here is a belt of wampum to show that I speak the truth. If your people are willing to be friendly, take it," and he held up the belt. The Cherokee chief stepped forward and said, "I will hold it in my hand, and to-morrow we will tell you what we decide." He then turned and said to the people, "Go home and bring food." They went and brought so much food that it made a great pile across the house, and all of both tribes ate together, but could not finish it.

Next day they ate together again, and when all were done the Cherokee chief said to the Seneca, "We have decided to be friendly and to bury our weapons, these knives and hatchets, so that no man may take them up again." The Seneca chief replied, "We are glad you have accepted our offer, and now we have all thrown our weapons in a pile together, and the white wampum hangs between us, and the belt shall be as long as a man and hang down to the ground."

Then the Cherokee chief said to his people, "Now is the time for any of you that wishes to adopt a relative from among the Seneca to do so." So some Cherokee women went and picked out one man and said, "You shall be our uncle," and some more took another for their brother, and so on until only Ga'na', the chief, was left, but the Cherokee chief said, "No one must take Ga'na', for a young man is here to claim him as his father." Then the young man came up to Ga'na' and said, "Father, I am glad to see you. Father, we will go home," and he led Ga'na' to his own mother's house, the house where Ga'na' had spent the first night. The young man was really his son, and when Ga'na' came to the house he recognized the woman as his wife who had been carried off long ago by the Cherokee.

While they were there a messenger came from the Seoqgwageono tribe, that lived near the great salt water in the east, to challenge the Cherokee to a ball play. He was dressed in skins which were so long that they touched the ground. He said that his people were already on the way and would arrive in a certain number of days. They came on the appointed day and the next morning began to make the bets with the Cherokee. The Seneca were still there. The strangers bet two very heavy and costly robes, besides other things. They began to play, and the Cherokee lost the game. Then the Seneca said, "We will try this time." Both sides bet heavily again, and the game began, but after a little running the Seneca carried the ball to their goal and made a point. Before long they made all the points and won the game. Then the bets were doubled, and the Seneca won again. When they won a third game also the Seoqgwageono said, "Let us try a race," and the Seneca agreed.

The course was level, and the open space was very wide. The Cherokee selected the Seneca runner, and it was agreed that they would run the first race without betting and then make their bets on the second race. They ran the first race, and when they reached the post the Seneca runner was just the measure of his body behind the other. His people asked him if he had done his best, but he said, "No; I have not," so they made their bets, and the second race—the real race—began. When they got to the middle the Seneca runner said to the other, "Do your best now, for I am going to do mine," and as he said it he pulled out and left the other far behind and won the race. Then the Seoqgwageono said, "There is one more race yet—the long race," and they got ready for it, but the Cherokee chief said to his own men, "We have won everything from these people. I think it will be best to let them have one race, for if they lose all, they may make trouble." They selected a Cherokee to run, and he was beaten, and the Seoqgwageono went home.

In a few days they sent a messenger to challenge the Cherokee to meet them halfway for a battle. When the Cherokee heard this they said to the Seneca, "There are so few of you here that we don't want to have you killed. It is better for you to go home." So the Seneca went back to their own country.

Three years later they came again to visit the Cherokee, who told them that the Seoqgwageono had won the battle, and that the chief of the enemy had said afterward, "I should like to fight the Seneca, for I am a double man." Before long the enemy heard that the Seneca were there and sent them a challenge to come and fight. The Seneca said, "We must try to satisfy them," so with Cherokee guides they set out for the country of the Seoqgwageono. They went on until they came to an opening in the woods within one day's journey of the first village. Then they stopped and got ready to send two messengers to notify the enemy, but the Cherokee said, "You must send them so as to arrive about sundown." They did this, and when the messengers arrived near the town they saw all the people out playing ball.

The two Seneca went around on the other side, and began throwing sumac darts as they approached, so that the others would think they were some of their own men at play. In this way they got near enough to kill a man who was standing alone. They scalped him, and then raising the scalp yell they rushed off through the woods, saying to each other as they ran, "Be strong—Be strong." Soon they saw the Seoqgwageono coming on horses, but managed to reach a dry creek and to hide under the bank, so that the enemy passed on without seeing them.

The next morning they came out and started on, but the enemy was still on the watch, and before long the two men saw the dust of the horses behind them. The others came up until they were almost upon them and began to shoot arrows at them, but by this time the two Seneca were near the opening where their own friends were hiding, drawn up on each side of the pass. As the pursuers dashed in the two lines of the Seneca closed in and every man of the Seoqgwageono was either killed or taken.

The Seneca went back to the Cherokee country and after about a month they returned to their own homes. Afterward the Cherokee told them, "We hear the Seoqgwageono think you dangerous people. They themselves are conjurers and can tell what other people are going to do, but they cannot tell what the Seneca are going to do. The Seneca medicine is stronger."—Arranged from Curtin, Seneca manuscript.

99. THE SHAWANO WARS

Among the most inveterate foes of the Cherokee were the Shawano, known to the Cherokee as Ani'-Sawănu'gĭ, who in ancient times, probably as early as 1680, removed from Savannah (i. e., Shawano) river, in South Carolina, and occupied the Cumberland river region in middle Tennessee and Kentucky, from which they were afterward driven by the superior force of the southern tribes and compelled to take refuge north of the Ohio. On all old maps we find the Cumberland marked as the "river of the Shawano." Although the two tribes were frequently, and perhaps for long periods, on friendly terms, the ordinary condition was one of chronic warfare, from an early traditional period until the close of the Revolution. This hostile feeling was intensified by the fact that the Shawano were usually the steady allies of the Creeks, the hereditary southern enemies of the Cherokee. In 1749, however, we find a party of Shawano from the north, accompanied by several Cherokee, making an inroad into the Creek country, and afterward taking refuge among the Cherokee, thus involving the latter in a new war with their southern neighbors (Adair, Am. Inds., 276, 1775). The Shawano made themselves respected for their fighting qualities, gaining a reputation for valor which they maintained in their later wars with the whites, while from their sudden attack and fertility of stratagem they came to be regarded as a tribe of magicians. By capture or intermarriage in the old days there is quite an admixture of Shawano blood among the Cherokee.

According to Haywood, an aged Cherokee chief, named the Little Cornplanter (Little Carpenter?), stated in 1772 that the Shawano had removed from the Savannah river a long time before in consequence of a disastrous war with several neighboring tribes, and had settled upon the Cumberland, by permission of his people. A quarrel having afterward arisen between the two tribes, a strong body of Cherokee invaded the territory of the Shawano, and, treacherously attacking them, killed a great number. The Shawano fortified themselves and a long war ensued, which continued until the Chickasaw came to the aid of the Cherokee, when the Shawano were gradually forced to withdraw north of the Ohio.

At the time of their final expulsion, about the year 1710, the boy Charleville was employed at a French post, established for the Shawano trade, which occupied a mound on the south side of Cumberland river, where now is the city of Nashville. For a long time the Shawano had been so hard pressed by their enemies that they had been withdrawing to the north in small parties for several years, until only a few remained behind, and these also now determined to leave the country entirely. In March the trader sent Charleville ahead with several loads of skins, intending himself to follow with the Shawano a few months later. In the meantime the Chickasaw, learning of the intended move, posted themselves on both sides of Cumberland river, above the mouth of Harpeth, with canoes to cut off escape by water, and suddenly attacked the retreating Shawano, killing a large part of them, together with the trader, and taking all their skins, trading goods, and other property. Charleville lived to tell the story nearly seventy years later. As the war was never terminated by any formal treaty of peace, the hostile warriors continued to attack each other whenever they chanced to meet on the rich hunting grounds of Kentucky, until finally, from mutual dread, the region was abandoned by both parties, and continued thus unoccupied until its settlement by the whites.[1]

According to Cherokee tradition, a body of Creeks was already established near the mouth of Hiwassee while the Cherokee still had their main settlements upon the Little Tennessee. The Creeks, being near neighbors, pretended friendship, while at the same time secretly aiding the Shawano. Having discovered the treachery, the Cherokee took advantage of the presence of the Creeks at a great dance at Itsâ'tĭ, or Echota, the ancient Cherokee capital, to fall suddenly upon them and kill nearly the whole party. The consequence was a war, with the final result that the Creeks were defeated and forced to abandon all their settlements on the waters of the Tennessee river.[2]

Haywood says that "Little Cornplanter" had seen Shawano scalps brought into the Cherokee towns. When he was a boy, his father, who was also a chief, had told him how he had once led a party against the Shawano and was returning with several scalps, when, as they were coming through a pass in the mountains, they ran into another party of Cherokee warriors, who, mistaking them for enemies, fired into them and killed several before they discovered their mistake.[3]

Schoolcraft also gives the Cherokee tradition of the war with the Shawano, as obtained indirectly from white informants, but incorrectly makes it occur while the latter tribe still lived upon the Savannah. "The Cherokees prevailed after a long and sanguinary contest and drove the Shawnees north. This event they cherish as one of their proudest achievements. 'What!' said an aged Cherokee chief to Mr Barnwell, who had suggested the final preservation of the race by intermarriage with the whites. 'What! Shall the Cherokees perish! Shall the conquerors of the Shawnees perish! Never!'"[4]

Tribal warfare as a rule consisted of a desultory succession of petty raids, seldom approaching the dignity of a respectable skirmish and hardly worthy of serious consideration except in the final result. The traditions necessarily partake of the same trivial character, being rather anecdotes than narratives of historical events which had dates and names. Lapse of time renders them also constantly more vague.

On the Carolina side the Shawano approach was usually made up the Pigeon river valley, so as to come upon the Cherokee settlements from behind, and small parties were almost constantly lurking about waiting the favorable opportunity to pick up a stray scalp. On one occasion some Cherokee hunters were stretched around the camp fire at night when they heard the cry of a flying squirrel in the woods—*tsu-u! tsu-u! tsu-u!* Always on the alert for danger, they suspected it might be the enemy's signal, and all but one hastily left the fire and concealed themselves. That one, however, laughed at their fears and, defiantly throwing some heavy logs on the fire, stretched himself out on his blanket

[1] Haywood, Nat. and Aborig. Hist. of Tennessee, pp. 222–224, 1823.
[2] Ibid, p. 241.   [3] Ibid, p. 222.   [4] Schoolcraft, Notes on Iroquois, p. 160, 1847.

and began to sing. Soon he heard a stealthy step coming through the bushes and gradually approaching the fire, until suddenly an enemy sprang out upon him from the darkness and bore him to the earth. But the Cherokee was watchful, and putting up his hands he seized the other by the arms, and with a mighty effort threw him backward into the fire. The dazed Shawano lay there a moment squirming upon the coals, then bounded to his feet and ran into the woods, howling with pain. There was an answering laugh from his comrades hidden in the bush, but although the Cherokee kept watch for some time the enemy made no further attack, probably led by the very boldness of the hunter to suspect some ambush.

On another occasion a small hunting party in the Smoky mountains heard the gobble of a turkey (in telling the story Swimmer gives a good imitation). Some eager young hunters were for going at once toward the game, but others, more cautious, suspected a ruse and advised a reconnaissance. Accordingly a hunter went around to the back of the ridge, and on coming up from the other side found a man posted in a large tree, making the gobble call to decoy the hunters within reach of a Shawano war party concealed behind some bushes midway between the tree and the camp. Keeping close to the ground, the Cherokee crept up without being discovered until within gunshot, then springing to his feet he shot the man in the tree, and shouting "Kill them all," rushed upon the enemy, who, thinking that a strong force of Cherokee was upon them, fled down the mountain without attempting to make a stand.

Another tradition of these wars is that concerning Tunâ'ĭ, a great warrior and medicine-man of old Itsâ'tĭ, on the Tennessee. In one hard fight with the Shawano, near the town, he overpowered his man and stabbed him through both arms. Running cords through the holes he tied his prisoner's arms and brought him thus into Itsâ'tĭ, where he was put to death by the women with such tortures that his courage broke and he begged them to kill him at once.

After retiring to the upper Ohio the Shawano were received into the protection of the Delawares and their allies, and being thus strengthened felt encouraged to renew the war against the Cherokee with increased vigor. The latter, however, proved themselves more than a match for their enemies, pursuing them even to their towns in western Pennsylvania, and accidentally killing there some Delawares who occupied the country jointly with the Shawano. This involved the Cherokee in a war with the powerful Delawares, which continued until brought to an end in 1768 at the request of the Cherokee, who made terms of friendship at the same time with the Iroquois. The Shawano being thus left alone, and being, moreover, roundly condemned by their friends, the Delawares, as the cause of the whole trouble, had no heart to continue the war and were obliged to make final peace.[1]

---

[1] Heckewelder, Indian Nations, p. 88, reprint of 1876.

100. THE RAID ON TĬKWĂLI'TSĬ

The last noted leader of the Shawano raiding parties was a chief known to the Cherokee as Tawa'lĭ-ukwanûñ'tĭ, "Punk-plugged-in," on account of a red spot on his cheek which looked as though a piece of punk (*tawa'lĭ*) had been driven into the flesh.

The people of Tĭkwăli'tsĭ town, on Tuckasegee, heard rumors that a war party under this leader had come in from the north and was lurking somewhere in the neighborhood. The Cherokee conjurer, whose name was Ĕtăwa'hă-tsistatla'skĭ, "Dead-wood-lighter," resorted to his magic arts and found that the Shawano were in ambush along the trail on the north side of the river a short distance above the town. By his advice a party was fitted out to go up on the south side and come in upon the enemy's rear. A few foolhardy fellows, however, despised his words and boldly went up the trail on the north side until they came to Deep Creek, where the Shawano in hiding at the ford took them " like fish in a trap" and killed nearly all of them.

Their friends on the other side of the river heard the firing, and crossing the river above Deep creek they came in behind the Shawano and attacked them, killing a number and forcing the others to retreat toward the Smoky mountains, with the Cherokee in pursuit. The invaders had with them two Cherokee prisoners who were not able to keep up with the rapid flight, so their captors took them, bound as they were, and threw them over a cliff. An old conjurer of their own party finding himself unable to keep up deliberately sat down against a tree near the same spot to wait for death. The pursuers coming up split his head with a hatchet and threw his body over the same cliff, which takes its name from this circumstance. The Shawano continued to retreat, with the Cherokee close behind them, until they crossed the main ridge at the gap just below Clingman's dome. Here the Cherokee gave up the pursuit and returned to their homes.

101. THE LAST SHAWANO INVASION

Perhaps a year after the raid upon Tĭkwăli'tsĭ, the Shawano again, under the same leader, came down upon the exposed settlement of Kanuga, on Pigeon river, and carried off a woman and two children whom they found gathering berries near the town. Without waiting to make an attack they hastily retreated with their prisoners. The people of Kanuga sent for aid to the other settlements farther south, and a strong party was quickly raised to pursue the enemy and recover the captives. By this time, however, the Shawano had had several days' start and it was necessary for the Cherokee to take a shorter course across the mountains to overtake them. A noted conjurer named Kâ'lanû, "The Raven," of Hiwassee town, was called upon to discover by his magic arts what direction the Shawano had taken and how far they had already gone. Calling the chiefs together he told them to fill the pipe and smoke and he would return with the information before the pipe was smoked out. They sat down in a circle around the fire and lighted the pipe, while he went out into the woods. Soon they heard the cry of an owl, and after some interval they heard it again, and the next moment the conjurer walked out from the trees before yet the first smoke was finished.

He reported that he had trailed the Shawano to their camp and that they were seven days ahead. The Cherokee at once followed as The Raven guided, and reached the place in seven days and found all the marks of a camp, but the enemy was already gone. Again and once again the conjurer went ahead in his own mysterious fashion to spy out the country, and they followed as he pointed the way. On returning the third time he reported that their enemies had halted beside the great river (the Ohio), and soon afterward he came in with the news that they were crossing it. The Cherokee hurried on to the river, but by this time the Shawano were on the other side. The pursuers hunted up and down until they found a favorable spot in the stream, and then waiting until it was dark they prepared to cross, using logs as rafts and tacking with the current, and managed it so well that they were over long before daylight without alarming the enemy.

The trail was now fresh, and following it they soon came upon the camp, which was asleep and all unguarded, the Shawano, thinking themselves now safe in their own country, having neglected to post sentinels. Rushing in with their knives and tomahawks, the Cherokee fell upon their sleeping foe and killed a number of them before the others could wake and seize their arms to defend themselves. Then there was a short, desperate encounter, but the Shawano were taken at a disadvantage, their leader himself being among the first killed, and in a few moments they broke and ran, every man for himself, to escape as best he could. The Cherokee released the captives, whom they found tied to trees, and after taking the scalps from the dead Shawano, with their guns and other equipments, returned to their own country.

102. THE FALSE WARRIORS OF CHILHOWEE

Some warriors of Chilhowee town, on Little Tennessee, organized a war party, as they said, to go against the Shawano. They started off north along the great war trail, but when they came to Pigeon river they changed their course, and instead of going on toward the Shawano country they went up the river and came in at the back of Cowee, one of the Middle settlements of their own tribe. Here they concealed themselves near the path until a party of three or four unsuspecting townspeople came by, when they rushed out and killed them, took their scalps and a gun belonging to a man named Gûñskäli'skĭ, and then

hurriedly made their way home by the same roundabout route to Chilhowee, where they showed the fresh scalps and the gun, and told how
they had met the Shawano in the north and defeated them without
losing a man.

According to custom, preparations were made at once for a great
scalp dance to celebrate the victory over the Shawano. The dance was
held in the townhouse and all the people of the settlement were there
and looked on, while the women danced with the scalps and the gun,
and the returned warriors boasted of their deeds. As it happened,
among those looking on was a visitor from Cowee, a gunstocker, who
took particular notice of the gun and knew it at once as one he had
repaired at home for Gûñskăli′skĭ. He said nothing, but wondered
much how it had come into possession of the Shawano.

The scalp dance ended, and according to custom a second dance was
appointed to be held seven days later, to give the other warriors also
a chance to boast of their own war deeds. The gunstocker, whose
name was Gûlsadihĭ′, returned home to Cowee, and there heard for the
first time how a Shawano war party had surprised some of the town
people, killed several, and taken their scalps and a gun. He understood it all then, and told the chief that the mischief had been done,
not by a hostile tribe, but by the false men of Chilhowee. It seemed
too much to believe, and the chief said it could not be possible, until
the gunstocker declared that he had recognized the gun as one he had
himself repaired for the man who had been killed. At last they were
convinced that his story was true, and all Cowee was eager for revenge.

It was decided to send ten of their bravest warriors, under the leadership of the gunstocker, to the next dance at Chilhowee, there to take
their own method of reprisal. Volunteers offered at once for the service.
They set out at the proper time and arrived at Chilhowee on the night
the dance was to begin. As they crossed the stream below the town
they met a woman coming for water and took their first revenge by
killing her. Men, women, and children were gathered in the townhouse, but the Cowee men concealed themselves outside and waited.

In this dance it was customary for each warrior in turn to tell the
story of some deed against the enemy, putting his words into a song
which he first whispered to the drummer, who then sang with him,
drumming all the while. Usually it is serious business, but occasionally, for a joke, a man will act the clown or sing of some extravagant
performance that is so clearly impossible that all the people laugh. One
man after another stepped into the ring and sang of what he had done
against the enemies of his tribe. At last one of the late war party rose
from his seat, and after a whisper to the drummer began to sing of how
they had gone to Cowee and taken scalps and the gun, which he carried
as he danced. The chief and the people, who knew nothing of the
treacherous act, laughed heartily at what they thought was a great joke.

But now the gunstocker, who had been waiting outside with the Cowee men, stripped off his breechcloth and rushed naked into the townhouse. Bending down to the drummer—who was one of the traitors, but failed to recognize Gûlsadihĭ'—he gave him the words, and then straightening up he began to sing, "*Hi!* Ask who has done this!" while he danced around the circle, making insulting gestures toward everyone there. The song was quick and the drummer beat very fast.

He made one round and bent down again to the drummer, then straightened up and sang, "*Yu!* I have killed a pregnant woman at the ford and thrown her body into the river!" Several men started with surprise, but the chief said, "He is only joking; go on with the dance," and the drummer beat rapidly.

Another round and he bent down again to the drummer and then began to sing, "We thought our enemies were from the north, but we have followed them and they are here!" Now the drummer knew at last what it all meant and he drummed very slowly, and the people grew uneasy. Then, without waiting on the drummer, Gûlsadihĭ' sang, "Cowee will have a ball play with you!"—and everyone knew this was a challenge to battle—and then fiercely: "But if you want to fight now my men are ready to die here!"

With that he waved his hand and left the townhouse. The dancers looked at each other uneasily and some of them rose to go. The chief, who could not understand it, urged them to go on with the dance, but it was of no avail. They left the townhouse, and as they went out they met the Cowee men standing with their guns ready and their hatchets in their belts. Neither party said anything, because they were still on friendly ground, but everyone knew that trouble was ahead.

The Cowee men returned home and organized a strong party of warriors from their own and all the neighboring Middle settlements to go and take vengeance on Chilhowee and on Kuwâ'hĭ, just below, which had also been concerned in the raid. They went down the Tennessee and crossed over the mountains, but when they came on the other side they found that their enemies had abandoned their homes and fled for refuge to the remoter settlements or to the hostile Shawano in the north.

103. COWEE TOWN

Cowee', properly Kawi'yĭ, abbreviated Kawi', was the name of two Cherokee settlements, one of which existed in 1755 on a branch of Keowee river, in upper South Carolina, while the other and more important was on Little Tennessee river, at the mouth of Cowee creek, about 10 miles below the present Franklin, in North Carolina. It was destroyed by the Americans in 1876, when it contained about a hundred houses, but was rebuilt and continued to be occupied until the cession of 1819. The name can not be translated, but may possibly mean "the place of the Deer clan" (Ani'-Kawĭ'). It was one of the oldest and largest of the Cherokee towns, and when Wafford visited it as a boy he found the trail leading to it worn so deep in places that, although on horseback, he could touch the ground with his feet on each side.

There is a story, told by Wafford as a fact, of a Shawano who had been a prisoner there, but had escaped to his people in the north, and after the peace between the two tribes wandered back into the neighborhood on a hunting trip. While standing on a hill overlooking the valley he saw several Cherokee on an opposite hill, and called out to them, "Do you still own Cowee?" They shouted in reply, "Yes; we own it yet." Back came the answer from the Shawano, who wanted to encourage them not to sell any more of their lands, "Well, it's the best town of the Cherokee. It's a good country; hold on to it."

104. THE EASTERN TRIBES

Besides the Iroquois and Shawano, the Cherokee remember also the Delawares, Tuscarora, Catawba, and Cheraw as tribes to the east or north with which they formerly had relations.

The Cherokee call the Delawares Anakwan'ki, in the singular Akwan'ki, a derivative formed according to usual Cherokee phonetic modification from Wapanaq'ki, "Easterners," the generic name by which the Delawares and their nearest kindred call themselves.

In the most ancient tradition of the Delawares the Cherokee are called Talega, Tallige, Tallige-wi, etc.[1] In later Delaware tradition they are called Kĭtu'hwa, and again we find the two tribes at war, for which their neighbors are held responsible. According to the Delaware account, the Iroquois, in one of their forays to the south, killed a Cherokee in the woods and purposely left a Delaware war club near the body to make it appear that the work had been done by men of that tribe. The Cherokee found the body and the club, and naturally supposing that the murder had been committed by the Delawares, they suddenly attacked the latter, the result being a long and bloody war between the two tribes.[2] At this time, i. e., about the end of the seventeenth century, it appears that a part at least of the Cherokee lived on the waters of the Upper Ohio, where the Delawares made continual inroads upon them, finally driving them from the region and seizing it for themselves about the year 1708.[3] A century ago the Delawares used to tell how their warriors would sometimes mingle in disguise with the Cherokee at their night dances until the opportunity came to strike a sudden blow and be off before their enemies recovered from the surprise.

Later there seems to have been peace until war was again brought on

---

[1] Brinton, Lenape and Their Legends, p. 130 et passim, 1885; Schoolcraft, Notes on Iroquois, pp. 147, 305 et passim, 1847; Heckewelder, Indian Nations, pp. 47–50, ed. 1876.

[2] Heckewelder, op. cit., p. 54.

[3] Loskiel, History of the [Moravian] Mission, pp. 124–127; London, 1794.

by the action of the Shawano, who had taken refuge with the Delawares, after having been driven from their old home on Cumberland river by the Cherokee. Feeling secure in their new alliance, the Shawano renewed their raids upon the Cherokee, who retaliated by pursuing them into the Delaware country, where they killed several Delawares by mistake. This inflamed the latter people, already excited by the sight of Cherokee scalps and prisoners brought back through their country by the Iroquois, and another war was the result, which lasted until the Cherokee, tired of fighting so many enemies, voluntarily made overtures for peace, in 1768, saluting the Delawares as Grandfather, an honorary title accorded them by all the Algonquian tribes. The Delawares then reprimanded the Shawano, as the cause of the trouble, and advised them to keep quiet, which, as they were now left to fight their battles alone, they were glad enough to do. At the same time the Cherokee made peace with the Iroquois, and the long war with the northern tribes came to an end. The friendly feeling thus established was emphasized in 1779, when the Cherokee sent a message of condolence upon the death of the Delaware chief White-eyes.[1]

The Tuscarora, formerly the ruling tribe of eastern North Carolina, are still remembered under the name Ani'-Skălä'lĭ, and are thus mentioned in the Feather dance of the Cherokee, in which some of the actors are supposed to be visiting strangers from other tribes.

As the majority of the Tuscarora fled from Carolina to the Iroquois country about 1713, in consequence of their disastrous war with the whites, their memory has nearly faded from the recollection of the southern Indians. From the scanty light which history throws upon their mutual relations, the two tribes seem to have been almost constantly at war with each other. When at one time the Cherokee, having already made peace with some other of their neighbors, were urged by the whites to make peace also with the Tuscarora, they refused, on the ground that, as they could not live without war, it was better to let matters stand as they were than to make peace with the Tuscarora and be obliged immediately to look about for new enemies with whom to fight. For some years before the outbreak of the Tuscarora war in 1711 the Cherokee had ceased their inroads upon this tribe, and it was therefore supposed that they were more busily engaged with some other people west of the mountains, these being probably the Shawano, whom they drove out of Tennessee about this time.[2] In the war of 1711–1713 the Cherokee assisted the whites against the Tuscarora. In 1731 the Cherokee again threatened to make war upon the remnant of that tribe still residing in North Carolina and the colonial government was compelled to interfere.[3]

---

[1] Heckewelder, Indian Nations, pp. 88–89, 1876.
[2] See Haywood, Nat. and Aborig. Hist. of Tennessee, pp. 220, 224, 237, 1823.
[3] North Carolina Colonial Records, III, pp. 153, 202, 345, 369, 393, 1886.

The Cheraw or Sara, ranging at different periods from upper South Carolina to the southern frontier of Virginia, are also remembered under the name of Ani'-Suwa'lĭ, or Ani'-Suwa'la, which agrees with the Spanish form Xuala of De Soto's chronicle, and Suala, or Sualy, of Lederer. The Cherokee remember them as having lived east of the Blue ridge, the trail to their country leading across the gap at the head of Swannanoa river, east from Asheville. The name of the stream and gap is a corruption of the Cherokee Suwa'lĭ-Nûññâ'hĭ, "Suwa'li trail." Being a very warlike tribe, they were finally so reduced by conflicts with the colonial governments and the Iroquois that they were obliged to incorporate with the Catawba, among whom they still maintained their distinct language as late as 1743.[1]

The Catawba are known to the Cherokee as Ani'ta'gwa, singular Ata'gwa, or Ta'gwa, the Cherokee attempt at the name by which they are most commonly known. They were the immediate neighbors of the Cherokee on the east and southeast, having their principal settlements on the river of their name, just within the limits of South Carolina, and holding the leading place among all the tribes east of the Cherokee country with the exception of the Tuscarora. On the first settlement of South Carolina there were estimated to be about 7,000 persons in the tribe, but their decline was rapid, and by war and disease their number had been reduced in 1775 to barely 500, including the incorporated remnants of the Cheraw and several smaller tribes. There are now, perhaps, 100 still remaining on a small reservation near the site of their ancient towns. Some local names in the old Cherokee territory seem to indicate the former presence of Catawba, although there is no tradition of any Catawba settlement within those limits. Among such names may be mentioned Toccoa creek, in northeastern Georgia, and Toccoa river, in north-central Georgia, both names being derived from the Cherokee Tagwâ'hĭ, "Catawba place." An old Cherokee personal name is Ta'gwădihĭ', "Catawba-killer."

The two tribes were hereditary enemies, and the feeling between them is nearly as bitter to-day as it was a hundred years ago. Perhaps the only case on record of their acting together was in the war of 1711–13, when they cooperated with the colonists against the Tuscarora. The Cherokee, according to the late Colonel Thomas, claim to have formerly occupied all the country about the head of the Catawba river, to below the present Morganton, until the game became scarce, when they retired to the west of the Blue ridge, and afterward "loaned" the eastern territory to the Catawba. This agrees pretty well with a Catawba tradition recorded in Schoolcraft, according to which the Catawba—who are incorrectly represented as comparatively recent immigrants from the north—on arriving at Catawba river found

---

[1] Mooney, Siouan Tribes of the East (bulletin of the Bureau of Ethnology), pp. 56, 61, 1894.

their progress disputed by the Cherokee, who claimed original ownership of the country. A battle was fought, with incredible loss on
both sides, but with no decisive result, although the advantage was
with the Catawba, on account of their having guns, while their opponents had only Indian weapons. Preparations were under way to
renew the fight when the Cherokee offered to recognize the river as
the boundary, allowing the Catawba to settle anywhere to the east.
The overture was accepted and an agreement was finally made by which
the Catawba were to occupy the country east of that river and the
Cherokee the country west of Broad river, with the region between
the two streams to remain as neutral territory. Stone piles were
heaped up on the battlefield to commemorate the treaty, and the Broad
river was henceforth called Eswau Huppeday (Line river), by the
Catawba, the country eastward to Catawba river being left unoccupied.[1]
The fact that one party had guns would bring this event within the
early historic period.

The Catawba assisted the whites against the Cherokee in the war
of 1760 and in the later Revolutionary struggle. About 100 warriors, nearly the whole fighting strength of the tribe, took part in
the first-mentioned war, several being killed, and a smaller number
accompanied Williamson's force in 1776.[2] At the battle fought under
Williamson near the present site of Franklin, North Carolina, the
Cherokee, according to the tradition related by Wafford, mistook the
Catawba allies of the troops for some of their own warriors, and were
fighting for some time under this impression before they noticed that
the Catawba wore deer tails in their hair so that the whites might not
make the same mistake. In this engagement, which was one of the
bloodiest Indian encounters of the Revolution, the Cherokee claim
that they had actually defeated the troops and their Catawba allies,
when their own ammunition gave out and they were consequently
forced to retire. The Cherokee leader was a noted war chief named
Tsanĭ (John).

About 1840 nearly the whole Catawba tribe moved up from South
Carolina and joined the eastern band of Cherokee, but in consequence
of tribal jealousies they remained but a short time, and afterward
returned to their former home, as is related elsewhere.

Other tribal names (of doubtful authority) are Ani'-Sa'nɪ and Ani'-
Sawahâ'nĭ, belonging to people said to have lived toward the north;
both names are perhaps intended for the Shawano or Shawnee, properly Ani'-Sawănu'gĭ. The Ani'-Gilĭ' are said to have been neighbors
of the Anin'tsĭ or Natchez; the name may possibly be a Cherokee form
for Congaree.

---

[1] Catawba MS from South Carolina official archives. Schoolcraft, Indian Tribes, III, pp. 293–4, 1853.
[2] Ibid., p. 294, 1853.

105. THE SOUTHERN AND WESTERN TRIBES

The nearest neighbors of the Cherokee to the south were the Creeks or Muscogee, who found mixed confederacy holding central and southern Georgia and Alabama. They were known to the Cherokee as Ani'-Ku'sa or Ani'-Gu'sa, from Kusa, the principal town of the Upper Creeks, which was situated on Coosa river, southwest from the present Talladega, Alabama. The Lower Creeks, residing chiefly on Chattahoochee river, were formerly always distinguished as Ani-Kawi'ta, from Kawita or Coweta, their ancient capital, on the west side of the river, in Alabama, nearly opposite the present Columbus, Georgia. In number the Creeks were nearly equal to the Cherokee, but differed in being a confederacy of cognate or incorporated tribes, of which the Muscogee proper was the principal. The Cherokee were called by them Tsal-gal'gi or Tsûlgûl'gi, a plural derivative from Tsa'lăgĭ', the proper name of the tribe.

The ordinary condition between the two tribes was one of hostility, with occasional intervals of good will. History, tradition, and linguistic evidence combine to show that the Creeks at one time occupied almost the whole of northern Georgia and Alabama, extending a considerable distance into Tennessee and perhaps North Carolina, and were dispossessed by the Cherokee pressing upon them from the north and northeast. This conquest was accomplished chiefly during the first half of the eighteenth century, and culminated with the decisive engagement of Tali'wă about 1755. In most of their early negotiations with the Government the Creeks demanded that the lands of the various tribes be regarded as common property, and that only the boundary between the Indians and the whites be considered. Failing in that, they claimed as theirs the whole region of the Chattahoochee and Coosa, north to the dividing ridge between those streams and the Tennessee, or even beyond to the Tennessee itself, and asserted that any Cherokee settlements within those limits were only by their own permission. In 1783 they claimed the Savannah river as the eastern boundary between themselves and the Cherokee, and asserted their own exclusive right of sale over all the territory between that river and the Oconee. On the other hand the Cherokee as stoutly claimed all to a point some 70 miles south of the present city of Atlanta, on the ground of having driven the Creeks out of it in three successive wars, and asserted that their right had been admitted by the Creeks themselves in a council held to decide the question between the two tribes before the Revolution. By mutual agreement, about 1816, members of either tribe were allowed to settle within the territory claimed by the other. The line as finally established through the mediation of the colonial and Federal governments ran from the mouth of Broad river on Savannah nearly due west across Georgia, passing about 10 miles north of Atlanta, to Coosa river in Alabama, and thence northwest to strike the west line of Alabama about 20 miles south of the Tennessee. [1]

Among the names which remain to show the former presence of Creeks north of this boundary are the following: Coweeta, a small creek entering the Little Tennessee above Franklin, North Carolina; Tomatola (Cherokee, Tama'lĭ), a former town site on Valley river, near Murphy, North Carolina, the name being that of a former Creek town on Chattahoochee; Tomotley (Cherokee, Tama'lĭ), a ford at another town site on Little Tennessee, above Tellico mouth, in Tennessee; Coosa (Cherokee, Kŭsă'), an upper creek of Nottely river, in Union county, Georgia; Chattooga (Cherokee, Tsatu'gĭ), a river in northwest Georgia; Chattooga (Cherokee, Tsatu'gĭ), another river, a head-stream of Savannah; Chattahoochee river (Creek, Chatu-huchi, "pictured rocks"); Coosawatee (Cherokee, Ku'să-weti'yĭ, "Old Creek place"), a river in northwestern Georgia; Tali'wă, the Cherokee form of a Creek name for a place on an upper branch of Etowah river in Georgia, probably from the Creek *ta'lua* or *ita'lua*, "town"; Euharlee (Cherokee, Yuha'lĭ, said by the Cherokee to be from Yufala or Eufaula, the name of several Creek towns), a creek flowing into lower Etowah river; Suwanee (Cherokee, Suwa'nĭ) a small creek on upper Chattahoochee, the site of a former Cherokee town with a name which the Cherokee say is Creek. Several other names within the same territory are said by the Cherokee to be of foreign origin, although perhaps not Creek, and may be from the Taskigi language.

According to Cherokee tradition as given to Haywood nearly eighty years ago the country about the mouth of Hiwassee river, in Tennessee, was held by the Creeks, while the Cherokee still had their main settlements farther to the north, on the Little Tennessee. In the Shawano war, about the year 1700, the Creeks pretended friendship for the Cherokee while secretly helping their enemies, the Shawano. The Cherokee discovered the treachery, and took occasion, when a party of Creeks was visiting a dance at Itsâ'tĭ (Echota), the Cherokee capital, to fall upon them and massacre nearly every man. The consequence was a war between the two tribes, with the final result that the Creeks were forced to abandon all their settlements upon the waters of the Tennessee, and to withdraw south to the Coosa and the neighborhood of the "Creek path," an old trading trail from South Carolina, which crossed at the junction of the Oostanaula and Etowah rivers, where now is the city of Rome, Georgia, and struck the Tennessee at the present Guntersville, Alabama.

As an incident of this war the same tradition relates how the Cherokee once approached a large Creek settlement "at the island on

[1] Royce, The Cherokee Nation of Indians, in Fifth Report of Bureau of Ethnology, pp. 205–208, 266–272, 1887; also (for 1783) Bartram, Travels, p. 483, 1792.

the Creek path," in Tennessee river, opposite Guntersville, and, concealing their main force, sent a small party ahead to decoy the Creeks
to an engagement.   The Creek warriors at once crossed over in their
canoes to the attack, when the Cherokee suddenly rose up from their
ambush, and surrounded the Creeks and defeated them after a desperate
battle.   Then, taking the captured canoes, they went over to the island
and destroyed all that was there.   The great leader of the Cherokee
in this war was a chief named Bullhead, renowned in tradition for his
bravery and skill in strategy.[1]   At about the same time, according to
Wafford, the Cherokee claim to have driven the Creeks and Shawano
from a settlement which they occupied jointly near Savannah, Georgia.

There was a tradition among the few old traders still living in upper
Georgia in 1890 that a large tract in that part of the State had been
won by the Cherokee from the Creeks in a ballplay.[2]   There are no
Indians now living in that region to substantiate the story.   As
originally told it may have had a veiled meaning, as among the Cherokee the expression "to play a ball game" is frequently used figur-
atively to denote fighting a battle.   There seems to be no good ground
for Bartram's statement that the Cherokee had been dispossessed by
the Creeks of the region between the Savannah and the Ocmulgee, in
southwestern Georgia, within the historic period.[3]   The territory is
south of any traditional Cherokee claim, and the statement is at
variance with what we know through history.   He probably had in
mind the Uchee, who did actually occupy that country until incorporated with the Creeks.

The victory was not always on one side, however, for Adair states
that toward the end of the last war between the two tribes the Creeks,
having easily defeated the Cherokee in an engagement, contemptuously
sent against them a number of women and boys.   According to this
writer, the "true and sole cause" of this last war was the killing of
some adopted relatives of the Creeks in 1749 by a party of northern
Shawano, who had been guided and afterward sheltered by the Cherokee.   The war, which he represents as a losing game for the Cherokee, was finally brought to an end through the efforts of the governor
of South Carolina, with the unfortunate result to the English that the
Creeks encouraged the Cherokee in the war of 1760 and rendered them
very essential help in the way of men and ammunition.[4]

The battle of Tali'wă, which decided in favor of the Cherokee the
long war between themselves and the Creeks, was fought about 1755
or a few years later at a spot on Mountain creek or Long-swamp
creek, which enters Etowah river above Canton, Georgia, near where

---

[1] Haywood, Nat. and Aborig. Hist. Tenn., p. 241, 1823. Bullhead may be intended for Doublehead,
an old Cherokee name.
[2] Mooney, The Cherokee Ball Play, in The American Anthropologist, III, p. 107, April, 1890.
[3] Bartram, Travels, p. 518, 1791.
[4] Adair, History of American Indians, pp. 227, 247, 252-256, 270, 276-279, 1775.

the old trail crossed the river about Long-swamp town. All our information concerning it is traditional, obtained from James Wafford, who heard the story when a boy, about the year 1815, from an old trader named Brian Ward, who had witnessed the battle sixty years before. According to his account, it was probably the hardest battle ever fought between the two tribes, about five hundred Cherokee and twice that number of Creek warriors being engaged. The Cherokee were at first overmatched and fell back, but rallied again and returned to the attack, driving the Creeks from cover so that they broke and ran. The victory was complete and decisive, and the defeated tribe immediately afterward abandoned the whole upper portion of Georgia and the adjacent part of Alabama to the conquerors. Before this battle the Creeks had been accustomed to shift about a good deal from place to place, but thereafter they confined themselves more closely to fixed home locations. It was in consequence of this defeat that they abandoned their town on Nottely river, below Coosa creek, near the present Blairsville, Georgia, their old fields being at once occupied by Cherokee, who moved over from their settlements on the head of Savannah river. As has been already stated, a peace was made about 1759, just in time to enable the Creeks to assist the Cherokee in their war with South Carolina. We hear little more concerning the relations of the two tribes until the Creek war of 1813–14, described in detail elsewhere; after this their histories drift apart.

The Yuchi or Uchee, called Ani'-Yu'tsĭ by the Cherokee, were a tribe of distinct linguistic stock and of considerable importance in early days; their territory bordered Savannah river on both sides immediately below the Cherokee country, and extended some distance westward into Georgia, where it adjoined that of the Creeks. They were gradually dispossessed by the whites, and were incorporated with the Creeks about the year 1740, but retain their separate identity and language to this day, their town being now the largest in the Creek Nation in Indian Territory.

According to the testimony of a Cherokee mixed-blood named Gansĕ'tĭ or Rattling-gourd, who was born on Hiwassee river in 1820 and came west with his people in 1838, a number of Yuchi lived, before the Removal, scattered among the Cherokee near the present Cleveland, Tennessee, and on Chickamauga, Cohutta, and Pinelog creeks in the adjacent section of Georgia. They had no separate settlements, but spoke their own language, which he described as "hard and grunting." Some of them spoke also Cherokee and Creek. They had probably drifted north from the Creek country before a boundary had been fixed between the tribes. When Tahlequah was established as the capital of the Cherokee Nation in the West in 1839 a few Yuchi were found already settled at the spot, being supposed to have removed from the East with some Creeks after the chief McIntosh was killed in

1825. They perished in the smallpox epidemic which ravaged the frontier in 1840, and their graves were still pointed out at Tahlequah in 1891. Shortly before the outbreak of the Civil war there was a large and prosperous Yuchi settlement on Cimarron river, in what was afterward the Cherokee strip.

Ramsey states that "a small tribe of Uchees" once occupied the country near the mouth of the Hiwassee, and was nearly exterminated in a desperate battle with the Cherokee at the Uchee Old Fields, in Rhea (now Meigs) county, Tennessee, the few survivors retreating to Florida, where they joined the Seminoles.[1] There seems to be no other authority for the statement.

Another broken tribe incorporated in part with the Creeks and in part with the Cherokee was that of the Na′′tsĭ, or Natchez, who originally occupied the territory around the site of the present town of Natchez in southern Mississippi, and exercised a leading influence over all the tribes of the region. In consequence of a disastrous war with the French in 1729–31 the tribe was disrupted, some taking refuge with the Chickasaw, others with the Creeks, either then or later, while others, in 1736, applied to the government of South Carolina for permission to settle on the Savannah river. The request was evidently granted, and we find the "Nachee" mentioned as one of the tribes living with the Catawba in 1743, but retaining their distinct language. In consequence of having killed some of the Catawba in a drunken quarrel they were forced to leave this region, and seem to have soon afterward joined the Cherokee, as we find them twice mentioned in connection with that tribe in 1755. This appears to be the last reference to them in the South Carolina records.[2]

Just here the Cherokee tradition takes them up, under the name of Anin′tsĭ, abbreviated from Ani′-Na′′tsĭ, the plural of Na′′tsĭ. From a chance coincidence with the word for pine tree, na′tsĭ′, some English speaking Indians have rendered this name as "Pine Indians." The Cherokee generally agree that the Natchez came to them from South Carolina, though some say that they came from the Creek country. It is probable that the first refugees were from Carolina and were joined later by others from the Creeks and the Chickasaw. Bienville states, in 1742, that some of them had gone to the Cherokee directly from the Chickasaw when they found the latter too hard pressed by the French to be able to care for them.[3] They seem to have been regarded by the Cherokee as a race of wizards and conjurers, a view which was probably due in part to their peculiar religious rites and in part to the interest which belonged to them as the remnant of an extirpated tribe. Although we have no direct knowledge on the subject, there is every

[1] Ramsey, Annals of Tennessee, pp. 81, 84, 1853.
[2] Mooney, Siouan Tribes of the East (bulletin of the Bureau of Ethnology), p. 83, 1894.
[3] Bienville, quoted in Gayarré, Louisiana.

reason to suppose that the two tribes had had communication with each other long before the period of the Natchez war.

According to the statement of James Wafford, who was born in 1806 near the site of .Clarkesville, Ga., when this region was still Indian country, the "Notchees" had their town on the north bank of Hiwassee, just above Peachtree creek, on the spot where a Baptist mission was established by the Rev. Evan Jones in 1821, a few miles above the present Murphy, Cherokee county, North Carolina. On his mother's side he had himself a strain of Natchez blood. His grandmother had told him that when she was a young woman, perhaps about 1755, she once.had occasion to go to this town on some business, which she was obliged to transact through an interpreter, as the Natchez had been there so short a time that only one or two spoke any Cherokee. They were all in the one town, which the Cherokee called Gwalʻgâʹhĭ, "Frog place," but he was unable to say whether or not it had a townhouse. In 1824, as one of the census takers for the Cherokee Nation, he went over the same section and found the Natchez then living jointly with the Cherokee in a town called Gûʻlăniʹyĭ at the junction of Brasstown and Gumlog creeks, tributary to Hiwassee, some 6 miles southeast of their former location and close to the Georgia line. The removal may have been due to the recent establishment of the mission at the old place. It was a large settlement, made up about equally from the two tribes, but by this time the Natchez were not distinguishable in dress or general appearance from the others, and nearly all spoke broken Cherokee, while still retaining their own language. As most of the Indians had come under Christian influences so far as to have quit dancing, there was no townhouse. Harry Smith, who was born about 1820, father of the late chief of the East Cherokee, also remembers them as living on Hiwassee and calling themselves Naʹʹtsĭ.

Gansĕʹʹtĭ, already mentioned, states that when he was a boy the Natchez were scattered among the Cherokee settlements along the upper part of Hiwassee, extending down into Tennessee. They had then no separate townhouses. Some of them, at least, had come up from the Creeks, and spoke Creek and Cherokee, as well as their own language, which he could not understand, although familiar with both of the others. They were great dance leaders, which agrees with their traditional reputation for ceremonial and secret knowledge. They went west with the Cherokee at the final removal of the tribe to Indian Territory in 1838. In 1890 there was a small settlement on Illinois river a few miles south of Tahlequah, Cherokee Nation, several persons in which still spoke their own language. Some of these may have come with the Creeks, as by an agreement between Creeks and Cherokee about the time of the Removal it had been arranged that citizens of either tribe living within the boundaries claimed by the other might remain without question if they so elected. There are still several persons claiming Natchez descent among the East Cherokee, but the last one said to have been of full Natchez blood, an old woman named Alkĭnĭ′, died about 1895. She was noted for her peculiarities, especially for a drawling tone, said to have been characteristic of her people, as old men remembered them years ago.

Haywood, the historian of Tennessee, says that a remnant of the Natchez lived within the present limits of the State as late as 1750, and were even then numerous. He refers to those with the Cherokee, and tells a curious story, which seems somehow to have escaped the notice of other writers. According to his statement, a portion of the Natchez, who had been parceled out as slaves among the French in the vicinity of their old homes after the downfall of their tribe, took advantage of the withdrawal of the troops to the north, in 1758, to rise and massacre their masters and make their escape to the neighboring tribes. On the return of the troops after the fall of Fort Du Quesne they found the settlement at Natchez destroyed and their Indian slaves fled. Some time afterward a French deserter seeking an asylum among the Cherokee, having made his way to the Great Island town, on the Tennessee, just below the mouth of Tellico river, was surprised to find there some of the same Natchez whom he had formerly driven as slaves. He lost no time in getting away from the place to find safer quarters among the mountain towns. Notchy creek, a lower affluent of Tellico, in Monroe county, Tennessee, probably takes its name from these refugees. Haywood states also that, although incorporated with the Cherokee, they continued for a long time a separate people, not marrying or mixing with other tribes, and having their own chiefs and holding their own councils; but in 1823 hardly anything was left of them but the name.[1]

Another refugee tribe incorporated partly with the Cherokee and partly with the Creeks was that of the Taskigi, who at an early period had a large town of the same name on the south side of the Little Tennessee, just above the mouth of Tellico, in Monroe county, Tennessee. Sequoya, the inventor of the Cherokee alphabet, lived here in his boyhood, about the time of the Revolution. The land was sold in 1819. There was another settlement of the name, and perhaps once occupied by the same people, on the north bank of Tennessee river, in a bend just below Chattanooga, Tennessee, on land sold also in 1819. Still another may have existed at one time on Tuskegee creek, on the south bank of Little Tennessee river, north of Robbinsville, in Graham county, North Carolina, on land which was occupied until the Removal in 1838. Taskigi town of the Creek country was on Coosa river, near the junction with the Tallapoosa, some distance above the present Montgomery,

---

[1] Haywood, Natural and Aboriginal History of Tennessee, pp. 105–107, 1823. For a sketch of the Natchez war and the subsequent history of the scattered fragments of the tribe, see the author's paper, The End of the Natchez, in the American Anthropologist for July, 1899.

Alabama. We find Tasquiqui mentioned as a town in the Creek country visited by the Spanish captain, Juan Pardo, in 1567. The name
is evidently the same, though we can not be sure that the location was
identical with that of the later town.

Who or what the Taskigi were is uncertain and can probably never
be known, but they were neither Cherokee nor Muscogee proper. It
would seem most probable that they were of Muskhogean affinity, but
they may have been an immigrant tribe from another section, or may
even have constituted a distinct linguistic stock, representing all that
was left of an ancient people whose occupation of the country antedated the coming of the Cherokee and the Creeks. The name may be
derived from *taska* or *taska'ya*, meaning "warrior" in several of the
Muskhogean dialects. It is not a Cherokee word, and Cherokee informants state positively that the Taskigi were a foreign people, with
distinct language and customs. They were not Creeks, Natchez,
Uchee, or Shawano, with all of whom the Cherokee were well
acquainted under other names. In the townhouse of their settlement
at the mouth of Tellico they had an upright pole, from the top of
which hung their protecting "medicine," the image of a human figure
cut from a cedar log. For this reason the Cherokee in derision sometimes called the place Atsĭnä'-k'taûñ, "Hanging-cedar place." Before
the sale of the land in 1819 they were so nearly extinct that the Cherokee had moved in and occupied the ground.

Adair, in 1775, mentions the Tae-keo-ge (*sic*—a double misprint) as
one of several broken tribes which the Creeks had "artfully decoyed" to
incorporate with them in order to strengthen themselves against hostile attempts. Milfort, about 1780, states that the Taskigi on Coosa
river were a foreign people who had been driven by wars to seek an
asylum among the Creeks, being encouraged thereto by the kind reception accorded to another fugitive tribe. Their request was granted by
the confederacy, and they were given lands upon which they built
their town. He puts this event shortly before the incorporation of
the Yuchi, which would make it early in the eighteenth century. In
1799, according to Hawkins, the town had but 35 warriors, "had lost
its ancient language," and spoke Creek. There is still a "white" or
peace town named Taskigi in the Creek Nation in Indian Territory.[1]

The nearest neighbors of the Cherokee on the west, after the expulsion of the Shawano, were the Chickasaw, known to the Cherokee as
Ani'-Tsĭ'ksû, whose territory lay chiefly between the Mississippi and
the Tennessee, in what is now western Kentucky and Tennessee and
the extreme northern portion of Mississippi. By virtue, however, of
conquest from the Shawano or of ancient occupancy they claimed a

---

[1] Adair, History of American Indians, p. 257, 1775. The other statements concerning the Taskigi
among the Creeks are taken from Gatschet's valuable study, A Migration Legend of the Creek
Indians, I, pp. 122, 145, 228, 1884.

large additional territory to the east of this, including all upon the
waters of Duck river and Elk creek. This claim was disputed by
the Cherokee. According to Haywood, the two tribes had been
friends and allies in the expulsion of the Shawano, but afterward,
shortly before the year 1769, the Cherokee, apparently for no sufficient reason, picked a quarrel with the Chickasaw and attacked them
in their town at the place afterward known as the Chickasaw Old
Fields, on the north side of Tennessee river, some twenty miles below
the present Guntersville, Alabama. The Chickasaw defended themselves so well that the assailants were signally defeated and compelled
to retreat to their own country.[1] It appears, however, that the
Chickasaw, deeming this settlement too remote from their principal
towns, abandoned it after the battle. Although peace was afterward
made between the two tribes their rival claim continued to be a subject of dispute throughout the treaty period.

The Choctaw, a loose confederacy of tribes formerly occupying
southern Mississippi and the adjacent coast region, are called Ani'-
Tsa'ta by the Cherokee, who appear to have had but little communication with them, probably because the intermediate territory was held
by the Creeks, who were generally at war with one or the other. In
1708 we find mention of a powerful expedition by the Cherokee,
Creeks, and Catawba against the Choctaw living about Mobile bay.[2]

Of the Indians west of the Mississippi those best known to the
Cherokee were the Ani'-Wasa'sĭ, or Osage, a powerful predatory tribe
formerly holding most of the country between the Missouri and Arkansas rivers, and extending from the Mississippi far out into the plains.
The Cherokee name is a derivative from Wasash', the name by which
the Osage call themselves.[3] The relations of the two tribes seem to
have been almost constantly hostile from the time when the Osage
refused to join in the general Indian peace concluded in 1768 (see
"The Iroquois Wars") up to 1822, when the Government interfered
to compel an end of the bloodshed. The bitterness was largely due to
the fact that ever since the first Cherokee treaty with the United
States, made at Hopewell, South Carolina, in 1785, small bodies of
Cherokee, resenting the constant encroachments of the whites, had
been removing beyond the Mississippi to form new settlements within
the territory claimed by the Osage, where in 1817 they already numbered between two and three thousand persons. As showing how new
is our growth as a nation, it is interesting to note that Wafford, when
a boy, attended near the site of the present Clarkesville, Georgia,
almost on Savannah river, a Cherokee scalp dance, at which the women

[1] Haywood, Natural and Aboriginal History of Tennessee, p. 24, 1823. From a contemporary reference
in Rivers, South Carolina, page 57, it appears that this war was in full progress in 1757.
[2] Margry, quoted in Gatschet, Creek Migration Legend, I, pp. 16, 87, 1884.
[3] Wasash, French Ouasage, corrupted by the Americans into Osage.

danced over some Osage scalps sent by their relatives in the west as trophies of a recent victory.

Other old Cherokee names for western tribes which can not be identified are Tayûñ′ksĭ, the untranslatable name of a tribe described simply as living in the West; Tsuniya′tigă, "Naked people," described as living in the far West; Gûn′-tsuskwa′′lĭ, "Short-arrows," who lived in the far West, and were small, but great fighters; Yûñ′wini′giskĭ, "Man-eaters," a hostile tribe west or north, possibly the cannibal Atakapa or Tonkawa, of Louisiana or Texas. Their relations with the tribes with which they have become acquainted since the removal to Indian Territory do not come within the scope of this paper.

106. THE GIANTS FROM THE WEST

James Wafford, of the western Cherokee, who was born in Georgia in 1806, says that his grandmother, who must have been born about the middle of the last century, told him that she had heard from the old people that long before her time a party of giants had come once to visit the Cherokee. They were nearly twice as tall as common men, and had their eyes set slanting in their heads, so that the Cherokee called them Tsunil′ kălû′, "The Slant-eyed people," because they looked like the giant hunter Tsul′kălû′ (see the story). They said that these giants lived very far away in the direction in which the sun goes down. The Cherokee received them as friends, and they stayed some time, and then returned to their home in the west. The story may be a distorted historical tradition.

107. THE LOST CHEROKEE

When the first lands were sold by the Cherokee, in 1721, a part of the tribe bitterly opposed the sale, saying that if the Indians once consented to give up any of their territory the whites would never be satisfied, but would soon want a little more, and a little again, until at last there would be none left for the Indians. Finding all they could say not enough to prevent the treaty, they determined to leave their old homes forever and go far into the West, beyond the Great river, where the white men could never follow them. They gave no heed to the entreaties of their friends, but began preparations for the long march, until the others, finding that they could not prevent their going, set to work and did their best to fit them out with pack horses loaded with bread, dried venison, and other supplies.

When all was ready they started, under the direction of their chief. A company of picked men was sent with them to help them in crossing the Great river, and every night until they reached it runners were sent back to the tribe, and out from the tribe to the marching band, to carry messages and keep each party posted as to how the other was getting along. At last they came to the Mississippi, and crossed it by the help of those warriors who had been sent with them. These then returned to the tribe, while the others kept on to the west. All communication was now at an end. No more was heard of the wanderers, and in time the story of the lost Cherokee was forgotten or remembered only as an old tale.

Still the white man pressed upon the Cherokee and one piece of land after another was sold, until as years went on the dispossessed people began to turn their faces toward the west as their final resting place, and small bands of hunters crossed the Mississippi to learn what might be beyond. One of these parties pushed on across the plains and there at the foot of the great mountains—the Rockies—they found a tribe speaking the old Cherokee language and living still as the Cherokee had lived before they had ever known the white man or his ways.

108. THE MASSACRE OF THE ANI′-KUTA′Nĭ

Among other perishing traditions is that relating to the Ani′-Kuta′nĭ or Ani′-Kwăta′nĭ, concerning whom the modern Cherokee know so little that their very identity is now a matter of dispute, a few holding that they were an ancient people who preceded the Cherokee and built the mounds, while others, with more authority, claim that they were a clan or society in the tribe and were destroyed long ago by pestilence or other calamity. Fortunately, we are not left to depend entirely upon surmise in the matter, as the tradition was noted by Haywood some seventy years ago, and by another writer some forty years later, while the connected story could still be obtained from competent authorities. From the various statements it would seem that the Ani′-Kuta′nĭ were a priestly clan, having hereditary supervision of all religious ceremonies among the Cherokee, until, in consequence of having abused their sacred privileges, they were attacked and completely exterminated by the rest of the tribe, leaving the priestly functions to be assumed thereafter by individual doctors and conjurers.

Haywood says, without giving name or details, "The Cherokees are addicted to conjuration to ascertain whether a sick person will recover. This custom arose after the destruction of their priests. Tradition states that such persons lived among their ancestors and were deemed superior to others, and were extirpated long ago, in consequence of the misconduct of one of the priests, who attempted to take the wife of a man who was the brother of the leading chief of the nation."[1]

A more detailed statement, on the authority of Chief John Ross and Dr J. B. Evans, is given in 1866 by a writer who speaks of the massacre as having occurred about a century before, although from the

---

[1] Nat. and Aborig. Hist. Tenn., p. 266.

dimness of the tradition it is evident that it must have been much earlier:

"The facts, though few, are interesting. The order was hereditary; in this respect peculiar, for among Indians seldom, and among the Cherokees never, does power pertain to any family as a matter of right. Yet the family of the Nicotani—for it seems to have been a family or clan—enjoyed this privilege. The power that they exercised was not, however, political, nor does it appear that chiefs were elected from among them.

"The Nicotani were a mystical, religious body, of whom the people stood in great awe, and seem to have been somewhat like the Brahmins of India. By what means they attained their ascendancy, or how long it was maintained, can never be ascertained. Their extinction by massacre is nearly all that can be discovered concerning them. They became haughty, insolent, overbearing, and licentious to an intolerable degree. Relying on their hereditary privileges and the strange awe which they inspired, they did not hesitate by fraud or violence to rend asunder the tender relations of husband and wife when a beautiful woman excited their passions. The people long brooded in silence over the oppressions and outrages of this high caste, whom they deeply hated but greatly feared. At length a daring young man, a member of an influential family, organized a conspiracy among the people for the massacre of the priesthood. The immediate provocation was the abduction of the wife of the young leader of the conspiracy. His wife was remarkable for her beauty, and was forcibly abducted and violated by one of the Nicotani while he was absent on the chase. On his return he found no difficulty in exciting in others the resentment which he himself experienced. So many had suffered in the same way, so many feared that they might be made to suffer, that nothing was wanted but a leader. A leader appearing in the person of the young brave whom we have named, the people rose under his direction and killed every Nicotani, young and old. Thus perished a hereditary secret society, since which time no hereditary privileges have been tolerated among the Cherokees."[1]

109. THE WAR MEDICINE

Some warriors had medicine to change their shape as they pleased, so that they could escape from their enemies. Once one of these medicine warriors who had been away from home came back and found a strong party of the enemy attacking the settlement while nearly all the men were off on a hunt. The town was on the other side of the river, but his grandmother was there, so he made up his mind to save her. Going down the stream a little way, he hunted until he found a

[1] MacGowan, Dr D. J., Indian Secret Societies, Historical Magazine, x, p. 139, 1866. Morrisania, N. Y.

mussel shell. With his medicine he changed this to a canoe, in which he crossed over to his grandmother's house, and found her sitting there, waiting for the enemy to come and kill her. Again he made medicine and put her into a small gourd which he fastened to his belt. Then climbing a tree he changed himself to a swamp woodcock, and with one cry he spread his wings and flew across to the other side of the river, where both took their natural shape again and made their way through the woods to another settlement.

There was another great Cherokee warrior, named Dasi'giya'gĭ, or Shoe-boots, as the whites called him, who lived on Hightower creek, in Georgia. He was so strong that it was said he could throw a corn mortar over a house, and with his magic power could clear a river at one jump. His war medicine was an uktena scale and a very large turtle shell which he got from the Shawano. In the Creek war he put this scale into water and bathed his body with the water, and also burned a piece of the turtle shell and drew a black line around his men with the coal, and he was never wounded and never had a man killed.

Some great warriors had a medicine by the aid of which they could dive under the ground as under water, come up among the enemy to kill and scalp one, then dive under the ground again and come up among their friends.

Some war captains knew how to put their lives up in the tree tops during a fight, so that even if they were struck by the enemy they could not be killed. Once, in a battle with the Shawano, the Chero- kee leader stood directly in front of the enemy and let the whole party shoot at him, but was not hurt until the Shawano captain, who knew this war medicine himself, ordered his men to shoot into the branches above the head of the other. They did this and the Cherokee leader fell dead.

110. INCIDENTS OF PERSONAL HEROISM

In the Cherokee war of 1760 when small bodies of the enemy, according to Haywood, were pushing their inroads eastward almost to Salisbury, a party of six or eight warriors was discovered, watched, and followed until they were seen to enter a deserted cabin to pass the night. The alarm was given, and shortly before daylight the whites surrounded the house, posting themselves behind the fodder stack and some outbuildings so as to command both the door and the wide chimney top. They then began to throw fire upon the roof to drive out the Indians, when, as the blaze caught the dry shingles, and death either by fire or bullet seemed certain, one of the besieged warriors called to his companions that it was better that one should be a sacrifice than that all should die, and that if they would follow his directions he would save them, but die himself. He proposed to sally out alone to draw the fire of the besiegers, while his friends stood ready to make for the woods as soon as the guns of the whites were empty. They agreed, and the door was opened, when he suddenly rushed forth, dodging and running in a zigzag course, so that every gun was emptied at him before he fell dead, covered with wounds. While the whites were reloading, the other warriors ran out and succeeded in reaching the woods before the besiegers could recover from their surprise. The historian adds, "How greatly it is to be regretted that the name of this hero is not known to the writer, that it might be recorded with this specimen of Cherokee bravery and patriotism, firmness and presence of mind in the hour of danger."[1]

More than once women seem to have shown the courage of warriors when the occasion demanded. At the beginning of the last century there was still living among the Cherokee a woman who had killed her husband's slayer in one of the Revolutionary engagements. For this deed she was treated with so much consideration that she was permitted to join the warriors in the war dance, carrying her gun and tomahawk. The Wahnenauhi manuscript has a tradition of an attack upon a Cherokee town and the killing of the chief by a hostile war party. His wife, whose name was Cuhtahlatah (Gatûñ'lătĭ, "Wild-hemp"?), on seeing her husband fall, snatched up his tomahawk, shouting, "Kill! Kill!" and rushed upon the enemy with such fury that the retreating Cherokee rallied and renewed the battle with so great courage as to gain a complete victory. This may be a different statement of the same incident.

In Rutherford's expedition against the Cherokee, in 1776, the Indians made a stand near Waya gap, in the Nantahala mountains, and a hard-fought engagement took place, with a loss to the Americans of nineteen men, although the enemy was finally driven from the ground. After the main body had retreated, an Indian was seen looking out from behind a tree, and was at once shot and killed by the soldiers, who, on going to the spot, found that it was a woman, painted and stripped like a warrior and armed with bow and arrows. She had already been shot through the thigh, and had therefore been unable to flee with the rest.

iii. THE MOUNDS AND THE CONSTANT FIRE: THE OLD SACRED THINGS

Some say that the mounds were built by anotner people. Others say they were built by the ancestors of the old Ani'-Kĭtu'hwagĭ for town-house foundations, so that the townhouses would be safe when freshets came. The townhouse was always built on the level bottom lands by the river in order that the people might have smooth ground for their dances and ballplays and might be able to go down to water during the dance.

---

[1] Haywood, Nat. and Aborig. Hist. Tenn., p. 239.

When they were ready to build the mound they began by laying a circle of stones on the surface of the ground. Next they made a fire in the center of the circle and put near it the body of some prominent chief or priest who had lately died—some say seven chief men from the different clans—together with an Ulûñsû′tï stone, an uktena scale or horn, a feather from the right wing of an eagle or great tlă′nuwă, which lived in those days, and beads of seven colors, red, white, black, blue, purple, yellow, and gray-blue. The priest then conjured all these with disease, so that, if ever an enemy invaded the country, even though he should burn and destroy the town and the townhouse, he would never live to return home.

The mound was then built up with earth, which the women brought in baskets, and as they piled it above the stones, the bodies of their great men, and the sacred things, they left an open place at the fire in the center and let down a hollow cedar trunk, with the bark on, which fitted around the fire and protected it from the earth. This cedar log was cut long enough to reach nearly to the surface inside the townhouse when everything was done. The earth was piled up around it, and the whole mound was finished off smoothly, and then the townhouse was built upon it. One man, called the fire keeper, stayed always in the townhouse to feed and tend the fire. When there was to be a dance or a council he pushed long stalks of the *ihyâ′ga* weed, which some call *atsil′-sûñ′tï*, "the fire maker" (*Erigeron canadense* or fleabane), down through the opening in the cedar log to the fire at the bottom. He left the ends of the stalks sticking out and piled lichens and punk around, after which he prayed, and as he prayed the fire climbed up along the stalks until it caught the punk. Then he put on wood, and by the time the dancers were ready there was a large fire blazing in the townhouse. After the dance he covered the hole over again with ashes, but the fire was always smoldering below. Just before the Green-corn dance, in the old times, every fire in the settlement was extinguished and all the people came and got new fire from the townhouse. This was called *atsi′la gălûñkw′ti′yu*, "the honored or sacred fire." Sometimes when the fire in a house went out, the woman came to the fire keeper, who made a new fire by rubbing an ihyâ′ga stalk against the under side of a hard dry fungus that grows upon locust trees.

Some say this everlasting fire was only in the larger mounds at Nĭkwăsĭ′, Kĭtu′hwa, and a few other towns, and that when the new fire was thus drawn up for the Green-corn dance it was distributed from them to the other settlements. The fire burns yet at the bottom of these great mounds, and when the Cherokee soldiers were camped near Kĭtu′hwa during the civil war they saw smoke still rising from the mound.

The Cherokee once had a wooden box, nearly square and wrapped up in buckskin, in which they kept the most sacred things of their old religion.   Upon every important expedition two priests carried it in turn and watched over it in camp so that nothing could come near to disturb it.   The Delawares captured it more than a hundred years ago, and after that the old religion was neglected and trouble came to the Nation.   They had also a great peace pipe, carved from white stone, with seven stem-holes, so that seven men could sit around and smoke from it at once at their peace councils.   In the old town of Keowee they had a drum of stone, cut in the shape of a turtle, which was hung up inside the townhouse and used at all the town dances.   The other towns of the Lower Cherokee used to borrow it, too, for their own dances.

All the old things are gone now and the Indians are different.

MISCELLANEOUS MYTHS AND LEGENDS

112. THE IGNORANT HOUSEKEEPER

An old man whose wife had died lived alone with his son.   One day he said to the young man, "We need a cook here, so you would better get married."   So the young man got a wife and brought her home. Then his father said, "Now we must work together and do all we can to help her.   You go hunting and bring in the meat and I'll look after the corn and beans, and then she can cook."   The young man went into the woods to look for a deer and his father went out into the field to attend to the corn.   When they came home at night they were hungry, and the young woman set out a bowl of walnut hominy (*kanā'ta-lu'hĭ*) before them.   It looked queer, somehow, and when the old man examined it he found that the walnuts had been put in whole.   "Why didn't you shell the walnuts and then beat up the kernels," said he to the young woman.   "I didn't know they had to be shelled," she replied.   Then the old man said, "You think about marrying and you don't know how to cook," and he sent her away.

113. THE MAN IN THE STUMP

A man who had a field of growing corn went out one day to see how it was ripening and climbed a tall stump to get a better view.   The stump was hollow and a bear had a nest of cubs in the bottom.   The man slipped and fell down upon the cubs, which set up such a squealing that the old she-bear heard them and came climbing down into the stump tail first, in bear fashion, to see what was the matter.   The man caught hold of her by the hind legs and the old bear was so frightened that she at once climbed out again, dragging the man, who thus got out of the stump, when the bear ran away.

114. TWO LAZY HUNTERS

A party of warriors once started out for a long hunting trip in the mountains.   They went on until they came to a good game region, when they set up their bark hut in a convenient place near the river side. Every morning after breakfast they scattered out, each man for himself, to be gone all day, until they returned at night with whatever game they had taken. There was one lazy fellow who went out alone every morning like the others, but only until he found a sunny slope, when he would stretch out by the side of a rock to sleep until evening, returning then to camp empty-handed, but with his moccasins torn and a long story of how he had tramped all day and found nothing. This went on until one of the others began to suspect that something was wrong, and made it his business to find it out. The next morning he followed him secretly through the woods until he saw him come out into a sunny opening, where he sat down upon a large rock, took off his moccasins, and began rubbing them against the rocks until he had worn holes in them. Then the lazy fellow loosened his belt, lay down beside the rock, and went to sleep. The spy set fire to the dry leaves and watched until the flame crept close up to the sleeping man, who never opened his eyes.

The spy went back to camp and told what he had seen. About supper time the lazy fellow came in with the same old story of a long day's hunt and no game started. When he had finished the others all laughed and called him a sleepyhead. He insisted that he had been climbing the ridges all day, and put out his moccasins to show how worn they were, not knowing that they were scorched from the fire, as he had slept on until sundown. When they saw the blackened moccasins they laughed again, and he was too much astonished to say a word in his defense; so the captain said that such a liar was not fit to stay with them, and he was driven from the camp.

     *   *   *   *   *   *   *

There was another lazy fellow who courted a pretty girl, but she would have nothing to do with him, telling him that her husband must be a good hunter or she would remain single all her life. One morning he went into the woods, and by a lucky accident managed to kill a deer. Lifting it upon his back, he carried it into the settlement, passing right by the door of the house where the girl and her mother lived. As soon as he was out of sight of the house he went by a roundabout course into the woods again and waited until evening, when he appeared with the deer on his shoulder and came down the trail past the girl's house as he had in the morning. He did this the next day, and the next, until the girl began to think he must be killing all the deer in the woods. So her mother—the old women are usually the matchmakers—got ready and went to the young man's mother to talk it over.

When she arrived and the greetings were done she said, "Your son must be a good hunter." "No," replied the old woman, "he seldom kills anything." "But he has been killing a great many deer lately." "I haven't seen any," said his mother. "Why, he has been carrying deer past our house twice a day for the last three days." "I don't know what he did with them," said the young man's mother; "he never brought them here." Then the girl's mother was sure there was something wrong, so she went home and told her husband, who followed up the young man's trail into the woods until it brought him to where the body of the deer was hidden, now so far decayed that it had to be thrown away.

115. THE TWO OLD MEN

Two old men went hunting. One had an eye drawn down and was called Uk-kwŭnăgi'ta, "Eye-drawn-down." The other had an arm twisted out of shape and was called Uk-ku'sûñtsûtĭ, "Bent-bow-shape." They killed a deer and cooked the meat in a pot. The second old man dipped a piece of bread into the soup and smacked his lips as he ate it. "Is it good?" said the first old man. Said the other, "*Hayŭ'! uk-kwŭnăgi'stĭ*—Yes, sir! It will draw down one's eye."

Thought the first old man to himself, "He means me." So he dipped a piece of bread into the pot, and smacked his lips as he tasted it. "Do you find it good?" said the other old man. Said his comrade, "*Hayŭ'! uk-ku'sûñtsûtĕtĭ'*—Yes, sir! It will twist up one's arm." Thought the second old man, "He means me"; so he got very angry and struck the first old man, and then they fought until each killed the other.

116. THE STAR FEATHERS

A long time ago a warrior of roving disposition went down into the white settlements toward the east, where for the first time he saw a peacock. The beautiful long feathers surprised and delighted him, and by trading some valuable Indian possession of his own he managed to buy a few of them, which he took with him to the mountains and hid, until he was ready to use them, in an old beaver lodge under the river bank. To get into the beaver lodge he had to dive under the water.

Then he set to work secretly and made himself a headdress, with the long peacock feathers in the front and trailing out behind and the shorter ones at the sides. At the next dance he wore the new headdress, and asserted that he had been up to the sky and that these were star feathers (see number 9, "What the stars are like"). He made a long speech also, which he pretended was a message he had received from the star spirits to deliver to the people.

Everyone wondered at the beautiful feathers, so different from any they had ever seen before. They made no doubt that he had been up to the sky and talked with spirits. He became a great prophet, and used to keep himself hidden all day in the beaver hole, and whenever there was a night gathering for a dance or a council he would suddenly appear among them wearing his feather headdress and give the people a new message from the sky. Then he would leave them again, pretending that he went up to heaven.

He grew famous and powerful among all the medicine men, until at last it happened that another Cherokee went down among the white settlements and saw there another peacock, and knew at once that the prophet was a fraud. On his return he quietly told some of his friends, and they decided to investigate. When the next night dance came around the prophet was on hand as usual with a new message fresh from the stars. The people listened reverently, and promised to do all that he commanded. Then he left them, saying that he must return at once to the sky, but as he went out from the circle the spies followed him in the darkness, and saw him go down to the river and dive under the water. They waited, but he did not come up again, and they went back and told the people. The next morning a party went to the spot and discovered the beaver lodge under the bank. One man dived and came up inside, and there he found the prophet sitting with the peacock feathers by his side.

117. THE MOTHER BEAR'S SONG

A hunter in the woods one day heard singing in a cave. He came near and peeped in, and it was a mother bear singing to her cubs and telling them what to do when the hunters came after them.

Said the mother bear to the cubs, "When you hear the hunters coming down the creek, then—

Tsâ′gĭ, tsâ′gĭ, hwĭ′lahĭ′;
Tsâ′gĭ, tsâ′gĭ, hwĭ′lahĭ.

Upstream, upstream, you (must) go;
Upstream, upstream, you (must) go.

"But if you hear them coming up the creek, children, then—

Ge′ĭ, ge′ĭ, hwĭ′lahĭ′;
Ge′ĭ, ge′ĭ, hwĭ′lahĭ′.

Downstream, downstream, you (must) go;
Downstream, downstream, you (must) go."

*   *   *   *   *   *   *

Another hunter out in the woods one day thought he heard a woman singing to a baby. He followed the sound up to the head of the branch until he came to a cave under the bushes, and inside was a mother bear rocking her cub in her paws and singing to it this baby song, which the Ani′-Tsâ′gûhĭ used to know before they were turned into bears:

Ha′-mama′, ha′-mama′, ha′-mama′, ha′-mama′;
Udâ′hale′yĭ hi′lûñnû, hi′lûñnû;
Udâ′hale′yĭ hi′lûñnû, hi′lûñnû.

Let me carry you on my back (four times);
On the sunny side go to sleep, go to sleep;
On the sunny side go to sleep, go to sleep.

118. BABY SONG, TO PLEASE THE CHILDREN

Ha′wiye′-hyuwe′, Ha′wiye′-hyuwe′,
Yu′wĕ-yuwĕhe′, Ha′wiyĕhyu′-uwe′—
Yâ′nû une′guhi′ tsana′sehâ′;
E′tï une′guhi′ tsana′sehâ′;
Yâ′nû nudûññelû′ tsa′nadiskâ′.

Ha′wiye′-hyuwe′, Ha′wiye′-hyuwe′,
Yu′wĕ-yuwĕhe′, Ha′wiyĕhyu′-uwe′—
The Bear is very bad, so they say;
Long time ago he was very bad, so they say;
The Bear did so and so, they say.

119. WHEN BABIES ARE BORN: THE WREN AND THE CRICKET

The little Wren is the messenger of the birds, and pries into everything. She gets up early in the morning and goes round to every house in the settlement to get news for the bird council. When a new baby is born she finds out whether it is a boy or girl and reports to the council. If it is a boy the birds sing in mournful chorus: "Alas! the whistle of the arrow! my shins will burn," because the birds know that when the boy grows older he will hunt them with his blowgun and arrows and roast them on a stick.

But if the baby is a girl, they are glad and sing: "Thanks! the sound of the pestle! At her home I shall surely be able to scratch where she sweeps," because they know that after a while they will be able to pick up stray grains where she beats the corn into meal.

When the Cricket hears that a girl is born, it also is glad, and says, "Thanks, I shall sing in the house where she lives." But if it is a boy the Cricket laments: *Gwe-he!* He will shoot me! He will shoot me! He will shoot me!" because boys make little bows to shoot crickets and grasshoppers.

When inquiring as to the sex of the new arrival the Cherokee asks, "Is it a bow or a (meal) sifter?" or, "Is it ballsticks or bread?"

120. THE RAVEN MOCKER

Of all the Cherokee wizards or witches the most dreaded is the Raven Mocker (*Kâ′lanû Ahyeli′skï*), the one that robs the dying man of life. They are of either sex and there is no sure way to know one, though they usually look withered and old, because they have added so many lives to their own.

At night, when some one is sick or dying in the settlement, the Raven Mocker goes to the place to take the life. He flies through the air in fiery shape, with arms outstretched like wings, and sparks trailing behind, and a rushing sound like the noise of a strong wind. Every little while as he flies he makes a cry like the cry of a raven when it "dives" in the air—not like the common raven cry—and those

who hear are afraid, because they know that some man's life will soon
go out. When the Raven Mocker comes to the house he finds others
of his kind waiting there, and unless there is a doctor on guard who
knows how to drive them away they go inside, all invisible, and
frighten and torment the sick man until they kill him. Sometimes to
do this they even lift him from the bed and throw him on the floor,
but his friends who are with him think he is only struggling for
breath.

After the witches kill him they take out his heart and eat it, and so
add to their own lives as many days or years as they have taken from
his. No one in the room can see them, and there is no scar where they
take out the heart, but yet there is no heart left in the body. Only
one who has the right medicine can recognize a Raven Mocker, and if
such a man stays in the room with the sick person these witches are
afraid to come in, and retreat as soon as they see him, because when
one of them is recognized in his right shape he must die within seven
days. There was once a man named Gûñskăli′skĭ, who had this medicine and used to hunt for Raven Mockers, and killed several. When
the friends of a dying person know that there is no more hope they
always try to have one of these medicine men stay in the house and
watch the body until it is buried, because after burial the witches do
not steal the heart.

The other witches are jealous of the Raven Mockers and afraid to
come into the same house with one. Once a man who had the witch
medicine was watching by a sick man and saw these other witches outside trying to get in. All at once they heard a Raven Mocker cry
overhead and the others scattered "like a flock of pigeons when the
hawk swoops." When at last a Raven Mocker dies these other witches
sometimes take revenge by digging up the body and abusing it.

The following is told on the reservation as an actual happening:

A young man had been out on a hunting trip and was on his way
home when night came on while he was still a long distance from the
settlement. He knew of a house not far off the trail where an old man
and his wife lived, so he turned in that direction to look for a place to
sleep until morning. When he got to the house there was nobody in
it. He looked into the âsĭ and found no one there either. He thought
maybe they had gone after water, and so stretched himself out in the
farther corner to sleep. Very soon he heard a raven cry outside, and
in a little while afterwards the old man came into the âsĭ and sat down
by the fire without noticing the young man, who kept still in the dark
corner. Soon there was another raven cry outside, and the old man
said to himself, "Now my wife is coming," and sure enough in a
little while the old woman came in and sat down by her husband.
Then the young man knew they were Raven Mockers and he was
frightened and kept very quiet.

Said the old man to his wife, "Well, what luck did you have?" "None," said the old woman, "there were too many doctors watching. What luck did you have?" "I got what I went for," said the old man, "there is no reason to fail, but you never have luck. Take this and cook it and let's have something to eat." She fixed the fire and then the young man smelled meat roasting and thought it smelled sweeter than any meat he had ever tasted. He peeped out from one eye, and it looked like a man's heart roasting on a stick.

Suddenly the old woman said to her husband, "Who is over in the corner?" "Nobody," said the old man. "Yes, there is," said the old woman, "I hear him snoring," and she stirred the fire until it blazed and lighted up the whole place, and there was the young man lying in the corner. He kept quiet and pretended to be asleep. The old man made a noise at the fire to wake him, but still he pretended to sleep. Then the old man came over and shook him, and he sat up and rubbed his eyes as if he had been asleep all the time.

Now it was near daylight and the old woman was out in the other house getting breakfast ready, but the hunter could hear her crying to herself. "Why is your wife crying?" he asked the old man. "Oh, she has lost some of her friends lately and feels lonesome," said her husband; but the young man knew that she was crying because he had heard them talking.

When they came out to breakfast the old man put a bowl of corn mush before him and said, "This is all we have—we have had no meat for a long time." After breakfast the young man started on again, but when he had gone a little way the old man ran after him with a fine piece of beadwork and gave it to him, saying, "Take this, and don't tell anybody what you heard last night, because my wife and I are always quarreling that way." The young man took the piece, but when he came to the first creek he threw it into the water and then went on to the settlement. There he told the whole story, and a party of warriors started back with him to kill the Raven Mockers. When they reached the place it was seven days after the first night. They found the old man and his wife lying dead in the house, so they set fire to it and burned it and the witches together.

121. HERBERT'S SPRING

"From the head of the southern branch of Savannah river it does not exceed half a mile to a head spring of the Missisippi water that runs through the middle and upper parts of the Cheerake nation about a northwest course, and, joining other rivers, they empty themselves into the great Missisippi. The above fountain is called 'Herbert's spring,' so named from an early commissioner of Indian affairs, and it was natural for strangers to drink thereof, to quench thirst, gratify their curiosity, and have it to say they had drank of the French waters.

Some of our people, who went only with the view of staying a short time, but by some allurement or other exceeded the time appointed, at their return reported, either through merriment or superstition, that the spring had such a natural bewitching quality that whosoever drank of it could not possibly quit the nation during the tedious space of seven years. All the debauchees readily fell in with this superstitious notion as an excuse for their bad method of living, when they had no proper call to stay in that country; and in process of time it became as received a truth as any ever believed to have been spoken by the Delphic oracle. One cursed, because its enchantment had marred his good fortune; another condemned his weakness for drinking down witchcraft, against his own secret suspicions; one swore he would never taste another such dangerous poison, even though he should be forced to go down to the Missisippi for water; and another comforted himself that so many years out of the seven were already passed, and wished that if ever he tasted it again, though under the greatest necessity, he might be confined to the Stygian waters. Those who had their minds more enlarged diverted themselves much at their cost, for it was a noted favorite place, on account of the name it went by; and, being a well situated and good spring, there all travelers commonly drank a bottle of choice. But now most of the pack-horse men, though they be dry, and also matchless sons of Bacchus, on the most pressing invitations to drink there, would swear to forfeit sacred liquor the better part of their lives rather than basely renew or confirm the loss of their liberty, which that execrable fountain occasions."—Adair, American Indians, p. 231, 1775.

122. LOCAL LEGENDS OF NORTH CAROLINA

Owing chiefly to the fact that the Cherokee still occupy western North Carolina, the existing local legends for that section are more numerous than for all the rest of their ancient territory. For the more important legends see the stories: Agân-unitsi's Search for the Uktena, Atagâ'hĭ, Hemp-carrier, Herbert's Spring, Kăna'sta, The Great Leech of Tlanusi'yĭ, The Great Yellow-jacket, The Nûñnĕ'hĭ, The Raid on Tĭkwali'tsĭ, The Removed Townhouses, The Spirit Defenders of Nĭkwăsĭ', The Uw'tsûñ'ta, Tsul'kălû', Tsuwe'năhĭ, The Uʻtlûñ'ta.

AKWĔʻTIʻYĬ: A spot on Tuckasegee river, in Jackson county, between Dick's creek and the upper end of Cowee tunnel. According to tradition there was a dangerous water monster in the river there. The meaning of the name is lost.

ATSI'LA-WA'ĭ: "Fire's relative," a peak, sometimes spoken of as Rattlesnake knob, east of Oconaluftee river and about 2 miles northeast of Cherokee or Yellow Hill, in Swain county. So called from a tradition that a ball of fire was once seen to fly through the air from

ON ONONALUFTEE RIVER

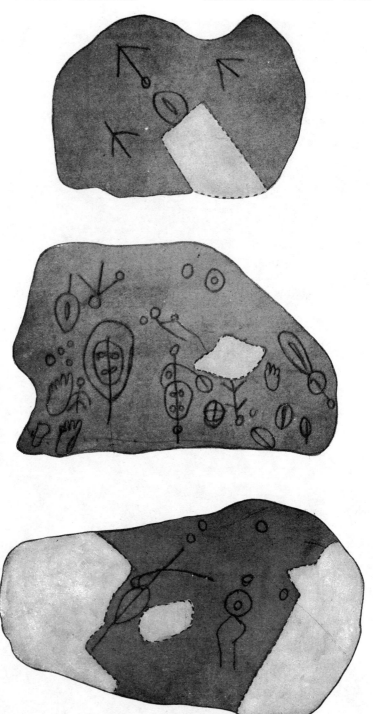

PETROGLYPHS AT TRACK-ROCK GAP, GEORGIA

(From sketches by the author, 1889.   Portions cut out by vandals are indicated by lighter shading)

the direction of Highlands, in Macon county, and alight upon this mountain. The Indians believe it to have been an ulûñsûtĭ (see number 50), which its owner had kept in a hiding place upon the summit, from which, after his death, it issued nightly to search for him.

BLACK ROCK: A very high bald peak toward the head of Scott's creek, northeast of Webster, on the line of Jackson and Haywood counties. Either this peak or the adjacent Jones knob, of equal height, is known to the Cherokee as Ûñ′wădâ-tsu‘gilasûñ′, "Where the storehouse was taken off," from a large flat rock, supported by four other rocks, so as to resemble a storehouse (ûñwădâ′lĭ) raised on poles, which was formerly in prominent view upon the summit until thrown down by lightning some fifty years ago.

BUFFALO CREEK, WEST: A tributary of Cheowa river, in Graham county. The Cherokee name is Yûnsâ′ĭ, "Buffalo place," from a tradition that a buffalo formerly lived under the water at its mouth (see Tsuta′tsinasûñ′yĭ).

CHEOWA MAXIMUM: A bald mountain at the head of Cheowa river, on the line between Graham and Macon counties. This and the adjoining peak, Swim bald, are together called Sehwate′yĭ, "Hornet place," from a monster hornet, which, according to tradition, formerly had its nest there, and could be seen flying about the tree tops or sunning itself on the bald spots, and which was so fierce that it drove away every one who came near the mountain. It finally disappeared.

DĂKWÂ′Ĭ: "Dăkwă′ place," in French Broad river, about 6 miles above Warm Springs, in Madison county, and 30 miles below Asheville. A dăkwă′ or monster fish is said to have lived in the stream at that point.

DA′ᴺAWA-(A) SA′ᵗTSÛÑYĬ: "War crossing," a ford in Cheowa river about 3 miles below Robbinsville, in Graham county. A hostile war party from the North, probably Shawano or Iroquois, after having killed a man on Cheowa, was pursued and crossed the river at this place.

DATLE′YĂSTA′Ĭ: "Where they fell down," on Tuckasegee river, at the bend above Webster, in Jackson county, where was formerly the old town of Gănsâ′gĭ (Conasauga). Two large uktenas, twined about each other as though in combat, were once seen to lift themselves from a deep hole in the river there and fall back into the water.

DÂTSI′YĬ: "Dâtsĭ place," just above Eagle creek, on Little Tennessee river, between Graham and Swain counties. So called from a traditional water monster of that name, said to have lived in a deep hole in the stream.

DEGAL‘GÛÑ′YĬ: "Where they are piled up," a series of cairns on both sides of the trail down the south side of Cheowa river, in Graham county. They extend along the trail for several miles, from below Santeetla creek nearly to Slick Rock creek, on the Tennessee line (the first being just above Disgâ'gisti'yĭ, q. v.), and probably mark the site of an ancient battle. One at least, nearly off Yellow creek, is reputed to be the grave of a Cherokee killed by the enemy. Every passing Indian throws an additional stone upon each heap, believing that some misfortune will befall him should he neglect this duty. Other cairns are on the west side of Slick Rock creek about a mile from Little Tennessee river, and others south of Robbinsville, near where the trail crosses the ridge to Valleytown, in Cherokee county.

DIDA'SKASTI'YĬ: "Where they were afraid of each other," a spot on the east side of Little Tennessee river, near the mouth of Alarka creek, in Swain county. A ball game once arranged to take place there, before the Removal, between rival teams from Qualla and Valleytown, was abandoned on account of the mutual fear of the two parties.

DISGÂ'GISTI'YĬ: "Where they gnaw," a spot where the trail down the south side of Cheowa river crosses a small branch about half way between Cockram creek and Yellow creek, in Graham county. Indians passing gnaw the twigs from the laurel bushes here, in the belief that if they should fail to do so they will encounter some misfortune before crossing the next ridge. Near by is a cairn to which each also adds a stone (see Degal'gûñ'yĭ).

DUDUÑ'LĔKSÛÑ'YĬ: "Where its legs were broken off," a spot on the east side of Tuckasegee river, opposite the mouth of Cullowhee river, a few miles above Webster, in Jackson county. The name suggests a tradition, which appears to be lost.

DULASTÛÑ'YĬ: "Potsherd place," a former settlement on Nottely river, in Cherokee county, near the Georgia line. A half-breed Cherokee ball captain who formerly lived there, John Butler or Tsan-uga'sĭtă (Sour John), having been defeated in a ball game, said, in contempt of his men, that they were of no more use than broken pots.

DUNIDÛ'LALÛÑYĬ: "Where they made arrows," on Straight creek, a head-stream of Oconaluftee river, near Cataluchee peak, in Swain county. A Shawano war party coming against the Cherokee, after having crossed the Smoky mountains, halted there to prepare arrows.

FRENCH BROAD RIVER: A magazine writer states that the Indians called this stream "the racing river." This is only partially correct. The Cherokee have no name for the river as a whole, but the district through which it flows about Asheville is called by them Un-ta'kiyasti'yĭ, "Where they race." The name of the city they translate as Kâsdu'yĭ, "Ashes place."

GAKATI'YĬ: "Place of setting free," a south bend in Tuckasegee river about 3 miles above Bryson City, in Swain county. It is sometimes put in the plural form, Diga'katiyĭ, "Place of setting them free." In one of their old wars the Cherokee generously released some prisoners there.

GATUTI'YĬ: "Town-building place," near the head of Santeetla creek, southwest from Robbinsville, in Graham county. High up on the slopes of the neighboring mountain, Stratton bald, is a wide "bench," where the people once started to build a settlement, but were frightened off by a strange noise, which they thought was made by an uktena.

GĬʻLĬ'-DINĔHŬÑ'YĬ: "Where the dogs live," a deep place in Oconaluftee river, Swain county, a short distance above Yellow Hill (Cherokee) and just below the mound. It is so named from a tradition that two "red dogs" were once seen there playing on the bank. They were supposed to live under the water.

GISEHŬÑ'YĬ: "Where the Female lives," on Tuckasegee river, about 2 miles above Bryson City, Swain county. There is a tradition that some supernatural "white people" were seen there washing clothes in the river and hanging them out upon the bank to dry. They were probably supposed to be the family of the Agis'-e'gwa, or "Great Female," a spirit invoked by the conjurers.

GREGORY BALD: A high peak of the Great Smoky mountains on the western border of Swain county, adjoining Tennessee. The Cherokee call it Tsistu'yĭ, "Rabbit place." Here the rabbits had their townhouse and here lived their chief, the Great Rabbit, and in the old times the people could see him. He was as large as a deer, and all the little rabbits were subject to him.

JOANNA BALD: A bald mountain near the head of Valley river, on the line between Graham and Cherokee counties. Called Diyâ'hăli'yĭ, "Lizard place," from a traditional great lizard, with glistening throat, which used to haunt the place and was frequently seen sunning itself on the rocky slopes.

JUTACULLA OLD FIELDS: A bald spot of perhaps a hundred acres on the slope of Tennessee bald (Tsulʻkălû' Tsunegûñ'yĭ), at the extreme head of Tuckasegee river, in Jackson county, on the ridge from which the lines of Haywood, Jackson, and Transylvania counties diverge. The giant Tsulʻkălû', or Jutaculla, as the name is corrupted by the whites, had his residence in the mountain (see story), and according to local legend among the whites, said to be derived from the Indians, this bald spot was a clearing which he made for a farm. Some distance farther to the west, on the north bank of Cany fork, about 1 mile above Moses creek and perhaps 10 miles above Webster, in the same county, is the Jutaculla rock, a large soapstone slab covered with rude carvings, which, according to the same tradition, are scratches made by the giant in jumping from his farm on the mountain to the creek below.

JUTACULLA ROCK: See Jutaculla old fields.

KÂL-DETSI'YÛÑYĬ: "Where the bones are," a ravine on the north side of Cheowa river, just above the mouth of East Buffalo creek, in Graham county. In the old time two Cherokee were killed here by the enemy, and their fate was unknown until, long afterward, their friends found their bones scattered about in the ravine.

NANTAHALA: A river and ridge of very steep mountains in Macon county, the name being a corruption of Nûñ'däye'′lĭ, applied to a former settlement about the mouth of Briertown creek, the townhouse being on the west side of the river, about the present Jarretts. The word means "middle sun," i. e., "midday sun," from *nûñdă'*, "sun," and *aye'′lĭ*, "middle," and refers to the fact that in places along the stream the high cliffs shut out the direct light of the sun until nearly noon. From a false idea that it is derived from *unûñtĭ*, "milk," it has been fancifully rendered, "Center of a woman's breast," "Maiden's bosom," etc. The valley was the legendary haunt of the Uw'tsûñ'ta (see number 45). As illustrating the steepness of the cliffs along the stream it was said of a noted hunter, Tsasta'wĭ, who lived in the old town, that he used to stand on the top of the bluff overlooking the settlement and throw down upon the roof of his house the liver of the freshly killed deer, so that his wife would have it cooked and waiting for him by the time he got down the mountain.

NUGĂTSA'NĬ: A ridge below Yellow Hill (Cherokee), on Oconaluftee river, in Swain county, said to be a resort of the Nûñnĕ'hĭ fairies. The word is an archaic form denoting a high ridge with a long, gradual slope.

QUALLA: A post-office and former trading station in Jackson county, on the border of the present East Cherokee reservation, hence sometimes called the Qualla reservation. The Cherokee form is Kwalĭ, or Kwalûñyĭ in the locative. According to Captain Terrell, the former trader at that place, it was named from Kwalĭ, i. e., Polly, an old Indian woman who lived there some sixty years ago.

SĂLIGU'GĬ: "Turtle place," a deep hole in Oconaluftee river, about half a mile below Adams creek, near Whittier, in Swain county, said to be the resort of a monster turtle.

SKWAN'-DIGŬ′GŬÑ'YĬ: For Askwan'-digû′gûñ'yĭ, "Where the Spaniard is in the water," on Soco creek, just above the entrance of Wright's creek, in Jackson county. According to tradition a party of Spaniards advancing into the mountains was attacked here by the Cherokee, who threw one of them (dead?) into the stream.

SOCO GAP: Ăhălu'na, Ă'hălunûñ'yĭ, or Uni'hălu'na, "Ambush," or "Where they ambushed"; at the head of Soco creek, on the line between Swain and Haywood counties. The trail from Pigeon river crosses this gap, and in the old times the Cherokee were accustomed to keep a lookout here for the approach of enemies from the north. On the occasion which gave it the name, they ambushed here, just below the gap, on the Haywood side, a large party of invading Shawano, and killed all but one, whose ears they cut off, after which, according to a common custom, they released him to carry the news back to his people.

STANDING INDIAN: A high bald peak at the extreme head of Nantahala river, in Macon county. The name is a rendering of the Cherokee name, Yûñ′wĭ-tsulenûñ′yĭ, "Where the man stood" (originally Yû′ñwĭ-dĭkatâgûñ′yĭ, "Where the man stands"), given to it on account of a peculiarly shaped rock formerly jutting out from the bald summit, but now broken off. As the old memory faded, a tradition grew up of a mysterious being once seen standing upon the mountain top.

STEKOA: A spot on Tuckasegee river, just above Whittier, in Swain county, better known as the Thomas farm, from its being the former residence of Colonel W. H. Thomas, for a long time the agent of the East Cherokee. The correct form is Stikâ′yĭ, the name of an ancient settlement at the place, as also of another on a creek of the same name in Rabun county, Georgia. The word has been incorrectly rendered "little grease," from *usdi′ga* or *usdi′*, "little," and *ka′ĭ*, "grease" or "oil," but the true meaning is lost.

SWANNANOA: A river joining the French Broad at Asheville, and the gap in the Blue ridge at its head. A magazine writer has translated this name "the beautiful." The word, however, is a corruption of Suwa′li-nûñnâ′(-hĭ), "Suwali trail," the Cherokee name, not of the stream, but of the trail crossing the gap toward the country of the Ani′-Suwa′lĭ or Cheraw (see number 104, "The Eastern Tribes").

SWIM BALD OR WOLF CREEK BALD. See Cheowa Maximum.

TSI′SKWUNSDI′-ADSISTI′YĬ: "Where they killed Little-bird," a place near the head of West Buffalo creek, southwest of Robbinsville, in Graham county. A trail crosses the ridge near this place, which takes its name from a man who was killed here by a hostile war party in the old fighting days.

TSU′DINÛÑTI′YĬ: "Throwing down place," the site of a former settlement in a bend on the west side of Nantahala river, just within the limits of Macon county. So called from a tradition that a Cherokee pursued by the enemy threw away his equipment there.

TSUKILÛÑNÛ′YĬ: "Where he alighted," two small bald spots on the side of the mountain at the head of Little Snowbird creek, southwest of Robbinsville, in Graham county. A mysterious being, having the form of a giant, with head blazing like the sun, was once seen to fly through the air, alight at this place, and stand for some time looking out over the landscape. It then flew away, and when the people came afterward to look, they found the herbage burned from the ground where it had stood. They do not know who it was, but some think it may have been the Sun.

TSULÂ′SINÛÑ′YĬ: "Where the footprint is," on Tuckasegee river, about a mile above Deep creek, in Swain county. From a rock now blasted out to make way for the railroad, on which were impressions said to have been the footprints of the giant Tsul'kălû' (see story) and a deer.

Tsunda'nilti'yĭ: "Where they demanded the debt from him," a fine camping ground, on the north side of Little Santeetla creek, about half-way up, west from Robbinsville, Graham county. Here a hunter once killed a deer, which the others of the party demanded in payment of a debt due them. The Cherokee commonly give the creek the same name.

Tsûta'ga Uweyûñ'ĭ: "Chicken creek," an extreme eastern head-stream of Nantahala river, entering about 4 miles above Clear branch, in Macon county. So called from a story that some hunters camping there for the night once heard a noise as of chickens constantly crow-ing upon a high rock farther up the stream.

Tsuta'tsinâsûñ'yĭ: "Where it eddies," a deep hole at the mouth of Cockram creek of Cheowa river, in Graham county, where is an eddy said to be caused by a buffalo which lives under the water at this spot, and which anciently lived at the mouth of West Buffalo creek, farther up the river.

Tusquittee bald: A bald mountain at the head of Tusquittee creek, eastward from Hayesville, in Clay county. The Cherokee name is Tsuwă'-uniyetsûñ'yĭ, "Where the water-dogs laughed," the water-dog of the southern Alleghenies, sometimes also called mud-puppy or hell-bender, being a large amphibious lizard or salamander of the genus *Menopoma*, frequenting muddy waters. According to the story, a hunter once crossing over the mountain in a very dry season, heard voices, and creeping silently toward the place from which the sound proceeded, peeped over a rock and saw two water-dogs walking together on their hind legs along the trail and talking as they went. Their pond had dried up and they were on the way over to Nantahala river. As he listened one said to the other, "Where's the water? I'm so thirsty that my apron (gills) hangs down," and then both water-dogs laughed.

Ukṭe'na-tsuganûñ'tatsûñ'yĭ: "Where the uktena got fastened," a spot on Tuckasegee river, about 2 miles above Deep creek, near Bryson City, in Swain county. There is a tradition that an uktena, trying to make his way upstream, became fastened here, and in his struggles pried up some large rocks now lying in the bed of the river, and left deep scratches upon other rocks along the bank.

Ukṭe'na-utansi'nastûñ'yĭ: "Where the uktena crawled," a large rock on the Hyatt farm, on the north bank of Tuckasegee river, about four miles above Bryson City, in Swain county. In the rock bed of the stream and along the rocks on the side are wavy depressions said to have been made by an uktena in going up the river.

Untlasgâsti'yĭ: "Where they scratched," at the head of Hyatt creek, of Valley river, in Cherokee county. According to hunting tradition, every animal on arriving at this spot was accustomed to scratch the ground like a turkey.

VENGEANCE CREEK: A south tributary of Valley river, in Cherokee county. So called by the first settlers from an old Indian woman who lived there and whom they nicknamed "Vengeance," on account of her cross looks. The Cherokee call the district Gănsaʻti′yĭ, "Robbing place," from their having robbed a trader there in the Revolution.

WAYA GAP: A gap in the Nantahala mountains, in Macon county, where the trail crosses from Laurel creek of Nantahala river to Cartoogajə creek of the Little Tennessee. The Cherokee call it A′tâhi′ta, "Shouting place." For the tradition see number 13. It was the scene of a stubborn encounter in the Revolution (see page 49). The name Waya appears to be from the Cherokee wă′ya, "wolf."

WEBSTER: The county seat of Jackson county, on Tuckasegee river. Known to the Cherokee as Unadanti′yĭ, "Where they conjured." The name properly belongs to a gap 3 miles east of Webster, on the trail going up Scotts creek. According to tradition, a war party of Shawano, coming from the direction of Pigeon river, halted here to "make medicine" against the Cherokee, but while thus engaged were surprised by the latter, who came up from behind and killed several, including the conjurer.

YÂ′NÛ-DINĔHÛÑ′YĬ: "Where the bears live," on Oconaluftee river, about a mile above its junction with Tuckasegee, in Swain county. A family of "water bears" is said to live at the bottom of the river in a deep hole at this point.

YÂ′NÛ-U′NĂTAWASTI′YĬ: "Where the bears wash," a small pond of very cold, purple water, which has no outlet and is now nearly dried up, in a gap of the Great Smoky mountains, at the extreme head of Raven fork of Oconaluftee, in Swain county. It was said to be a favorite bear wallow, and according to some accounts its waters had the same virtues ascribed to those of Atagâ′hĭ (see number 69).

YAWÂ′Ĭ: "Yawa place," a spot on the south side of Yellow creek of Cheowa river, in Graham county, about a mile above the trail crossing near the mouth of the creek. The legend is that a mysterious personage, apparently a human being, formerly haunted a round knob near there, and was sometimes seen walking about the top of the knob and crying, Yawă′! Yawă′! while the sound of invisible guns came from the hill, so that the people were afraid to go near it.

123. LOCAL LEGENDS OF SOUTH CAROLINA

As the Cherokee withdrew from all of South Carolina except a small strip in the extreme west as early as 1777, the memory of the old legends localized within the state has completely faded from the tribe. There remain, however, some local names upon which the whites who succeeded to the inheritance have built traditions of more or less doubtful authenticity.

In Pickens and Anderson counties, in the northwest corner of the state, is a series of creeks joining Keowee river and named, respectively in order, from above downward, Mile, Six-mile, Twelve-mile, Eighteen-mile, Twenty-three-mile, and Twenty-six-mile. According to the local story, they were thus christened by a young woman, in one of the early Indian wars, as she crossed each ford on a rapid horseback flight to the lower settlements to secure help for the beleaguered garrison of Fort Prince George. The names really date back almost to the first establishment of the colony, and were intended to indicate roughly the distances along the old trading path from Fort Ninety-six, on Henleys creek of Saluda river, to Keowee, at that time the frontier town of the Cherokee Nation, the two points being considered 96 miles apart as the trail ran. Fort Prince George was on the east bank of Keowee river, near the entrance of Crow creek, and directly opposite the Indian town.

CONNEROSS: The name of a creek which enters Keowee (or Seneca) river from the west, in Anderson county; it is a corruption of the Lower Cherokee dialectic form, Kăwân'-urâ'sûñyĭ or Kăwân'-tsurâ'-sûñyĭ, "Where the duck fell off." According to the still surviving Cherokee tradition, a duck once had her nest upon a cliff overlooking the stream in a cave with the mouth so placed that in leaving the nest she appeared to fall from the cliff into the water. There was probably an Indian settlement of the same name.

TOXAWAY: The name of a creek and former Cherokee settlement at the extreme head of Keowee river; it has been incorrectly rendered "Place of shedding tears," from daksăwa'ihû, "he is shedding tears." The correct Cherokee form of the name is Dûksa'ĭ or Dûkw'sa'ĭ, a word which can not be analyzed and of which the meaning is now lost.

124. LOCAL LEGENDS OF TENNESSEE

For the more important legends localized in Tennessee see the stories The Hunter in the Dăkwă', The Nest of the Tlă'nuwă, The Removed Townhouses, The Haunted Whirlpool, Ûñtsaiyĭ', and Uʻtlûñ'ta.

BUFFALO TRACK ROCK: This rock, of which the Indian name is now lost, is indefinitely mentioned as located southwest from Cumberland gap, on the northern border of the state. According to Wafford, it was well known some eighty years ago to the old Cherokee hunters, who described it as covered with deep impressions made by buffalo running along the rock and then butting their heads, as though in mad fury, against a rock wall, leaving the prints of their heads and horns in the stone.

CHATTANOOGA: This city, upon Tennessee river, near the entrance of the creek of the same name in Hamilton county, was incorporated in 1848. So far as is known there was no Cherokee settlement at the place, although some prominent men of the tribe lived in the vicinity. The name originally belonged to some location upon the creek. The Cherokee pronounce it Tsatănu'gĭ, but say that it is not a Cherokee word and has no meaning in their language. The best informants express the opinion that it was from the Chickasaw (Choctaw) language, which seems possible, as the Chickasaw country anciently extended a considerable distance up the Tennessee, the nearest settlement being within 80 miles of the present city. The Cherokee sometimes call the city A'tlă'nuwă', "Tlă'nuwă (Hawk) hole," that being their old name for a bluff on the south side of the river at the foot of the present Market street. From this circumstance probably originated the statement by a magazine writer that the name Chattanooga signifies "The crow's nest."

CHICKAMAUGA: The name of two creeks in Hamilton county, entering Tennessee river from opposite sides a few miles above Chattanooga. A creek of the same name is one of the head-streams of Chattahoochee river, in White county, Georgia. The Cherokee pronounce it Tsĭkăma'gĭ, applying the name in Tennessee to the territory about the mouth of the southern, or principal, stream, where they formerly had a town, from which they removed in 1782. They state, however, that it is not a Cherokee word and has no meaning in their language. Filson, in 1793, erroneously states that it is from the Cherokee language and signifies "Boiling pot," referring to a dangerous whirlpool in the river near by, and later writers have improved upon this by translating it to mean "Whirlpool." The error arises from confounding this place with The Suck, a whirlpool in Tennessee river 15 miles farther down and known to the Cherokee as Ûñtiguhĭ', "Pot in the water" (see number 63, "Ûñtsaiyĭ', the Gambler"). On account of the hard fighting in the neighborhood during the Civil war, the stream was sometimes called, poetically, "The River of Death," the term being frequently given as a translation of the Indian word. It has been suggested that the name is derived from an Algonquian word referring to a fishing or fish-spearing place, in which case it may have originated with the Shawano, who formerly occupied middle Tennessee, and some of whom at a later period resided jointly with the Cherokee in the settlements along this part of the river. If not Shawano it is probably from the Creek or Chickasaw.

Concerning "Chickamauga gulch," a canyon on the northern stream of that name, a newspaper writer gives the following so-called legend, which it is hardly necessary to say is not genuine:

The Cherokees were a tribe singularly rich in tradition, and of course so wild, gloomy, and remarkable a spot was not without its legend. The descendants of the expatriated semi-barbarians believe to this day that in ages gone a great serpent made its den in the gulch, and that yearly he demanded of the red men ten of their most beautiful maidens as a sacrificial offering. Fearful of extermination, the demand was always complied with by the tribe, amid weeping and wailing by the women. On the day before the tribute was due the serpent announced its presence by a demoniacal hiss, and the next morning the fair ones who had been chosen to save the tribe were taken to the summit of a cliff and left to be swallowed by the scaly Moloch.

CHILHOWEE: A mountain and station on the north side of Little Tennessee river, in Blount county. The correct Cherokee form is Tsû′lûñwe′ĭ, applied to the lower part of Abrams creek, which enters the river from the north just above. The meaning of the word is lost, although it may possibly have a connection with *tsû′lû*, "king-fisher." It has been incorrectly rendered "fire deer," an interpretation founded on the false assumption that the name is compounded from *atsi′la*, "fire," and *a'wĭ′*, "deer," whence Chil-howee. For legends localized in this vicinity, see the stories noted above. Chilhowee occurs also as the name of a stream in the mountains of southwestern Virginia.

LENOIR: On the north bank of the main Tennessee, at the junction of the Little Tennessee, in Loudon county. The Cherokee name is Wa′gĭnsĭ′, of which the meaning is lost, and was applied originally to an eddy in the stream, where, it was said, there dwelt a large serpent, to see which was an omen of evil. On one occasion a man crossing the river at this point saw the snake in the water and soon afterward lost one of his children.

MORGANTON: On a rocky hill on the old Indian trail on the west side of Little Tennessee river, above and nearly opposite Morganton, in Loudon county, are, or were a few years ago, four trees blazed in a peculiar manner, concerning which the Indians had several unsatisfactory stories, the most common opinion being that the marks were very old and had been made by Indians to indicate the position of hidden mines.

NASHVILLE: The state capital, in Davidson county. The Cherokee name is Dăgû′năwelâ′hĭ, "Mussel-liver place," which would seem to have originated in some now forgotten legend.

NICKAJACK: A creek entering Tennessee river from the south about 15 miles below Chattanooga. Near its mouth is a noted cave of the same name. The Cherokee form is Nĭkutse′gĭ, the name of a former settlement of that tribe at the mouth of the creek; but the word has no meaning in that language, and is probably of foreign, perhaps Chickasaw, origin. The derivation from a certain "Nigger Jack," said to have made the cave his headquarters is purely fanciful.

SAVANNAH: A farm on the north bank of Hiwassee river at a ford of the same name, about 5 miles above Conasauga creek and Columbus, in Polk county. Here are extensive remains of an ancient settlement, including mounds, cemetery, and also, some seventy years ago, a small square inclosure or "fort" of undressed stone. According to a tradition given to Wafford, the Cherokee once prepared an ambush here for a hostile war party which they were expecting to come up the river, but were themselves defeated by the enemy, who made a detour around the Black mountain and came in upon their rear.

TENNESSEE: The Cherokee form is Tănăsĭ′, and was applied to several localities within the old territory of the tribe. The most important town of this name was on the south bank of Little Tennessee river, halfway between Citico and Toco creeks, in Monroe county, Tennessee. Another was on the south side of Hiwassee, just above the junction of Ocoee, in Polk county, Tennessee. A third district of the same name was on Tennessee creek, the extreme easterly head of Tuckasegee river, in Jackson county, North Carolina. The meaning of the name is lost. It was not the Indian name of the river, and does not mean "Big spoon," as has been incorrectly asserted.

125. LOCAL LEGENDS OF GEORGIA

For more important legends localized in Georgia see the stories Yahula, The Nûñnĕhĭ, The Ustû′tlĭ, Âgan-uni′tsĭ's Search for the Uktena, and The Man who Married the Thunder's Sister. White's Historical Collections of Georgia is responsible for a number of pseudo-myths.

CHOPPED OAK: A noted tree, scarred with hundreds of hatchet marks, formerly in Habersham county, 6 miles east of Clarkesville, on the summit of Chattahoochee ridge, and on the north side of the road from Clarkesville to Toccoa creek. The Cherokee name is Digălu′yătûñ′yĭ, "Where it is gashed with hatchets." It was a favorite assembly place for the Indians, as well as for the early settlers, according to whom the gashes were tally marks by means of which the Indians kept the record of scalps taken in their forays. The tradition is thus given by White (Historical Collections of Georgia, p. 489, 1855) on some earlier authority:

Among the curiosities of this country was the Chopped Oak, a tree famous in Indian history and in the traditions of the early settlers. This tree stood about 6 miles southeast of Clarkesville, and was noted as being the Law Ground, or place of holding company musters and magistrates' courts. According to tradition, the Chopped Oak was a celebrated rendezvous of the Indians in their predatory excursions, it being at a point where a number of trails met. Here their plans of warfare were laid; here the several parties separated; and here, on their return, they awaited each other; and then, in their brief language, the result of their enterprise was stated, and for every scalp taken a gash cut in the tree. If tradition tells the truth, and every scar on the blasted oak counts for a scalp, the success of their scouting parties must have been great. This tree was alive a few years since when a young man, possessing all the prejudices of his countrymen, and caring less for the traditions of the Indians than his own revenge, killed the tree by girdling it, that it might be no longer a living monument of the cruelties of the savages. The stump is still standing.

DEAD MAN'S GAP: One mile below Tallulah falls, on the west side of
the railroad, in Habersham county. So called from a former reputed
Indian grave, now almost obliterated. According to the story, it was
the grave of an Indian who was killed here while eloping with a white
woman, whom he had stolen from her husband.

FROGTOWN: A creek at the head of Chestatee river, north of Dahlonega, in Lumpkin county. The Cherokee name is Walâsi'yĭ, "Frog
place." The name was originally applied to a mountain to the northeast (Rock mountain ?), from a tradition that a hunter had once seen
there a frog as large as a house. The Indian settlement along the
creek bore the same name.

HIWASSEE: A river having its source in Towns county, of northern
Georgia, and flowing northwestward to join the Tennessee. The correct Cherokee form, applied to two former settlements on the stream, is
Ayuhwa'sĭ (meaning "A savanna"). Although there is no especial
Cherokee story connected with the name, White (Historical Collections
of Georgia, p. 660) makes it the subject of a long pseudo-myth, in
which Hiwassee, rendered "The Pretty Fawn," is the beautiful
daughter of a Catawba chief, and is wooed, and at last won, by a
young Cherokee warrior named Notley, "The Daring Horseman,"
who finally becomes the head chief of the Cherokee and succeeds in
making perpetual peace between the two tribes. The story sounds
very pretty, but is a pure invention.

NACOOCHEE: A village on the site of a former Cherokee settlement,
in a beautiful and fertile valley of the same name at the head of Chattahoochee river, in White county. The Cherokee form is Nagu'tsĭ',
but the word has no meaning in that language and seems to be of foreign, perhaps Creek, origin. About 2 miles above the village, on the
east bank of the river, is a large mound. White (Historical Collections of Georgia, p. 486) quotes a fictitious legend, according to which
Nacoochee, "The Evening Star," was a beautiful Indian princess, who
unfortunately fell in love with a chieftain of a hostile tribe and was
killed, together with her lover, while fleeing from the vengeance of
an angry father. The two were buried in the same grave and the
mound was raised over the spot. The only grain of truth in the story
is that the name has a slight resemblance to *năkwĭsĭ'*, the Cherokee
word for "star."

NOTTELY: A river rising in Union county and flowing northwestward into Hiwassee. The Cherokee form is Na'dû'lĭ', applied to a
former settlement on the west side of the river, in Cherokee county,
North Carolina, about a mile from the Georgia line. Although suggestive of *na'tû'lĭ*, "spicewood," it is a different word and has no meaning in the Cherokee language, being apparently of foreign, perhaps
Creek, origin. For a pseudo-myth connected with the name, see the
preceding note on Hiwassee.

TALKING ROCK: A creek in upper Georgia flowing northward to join Coosawatee river. The Indian settlements upon it were considered as belonging to Sanderstown, on the lower part of the creek, the townhouse being located about a mile above the present Talking Rock station on the west side of the railroad. The name is a translation of the Cherokee Nûñyû′-gûñwani′skĭ, "Rock that talks," and refers, according to one informant, to an echo rock somewhere upon the stream below the present railroad station. An old-time trader among the Cherokee in Georgia says that the name was applied to a rock at which the Indians formerly held their councils, but the etymology of the word is against this derivation.

TALLULAH: A river in Rabun county, northeastern Georgia, which flows into the Tugaloo, and has a beautiful fall about 2 miles above its mouth. The Cherokee form is Tălulŭ′ (Tărurĭ′ in the lower Cherokee dialect), the name of an ancient settlement some distance above the falls, as also of a creek and district at the head of Cheowa river, in Graham county, North Carolina. The name can not be translated. A magazine writer has rendered it "The Terrible," for which there is no authority. Schoolcraft, on the authority of a Cherokee lady, renders it "There lies your child," derived from a story of a child having been carried over the falls. The name, however, was not applied to the falls, but to a district on the stream above, as well as to another in North Carolina. The error arises from the fact that a word of somewhat similar sound denotes "having children" or "being pregnant," used in speaking of a woman. One informant derives it from tălulŭ′, the cry of a certain species of frog known as dulusĭ, which is found in that neighborhood, but not upon the reservation, and which was formerly eaten as food. A possible derivation is from a′tălulŭ′, "unfinished, premature, unsuccessful." The fall was called Ugûñ′yĭ, a name of which the meaning is lost, and which was applied also to a locality on Little Tennessee river near Franklin, North Carolina. For a myth localized at Tallulah falls, see number 84, "The Man who Married the Thunder's Sister."

In this connection Lanman gives the following story, which, notwithstanding its white man's dress, appears to be based upon a genuine Cherokee tradition of the Nûññĕ′hĭ:

During my stay at the Falls of Tallulah I made every effort to obtain an Indian legend or two connected with them, and it was my good fortune to hear one which has never yet been printed. It was originally obtained by the white man who first discovered the falls from the Cherokees, who lived in the region at the time. It is in substance as follows: Many generations ago it so happened that several famous hunters, who had wandered from the West toward what is now the Savannah river, in search of game, never returned to their camping grounds. In process of time the curiosity as well as the fears of the nation were excited, and an effort was made to ascertain the cause of their singular disappearance, whereupon a party of medicine men were deputed to make a pilgrimage toward the great river. They were absent a whole moon, and, on returning to their friends, they reported that they had discovered a dreadful fissure in an unknown part of the country, through which a mountain torrent took its way with a deafening noise. They said that it was an exceedingly wild place, and that its inhabitants were a species of little men and women, who dwelt in the crevices of the rocks and in grottoes under the waterfalls. They had attempted by every artifice in their power to hold a council with the little people, but all in vain; and, from the shrieks they frequently uttered, the medicine men knew that they were the enemies of the Indian race, and, therefore, it was concluded in the nation at large that the long-lost hunters had been decoyed to their death in the dreadful gorge, which they called Tallulah. In view of this little legend, it is worthy of remark that the Cherokee nation, previous to their departure for the distant West, always avoided the Falls of Tallulah, and were seldom found hunting or fishing in their vicinity.[1]

TOCCOA: (1) A creek flowing into Tugaloo river, in Habersham county, with a fall upon its upper course, near the village of the same name. (2) A river in upper Georgia, flowing northwestward into Hiwassee. The correct Cherokee form applied to the former settlement on both streams is Tagwâ'hĭ, "Catawba place," implying the former presence of Indians of that tribe. The lands about Toccoa falls were sold by the Cherokee in 1783 and were owned at one time by Wafford's grandfather. According to Wafford, there was a tradition that when the whites first visited the place they saw, as they thought, an Indian woman walking beneath the surface of the water under the falls, and on looking again a moment after they saw her sitting upon an overhanging rock 200 feet in the air, with her feet dangling over. Said Wafford, "She must have been one of the Nûñně'hĭ."

TRACK ROCK GAP: A gap about 5 miles east of Blairsville, in Union county, on the ridge separating Brasstown creek from the waters of Nottely river. The micaceous soapstone rocks on both sides of the trail are covered with petroglyphs, from which the gap takes its name. The Cherokee call the place Datsu'nalâsgûñ'yĭ, "Where there are tracks," or Degayelûñ'hă, "Printed (Branded) place." The carvings are of many and various patterns, some of them resembling human or animal footprints, while others are squares, crosses, circles, "bird tracks," etc., disposed without any apparent order. On the authority of a Doctor Stevenson, writing in 1834, White (Historical Collections of Georgia, p. 658, 1855), and after him Jones (Antiquities of the Southern Indians, 1873), give a misleading and greatly exaggerated account of these carvings, without having taken the trouble to investigate for themselves, although the spot is easily accessible. No effort, either state or local, is made to preserve the pictographs from destruction, and many of the finest have been cut out from the rock and carried off by vandals, Stevenson himself being among the number, by his own confession. The illustration (plate XX) is from a rough sketch made by the author in 1890.

The Cherokee have various theories to account for the origin of the carvings, the more sensible Indians saying that they were made by

---

[1] Letters from the Alleghany Mountains, pages 41–42.

hunters for their own amusement while resting in the gap. Another tradition is that they were made while the surface of the newly created earth was still soft by a great army of birds and animals fleeing through the gap to escape some pursuing danger from the west—some say a great "drive hunt" of the Indians. Haywood confounds them with other petroglyphs in North Carolina connected with the story of the giant Tsul'kălû' (see number 81).

The following florid account of the carvings and ostensible Indian tradition of their origin is from White, on the authority of Stevenson:

> The number visible or defined is 136, some of them quite natural and perfect, and others rather rude imitations, and most of them from the effects of time have become more or less obliterated. They comprise human feet from those 4 inches in length to those of great warriors which measure 17½ inches in length and 7¾ in breadth across the toes. What is a little curious, all the human feet are natural except this, which has 6 toes, proving him to have been a descendant of Titan. There are 26 of these impressions, all bare except one, which has the appearance of having worn moccasins. A fine turned hand, rather delicate, occupied a place near the great warrior, and probably the impression of his wife's hand, who no doubt accompanied her husband in all his excursions, sharing his toils and soothing his cares away. Many horse tracks are to be seen. One seems to have been shod, some are very small, and one measures 12½ inches by 9½ inches. This the Cherokee say was the footprint of the great war horse which their chieftain rode. The tracks of a great many turkeys, turtles, terrapins, a large bear's paw, a snake's trail, and the footprints of two deer are to be seen. The tradition respecting these impressions varies. One asserts that the world was once deluged with water, and men with all animated beings were destroyed, except one family, together with various animals necessary to replenish the earth; that the Great Spirit before the floods came commanded them to embark in a big canoe, which after long sailing was drawn to this spot by a bevy of swans and rested there, and here the whole troop of animals was disembarked, leaving the impressions as they passed over the rock, which being softened by reason of long submersion kindly received and preserved them.

WAR WOMAN'S CREEK: Enters Chattooga river in Rabun county, northeastern Georgia, in the heart of the old Lower Cherokee country. The name seems to be of Indian origin, although the Cherokee name is lost and the story has perished. A writer quoted by White (Historical Collections of Georgia, p. 444) attempts to show its origin from the exploit of a certain Revolutionary amazon, in capturing a party of Tories, but the name occurs in Adair (note, p. 185) as early as 1775. There is some reason for believing that it refers to a former female dignitary among the Cherokee, described by Haywood under the title of the "Pretty Woman" as having authority to decide the fate of prisoners of war. Wafford once knew an old woman whose name was Da'nă-gâ'stă, an abbreviated form for Da'năwă-gâsta'yă, "Sharp war," understood to mean "Sharp (i., e., Fierce) warrior." Several cases of women acting the part of warriors are on record among the Cherokee.

126. PLANT LORE

The Cherokee have always been an agricultural people, and their old country is a region of luxuriant flora, with tall trees and tangled undergrowth on the slopes and ridges, and myriad bright-tinted blossoms and sweet wild fruits along the running streams. The vegetable kingdom consequently holds a far more important place in the mythology and ceremonial of the tribe than it does among the Indians of the treeless plains and arid sage deserts of the West, most of the beliefs and customs in this connection centering around the practice of medicine, as expounded by the priests and doctors in every settlement. In general it is held that the plant world is friendly to the human species, and constantly at the willing service of the doctors to counteract the jealous hostility of the animals. The sacred formulas contain many curious instructions for the gathering and preparation of the medicinal roots and barks, which are selected chiefly in accordance with the theory of correspondences.

The Indians are close observers, and some of their plant names are peculiarly apt. Thus the mistletoe, which never grows alone, but is found always with its roots fixed in the bark of some supporting tree or shrub from which it draws its sustenance, is called by a name which signifies "it is married" (*uda'lĭ*). The violet is still called by a plural name, *dinda'skwate'skĭ*, "they pull each other's heads off," showing that the Cherokee children have discovered a game not unknown among our own. The bear-grass (*Eryngium*), with its long, slender leaves like diminutive blades of corn, is called *sălikwâ'yĭ*, "greensnake," and the larger grass known as Job's tears, on account of its glossy, rounded grains, which the Indian children use for necklaces, is called *sel-utsĭ'*, "the mother of corn." The black-eyed Susan (*Rudbeckia*) of our children is the "deer-eye" (*a'wĭ'-aktă'*) of the Cherokee, and our lady-slipper (*Cypripedium*) is their "partridge moccasin" (*gŭgwĕ'-ulasu'la*). The May-apple (*Podophyllum*), with its umbrella-shaped top, is called *u'niskwetu'gĭ*, meaning "it wears a hat," while the white puffball fungus is *năkwĭsĭ'-usdĭ'*, "the little star," and the common rock lichen bears the musical, if rather unpoetic, name of *utsăle'ta*, "pot scrapings." Some plants are named from their real or supposed place in the animal economy, as the wild rose, *tsist-uni'gistĭ*, "the rabbits eat it"—referring to the seed berries—and the shield fern (*Aspidium*), *yân-utse'stû*, "the bear lies on it." Others, again, are named from their domestic or ceremonial uses, as the fleabane (*Erigeron canadense*), called *atsil'-sûñ'tĭ*, "fire maker," because its dried stalk was anciently employed in producing fire by friction, and the bugle weed (*Lycopus virginicus*), known as *aniwani'skĭ*, "talkers," because the chewed root, given to children to swallow, or rubbed upon their lips, is supposed to endow them with the gift of eloquence. Some few, in addition to the ordinary term in use among the common people, have a sacred or symbolic name, used only by the priests and doctors in the prayer formulas. Thus ginseng, or "sang," as it is more often called by the white mountaineers, is known to the laity as â'talĭ-gûlĭ', "the mountain climber," but is addressed in the formulas as Yûñwĭ Usdi', "Little Man," while selu (corn) is invoked under the name of Agawe'la, "The Old Woman." One or two plant names have their origin in myths, as, for instance, that of Prosartes lanuginosa, which bears the curious name of walâs'-unûl'stĭ, "frogs fight with it," from a story that in the long ago—hĭlahi'yu—two quarrelsome frogs once fought a duel, using its stalks as lances. In the locative form this was the name of a former Cherokee settlement in Georgia, called by the whites Fighting-town, from a misapprehension of the meaning of the word. Of the white clover, the Cherokee say that "it follows the white man."

The division of trees into evergreen and deciduous is accounted for by a myth, related elsewhere, according to which the loss of their leaves in winter time is a punishment visited upon the latter for their failure to endure an ordeal to the end. With the Cherokee, as with nearly all other tribes east and west, the cedar is held sacred above other trees. The reasons for this reverence are easily found in its ever-living green, its balsamic fragrance, and the beautiful color of its fine-grained wood, unwarping and practically undecaying. The small green twigs are thrown upon the fire as incense in certain ceremonies, particularly to counteract the effect of asgina dreams, as it is believed that the anisgi'na or malevolent ghosts can not endure the smell; but the wood itself is considered too sacred to be used as fuel. In the war dance, the scalp trophies, stretched on small hoops, were hung upon a cedar sapling trimmed and decorated for the occasion. According to a myth the red color comes originally from the blood of a wicked magician, whose severed head was hung at the top of a tall cedar. The story is now almost forgotten, but it was probably nearly identical with one still existing among the Yuchi, former neighbors of the Cherokee. According to the Yuchi myth, a malevolent magician disturbed the daily course of the sun until at last two brave warriors sought him out and killed him in his cave. They cut off his head and brought it home with them to show to the people, but it continued still alive. To make it die they were advised to tie it in the topmost branches of a tree. This they did, trying one tree after another, but each morning the head was found at the foot of the tree and still alive. At last they tied it in a cedar, and there the head remained until it was dead, while the blood slowly trickling down along the trunk gave the wood its red color, and henceforth the cedar was a "medicine" tree.[1]

The linn or basswood (Tilia) is believed never to be struck by lightning, and the hunter caught in one of the frequent thunderstorms of

---

[1] Gatschet, Some Mythic Stories of the Yuchi Indians, in American Anthropologist, VI, p. 281, July, 1893.

the southern mountains always seeks its shelter. From its stringy bark are twisted the hunting belts worn about the waist. Sourwood (*Oxydendrum*) is used by the hunters for barbecue sticks to roast meat before the fire, on account of the acid flavor of the wood, which they believe to be thus communicated to the meat. Spoons and combs are also carved from the wood, but it is never burned, from an idea that lye made from the ashes will bring sickness to those who use it in preparing their food. It is said also that if one should sleep beside a fire containing sourwood sticks the sourwood "will barbecue him," which may possibly mean that he will have hot or feverish pains thereafter.

The laurel, in its two varieties, large and small (*Rhododendron* and *Kalmia*, or "ivy"), is much used for spoons and combs, on account of its close grain, as also in medicine, but is never burned, as it is believed that this would bring on cold weather, and would furthermore destroy the medicinal virtues of the whole species. The reason given is that the leaves, when burning, make a hissing sound suggestive of winter winds and falling snow. When the doctor is making up a compound in which any part of the laurel is an ingredient, great precautions are taken to prevent any of the leaves or twigs being swept into the fire, as this would render the decoction worthless. Sassafras is tabued as fuel among the Cherokee, as also among their white neighbors, perhaps for the practical reason that it is apt to pop out of the fire when heated and might thus set the house on fire.

Pounded walnut bark is thrown into small streams to stupefy the fish, so that they may be easily dipped out in baskets as they float on the surface of the water. Should a pregnant woman wade into the stream at the time, its effect is nullified, unless she has first taken the precaution to tie a strip of the bark about her toe. A fire of post-oak and the wood of the *telûñ'lătĭ* or summer grape (*Vitis æstivalis*) is believed to bring a spell of warm weather even in the coldest winter season.

Mysterious properties attach to the wood of a tree which has been struck by lightning, especially when the tree itself still lives, and such wood enters largely into the secret compounds of the conjurers. An ordinary person of the laity will not touch it, for fear of having cracks come upon his hands and feet, nor is it burned for fuel, for fear that lye made from the ashes will cause consumption. In preparing ballplayers for the contest, the medicine-man sometimes burns splinters of it to coal, which he gives to the players to paint themselves with in order that they may be able to strike their opponents with all the force of a thunderbolt. Bark or wood from a tree struck by lightning, but still green, is beaten up and put into the water in which seeds are soaked before planting, to insure a good crop, but, on the other hand, any lightning-struck wood thrown into the field will cause the crop to wither, and it is believed to have a bad effect even to go into the field immediately after having been near such a tree.

Among all vegetables the one which holds first place in the household economy and ceremonial observance of the tribe is *selu*, "corn," invoked in the sacred formulas under the name of Agawe'la, "The Old Woman," in allusion to its mythic origin from the blood of an old woman killed by her disobedient sons (see number 3, "Kana'tĭ and Selu"). In former times the annual thanksgiving ceremony of the Green-corn dance, preliminary to eating the first new corn, was the most solemn tribal function, a propitiation and expiation for the sins of the past year, an amnesty for public criminals, and a prayer for happiness and prosperity for the year to come. Only those who had properly prepared themselves by prayer, fasting, and purification were allowed to take part in this ceremony, and no one dared to taste the new corn until then. Seven ears from the last year's crop were always put carefully aside, in order to *attract the corn* until the new crop was ripened and it was time for the dance, when they were eaten with the rest. In eating the first new corn after the Green Corn dance, care was observed not to blow upon it to cool it, for fear of causing a wind storm to beat down the standing crop in the field.

Much ceremony accompanied the planting and tending of the crop. Seven grains, the sacred number, were put into each hill, and these were not afterward thinned out. After the last working of the crop, the priest and an assistant—generally the owner of the field—went into the field and built a small inclosure (*detsănûñ'lĭ*) in the center. Then entering it, they seated themselves upon the ground, with heads bent down, and while the assistant kept perfect silence the priest, with rattle in hand, sang songs of invocation to the spirit of the corn. Soon, according to the orthodox belief, a loud rustling would be heard outside, which they would know was caused by the "Old Woman" bringing the corn into the field, but neither must look up until the song was finished. This ceremony was repeated on four successive nights, after which no one entered the field for seven other nights, when the priest himself went in, and, if all the sacred regulations had been properly observed, was rewarded by finding young ears upon the stalks. The corn ceremonies could be performed by the owner of the field himself, provided he was willing to pay a sufficient fee to the priest in order to learn the songs and ritual. Care was always taken to keep a clean trail from the field to the house, so that the corn might be encouraged to stay at home and not go wandering elsewhere. Most of these customs have now fallen into disuse excepting among the old people, by many of whom they are still religiously observed.

Another curious ceremony, of which even the memory is now almost forgotten, was enacted after the first working of the corn, when the owner or priest stood in succession at each of the four corners of the field and wept and wailed loudly. Even the priests are now unable to give a reason for this performance, which may have been a lament for the bloody death of Selu, as the women of Byblos were wont to weep for Adonis.

Next to corn, the bean (*tuya*) is the most important food plant of the Cherokee and other southern Indians, with whom it is probably native, but there does not appear to be much special ceremony or folklore in connection with it. Beans which crack open in cooking are sometimes rubbed by mothers on the lips of their children in order to make them look smiling and good-tempered. The association of ideas seems to be the same as that which in Ireland causes a fat mealy potato, which cracks open in boiling, to be called a "laughing" potato. Melons and squashes must not be counted or examined too closely, while still growing upon the vine, or they will cease to thrive; neither must one step over the vine, or it will wither before the fruit ripens. One who has eaten a May-apple must not come near the vines under any circumstances, as this plant withers and dries up very quickly, and its presence would make the melons wither in the same way.

Tobacco was used as a sacred incense or as the guarantee of a solemn oath in nearly every important function—in binding the warrior to take up the hatchet against the enemy, in ratifying the treaty of peace, in confirming sales or other engagements, in seeking omens for the hunter, in driving away witches or evil spirits, and in regular medical practice. It was either smoked in the pipe or sprinkled upon the fire, never rolled into cigarettes, as among the tribes of the Southwest, neither was it ever smoked for the mere pleasure of the sensation. Of late years white neighbors have taught the Indians to chew it, but the habit is not aboriginal. It is called *tsâlû*, a name which has lost its meaning in the Cherokee language, but is explained from the cognate Tuscarora, in which *charhû'*, "tobacco," can still be analyzed as "fire to hold in the mouth," showing that the use is as old as the knowledge of the plant. The tobacco originally in use among the Cherokee, Iroquois, and other eastern tribes was not the common tobacco of commerce (*Nicotiana tabacum*), which has been introduced from the West Indies, but the *Nicotiana rustica*, or wild tobacco, now distinguished by the Cherokee as *tsâl-agăyûñ'li*, "old tobacco," and by the Iroquois as "real tobacco." Its various uses in ritual and medicine are better described under other headings. For the myth of its loss and recovery see number 6, "How They Brought Back the Tobacco." The cardinal flower (*Lobelia*), mullein (*Verbascum*), and one or two related species are called *tsâliyu'stĭ*, "like tobacco," on account of their general resemblance to it in appearance, but they were never used in the same way.

The poisonous wild parsnip (*Peucedanum*?) bears an unpleasant reputation on account of its frequent use in evil spells, especially those intended to destroy the life of the victim. In one of these conjurations seven pieces of the root are laid upon one hand and rubbed gently with the other, the omen being taken from the position of the pieces when the hand is removed. It is said also that poisoners mix it secretly with the food of their intended victim, when, if he eats, he soon becomes drowsy, and, unless kept in motion until the effect wears off, falls asleep, never to wake again. Suicides are said to eat it to procure death. Before starting on a journey a small piece of the root is sometimes chewed and blown upon the body to prevent sickness, but the remedy is almost as bad as the disease, for the snakes are said to resent the offensive smell by biting the one who carries it. In spite of its poisonous qualities, a decoction of the root is much used for steaming patients in the sweat bath, the idea seeming to be that the smell drives away the disease spirits.

The poison oak or poison ivy (*Rhus radicans*), so abundant in the damp eastern forests, is feared as much by Indians as by whites. When obliged to approach it or work in its vicinity, the Cherokee strives to conciliate it by addressing it as "My friend" (*hi'ginalĭi*). If poisoned by it, he rubs upon the affected part the beaten flesh of a crawfish.

One variety of brier (*Smilax*) is called *di″nŭ'skĭ*, "the breeder," from a belief that a thorn of it, if allowed to remain in the flesh, will breed others in a day or two.

Ginseng, which is sold in large quantities to the local traders, as well as used in the native medical practice, is called *âtalĭ-gûlĭ'*, "the mountain climber," but is addressed by the priests as Yûñwĭ Usdi', "Little Man," or Yûñwi Usdi'ga Ada'wehi'yu, "Little Man, Most Powerful Magician," the Cherokee sacred term, like the Chinese name, having its origin from the frequent resemblance of the root in shape to the body of a man. The beliefs and ceremonies in connection with its gathering and preparation are very numerous. The doctor speaks constantly of it as of a sentient being, and it is believed to be able to make itself invisible to those unworthy to gather it. In hunting it, the first three plants found are passed by. The fourth is taken, after a preliminary prayer, in which the doctor addresses it as the "Great Ada'wehĭ," and humbly asks permission to take a small piece of its flesh. On digging it from the ground, he drops into the hole a bead and covers it over, leaving it there, by way of payment to the plant spirit. After that he takes them as they come without further ceremony.

The catgut or devil's shoestring (*Tephrosia*) is called *distai'yĭ*, "they are tough," in allusion to its stringy roots, from which Cherokee women prepare a decoction with which to wash their hair in order to impart to it the strength and toughness of the plant, while a preparation of the leaves is used by ballplayers to wash themselves in order to toughen their limbs. To enable them to spring quickly to their feet if thrown to the ground, the players bathe their limbs also with a decoction of the small rush (*Juncus tenuis*), which, they say, always recovers its erect position, no matter how often trampled down. The white seeds of the viper's bugloss (*Echium vulgare*) were formerly used in many important ceremonies of which the purpose was to look into the future, but have now been superseded by the ordinary glass beads of the traders. The culver root (*Leptandra*) is used in love conjurations, the omen being taken from the motion of the root when held in the hand. The campion (*Silene stellata*), locally known as "rattlesnake's master," is called *ganidawâ'skĭ*, "it disjoints itself," because the dried stalk is said to break off by joints, beginning at the top. As among the white mountaineers, the juice is held to be a sovereign remedy for snake bites, and it is even believed that the deadliest snake will flee from one who carries a small portion of the root in his mouth.

Almost all varieties of burs, from the Spanish needle up to the cocklebur and Jimsonweed, are classed together under the generic name of *u'nistilûñ'istĭ*, which may be freely rendered as "stickers." From their habit of holding fast to whatever object they may happen to touch, they are believed to have an occult power for improving the memory and inducing stability of character. Very soon after a child is born, one of the smaller species, preferably the *Lespedeza repens*, is beaten up and a portion is put into a bowl of water taken from a fall or cataract, where the stream makes a constant noise. This is given to the child to drink on four successive days, with the intention of making him quick to learn and retain in memory anything once heard. The noise of the cataract from which the water is taken is believed to be the voice of Yûñwĭ Gûnahi'ta, the "Long Man," or river god, teaching lessons which the child may understand, while the stream itself is revered for its power to seize and hold anything cast upon its surface. A somewhat similar ceremony is sometimes used for adults, but in this case the matter is altogether more difficult, as there are tabus for four or seven days, and the mind must be kept fixed upon the purpose of the rite throughout the whole period, while if the subject so far forgets himself as to lose his temper in that time he will remain of a quarrelsome disposition forever after.

A flowering vine, known as *nuniyu'stĭ*, "potato-like," which grows in cultivated fields, and has a tuberous root somewhat resembling a potato, is used in hunting conjurations. The bruised root, from which a milky juice oozes, is rubbed upon the deer bleat, *a'wĭ'-ahyelĭ'skĭ*, with which the hunter imitates the bleating of the fawn, under the idea that the doe, hearing it, will think that her offspring desires to suck, and will therefore come the sooner. The putty-root (Adam-and-Eve, *Aplectrum hiemale*), which is of an oily, mucilaginous nature, is carried by the deer hunter, who, on shooting a deer, puts a small piece of the chewed root into the wound, expecting as a necessary result to find the animal unusually fat when skinned. Infants which seem to pine and grow thin are bathed with a decoction of the same root in order to fatten them. The root of the rare plant known as Venus' flytrap (*Dionæa*), which has the remarkable property of catching and digesting insects which alight upon it, is chewed by the fisherman and spit upon the bait that no fish may escape him, and the plant is tied upon the fish trap for the same purpose.

The root of a plant called *unatlûñwe'hitû*, "having spirals," is used in conjurations designed to predispose strangers in favor of the subject. The priest "takes it to water"—i. e., says certain prayers over it while standing close to the running stream, then chews a small piece and rubs and blows it upon the body and arms of the patient, who is supposed to be about to start upon a journey, or to take part in a council, with the result that all who meet him or listen to his words are at once pleased with his manner and appearance, and disposed to give every assistance to his projects.

NOTES AND PARALLELS TO MYTHS

In the preparation of the following notes and parallels the purpose has been to incorporate every Cherokee variant or pseudomyth obtainable from any source, and to give some explanation of tribal customs and beliefs touched upon in the myths, particularly among the Southern tribes. A certain number of parallels have been incorporated, but it must be obvious that this field is' too vast for treatment within the limits of a single volume. Moreover, in view of the small number of tribes that have yet been studied, in comparison with the great number still unstudied, it is very doubtful whether the time has arrived for any extended treatment of Indian mythology. The most complete index of parallels that has yet appeared is that accompanying the splendid collection by Dr Franz Boas, Indianische Sagen von der nordpacifischen Küste Amerikas.[1] In drawing the line it has been found necessary to restrict comparisons, excepting in a few special cases, to the territory of the United States or the immediate border country, although this compels the omission of several of the best collections, particularly from the northwest coast and the interior of British America. Enough has been given to show that our native tribes had myths of their own without borrowing from other races, and that these were so widely and constantly disseminated by trade and travel and interchange of ceremonial over wide areas as to make the Indian myth system as much a unit in this country as was the Aryan myth structure in Europe and Asia. Every additional tribal study may be expected to corroborate this result.

A more special study of Cherokee myths in their connection with the medical and religious ritual of the tribe is reserved for a future paper, of which preliminary presentation has been given in the author's Sacred Formulas of the Cherokees, in the Seventh Annual Report of the Bureau of Ethnology.

STORIES AND STORY TELLERS (p. 229): *Migration legend*—In Buttrick's Antiquities[2] we find some notice of this migration legend, which, as given by the missionary, is unfortunately so badly mixed up with the Bible story that it is almost impossible to isolate the genuine. He starts them under the leadership of their "greatest prophet," Wâsĭ—who is simply Moses—in search of a far distant country where they may be safe from their enemies. Who these enemies are, or in what quarter they live, is not stated. Soon after setting out they come to a great water, which

---

[1] Asher & Co., Berlin, 1895.

[2] Antiquities of the Cherokee Indians, compiled from the collection of Reverend Sabin Buttrick, their missionary from 1817 to 1847, as presented in the Indian Chieftain; Vinita, Indian Territory, 1884.

Wâsĭ strikes with his staff; the water divides so that they pass through safely, and then rolls back and prevents pursuit by their enemies. They then enter a wilderness and come to a mountain, and we are treated to the Bible story of Sinai and the tables of stone. Here also they receive sacred fire from heaven, which thereafter they carry with them until the house in which it is kept is at last destroyed by a hostile invasion. This portion of the myth seems to be genuine Indian (see notes to number 111, "The Mounds and the Constant Fire").

In this journey "the tribes marched separately and also the clans. The clans were distinguished by having feathers of different colors fastened to their ears. They had two great standards, one white and one red. The white standard was under the control of the priests, and used for civil purposes; but the red standard was under the direction of the war priests, for purposes of war and alarm. These were carried when they journeyed, and the white standard erected in front of the building above mentioned [the ark or palladium], when they rested."

They cross four rivers in all—which accords with the Indian idea of the sacred four—and sit down at last beyond the fourth, after having been for many years on the march. "Their whole journey through this wilderness was attended with great distress and danger. At one time they were beset by the most deadly kind of serpents, which destroyed a great many of the people, but at length their leader shot one with an arrow and drove them away. Again, they were walking along in single file, when the ground cracked open and a number of people sank down and were destroyed by the earth closing upon them. At another time they came nigh perishing for water. Their head men dug with their staves in all the low places, but could find no water. At length their leader found a most beautiful spring coming out of a rock."[1]

At one point in this migration, according to a tradition given to Schoolcraft by Stand Watie, they encountered a large river or other great body of water, which they crossed upon a bridge made by tying grapevines together.[2] This idea of a vine bridge or ladder occurs also in the traditions of the Iroquois, Mandan, and other tribes.

Farther on the missionary already quoted says: "Shield-eater once inquired if I ever heard of houses with flat roofs, saying that his father's great grandfather used to say that once their people had a great town, with a high wall about it; that on a certain occasion their enemies broke down a part of this wall; that the houses in this town had flat roofs—though, he used to say, this was so long ago it is not worth talking about now."[3]

Fire of cane splints—Bartram thus describes the method as witnessed by him at Attasse (Autossee) among the Creeks about 1775. The fire which blazed up so mysteriously may have been kept constantly smoldering below, as described in number 111:

"As their virgils [sic] and manner of conducting their vespers and mystical fire in this rotunda, are extremely singular, and altogether different from the customs and usages of any other people, I shall proceed to describe them. In the first place, the governor or officer who has the management of this business, with his servants attending, orders the black drink to be brewed, which is a decoction or infusion of the leaves and tender shoots of the cassine. This is done under an open shed or pavilion, at twenty or thirty yards distance, directly opposite the door of the council-house. Next he orders bundles of dry canes to be brought in: these are previously split and broken in pieces to about the length of two feet, and then placed obliquely crossways upon one another on the floor, forming a spiral circle round about the great centre pillar, rising to a foot or eighteen inches in height from the ground; and this circle spreading as it proceeds round and round, often repeated from right to

---

[1] Buttrick, Antiquities of the Cherokee Indians, pp. 9–10.
[2] Schoolcraft, Notes on the Iroquois, p. 359, 1847.
[3] Buttrick, op. cit., p. 10.

left, every revolution increases its diameter, and at length extends to the distance of ten or twelve feet from the centre, more or less, according to the length of time the assembly or meeting is to continue. By the time these preparations are accomplished, it is night, and the assembly have taken their seats in order. The exterior or outer end of the spiral circle takes fire and immediately rises into a bright flame (but how this is effected I did not plainly apprehend; I saw no person set fire to it; there might have been fire left on the earth; however I neither saw nor smelt fire or smoke until the blaze instantly ascended upwards), which gradually and slowly creeps round the centre pillar, with the course of the sun, feeding on the dry canes, and affords a cheerful, gentle and sufficient light until the circle is consumed, when the council breaks up." [1]

1. How THE WORLD WAS MADE (p. 239): From decay of the old tradition and admixture of Bible ideas the Cherokee genesis myth is too far broken down to be recovered excepting in disjointed fragments. The completeness of the destruction may be judged by studying the similar myth of the Iroquois or the Ojibwa. What is here preserved was obtained chiefly from Swimmer and John Ax, the two most competent authorities of the eastern band. The evergreen story is from Ta'gwădihĭ'. The incident of the brother striking his sister with a fish to make her pregnant was given by Ayâsta, and may have a phallic meaning. John Ax says the pregnancy was brought about by the "Little People," Yuñwĭ Tsunsdi', who commanded the woman to rub spittle (of the brother?) upon her back, and to lie upon her breast, with her body completely covered, for seven days and nights, at the end of which period the child was born, and another thereafter every seven days until the period was made longer. According to Wafford the first man was created blind and remained so for some time. The incident of the buzzard shaping the mountains occurs also in the genesis myth of the Creeks [2] and Yuchi, [3] southern neighbors of the Cherokee, but by them the first earth is said to have been brought up from under the water by the crawfish. Among the northern tribes it is commonly the turtle which continues to support the earth upon its back. The water beetle referred to is the *Gyrinus*, locally known as mellow bug or apple beetle. One variant makes the *dilsta'ya'tĭ*, waterspider ("scissors," *Dolomedes*), help in the work. Nothing is said as to whence the sun is obtained. By some tribes it is believed to be a gaming wheel stolen from a race of superior beings. See also number 7, "The Journey to the Sunrise."

The missionaries Buttrick and Washburn give versions of the Cherokee genesis, both of which are so badly warped by Bible interpretation as to be worthless. No native cosmogonic myth yet recorded goes back to the first act of creation, but all start out with a world and living creatures already in existence, though not in their final form and condition.

Hand-breadth—The Cherokee word is *utawá'hilú*, from *uwáyĭ*, hand. This is not to be taken literally, but is a figurative expression much used in the sacred formulas to denote a serial interval of space. The idea of successive removals of the sun, in order to modify the excessive heat, is found with other tribes. Buttrick, already quoted, says in his statement of the Cherokee cosmogony: "When God created the world he made a heaven or firmament about as high as the tops of the mountains, but this was too warm. He then created a second, which was also too warm. He thus proceeded till he had created seven heavens and in the seventh fixed His abode. During some of their prayers they raise their hands to the first, second, third, fourth, fifth, sixth and seventh heaven," etc. [4]

---

[1] Travels, pp. 449–450.

[2] W. O. Tuggle, Myths of the Creeks, MS, 1887. Copy in archives of the Bureau of American Ethnology.

[3] A. S. Gatschet, Some Mythic Stories of the Yuchi Indians, in American Anthropologist, VI, p. 281, July, 1893.

[4] Antiquities.

In Hindu cosmogony also we find seven heavens or stages, increasing in sanctity as they ascend; the Aztecs had nine, as had also the ancient Scandinavians.[1] Some Polynesian tribes have ten, each built of azure stone, with apertures for intercommunication. The lowest originally almost touched the earth and was elevated to its present position by successive pushes from the gods Ru and Matti, resting first prostrate upon the ground, then upon their knees, then lifting with their shoulders, their hands, and their finger tips, until a last supreme effort sent it to its present place.[2]

Seven: The sacred numbers—In every tribe and cult throughout the world we find sacred numbers. Christianity and the Christian world have three and seven. The Indian has always four as the principal sacred number, with usually another only slightly subordinated. The two sacred numbers of the Cherokee are four and seven, the latter being the actual number of the tribal clans, the formulistic number of upper worlds or heavens, and the ceremonial number of paragraphs or repetitions in the principal formulas. Thus in the prayers for long life the priest raises his client by successive stages to the first, second, third, fourth, and finally to the seventh heaven before the end is accomplished. The sacred four has direct relation to the four cardinal points, while seven, besides these, includes also "above," "below," and "here in the center." In many tribal rituals color and sometimes sex are assigned to each point of direction. In the sacred Cherokee formulas the spirits of the East, South, West, and North are, respectively, Red, White, Black, and Blue, and each color has also its own symbolic meaning of Power (War), Peace, Death, and Defeat.

2. THE FIRST FIRE (p. 240): This myth was obtained from Swimmer and John Ax. It is noted also in Foster's "Sequoyah"[3] and in the Wahnenauhi manuscript.[4] The uksu'hĭ and the gûle'gĭ are, respectively, the *Coluber obsoletus* and *Bascanion constrictor*. The water-spider is the large hairy species *Argyroneta*.

In the version given in the Wahnenauhi manuscript the Possum and the Buzzard first make the trial, but come back unsuccessful, one losing the hair from his tail, while the other has the feathers scorched from his head and neck. In another version the Dragon-fly assists the Water-spider by pushing the tusti from behind. In the corresponding Creek myth, as given in the Tuggle manuscript, the Rabbit obtains fire by the stratagem of touching to the blaze a cap trimmed with sticks of rosin, while pretending to bend low in the dance. In the Jicarilla myth the Fox steals fire by wrapping cedar bark around his tail and thrusting it into the blaze while dancing around the circle.[5]

3. KANA'TĬ AND SELU: ORIGIN OF CORN AND GAME (p. 242): This story was obtained in nearly the same form from Swimmer and John Ax (east) and from Wafford (west), and a version is also given in the Wahnenauhi manuscript. Hagar notes it briefly in his manuscript Stellar Legends of the Cherokee. So much of belief and custom depend upon the myth of Kana'tĭ that references to the principal incidents are constant in the songs and formulas. It is one of those myths held so sacred that in the old days one who wished to hear it from the priest of the tradition must first purify himself by "going to water," i. e., bathing in the running stream before daylight when still fasting, while the priest performed his mystic ceremonies upon the bank.

In his Letters from the Alleghany Mountains, written more than fifty years ago, Lanman gives (pp. 136, 137) a very fair synopsis of this myth, locating the game

[1] E. G. Squier, The Serpent Symbol and the Worship of the Reciprocal Principles of Nature in America (Am. Archæological Researches, 1); New York, 1851.
[2] Rev. Wm. W. Gill, Myths and Songs from the South Pacific, with a preface by F. Max Müller; London, 1876, pp. 18, 21, 58, 71.
[3] G. E. Foster, Sequoyah, the American Cadmus and Modern Moses; Philadelphia, Indian Rights Association, 1885.
[4] Historical Sketches of the Cherokees, together with some of their Customs, Traditions, and Superstitions, by Wahnenauhi, a Cherokee Indian; MS in archives of the Bureau of American Ethnology.
[5] Frank Russell, Myths of the Jicarilla Apaches, in Journal of Am. Folklore, October, 1898.

preserve of Kana'tĭ, whom he makes an old Cherokee chief, in a (traditional) cave on the north side of the Black mountain, now Mount Mitchell, in Yancey county, North Carolina, the highest peak east of the Rocky mountains. After his father had disappeared, and could not be found by long search, "The boy fired an arrow towards the north, but it returned and fell at his feet, and he knew that his father had not travelled in that direction. He also fired one towards the east and the south and the west, but they all came back in the same manner. He then thought that he would fire one directly above his head, and it so happened that this arrow never returned, and so the boy knew that his father had gone to the spirit land. The Great Spirit was angry with the Cherokee nation, and to punish it for the offense of the foolish boy he tore away the cave from the side of the Black mountain and left only a large cliff in its place, which is now a conspicuous feature, and he then declared that the time would come when another race of men should possess the mountains where the Cherokees had flourished for many generations."

The story has numerous parallels in Indian myth, so many in fact that almost every important concept occurring in it is duplicated in the North, in the South, and on the plains, and will probably be found also west of the mountains when sufficient material of that region shall have been collected. The Ojibwa story of "The Ween-digoes,"[1] in particular, has many striking points of resemblance; so, also, the Omaha myth, "Two-faces and the Twin Brothers," as given by Dorsey.[2]

His wife was Selu, "Corn"—In Cherokee belief, as in the mythologies of nearly every eastern tribe, the corn spirit is a woman, and the plant itself has sprung originally from the blood drops or the dead body of the Corn Woman. In the Cherokee sacred formulas the corn is sometimes invoked as Agawe'la, "The Old Woman," and one myth (number 72, "The Hunter and Selu") tells how a hunter once witnessed the transformation of the growing stalk into a beautiful woman.

In the Creek myth "Origin of Indian Corn," as given in the Tuggle manuscript, the corn plant appears to be the transformed body of an old woman whose only son, endowed with magic powers, has developed from a single drop of her (menstrual?) blood.

In Iroquois legend, according to Morgan, the corn plant sprang from the bosom of the mother of the Great Spirit (*sic*) after her burial. The spirits of corn, bean, and squash are represented as three sisters. "They are supposed to have the forms of beautiful females, to be very fond of each other, and to delight to dwell together. This last belief is illustrated by a natural adaptation of the plants themselves to grow up together in the same field and perhaps from the same hill." [3]

Sprang from blood—This concept of a child born of blood drops reappears in the Cherokee story of Tsul'kälû' (see number 81). Its occurrence among the Creeks has just been noted. It is found also among the Dakota (Dorsey, "The Blood-clots Boy," in Contributions to North American Ethnology, IX, 1893), Omaha (Dorsey, "The Rabbit and the Grizzly Bear," Cont. to N. A. Eth., VI, 1890), Blackfeet ("Kutoyis," in Grinnell, "Blackfoot Lodge Tales"; New York, 1892), and other tribes. Usually the child thus born is of wilder and more mischievous nature than is common.

Deer shut up in hole—The Indian belief that the game animals were originally shut up in a cave, from which they were afterward released by accident or trickery, is very widespread. In the Tuggle version of the Creek account of the creation of the earth we find the deer thus shut up and afterward set free. The Iroquois "believed that the game animals were not always free, but were enclosed in a cavern

---

[1] H. R. Schoolcraft, Algic Researches, Comprising Inquiries Respecting the Mental Characteristics of the North American Indians; first series, Indian Tales and Legends (two volumes); New York, 1839.

[2] The Dhegiha Language, in Contributions to North American Ethnology, VI (Department of the Interior, U. S. Geographical and Geological Survey of the Rocky Mountain Region. J. W. Powell in charge), Washington, D. C.

[3] League of the Iroquois, pp. 161, 162, and 199.

where they had been concealed by Tawiskara'; but that they might increase and fill the forest Yoskehă' gave them freedom."[1]   The same idea occurs in the Omaha story of "Ictinike, the Brothers and Sister" (Dorsey, in Contributions to North American Ethnology, VI, 1890).   The Kiowa tell how the buffalo were kept thus imprisoned by the Crow until released by Sinti when the people were all starving for want of meat.   When the buffalo so suddenly and completely disappeared from the plains about twenty-five years ago, the prairie tribes were unable to realize that it had been exterminated, but for a long time cherished the belief that it had been again shut up by the superior power of the whites in some underground prison, from which the spells of their own medicine men would yet bring it back (see references in the author's Calendar History of the Kiowa Indians, in Seventeenth Annual Report of the Bureau of American Ethnology, part 1, 1901).   The Kiowa tradition is almost exactly paralleled among the Jicarilla (Russell, Myths of the Jicarilla Apaches, in Journal of American Folk-Lore, Oct., 1898).

Storehouse—The unwadă′lĭ, or storehouse for corn, beans, dried pumpkins, and other provisions, was a feature of every Cherokee homestead and was probably common to all the southern tribes.   Lawson thus describes it among the Santee in South Carolina about the year 1700:

"They make themselves cribs after a very curious manner, wherein they secure their corn from vermin, which are more frequent in these warm climates than in countries more distant from the sun.   These pretty fabrics are commonly supported with eight feet or posts about seven feet high from the ground, well daubed within and without upon laths, with loam or clay, which makes them tight and fit to keep out the smallest insect, there being a small door at the gable end, which is made of the same composition and to be removed at pleasure, being no bigger than that a slender man may creep in at, cementing the door up with the same earth when they take the corn out of the crib and are going from home, always finding their granaries in the same posture they left them—theft to each other being altogether unpracticed."[2]

Rubbed her stomach—This miraculous procuring of provisions by rubbing the body occurs also in number 76, "The Bear Man."

Knew their thoughts—Mind reading is a frequent concept in Indian myth and occurs in more than one Cherokee story.

Seven times—The idea of sacred numbers has already been noted, and the constant recurrence of seven in the present myth exemplifies well the importance of that number in Cherokee ritual.

A tuft of down—In the Omaha story, "The Corn Woman and the Buffalo Woman" (Dorsey, Contributions to North American Ethnology, VI, 1890), the magician changes himself into a feather and allows himself to be blown about by the wind in order to accomplish his purpose.   The wolf does the same in a Thompson River myth.[3]   The self-transformation of the hero into a tuft of bird's down, a feather, a leaf, or some other light object, which is then carried by the wind wherever he wishes to go, is very common in Indian myth.

Play ball against them—This is a Cherokee figurative expression for a contest of any kind, more particularly a battle.

Left an open space—When the Cherokee conjurer, by his magic spells, coils the great (invisible) serpent around the house of a sick man to keep off the witches, he is always careful to leave a small space between the head and tail of the snake, so that the members of the family can go down to the spring to get water.

---

[1] Hewitt, Cosmogonic Gods of the Iroquois, in Proc. Am. Ass. Adv. Sci., XLIV, 1895.

[2] History of Carolina, ed. 1860, p. 35.

[3] Traditions of the Thompson River Indians of British Columbia, collected and annotated by James Teit, with introduction by Franz Boas (Memoirs of the American Folk-Lore Society, VI); Boston and New York, 1898, p. 74.

Wolves—The wolf is regarded as the servant and watchdog of Kana′tĭ. See number 15, "The Fourfooted Tribes."

From these have come all—In nearly every Indian mythology we find the idea of certain animal tribes being descended from a single survivor of some great slaughter by an early hero god or trickster. Thus the Kiowa say that all the prairie dogs on the plains are descended from a single little fellow who was too wary to close his eyes, as his companions did, when the hungry vagrant Sinti was planning to capture them all for his dinner under pretense of teaching them a new dance.

A gaming wheel—This was the stone wheel or circular disk used in the wheel-and-stick game called by the Cherokee gatayûstĭ, and which in one form or another was practically universal among the tribes. It was the game played by the great mythic gambler Ûñtsaiyĭ′ (see number 63). It has sometimes been known in the north as the "snow-snake," while to the early southern traders it was known as *chuñki* or *chungkey*, a corruption of the Creek name. Timberlake (page 77) mentions it under the name of *nettecawaw*—for which there seems to be no other authority—as he saw it among the Cherokee in 1762.[1] It was also noted among the Carolina tribes by Lederer in 1670 and Lawson in 1701. John Ax, the oldest man now living among the East Cherokee, is the only one remaining in the tribe who has ever played the game, having been instructed in it when a small boy by an old man who desired to keep up the memory of the ancient things. The sticks used have long since disappeared, but the stones remain, being frequently picked up in the plowed fields, especially in the neighborhood of mounds. The best description of the southern game is given by Adair:

"They have near their state house a square piece of ground well cleaned, and fine sand is carefully strewed over it, when requisite, to promote a swifter motion to what they throw along the surface. Only one, or two on a side, play at this ancient game. They have a stone about two fingers broad at the edge and two spans round. Each party has a pole of about eight feet long, smooth, and tapering at each end, the points flat. They set off abreast of each other at 6 yards from the end of the playground; then one of them hurls the stone on its edge, in as direct a line as he can, a considerable distance toward the middle of the other end of the square. When they have ran [*sic*] a few yards each darts his pole, anointed with bear's oil, with a proper force, as near as he can guess in proportion to the motion of the stone, that the end may lie close to the stone. When this is the case, the person counts two of the game, and in proportion to the nearness of the poles to the mark, one is counted, unless by measuring both are found to be at an equal distance from the stone. In this manner the players will keep running most part of the day at half speed, under the violent heat of the sun, staking their silver ornaments, their nose, finger and ear rings; their breast, arm and wrist plates, and even all their wearing apparel except that which barely covers their middle. All the American Indians are much addicted to this game, which to us appears to be a task of stupid drudgery. It seems, however, to be of early origin, when their forefathers used diversions as simple as their manners. The hurling stones they use at present were time immemorial rubbed smooth on the rocks, and with prodigious labour. They are kept with the strictest religious care from one generation to another, and are exempted from being buried with the dead. They belong to the town where they are used, and are carefully preserved."[2]

In one version of the Kana′tĭ myth the wheel is an arrow, which the wild boy shoots toward the four cardinal points and finally straight upward, when it comes back no more. When they get above the sky they find Kana′tĭ and Selu sitting together, with the arrow sticking in the ground in front of them. In the Creek story, "The Lion [Panther?] and the Little Girl," of the Tuggle collection, the lion has a wheel "which could find anything that was lost."

---

[1] Memoirs, p. 77.
[2] History of the American Indians, p. 401.

The twilight land—Usûñhi′yĭ, "Where it is always growing dark," the spirit land in the west. This is the word constantly used in the sacred formulas to denote the west, instead of the ordinary word Wude′ligûñ′yĭ, "Where it sets." In the same way Nûñdâ′yĭ, or Nûñdâgûñ′yĭ, the "Sun place, or region," is the formulistic name for the east instead of Digălûñgûñ′yĭ, "Where it [i. e., the sun] comes up," the ordinary term. These archaic expressions give to myths and formulas a peculiar beauty which is lost in the translation. As the interpreter once said, "I love to hear these old words."

Struck by lightning—With the American tribes, as in Europe, a mysterious potency attaches to the wood of a tree which has been struck by lightning. The Cherokee conjurers claim to do wonderful things by means of such wood. Splinters of it are frequently buried in the field to make the corn grow. It must not be forgotten that the boys in this myth are Thunder Boys.

The end of the world—See notes to number 7, "The Journey to the Sunrise."

Anisga′ya Tsunsdi′—Abbreviated from Anisga′ya Tsunsdi′ga, "Little Men." These two sons of Kana′ti, who are sometimes called Thunder Boys and who live in in Usûñhi′yĭ above the sky vault, must not be confounded with the Yûñwĭ Tsunsdi′, or "Little People," who are also Thunderers, but who live in caves of the rocks and cause the short, sharp claps of thunder. There is also the Great Thunderer, the thunder of the whirlwind and the hurricane, who seems to be identical with Kana′tĭ himself.

Deer songs—The Indian hunters of the olden time had many songs intended to call up the deer and the bear. Most of these have perished, but a few are still remembered. They were sung by the hunter, with some accompanying ceremony, to a sweetly plaintive tune, either before starting out or on reaching the hunting ground.

One Cherokee deer song, sung with repetition, may be freely rendered:

> O Deer, you stand close by the tree,
> You sweeten your saliva with acorns,
> Now you are standing near,
> You have come where your food rests on the ground.

Gatschet, in his Creek Migration Legend (i, p. 79), gives the following translation of a Hichitee deer hunting song:

> Somewhere (the deer) lies on the ground, I think; I walk about.
>> Awake, arise, stand up!
> It is raising up its head, I believe; I walk about.
>> Awake, arise, stand up!
> It attempts to rise, I believe; I walk about.
>> Awake, arise, stand up!
> Slowly it raises its body, I think; I walk about.
>> Awake, arise, stand up!
> It has now risen on its feet, I presume; I walk about.
>> Awake, arise, stand up!

4. ORIGIN OF DISEASE AND MEDICINE (p. 250): This myth was obtained first from Swimmer, as explaining the theory upon which is based the medical practice of the Cherokee doctor. It was afterward heard, with less detail, from John Ax (east) and James Wafford (west). It was originally published in the author's Sacred Formulas of the Cherokees, in the Seventh Annual Report of the Bureau of Ethnology.

In the mythology of most Indian tribes, as well as of primitive peoples generally, disease is caused by animal spirits, ghosts, or witchcraft, and the doctor's efforts are directed chiefly to driving out the malevolent spirit. In Creek belief, according to the Tuggle manuscript, "all disease is caused by the winds, which are born in the air and then descend to the earth." It is doubtful, however, if this statement is intended to apply to more than a few classes of disease, and another myth in the same collection recites that "once upon a time the beasts, birds, and reptiles held a council to devise means to destroy the enemy, man." For an extended discussion of the Indian medical theory, see the author's paper mentioned above.

Animal chiefs and tribes—For an exposition of the Cherokee theory of the tribal organization of the animals, with townhouses and councils, under such chiefs as the White Bear, the Little Deer, etc., see number 15, "The Fourfooted Tribes."

Kuwa'hĭ mountain—"The Mulberry place," one of the high peaks in the Great Smoky mountains, on the dividing line between Swain county, North Carolina, and Sevier county, Tennessee. The bears have a townhouse under it.

Ask the bear's pardon—See number 15, "The Fourfooted Tribes," and notes.

The ground squirrel's stripes—According to a Creek myth in the Tuggle collection the stripes on the back of the ground squirrel were made by the bear, who scratched the little fellow in anger at a council held by the animals to decide upon the proper division of day and night. Precisely the same explanation is given by the Iroquois of New York state[1] and by the Thompson River Indians of British Columbia.[2]

5. THE DAUGHTER OF THE SUN: ORIGIN OF DEATH (p. 252): This is one of the principal myths of the Cherokee, and like most of its class, has several variants. The sequel has an obvious resemblance to the myth of Pandora. It was obtained in whole or in part from Swimmer, John Ax, James Blythe, and others of the eastern band. The version mainly followed is that of Swimmer, which differs in important details from that of John Ax.

As told by John Ax, it is the Sun herself, instead of her daughter, who is killed, the daughter having been assigned the duty of lighting the earth after the death of her mother, the original Sun. The only snakes mentioned are the Spreading Adder and the Rattlesnake, the first being a transformed man, while the other is a stick, upon which the Little Men cut seven rings before throwing it in the pathway of the Sun, where it becomes a rattlesnake. The seven rods or staves of the Swimmer version are with John Ax seven corncobs, which are thrown at the girl as she passes in the dance (cf. Hagar variant of number 8 in notes). The Little Men (see number 3, "Kana'tĭ and Selu," and other stories) belong to the John Ax version. The others have only a conjurer or chief to direct proceedings.

This myth is noted in the Payne manuscript, of date about 1835, quoted in Squier, Serpent Symbol, page 67: "The Cherokees state that a number of beings were engaged in the creation. The Sun was made first. The intention of the creators was that men should live always. But the Sun, when he passed over, told them that there was not land enough and that people had better die. At length the daughter of the Sun, who was with them, was bitten by a snake and died. The Sun, on his return, inquired for her and was told that she was dead. He then consented that human beings might live always, and told them to take a box and go where the spirit of his daughter was and bring it back to her body, charging them that when they got her spirit they should not open the box until they had arrived where her body was. However, impelled by curiosity, they opened it, contrary to the injunction of the Sun, and the spirit escaped; and then the fate of all men was decided, that they must die." This is copied without credit by Foster, Sequoyah, page 241.

Another version is thus given by the missionary Buttrick, who died in 1847, in his Antiquities of the Cherokee Indians, page 3: "Soon after the creation one of the family was bitten by a serpent and died. All possible means were resorted to to bring back life, but in vain. Being overcome in this first instance, the whole race was doomed to follow, not only to death, but to misery afterwards, as it was supposed

---

[1] Erminnie Smith, Myths of the Iroquois, in Second Annual Report of the Bureau of Ethnology, p. 86.

[2] Teit, Thompson River Traditions, p. 61.

that that person went to misery. Another tradition says that soon after the creation a young woman was bitten by a serpent and died, and her spirit went to a certain place, and the people were told that if they would get her spirit back to her body that the body would live again, and they would prevent the general mortality of the body. Some young men therefore started with a box to catch the spirit. They went to a place and saw it dancing about, and at length caught it in the box and shut the lid, so as to confine it, and started back. But the spirit kept constantly pleading with them to open the box, so as to afford a little light, but they hurried on until they arrived near the place where the body was, and then, on account of her peculiar urgency, they removed the lid a very little, and out flew the spirit and was gone, and with it all their hopes of immortality."

In a variant noted by Hagar the messengers carry four staves and are seven days traveling to the ghost country. "They found her dancing in the land of spirits. They struck her with the first 'stick,' it produced no effect—with the second, and she ceased to dance—with the third, and she looked around—with the fourth, and she came to them. They made a box and placed her in it." He was told by one informant: "Only one man ever returned from the land of souls. He went there in a dream after a snake had struck him in the forehead. He, Turkey-head, came back seven days after and described it all. The dead go eastward at first, then westward to the Land of Twilight. It is in the west in the sky, but not amongst the stars" (Stellar Legends of the Cherokee, MS, 1898).

In a Shawano myth a girl dies, and, after grieving long for her, her brother sets out to bring her back from the land of shadows. He travels west until he reaches the place where the earth and sky meet; then he goes through and climbs up on the other side until he comes to the house of a great beneficent spirit, who is designated, according to the Indian system of respect, as grandfather. On learning his errand this helper gives him "medicine" by which he will be able to enter the spirit world, and instructs him how and in what direction to proceed to find his sister. " He said she would be at a dance, and when she rose to join in the movement he must seize and ensconce her in the hollow of a reed with which he was furnished, and cover the orifice with the end of his finger." He does as directed, secures his sister, and returns to the house of his instructor, who transforms both into material beings again, and, after giving them sacred rituals to take back to their tribe, dismisses them by a shorter route through a trapdoor in the sky.[1]

In an Algonquian myth of New Brunswick a bereaved father seeks his son's soul in the spirit domain of Papkootpawut, the Indian Pluto, who gives it to him in the shape of a nut, which he is told to insert in his son's body, when the boy will come to life. He puts it into a pouch, and returns with the friends who had accompanied him. Preparations are made for a dance of rejoicing. "The father, wishing to take part in it, gave his son's soul to the keeping of a squaw who stood by. Being curious to see it, she opened the bag, on which it escaped at once and took its flight for the realms of Papkootpawut."[2] In a myth from British Columbia two brothers go upon a similar errand to bring back their mother's soul. After crossing over a great lake they approach the shore of the spirit world and hear the sound of singing and dancing in the distance, but are stopped at the landing by a sentinel, who tells them: " Your mother is here, but you cannot enter alive to see her, neither can you take her away." One of them said, "I must see her!" Then the man took his body or mortal part away from him and he entered. The other brother came back.[3]

---

[1] Josiah Gregg, The Commerce of the Prairies, or The Journal of a Santa Fe Trader During Eight Expeditions across the Great Western Prairies and a Residence of Nearly Nine Years in Northern Mexico; vol. II, pp. 239–240; New York and London, 1844.

[2] Francis Parkman, The Jesuits in North America in the Seventeenth Century, second edition, p. lxxxiii (quoting Le Clerc); Boston, 1867.

[3] Teit, Thompson River Traditions, p. 85.

In the ancient Egyptian legend of Râ and Isis, preserved in a Turin papyrus dating from the twentieth dynasty, the goddess Isis, wishing to force from the great god Râ, the sun, the secret of his power, sends a serpent to bite him, with the intention of demanding the secret for herself as the price of assistance. Taking some of her spittle, "Isis with her hand kneaded it together with the earth that was there. She made thereof a sacred serpent unto which she gave the form of a spear. She . . . cast it on the way which the great god traversed in his double kingdom whenever he would. The venerable god advanced, the gods who served him as their Pharaoh followed him, he went forth as on every day. Then the sacred serpent bit him. The divine god opened his mouth and his cry reached unto heaven . . . The poison seized on his flesh," etc.[1]

The sky vault—See other references in number 1, " How the World was Made;" number 3, "Kanati,and Selu," and number 7, "The Journey to the Sunrise."

My grandchildren—The Sun calls the people *tsûñgili′sĭ*, "my grandchildren," this being the term used by maternal grandparents, the corresponding term used by paternal grandparents being *tsûñgini′sĭ*. The Moon calls the people *tsûñkina′tlĭ*, "my younger brothers," the term used by a male speaking, the Moon being personified as a man in Cherokee mythology. The corresponding term used by a female is *tsûñkită′*.

The Little Men—The Thunder Boys, sons of Kana′tĭ (see number 3, "Kana′tĭ and Selu"). They are always represented as beneficent wonder workers, of great power.

Changed to snakes—The Cherokee names of the rattlesnake (*Crotalus*), copperhead (*Trigonocephalus*), and spreading adder (*Heterodon*) are, respectively, *utsa′natĭ*, "he has a bell" (?); *wă′dige′ĭ askă′lĭ*, "red-brown head"; and *da′lĭkstă′*, "vomiter," from its habit of vomiting yellow slime, as is told in the story. For more concerning the Uktena see number 50, "The Uktena and the Ulûñsû′tĭ."

Hand-breadth—See note to number 1, "How the World was Made."

6. How they brought back the tobacco (p. 254): The first version of this myth as here given was obtained from Swimmer, and agrees with that of John Ax, except that for the humming bird the latter substitutes the *wasulû*, or large red-brown moth, which flies about the tobacco flower in the evening, and states that it was selected because it could fly so quietly that it would not be noticed. The second version was obtained from Wafford, in the Cherokee Nation west, who heard it from his greatuncle nearly ninety years ago, and differs so much from the other that it has seemed best to give it separately. The incident of the tree which grows taller as the man climbs it has close parallels in the mythology of the Kiowa and other Western tribes, but has no obvious connection with the story, and is probably either one of a series of adventures originally belonging to the trip or else a fragment from some otherwise forgotten myth. It may be mentioned that Wafford was a man of rather practical character, with but little interest or memory for stories, being able to fill in details of but few of the large number which he remembered having heard when a boy.

In his Letters from the Alleghany Mountains, pages 119–121, Lanman gives the story as he obtained it in 1848 from Chief Kâlahû (see p. 173), still well remembered by those who knew him as an authority upon tribal traditions and ritual. In the Kâlahû version the story is connected with Hickorynut gap, a remarkable pass in the Blue ridge southeast from Asheville, North Carolina, and a comparison with the later versions shows clearly how much has been lost in fifty years. The whole body of Cherokee tradition has probably suffered a proportionate loss.

"Before visiting this remarkable passage through the mountains [Hickorynut gap], I endeavored to ascertain, from the Cherokees of Qualla town, its original Indian

---

[1] Alfred Wiedemann, Religion of the Ancient Egyptians; New York, 1897, p. 55.

name, but without succeeding.   It was my good fortune, however, to obtain a romantic legend connected therewith.   I heard it from the lips of a chief who glories in the two names of All-bones and Flying-squirrel, and, though he occupied no less than two hours in telling the story, I will endeavor to give it to my readers in about five minutes.

"There was a time when the Cherokees were without the famous *tso-lungh*, or tobacco weed, with which they had previously been made acquainted by a wandering stranger from the far east.   Having smoked it in their large stone pipes, they became impatient to obtain it in abundance.   They ascertained that the country where it grew in the greatest quantities was situated on the big waters, and that the gateway to that country (a mighty gorge among the mountains) was perpetually guarded by an immense number of little people or spirits.   A council of the bravest men in the nation was called, and, while they were discussing the dangers of visiting the unknown country, and bringing therefrom a large knapsack of the fragrant tobacco, a young man stepped boldly forward and said that he would undertake the task.   The young warrior departed on his mission and never returned.   The Cherokee nation was now in great tribulation, and another council was held to decide upon a new measure.   At this council a celebrated magician rose and expressed his willingness to relieve his people of their difficulties, and informed them that he would visit the tobacco country and see what he could accomplish.   He turned himself into a mole, and as such made his appearance eastward of the mountains; but having been pursued by the guardian spirits, he was compelled to return without any spoil.   He next turned himself into a humming-bird, and thus succeeded, to a very limited extent, in obtaining what he needed.   On returning to his country he found a number of his friends at the point of death, on account of their intense desire for the fragrant weed; whereupon he placed some of it in a pipe, and, having blown the smoke into the nostrils of those who were sick, they all revived and were quite happy.   The magician now took into his head that he would revenge the loss of the young warrior, and at the same time become the sole possessor of all the tobacco in the unknown land.   He therefore turned himself into a whirlwind, and in passing through the Hickorynut gorge he stripped the mountains of their vegetation, and scattered huge rocks in every part of the narrow valley; whereupon the little people were all frightened away, and he was the only being in the country eastward of the mountains.   In the bed of a stream he found the bones of the young warrior, and having brought them to life, and turned himself into a man again, the twain returned to their own country heavily laden with tobacco; and ever since that time it has been very abundant throughout the entire land."

In the Iroquois story of "The Lad and the Chestnuts," the Cherokee myth is paralleled with the substitution of a chestnut tree guarded by a white heron for the tobacco plant watched by the dagûl'kû geese (see Smith, Myths of the Iroquois, in Second Annual Report Bureau of Ethnology, 1883).

Tobacco—Tobacco, as is well known, is of American origin and is sacred among nearly all our tribes, having an important place in almost every deliberative or religious ceremony.   The tobacco of commerce (*Nicotiana tabacum*) was introduced from the West Indies.   The original tobacco of the Cherokee and other eastern tribes was the "wild tobacco" (*Nicotiana rustica*), which they distinguish now as *tsâl-agayûñ'li*, "old tobacco."   By the Iroquois the same species is called the "real tobacco."

Dagûl'kû geese.—The dagûl'kû is the American white-fronted goose (*Anser albifrons gambeli*).   It is said to have been of bluish-white color, and to have been common in the low country toward the coast, but very rare in the mountains.   About the end of September it goes south, and can be heard at night flying far overhead and crying *dugalŭ! dugalŭ! dugalŭ!*   Swimmer had heard them passing over, but had never seen one.

7. The journey to the sunrise (p. 255): This story, obtained from John Ax, with additional details by Swimmer and Wafford. has parallels in many tribes. Swimmer did not know the burial incident, but said—evidently a more recent interpolation—that when they came near the sunrise they found there a race of black men at work. It is somewhat remarkable that the story has nothing to say of the travelers reaching the ocean, as the Cherokee were well aware of its proximity.

What the Sun is like—According to the Payne manuscript, already quoted, the Cherokee anciently believed that the world, the first man and woman, and the sun and moon were all created by a number of beneficent beings who came down for the purpose from an upper world, to which they afterward returned, leaving the sun and moon as their deputies to finish and rule the world thus created. "Hence whenever the believers in this system offer a prayer to their creator, they mean by the creator rather the Sun and Moon. As to which of these two was supreme, there seems to have been a wide difference of opinion. In some of their ancient prayers, they speak of the Sun as male, and consider, of course, the Moon as female. In others, however, they invoke the Moon as male and the Sun as female; because, as they say, the Moon is vigilant and travels by night. But both Sun and Moon, as we have before said, are adored as the creator. . . . The expression, 'Sun, my creator,' occurs frequently in their ancient prayers. Indeed, the Sun was generally considered the superior in their devotions" (quoted in Squier, Serpent Symbol, p. 68). Haywood, in 1823, says: "The sun they call the day moon or female, and the night moon the male" (Nat. and Aborig. Hist. Tenn., p. 266). According to Swimmer, there is also a tradition that the Sun was of cannibal habit, and in human form was once seen killing and devouring human beings. Sun and Moon are sister and brother. See number 8, "The Moon and the Thunders."

The Indians of Thompson river, British Columbia, say of the sun that formerly "He was a man and a cannibal, killing people on his travels every day. . . . He hung up the people whom he had killed during his day's travel when he reached home, taking down the bodies of those whom he had hung up the night before and eating them." He was finally induced to abandon his cannibal habit (Teit, Thompson River Traditions, p. 53).

In the same grave—This reminds us of the adventure in the voyage of Sinbad the Sailor, as narrated in the Arabian Nights. The sacrifice of the wife at her husband's funeral was an ancient custom in the Orient and in portions of Africa, and still survives in the Hindu suttee. It may once have had a counterpart in America, but so far as known to the author the nearest approach to it was found in the region of the lower Columbia and adjacent northwest coast, where a slave was frequently buried alive with the corpse.

Vault of solid rock—The sky vault which is constantly rising and falling at the horizon and crushes those who try to go beyond occurs in the mythologies of the Iroquois of New York, the Omaha and the Sioux of the plains, the Tillamook of Oregon, and other widely separated tribes. The Iroquois concept is given by Hewitt, "Rising and Falling of the Sky," in Iroquois Legends, in the American Anthropologist for October, 1892. In the Omaha story of "The Chief's Son and the Thunders" (Dorsey, Contributions to North American Ethnology, VI, 1890), a party of travelers in search of adventures "came to the end of the sky, and the end of the sky was going down into the ground." They tried to jump across, and all succeeded excepting one, who failed to clear the distance, and "the end of the sky carried him away under the ground." The others go on behind the other world and return the same way. In the Tillamook myth six men go traveling and reach "the lightning door, which opened and closed with great rapidity and force." They get through safely, but one is caught on the return and has his back cut in half by the descending sky (Boas, Traditions of the Tillamook Indians, in Journal of American Folk-Lore, Jan., 1898). See also number 1, "How the World was Made" and number 3, "Kana'tï and Selu."

8. THE MOON AND THE THUNDERS (p. 256): The story of the sun and the moon, as here given, was obtained first from Swimmer and afterward from other inform- ants. It is noted by Hagar, in his manuscript Stellar Legends of the Cherokee, one narrator making the girl blacken her brother's face with seven (charred?) corn cobs (cf. John Ax's version of number 5 in notes). Exactly the same myth is found with the native tribes of Greenland, Panama, Brazil, and Northern India. Among the Khasias of the Himalaya mountains "the changes of the moon are accounted for by the theory that this orb, who is a man, monthly falls in love with his wife's mother, who throws ashes in his face. The sun is female." On some northern branches of the Amazon "the moon is represented as a maiden who fell in love with her brother and visited him at night, but who was finally betrayed by his passing his blackened hand over her face." With the Greenland Eskimo the Sun and Moon are sister and brother, and were playing in the dark, "when Malina, being teased in a shameful manner by her brother Anninga, smeared her hands with the soot of the lamp and rubbed them over the face and hands of her persecutor, that she might recognize him by daylight. Hence arise the spots in the moon (see Timothy Har- ley, Moon Lore, London, 1885, and the story "The Sun and the Moon," in Henry Rink's Tales and Traditions of the Eskimo, London, 1875). In British Columbia the same incident occurs in the story of a girl and her lover, who was a dog trans- formed to the likeness of a man (Teit, Thompson River Traditions, p. 62). A very similar myth occurs among the Cheyenne, in which the chief personages are human, but the offspring of the connection become the Pleiades (A. L. Kroeber, Cheyenne Tales, in Journal of American Folk-Lore, July, 1900). In nearly all mythologies the Sun and Moon are sister and brother, the Moon being generally masculine, while the Sun is feminine (cf. German, Der Mond, Die Sonne).

The myth connecting the moon with the ballplay is from Haywood (Natural and Aboriginal History of Tennessee, p. 285), apparently on the authority of Charles Hicks, a mixed-blood chief.

Eclipse—Of the myth of the eclipse monster, which may be frightened away by all sorts of horrible noises, it is enough to say that it is universal (see Harley, Moon Lore). The Cherokee name for the phenomenon is *nûñdă' wală'sĭ u'gĭskă'*, "the frog is swallowing the sun or moon." Says Adair (History of the American Indians p. 65): "The first lunar eclipse I saw after I lived with the Indians was among the Cherokee, An. 1736, and during the continuance of it their conduct appeared very surprizing to one who had not seen the like before. They all ran wild, this way and that way, like lunatics, firing their guns, whooping and hallooing, beating of kettles, ringing horse bells, and making the most horrid noises that human beings possibly could. This was the effect of their natural philosophy and done to assist the suffering moon."

Sun and moon names—In probably every tribe both sun and moon are called by the same name, accompanied by a distinguishing adjective.

The Thunders—The Cherokee name for Thunder, Ani'-Hyûñ'tĭkwălă'skĭ, is an animate plural form and signifies literally, "The Thunderers" or "They who make the Thunder." The great Thunderers are Kana'tĭ and his sons (see the story), but inferior thunder spirits people all the cliffs and mountains, and more particularly the great waterfalls, such as Tallulah, whose never-ceasing roar is believed to be the voice of the Thunderers speaking to such as can understand. A similar conception prevailed among the Iroquois and the eastern tribes generally. Adair says (History of the American Indians, p. 65), speaking of the southern tribes: "I have heard them say, when it rained, thundered, and blew sharp for a considerable time, that the beloved or holy people were at war above the clouds; and they believe that the war at such times is moderate or hot in proportion to the noise and violence of the storm." In Portuguese West Africa also the Thunderers are twin brothers who quarreled and went, one to the east, the other to the west, whence each answers the other whenever a great storm arises.[1]   Among the plains tribes both thunder and lightning are caused by a great bird.

Rainbow—The conception of the rainbow as the beautiful dress of the Thunder god occurs also among the South Sea islanders.   In Mangaia it is the girdle of the god Tangaroa, which he loosens and allows to hang down until the end reaches to the earth whenever he wishes to descend (Gill, Myths and Songs of the South Pacific, p. 44).   For some unexplained reason the dread of pointing at the rainbow, on penalty of having the finger wither or become misshapen, is found among most of the tribes even to the Pacific coast.   The author first heard of it from a Puyallup boy of Puget sound, Washington.

9.   WHAT THE STARS ARE LIKE (p. 257): This story, told by Swimmer, embodies the old tribal belief.   By a different informant Hagar was told: "Stars are birds. We know this because one once shot from the sky to the ground, and some Cherokee who looked for it found a little bird, about the size of a chicken just hatched, where it fell" (MS Stellar Legends of the Cherokee, 1898).

The story closely resembles something heard by Lawson among the Tuscarora in eastern North Carolina about the year 1700.   An Indian having been killed by lightning, the people were assembled for the funeral, and the priest made them a long discourse upon the power of lightning over all men, animals, and plants, save only mice and the black-gum tree.   "At last he began to tell the most ridiculous absurd parcel of lies about lightning that could be; as that an Indian of that nation had once got lightning in the likeness of a partridge; that no other lightning could harm him whilst he had that about him; and that after he had kept it for several years it got away from him, so that he then became as liable to be struck with lightning as any other person.   There was present at the same time an Indian that had lived from his youth chiefly in an English house, so I called to him and told him what a parcel of lies the conjurer told, not doubting but he thought so as well as I; but I found to the contrary, for he replied that I was much mistaken, for the old man—who, I believe, was upwards of an hundred years old—did never tell lies; and as for what he said, it was very true, for he knew it himself to be so.   Thereupon seeing the fellow's ignorance, I talked no more about it" (History of Carolina, page 346).

According to Hagar a certain constellation of seven stars, which he identifies as the Hyades, is called by the Cherokee "The Arm," on account of its resemblance to a human arm bent at the elbow, and they say that it is the broken arm of a man who went up to the sky because, having been thus crippled, he was of no further use upon earth.

A meteor, and probably also a comet, is called *Atsil'-Tluñtû'tsĭ*, "Fire-panther," the same concept being found among the Shawano, embodied in the name of their great chief, Tecumtha (see p. 215).

10.   ORIGIN OF THE PLEIADES AND THE PINE (p. 258): This myth is well known in the tribe, and was told in nearly the same form by Swimmer, Ta'gwadihĭ' and Suyeta. The Feather dance, also called the Eagle dance, is one of the old favorites, and is the same as the ancient Calumet dance of the northern tribes.   For a description of the gatayû'stĭ game, see note to number 3, "Kana'ti and Selu."   In a variant recorded by Stansbury Hagar (MS Stellar Legends of the Cherokee) the boys spend their time shooting at cornstalks.

According to Squier (Serpent Symbol, p. 69), probably on the authority of the Payne manuscript, "The Cherokees paid a kind of veneration to the morning star, and also to the seven stars, with which they have connected a variety of legends, all of which, no doubt, are allegorical, although their significance is now unknown."

---

[1] Heli Chatelain, Folktales of Angola: Fifty Tales, with Ki-mbundu text, literal English translation, introduction, and notes (Memoirs of the American Folk-Lore Society, I); Boston and New York. 1894.

The corresponding Iroquois myth below, as given by Mrs Erminnie Smith in her Myths of the Iroquois (Second Annual Report of Bureau of Ethnology, p. 80), is practically the same so far as it goes, and the myth was probably once common over a wide area in the East:

"Seven little Indian boys were once accustomed to bring at eve their corn and beans to a little mound, upon the top of which, after their feast, the sweetest of their singers would sit and sing for his mates who danced around the mound. On one occasion they resolved on a more sumptuous feast, and each was to contribute towards a savory soup. But the parents refused them the needed supplies, and they met for a feastless dance. Their heads and hearts grew lighter as they flew around the mound, until suddenly the whole company whirled off into the air. The inconsolable parents called in vain for them to return, but it was too late. Higher and higher they arose, whirling around their singer, until, transformed into bright stars, they took their places in the firmament, where, as the Pleiades, they are dancing still, the brightness of the singer having been dimmed, however, on account of his desire to return to earth."

In an Eskimo tale a hunter was pursued by enemies, and as he ran he gradually rose from the ground and finally reached the sky, where he was turned into a star (Kroeber, Tales of the Smith Sound Eskimo, in Journal of American Folk-Lore). This transformation of human beings into stars and constellations is one of the most common incidents of primitive myth.

11. THE MILKY WAY (p. 259): This story, in slightly different forms, is well known among the Cherokee east and west. The generic word for mill is *dista'stĭ*, including also the self-acting pound-mill or *ŭlskwûlte'gĭ*. In the original version the mill was probably a wooden mortar, such as was commonly used by the Cherokee and other eastern and southern tribes.

In a variant recorded in the Hagar Cherokee manuscript there are two hunters, one living in the north and hunting big game, while the other lives in the south and hunts small game. The former, discovering the latter's wife grinding corn, seizes her and carries her far away across the sky to his home in the north. Her dog, after eating what meal is left, follows the pair across the sky, the meal falling from his mouth as he runs, making the Milky Way.

With the Kiowa, Cheyenne, and other plains tribes the Milky Way is the dusty track along which the Buffalo and the Horse once ran a race across the sky.

12. ORIGIN OF STRAWBERRIES (p. 259): This myth, as here given, was obtained from Ta'gwadihĭ', who said that all the fruits mentioned were then for the first time created, and added, "So some good came from the quarrel, anyhow." The Swimmer version has more detail, but seems overdressed.

13. THE GREAT YELLOW-JACKET: ORIGIN OF FISH AND FROGS (p. 260): This story, obtained from Swimmer, is well known in the tribe, and has numerous parallels in other Indian mythologies. In nearly every tribal genesis we find the primitive world infested by ferocious monster animals, which are finally destroyed or rendered harmless, leaving only their descendants, the present diminutive types. Conspicuous examples are afforded in Matthew's Navaho Legends[1] and in the author's story of the Jicarilla genesis in the American Anthropologist for July, 1898.

Another version of the Cherokee legend is given by Lanman in his Letters from the Alleghany Mountains, pages 73–74:

"The Cherokees relate that there once existed among those mountains [about Nantahala and Franklin] a very large bird, which resembled in appearance the green-winged hornet, and this creature was in the habit of carrying off the younger children of the nation who happened to wander into the woods. Very many children had mysteriously disappeared in this manner, and the entire people declared a

---

[1] Memoirs of American Folk-Lore Society, v; Boston and New York, 1897.

warfare against the monster. A variety of means were employed for his destruction, but without success. In process of time it was determined that the wise men (or medicine-men) of the nation should try their skill in the business. They met in council and agreed that each one should station himself on the summit of a mountain, and that, when the creature was discovered, the man who made the discovery should utter a loud halloo, which shout should be taken up by his neighbor on the next mountain, and so continued to the end of the line, that all the men might have a shot at the strange bird. This experiment was tried and resulted in finding out the hiding place of the monster, which was a deep cavern on the eastern side of the Blue ridge and at the fountain-head of the river Too-ge-lah [Tugaloo river, South Carolina]. On arriving at this place, they found the entrance to the cavern entirely inaccessible by mortal feet, and they therefore prayed to the Great Spirit that he would bring out the bird from his den, and place him within reach of their arms. Their petition was granted, for a terrible thunder-storm immediately arose, and a stroke of lightning tore away one half of a large mountain, and the Indians were successful in slaying their enemy. The Great Spirit was pleased with the courage manifested by the Cherokees during this dangerous fight, and, with a view of rewarding the same, he willed it that all the highest mountains in their land should thereafter be destitute of trees, so that they might always have an opportunity of watching the movements of their enemies.

As a sequel to this legend, it may be appropriately mentioned, that at the head of the Too-ge-lah is to be found one of the most remarkable curiosities of this mountain-land. It is a granite cliff with a smooth surface or front, half a mile long, and twelve hundred feet high, and generally spoken of in this part of the country as the *White-side mountain,* or *the Devil's court-house.* To think of it is almost enough to make one dizzy, but to see it fills one with awe. Near the top of one part of this cliff is a small cave, which can be reached only by passing over a strip of rock about two feet wide. One man only has ever been known to enter it, and when he performed the deed he met at the entrance of the cave a large bear, which animal, in making its escape, slipped off the rock, fell a distance of near a thousand feet, and was of course killed. When the man saw this, he became so excited that it was some hours before he could quiet his nerves sufficiently to retrace his dangerous pathway."

The Cherokee myth has a close parallel in the Iroquois story of the great mosquito, as published by the Tuscarora traditionist, Cusick, in 1825, and quoted by Schoolcraft, Indian Tribes, v, page 638:

"About this time a great musqueto invaded the fort Onondaga; the musqueto was mischievous to the people, it flew about the fort with a long stinger, and sucked the blood of a number of lives; the warriors made several oppositions to expel the monster, but failed; the country was invaded until the Holder of the Heavens was pleased to visit the people; while he was visiting the king at the fort Onondaga, the musqueto made appearance as usual and flew about the fort, the Holder of the Heavens attacked the monster, it flew so rapidly that he could hardly keep in sight of it, but after a few days chase the monster began to fail, he chased on the borders of the great lakes towards the sun-setting, and round the great country, at last he overtook the monster and killed it near the salt lake Onondaga, and the blood became small musquetos."

U'la'gü'—This is not the name of any particular species, but signifies a leader, principal, or colloquially, "boss," and in this sense is applied to the large queen yellow-jacket seen in spring, or to the leader of a working gang. The insect of the story is described as a monster yellow-jacket.

14. The Deluge (p. 261): This story is given by Schoolcraft in his Notes on the Iroquois, page 358, as having been obtained in 1846 from the Cherokee chief, Stand Watie. It was obtained by the author in nearly the same form in 1890 from James Wafford, of Indian Territory, who had heard it from his grandmother nearly eighty

years before. The incident of the dancing skeletons is not given by Schoolcraft, and seems to indicate a lost sequel to the story. Haywood (Nat. and Aborig. Hist. Tenn., p. 161) mentions the Cherokee deluge myth and conjectures that the petroglyphs at Track Rock gap in Georgia may have some reference to it. The versions given by the missionaries Buttrick and Washburn are simply the Bible narrative as told by the Indians. Washburn's informant, however, accounted for the phenomenon by an upheaval and tilting of the earth, so that the waters for a time overflowed the inhabited parts (Reminiscences, pp. 196–197). In a variant related by Hagar (MS Stellar Legends of the Cherokee) a star with fiery tail falls from heaven and becomes a man with long hair, who warns the people of the coming deluge.

It is not in place here to enter into a discussion of the meaning and universality of the deluge myth, for an explanation of which the reader is referred to Bouton's Bible Myths and Bible Folklore.[1] Suffice it to say that such a myth appears to have existed with every people and in every age. Among the American tribes with which it was found Brinton enumerates the Athapascan, Algonquian, Iroquois, Cherokee, Chickasaw, Caddo, Natchez, Dakota, Apache, Navaho, Mandan, Pueblo, Aztec, Mixtec, Zapotec, Tlascalan, Michoacan, Toltec, Maya, Quiche, Haitian, Darien, Popayan, Muysca, Quichua, Tupinamba, Achagua, Auraucanian, "and doubtless others."[2] It is found also along the Northwest coast, was known about Albemarle sound, and, as has been said, was probably common to all the tribes.

In one Creek version the warning is given by wolves; in another by cranes (see Bouton, cited above).

15. THE FOUR-FOOTED TRIBES (p. 261): *No essential difference*—"I have often reflected on the curious connexion which appears to subsist in the mind of an Indian between man and the brute creation, and found much matter in it for curious observation. Although they consider themselves superior to all other animals and are very proud of that superiority; although they believe that the beasts of the forest, the birds of the air, and the fishes of the waters were created by the Almighty Being for the use of man; yet it seems as if they ascribe the difference between themselves and the brute kind, and the dominion which they have over them, more to their superior bodily strength and dexterity than to their immortal souls. All being endowed by the Creator with the power of volition and self motion, they view in a manner as a great society of which they are the head, whom they are appointed, indeed, to govern, but between whom and themselves intimate ties of connexion and relationship may exist, or at least did exist in the beginning of time. They are, in fact, according to their opinions, only the first among equals, the legitimate hereditary sovereigns of the whole animated race, of which they are themselves a constituent part. Hence, in their languages, these inflections of their nouns, which we call *genders*, are not, as with us, descriptive of the *masculine* and *feminine* species, but of the *animate* and *inanimate* kinds. Indeed, they go so far as to include trees, and plants within the first of these descriptions. All animated nature, in whatever degree, is in their eyes a great whole from which they have not yet ventured to separate themselves. They do not exclude other animals from their world of spirits, the place to which they expect to go after death."[3]

According to the Ojibwa the animals formerly had the faculty of speech, until it was taken from them by Nanibojou as a punishment for having conspired against the human race.[4]

Animal chiefs and councils—In Pawnee belief, according to Grinnell, the animals,

[1] J. W. Bouton, Bible Myths and their Parallels in Other Religions; 2d ed., New York, 1883; Bible Folklore, A Study in Comparative Mythology; New York, 1884.

[2] The Myths of the New World, A Treatise on the Symbolism and Mythology of the Red Race of America; 3d ed., Philadelphia, 1896.

[3] Heckewelder, Indian Nations, p. 254, ed. 1876.

[4] Henry, Travels and Adventures in Canada, etc., pp. 212–213, New York, 1809.

or Nahurac, possess miraculous attributes given them by the great creator, Tirawa. "The Pawnees know of five places where these animals meet to hold council—five of these Nahurac lodges." He gives a detailed description of each. The fourth is a mound-shaped hill, on the top of which is a deep well or water hole, into which the Pawnee throw offerings. The fifth is a rock hill in Kansas, known to the whites as Guide rock, and "in the side of the hill there is a great hole where the Nahurac hold councils." [1]

The same belief is noted by Chatelain in Angola, West Africa: "In African folk tales the animal world, as also the spirit world, is organized and governed just like the human world. In Angola the elephant is the supreme king of all animal creation, and the special chief of the edible tribe of wild animals. Next to him in rank the lion is special chief of the tribe of ferocious beasts and highest vassal of the elephant. Chief of the reptile tribe is the python. Chief of the finny tribe is, in the interior, the *di-lenda*, the largest river fish. Chief of the feathery tribe is the *kakulu ka humbi*, largest of the eagles. Among the domestic animals the sceptre belongs to the bull; among the locusts to the one called *di-ngundu*. Even the ants and termites have their kings or queens. Every chief or king has his court, consisting of the *ngolambole, tandala*, and other officers, his parliament of *ma-kota* and his plebeian subjects, just like any human African *saba*" (Folk tales of Angola, p. 22).

Asking pardon of animals—For other Cherokee references see remarks upon the Little Deer, the Wolf, and the Rattlesnake; also number 4, "Origin of Disease and Medicine," and number 58, "The Rattlesnake's Vengeance." This custom was doubtless general among the tribes, as it is thoroughly in consonance with Indian idea. The trader Henry thus relates a characteristic instance among the Ojibwa in 1764 on the occasion of his killing a bear near the winter camp:

"The bear being dead, all my assistants approached, and all, but more particularly my old mother (as I was wont to call her), took his head in their hands, stroking and kissing it several times; begging a thousand pardons for taking away her life; calling her their relation and grandmother; and requesting her not to lay the fault upon them, since it was truly an Englishman that had put her to death.

"This ceremony was not of long duration; and if it was I that killed their grandmother, they were not themselves behind-hand in what remained to be performed. The skin being taken off, we found the fat in several places six inches deep. This, being divided into two parts, loaded two persons; and the flesh parts were as much as four persons could carry. In all, the carcass must have exceeded five hundred weight.

"As soon as we reached the lodge, the bear's head was adorned with all the trinkets in the possession of the family, such as silver arm-bands and wrist-bands, and belts of wampum; and then laid upon a scaffold, set up for its reception, within the lodge. Near the nose was placed a large quantity of tobacco.

"The next morning no sooner appeared, than preparations were made for a feast to the manes. The lodge was cleaned and swept; and the head of the bear lifted up, and a new stroud of blanket, which had never been used before, spread under it. The pipes were now lit; and Wawatam blew tobacco smoke into the nostrils of the bear, telling me to do the same, and thus appease the anger of the bear on account of my having killed her. I endeavored to persuade my benefactor and friendly adviser, that she no longer had any life, and assured him that I was under no apprehension from her displeasure; but, the first proposition obtained no credit, and the second gave but little satisfaction.

"At length, the feast being ready, Wawatam commenced a speech, resembling, in many things, his address to the manes of his relations and departed companions; but, having this peculiarity, that he here deplored the necessity under which men

---

[1] G. B. Grinnell, Pawnee Hero Stories and Folktales, with Notes on the Origin, Customs, and Character of the Pawnee People; New York, 1889, pp. 358–359.

labored thus to destroy their *friends*. He represented, however, that the misfortune was unavoidable, since without doing so, they could by no means subsist. The speech ended, we all ate heartily of the bear's flesh; and even the head itself, after remaining three days on the scaffold, was put into the kettle."—Travels, pp. 143–145.

The Rabbit—The part played by the Rabbit or Hare and his symbolic character in Indian myth has been already noted (see "Stories and Story Tellers"). In his purely animal character, as an actor among the fourfooted creatures, the same attributes of trickery and surpassing sagacity are assigned him in other parts of the world. In the folktales of Angola, West Africa, "The Hare seems to surpass the fox in shrewdness," and "The Hare has the swiftness and shrewdness of the Monkey, but he is never reckless, as the Monkey sometimes appears to be" (Chatelain, Folktales of Angola, pp. 295, 300). In farthest Asia also "The animals, too, have their stories, and in Korea, as in some other parts of the world, the Rabbit seems to come off best, as a rule" (H. N. Allen, Korean Tales, p. 34; New York and London, 1889).

The buffalo—Timberlake repeatedly remarks upon the abundance of the buffalo in the Cherokee country of East Tennessee in 1762. On one occasion, while in camp, they heard rapid firing from their scouts and "in less than a minute seventeen or eighteen buffaloes ran in amongst us, before we discovered them, so that several of us had like to have been run over, especially the women, who with some difficulty sheltered themselves behind the trees. Most of the men fired, but firing at random, one only was killed, tho' several more wounded" (Memoirs, p. 101). According to a writer in the Historical Magazine, volume VIII, page 71, 1864, the last two wild buffalo known in Ohio were killed in Jackson county in 1800.

The elk—This animal ranged in eastern Carolina in 1700. "The elk is a monster of the venison sort. His skin is used almost in the same nature as the buffelo's [*sic*]. . . . His flesh is not so sweet as the lesser deer's. His hams exceed in weight all creatures which the new world affords. They will often resort and feed with the buffalo, delighting in the same range as they do" (Lawson, Carolina, p. 203).

Cuts out the hamstring—No satisfactory reason has been obtained for this custom, which has been noted for more than a century. Buttrick says of the Cherokee: "The Indians never used to eat a certain sinew in the thigh. . . . Some say that if they eat of the sinew they will have cramp in it on attempting to run. It is said that once a woman had cramp in that sinew and therefore none must eat it" (Antiquities, p. 12). Says Adair, speaking of the southern tribes generally: "When in the woods the Indians cut a small piece out of the lower part of the thigh of the deer they kill, lengthways and pretty deep. Among the great number of venison hams they bring to our trading houses I do not remember to have observed one without it" (History of the American Indians, pp. 137–138).

White animals sacred—According to a formula in the Tuggle manuscript for curing the "deer sickness," the "White Deer" is chief of his tribe in Creek mythology also. Peculiar sacredness always attaches, in the Indian mind, to white and albino animals, partly on account of the symbolic meaning attached to the color itself and partly by reason of the mystery surrounding the phenomenon of albinism. Among the Cherokee the chiefs both of the Deer and of the Bear tribe were white. On the plains the so-called white buffalo was always sacred. Among the Iroquois, according to Morgan (League of the Iroquois, p. 210), "the white deer, white squirrel and other chance animals of the albino kind, were regarded as consecrated to the Great Spirit." One of their most solemn sacrifices was that of the White Dog.

The bear—A reverence for the bear and a belief that it is half human is very general among the tribes, and is probably based in part upon the ability of the animal to stand upright and the resemblance of its tracks to human footprints. According to Grinnell (Blackfoot Lodge Tales, p. 260), "The Blackfeet believe it to be part brute and part human, portions of its body, particularly the ribs and feet, being like those of a man." In a note upon a Navaho myth Matthews says (Navaho Legends,

p. 249): "The bear is a sacred animal with the Navahoes; for this reason the hero did not skin the bears or eat their flesh. The old man, being a wizard, might do both."

The Ojibwa idea has been noted in connection with the ceremony of asking pardon of the slain animal. A curious illustration of the reverse side of the picture is given by Heckewelder (Indian Nations, p. 255):

"A Delaware hunter once shot a huge bear and broke its backbone. The animal fell and set up a most plaintive cry, something like that of the panther when he is hungry. The hunter instead of giving him another shot, stood up close to him, and addressed him in these words: 'Hark ye! bear; you are a coward and no warrior as you pretend to be. Were you a warrior, you would shew it by your firmness, and not cry and whimper like an old woman. You know, bear, that our tribes are at war with each other, and that yours was the aggressor [probably alluding to a tradition which the Indians have of a very ferocious kind of bear, called the *naked bear*, which they say once existed, but was totally destroyed by their ancestors] . . . You have found the Indians too powerful for you, and you have gone sneaking about in the woods, stealing their hogs; perhaps at this time you have hog's flesh in your belly. Had you conquered me, I would have borne it with courage and died like a brave warrior; but you, bear, sit here and cry, and disgrace your tribe by your cowardly conduct.' I was present at the delivery of this curious invective. When the hunter had despatched the bear, I asked him how he thought that poor animal could understand what he said to it? 'Oh,' said he in answer, 'the bear understood me very well; did you not observe how ashamed he looked while I was upbraiding him?'"

The wolf and wolf killer—Speaking of the Gulf tribes generally, Adair says: "The wolf, indeed, several of them do not care to meddle with, believing it unlucky to kill them, which is the sole reason that few of the Indians shoot at that creature, through a notion of spoiling their guns" (History of the American Indians, p. 16). The author has heard among the East Cherokee an incident of a man who, while standing one night upon a fish trap, was scented by a wolf, which came so near that the man was compelled to shoot it. He at once went home and had the gun exorcised by a conjurer. Wafford, when a boy in the old Nation, knew a professional wolf killer. It is always permissible to hire a white man to kill a depredating wolf, as in that case no guilt attaches to the Indian or his tribe.

16. THE RABBIT GOES DUCK HUNTING (p. 266): This story was heard from Swimmer, John Ax, Suyeta (east), and Wafford (west). Discussions between animals as to the kind of food eaten are very common in Indian myth, the method chosen to decide the dispute being usually quite characteristic. The first incident is paralleled in a Creek story of the Rabbit and the Lion (Panther?) in the Tuggle manuscript collection and among the remote Wallawalla of Washington (see Kane, Wanderings of an Artist among the Indians of North America, p. 268; London, 1859). In an Omaha myth, Ictinike and the Buzzard, the latter undertakes to carry the trickster across a stream, but drops him into a hollow tree, from which he is chopped out by some women whom he has persuaded that there are raccoons inside (Dorsey, Contributions to North American Ethnology, VI). In the Iroquois tale, "A Hunter's Adventures," a hunter, endeavoring to trap some geese in the water, is carried up in the air and falls into a hollow stump, from which he is released by women (Smith, Myths of the Iroquois, in Second Annual Report of Bureau of Ethnology). In the Uncle Remus story, "Mr. Rabbit Meets His Match Again," the Buzzard persuades the Rabbit to get upon his back in order to be carried across a river, but alights with him upon a tree overhanging the water and thus compels the Rabbit, by fear of falling, to confess a piece of trickery.[1]

---

[1] Joel C. Harris, Uncle Remus, His Songs and His Sayings; New York, 1886.

17. How the Rabbit stole the Otter's coat (p. 267): This story is well known in the tribe and was heard from several informants, both east and west. Nothing is said as to how the Otter recovered his coat. It has exact parallels in the Creek myths of the Tuggle collection, in one of which the Rabbit tries to personate a boy hero by stealing his coat, while in another he plays a trick on the Lion (Panther) by throwing hot coals over him while asleep, at a creek which the Rabbit says is called "Throwing-hot-ashes-on-you."

18. Why the Possum's tail is bare (p. 269): This story was heard from several informants, east and west. In one variant the hair clipping was done by the Moth, and in another by the spells of the Snail, who is represented as a magician. The version here given is the most common, and agrees best with the Cherokee folklore concerning the Cricket (see number 59, "The Smaller Reptiles, Fishes, and Insects").

In the Creek myth, as given in the Tuggle collection, the Opossum burned the hair from his tail in trying to put rings upon it like those of the Raccoon's tail, and grins from chewing a bitter oak ball which he mistook for a ripened fruit.

The anatomical peculiarities of the opossum, of both sexes, have occasioned much speculation among the Indians, many of whom believe that the female produces her young without any help from the male. The Creeks, according to the Tuggle manuscript, believe that the young are born in the pouch, from the breathing of the female against it when curled up, and even Lawson and Timberlake assert that they are born at the teat, from which they afterward drop off into the pouch.

A council and a dance—In the old days, as to-day among the remote Western tribes, every great council gathering was made the occasion of a series of dances, accompanied always by feasting and a general good time.

19. How the Wildcat caught the Gobbler (p. 269): This story was heard from John Ax and David Blythe (east) and from Wafford and Boudinot (west). The version given below, doctored to suit the white man's idea, appears without signature in the Cherokee Advocate of December 18, 1845:

"There was once a flock of wild turkeys feeding in a valley. As they fed they heard a voice singing. They soon discovered that the musician was a hare, and the burden of his song was that he had a secret in his breast which he would on no account divulge. The curiosity of the turkeys was excited, and they entreated the hare to tell them the secret. This he finally consented to do if they would procure for him the king's daughter for his wife and go with him and dance around their enemy. They engaged to do all, and the hare led them to where a wildcat lay apparently dead. The hare prevailed upon them to close their eyes as they danced. The wildcat meanwhile silently arose and killed several of them before the rest found out what a snare they had been caught in. By this artifice on the part of the wildcat, seconded by the hare, the former had a sumptuous repast."

This, with its variants, is one of the most widespread of the animal myths. The same story told by the Cherokee, identical even to the song, is given in the Creek collection of Tuggle, with the addition that the Rabbit's tail is afterward bitten off by the enraged Turkeys. In another Creek version, evidently a later invention, the Raccoon plays a similar trick upon the Deer for the benefit of the Panther. The Kiowa of the southern plains tell how the hungry trickster, Sinti, entices a number of prairie dogs to come near him, under pretense of teaching them a new dance, and then kills all but one, while they are dancing around him, according to instruction, with their eyes shut. With the Omaha the Rabbit himself captures the Turkeys while they dance around, with closed eyes, to his singing (Dorsey, "The Rabbit and the Turkeys," and "Ictinike, the Turkeys, Turtle, and Elk," in Contributions to North American Ethnology, vi). The same stratagem, with only a change of names, recurs in another Omaha story, "The Raccoon and the Crabs," of the same collection, and in a Cheyenne story of White-man (A. L. Kroeber, Cheyenne Tales, in Journal

of American Folk-Lore, July, 1900), and in the Jicarilla story of "The Fox and
the Wildcat" (Russell, Myths of the Jicarilla, ibid., October, 1898). The Southern
negro version, which lacks the important song and dance feature, is given by Harris
in his story of "Brother Rabbit and Mr Wildcat." [1]

20. How the Terrapin beat the Rabbit (p. 270): This story was obtained from
John Ax and Suyeta and is well known in the tribe. It is sometimes told with the
Deer instead of the Rabbit as the defeated runner, and in this form is given by Lanman, who thus localizes it: "The race was to extend from the Black mountain to the
summit of the third pinnacle extending to the eastward" (Letters, p. 37).

In the Creek collection of Tuggle the same story is given in two versions, in one of
which the Deer and in the other the Wolf is defeated by the stratagem of the Terrapin. The Southern negro parallel is given by Harris (Uncle Remus, His Songs and
His Sayings) in the story, "Mr Rabbit Finds His Match at Last." It seems almost
superfluous to call attention to the European folklore version, the well-known story
of the race between the Hare and the Tortoise.

21. The Rabbit and the tar wolf (p. 271): This story was obtained in the
Indian Territory from James Wafford, who said he had repeatedly heard it in boyhood about Valley river, in the old Nation, from Cherokee who spoke no English.

The second version, from the Cherokee Advocate, December 18, 1845, is given,
together with the story of "How the Wildcat caught the Gobbler," with this introduction:

"*Indian Fables.* Mr William P. Ross: I have recently stumbled on the following
Cherokee fables, and perhaps you may think them worth inserting in the Advocate
for the sake of the curious. I am told that the Cherokees have a great many fables.
If I understand the following, the intention seems to be to teach cunning and artifice
in war. Æsop." The newspaper paragraph bears the pencil initials of S[amuel]
W[orcester] B[utler].

Other Indian versions are found with the Jicarilla ("Fox and Rabbit," Myths of
the Jicarilla, by Frank Russell, in Journal of American Folk-Lore, October, 1898)
and Sioux (S. D. Hinman, cited in Transactions of the Anthropological Society of
Washington, I, p. 103, Washington, 1882). The southern negro variant, "The Wonderful Tar-Baby Story," is the introductory tale in Harris's Uncle Remus, His Songs
and His Sayings. A close parallel occurs in the West African story of "Leopard,
Monkey, and Hare" (Chatelain, Folktales of Angola).

22. The Rabbit and the Possum after a wife (p. 273): This specimen of Indian
humor was obtained at different times from Swimmer, John Ax, Suyeta (east), and
Wafford (west), and is well known in the tribe. Wafford, in telling the story,
remarked that the Rabbit was the chief's runner, and according to custom was
always well entertained wherever he went.

23. The Rabbit dines the Bear (p. 273): This favorite story with the Cherokee
east and west is another of the animal myths of wide distribution, being found with
almost every tribe from Maine to the Pacific. Beans and peas in several varieties
were indigenous among the agricultural tribes.

In the Creek version, in the Tuggle manuscript, "The Bear invited the Rabbit to
dinner. When he came the Bear called his wife and said, 'Have peas for dinner:
the Rabbit loves peas.' 'But there is no grease,' said the Bear's wife, 'to cook them
with.' 'O,' said the Bear, 'that's no trouble, bring me a knife.' So she brought
the knife and the Bear took it and split between his toes, while the Rabbit looked
on in wonder. 'No grease between my toes! Well, I know where there is some,'
so he cut a gash in his side and out ran the grease. His wife took it and cooked the
peas and they had a fine dinner and vowed always to be good friends," etc. The

[1] J. C. Harris, Nights with Uncle Remus: Myths and Legends of the Old Plantation; Boston, 1883.

wounded Rabbit is put under the care of the Buzzard, who winds up by eating his patient.

In the Passamaquoddy version, "The Rabbit's Adventure with Mooin, the Bear," the Bear cuts a slice from his foot and puts it into the pot. The Rabbit invites the Bear to dinner and attempts to do the same thing, but comes to grief.[1] In a Jicarilla myth a somewhat similar incident is related of the Fox (Coyote?) and the Prairie-dog (Russell, Myths of the Jicarilla, in Journal of American Folk-Lore, October, 1898). In a British Columbian myth nearly the same thing happens when the Coyote undertakes to return the hospitality of the Black Bear (Teit, Thompson River Indian Traditions, p. 40).

24. THE RABBIT ESCAPES FROM THE WOLVES (p. 274): This story was obtained from James Wafford, in Indian Territory. Compare number 19, "How the Wildcat Caught the Gobbler."

25. FLINT VISITS THE RABBIT (p. 274): This story was told in slightly different form by John Ax and Swimmer (east) and was confirmed by Wafford (west). Although among the Cherokee it has degenerated to a mere humorous tale for the amusement of a winter evening, it was originally a principal part of the great cosmogonic myth common to probably all the Iroquoian and Algonquian tribes, and of which we find traces also in the mythologies of the Aztec and the Maya. Among the northern Algonquian tribes "the West was typified as a flint stone, and the twin brother of Michabo, the Great Rabbit. The feud between them was bitter, and the contest long and dreadful. . . . At last Michabo mastered his fellow twin and broke him into pieces. He scattered the fragments over the earth. . . ." Among the Iroquoian tribes, cognate with the Cherokee, the name is variously Tăwiskaroñ, Tăwiskară, and sometimes Ohaa, all of which are names both for flint and for hail or ice. Tăwiskara is the evil-working god, in perpetual conflict with his twin brother Yoskeha, the beneficent god, by whom he is finally overpowered, when the blood that drops from his wounds is changed into flint stones. Brinton sees in the Great Rabbit and the Flint the opposing forces of day and night, light and darkness, locally personified as East and West, while in the twin gods of the Iroquois Hewitt sees the conflicting agents of heat and cold, summer and winter. Both conceptions are identical in the final analysis. Hewitt derives the Iroquois name from a root denoting "hail, ice, glass"; in Cherokee we have tăwiskalûñ'ĭ, tăwi'skălă, "flint," tăwi'skă, "smooth," une'stălûñ, "ice." (See Brinton, American Hero Myths, pp. 48, 56, 61; Hewitt, The Cosmogonic Gods of the Iroquois, in Proc. Am. Ass. Adv. Sci., XLIV, 1895.)

In one of the Cherokee sacred formulas collected by the author occurs the expression: "The terrible Flint is coming. He has his paths laid down in this direction. He is shaking the red switches threateningly. Let us run toward the Sun land."

Siyu'—This word, abbreviated from ásiyu', "good," is the regular Cherokee salutation. With probably all the tribes the common salutation is simply the word "good," and in the sign language of the plains the gesture conveying that meaning is used in the same way. The ordinary good-bye is usually some equivalent of "I go now."

26. HOW THE DEER GOT HIS HORNS (p. 275): This story was heard from Swimmer, Suyeta, and others, and is well known in the tribe.

In a parallel Pawnee myth, "How the Deer Lost His Gall," the Deer and Antelope wager their galls in a race, which the Antelope wins, but in sympathy takes off his own dewclaws and gives them to the Deer. In the Blackfoot variant the Deer and the Antelope run two races. The first, which is over the prairie, the Antelope wins and takes the Deer's gall, while in the second, which the Deer stipulates shall be run through the timber, the Deer wins and takes the Antelope's dewclaws (Grinnell, Pawnee Hero Tales, pp. 204, 205).

---

[1] C. G. Leland, Algonquin Legends of New England, p. 212; Boston, 1884.

27. WHY THE DEER'S TEETH ARE BLUNT (p. 276): This story follows the last in regular sequence and was told by the same informants.

In a Jicarilla myth the Fox kills a dangerous Bear monster under pretense of trimming down his legs so that he can run faster (Russell, Myth of the Jicarilla, in Journal of American Folk-Lore, p. 262, October, 1898).

28. WHAT BECAME OF THE RABBIT (p. 277): This version was obtained from Suyeta, who says the Rabbit never went up, because he was "too mean" to be with the other animals. Swimmer, however, says that he did afterward go up to Gălûñ'lătĭ. The belief in a large rabbit still existing beyond a great river may possibly have its origin in indirect reports of the jack-rabbit west of the Missouri.

The myth has close parallel in the southern negro story of "The Origin of the Ocean" (Harris, Nights with Uncle Remus), in which the Rabbit by a stratagem persuades the Lion to jump across a creek, when the Rabbit "cut de string w'at hol' de banks togedder. . . . Co'se wen Brer Rabbit tuck'n cut de string, de banks er de creek, de banks dey fall back, dey did, en Mr Lion can't jump back. De banks dey keep on fallin' back, en de creek keep on gittin' wider en wider, twel bimeby Brer Rabbit en Mr Lion ain't in sight èr one er n'er, en fum dat day to dis de big waters bin rollin' 'twix um."

Kû!—A Cherokee exclamation used as a starting signal and in introducing the paragraphs of a speech. It might be approximately rendered, *Now!*

29. WHY THE MINK SMELLS (p. 277): Obtained from John Ax.

30. WHY THE MOLE LIVES UNDERGROUND (p. 277): This story, from John Ax, not only accounts for the Mole's underground habit, but illustrates a common Cherokee witchcraft belief, which has parallels all over the world.

31. THE TERRAPIN'S ESCAPE FROM THE WOLVES (p. 278): This story, of which the version here given, from Swimmer and John Ax, is admittedly imperfect, is known also among the western Cherokee, having been mentioned by Wafford and others in the Nation, although for some reason none of them seemed able to fill in the details. A somewhat similar story was given as belonging to her own tribe by a Catawba woman married among the East Cherokee. It suggests number 21, "The Rabbit and the tar wolf," and has numerous parallels.

In the Creek version, in the Tuggle manuscript, the Terrapin ridicules a woman, who retaliates by crushing his shell with a corn pestle. He repairs the injury by singing a medicine song, but the scars remain in the checkered spots on his back. In a variant in the same collection the ants mend his shell with tar, in return for his fat and blood. Other parallels are among the Omaha, "How the Big Turtle went on the Warpath" (Dorsey, Contributions to North American Ethnology, vi, p. 275), and the Cheyenne, "The Turtle, the Grasshopper, and the Skunk" (Kroeber, Cheyenne Tales, in Journal of American Folk-Lore, July, 1900). The myth is recorded also from west Africa by Chatelain ("The Man and the Turtle," in Folktales of Angola, 1894).

Kanahe'na.—This is a sour corn gruel, the *tamfuli* or "Tom Fuller" of the Creeks, which is a favorite food preparation among all the southern tribes. A large earthern jar of kanahe'na, with a wooden spoon upright in it, is always upon a bench just inside the cabin door, for every visitor to help himself.

32. ORIGIN OF THE GROUNDHOG DANCE (p. 279): This story is from Swimmer, the supplementary part being added by John Ax. The Groundhog dance is one of those belonging to the great thanksgiving ceremony, Green-corn dance. It consists of alternate advances and retreats by the whole line of dancers in obedience to signals by the song leader, who sings to the accompaniment of a rattle. The burden of the song, which is without meaning, is

Ha'wiye'ĕhi' Yaha'wiye'ĕhi [twice] *Yu-u*
Hi'yagu'wĕ Hahi'yagu'wĕ [twice] *Yu-yu.*

33. The migration of the animals (p. 280): This little story is given just as related by Ayâsta, the only woman privileged to speak in council among the East Cherokee. A similar incident occurs in number 76, "The Bear Man." According to one Cherokee myth concerning the noted Track Rock gap, near Blairsville in upper Georgia, the pictographs in the rocks there are the footprints of all sorts of birds and animals which once crossed over the gap in a great migration toward the south.

34. The Wolf's revenge: The Wolf and the Dog (p. 280): These short stories from Swimmer illustrate the Cherokee belief that if a wolf be injured his fellows will surely revenge the injury. See also note to number 15, "The Fourfooted Tribes," and number 3, "Kana′tĭ and Selu."

In a West African tale recorded by Chatelain (Folktales of Angola, 1894) the dog and the jackal are kinsmen, who live together in the bush until the jackal sends the dog to the village for fire. The dog goes, enters a house and is fed by a woman, and thereupon concludes to stay in the village, where there is always food.

35. The bird tribes (p. 280): *The eagle killer*—Of the Southern tribes generally Adair says: "They use the feathers of the eagle's tail in certain friendly and religious dances, but the whole town will contribute, to the value of 200 deerskins, for killing a large eagle—the bald eagle they do not esteem—and the man also gets an honorable title for the exploit, as if he had brought in the scalp of an enemy." [1]

Timberlake says that the Cherokee held the tail of an eagle in the greatest esteem, as these tails were sometimes given with the wampum in their treaties, and none of their warlike ceremonies could be performed without them (Memoirs, p. 81). The figurative expression, "a snowbird has been killed," used to avoid offending the eagle tribe, is paralleled in the expression, "he has been scratched by a brier," used by the Cherokee to mean, "he has been bitten by a snake." Professional eagle killers existed among many tribes, together with a prescribed ceremonial for securing the eagle. The most common method was probably that described in a note to number 98, "Gana's Adventures among the Cherokee." A detailed account of the Blackfoot method is given by Grinnell, in his Blackfoot Lodge Tales, pp. 236–240. The eagle, being a bird of prey, as well as a sacred bird, was never eaten.

The shifting of responsibility for the killing to a vicarious victim is a common feature of Indian formulas for obtaining pardon, especially for offenses against the animal tribe or the spirits of the dead. A remarkable parallel to the Cherokee prayer, from the Quichua of Peru, is given by Dr G. A. Dorsey. Having started, with a party of Indian laborers and a Spanish gentleman who was well acquainted with the native language, to examine some cave tombs near the ancient city of Cuzco, they had arrived at the spot and he was about to give the order to begin operations, when the Indians, removing their blankets and hats, knelt down and recited in unison in their own language a prayer to the spirits of the dead, of which the following translation is an extract:

"Chiefs, sons of the sun, you and we are brothers, sons of the great Pachacamac. You only know this, but we know that three persons exist, the Father, the Son, and the Holy Ghost. This is the only difference between you and us. . . . Chiefs, sons of the sun, we have not come to disturb your tranquil sleep in this, your abode. We come only because we have been compelled by our superiors; toward them may you direct your vengeance and your curses."

Then followed sacrifices of coca leaves, aguardiente, and chicha, after which they called upon the snow-capped mountain to witness their affection for their ancestors, and were then ready to begin work (Dorsey, A Ceremony of the Quichuas of Peru, in Journal of American Folk-Lore, October, 1894).

Night birds—Says Adair of the Southern tribes (History of the American Indians, p. 130, 1775): "They reckon all birds of prey, and birds of night, to be unclean and

---

[1] History of the American Indians, p. 30.

unlawful to be eaten." The mixed feeling of fear and reverence for all night birds is universal among the Western tribes. Owls particularly are believed to bring prophetic tidings to the few great conjurers who can interpret their language.

The hawk—This, being a bird of prey, was never eaten. The following incident is related by Adair, probably from the Chickasaw: "Not long ago when the Indians were making their winter's hunt and the old women were without flesh meat at home, I shot a small fat hawk and desired one of them to take and dress it; but though I strongly importuned her by way of trial, she as earnestly refused it for fear of contracting pollution, which she called the 'accursed sickness,' supposing disease would be the necessary effect of such an impurity" (Hist. Am. Indians, p. 130).

Chickadee and titmouse—Adair speaks,of having once observed a party of Southern Indians "to be intimidated at the voice of a small uncommon bird, when it pitched and chirped on a tree over their camp" (op. cit., p. 26). At a conference with the Six Nations at Albany in 1775 the Oneida speaker said: "We, the Six Nations, have heard the voice of a bird called Tskleleli (*Tsĭkĭlĭlĭ′*?), a news carrier, that came among us. It has told us that the path at the western connection, by Fort Stanwix, would be shut up by either one party or the other." In reply, the commissioners said: "We apprehend the bird Tskleleli has been busy again; he seems to be a mischievous bird and ought not to be nourished or entertained" (New York Colonial Documents, viii, pp. 612, 628, 1857). The bird name is in the Oneida dialect. Bruyas gives *teksereri* as the Mohawk name for the tomtit.

36. The ball game of the birds and animals (p. 286): This is one of the best-known animal stories and was heard with more or less of detail from John Ax, Swimmer, Suyeta, and A′wani′ta in the east, and from Wafford in the Territory.

The Creeks and the Seminoles also, as we learn from the Tuggle manuscript collection, have stories of ball games by the birds against the fourfooted animals. In one story the bat is rejected by both sides, but is finally accepted by the fourfooted animals on account of his having teeth, and enables them to win the victory from the birds.

The ballplay—The ballplay, *a′ne′tsâ*, is the great athletic game of the Cherokee and the Gulf tribes, as well as with those of the St Lawrence and Great lakes. It need hardly be stated that it is not our own game of base ball, but rather a variety of tennis, the ball being thrown, not from the hand, but from a netted racket or pair of rackets. The goals are two sets of upright poles at either end of the ball ground, which is always a level grassy bottom beside a small stream. There is much accompanying ceremonial and conjuration, with a ball dance, in which the women take part, the night before. It is the same game by which the hostile tribes gained entrance to the British post at Mackinaw in 1763, and under the name of lacrosse has become the national game of Canada. It has also been adopted by the French Creoles of Louisiana under the name of raquette. In British Columbia it is held to be the favorite amusement of the people of the underworld (Teit, Thompson River Traditions, p. 116). In the southern states the numerous localities bearing the names of "Ballplay," "Ball flat," and "Ball ground," bear witness to the Indian fondness for the game. Large sums were staked upon it, and there is even a tradition that a considerable territory in northern Georgia was won from the Creeks by the Cherokee in a ball game. For an extended description see the the author's article "The Cherokee Ball Play," in the American Anthropologist for April, 1890.

Won the game—On account of their successful work on this occasion the Cherokee ballplayer invokes the aid of the bat and the flying squirrel, and also ties a small piece of the bat's wing to his ball stick or fastens it to the frame over which the sticks are hung during the preliminary dance the night before.

Gave the martin a gourd—The black house-martin is a favorite with the Cherokee, who attract it by fastening hollow gourds to the tops of long poles set up near their houses so that the birds may build their nests in them. In South Carolina, as far back as 1700, according to Lawson: "The planters put gourds on standing holes [poles] on purpose for these fowl to build in, because they are a very warlike bird and beat the crows from the plantations" (History of Carolina, p. 238).

37. HOW THE TURKEY GOT HIS BEARD (p. 287): This story is well known in the tribe and was heard from several informants.

According to a Creek myth in the Tuggle collection the Turkey was once a warrior and still wears his last scalp from his neck. In another story of the same collection it is a man's scalp which he seized from the Terrapin and accidentally swallowed as he ran off, so that it grew out from his breast.

38. WHY THE TURKEY GOBBLES (p. 288): This story was first heard from John Ax (east) and afterward from Wafford (west). The grouse is locally called "partridge" in the southern Alleghenies.

39. HOW THE KINGFISHER GOT HIS BILL (p. 288): The first version is from John Ax, the other from Swimmer.

Yûñwĭ tsunsdi'—"Little People," another name for the Nuññĕ'hĭ (see number 78). These are not to be confounded with the Anisga'ya Tsunsdi', "Little Men," or Thunder Boys.

Tugălû'nă—A small slender-bodied spotted fish about four inches in length, which likes to lie upon the rocks at the bottom of the larger streams. The name refers to a gourd, from a fancied resemblance of the long nose to the handle of a gourd.

40. HOW THE PARTRIDGE GOT HIS WHISTLE (p. 289): This little story is well known in the tribe.

Whistles and flutes or flageolets are in use among nearly all tribes for ceremonial and amusement purposes. The whistle, usually made from an eagle bone, was worn suspended from the neck. The flute or flageolet was commonly made from cedar wood.

41. HOW THE REDBIRD GOT HIS COLOR (p. 289): This short story was obtained from Cornelius Boudinot, a prominent mixed-blood of Tahlequah, and differs from the standard Cherokee myth, according to which the redbird is the transformed daughter of the Sun (see number 5, "The Daughter of the Sun").

Red paint—Much sacredness attaches, in the Indian mind, to red paint, the color being symbolic of war, strength, success, and spirit protection. The word paint, in any Indian language, is generally understood to mean red paint, unless it is otherwise distinctly noted. The Indian red paint is usually a soft hematite ore, found in veins of hard-rock formation, from which it must be dug with much labor and patience. In the western tribes everyone coming thus to procure paint makes a prayer beside the rock and hangs a small sacrifice upon a convenient bush or stick before beginning operations.

42. THE PHEASANT BEATING CORN; THE PHEASANT DANCE (p. 290): The first of these little tales is from John Ax, the second from Swimmer. The pheasant (*Bonasa umbella;* Cherokee *tluñti'stĭ*) is also locally called grouse or partridge.

43. THE RACE BETWEEN THE CRANE AND THE HUMMINGBIRD (p. 290): This story is a favorite one in the tribe, and was heard from several informants, both East and West. The sequel may surprise those who have supposed that woman has no rights in Indian society.

In a Creek story under the same title, in the Tuggle collection, the rivals agree to fly from a certain spot on a stream to the spring at its head. The humming bird is obliged to follow the windings of the stream, but the crane takes a direct course above the trees and thus wins the race.

Fly around the world—Not around a globe, but around the circumference of a disk, according to the Indian idea.

44. The Owl gets married (p. 291): Told by Swimmer. The three owls of the Cherokee country are known, respectively, as *tskĭlĭ'* (i. e., "witch," *Bubo virginianus saturatus*, great, dusky-horned owl), *wa'huhu'* (*Megascops asio*, screech owl), and *uguku'* (*Syrnium nebulosum*, hooting or barred owl). There is no generic term. The Cherokee say that there is almost no flesh upon the body of the hooting owl except upon the head.

45. The Huhu gets married (p. 292): This story was heard at different times from Swimmer, John Ax, and Ta'gwadihĭ'. The first named always gave in the proper place a very good imitation of the huhu call, drawing out the *sau-h* slowly, giving the *hŭ, hŭ, hŭ, hŭ, hŭ, hŭ* in quick, smothered tones, and ending with three chirps and a long whistle. From this and one or two other stories of similar import it would seem that the woman is the ruling partner in the Cherokee domestic establishment. Matches were generally arranged by the mother, and were conditional upon the consent of the girl (see notes to number 84, "The Man who Married the Thunder's Sister ").

The huhu of the Cherokee, so called from its cry, is the yellow-breasted chat (*Icteria virens*), also known as the yellow mocking bird on account of its wonderful mimic powers.

46. Why the Buzzard's head is bare (p. 293): This story was told by Swimmer and other informants, and is well known. It has an exact parallel in the Omaha story of "Ictinike and the Buzzard" (Dorsey, in Contributions to North American Ethnology, vi).

47. The Eagle's revenge (p. 293): This story, told by John Ax, illustrates the tribal belief and custom in connection with the eagle and the eagle dance, as already described in number 35, "The Bird Tribes," and the accompanying notes.

Drying pole—A pole laid horizontally in the forks of two upright stakes, planted firmly in the ground, for the purpose of temporarily hanging up game and fresh meat in the hunting camp, to protect it from wolves and other prey animals or to allow it to dry out before the fire.

48. The Hunter and the Buzzard (p. 294): Told by Swimmer. The custom of lending or exchanging wives in token of hospitality and friendship, on certain ceremonial occasions, or as the price of obtaining certain secret knowledge, was very general among the tribes, and has been noted by explorers and other observers, east and west, from the earliest period.

49. The snake tribe (p. 294): *Rattlesnake*—The custom of asking pardon of slain or offended animals has already been noted under number 15, "The Fourfooted Tribes," and number 35, "The Bird Tribes" (eagle). Reverence for the rattlesnake was universal among the Indians, and has been repeatedly remarked by travelers in every part of the country. To go into a dissertation upon the great subject of serpent worship is not a part of our purpose.

The missionary Washburn tells how, among the Cherokee of Arkansas, he was once riding along, accompanied by an Indian on foot, when they discovered a poisonous snake coiled beside the path. "I observed Blanket turned aside to avoid the serpent, but made no signs of attack, and I requested the interpreter to get down and kill it. He did so, and I then inquired of Blanket why he did not kill the serpent. He answered, 'I never kill snakes and so the snakes never kill me; but I will tell you about it when you next come to see me.'" He kept his word soon after by relating as a personal experience (probably, in fact, an Indian dream) a long story of having once been conducted by a rattlesnake to an underground council of the rattlesnake tribe, where he found all the snakes lamenting over one of their number who had been recently killed by an Indian, and debating the method of punishment, which was executed a day or two later by inflicting a fatal bite upon the offender while engaged in the ballplay (Reminiscences, pp. 208–212). As told by the missionary, the story is very much dressed up, but strikingly resembles number 58, "The Rattle-snake's Vengeance."

Adair, evidently confusing several Cherokee snake myths, speaks of some reputed gigantic rattlesnakes in the Cherokee mountains, with beautiful changing colors and great power of fascination, by which they drew into their jaws any living creature coming within their vision, and continues: "They call them and all of the rattle-snake kind, kings or chieftains of the snakes, and they allow one such to every dif-ferent species of the brute creation. An old trader of Cheeowhee told me that for the reward of two pieces of stroud cloth he engaged a couple of young warriors to show him the place of their resort; but the headmen would not by any means allow it, on account of a superstitious tradition—for they fancy the killing of them would expose them to the danger of being bit by the other inferior species of the serpentine tribe, who love their chieftains and know by instinct those who maliciously killed them, as they fight only in their own defense and that of their young ones, never biting those who do not disturb them." He mentions also an instance of a Chicka-saw priest who, after having applied to his hands the juice of a certain plant, took up a rattlesnake without damage and laid it carefully in a hollow tree to prevent Adair's killing it (History of the American Indians, pp. 237–238).

Of the Carolina tribes generally, Lawson, in 1701, says: "As for killing of snakes, they avoid it if they lie in their way, because their opinion is that some of the ser-pents' kindred would kill some of the savage's relations that should destroy him" (History of Carolina, p. 341).

Bartram says of the Seminoles, about 1775: "These people never kill the rattlesnake or any other serpent, saying, if they do so, the spirit of the killed snake will excite or influence his living kindred or relatives to revenge the injury or violence done to him when alive." He recounts an amusing incident of his own experience where the Indians sent for him to come and kill a rattlesnake which had invaded their camp ground, and which they were afraid to disturb. Their request having been complied with, the Indians then insisted upon scratching him, according to the Indian custom, in order to let out some of his superabundant blood and courage, but were finally, with some difficulty, dissuaded from their purpose. "Thus it seemed that the whole was a ludicrous farce to satisfy their people and appease the manes of the dead rattlesnake" (Travels, pp. 258–261).

The trader Henry (Travels, pp. 176–179) narrates a most interesting instance from among the Ojibwa of Lake Superior in 1764. While gathering wood near the camp he was startled by a sudden rattle, and looking down discovered a rattlesnake almost at his feet, with body coiled and head raised to strike.

"I no sooner saw the snake, than I hastened to the canoe, in order to procure my gun; but, the Indians observing what I was doing, inquired the occasion, and being informed, begged me to desist. At the same time, they followed me to the spot, with their pipes and tobacco-pouches in their hands. On returning, I found the snake still coiled.

"The Indians, on their part, surrounded it, all addressing it by turns, and calling it their *grandfather;* but yet keeping at some distance. During this part of the cere-mony, they filled their pipes; and now each blew the smoke toward the snake, who, as it appeared to me, really received it with pleasure. In a word, after remaining coiled, and receiving incense, for the space of half an hour, it stretched itself along the ground, in visible good humor. Its length was between four and five feet. Having remained outstretched for some time, at last it moved slowly away, the Indians fol-lowing it, and still addressing it by the title of grandfather, beseeching it to take care of their families during their absence, and to be pleased to open the heart of Sir Wil-liam Johnson [the British Indian agent, whom they were about to visit], so that he might *show them charity,* and fill their canoe with rum. One of the chiefs added a petition, that the snake would take no notice of the insult which had been offered him by the Englishman, who would even havé put him to death, but for the interference of the Indians, to whom it was hoped he would impute no part of the offence. They further requested, that he would remain, and inhabit their country, and not return among the English; that is, go eastward.''

He adds that the appearance of the rattlesnake so far north was regarded as an extraordinary omen, and that very little else was spoken of for the rest of the evening. The next day, while steering across Lake Huron in their canoe, a terrible storm came up.

''The Indians, beginning to be alarmed, frequently called on the rattlesnake to come to their assistance. By degrees the waves grew high; and at 11 o'clock it blew a hurricane, and we expected every moment to be swallowed up. From prayers, the Indians now proceeded to sacrifices, both alike offered to the god-rattlesnake, or *manito-kinibic*. One of the chiefs took a dog, and after tying its forelegs together, threw it overboard, at the same time calling on the snake to preserve us from being drowned, and desiring him to satisfy his hunger with the carcass of the dog. The snake was unpropitious, and the wind increased. Another chief sacrificed another dog, with the addition of some tobacco. In the prayer which accompanied these gifts, he besought the snake, as before, not to avenge upon the Indians the insult which he had received from myself, in the conception of a design to put him to death. He assured the snake, that I was absolutely an Englishman, and of kin neither to him nor to them. At the conclusion of this speech, an Indian, who sat near me, observed, that if we were drowned it would be for my fault alone, and that I ought myself to be sacrificed, to appease the angry manito, nor was I without apprehensions, that in case of extremity, this would be my fate; but, happily for me, the storm at length abated, and we reached the island safely.''

The Delawares also, according to Heckewelder, called the rattlesnake grandfather and refrained from injuring him. He says: ''One day, as I was walking with an elderly Indian on the banks of the Muskingum, I saw a large rattlesnake lying across the path, which I was going to kill. The Indian immediately forbade my doing so; 'for,' said he, 'the rattlesnake is grandfather to the Indians, and is placed here on purpose to guard us, and to give us notice of impending danger by his rattle, which is the same as if he were to tell us, '*look about.*' 'Now,' added he, 'if we were to kill one of those, the others would soon know it, and the whole race would rise upon us and bite us.' I observed to him that the white people were not afraid of this; for they killed all the rattlesnakes that they met with. On this he enquired whether any white man had been bitten by these animals, and of course I answered in the affirmative. ' No wonder, then!' replied he, ' you have to blame yourselves for that. You did as much as declaring war against them, and you will find them in *your* country, where they will not fail to make frequent incursions. They are a very dangerous enemy; take care you do not irritate them in *our* country; they and their grandchildren are on good terms, and neither will hurt the other.' These ancient notions have, however in a great measure died away with the last generation, and the Indians at present kill their grandfather, the rattlesnake, without ceremony, whenever they meet with him'' (Indian Nations, p. 252).

Sălikwăyĭ—''The old Tuscaroras had a custom, which they supposed would keep their teeth white and strong through life. A man caught a snake and held it by its head and tail. Then he bit it through, all the way from the head to the tail, and this kept the teeth from decay'' (W. M. Beauchamp, Iroquois Notes, in Journal of American Folk-Lore, July, 1892).

Send torrents of rain—The belief in a connection between the serpent and the rain-gods is well-nigh universal among primitive peoples, and need only be indicated here.

50. THE UKTENA AND THE ULŬÑSŬ'TĬ (p. 297): The belief in the great Uktena and the magic power of the Ulŭñsŭ'tĭ is firmly implanted in the Cherokee breast. The Uktena has its parallel in the Gitchi-Kenebig or Great Horned Serpent of the

northern Algonquian tribes, and is somewhat analogous to the Zemo'gu'ani or Great Horned Alligator of the Kiowa. Myths of a jewel in the head of a serpent or of a toad are so common to all Aryan nations as to have become proverbial. Talismanic and prophetic stones, which are carefully guarded, and to which prayer and sacrifice are offered, are kept in many tribes (see Dorsey, Teton Folklore, in American Anthropologist, April, 1889). The name of the serpent is derived from akta, "eye," and may be rendered "strong looker," i. e., "keen eyed," because nothing within the range of its vision can escape discovery. From the same root is derived akta'tĭ, "to look into," "to examine closely," the Cherokee name for a field glass or telescope. By the English-speaking Indians the serpent is sometimes called the diamond rattlesnake. The mythic diamond crest, when in its proper place upon the snake's head, is called ulstĭtlû', literally, "it is on his head," but when detached and in the hands of the conjurer it becomes the Ulûñsû'tĭ, "Transparent," the great talisman of the tribe. On account of its glittering brightness it is sometimes called Igăgû'tĭ, "Daylight." Inferior magic crystals are believed to be the scales from the same serpent, and are sometimes also called ulûñsû'tĭ.

The earliest notice of the Ulûñsû'tĭ is given by the young Virginian officer, Timberlake, who was sent upon a peace mission to the Cherokee in 1762, shortly after the close of their first war with the whites. He says (Memoirs, pp. 47–49):

"They have many beautiful stones of different colours, many of which, I am apt to believe, are of great value; but their superstition has always prevented their disposing of them to the traders, who have made many attempts to that purpose; but as they use them in their conjuring ceremonies, they believe their parting with them or bringing them from home, would prejudice their health or affairs. Among others there is one in the possession of a conjurer, remarkable for its brilliancy and beauty, but more so for the extraordinary manner in which it was found. It grew, if we may credit the Indians, on the head of a monstrous serpent, whose retreat was, by its brilliancy, discovered; but a great number of snakes attending him, he being, as I suppose by his diadem, of a superior rank among the serpents, made it dangerous to attack him. Many were the attempts made by the Indians, but all frustrated, till a fellow more bold than the rest, casing himself in leather, impenetrable to the bite of the serpent or his guards, and watching a convenient opportunity, surprised and killed him, tearing his jewel from his head, which the conjurer has kept hid for many years, in some place unknown to all but two women, who have been offered large presents to betray it, but steadily refused, lest some signal judgment or mischance should follow. That such a stone exists, I believe, having seen many of great beauty; but I cannot think it would answer all the encomiums the Indians bestow upon it. The conjurer, I suppose, hatched the account of its discovery; I have however given it to the reader, as a specimen of an Indian story, many of which are much more surprising."

A few years later Adair gives us an account of the serpent and the stone. According to his statement the uktenas had their home in a deep valley between the heads of the Tuckasegee and the "northern branch of the lower Cheerake river" (i. e., the Little Tennessee), the valley being the deep defile of Nantahala, where, by reason of its gloomy and forbidding aspect, Cherokee tradition locates more than one legendary terror. With pardonable error he confounds the Uktena with the Chief of the Rattlesnakes. The two, however, are distinct, the latter being simply the head of the rattlesnake tribe, without the blazing carbuncle or the immense size attributed to the Uktena.

"Between two high mountains, nearly covered with old mossy rocks, lofty cedars and pines, in the valleys of which the beams of the sun reflect a powerful heat, there are, as the natives affirm, some bright old inhabitants or rattlesnakes, of a more enormous size than is mentioned in history. They are so large and unwieldy, that they take a circle almost as wide as their length to crawl around in their shortest orbit; but bountiful nature compensates the heavy motion of their bodies, for, as they say,

no living creature moves within the reach of their sight, but they can draw it to
them. . . .

"The description the Indians give us of their colour is as various as what we are
told of the camelion, that seems to the spectator to change its colour, by every different
position he may view it in; which proceeds from the piercing rays of the light that
blaze from their foreheads, so as to dazzle the eyes, from whatever quarter they post
themselves—for in each of their heads, there is a large carbuncle, which not only
repels, but they affirm, sullies the meridian beams of the sun. They reckon it so
dangerous to disturb these creatures, that no temptation can induce them to betray
their secret recess to the prophane. They call them and all of the rattlesnake kind,
kings, or chieftains of the snakes, and they allow one such to every different species
of the brute creation. An old trader of Cheeowhee told me, that for the reward of
two pieces of stroud cloth, he engaged a couple of young warriors to shew him the
place of their resort, but the head-men would not by any means allow it, on account
of a superstitious tradition—for they fancy the killing of them would expose them to
the danger of being bit by the other inferior species of that serpentine tribe, who love
their chieftains, and know by instinct those who maliciously killed them, as they
fight only in their own defence and that of their young ones, never biting those who
do not disturb them."—History of the American Indians, pp. 237–238.

In another place (page 87) he tells us of an ulûñsûtĭ owned by a medicine-man
who resided at Tymahse (Tomassee), a former Cherokee town on the creek of the
same name near the present Seneca, South Carolina. "The above Cheerake prophet
had a carbuncle near as big as an egg, which they said he found where a great
rattlesnake lay dead, and that it sparkled with such surprising lustre as to illumi-
nate his dark winter house, like strong flashes of continued lightning, to the great
terror of the weak, who durst not upon any account approach the dreadful fire-dart-
ing place, for fear of sudden death. When he, died it was buried along with him,
according to custom, in the town of Tymahse, under the great beloved cabbin [seat],
which stood in the westernmost part of that old fabric, where they who will run the
risk of searching may luckily find it."

Hagar also mentions the "Oolunsade," and says, on the authority of John Ax:
"He who owns a crystal can call one of the Little People to him at any time and
make him do his bidding. Sometimes when people are ill it is because some evil
invisible being has taken possession of him. Then the Little Man called up by the
crystal can be placed on guard near the ill man to prevent the evil spirit from
re-entering after it has been expelled" (MS Stellar Legends of the Cherokee).

The Southern Alleghenies, the old Cherokee country, abound with crystals of
various kinds, as well as with minerals. The Ulûñsû'tĭ is described as a triangular
crystal about two inches long, flat on the bottom, and with slightly convex sides
tapering up to a point, and perfectly transparent with the exception of a single red
streak running through the center from top to bottom. It is evidently a rare and
beautiful specimen of rutile quartz, crystals of which, found in the region, may be
seen in the National Museum at Washington.

Other small stones of various shapes and color are in common use among the
Cherokee conjurers to discover lost articles or for other occult purposes. These
also are frequently called by the same name, and are said to have been originally
the scales of the Uktena, but the Ulûñsû'tĭ—the talisman from the forehead of the
serpent—is the crystal here described, and is so exceedingly rare that so far as is known
only one remained among the East Cherokee in 1890. Its owner, a famous hunter,
kept it hidden in a cave, wrapped up in a deerskin, but refused all inducements to
show it, much less to part with it, stating that if he should expose it to the gaze of a
white man he could kill no more game, even were he permitted to live after such
a sacrilege.

The possession of the talisman insures success in hunting, love, rain making, and all other undertakings, but its great use is in life divination, and when it is invoked for this purpose by its owner the future is mirrored in the transparent crystal as a tree is reflected in the quiet stream below.

When consulting it the conjurer gazes into the crystal, and after some little time sees in its transparent depths a picture of the person or event in question. By the action of the specter, or its position near the top or bottom of the crystal, he learns not only the event itself, but also its nearness in time or place.

Many of the East Cherokee who enlisted in the Confederate service during the late war consulted the Ulûñsû′tĭ before starting, and survivors declare that their experiences verified the prediction. One of these had gone with two others to consult the fates. The conjurer, placing the three men facing him, took the talisman upon the end of his outstretched finger and bade them look intently into it. After some moments they saw their own images at the bottom of the crystal. The images gradually ascended along the red line. Those of the other two men rose to the middle and then again descended, but the presentment of the one who tells the story continued to ascend until it reached the top before going down again. The conjurer then said that the other two would die in the second year of the war, but the third would survive through hardships and narrow escapes and live to return home. As the prophecy, so the event.

When consulted by the friends of a sick man to know if he will recover, the conjurer shows them the image of the sick man lying at the bottom of the Ulûñsû′tĭ. He then tells them to go home and kill some game (or, in these latter days, any food animal) and to prepare a feast. On the appointed day the conjurer, at his own home, looks into the crystal and sees there the picture of the party at dinner. If the image of the sick man rises and joins them at the feast the patient will recover; if otherwise, he is doomed.

51. ÂGAN-UNI′TSĬ'S SEARCH FOR THE UKTENA (p. 248): This is one of the most important of the Cherokee traditions, for the reason that it deals with the mythic monster, the Uktena, and explains the origin of the great talisman, the Ulûñsû′tĭ. As here given it was obtained from Swimmer (east) with additions and variants from Wafford (west) and others. It is recorded by Ten Kate as obtained by him in the Territory (Legends of the Cherokees, in Journal of American Folk-Lore, January, 1889), and is mentioned in connection with the Ulûñsû′tĭ, by Adair, in 1775, and by Timberlake as early as 1762 (see notes to number 50, "The Uktena and the Ulûñsû′tĭ"). One variant makes the Ulûñsû′tĭ a scale from the seventh ring of the serpent.

The Shawano, who at one time occupied the Cumberland region of Tennessee immediately adjoining the Cherokee, were regarded as wizards by all the southern tribes. Brinton says: "Among the Algonkins the Shawnee tribe did more than all others combined to introduce and carry about religious legends and ceremonies. From the earliest times they seem to have had peculiar aptitude for the ecstacies, deceits, and fancies that make up the spiritual life of their associates. Their constantly roving life brought them in contact with the myths of many nations, and it is extremely probable that they first brought the tale of the horned serpent from the Creeks and Cherokees" (Myths of the New World, p. 137).

Localities—Utăwagûn′ta mountain, Walâsi′yĭ gap, Duniskwa′lgûñ′yĭ gap and Atagâ′hĭ (mythic) lake, are all points in the Great Smoky range, which forms the dividing line between North Carolina and Tennessee. Tlanusi′yĭ is the native name for the site of Murphy, at the junction of Hiwassee and Valley rivers, North Carolina. Gahû′tĭ is Cohutta mountain in Murray county, Georgia. According to Wafford there are on the sides of this mountain several stone inclosures which were built by Âgan-uni′tsĭ for shelter places before attacking the Uktena (see also Glossary).

52. THE RED MAN AND THE UKTENA (p. 300): This story was obtained from John

Ax. Swimmer had heard it also, but remembered only a part of it. For more in regard to the Uktena and the talisman derived from it, see numbers 50 and 51, with notes.

Asga'ya Gi'gage'ĭ—The "Red Man," or lightning spirit, who is frequently invoked in the sacred formulas.

Struck by lightning—As has been explained elsewhere, the wood of a tree that has been struck by lightning plays an important part in Cherokee folklore.

Strong and dangerous—It is a common article of Indian belief that the presence of a powerful talisman, no matter how beneficent in itself, is enervating or positively dangerous to those in its vicinity unless they be fortified by some ceremonial tonic. For this reason every great "medicine" is usually kept apart in a hut or tipi built for the purpose, very much as we are accustomed to store explosives at some distance from the dwelling or business house.

53. The Hunter and the Uksu'hĭ (p. 301): This story was told by Swimmer and John Ax as an actual fact. The uksu'hĭ is the mountain blacksnake or black racer (*Coluber obsoletus*). The name seems to refer to some peculiarity of the eye, aktă (cf. uktena). Hickory-log, properly Wane'asûñ'tlûñyi, "Hickory footlog," was a Cherokee settlement on Hiwassee river, near the present Hayesville, Clay county, North Carolina. Another of the same name was on Etowah river in Georgia.

Perspiration—The Indian belief may or may not have foundation in fact.

54. The Ustû'tlĭ (p. 302): This story was told by Swimmer and John Ax (east) and by Wafford (west), and is a common tradition throughout the tribe. The name ustû'tlĭ refers to the sole of the foot, and was given to the serpent on account of its peculiar feet or "suckers." The same name is given to the common hoop-snake of the south (*Abastor erythrogrammus*), about which such wonderful tales are told by the white mountaineers. Cohutta (Gahû'tĭ) mountain, in Murray county, Georgia, was also the traditional haunt of the Uktena (see number 51, "Âgan-Uni'tsĭ's search for the Uktena," and compare also number 55, "The Uw'tsûñ'ta.")

55. The Uw'tsûñ'ta (p. 303): This story was obtained from James Blythe. Nûñ-daye'lĭ, whence Nantahala, was on the river of that name below the present Jarrett's station.

56. The Snake Boy (p. 304): This myth was told by Swimmer.

Âsĭ—The Cherokee âsĭ, or "hot-house," as it was called by the old traders, is the equivalent of the sweat-house of the western tribes. It is a small hut of logs plastered over with clay, with a shed roof, and just tall enough to permit a sitting or reclining, but not a standing, position inside. It is used for sweat-bath purposes, and as it is tight and warm, and a fire is usually kept smoldering within, it is a favorite sleeping place for the old people in cold weather. It is now nearly obsolete.

57. The Snake Man (p. 304): This myth, obtained from Chief Smith, seems designed to impress upon the laity the importance of a strict observance of the innumerable gaktûñ'ta, or tabus, which beset the daily life of the Cherokee, whether in health or sickness, hunting, war, or arts of peace (see the author's "Sacred Formulas of the Cherokees," in the Seventh Annual Report of the Bureau of Ethnology).

Similar transformation myths are found all over the world. One of the most ancient is the story of Cadmus, in Ovid's "Metamorphoses," with the despair of the wife as she sees the snaky change come over her husband. "Cadmus, what means this? Where are thy feet? Where are both thy shoulders and thy hands? Where is thy color? and, while I speak, where all else besides?"

In a Pawnee story given by Grinnell two brothers, traveling, camp for the night. The elder eats some tabued food, and wakes from his sleep to find that he is changing into a great rattlesnake, the change beginning at his feet. He rouses his brother and gives him his last instructions:

"When I have changed into a snake, take me in your arms and carry me over to that hole. That will be my home, for that is the house of the snakes.'' Having still a man's mind, he continues to talk as the metamorphosis extends upward, until at last his head changes to that of a snake, when his brother takes him up and carries him to the hole. The relatives make frequent visits to the place to visit the snake, who always comes out when they call, and the brother brings it a share of his war trophies, including a horse and a woman, and receives in return the protection of the snake man (Pawnee Hero Stories, pp. 171–181). A close Omaha variant is given by Dorsey (''The warriors who were changed to snakes,'' in Contributions to North American Ethnology, vi).

58. The Rattlesnake's vengeance (p. 305): This story, told by Swimmer, exemplifies the Indian reverence for the rattlesnake and dread of offending it already explained in number 49, ''The Snake Tribe,'' and the accompanying notes. .

Prayer song—See other references under number 3, '' Kana'ti and Selu.'' Many of the Indian ceremonial prayers and invocations are in the form of songs or chants.

59. The smaller reptiles, fishes, and insects (p. 306): *Gi'gă-tsuha′lĭ*—This lizard is probably the *Pleistodon erythrocephalus*, which is described in Holbrook's ''Herpetology'' as being about 11 to 13 inches long, with bright red head, olive-brown body and tail, and yellowish-white throat and abdomen. ''The *Pleistodon erythrocephalus* chooses his residence in deep forests, and is commonly found about hollow trees, often at a height of 30 or 40 feet from the ground, sometimes taking up his abode in the last year's nest of the woodpecker, out of which he thrusts his bright red head in a threatening manner to those who would disturb his home. He never makes his habitation on or near the ground, and in fact seldom descends from his elevation unless in search of food or water. Though shy and timid, he is very fierce when taken, and bites severely, owing to the great strength of his jaws, as well as the size and firmness of the teeth. The bite, however, though sharp and painful, is not, as is commonly supposed, venomous.'' [1]

Large horned beetle—This beetle, variously called by the Cherokee crawfish, deer or buck, on account of its branching horns, is probably the ''flying stag'' of early travelers. Says Timberlake: '' Of insects, the flying stag is almost the only one worthy of notice. It is about the shape of a beetle, but has very large, beautiful, branching horns, like those of a stag, from whence it took its name '' (Memoirs p. 46). Lawson, about 1700, also mentions ''the flying stags, with horns,'' among the insects of eastern Carolina.

60. Why the Bullfrog's head is striped (p. 310): The first version is from John Ax, the second from Swimmer, who had forgotten the details.

61. The Bullfrog lover (p. 310): The first amusing little tale was heard from several story-tellers. The warning words are sometimes given differently, but always in a deep, gruff, singing tone, which makes a very fair imitation of a bullfrog's note. The other stories were told by Tsĕsa'ni (Jessan) and confirmed by Swimmer.

In a Creek variant of the first story, in the Tuggle collection, it is a pretty girl, who is obdurate until her lover, the Rabbit, conceals himself in the same way near the spring, with a blowgun for a trumpet, and frightens her into consent by singing out: ''The girl who stays single will die, will die, will die.''

62. The Katydid's warning (p. 311): Told by Swimmer and James Blythe.

63. Ûñtsaiyĭ', the Gambler (p. 311): This story was obtained from Swimmer and John Ax (east), and confirmed also by James Wafford (west), who remembered, however, only the main points of the pursuit and final capture at Kâgûñ'yĭ. The two versions corresponded very closely, excepting that Ax sends the boy to the Sunset land to play against his brothers, while Swimmer brings them to meet him

---

[1] J. E. Holbrook, North American Herpetology, or a Description of the Reptiles inhabiting the United States, ii, p. 119; Phila., 1842.

at their father's house. In the Ax version, also, the gambler flees directly to the west, and as often as the brothers shoot at him with their arrows the thunder rolls and the lightning flashes, but he escapes by sinking into the earth, which opens for him, to reappear in another form somewhere else. Swimmer makes the Little People help in the chase. In Cherokee figure an invitation to a ball contest is a challenge to battle. Thunder is always personified in the plural, Ani'-Hyûñ'tikwălâ'skĭ, "The Thunderers." The father and the two older sons seem to be Kana'tĭ and the Thunder Boys (see number 3, "Kana'tĭ and Selu"), although neither informant would positively assert this, while the boy hero, who has no other name, is said to be the lightning. Nothing is told of his after career.

Ûñtsaiyĭ'—In this name (sometimes E'tsaiyĭ' or Tsaiyĭ') the first syllable is almost silent and the vowels are prolonged to imitate the ringing sound produced by striking a thin sheet of metal. The word is now translated "brass," and is applied to any object made of that metal. The mythic gambler, who has his counterpart in the mythologies of many tribes, is the traditional inventor of the wheel-and-stick game, so popular among the southern and eastern Indians, and variously known as gatayûstĭ, chenco, or chûnki (see note under number 3, "Kana'tĭ and Selu"). He lived on the south side of Tennessee river, at Ûñ'tiguhĭ'.

Ûñ'tiguhĭ' or The Suck—The noted and dangerous rapid known to the whites as "The Suck" and to the Cherokee as Ûñ'tiguhĭ', "Pot in the water," is in Tennessee river, near the entrance of Suck creek, about 8 miles below Chattanooga, at a point where the river gathers its whole force into a contracted channel to break through the Cumberland mountain. The popular name, Whirl, or Suck, dates back at least to 1780, the upper portion being known at the same time as "The boiling pot" (Donelson diary, in Ramsey, Tennessee, p. 71),[1] a close paraphrase of the Indian name. In the days of pioneer settlement it was a most dangerous menace to navigation, but some of the most serious obstacles in the channel have now been removed by blasting and other means. The Cherokee name and legend were probably suggested by the appearance of the rapids at the spot. Close to where Ûñtsaiyĭ' lived, according to the Indian account, may still be seen the large flat rock upon which he was accustomed to play the gatayûstĭ game with all who accepted his challenge, the lines and grooves worn by the rolling of the wheels being still plainly marked, and the stone wheels themselves now firmly attached to the surface of the rock. A similarly grooved or striped rock, where also, it is said, Ûñtsaiyĭ' used to roll his wheel, is reported to be on the north side of Hiwassee, just below Calhoun, Tennessee.

The Suck is thus described by a traveler in 1818, while the whole was still Indian country and Chattanooga was yet undreamed of:

"And here, I cannot forbear pausing a moment to call your attention to the grand and picturesque scenery which opens to the view of the admiring spectator. The country is still possessed by the aborigines, and the hand of civilization has done but little to soften the wild aspect of nature. The Tennessee river, having concentrated into one mass the numerous streams it has received in its course of three or four hundred miles, glides through an extended valley with a rapid and overwhelming current, half a mile in width. At this place, a group of mountains stand ready to dispute its progress. First, the 'Lookout,' an independent range, commencing thirty miles below, presents, opposite the river's course, its bold and rocky termination of two thousand feet. Around its brow is a pallisade [sic] of naked rocks, from seventy to one hundred feet. The river flows upon its base, and instantly twines to the right. Passing on for six miles farther it turns again, and is met by the side of the Rackoon mountain. Collecting its strength into a channel of seventy yards, it severs the mountain, and rushes tumultuously through the rocky defile, wafting the trembling navigator at the rate of a mile in two or three minutes. The passage is called 'The

<hr/>

[1] J. G. M. Ramsey, The Annals of Tennessee to the end of the Eighteenth Century, etc., Philadelphia, 1853.

Suck.' The summit of the Lookout mountain overlooks the whole country. And to those who can be delighted with the view of an interminable forest, penetrated by the windings of a bold river, interspersed with hundreds of verdant prairies, and broken by many ridges and mountains, furnishes in the month of May, a landscape, which yields to few others, in extent, variety or beauty."—Rev. Elias Cornelius, in (Silliman's) American Journal of Science, I, p. 223, 1818.

Bet even his life—The Indian was a passionate gambler and there was absolutely no limit to the risks which he was willing to take, even to the loss of liberty, if not of life. Says Lawson (History of Carolina, p. 287): "They game very much and often strip one another of all they have in the world; and what is more, I have known several of them play themselves away, so that they have remained the winners' servants till their relations or themselves could pay the money to redeem them."

His skin was clean—The idea of purification or cleansing through the efficacy of the sweat-bath is very common in Indian myth and ceremonial. In an Omaha story given by Dorsey the hero has been transformed, by witchcraft, into a mangy dog. He builds a sweat lodge, goes into it as a dog and sweats himself until, on his command, the people take off the blankets, when "Behold, he was not a dog; he was a very handsome man" ("Adventures of Hingpe-agce," in Contributions to North American Ethnology, VI, p. 175).

From the bottom—The choice of the most remote or the most insignificant appearing of several objects, as being really the most valuable, is another common incident in the myths.

Honey-locust tree—The favorite honey-locust tree and the seat with thorns of the same species in the home of the Thunder Man may indicate that in Indian as in Aryan thought there was an occult connection between the pinnated leaves and the lightning, as we know to be the case with regard to the European rowan or mountain ash.

All kinds of snakes—It will be remembered that the boy's father was a thunder god. The connection between the snake and the rain or thunder spirit has already been noted. It appears also in number 84, "The Man who Married the Thunder's Sister."

Elder brother—My elder brother (male speaking), *ûñgini'lï;* my elder brother (female speaking), *ûñgidä';* thy two elder brothers (male speaking), *tsetsăni'lï.*

Sunset land—The Cherokee word here used is *Wusûhihûñ'yï,* "there where they stay over night." The usual expression in the sacred formula is *usûñhi'yï,* "the darkening, or twilight place"; the common word is *wude'ligûñ'yï,* "there where it (the sun) goes down."

Lightning at every stroke—In the Omaha myth of "The Chief's Son and the Thunders," given by Dorsey, some young men traveling to the end of the world meet a Thunder Man, who bids the leader select one of four medicine bags. Having been warned in advance, he selects the oldest, but most powerful, and is then given also a club which causes thunder whenever flourished in the air (Contributions to North American Ethnology, VI, p. 185).

Strike the rock—This method of procuring water is as old at least as the book of Exodus.

The brass rubbed off—The beautiful metallic luster on the head of *Phanæus carni-fex* is thus accounted for. The common roller beetle is called "dung roller," but this species is distinguished as the "horned, brass" beetle. It is also sometimes spoken of as the dog of the Thunder Boys.

Beavers gnaw at the grapevine—Something like this is found among the Cheyenne: "The earth rests on a large beam or post. Far in the north there is a beaver as white as snow who is a great father of all mankind. Some day he will gnaw through the support at the bottom. We shall be helpless and the earth will fall. This will happen when he becomes angry. The post is already partly eaten through. For this reason one band of the Cheyenne never eat beaver or even touch the skin. If they do touch it, they become sick" (Kroeber, Cheyenne Tales, in Journal of American Folk-Lore, July, 1900).

64. The nest of the Tlă′nuwă (p. 315): This story was obtained first from John Ax and Ta′gwadihi′, and was afterward heard of frequently in connection with the cave at Citico. It is mentioned by Ten Kate in "Legends of the Cherokees," obtained in the Indian Territory, in the Journal of American Folk-Lore, January, 1889.

Tlă′nuwă—The Tlă′nuwă (Tsă′nuwă or Sû′năwă in the Middle dialect) is a mythic bird, described as a great hawk, larger than any bird now existing. There is a small hawk called tlă′nuwă usdi′, "little tlă′nuwă," which is described as its smaller counterpart or image, and which the Cherokee say accompanies flocks of wild pigeons, occasionally when hungry swooping down and killing one by striking it with its sharp breast bone. It is probably the goshawk (*Astur atricapillus*). The great Tlă′nuwă, like the other animals, "went up." According to Adair (History of the American Indians, p. 17) the Cherokee used to compare a miserly person to a "sinnawah." When John Ax first recited the story he insisted that the whites must also believe it, as they had it pictured on their money, and holding up a silver coin, he triumphantly pointed out what he claimed was the figure of the Tlă′nuwă, holding in its talons the arrows and in its beak the serpent. He was not so far wrong, as it is well known that the Mexican coat of arms, stamped upon the coins of the republic, has its origin in a similar legend handed down from the Aztec. Myths of dangerous monster serpents destroyed by great birds were common to a number of tribes. The Tuscarora, formerly eastern neighbors of the Cherokee, told "a long tale of a great rattlesnake, which, a great while ago, lived by a creek in that river, which was Neus, and that it killed abundance of Indians; but at last a bald eagle killed it, and they were rid of a serpent that used to devour whole canoes full of Indians at a time" (Lawson, Carolina, p. 346).

Tlă′nuwa′i—"Tlă′nuwă place," the cliff so called by the Cherokee, with the cave half way up its face, is on the north bank of Little Tennessee river, a short distance below the entrance of the Citico creek, on land formerly belonging to Colonel John Lowrey, one of the Cherokee officers at the battle of the Horseshoe bend (Wafford). Just above, but on the opposite side of the river, is U′tlûñti′yĭ, the former haunt of the cannibal liver eater (see number 66, "U′tlûñta, the Spear-finger").

Soon after the creation—As John Ax put it, adopting the Bible expression, *Hĭlahi′yu dine′tlănă a′nigwa*—"A long time ago the creation soon after."

Rope of linn bark—The old Cherokee still do most of their tying and packing with ropes twisted from the inner bark of trees. In one version of the story the medicine-man uses a long udâ′ĭ or cohosh (*Actæa?*) vine.

Holes are still there—The place which the Cherokee call Tlă′nuwă-a′tsiyelûñisûñ′yĭ, "Where the Tlă′nuwă cut it up," is nearly opposite Citico, on Little Tennessee river, just below Talassee ford, in Blount county, Tennessee. The surface of the rock bears a series of long trenchlike depressions, extending some distance, which, according to the Indians, are the marks where the pieces bitten from the body of the great serpent were dropt by the Tlă′nuwă.

65. The hunter and the Tlă′nuwă (p. 316): This myth was told by Swimmer.

66. U′tlûñ′ta, the Spear-finger (p. 316): This is one of the most noted among the Cherokee myths, being equally well known both east and west. The version here given was obtained from John Ax, with some corrections and additions from Swimmer, Wafford (west) and others. A version of it, "The Stone-shields," in which the tomtit is incorrectly made a jay, is given by Ten Kate, in his "Legends of the Cherokees," in the Journal of American Folk-Lore for January, 1889, as obtained from a mixed-blood informant in Tahlequah. Another version, "The Demon of

Consumption," by Capt. James W. Terrell, formerly a trader among the East Cherokee, appears in the same journal for April, 1892. Still another 'variant, apparently condensed from Terrell's information, is given by Zeigler and Grosscup, "Heart of the Alleghanies," page 24 (Raleigh and Cleveland, 1883). In Ten Kate's version the stone coat of mail broke in pieces as soon as the monster was killed, and the fragments were gathered up and kept as amulets by the people.

There is some confusion between this story of U'tlûñ'ta and that of Nûñ'yunu'wĭ (number 67). According to some myth tellers the two monsters were husband and wife and lived together, and were both alike dressed in stone, had awl fingers and ate human livers, the only difference being that the husband waylaid hunters, while his female partner gave her attention to children.

This story has a close parallel in the Creek myth of the Tuggle collection, "The Big Rock Man," in which the people finally kill the stony monster by acting upon the advice of the Rabbit to shoot him in the ear.

Far away, in British Columbia, the Indians tell how the Coyote transformed himself to an Elk, covering his body with a hard shell. "Now this shell was like an armor, for no arrow could pierce it; but being hardly large enough to cover all his body, there was a small hole left underneath his throat." He attacks the people, stabbing them with his antlers and trampling them under foot, while their arrows glance harmlessly from his body, until 'the Meadow-lark, who was a great telltale, appeared and cried out, 'There is just a little hole at his throat!'" A hunter directs his arrow to that spot and the Elk falls dead (Teit, Thompson River Traditions, pp. 33–34).

U'tlûñ'ta—The word means literally "he (or she) has it sharp," i. e., has some sharp part or organ. It might be used of a tooth or finger nail or some other attached portion of the body, but here refers to the awl-like finger. Ten Kate spells the name Uilata. On Little Tennessee river, nearly opposite the entrance of Citico creek, in Blount county, Tennessee, is a place which the Cherokee call U'tlûñtûñ'yĭ, "Sharp-finger place," because, they say, U'tlûñ'ta used to frequent the spot.

Nûñyû'-tlu'gûñ'ĭ—"Tree rock," so called on account of its resemblance to a standing tree trunk; a notable monument-shape rock on the west side of Hiwassee river, about four miles above Hayesville, North Carolina, and nearly on the Georgia line.

Whiteside mountain—This noted mountain, known to the Cherokee as Sanigilâ'gĭ, a name for which they have no meaning, is one of the prominent peaks of the Blue ridge, and is situated southeast from Franklin and about four miles from Highlands, or the dividing line between Macon and Jackson counties, North Carolina. It is 4,900 feet high, being the loftiest elevation on the ridge which forms the watershed between the tributaries of the Little Tennessee and the Chattooga branch of Savannah. It takes its name from the perpendicular cliff on its western exposure, and is also known sometimes as the Devil's courthouse. The Indians compare the appearance of the cliff to that of a sheet of ice, and say that the western summit was formerly crowned by a projecting rock, since destroyed by lightning, which formed a part of the great bridge which U'tlûñ'ta attempted to build across the valley. Lanman's description of this mountain, in 1848, has been quoted in the notes to number 13, "The Great Yellow-jacket." Following is a notice by a later writer:

"About five miles from Highlands is that huge old cliff, Whitesides, which forms the advanced guard of all the mountain ranges trending on the south. It is no higher than the Righi, but, like it, rising direct from the plain, it overpowers the spectator more than its loftier brethren. Through all the lowlands of upper Georgia and Alabama this dazzling white pillar of rock, uplifting the sky, is an emphatic and significant landmark. The ascent can be made on horseback, on the rear side of the mountain, to within a quarter of a mile of the summit. When the top is reached, after a short stretch of nearly perpendicular climbing, the traveler finds himself on the edge of a sheer white wall of rock, over which, clinging for life to a protecting hand, he can look, if he chooses, two thousand feet down into the dim valley below. A pebble dropped from his hand will fall straight as into a well. On the vast plain below he can see the wavelike hills on which the great mountain ranges which have stretched from Maine along the continent ebb down finally into the southern plains"—Rebecca H. Davis, Bypaths in the Mountains, in Harper's Magazine, LXI, p. 544, September, 1880.

Picking strawberries—For more than a hundred years, as readers of Bartram will remember, the rich bottom lands of the old Cherokee country have been noted for their abundance of strawberries and other wild fruits.

My grandchildren—As in most Indian languages, Cherokee kinship terms are usually specialized, and there is no single term for grandchild. "My son's child" is *ûñgini'sĭ*, plural *tsûñgini'sĭ;* "my daughter's child" is *ûñgili'sĭ*, plural *tsûñgili'sĭ.* The use of kinship terms as expressive of affection or respect is very common among Indians.

Taking the appearance—This corresponds closely with the European folk-belief in fairy changelings.

To burn the leaves—The burning of the fallen leaves in the autumn, in order to get at the nuts upon the ground below, is still practiced by the white mountaineers of the southern Alleghenies. The line of fire slowly creeping up the mountain side upon a dark night is one of the picturesque sights of that picturesque country.

The song—As rendered by Swimmer, the songs seem to be intended for an imitation of the mournful notes of some bird, such as the turtle dove, hidden in the deep forests.

Pitfall—The pitfall trap for large game was known among nearly all the tribes, but seems not to have been in frequent use.

Chickadee and tomtit—These two little birds closely resemble each other, the Carolina chickadee (*Parus carolinensis*) or tsĭkĭlilĭ being somewhat smaller than the tufted titmouse (*Parus bicolor*) or utsu'gĭ, which is also distinguished by a topknot or crest. The belief that the tsĭkĭlilĭ foretells the arrival of an absent friend is general among the Cherokee, and has even extended to their neighbors, the white mountaineers. See also number 35, "The Bird Tribes," and accompanying notes.

Her heart—The conception of a giant or other monster whose heart or "life" is in some unaccustomed part of the body, or may even be taken out and laid aside at will, so that it is impossible to kill the monster by ordinary means, is common in Indian as well as in European and Asiatic folklore.

In a Navaho myth we are told that the Coyote "did not, like other beings, keep his vital principle in his chest, where it might easily be destroyed. He kept it in the tip of his nose and in the end of his tail, where no one would expect to find it." He meets several accidents, any one of which would be sufficient to kill an ordinary creature, but as his nose and tail remain intact he is each time resurrected. Finally a girl whom he wishes to marry beats him into small pieces with a club, grinds the pieces to powder, and scatters the powder to the four winds. "But again she neglected to crush the point of the nose and the tip of the tail," with the result that the Coyote again comes to life, when of course they are married and live happily until the next chapter (Matthews, Navaho Legends, pp. 91–94).

In a tale of the Gaelic highlands the giant's life is in an egg which he keeps concealed in a distant place, and not until the hero finds and crushes the egg does the giant die. The monster or hero with but one vulnerable spot, as was the case with Achilles, is also a common concept.

67. Nûñyunu'wĭ, THE STONE MAN (p. 319): This myth, although obtained from Swimmer, the best informant in the eastern band, is but fragmentary, for the reason that he confounded it with the somewhat similar story of U'tlûñ'ta (number 66). It was mentioned by Ayâsta and others (east) and by Wafford (west) as a very old

and interesting story, although none of these could recall the details in connected form. It is noted as one of the stories heard in the Territory by Ten Kate (Legends of the Cherokees, in Journal of American Folk-Lore, January, 1889), who spells the name Nayunu'wi.

Nûñyunu'wĭ, "Dressed in stone"; *adä'lanûñstĭ*, a staff or cane; *asûñ'tlĭ, asûñ'tlûñĭ*, a foot log or bridge; *ada'wehĭ*, a great magician or supernatural wonder-worker; see the glossary.

A very close parallel is found among the Iroquois, who have traditions of an invasion by a race of fierce cannibals known as the Stonish Giants, who, originally like ordinary humans, had wandered off into the wilderness, where they became addicted to eating raw flesh and wallowing in the sand until their bodies grew to gigantic size and were covered with hard scales like stone, which no arrow could penetrate (see Cusick, in Schoolcraft, Indian Tribes, v, p. 637). One of these, which preyed particularly upon the Onondaga, was at last taken in a pitfall and thus killed. Another, in tracking his victims used "something which looked like a finger, but was really a pointer made of bone. With this he could find anything he wished." The pointer was finally snatched from him by a hunter, on which the giant, unable to find his way without it, begged piteously for its return, promising to eat no more men and to send the hunter long life and good luck for himself and all his friends. The hunter thereupon restored it and the giant kept his promises (Beauchamp, W. M., Iroquois Notes, in Journal of American Folk-Lore, Boston, July, 1892.) As told by Mrs Smith ("The Stone Giant's Challenge," Myths of the Iroquois, in Second Annual Report of the Bureau of Ethnology, 1883), the pointer was a human finger. "He placed it upright upon his hand, and it immediately pointed the way for him to go."

Menstrual woman—Among all our native tribes it is believed that there is something dangerous or uncanny in the touch or presence of a menstrual woman. Hence the universal institution of the "menstrual lodge," to which the woman retires at such periods, eating, working, and sleeping alone, together with a host of tabus and precautions bearing upon the same subject. Nearly the same ideas are held in regard to a pregnant woman.

Sourwood stakes—Cherokee hunters impale meat upon sourwood (*Oxydendrum*) stakes for roasting, and the wood is believed, also, to have power against the spells of witches.

Began to talk—The revealing of "medicine" secrets by a magician when in his final agony is a common incident in Indian myths.

Whatever he prayed for—Swimmer gives a detailed statement of the particular petition made by several of those thus painted. Painting the face and body, especially with red paint, is always among Indians a more or less sacred performance, usually accompanied with prayers.

68. THE HUNTER IN THE DÄKWÄ'—This story was told by Swimmer and Ta'gwadihĭ' and is well known in the tribe. The version from the Wahnenauhi manuscript differs considerably from that here given. In the Bible translation the word däkwä' is used as the equivalent of whale. Haywood thus alludes to the story (Nat. and Aborig. Hist. Tenn., p. 244): "One of the ancient traditions of the Cherokees is that once a whale swallowed a little boy, and after some time spewed him upon the land."

It is pretty certain that the Cherokee formerly had some acquaintance with whales, which, about the year 1700, according to Lawson, were "very numerous" on the coast of North Carolina, being frequently stranded along the shore, so that settlers derived considerable profit from the oil and blubber. He enumerates four species there known, and adds a general statement that "some Indians in America" hunted them at sea (History of Carolina, pp. 251–252).

In almost every age and country we find a myth of a great fish swallowing a man, who afterward finds his way out alive. Near to the Cherokee myth are the Bible story of Jonah, and the Greek story of Hercules, swallowed by a fish and coming out afterward alive, but bald. For parallels and theories of the origin and meaning of the myth among the ancient nations, see chapter IX of Bouton's Bible Myths.

In an Ojibwa story, the great Manabozho is swallowed, canoe and all, by the king of the fishes. With his war club he strikes repeated blows upon the heart of the fish, which attempts to spew him out. Fearing that he might drown in deep water, Manabozho frustrates the endeavor by placing his canoe crosswise in the throat of the fish, and continues striking at the heart until the monster makes for the shore and there dies, when the hero makes his escape through a hole which the gulls have torn in the side of the carcass (Schoolcraft, Algic Researches, I, pp. 145–146).

69. ATAGÂ′HI, THE ENCHANTED LAKE (p. 321): This story was heard from Swimmer, Ta′gwadih̆′, and others, and is a matter of familiar knowledge to every hunter among the East Cherokee. If Indian testimony be believed there is actually a large bare flat of this name in the difficult recesses of the Great Smoky mountains on the northern boundary of Swain county, North Carolina, somewhere between the heads of Bradleys fork and Eagle creek. It appears to be a great resort for bears and ducks, and is perhaps submerged at long intervals, which would account for the legend.

Prayer, fasting, and vigil—In Indian ritual, as among the Orientals and in all ancient religions, these are prime requisites for obtaining clearness of spiritual vision. In almost every tribe the young warrior just entering manhood voluntarily subjected himself to an ordeal of this kind, of several days' continuance, in order to obtain a vision of the "medicine" which was to be his guide and protector for the rest of his life.

70. THE BRIDE FROM THE SOUTH (p. 322): This unique allegory was heard from both Swimmer and Ta′gwădihĭ′ in nearly the same form. Hagar also (MS Stellar Legends of the Cherokee) heard something of it from Ayâsta, who, however, confused it with the Hagar variant of number 11, "The Milky Way" (see notes to number 11).

In a myth from British Columbia, "The Hot and the Cold Winds," the cold-wind people of the north wage war with the hot-wind people of the south, until the Indians, whose country lay between, and who constantly suffer from both sides, bring about a peace, to be ratified by a marriage between the two parties. Accordingly, the people of the south send their daughter to marry the son of the north. The two are married and have one child, whom the mother after a time decides to take with her to visit her own people in the north. Her visit ended, she starts on her return, accompanied by her elder brother. "They embarked in a bark canoe for the country of the cold. Her brother paddled. After going a long distance, and while crossing a great lake, the cold became so intense that her brother could not endure it any longer. He took the child from his sister and threw it into the water. Immediately the air turned warm and the child floated on the water as a lump of ice."—Teit, Traditions of the Thompson River Indians, pp. 55, 56.

71. THE ICE MAN (p. 322): This story, told by Swimmer, may be a veiled tradition of a burning coal mine in the mountains, accidentally ignited in firing the woods in the fall, according to the regular Cherokee practice, and finally extinguished by a providential rainstorm. One of Buttrick's Cherokee informants told him that "a great while ago a part of the world was burned, though it is not known now how, or by whom, but it is said that other land was formed by washing in from the mountains" (Antiquities, p. 7).

When the French built Fort Caroline, near the present Charleston, South Carolina, in 1562, an Indian villlage was in the vicinity, but shortly afterward the chief, with all his people, removed to a considerable distance in consequence of a strange accident—"a large piece of peat bog [was] kindled by lightning and consumed, which he supposed to be the work of artillery."[1]

Volcanic activities, some of very recent date, have left many traces in the Carolina mountains. A mountain in Haywood county, near the head of Fines creek, has been noted for its noises and quakings for nearly a century, one particular explosion having split solid masses of granite as though by a blast of gunpowder. These shocks and noises used to recur at intervals of two or three years, but have not now been noticed for some time. In 1829 a violent earthquake on Valley river split open a mountain, leaving a chasm extending for several hundred yards, which is still to be seen. Satoola mountain, near Highlands, in Macon county, has crevices from which smoke is said to issue at intervals. In Madison county there is a mountain which has been known to rumble and smoke, a phenomenon with which the Warm springs in the same county may have some connection. Another peak, known as Shaking or Rumbling bald, in Rutherford county, attracted widespread attention in 1874 by a succession of shocks extending over a period of six months (see Zeigler and Grosscup, Heart of the Alleghanies, pp. 228–229).

72. THE HUNTER AND SELU (p. 323): The explanation of this story, told by Swimmer, lies in the myth which derives corn from the blood of the old woman Selu (see number 3, "Kana'tï and Selu").

In Iroquois myth the spirits of Corn, Beans, and Squash are three sisters. Corn was originally much more fertile, but was blighted by the jealousy of an evil spirit. "To this day, when the rustling wind waves the corn leaves with a moaning sound, the pious Indian fancies that he hears the Spirit of Corn, in her compassion for the red man, still bemoaning with unavailing regrets her blighted fruitfulness" (Morgan, League of the Iroquois, p. 162). See number 126, "Plant Lore," and accompanying notes.

73. THE UNDERGROUND PANTHERS (p. 324): This story was told by John Ax. For an explanation of the Indian idea concerning animals see number 15, "The Four-footed Tribes," and number 76, "The Bear Man."

Several days—The strange lapse of time, by which a period really extending over days or even years seems to the stranger under the spell to be only a matter of a few hours, is one of the most common incidents of European fairy recitals, and has been made equally familiar to American readers through Irving's story of Rip Van Winkle.

74. THE TSUNDIGE'WĪ (p. 325): This curious story was told by Swimmer and Ta'gwădihī' (east) and Wafford (west). Swimmer says the dwarfs lived in the west, but Ta'gwădihī' and Wafford locate them south from the Cherokee country.

A story which seems to be a variant of the same myth was told to the Spanish adventurer Ayllon by the Indians on the South Carolina coast in 1520, and is thus given in translation from Peter Martyr's Decades, in the Discovery and Conquest of Florida, ninth volume of the Hakluyt Society's publications, pages xv–xvi, London, 1851.

"Another of Ayllon's strange stories refers to a country called Inzignanin, . . . The inhabitauntes, by report of their ancestors, say, that a people as tall as the length of a man's arme, with tayles of a spanne long, sometime arrived there, brought thither by sea, which tayle was not movable or wavering, as in foure-footed beastes, but solide, broad above, and sharpe beneath, as wee see in fishes and crocodiles, and extended into a bony hardness. Wherefore, when they desired to sitt, they used seates with holes through them, or wanting them, digged upp the earth a spanne deepe or little more, they must convay their tayle into the hole when they rest them."

---

[1] Buckingham Smith, Letter of Hernando de Soto and Memoir of Hernando de Escalante, translated from the Spanish; Washington, 1854, p. 46.

It is given thus in Barcia, Ensayo, page 5: "Tambien llegaron a la Provincia de Yncignavin adonde les contaron aquellos Indios, que en cierto tiempo, avian aportado à ella, unas Gentes, que tenian Cola . . . de una quarta de largo, flexible, que les estorvaba tanto, que para sentarse agujereaban los asientos: que el Pellejo era mui aspero, y como escamoso, y que comìan solo Peces crudos: y aviendo estos muerļo, se acabò esta Nacion, y la Verdad del Caso, con ella "

A close parallel to the Cherokee story is found among the Nisqualli of Washington, in a story of three [four?] brothers, who are captured by a mircaculously strong dwarf who ties them and carries them off in his canoe. "Having rounded the distant point, where they had first descried him, they came to a village inhabited by a race of people as small as their captor, their houses, boats and utensils being all in proportion to themselves. The three brothers were then taken out and thrown, bound as they were, into a lodge, while a council was convened to decide upon their fate. During the sitting of the council an immense flock of birds, resembling geese, but much larger, pounced down upon the inhabitants and commenced a violent attack. These birds had the power of throwing their sharp quills like the porcupine, and although the little warriors fought with great valour, they soon became covered with the piercing darts and all sunk insensible on the ground. When all resistance has ceased, the birds took to flight and disappeared. The brothers had witnessed the conflict from their place of confinement, and with much labour had succeeded in releasing themselves from their bonds, when they went to the battle ground, and commenced pulling the quills from the apparently lifeless bodies; but no sooner had they done this, than all instantly returned to consciousness" (Kane, Wanderings of an Artist, pp. 252–253).

75. ORIGIN OF THE BEAR (p. 325): This story was told by Swimmer, from whom were also obtained the hunting songs, and was frequently referred to by other informants. The Ani'-Tsâ'gûhĭ are said to have been an actual clan in ancient times. For parallels, see number 76, "The Bear Man."

Had not taken human food—The Indian is a thorough believer in the doctrine that "man is what he eats." Says Adair (History of the American Indians, p. 133): "They believe that nature is possessed of such a property as to transfuse into men and animals the qualities, either of the food they use or of those objects that are presented to their senses. He who feeds on venison is, according to their physical system, swifter and more sagacious than the man who lives on the flesh of the clumsy bear or helpless dunghill fowls, the slow-footed tame cattle, or the heavy wallowing swine. This is the reason that several of their old men recommend and say that formerly their greatest chieftains observed a constant rule in their diet, and seldom ate of any animal of a gross quality or heavy motion of body, fancying it conveyed a dullness through the whole system and disabled them from exerting themselves with proper vigour in their martial, civil, and religious duties." A continuous adherence to the diet commonly used by a bear will finally give to the eater the bear nature, if not also the bear form and appearance. A certain term of "white man's food" will give the Indian the white man's nature, so that neither the remedies nor the spells of the Indian doctor will have any effect upon him (see the author's "Sacred Formulas of the Cherokees," in Seventh Annual Report of the Bureau of Ethnology, 1891).

Shall live always—For explanation of the doctrine of animal reincarnation, see number 15, "The Four-footed Tribes."

The songs—These are fair specimens of the hunting songs found in every tribe, and intended to call up the animals or to win the favor of the lords of the game (see also deer songs in notes to number 3, "Kana'tĭ and Selu"). As usual, the word forms are slightly changed to suit the requirements of the tune. The second song was first published by the author in the paper on sacred formulas, noted above. Tsistu'yĭ,

Kuwâ′hǐ, Uya′hye, and Gâte′gwâ (-hǐ) are four mountains, under each of which the bears have a townhouse in which they hold a dance before retiring to their dens for their winter sleep. At Tsistu′yǐ, "Rabbit place," known to us as Gregory bald, in the Great Smoky range, dwells the Great Rabbit, the chief of the rabbit tribe. At Kuwâ′hǐ, "Mulberry place," farther northeast along the same range, resides the White Bear, the chief of the bear tribe, and near by is the enchanted lake of Ata-gâ′hǐ, to which wounded bears go to bathe and be cured (see number 15, "The Four-footed Tribes," and number 69, "Atagâ′hǐ, the Enchanted Lake"). Uyâhye is also a peak of the Great Smokies, while Gâtegwâ′hǐ, "Great swamp or thicket (?)," is southeast of Franklin, North Carolina, and is perhaps identical with Fodderstack mountain (see also the glossary).

76. THE BEAR MAN (p. 327): This story was obtained first from John Ax, and has numerous parallels in other tribes, as well as in European and oriental folklore. The classic legend of Romulus and Remus and the stories of "wolf boys" in India will at once suggest themselves. Swimmer makes the trial of the hunter's weapons by the bears a part of his story of the origin of disease and medicine (number 4), but says that it may have happened on this occasion (see also number 15, "The Four-footed Tribes," and notes to number 75, "Origin of the Bear").

In a strikingly similar Creek myth of the Tuggle collection, "Origin of the Bear Clan," a little girl lost in the woods is adopted by a she-bear, with whom she lives for four years, when the bear is killed by the hunter and the girl returns to her people to become the mother of the Bear clan.

The Iroquois have several stories of children adopted by bears. In one, "The Man and His Stepson," a boy thus cared for is afterward found by a hunter, who tames him and teaches him to speak, until in time he almost forgets that he had lived like a bear. He marries a daughter of the hunter and becomes a hunter himself, but always refrains from molesting the bears, until at last, angered by the taunts of his mother-in-law, he shoots one, but is himself killed by an accident while on his return home (Smith, Myths of the Iroquois, in Second Annual Report Bureau of Ethnology). In line with this is the story of a hunter who had pursued a bear into its den. "When some distance in he could no longer see the bear, but he saw a fire and around it sat several men. The oldest of the three men looked up and asked, 'Why did you try to shoot one of my men. We sent him out to entice you to us'" (Curtin, Seneca MS in Bureau of American Ethnology archives).

In a Pawnee myth, "The Bear Man," a boy whose father had put him under the protection of the bears grows up with certain bear traits and frequently prays and sacrifices to these animals. On a war party against the Sioux he is killed and cut to pieces, when two bears find and recognize the body, gather up and arrange the pieces and restore him to life, after which they take him to their den, where they care for him and teach him their secret knowledge until he is strong enough to go home (Grinnell, Pawnee Hero Stories, pp. 121–128).

In a Jicarilla myth, "Origin and Destruction of the Bear," a boy playing about in animal fashion runs into a cave in the hillside. "When he came out his feet and hands had been transformed into bear's paws." Four times this is repeated, the change each time mounting higher, until he finally emerges as a terrible bear monster that devours human beings (Russell, Myths of the Jicarilla, in Journal of American Folk-Lore, October, 1898).

Read the thoughts—Thought reading is a very common feature of Indian myths. Certain medicine ceremonies are believed to confer the power upon those who fulfil the ordeal conditions.

Food was getting scarce—Several references in the myths indicate that, through failure of the accustomed wild crops, famine seasons were as common among the animal tribes as among the Indians (see number 33, "The Migration of the Animals").

Kalás'-Gúnahi'ta—See number 15, "The Four-footed Tribes."

Rubbed his stomach—This very original method of procuring food occurs also in number 3, "Kana'tĭ and Selu."

Topknots and Splitnoses—Tsunĭ'stsăhĭ', "Having topknots"—i. e., Indians, in allusion to the crests of upright hair formerly worn by warriors of the Cherokee and other eastern tribes. Timberlake thus describes the Cherokee warrior's headdress in 1762: "The hair of their head is shaved, tho' many of the old people have it plucked out by the roots, except a patch on the hinder part of the head about twice the bigness of a crown piece, which is ornamented with beads, feathers, wampum, stained deer's hair, and such like baubles" (Memoirs, p. 49). Tsunû'liyû' sŭnĕ-stlâ'tă, "they have split noses"—i. e., dogs.

Cover the blood—The reincarnation of the slain animal from the drops of blood spilt upon the ground or from the bones is a regular part of Cherokee hunting belief, and the same idea occurs in the folklore of many tribes. In the Omaha myth, "Ictinike and the Four Creators," the hero visits the Beaver, who kills and cooks one of his own children to furnish the dinner. When the meal was over "the Beaver gathered the bones and put them into a skin, which he plunged beneath the water. In a moment the youngest beaver came up alive out of the water" (Dorsey, in Contributions to North American Ethnology, VI, p. 557).

Like a man again—It is a regular article of Indian belief, which has its parallels in European fairy lore, that one who has eaten the food of the spirit people or supernaturals can not afterward return to his own people and live, unless at once, and sometimes for a long time, put under a rigid course of treatment intended to efface the longing for the spirit food and thus to restore his complete human nature. See also number 73, "The Underground Panthers." In "A Yankton Legend," recorded by Dorsey, a child falls into the water and is taken by the water people. The father hears the child crying under the water and employs two medicine men to bring it back. After preparing themselves properly they go down into the deep water, where they find the child sitting beside the water spirit, who, when they declare their message, tells them that if they had come before the child had eaten anything he might have lived, but now if taken away "he will desire the food which I eat; that being the cause of the trouble, he shall die." They return and report: "We have seen your child, the wife of the water deity has him. Though we saw him alive, he had eaten part of the food which the water deity eats, therefore the water deity says that if we bring the child back with us out of the water he shall die," and so it happened. Some time after the parents lose another child in like manner, but this time "she did not eat any of the food of the water deity and therefore they took her home alive." In each case a white dog is thrown in to satisfy the water spirits for the loss of the child (Contributions to North American Ethnology, VI, p. 357).

77. THE GREAT LEECH OF TLANUSI'YĬ (p. 329): This legend was heard first from Swimmer and Chief Smith, the latter of whom was born near Murphy; it was confirmed by Wafford (west) and others, being one of the best known myths in the tribe and embodied in the Cherokee name for Murphy. It is apparently founded upon a peculiar appearance, as of something alive or moving, at the bottom of a deep hole in Valley river, just below the old Unicoi turnpike ford, at Murphy, in Cherokee county, North Carolina. It is said that a tinsmith of the town once made a tin bomb which he filled with powder and sank in the stream at this spot with the intention of blowing up the strange object to see what it might be, but the contrivance failed to explode. The hole is caused by a sudden drop or split in the rock bed of the stream, extending across the river. Wafford, who once lived on Nottely river, adds the incident of the two women and says that the Leech had wings and could fly. He asserts also that he found rich lead ore in the hole, but that the swift current prevented working it. About two miles above the mouth of Nottely river a bend of the stream brings it within about the same distance of the Hiwassee at Murphy.

This nearest point of approach on Nottely is also known to the Cherokee as Tlanusi′yĭ, "leech place," and from certain phenomena common to both streams it is a general belief among Indians and whites that they are connected here by a subterranean water way. The legend and the popular belief are thus noted in 1848 by Lanman, who incorrectly makes the leech a turtle:

"The little village of Murphy, whence I date this letter, lies at the junction of the Owassa and Valley rivers, and in point of location is one of the prettiest places in the world. Its Indian name was Klausuna, or the Large Turtle. It was so called, says a Cherokee legend, on account of its being the sunning place of an immense turtle which lived in its vicinity in ancient times. The turtle was particularly famous for its repelling power, having been known not to be at all injured by a stroke of lightning. Nothing on earth had power to annihilate the creature; but, on account of the many attempts made to take its life, when it was known to be a harmless and inoffensive creature, it became disgusted with this world, and burrowed its way into the middle of the earth, where it now lives in peace.

"In connection with this legend, I may here mention what must be considered a remarkable fact in geology. Running directly across the village of Murphy is a belt of marble, composed of the black, grey, pure white and flesh-colored varieties, which belt also crosses the Owassa river. Just above this marble causeway the Owassa, for a space of perhaps two hundred feet, is said to be over one hundred feet deep, and at one point, in fact, a bottom has never been found. All this is simple truth, but I have heard the opinion expressed that there is a subterranean communication between this immense hole in Owassa and the river Notely, which is some two miles distant. The testimony adduced in proof of this theory is, that a certain log was once marked on the Notely, which log was subsequently found floating in the pool of the Deep Hole in the Owassa" (Letters, pp. 63–64).

78. THE NŬÑNĔ′HĬ AND OTHER SPIRIT FOLK (p. 330): The belief in fairies and kindred spirits, frequently appearing as diminutive beings in human form, is so universal among all races as to render citation of parallels unnecessary. Every Indian tribe has its own spirits of the woods, the cliffs, and the waters, usually benevolent and kindly when not disturbed, but often mischievous, and in rare cases malicious and revengeful. These invisible spirit people are regarded as a sort of supernatural human beings, entirely distinct from ghosts and from the animal and plant spirits, as well as from the godlike beings who rule the sun, the rain, and the thunder. Most of the Nŭññĕ′hĭ stories here given were told by Wafford, who believed them all firmly in spite of his white man's blood and education. The others, excepting that of the offended spirits (Wahnenauhi MS) and the Fire-carrier (Wafford), were heard from various persons upon the reservation. For other Nŭññĕ′hĭ references see the stories of Tsuwe′năhĭ, Kăna′sta, Yahula, etc.

Nŭññĕ′hĭ—This word (*gŭññĕ′hĭ* in a dialectic form and *nayĕ′hĭ* in the singular) may be rendered "dwellers anywhere" or "those who live anywhere," but is understood to mean "those who live forever," i. e., Immortals. It is spelled *Nanehi* by Buttrick and *Nuhnayie* in the Wahnenauhi manuscript. The singular form, *Nayĕ′hĭ*, occurs also as a personal name, equivalent to *Edâ′hĭ*, "One who goes about."

Some invisible townhouse—The ancient Creek town of Okmulgee, where now is the city of Macon, in Georgia, was destroyed by the Carolina people about the time of the Yamassee war. Sixty years later Adair says of the Creeks: "They strenuously aver that when the necessity forces them to encamp there, they always hear at the dawn of the morning the usual noise of Indians singing their joyful religious notes and dancing, as if going down to the river to purify themselves, and then returning to the old townhouse; with a great deal more to the same effect. Whenever I have been there, however, all hath been silent . . . But they say this was 'because I am an obdurate infidel that way' " (Hist. Am. Indians, p. 36).

Nottely town—Properly Na′dŭ′lĭ, was on Nottely river, a short distance above

Raper creek in Cherokee county, North Carolina. The old townhouse was upon a large mound on the west side of the river and about five miles below the Georgia line. The town was practically deserted before the removal in 1838 (see glossary).

Hemptown—Properly Gatûñlti′yĭ, "Hemp place," existed until the Removal, on Hemptown creek, a branch of Toccoa river, a few miles north of the present Morganton, in Fannin county, Georgia.

Noted circular depression—This may have been a circular earthwork of about thirty feet diameter, described as existing in 1890 a short distance east of Soquee post-office near the head of Soquee creek, about ten miles northwest of Clarkesville, Habersham county, Georgia. There are other circular structures of stone on elevated positions within a few miles of Clarkesville (see author's manuscript notes on Cherokee archeology, in Bureau of American Ethnology archives). The same story about throwing logs and stones into one of these sacred places, only to have them thrown out again by invisible hands, is told by Zeigler and Grosscup, in connection with the Jutaculla old fields (see note under number 81, "Tsul′kălû′").

Bewildered—"Crazy persons were supposed to be possessed with the devil or afflicted with the Nanehi" (Buttrick, Antiquities, p. 14). According to Hagar's informant: "The little people cause men to lose their minds and run away and wander in the forests. They wear very long hair, down to their heels" (MS Stellar Legends of the Cherokee). In Creek belief, according to the Tuggle manuscript, "Fairies or little people live in hollow trees and on rocky cliffs. They often decoy people from their homes and lose them in the woods. When a man's mind becomes bewildered—not crazy—this is caused by the little people."

Loaves seemed to shrink—The deceptive and unsatisfactory character of all fairy belongings when the spell is lifted is well known to the European peasantry.

Tsăwa′sĭ and Tsăga′sĭ—These sprites are frequently named in the hunting prayers and other sacred formulas.

Scratching—This is a preliminary rite of the ballplay and other ceremonies, as well as the doctor's method of hypodermic injection. As performed in connection with the ballplay it is a painful operation, being inflicted upon the naked skin with a seven-toothed comb of turkey bone, the scratches being drawn in parallel lines upon the breast, back, arms and legs, until the sufferer is bleeding from head to foot. In medical practice, in order that the external application may take hold more effectually, the scratching is done with a rattlesnake's tooth, a brier, a flint, or a piece of glass. See author's Cherokee Ball Play, in American Anthropologist, April, 1890, and Sacred Formulas of the Cherokees, in Seventh Annual Report Bureau of Ethnology, 1891. The practice seems to have been general among the southern tribes, and was sometimes used as a punishment for certain delinquents. According to Adair the doctor bled patients by scratching them with the teeth of garfish after the skin had been first well softened by the application of warm water, while any unauthorized person who dared to intrude upon the sacred square during ceremonial performances "would be dry-scratched with snakes' teeth, fixed in the middle of a split reed or piece of wood, without the privilege of warm water to supple the stiffened skin" (Hist. Am. Indians, pp. 46, 120).

The Fire-carrier—This is probably the gaseous phenomenon known as the will-o'-the-wisp, which has been a thing of mystery and fear to others beside Indians.

79. THE REMOVED TOWNHOUSES (p. 335): The first of these stories was told by John Ax. The second was obtained from Salâ′lĭ, "Squirrel," mentioned elsewhere as a self-taught mechanic of the East Cherokee. Wafford (west) had also heard it, but confused it with that of Tsul′kălû′ (number 81).

Excepting Gustĭ′, the localities are all in western North Carolina. The large mound of Sĕ′tsĭ is on the south side of Valley river, about three miles below Valleytown, in Cherokee county. Anisgaya′yĭ town is not definitely located by the story teller, but was probably in the same neighborhood. Tsudaye′lûñ′yĭ, literally "where it is isolated," or "isolated place," is a solitary high peak near Cheowa Maximum, a few miles northeast of Robbinsville, in Graham county, on the summit of which there is said to be a large rock somewhat resembling in appearance a circular town-house with a part wanting from one side. Du′stiya′lûñ′yĭ, "Where it was shot," i. e., "Where it was struck by lightning," is the territory on Hiwassee river, about the mouth of Shooting creek, above Hayesville, in Clay county (see also glossary).

No one must shout—The same injunction occurs in the legend of Tsul′kălû′ (number 81). The necessity for strict silence while under the conduct of fairy guides is constantly emphasized in European folklore.

Townhouse in the water below—Breton legend tells of a submerged city which rises out of the sea at long intervals, when it can be seen by those who possess the proper talisman, and we know that in Ireland

> "On Lough Neagh's banks as the fisherman strays,
> When the clear cold eve's declining,
> He sees the round towers of other days
> In the wave beneath him shining."

80. THE SPIRIT DEFENDERS OF NĬKWĂSĬ′ (p. 336): This story was obtained from Swimmer. Nĭkwăsĭ′ or Nĭkw'sĭ′, one of the most ancient settlements of the Cherokee, was on the west bank of Little Tennessee river, where is now the town of Franklin, in Macon county, North Carolina. The mound upon which the townhouse stood, in a field adjoining the river, is probably the largest in western Carolina and has never been explored. The Cherokee believe that it is the abode of the Nûñnĕ′hĭ or Immortals (see number 78) and that a perpetual fire burns within it. The name, which can not be translated, appears as Nucassee in old documents. The British agent held a council here with the Cherokee as early as 1730. Although twice destroyed, the town was rebuilt and continued to be occupied probably until the land was sold in 1819.

Bring the news home—It was a frequent custom in Indian warfare to spare a captive taken in battle in order that he might carry back to his people the news of the defeat. After the disastrous defeat of the French under D'Artaguette by the Chickasaw in upper Mississippi in 1736, D'Artaguette, Lieutenant Vincennes, Father Senac, and fifteen others were burned at the stake by the victors, but "one of the soldiers was spared to carry the news of the triumph of the Chickasaws and the death of these unhappy men to the mortified Bienville" (Pickett, History of Alabama, p. 298, ed. 1896).

81. TSUL′KĂLÛ′, THE SLANT-EYED GIANT (p. 337): The story of Tsul′kălû′ is one of the finest and best known of the Cherokee legends. It is mentioned as early as 1823 by Haywood, who spells the name Tuli-cula, and the memory is preserved in the local nomenclature of western Carolina. Hagar also alludes briefly to it in his manuscript Stellar Legends of the Cherokee. The name signifies literally "he has them slanting," being understood to refer to his eyes, although the word eye (*aktă′*, plural *diktă′*) is not a part of it. In the plural form it is also the name of a traditional race of giants in the far west (see number 106, "The Giants from the West"). Tsul′kălû′ lives in Tsuneguñ′yĭ and is the great lord of the game, and as such is frequently invoked in the hunting formulas. The story was obtained from Swimmer and John Ax, the Swimmer version being the one here followed. For parallels to the incident of the child born from blood see notes to number 3, "Kana′tĭ and Selu."

In the John Ax version it is the girl's father and mother, instead of her mother and brother, who try to bring her back. They are told they must fast seven days to succeed. They fast four days before starting, and then set out and travel two days, when they come to the mouth of the cave and hear the sound of the drum and the dance within. They are able to look over the edge of the rock and see their daughter among the dancers, but can not enter until the seventh day is arrived. Unluckily the man is very hungry by this time, and after watching nearly all night he insists that it is so near daylight of the seventh morning that he may safely take a small bite. His wife begs him to wait until the sun appears, but hunger overcomes him and he takes a bite of food from his pouch. Instantly the cave and the dancers disappear, and the man and his wife find themselves alone on the mountain. John Ax was a very old man at the time of the recital, with memory rapidly failing, and it is evident that his version is only fragmentary.

Haywood notes the story on the authority of Charles Hicks, an educated halfbreed (Nat. and Aborig. Hist. Tenn., p. 280): "They have a fabulous tradition respecting the mounds, which proves that they are beyond the events of their history. The mounds, they say, were caused by the quaking of the earth and great noise with it, a ceremony used for the adoption of their people into the family of Tuli-cula, who was an invisible person and had taken a wife of one of their town's people. And at the time when his first son was born the quaking of the earth and noise had commenced, but had ceased at the alarm whoop, which had been raised by two imprudent young men of the town, in consequence of which the mounds had been raised by the quaking noise. Whereupon the father took the child and mother and removed to near Brasstown, and had made the tracks in the rocks which are to be seen there."

From Buttrick we get the following version of the tradition, evidently told for the missionary's special benefit: "God directed the Indians to ascend a certain mountain—that is, the warriors—and he would there send them assistance. They started and had ascended far up the mountain, when one of the warriors began to talk about women. His companion immediately reproved him, but instantly a voice like thunder issued from the side of the mountain and God spoke and told them to return, as he could not assist them on account of that sin. They put the man to death, yet the Lord never returned to them afterwards" (Antiquities, p. 14). On the next page he tells it in a somewhat different form: "It is said that before coming to this continent, while in their own country, they were in great distress from their enemies, and God told them to march to the top of a certain mountain and He would come down and afford them relief. They ascended far up the mountain and thought they saw something coming down from above, which they supposed was for their aid. But just then one of the warriors," etc.

Zeigler and Grosscup give another version, which, although dressed up for advertising purposes, makes a fairly good story:

"But there is another legend of the Balsams more significant than any of these. It is the Paradise Gained of Cherokee mythology, and bears some distant resemblance to the Christian doctrine of mediation. The Indians believed that they were originally mortal in spirit as well as body, but above the blue vault of heaven there was, inhabited by a celestial race, a forest into which the highest mountains lifted their dark summits. * * *

"The mediator, by whom eternal life was secured for the Indian mountaineers, was a maiden of their own tribe. Allured by the haunting sound and diamond sparkle of a mountain stream, she wandered far up into a solitary glen, where the azalea, the kalmia, and the rhododendron brilliantly embellished the deep, shaded slopes, and filled the air with their delicate perfume. The crystal stream wound its crooked way between moss-covered rocks over which tall ferns bowed their graceful stems. Enchanted by the scene, she seated herself upon the soft moss, and, overcome by fatigue, was soon asleep. The dream picture of a fairyland was presently broken by the soft touch of a strange hand. The spirit of her dream occupied a place at her side, and, wooing, won her for his bride.

"Her supposed abduction caused great excitement among her people, who made diligent search for her recovery in their own villages. Being unsuccessful, they made war upon the neighboring tribes in the hope of finding the place of her concealment. Grieved because of so much bloodshed and sorrow, she besought the great chief of the eternal hunting grounds to make retribution. She was accordingly appointed to call a council of her people at the forks of the Wayeh (Pigeon) river. She appeared unto the chiefs in a dream, and charged them to meet the spirits of the hunting ground with fear and reverence.

"At the hour appointed the head men of the Cherokees assembled. The high Balsam peaks were shaken by thunder and aglare with lightning. The cloud, as black as midnight, settled over the valley, then lifted, leaving upon a large rock a cluster of strange men, armed and painted as for war. An enraged brother of the abducted maiden swung his tomahawk and raised the war whoop, but a swift thunderbolt dispatched him before the echo had died in the hills. The chiefs, terror-stricken, fled to their towns.

"The bride, grieved by the death of her brother and the failure of the council, prepared to abandon her new home and return to her kindred in the valleys. To reconcile her the promise was granted that all brave warriors and their faithful women should have an eternal home in the happy hunting ground above, after death. The great chief of the forest beyond the clouds became the guardian spirit of the Cherokees. All deaths, either from wounds in battle or disease, were attributed to his desire to make additions to the celestial hunting ground, or, on the other hand, to his wrath, which might cause their unfortunate spirits to be turned over to the disposition of the evil genius of the mountain tops."—Heart of the Alleghanies, pp. 22–24.

Kănu'ga—An ancient Cherokee town on Pigeon river, in the present Haywood county, North Carolina. It was deserted before the beginning of the historic period, but may have been located about the junction of the two forks of Pigeon river, a few miles east of Waynesville, where there are still a number of mounds and ancient cemeteries extending for some miles down the stream. Being a frontier town, it was probably abandoned early on account of its exposed position. The name, signifying "scratcher," is applied to a comb, used for scratching the ballplayers, and is connected with *kănugû'lă* or *nugû'lă*, a blackberry bush or brier. There are other mounds on Richland creek, in the neighborhood of Waynesville.

Tsul'kălû' Tsunegûñ'yĭ—Abbreviated Tsunegûñ'yĭ; the mountain in which the giant is supposed to have his residence, is Tennessee bald, in North Carolina, where the Haywood, Jackson, and Transylvania county lines come together, on the ridge separating the waters of Pigeon river from those flowing into Tennessee creek and Cany fork of the Tuckasegee, southeastward from Waynesville and Webster. The name seems to mean, "at the white place," from *une'ga*, "white," and may refer to a bald spot of perhaps a hundred acres on the top, locally known among the whites as Jutaculla old fields, from a tradition, said to be derived from the Indians, that it was a clearing made by "Jutaculla" (i. e., Tsul'kălû') for a farm. Some distance farther west, on the north side of Cany fork and about ten miles above Webster, in Jackson county, is a rock known as Jutaculla rock, covered with various rude carvings, which, according to the same tradition, are scratches made by the giant in jumping from his farm on the mountain to the creek below. Zeigler and Grosscup refer to the mountain under the name of "Old Field mountain" and mention a tradition among the pioneers that it was regarded by the Indians as the special abode of the Indian Satan!

"On the top of the mountain there is a prairie-like tract, almost level, reached by steep slopes covered with thickets of balsam and rhododendron, which seem to garrison the reputed sacred domain. It was understood among the Indians to be forbidden territory, but a party one day permitted their curiosity to tempt them. They forced a way through the entangled thickets, and with merriment entered the open ground. Aroused from sleep and enraged by their audacious intrusion, the devil, taking the form of an immense snake, assaulted the party and swallowed fifty of them before the thicket could be gained. Among the first whites who settled among the Indians, and traded with them, was a party of hunters who used this superstition to escape punishment for their reprehensible conduct. They reported that they were in league with the great spirit of evil, and to prove that they were, frequented this 'old field.' They described his bed, under a large overhanging rock, as a model of neatness. They had frequently thrown into it stones and brushwood during the day, while the master was out, but the place was invariably as clean the next morning 'as if it had been brushed with a bunch of feathers'" (Heart of the Alleghanies, p. 22).

The footprints can still be seen—Shining rock or Cold mountain, between the Forks of Pigeon river, in Haywood county, North Carolina, is known to the Cherokee as Datsu′nălâsgûñ′yĭ, "where their tracks are this way," on account of a rock at its base, toward Sonoma and three miles south of the trail, upon which are impressions said to be the footprints made by the giant and his children on their way to Tsunegûñ′yĭ. Within the mountain is also the legendary abode of invisible spirits. Haywood confounds this with Track Rock gap, near Blairsville, Georgia, where are other noted petroglyphs (see number 125, Minor Legends of Georgia).

The rapid growth of the two children is paralleled in many other tribal mythologies. The sequence of growth as indicated by the footprints reminds us of the concluding incident of the Arabian Nights, when Queen Scheherazade stands before the king to make a last request: "And the king answered her, ' Request, thou shalt receive, O Scheherazade.' So thereupon she called out to the nurses and the eunuchs and said to them, ' Bring ye my children.' Accordingly they brought them to her quickly, and they were three male children; one of them walked, and one crawled, and one was at the breast."

Must not raise the war whoop—See note under number 79, "The Removed Townhouses."

82. Kăna′sta, the lost settlement (p. 341): This story, obtained from Swimmer, bears resemblance to those of Tsul′kălû′, Tsuwe′năhĭ, The Removed Townhouses, and others, in which individuals, or even whole settlements, elect to go with the invisible spirit people in order to escape hardships or coming disaster.

Kăna′sta—Abbreviated from Kănastûñ′yĭ, a name which can not be translated, is described as an ancient Cherokee town on the French Broad where the trail from Tennessee creek of the Tuckasegee comes in, near the present Brevard, in Transylvania county, North Carolina. No mounds are known there, and we find no notice of the town in history, but another of the same name existed on Hiwassee and was destroyed in 1776.

Tsuwa′tel′da—Abbreviated from Tsuwa′teldûñ′yĭ, and known to the whites as Pilot knob, is a high mountain in Transylvania county, about eight miles north of Brevard. On account of the peculiar stratified appearance of the rocks, the faces of the cliffs are said frequently to present a peculiar appearance under the sun's rays, as of shining walls with doors, windows, and shingled roofs.

Datsu′nălâsgûñ′yĭ—Shining rock. See note under number 81, "Tsul′kălû′."

Fast seven days—This injunction of a seven days' fast upon those who would join the spirit people appears in several Cherokee myths, the idea being, as we learn from the priests, to spiritualize the human nature and quicken the spiritual vision by abstinence from earthly food. The doctrine is exemplified in an incident of the legend of Tsuwe′năhĭ, q. v. In a broader application, the same idea is a foundation principle of every ancient religion. In ordinary Cherokee ceremonial the fast is kept for one day—i. e., from midnight to sunset. On occasions of supreme importance it continues four or even seven days. Among the plains tribes those who voluntarily enter the Sun dance to make supplication and sacrifice for their people abstain entirely from food and drink during the four days and nights of the ceremony.

The Thunders—See number 3, "Kana′tĭ and Selu" and notes, and number 8, "The Moon and the Thunders," with notes.

83. Tsuwe′năhĭ, a legend of Pilot knob (p. 343): This story, from Swimmer,

is of the same order as the legends of Tsul'kälû', Kăna'sta, etc. The people whom the hunter met inside the enchanted mountain are evidently the same described in the last-named story (number 82), with the guests from the lost settlement.

The name Tsuwe'năhĭ can not be translated, but may possibly have a connection with *uwe'năhĭ*, "rich."

Kanu'ga and Tsuwa'tel'da—See notes under number 81, "Tsul'kälû'," and number 82, "Kăna'sta."

Parched corn—This was the standard provision of the warrior when on the march among all the tribes east of the Mississippi and probably among all the corn-growing tribes of America. It is the pinole of the Tarumari and other Mexican tribes. The Cherokee call it *găhăwĭ'sita*. Hawkins thus describes it as seen with his Cherokee guides in 1796: "They are small eaters, use no salt and but little bread. They carry their parched corn meal, *wissactaw*, and mix a handful in a pint of water, which they drink. Although they had plenty of corn and fowls, they made no other provision than a small bag of this for the path. I have plenty of provisions and give them some at every meal. I have several times drank of the wissactaw, and am fond of it with the addition of some sugar. To make of the best quality, I am told the corn should first be boiled, then parched in hot ashes, sifted, powdered, and made into flour."[1]

The seat was a turtle—This incident also occurs in number 84, "The Man who Married the Thunder's Sister." The species meant is the săligu'gĭ or common water turtle.

Like dogs' paws—No reason is given for this peculiarity, which is nowhere else mentioned as a characteristic of the mountain spirits.

Old tobacco—Tsâl-agăyûñ'li, "ancient tobacco," the *Nicotiana rustica*, sacred among all the eastern tribes. See number 6, "How they Brought back the Tobacco," and number 126, "Plant Lore."

Thorns of honey locust—This incident occurs also in number 63, "Ûñtsaiyĭ', The Gambler."

84. THE MAN WHO MARRIED THE THUNDER'S SISTER (p. 345): This story was heard first from John Ax, and afterward with additions and variants from Swimmer and others. It is also briefly noted in Hagar's manuscript "Stellar Legends of the Cherokee."

As explained elsewhere, the Thunder spirits are supposed to have their favorite residence under cataracts, of which Tallulah falls is probably the greatest in the Cherokee country. The connection of Thunder and Rain spirits with snakes and water animals is a matter of universal primitive belief and has already been noted. One Cherokee informant told Hagar (see above) that "Thunder is a horned snake (?), and lightning its tongue, and it lives with water and rains." It is hardly necessary to state that the dance was, and is, among all the tribes, not only the most frequent form of social amusement, but also an important part of every great religious or other ceremonial function.

Săkwi'yĭ—Abbreviated Săkwi', an ancient town about on the site of the present village of Soquee on the creek of the same name near Clarkesville, in Habersham county, Georgia.

Marry him—Among nearly all the tribes, with the exception of the Pueblo, the marriage ceremony was simple, consisting chiefly of the giving, by the lover, of certain presents to the parents of the intended bride, by way of compensating them for the loss of their daughter, after she herself had first signified her consent to the union. Although this has been represented as a purchase, it was really only a formal ratification of the contract, which the girl was free to accept or reject as she chose. On the other hand, should the presents be insufficient to satisfy the parents, they were

---

[1] Manuscript Journal, 1796, with Georgia Historical Society, Savannah.

refused or returned and the marriage could not take place, however willing the girl might be. The young man usually selected a friend to act as go-between with the girl's family, and in all tribes—as now in the West—the result seems to have been largely at the disposal of her brother, who continued to exercise some supervision and claim over her even after her marriage.

Lawson's statement concerning the eastern Carolina tribes in 1700 will hold almost equally good to-day in any part of the West: "As for the Indian marriages, I have read and heard of a great deal of form and ceremony used, which I never saw; nor yet could learn in the time I have been amongst them any otherwise than I shall here give you an account of, which is as follows:

"When any young Indian has a mind for such a girl to his wife, he, or some one for him, goes to the young woman's parents, if living; if not, to her nearest relations, where they make offers of the match betwixt the couple. The relations reply, they will consider of it; which serves for a sufficient answer, till there be a second meeting about the marriage, which is generally brought into debate before all the relations that are old people, on both sides, and sometimes the king with all his great men give their opinions therein. If it be agreed on and the young woman approve thereof—for these savages never give their children in marriage without their own consent—the man pays so much for his wife, and the handsomer she is the greater price she bears" (History of Carolina, pp. 302–303).

According to Adair, who makes it a little more formal among the Gulf tribes, "When an Indian makes his first address to the young woman he intends to marry, she is obliged by ancient custom to sit by him till he hath done eating and drinking, whether she likes or dislikes him; but afterward she is at her own choice whether to stay or retire" (Hist. Am. Indians, p. 139).

Would surely die—In Cherokee myth and ritual we frequently meet the idea that one who reveals supernatural secrets will die. Sometimes the idea is reversed, as when the discovery of the nefarious doings of a wizard or conjurer causes his death. The latter belief has its parallel in Europe.

Smooth as a pumpkin—This is the rendering of the peculiar tautologic Cherokee expression, *i'ya iya'-tăwi'skage--tăwi'skage i'ya-iyu'stĭ*, literally, "pumpkin, of pumpkin smoothness—smooth like a pumpkin." The rendering is in line with the repetition in such children's stories as that of "The House that Jack Built," but the translation fails to convey the amusing sound effect of the original.

A large turtle—This incident occurs also in number 83, "Tsuwe'năhĭ."

A horse—Although the reference to the horse must be considered a more modern interpolation it may easily date back two centuries, or possibly even to De Soto's expedition in 1540. Among the plains tribes the horse quickly became so essential a part of Indian life that it now enters into their whole social and mythic system.

The bracelets were snakes—The same concept appears also in number 63, "Ûñtsaiyĭ'," when the hero visits his father, the Thunder god.

85. THE HAUNTED WHIRLPOOL (p. 347): This legend was related by an East Cherokee known to the whites as Knotty Tom. For a description of the whirlpool rapids known as Thé Suck, see notes under number 63, "Ûñtsaiyĭ', the Gambler."

86. YAHULA (p. 347): This fine myth was obtained in the Territory from Wafford, who had it from his uncle, William Scott, a halfbreed who settled upon Yahoola creek shortly after the close of the Revolution. Scott claimed to have heard the bells and the songs, and of the story itself Wafford said, "I've heard it so often and so much that I'm inclined to believe it." It has its explanation in the beliefs connected with the Nûñnĕ'hĭ (see number 78 and notes), in whom Wafford had firm faith.

Yahula—This is a rather frequent Cherokee personal name, but seems to be of Creek origin, having reference to the song used in the "black drink" or "busk" ceremony of that tribe, and the songs which the lost trader used to sing may have been those of that ceremony. See the glossary.

Tinkling of the bells—Among the southern tribes in the old days the approach of a trader's cavalcade along the trail was always heralded by the jingling of bells hung about the necks of the horses, somewhat in the manner of our own winter sleighing parties. Among the plains tribes the children's ponies are always equipped with collars of sleigh bells.

In his description of a trader's pack-train before the Revolution, Bartram says (Travels, p. 439): "Every horse has a bell on, which being stopped, when we start in the morning, with a twist of grass or leaves, soon shakes out, and they are never stopped again during the day. The constant ringing and clattering of the bells, smacking of the whips, whooping and too frequent cursing these miserable quadrupeds, cause an incessant uproar and confusion inexpressibly disagreeable."

87. THE WATER CANNIBALS (p. 349): This story was obtained from Swimmer and contains several points of resemblance to other Cherokee myths. The idea of the spirit changeling is common to European fairy lore.

Tĭkwǎlĭ'tsĭ—This town, called by the whites Tuckalechee, was on Tuckasegee river, at the present Bryson City, in Swain county, North Carolina, where traces of the mound can still be seen on the south side of the river.

Afraid of the witches—See number 120, "The Raven Mocker," and notes.

88. FIRST CONTACT WITH WHITES (p. 350): The story of the jug of whisky left near a spring was heard first from Swimmer; the ulûñsû'tĭ story from Wafford; the locomotive story from David Blythe. Each was afterward confirmed from other sources.

The story of the book and the bow, quoted from the Cherokee Advocate of October 26, 1844, was not heard on the reservation, but is mentioned by other authorities. According to an old Cherokee quoted by Buttrick, "God gave the red man a book and a paper and told him to write, but he merely made marks on the paper, and as he could not read or write, the Lord gave him a bow and arrows, and gave the book to the white man." Boudinot, in "A Star in the West,"[1] quoted by the same author, says: "They have it handed down from their ancestors, that the book which the white people have was once theirs; that while they had it they prospered exceedingly; but that the white people bought it of them and learned many things from it, while the Indians lost credit, offended the Great Spirit, and suffered exceedingly from the neighboring nations; that the Great Spirit took pity on them and directed them to this country," etc. It is simply another version of the common tale of decadent nations, "We were once as great as you."

89. THE IROQUOIS WARS (p. 351): *The Iroquois league*—The Iroquois league consisted originally of a confederacy of five kindred tribes, the Mohawk, Oneida, Onondaga, Cayuga, and Seneca, in what is now the state of New York; to these were added the cognate Tuscarora after their expulsion from Carolina about 1715. The name Iroquois, by which they were known to the French, is supposed to be a derivative from some Indian term. To the English they were known as the Five, afterward the Six Nations. They called themselves by a name commonly spelt Hodenosaunee, and interpreted "People of the Long House." Of this symbolic long house the Mohawk guarded the eastern door, while the Seneca protected the western. Their remarkable governmental and clan system is still well preserved, each tribe, except the Mohawk and Oneida, having eight clans, arranged in two groups or phratries. The Mohawk and Oneida are said to have now but three clans apiece, probably because of their losses by withdrawals to the French missions. The Seneca clans, which are nearly the same for the other tribes, are the Wolf, Bear, Turtle, Beaver, Deer, Snipe, Heron, and Hawk. The confederacy is supposed to have been formed about the middle of the sixteenth century, and by 1680 the Iroquois had conquered and destroyed or incorporated all the surrounding tribes, and had asserted a paramount

---

[1] Dr Elias Boudinot, A Star in the West, or a Humble Attempt to Discover the Long Lost Ten Tribes of Israel, Preparatory to Their Return to Their Beloved City, Jerusalem; Trenton, N. J., 1816.

claim over the whole territory from the Cherokee border to Hudson bay and from southern New England to the Mississippi. According to a careful estimate in 1677 the Five Nations then numbered 2,150 warriors, or about 10,750 persons. The Tuscarora in Carolina were estimated a few years later at 1,200 warriors, or 5,000 persons, but this is probably an exaggeration. The league afterward lost heavily by wars with the French, and still more by withdrawals of Christianized Indians to the French Catholic mission colonies at Caughnawaga, Saint Regis, and elsewhere, the Mohawk being the chief sufferers. The Revolution brought about another separation, when about two-fifths of those remaining, including nearly all of the Mohawk and Cayuga, removed in a body to Canada. A mixed band of Seneca and Cayuga, known as the "Seneca of Sandusky," had previously settled in Ohio, whence they removed in 1831 to Indian Territory. Between 1820 and 1826 the greater portion of the Oneida removed from New York to lands in Wisconsin purchased from the Menomini. In spite, however, of wars and removals the Iroquois have held their own with a tenacity and a virility which mark their whole history, and both in this country and in Canada they are fairly prosperous and are increasing in population, being apparently more numerous to-day than at any former period. Those in New York and Pennsylvania, except the Saint Regis, and on the Grand River reservation in Canada, constituting together about one-half of the whole number, still keep up the forms and ceremonies of the ancient league.

According to a special bulletin of the census of 1890 the total number of Indians then belonging to the tribes originally constituting the Six Nations was 15,833, of whom 8,483 were living in Canada and 7,350 in the United States, excluding from the latter count 37 resident members of other tribes. Those in the United States were on six reservations in the State of New York, one in Pennsylvania, one in Wisconsin, and one in the Indian Territory, and were classed as follows:

Mohawk (including Indians of Saint Regis and Caughnawaga): in New York. 1,162
Oneida: in New York, 212; at Green Bay agency, Wisconsin, 1,716........... 1,928
Onondaga: in New York, 470; on Cornplanter reservation, Pennsylvania, 11 . 481
Cayuga: in New York 183
Seneca: in New York, 2,680; on Cornplanter reservation, Pennsylvania, 87... 2,767
Tuscarora: in New York.. 408
Iroquois mixed bloods, separately enumerated, on reservations in New York.. 87
Iroquois outside reservations in New York, Connecticut, and Massachusetts .. 79
Mixed Seneca and Cayuga at Quapaw agency, Indian Territory.............. 255
                                                                        _____
                                                                         7,350

Those in Canada were at the same time officially reported thus:

Mohawk: at Caughnawaga, 1,722; at Saint Regis, 1,190; on Grand River reservation, 1,344; at Bay of Quinte, 1,056..................................... 5,312
Oneida: on Thames river, 715; on Grand River reservation, 244............. 959
Onondaga: on Grand River reservation..................................... 325
Cayuga: on Grand River reservation 865
Seneca: on Grand River reservation 183
Tuscarora: on Grand River reservation 327
Iroquois of Lake of Two Mountains.. 375
Iroquois of Gibson 137
                                                                        _____
                                                                         8,483

A few Algonkin are included among the Iroquois of Caughnawaga and Saint Regis, the Iroquois of these two settlements having been originally Catholic emigrants from the Mohawk villages in New York, with a few Oneida and Onondaga. When the boundary line between New York and Canada was run it cut the Saint Regis reservation in two. The report of the Commissioner of Indian Affairs for 1900 shows

7,700 Iroquois living on the reservations in New York, Wisconsin, and Indian Territory, an increase within these limits of 527 in nine years. Assuming the same rate of increase in Pennsylvania and on the Canada side, the whole number of Iroquois to-day would be approximately 17,000. For detailed information see Colden, History of the Five Nations; Schoolcraft, Notes on the Iroquois; Morgan, League of the Hodenosaunee or Iroquois; Parkman's works; reports of the commissioners of Indian affairs for both the United States and Canada, and the excellent report on "The Six Nations of New York," by Donaldson and Carrington, contained in an extra bulletin of the Eleventh Census of the United States.

Seneca town, South Carolina—The statement given by Schoolcraft (Notes on Iroquois, 161), on the authority of Calhoun, that the Seneca once lived at Seneca town, in South Carolina, has probably no foundation in fact, the story having evidently arisen from a supposed similarity of name. The Cherokee call it *I'sû'nigû'*, and do not connect it in any way with *A-Sĕ'nikă* or *Anĭ'-Sĕ'nikă*, their name for the northern tribe.

The Cherokee war—The Iroquois story of the war between themselves and the Cherokee is from Schoolcraft, Notes on Iroquois, pages 252 and 256.

Five days' journey—This statement is on Morgan's authority, but the distance was certainly greater, unless we are to understand only the distance that separated their extreme accustomed hunting ranges, not that between the permanent settlements of the two peoples.

The Tennessee river boundary—The statement from Morgan (League of the Iroquois, p. 337) in regard to the truce line established at Tennessee river seems to find confirmation in incidental references in early documents. Boundaries beyond which war parties might not go, or neutral grounds where hereditary enemies met in peace, were a regular institution in ancient Indian society, the most notable instance being perhaps the famous pipestone quarry in Minnesota. Notwithstanding the claim of the Iroquois, backed by Sir William Johnson, to all the country north of the Tennessee river, it is very plain from history and the treaties that the Cherokee asserted a more or less valid claim as far north as the Ohio. Their actual settlements, however, were all south of the main Tennessee.

The Buffalo dance—The origin ascribed to the Buffalo dance of the Iroquois (Morgan, League of the Iroquois, p. 287) is in agreement with the common Indian idea, according to which dances named from animals are performed in imitation of the peculiar actions and cries of these animals, or in obedience to supposed commands from the ruling spirit animals.

The peace embassy—The story of the proposed intertribal alliance, with the statements as to Cherokee captives among the Seneca, are from Schoolcraft (Notes on Iroquois, pp. 158, 252, 257). The records of the conference at Johnson Hall in 1768 are published in the New York Colonial Documents. The account of the Iroquois peace embassy to Echota was given to Wafford by two eyewitnesses, one of whom was his mother's cousin, Sequoya. As the old man said, "Sequoya told me all about it." As stated in the narrative, Wafford himself had also seen the belts brought out and explained in a great intertribal council at Tahlequah. By common tribal custom ambassadors of peace were secure from molestation, whatever might be the result of the negotiations, although, as among more civilized nations, this rule was sometimes violated. According to tradition, the ancient peace pipe of the Cherokee, and probably of other eastern tribes, was of white stone, white being the universal peace color. The red stone pipe of the Sioux was also used in peace ceremonials, from the peculiar sacredness attached to it among the western tribes.

The accuracy of Wafford's statement from memory in 1891 is strikingly confirmed by a contemporary account of the great intertribal council at Tahlequah in 1843, by the artist, Stanley, who was present and painted a number of portraits on that occasion. The council was convened by John Ross in June and remained in session four weeks, some ten thousand Indians being in attendance, representing seventeen tribes. "During the whole session the utmost good feeling and harmony prevailed. The business was brought to a close at sundown, after which the various tribes joined in dancing, which was usually kept up to a late hour." The wampum belt was explained, according to Stanley's account, by Major George Lowrey (*Agi'lĭ,* "Rising"), second chief of the Nation, who thus recited the tradition of its coming from the Seneca [i. e. Iroquois]. The talk abounds in Indian reference and symbolism:

"You will now hear a talk from our forefathers. You must not think hard if we make a few mistakes in describing our wampum. If we do, we will try and rectify them.

"My Brothers, you will now hear what our forefathers said to us.

"In the first place, the Senecas, a great many years ago, devised a plan for us to become friends. When the plan was first laid, the Seneca rose up and said, I fear the Cherokee, because the tomahawk is stuck in several parts of his head. The Seneca afterwards remarked, that he saw the tomahawk still sticking in all parts of the Cherokee's head, and heard him whooping and hallooing say [*sic*] that he was too strong to die. The Seneca further said, Our warriors in old times used to go to war; when they did go, they always went to fight the Cherokees; sometimes one or two would return home—sometimes none. He further said, The Great Spirit must love the Cherokees, and we must be in the wrong, going to war with them. The Seneca then said, Suppose we make friends with the Cherokee, and wash his wounds and cause them to heal up, that he may grow larger than he was before. The Seneca, after thus speaking, sat down. The Wyandot then rose and said, You have done right, and let it be. I am your youngest brother, and you our oldest. This word was told to the Shawnees; They replied, We are glad, let it be; you are our elder brothers. The Senecas then said, they would go about and pray to the Great Spirit for four years to assist them in making peace, and that they would set aside a vessel of water and cover it, and at the end of every year they would take the cover off, and examine the water, which they did; every time they opened it they found it was changed; at the end of four years they uncovered the vessel and found that the water had changed to a colour that suited them. The Seneca then said, The Great Spirit has had mercy upon us, and the thing has taken place just as we wished it.

"The Shawnee then said, We will make straight paths; but let us make peace among our neighbouring tribes first, before we make this path to those afar off.

"The Seneca then said, Before we make peace, we must give our neighboring tribes some fire; for it will not do to make peace without it,—they might be traveling about, and run against each other, and probably cause them to hurt each other. These three tribes said, before making peace, that this fire which was to be given to them should be kindled in order that a big light may be raised, so they may see each other at a long distance; this is to last so long as the earth stands; They said further, that this law of peace shall last from generation to generation—so long as there shall be a red man living on this earth: They also said, that the fire shall continue among us and shall never be extinguished as long as one remains. The Seneca further said to the Shawnees, I have put a belt around you, and have tied up the talk in a bundle, and placed it on your backs; we will now make a path on which we will pass to the Sioux. The Seneca said further, You shall continue your path until it shall reach the lodge of the Osage. When the talk was brought to the Sioux, they replied, we feel thankful to you and will take your talk; we can see a light through the path you have made for us.

"When the Shawnees brought the talk to the Osages, they replied, By to-morrow, by the middle of the day, we shall have finished our business. The Osage said further, The Great Spirit has been kind to me. He has brought something to me, I being fatigued hunting for it. When the Shawnees returned to the lodge of the Osages, they were informed that they were to be killed, and they immediately made their escape.

"When the Shawnees returned to their homes whence they came, they said they had been near being killed.

"The Seneca then said to the Shawnees, that the Osages must be mistaken. The Shawnees went again to see the Osages—they told them their business. The Osages remarked, The Great Spirit has been good to us,—to-morrow by the middle of the day he will give us something without fatigue. When the Shawnees arrived at the lodge, an old man of the Osages told them that they had better make their escape; that if they did not, by the middle of the following day, they were all to be destroyed, and directed them to the nearest point of the woods. The Shawnees made their escape about midday. They discovered the Osages following them, and threw away their packs, reserving the bag their talk was in, and arrived at their camp safe. When the Shawnees arrived home, they said they had come near being killed, and the Osages refused to receive their talk. The Seneca then said, If the Osages will not take our talk, let them remain as they are; and when the rising generation shall become as one, the Osages shall be like some herb standing alone. The Seneca further said, The Osages shall be like a lone cherry-tree, standing in the prairies, where the birds of all kinds shall light upon it at pleasure. The reason this talk was made about the Osages was, that they prided themselves upon their warriors and manhood, and did not wish to make peace.

"The Seneca further said, we have succeeded in making peace with all the Northern and neighbouring tribes. The Seneca then said to the Shawnees, You must now turn your course to the South: you must take your path to the Cherokees, and even make it into their houses. When the Shawnees started at night they took up their camp and sat up all night, praying to the Great Spirit to enable them to arrive in peace and safety among the Cherokees. The Shawnees still kept their course, until they reached a place called Tah-le-quah, where they arrived in safety, as they wished, and there met the chiefs and warriors of the Cherokees. When they arrived near Tah-le-quah, they went to a house and sent two men to the head chiefs. The chief's daughter was the only person in the house. As soon as she saw them, she went out and met them, and shook them by the hand and asked them into the house to sit down. The men were all in the field at work—the girl's father was with them. She ran and told him that there were two men in the house, and that they were enemies. The chief immediately ran to the house and shook them by the hand, and stood at the door. The Cherokees all assembled around the house, and said, Let us kill them, for they are enemies. Some of the men said, No, the chief's daughter has taken them by the hand; so also has our chief. The men then became better satisfied. The chief asked the two men if they were alone. They answered, No; that there were some more with them. He told them to go after them and bring them to his house. When these two men returned with the rest of their people, the chief asked them what their business was. They then opened this valuable bundle, and told him that it contained a talk for peace. The chief told them, I cannot do business alone; all the chiefs are assembled at a place called Cho-qua-ta [for E-cho-ta], where I will attend to your business in general council. When the messengers of peace arrived at Cho-qua-ta, they were kindly received by the chiefs, who told them they would gladly receive their talk of peace. The messengers of peace then said to the Cherokees, We will make a path for you to travel in, and the rising generation may do the same,—we also will keep it swept clean and white, so that the rising generation may travel in peace. The Shawnee further said, We will keep the doors of our houses open, so that when the rising generation come among us they shall be welcome. He further said, This talk is intended for all the different tribes of our red brothers, and is to last to the end of time. He further said, I have made a fire out of the dry elm—this fire is for all the different tribes to see by. I have put one chunk toward the rising sun, one toward the north, and one toward the south. This fire is not to be extinguished so long as time lasts. I shall stick up a stick close by this fire, in order that it may frequently be stirred, and raise a light for the rising generation to see by; if any one should turn in the dark, you must catch him by the hand, and lead him to the light, so that he can see that he was wrong.

"I have made you a fire-light, I have stripped some white hickory bark and set it up against the tree, in order that when you wish to remove this fire, you can take it and put it on the bark; when you kindle this fire it will be seen rising up toward the heavens. I will see it and know it; I am your oldest brother. The messenger of peace further said, I have prepared white benches for you, and leaned the white pipe against them, and when you eat you shall have but one dish and one spoon. We have done everything that was good, but our warriors still hold their tomahawks in their hands, as if they wished to fight each other. We will now take their tomahawks from them and bury them; we must bury them deep under the earth where there is water; and there must be winds, which we wish to blow them so far that our warriors may never see them again.

"The messenger further said, Where there is blood spilt I will wipe it up clean— wherever bones have been scattered, I have taken them and buried them, and covered them with white hickory bark and a white cloth—there must be no more blood spilt; our warriors must not recollect it any more. Our warriors said that the Cherokees were working for the rising generation by themselves; we must take hold and help them.

"The messengers then said that you Cherokees are placed now under the centre of the sun; this talk I leave with you for the different tribes, and when you talk it, our voice shall be loud enough to be heard over this island. This is all I have to say." [1]

Wampum—The celebrated wampum was a species of bead cut from the shell of the clam, conch, or other shell-bearing mollusk of the coast or the larger streams. The common name is derived from an Algonquian word signifying *white*, and was properly applied only to one variety, the generic term varying with the tribe. The beads were rather cylindrical than globular, and were of two colors, white and purple or dark. They were rated at definite values. The wampum was manufactured by the coast tribes, being traded by them to those of the interior, and was largely used everywhere east of the Mississippi for necklaces, collars, belts, and other purposes of personal adornment, as well as in connection with the noted wampum belts, by means of which the memory of treaties and tribal traditions was handed down. These belts were woven with various designs in wampum, either pictographic or symbolic, the meaning of which was preserved and explained on public occasions by an officer appointed to that duty. In ancient times no treaty or covenant was considered binding, and no tribal embassy was recognized as official, without the delivery of a wampum belt as a guaranty and memorial. The colonial documents are full of references to this custom. Up to the end of the last century the Cherokee still tendered such belts in their treaties with the Government, and one was delivered in the same manner so late as the treaty of Prairie des Chiens in 1825. The Iroquois still preserve several ancient belts, of which a good idea is afforded by the illustration and accompanying description (figure 2, page 354). On account of the high estimation in which these shell beads were held they were frequently used in the East as a standard of exchange, as eagle feathers were in the West, and among the Cherokee the same word, *atela*, is used alike for bead and for money. On the Pacific coast,

---

[1] J. M. Stanley, Portraits of North American Indians, with sketches of scenery, etc., painted by J. M. Stanley, deposited with the Smithsonian Institution. Washington: Smithsonian Institution, December, 1852; pp. 18–22. The Stanley account was not seen by the present author until after the Wafford tradition was in proofs.

shells were more generally shaped into pendants and gorgets. For a good eye-witness account of the manufacture and use of wampum and gorgets of shell among the South Atlantic tribes, see Lawson, History of Carolina, 315–316.

90. HIADEONI, THE SENECA (p. 356): Of this story Schoolcraft says: "The following incident in the verbal annals of Iroquois hardihood and heroism was related to me by the intelligent Seneca, Tetoyoah, William Jones of Cattaraugus, along with other reminiscences of the ancient Cherokee wars." Hewitt thinks the proper Seneca form of the name may be Hăia'di'oñnĭ', signifying " His body lies supine."

92. ESCAPE OF THE SENECA BOYS (p. 359): The manuscript notes from which this and several following traditions are arranged are in the archives of the Bureau of American Ethnology, and were obtained in 1886–87 among the Seneca Indians of New York by Mr Jeremiah Curtin, since noted as the author of several standard collections of Indian and European myths and the translator of the works of the Polish novelist, Sienkiewicz.

Gowe'!—This is a long drawn halloo without significance except as a signal to arrest attention. It strikingly resembles the Australian "bush cry" *Coowee'!* used for the same purpose.

93. THE UNSEEN HELPERS (p. 359): The meaning of the Seneca name can not be given.

Animal Protectors—The leading incident of this tale is closely paralleled by a Kiowa story, told by the old men as an actual occurrence of some fifty years ago, concerning a warrior who, having been desperately wounded in an engagement with Mexican troops in southern Texas, was abandoned to die by his retreating comrades. At night, while lying upon the ground awaiting death, and unable to move, he heard a long howl in the distance, which was repeated nearer and nearer, until at last he heard the patter of feet in the sand, and a wolf came up and licked the festering wounds of the warrior with such soothing effect that he fell asleep. This was repeated several times until the man was able to sit up, when the wolf left him, after telling him—not in the vision of a dream, but as a companion face to face—that he must keep up his courage, and that he would get back in safety to his tribe. Soon afterward the wounded warrior was found by a party of Comanche, who restored him to his people. At the next Sun dance he made public thanksgiving for his rescue (see the author's Calendar History of the Kiowa Indians, in Seventeenth Annual Report Bureau of American Ethnology, part 1, 1901). The story is not impossible. A wolf may easily have licked the wounded man's sores, as a dog might do, and through the relief thus afforded, if not by sympathy of companionship, have enabled him to hold out until rescued by friends. The rest is easy to the imagination of an Indian, who believes that there is no essential difference between himself and other animals.

The War Woman—The women described as having power to decide the fate of captives, mentioned also in the next story (number 94), are evidently the female dignitaries among the ancient Cherokee known to early writers as "War Women" or "Pretty Women." Owing to the decay of Cherokee tradition and custom it is now impossible to gather anything positive on the subject from Indian informants, but from documentary references it is apparent that there existed among the Cherokee a custom analogous to that found among the Iroquois and probably other Eastern tribes, by which the decision of important questions relating to peace and war was left to a vote of the women. Among the Iroquois this privilege was exercised by a council of matrons, the mothers of the tribes. It may have been the same among the Cherokee, with the "Pretty Woman" to voice the decision of the council, or the final rendering may have been according to the will of the "Pretty Woman" herself. The institution served in a measure to mitigate the evils of war and had its origin in the clan system. Under this system a captive enemy was still an enemy until he had been adopted into the tribe, which could only be done through adoption into a clan and family. As clan descent was reckoned through the women it rested with them to decide the question of adoption. If they were favorable all was well, and the captive became at once a member of a family and clan and of the tribe at large. Otherwise, as a public enemy, only death remained to him, unless he was ransomed by friends. The proper Cherokee title of this female arbiter of life and death is unknown. The clan of the Ani′-Gilâ′hĭ, or "Long-hairs," is sometimes spoken of as the Pretty-woman clan, and the office may have been hereditary in that clan. The Seneca stories imply that there were two of these female officers, but from Haywood's account there would seem to have been but one. An upper tributary of Savannah rᵛᵉʳ in Georgia bears the name War-woman creek.

Timberlake says in 1765 (Memoirs, p. 70): "These chiefs or headmen likewise compose the assemblies of the nation, into which the war women are admitted, . many of the Indian women being as famous in war as powerful in the council."

At the Hopewell treaty conference in 1785 the principal chief of Echota, after an opening speech, said: "I have no more to say, but one of our beloved women has, who has borne and raised up warriors." After delivering a string of wampum to emphasize the importance of the occasion, "the war woman of Chota then addressed the commissioners." Having expressed her pleasure at the peace, she continued: "I have a pipe and a little tobacco to give to the commissioners to smoke in friendship. I look on you and the red people as my children. Your having determined on peace is most pleasing to me, for I have seen much trouble during the late war. I am old, but I hope yet to bear children, who will grow up and people our nation, as we are now to be under the protection of Congress and shall have no more disturbance. The talk I have given is from the young warriors I have raised in my town, as well as myself. They rejoice that we have peace, and we hope the chain of friendship will never more be broken." Two strings of wampum, a pipe, and some tobacco accompanied her words (American State Papers; Indian Affairs, ɪ, p. 41, 1832).

Haywood says in 1823: "The Cherokees had the law or custom of assigning to a certain woman the office of declaring what punishment should be inflicted on great offenders; whether, for instance, burning or other death, or whether they should be pardoned. This woman they called the pretty woman. Mrs Ward exercised this office when Mrs Bean, about the year 1776, was taken from the white settlements on the upper parts of Holston. Being bound and about to be burned on one of the mounds, the pretty woman interfered and pronounced her pardon" (Nat. and Aborig. Hist. Tenn., p. 278). See also historical note 20, "Peace Towns and Towns of Refuge."

Between two lines of people—This custom, known to colonial writers as "running the gauntlet," was very common among the eastern tribes, and was intended not so much to punish the captive as to test his courage and endurance, with a view to adoption if he proved worthy. It was practiced only upon warriors, never upon women or children, and although the blows were severe they were not intended to be fatal. The prisoner was usually unbound and made to run along a cleared space in the center of the village toward a certain goal, and was safe for the time being if he succeeded in reaching it.

94. HᴀᴛᴄɪɴᴏṄᴅᴏṄ's ᴇꜱᴄᴀᴘᴇ ꜰʀᴏᴍ ᴛʜᴇ Cʜᴇʀᴏᴋᴇᴇ (p. 362): The Seneca name is not translatable.

Canebrake—The tall cane reed (*Arundinaria*), called i′hya by the Cherokee, is common along the southern streams, as such names as Cany fork, Cut-cane creek, and Young-cane creek testify. It was greatly valued among the Indians for fishing rods, blowguns, and baskets, as well as for fodder for stock. The best canebrakes were famous far and wide, and were resorted to from long distances in the gathering season. Most of the cane now used by the East Cherokee for blowguns and baskets is procured by long journeys on foot to the streams of upper South Carolina, or to points on the French Broad above Knoxville, Tennessee.

Sky vault—See notes to number 1, "How the World was Made."

Hawĕñni'o—The Seneca name for the Thunder god is in the singular form. In the Cherokee language Thunder and the Thunder spirits are always spoken of in the plural. The messengers in the story may have been Thunder spirits.

Thought reading—See notes to number 76, "The Bear Man."

Woman arbiters—See the preceding story, number 93, and the note on the "The War Woman."

My grandson—Among all the eastern and plains tribes this is a term of affectionate address to a dependent or inferior, as "grandfather" is a respectful address to one occupying a superior station, or venerable by reason of age or dignity, both words being thus used without any reference to kinship. In tribal councils nearly all the eastern tribes except the Iroquois addressed the Delaware representatives as "grandfather," and in an Arapaho song of the Ghost dance the Whirlwind is thus addressed.

95. HEMP-CARRIER (p. 364): This story of the old wars was obtained from Colonel William H. Thomas, who says that Tâle'danigi'skĭ was a chief formerly living near Valleytown, in Cherokee county. The name is variously rendered "Hemp-carrier," "Nettle-carrier," or "Flax-toter," from *tâle'ta*, the richweed (*Pilea pumila*), a plant with a fibrous stalk from which the Indians wove thread and cordage. The trail along which the Seneca came ran from Valley river across the ridge to Cheowa (Robbinsville) and thence northwest to connect with the "great war path" in Tennessee (see historical note 19).

Cairns—Stone cairns were formerly very common along the trails throughout the Cherokee country, but are now almost gone, having been demolished by treasure hunters after the occupation of the country by the whites. They were usually sepulchral monuments built of large stones piled loosely together above the body to a height of sometimes 6 feet or more, with a corresponding circumference. This method of interment was used only when there was a desire to commemorate the death, and every passer-by was accustomed to add a stone to the heap. The custom is ancient and world-wide, and is still kept up in Mexico and in many parts of Europe and Asia. Early references to it among the southern tribes occur in Lederer (1670), Travels, page 10, ed. 1891, and Lawson (1700), History of Carolina, pages 43 and 78, ed. 1860. The latter mentions meeting one day "seven heaps of stones, being the monuments of seven Indians that were slain in that place by the Sinnagers or Troquois [Iroquois]. Our Indian guide added a stone to each heap." The common name is the Gaelic term, meaning literally "a pile."

Seven wives—Polygamy was common among the Cherokee, as among nearly all other tribes, although not often to such an exaggerated extent as in this instance. The noted chief Yânûgûñskĭ, who died in 1839, had two wives. With the plains tribes, and perhaps with others, the man who marries the eldest of several daughters has prior claim upon her unmarried sisters.

96. THE SENECA PEACEMAKERS (p. 365): This story was told to Schoolcraft by the Seneca more than fifty years ago. A somewhat similar story is related by Adair (Hist. American Indians, p. 392) of a young "Anantooeah" (i. e., Nûndăwegĭ or Seneca) warrior taken by the Shawano.

Death song—It seems to have been a chivalrous custom among the eastern tribes to give to the condemned prisoner who requested it a chance to recite his warlike deeds and to sing his death song before proceeding to the final torture. He was allowed the widest latitude of boasting, even at the expense of his captors and their tribe. The death song was a chant belonging to the warrior himself or to the war society of which he was a member, the burden being farewell to life and defiance to death. When the great Kiowa war chief, Set-ängya, burst his shackles at Fort Sill and sprang upon the soldiers surrounding him, with the deliberate purpose to sell his life rather than to remain a prisoner, he first sang the war song of his order, the

Kâitseñ'ko, of which the refrain is: "O earth, you remain forever, but we Kâitseñ'ko must die" (see the author's Calendar History of the Kiowa Indians, in Seventeenth Annual Report of the Bureau American Ethnology, part 1, 1901).

97. ORIGIN OF THE YONTOÑWISAS DANCE (p. 365): This is evidently the one called by Morgan (League of Iroquois, p. 290) the Untowesus. He describes both this and the Oaskanea as a "shuffle dance" for women only. The spelling of the Seneca names in the story is that given in the manuscript.

Not to go after—Morgan, in his work quoted above, asserts that the Iroquois never made any effort to recover those of their people who have been captured by the enemy, choosing to consider them thenceforth as lost to their tribe and kindred. This, if true, is doubly remarkable, in view of the wholesele adoption of prisoners and subjugated tribes by the Iroquois.

Blazing pine knots—Torches of seasoned pine knots are much in use among the Cherokee for lighting up the way on journeys along the difficult mountain trails by night. Owing to the accumulation of resin in the knots they burn with a bright and enduring flame, far surpassing the cloudy glow of a lantern.

Wild potatoes—As is well known, the potato is indigenous to America, and our first knowledge of it came to us from the Indians. Many other native tubers were in use among the tribes, even those which practiced no agriculture, but depended almost entirely upon the chase. Favorites among the Cherokee are the *Cynara scolymus* or wild artichoke, and the *Phaseolus* or pig potato, the name of the latter, *nuna*, being now used to designate the cultivated potato.

Sky people—These spirit messengers are mentioned also in the story of Hatcinofidoñ (number 94), another Seneca tradition. Every tribe has its own spirit creation.

Must do all this—Every sacred dance and religious rite, as well as almost every important detail of Indian ceremonial, is supposed to be in accordance with direct instruction from the spirit world as communicated in a vision.

98. GA'NA'S ADVENTURES AMONG THE CHEROKEE (p. 367): This story, from Curtin's Seneca manuscript, is particularly rich in Indian allusion. The purificatory rite, the eagle capture, the peace ceremonial, the ballplay, the foot race, and the battle are all described in a way that gives us a vivid picture of the old tribal life. The name of the Seneca hero, Ga'na', signifies, according to Hewitt, "Arrow" (cf. Cherokee *gûnĭ*, "arrow"), while the name of the great eagle, Shada'gea, may, according to the same authority, be rendered "Cloud-dweller." The Seoqgwageono, living east of the Cherokee and near the ocean, can not be identified. They could not have been the Catawba, who were known to the Iroquois as Toderigh-rono, but they may possibly have been the Congaree, Santee, or Sewee, farther down in South Carolina. In the Seneca form, as here given, *ge* (*ge'*) is a locative, and *ono* (*oñnoñ*) a tribal suffix qualifying the root of the word, the whole name signifying "people of, or at, Seoqgwa" (cf. Oyadageono, etc., i. e., Cherokee, p. 186).

Go to water—This rite, as practiced among the Cherokee, has been already noted in the chapter on stories and story tellers. Ceremonial purification by water or the sweat bath, accompanied by prayer and fasting, is almost universal among the tribes as a preliminary to every important undertaking. With the Cherokee it precedes the ballplay and the Green-corn dance, and is a part of the ritual for obtaining long life, for winning the affections of a woman, for recovering from a wasting sickness, and for calling down prosperity upon the family at each return of the new moon.

Get the eagle feathers—The Cherokee ritual for procuring eagle feathers for ceremonial and decorative purposes has been described in number 35, "The Bird Tribes." The Seneca method, as here described, is practically that in use among all the Indians of the plains, although the hunter is not usually satisfied with a single feather at a capture. Among certain western tribes the eagle was sometimes strangled before being stripped of its feathers, but it was essential that the body must not be mangled or any blood be drawn. The Pueblos were sometimes accustomed to take the young eagles from the nest and keep them in cages for their feathers. A full tail contains twelve large feathers of the kind used for war bonnets and on the wands of the Eagle dance.

Stockade—Stockaded villages were common to the Iroquois and most of the tribes along the Atlantic coast. They are mentioned also among the Cherokee in some of the exaggerated narratives of the early Spanish period, but were entirely unknown within the later colonial period, and it is very doubtful if the nature of the country would permit such compact mode of settlement.

Dancers went forward—The method of ceremonial approach here described was probably more or less general among the eastern tribes. On the plains the visitors usually dismount in sight of the other camp and advance on foot in slow procession, chanting the "visiting song," while the leader holds out the red stone pipe, which is the symbol of truce or friendship. For a good description of such a ceremonial, reproduced from Battey, see the author's Calendar History of the Kiowa Indians, in the Seventeenth Annual Report of the Bureau of American Ethnology. In this instance the visiting Pawnee carried a flag in lieu of a pipe.

The Cherokee ceremonial is thus described by Timberlake as witnessed at Citico in 1762: 'About 100 yards from the town-house we were received by a body of between three and four hundred Indians, ten or twelve of which were entirely naked, except a piece of cloth about their middle, and painted all over in a hideous manner, six of them with eagles' tails in their hands, which they shook and flourished as they advanced, danced in a very uncommon figure, singing in concert with some drums of their own make, and those of the late unfortunate Capt. Damere; with several other instruments, uncouth beyond description. Cheulah, the headman of the town, led the procession, painted blood-red, except his face, which was half black, holding an old rusty broad-sword in his right hand, and an eagle's tail in his left. As they approached, Cheulah, singling himself out from the rest, cut two or three capers, as a signal to the other eagle-tails, who instantly followed his example. This violent exercise, accompanied by the band of musick, and a loud yell from the mob, lasted about a minute, when the headman, waving his sword over my head, struck it into the ground, about two inches from my left foot; then directing himself to me, made a short discourse (which my interpreter told me was only to bid me a hearty welcome) and presented me with a string of beads. We then proceeded to the door, where Cheulah, and one of the beloved men, taking me by each arm, led me in, and seated me in one of the first seats; it was so dark that nothing was perceptible till a fresh supply of canes were brought, which being burnt in the middle of the house answers both purposes of fuel and candle. I then discovered about five hundred faces; and Cheulah addressing me a second time, made a speech much to the same effect as the former, congratulating me on my safe arrival thro' the numerous parties of northern Indians, that generally haunt the way I came. He then made some professions of friendship, concluding with giving me another string of beads, as a token of it. He had scarce finished, when four of those who had exhibited at the procession made their second appearance, painted in milk-white, their eagle-tails in one hand, and small gourds with beads in them in the other, which they rattled in time to the musick. During this dance the peace-pipe was prepared."— Timberlake, Memoirs, pp. 36–39.

Adair also makes brief mention of the ceremony among the Gulf tribes (Hist. Am. Indians, p. 260), but his account is too badly warped by theorizing to have much value.

Adopt a relative—This seems to point to a custom which has escaped the notice of earlier writers on the eastern tribes, but which is well known in Africa and other parts of the world, and is closely analogous to a still existing ceremony among the plains Indians by which two young men of the same tribe formally agree to become brothers, and ratify the compact by a public exchange of names and gifts.

White wampum—As is well known, white was universally typical of peace. The traditional peace-pipe of the Cherokee was of white stone and the word itself is symbolic of peace and happiness in their oratory and sacred formulas. Thus the speaker at the Green-corn dance invites the people to come along the white path and enter the white house of peace to partake of the new white food.

Held up the belt—As already noted, every paragraph of an ambassador's speech was accompanied by the delivery of a string or belt of wampum to give authority to his words, and to accept the belt was to accept the condition or compact which it typified. On the plains the red stone pipe took the place of the wampum.

Try a race—Public foot races were common among many tribes, more particularly in the West among the Pueblos, the Apache, and the Wichita, either as simple athletic contests or in connection with religious ceremonials. On the plains the horse race is more in favor and is always the occasion of almost unlimited betting.

Throwing sumac darts—The throwing of darts and arrows, either at a mark or simply to see who can throw farthest, is a favorite amusement among the young men and boys. The arrows used for this purpose are usually longer and heavier than the ordinary ones, having carved wooden heads and being artistically painted. They are sometimes tipped with the end of a buffalo horn.

99. THE SHAWANO WARS (p. 370): The chief authority as to the expulsion of the Shawano from Tennessee is Haywood (Natural and Aboriginal History of Tennessee, pp. 222–224). The Schoolcraft reference is from Notes on the Iroquois, p. 160, and the notice of the Cherokee-Delaware war from Loskiel, Mission of United Brethren, p. 128, and Heckewelder, Indian Nations, p. 88. The Tunâ′ĭ story is from Wafford; the other incidents from Swimmer.

Shawano—The Shawano or Shawnee were one of the most important of the Algonquian tribes. Their most noted chief was the great Tecumtha. The meaning of the name is doubtful. It is commonly interpreted "Southerners," from the Algonquian *shawan*, "the south," but may have come from another Algonquian word signifying "salt" (*siutagan, sewetagan*, etc., from *sewan*, "sweet, pungent"). Unlike the southern Indians generally, the Shawano were great salt users, and carried on an extensive salt manufacture by boiling at the salt springs of southwestern Virginia, furnishing the product in trade to other tribes. They have thirteen clans—Wolf, Loon, Bear, Buzzard, Panther, Owl, Turkey, Deer, Raccoon, Turtle, Snake, Horse, and Rabbit (Morgan), the clan of the individual being indicated by his name. They are organized also into four divisions or bands, perhaps originally independent allied tribes, viz, Piqua, Mequachake, Kiscopocoke, and Chilicothe. To the second of these belonged the hereditary priesthood, but the first was most prominent and apparently most numerous. The Shawano were of very wandering and warlike habit. Their earliest historical habitat appears to have been on the middle Savannah river, which takes its name from them, but before the end of the seventeenth century we find a portion of them, apparently the main body, occupying the basin of the Cumberland river in Tennessee and the adjacent region of Kentucky. About the year 1692 most of those remaining in South Carolina moved northward and settled upon the upper Delaware river, with their relatives and friends the Delaware and Mahican. These emigrants appear to have been of the Piqua division. Up to about the year 1730 the Shawano still had a town on Savannah river, near Augusta, from which they were finally driven by the Cherokee. From their former intimate association with the Uchee, living in the same neighborhood, some early writers have incorrectly supposed the two tribes to be the same. A part of the Shawano joined the Creek confederary, and up to the beginning of the last century, and probably until the final removal to the West, occupied a separate town and retained their distinct language. Those settled upon the Cumberland were afterward expelled by the Cherokee and Chickasaw, and retired to the upper waters of the Ohio under protection of the Delaware, who had given refuge to the original emigrants from South

Carolina. With the advance of the white settlements the two tribes moved westward into Ohio, the Shawano fixing themselves in the vicinity of the present Piqua and Chillicothe about the year 1750. They took a leading part in the French and Indian war, Pontiac's war, the Revolution, and the war of 1812. In 1793 a considerable band settled in Missouri upon lands granted by the Spanish government. As a result of successive sales and removals all that remain of the tribe are now established in Indian Territory, about one-half being incorporated with the Cherokee Nation. In 1900 they numbered about 1,580, viz, in Cherokee Nation (in 1898), 790; Absentee Shawnee of Sac and Fox Agency, 509; Absentee Shawnee of Big Jim's band, special agency, 184; Eastern Shawnee of Quapaw Agency, 93. There are also a few scattered among other tribes. For detailed information consult Drake, Life of Tecumseh; Heckewelder, Indian Nations; Brinton, Lenâpé and Their Legends; American State Papers: Indian Affairs, ɪ and ɪɪ; Annual Reports of the Commissioner of Indian Affairs.

100. THE RAID ON TĬKWĂLI′TSĬ (p. 374): Swimmer, from whom this story was obtained, was of opinion that the event occurred when his mother was a little girl, say about 1795, but it must have been earlier.

The locations are all in Swain county, North Carolina. Tĭkwăli′tsĭ town was on Tuckasegee river, at the present Bryson City, immediately below and adjoining the more important town of Kituhwa. Deep creek enters the Tuckasegee from the north, about a mile above Bryson City. The place where the trail crossed is called Uniga′yata′ti′yĭ, "Where they made a fish trap," a name which may have suggested the simile used by the story teller. The place where the Cherokee crossed, above Deep creek, is called Uniyâ′hitûñ′yĭ, "Where they shot it." The cliff over which the prisoners were thrown is called Kala′ăsûñyĭ, "Where he fell off," near Cold Spring knob, west of Deep creek. The Cherokee halted for a night at Agitsta′ti′yĭ, "Where they staid up all night," a few miles beyond, on the western head fork of Deep creek. They passed Kûnstûtsi′yĭ, "Sassafras place," a gap about the head of Noland creek, near Clingman's dome, and finally gave up the pursuit where the trail crossed into Tennessee, at a gap on the main ridge, just below Clingman's dome, known as Duniya″tă′lûñ′yĭ, "Where there are shelves," so called from an exposure of flat rock on the top of the ridge (see the glossary).

Magic arts—It is almost superfluous to state that no Indian war party ever started out without a vast deal of conjuring and "making medicine" to discover the whereabouts and strength of the enemy and to insure victory and safe return to the departing warriors.

Wait for death—The Indian usually meets inevitable fate with equanimity, and more than once in our Indian wars an aged warrior or helpless woman, unable to escape, has sat down upon the ground, and, with blanket drawn over the head, calmly awaited the fatal bullet or hatchet stroke.

101. THE LAST SHAWANO INVASION (p. 374): This story also is from Swimmer, whose antiquarian interest in the history of these wars may have been heightened by the fact that he had a slight strain of Shawano blood himself. The descendants of the old chief Sawanu′gi and his brothers, originally of Shawano stock, as the name indicates, have been prominent in the affairs of the East Cherokee for more than half a century, and one of them, bearing the ancestral name, is now second chief of the band and starter of the game at every large ballplay.

The cry of an owl—One of the commonest claims put forth by the medicine men is that of ability to understand the language of birds and to obtain supernatural knowledge from them, particularly from the owl, which is regarded with a species of fear by the laity, as the embodiment of a human ghost, on account of its nocturnal habit and generally uncanny appearance. A medicine man who died a few years ago among the Kiowa claimed to derive his powers from that bird. The body of an owl, wrapped in red cloth and decorated with various trinkets, was kept constantly suspended from a tall pole set up in front of his tipi, and whenever at night the warning cry sounded from the thicket he was accustomed to leave his place at the fire and go out, returning in a short while with a new revelation.

Rafts—The Cherokee canoe is hewn from a poplar log and is too heavy to be carried about like the bark canoe of the northern tribes. As a temporary expedient they sometimes used a bear or buffalo skin, tying the legs together at each end to fashion a rude boat. Upon this the baggage was loaded, while the owner swam behind, pushing it forward through the water.

102. THE FALSE WARRIORS OF CHILHOWEE (p. 375): This story was given by Swimmer and corroborated by others as that of an actual incident of the old times. The middle Cherokee (Kituhwa) settlements, on the head-streams of the Little Tennessee, were separated from the upper settlements, about its junction with the main Tennessee, by many miles of extremely rough mountain country. Dialectic differences and local jealousies bred friction, which sometimes brought the two sections into collision and rendered possible such an occurrence as is here narrated. On account of this jealousy, according to Adair, the first Cherokee war, which began in 1760, concerned for some time only a part of the tribe. "According to the well-known temper of the Cheerake in similar cases it might either have remained so, or soon have been changed into a very hot civil war, had we been so wise as to have improved the favourable opportunity. There were seven northern towns, opposite to the middle parts of the Cheerake country, who from the beginning of the unhappy grievances, firmly dissented from the hostile intentions of their suffering and enraged countrymen, and for a considerable time before bore them little good will, on account of some family disputes which occasioned each party to be more favourable to itself than to the other. These would readily have gratified their vindictive disposition either by a neutrality or an offensive alliance with our colonists against them" (History of the American Indians, page 248).

Chilhowee (properly Tsŭ'lûñ'we or Tsû'la'wĭ) was a noted settlement on the south bank of Little Tennessee river, opposite the present Chilhowee, in Monroe county, Tennessee. Cowee (properly Kawi'yĭ, abbreviated Kawi') was the name of two or more former settlements. The one here meant was at the junction of Cowee creek with Little Tennessee river, a short distance below the present Franklin, in Macon county, North Carolina. Neither name can be analyzed. The gunstocker's name, Gûlsădi'hĭ or Gûltsădi'hĭ, and that of the original owner of the gun, Gûñskăli'skĭ, are both of doubtful etymology.

Great war trail—See historical note 19.

Scalp dance—This dance, common to every tribe east of the Rocky mountains, was held to celebrate the taking of fresh scalps from the enemy. The scalps, painted red on the fleshy side, decorated and stretched in small hoops attached to the ends of poles, were carried in the dance by the wives and sweethearts of the warriors, while in the pauses of the song each warrior in turn recited his exploits in minute detail. Among the Cherokee it was customary for the warrior as he stepped into the center of the circle to suggest to the drummer an improvised song which summed up in one or two words his own part in the encounter. A new "war name" was frequently assumed after the dance (see sketch of Tsunu'lăhûñ'skĭ, page 164). Dances were held over the same scalps on consecutive nights or sometimes at short intervals for weeks together.

Coming for water—The getting of water from the neighboring stream or spring was a daily duty of the women, and accordingly we find in Indian stories constant allusion to ambuscades or lovers' appointments at such places.

To have a ballplay—See note under number 3, Kana'tĭ and Selu.

103. COWEE TOWN: See the preceeding note.

104. The eastern tribes (p. 378): *Delaware*—The Delawares derive their popular name from the river upon which, in the earliest colonial period, they had their principal settlements. They call themselves *Lena'pe* or *Leni-lena'pe*, a term apparently signifying "real, or original men," or "men of our kind." To the cognate tribes of the Ohio valley and the lakes they were known as *Wapanaq'ki*, "easterners," the name being extended to include the closely related tribes, the Mahican, Wappinger (i. e. Wapanaq'ki), Nanticoke, and Conoy. By all the widespread tribes of kindred Algonquian stock, as well as by the Winnebago, Wyandot, and Cherokee, they were addressed under the respectful title of "grandfather," the domineering Iroquois alone refusing to them any higher designation than "nephew."

Their various bands and subtribes seem originally to have occupied the whole basin of Delaware river, together with all of New Jersey, extending north to the watershed of the Hudson and west and southwest to the ridge separating the waters of the Delaware and Susquehanna. Immediately north of them, along the lower Hudson and extending into Massachusetts and Connecticut, were the closely affiliated Mahican and Wappinger, while to the south were their friends and kindred, the Nanticoke and Conoy, the former in Delaware and on the eastern shore of Maryland, the latter between Chesapeake bay and the lower Potomac. All of these, although speaking different languages of the common Algonquian stock, asserted their traditional origin from the Delawares, with whom, in their declining days, most of them were again merged. The Delawares proper were organized into three divisions, which, according to Brinton, were subtribes and not clans, although each of the three had a totemic animal by whose name it was commonly known. These three subtribes were: (1) The Minsi or Munsee (people of the "stony country"?), otherwise known as the Wolf tribe, occupying the hill country about the head of the Delaware; (2) the Unami (people "downstream"), or Turtle tribe, on the middle Delaware, and (3) the Unalachtgo (people "near the ocean"?), or Turkey tribe, in the southern part of the common territory. Of these the Turtle tribe assumed precedence in the council, while to the Wolf tribe belonged the leadership in war. Each of these three was divided into twelve families, or embryonic clans, bearing female names. In this connection it may be mentioned that the Delawares now residing with the Wichita, in Oklahoma, still use the figure of a turtle as their distinctive cattle brand.

Of the history of the Delawares it is only possible to say a very few words here. Their earliest European relations were with the Dutch and Swedes. In 1682 they made the famous treaty with William Penn, which was faithfully observed on both sides for sixty years. Gradually forced backward by the whites, they retired first to the Susquehanna, then to the upper Ohio, where, on the breaking out of the French and Indian war in 1754, they ranged themselves on the side of the French. They fought against the Americans in the Revolution, and in the war of 1812, having by that time been driven as far west as Indiana. In 1818 they ceded all their lands in that State and were assigned to a reservation in Kansas, where they were joined by a considerable body that had emigrated to Missouri, in company with a band of Shawano, some years before, by permission of the Spanish government. About the close of the Revolution another portion of the tribe, including most of those who had been Christianized by Moravian missionaries, had fled from Ohio and taken up a permanent abode on Canadian soil. In 1867 the main body of those in Kansas removed to Indian Territory and became incorporated with the Cherokee Nation. A smaller band settled on the Wichita reservation in Oklahoma. The present number of Delawares is, approximately, 1,600, viz: "Moravians and Munsees of the Thames," Ontario, 475; incorporated in Cherokee Nation, 870 (in 1898); on Wichita reservation, 95; Munsee in Kansas and incorporated with Stockbridges in Wisconsin, perhaps 100; Delawares, etc., with Six Nations, in New York, 50.

Of their former allies, the Wappinger and Conoy have long since disappeared through absorption into other tribes; the Mahican are represented by a band of about 530 Stockbridge Indians, including a number of Munsee, in Wisconsin, while about 70 mixed bloods still keep up the Nanticoke name in southern Delaware.

Tuscarora—The Tuscarora, a southern tribe of the Iroquoian stock, formerly occupied an extensive territory upon Neuse river and its branches, in eastern North Carolina, and, like their northern cousins, seem to have assumed and exercised a certain degree of authority over all the smaller tribes about them. As early as 1670 Lederer described the Tuscarora "emperor" as the haughtiest Indian he had ever met. About the year 1700 Lawson estimated them at 1,200 warriors (6,000 souls?) in 15 towns. In 1711 they rose against the whites, one of their first acts of hostility being the killing of Lawson himself, who was engaged in surveying lands which they claimed as their own. In a struggle extending over about two years they were so terribly decimated that the greater portion fled from Carolina and took refuge with their kinsmen and friends, the Iroquois of New York, who were henceforth known as the Six Nations. The so-called "friendly" party, under Chief Blount, was settled upon a small reservation north of Roanoke river in what is now Bertie county, North Carolina. Here they gradually decreased by disease and emigration to the north, until the few who were left sold their last remaining lands in 1804. The history of the tribe after the removal to the north is a part of the history of the Iroquois or Six Nations. They number now about 750, of whom about 380 are on the Tuscarora reservation in New York, the others upon the Grand River reservation in Ontario.

Xuala, Suwali, Sara or Cheraw—For the identification and earliest notices of the Sara see historical note 8, "De Soto's Route." Their later history is one of almost constant hostility to the whites until their final incorporation with the Catawba, with whom they were probably cognate, about the year 1720. In 1743 they still preserved their distinct language, and appear to be last mentioned in 1768, when they numbered about 50 souls living among the Catawba. See Mooney, Siouan Tribes of the East, bulletin of the Bureau of Ethnology, 1894.

Catawba—The origin and meaning of this name, which dates back at least two centuries, are unknown. It may possibly come from the Choctaw through the Mobilian trade jargon. They call themselves Nieye, which means simply "people" or "Indians." The Iroquois call them and other cognate tribes in their vicinity Toderigh-rono, whence Tutelo. In the seventeenth century they were often known as Esaw or Ushery, apparently from *iswă'*, river, in their own language. The Cherokee name Ata'gwa, plural Ani'ta'gwa, is a corruption of the popular form. Their linguistic affinity with the Siouan stock was established by Gatschet in 1881. See Mooney, Siouan Tribes of the East.

105. The SOUTHERN AND WESTERN TRIBES (p. 382): *The Creek confederacy*—Next in importance to the Cherokee, among the southern tribes, were the Indians of the Creek confederacy, occupying the greater portion of Georgia and Alabama, immediately south of the Cherokee. They are said to have been called Creeks by the early traders on account of the abundance of small streams in their country. Before the whites began to press upon them their tribes held nearly all the territory from the Atlantic westward to about the watershed between the Tombigby and the Pearl and Pascagoula rivers, being cut off from the Gulf coast by the Choctaw tribes, and from the Savannah, except near the mouth, by the Uchee, Shawano, and Cherokee. About the year 1800 the confederacy comprised 75 towns, the people of 47 of which were the Upper Creeks, centering about the upper waters of the Alabama, while those of the remaining 28 were the Lower Creeks, upon the lower Chattahoochee and its branches (Hawkins). Among them were represented a number of tribes formerly distinct and speaking distinct languages. The ruling tribe and language was the Muscogee (plural, Muscogûlgee), which frequently gave its name to the confederacy. Other languages were the Alabama, Koasati, Hichitee, Taskigi, Uchee, Natchee, and Sawanugi

or Shawano. The Muscogee, Alabama, Koasati, Hichitee, and Taskigi (?) belonged to the Muskhogean stock, the Alabama and Koasati, however, being nearer linguistically to the Choctaw than to the Muscogee. The Hichitee represent the conquered or otherwise incorporated Muskhogean tribes of the Georgia coast region. The Apalachi on Appalachee bay in Florida, who were conquered by the English about 1705 and afterward incorporated with the Creeks, were dialectically closely akin to the Hichitee; the Seminole also were largely an offshoot from this tribe. Of the Taskigi all that is known has been told elsewhere (see number 105).

The Uchee, Natchee, and Sawanugi were incorporated tribes, differing radically in language from each other and from the Muskhogean tribes. The territory of the Uchee included both banks of the middle Savannah, below the Cherokee, and extended into middle Georgia. They had a strong race pride, claiming to be older in the country than the Muscogee, and are probably identical with the people of Cofitachiqui, mentioned in the early Spanish narratives. According to Hawkins, their incorporation with the Creeks was brought about in consequence of intermarriages about the year 1729. The Natchee or Natchez were an important tribe residing in lower Mississippi, in the vicinity of the present town of that name, until driven out by the French about the year 1730, when most of them took refuge with the Creeks, while others joined the Chickasaw and Cherokee. The Sawanugi were Shawano who kept their town on Savannah river, near the present Augusta, after the main body of their tribe had removed to the north about 1692. They probably joined the Creeks about the same time as their friends, the Uchee. The Uchee still constitute a compact body of about 600 souls in the Creek Nation, keeping up their distinct language and tribal character. The Natchee are reduced to one or two old men, while the Sawanugi have probably lost their identity long ago.

According to Morgan, the Muscogee proper, and perhaps also their incorporated tribes, have 22 clans. Of these the Wind appears to be the leading one, possessing privileges accorded to no other clan, including the hereditary guardianship of the ancient metal tablets which constitute the palladium of the tribe. By the treaty of Washington in 1832, the Creeks sold all of their remaining lands in their old country and agreed to remove west of the Mississippi to what is now the Creek Nation in the Indian Territory. The removal extended over a period of several years and was not finally accomplished until 1845. In 1898 the citizen population of the Creek Nation numbered 14,771, of whom 10,014 were of Indian blood and the remainder were negroes, their former slaves. It appears that the Indian population included about 700 from other tribes, chiefly Cherokee. There are also about 300 Alabama, "Cushatta" (Koasati), and Muscogee in Texas. See also Hawkins, Sketch of the Creek Country; Gatschet, Creek Migration Legend; Adair, History of the American Indians; Bartram, Travels; The Five Civilized Tribes, Bulletin of the Eleventh Census; Wyman, in Alabama Historical Society Collections.

Chickasaw—This tribe, of Muskhogean stock, formerly occupied northern Mississippi and adjacent portions of Alabama and Tennessee, and at an early period had incorporated also several smaller tribes on Yazoo river in central Mississippi, chief among which were the cognate Chokchuma. The name occurs first in the De Soto narrative. The Chickasaw language was simply a dialect of Choctaw, although the two tribes were hereditary enemies and differed widely in character, the former being active and warlike, while the latter were notoriously sluggish. Throughout the colonial period the Chickasaw were the constant enemies of the French and friends of the English, but they remained neutral in the Revolution. By the treaty of Pontotoc in 1832 they sold their lands east of the Mississippi and agreed to remove to Indian Territory, where they are now organized as the Chickasaw Nation. According to Morgan they have 12 clans grouped into two phratries. In 1890, the citizen population of the Nation (under Chickasaw laws) consisted of 3,941 full-blood and mixed-blood Chickasaw, 681 adopted whites, 131 adopted negroes, and 946 adopted Indians from other tribes, chiefly Choctaws. Under the present law, by which citizenship claims are decided by a Government commission, "Chickasaw by blood" are reported in 1898 to number 4,230, while "white and negro" citizens are reported at 4,818. See also Gatschet, Creek Migration Legend; The Five Civilized Tribes, Bulletin of Eleventh Census.

The Choctaw confederacy—This was a loose alliance of tribes, chiefly of Muskhogean stock, occupying southern Alabama and Mississippi, with the adjacent Gulf coast of western Florida and eastern Louisiana. The Choctaw proper, of Muskhogean stock, occupying south central Mississippi, was the dominant tribe. Smaller tribes more or less closely affiliated were the Mobilian, Tohome, Mugulasha, Pascagoula, Biloxi, Acolapissa, Bayagoula, Houma, with others of less note. It had been assumed that all of these were of Muskhogean stock until Gatschet in 1886 established the fact that the Biloxi were of Siouan affinity, and it is quite probable that the Pascagoula also were of the same connection. All the smaller tribes excepting the Biloxi were practically extinct, or had entirely lost their identity, before the year 1800.

The Choctaw were one of the largest of the eastern tribes, being exceeded in numbers, if at all, only by the Cherokee; but this apparent superiority was neutralized by their unwarlike character and lack of cohesion. According to Morgan, whose statement has, however, been challenged, they had eight clans grouped into two phratries. There was also a geographic division into "Long towns," "Potato-eating towns," and "Six towns," the last named differing considerably in dialect and custom from the others. By treaties in 1820 and 1830 the Choctaw sold all their lands east of the Mississippi and agreed to remove to Indian Territory, where they now constitute the Choctaw Nation. A considerable number of vagrant Choctaw who had drifted into Louisiana and Arkansas at an early period have since joined their kindred in Indian Territory, but from 1,000 to 2,000 are still scattered along the swampy Gulf coast of Mississippi. In 1890 those of pure or mixed Choctaw blood in the Choctaw Nation were officially reported to number 10,211. In 1899, under different conditions of citizenship, the "Choctaw by blood" were put at 14,256, while the adopted whites and negroes numbered 5,150. See also Gatschet, Creek Migration Legend; The Five Civilized Tribes, Bulletin of Eleventh Census.

The Osage—The popular name is a corruption of Ouasage, the French spelling of Wasash, the name used by themselves. The Osage were the principal southern Siouan tribe, claiming at one time nearly the whole territory from the Missouri to the Arkansas and from the Mississippi far out into the plains. Their geographic position brought them equally into contact with the agricultural and sedentary tribes of the eastern country and the roving hunters of the prairie, and in tribal habit and custom they formed a connecting link between the two. Whether or not they deserved the reputation, they were considered by all their neighbors as particularly predatory and faithless in character, and had consequently few friends, but were generally at war with all tribes alike. They made their first treaty with the Government in 1808. In 1825 they ceded all their claims in Missouri and Arkansas, together with considerable territory in what is now Kansas. They have decreased terribly from war and dissipation, and are now, to the number of about 1,780, gathered upon a reservation in Oklahoma just west of the Cherokee and south of the Kansas line.

106. THE GIANTS FROM THE WEST (p. 391): This may be an exaggerated account of a visit from some warriors of a taller tribe from the plains, where it is customary to pluck out the eyebrows and to wear the hair in two long side pendants, wrapped round with otter skin and reaching to the knees, thus giving a peculiar expression to the eyes and an appearance of tallness which is sometimes deceptive. The Osage warriors have, however, long been noted for their height.

With the exception of Tsul'kalû′ there seem to be no giants in the mythology of the Cherokee, although all their woods and waters are peopled by invisible fairy tribes. This appears to be characteristic of Indian mythologies generally, the giants being comparatively few in number while the "little people" are legion. The Iroquois have a story of an invasion by a race of stony-skinned cannibal giants from the west (Schoolcraft, Notes on Iroquois, p. 266). Giant races occur also in the mythologies of the Navaho (Matthews, Navaho Legends), Choctaw (Gatschet, Creek Migration Legend), and other tribes. According to the old Spanish chroniclers, Ayllon in 1520 met on the coast of South Carolina a tribe of Indians whose chiefs were of gigantic size, owing, as he was told, to a special course of dieting and massage to which they were subjected in infancy.

107. THE LOST CHEROKEE (p. 391): This tradition as here given is taken chiefly from the Wahnenauhi manuscript. There is a persistent belief among the Cherokee that a portion of their people once wandered far to the west or southwest, where they were sometimes heard of afterward, but were never again reunited with their tribe. It was the hope of verifying this tradition and restoring his lost kinsmen to their tribe that led Sequoya to undertake the journey on which he lost his life. These traditional lost Cherokee are entirely distinct from the historic emigrants who removed from the East shortly after the Revolution.

Similar stories are common to nearly all the tribes. Thus the Kiowa tell of a chief who, many years ago, quarreled over a division of game and led his people far away across the Rocky mountains, where they are still living somewhere about the British border and still keeping their old Kiowa language. The Tonkawa tell of a band of their people who in some way were cut off from the tribe by a sudden inroad of the sea on the Texas coast, and, being unable to return, gradually worked their way far down into Mexico. The Tuscarora tell how, in their early wanderings, they came to the Mississippi and were crossing over to the west side by means of a grapevine, when the vine broke, leaving those on the farther side to wander off until in time they became enemies to those on the eastern bank. See Mooney, Calendar History of the Kiowa Indians, Seventeenth Annual Report Bureau of American Ethnology, part 1, and The Last of Our Cannibals, in Harper's Magazine, August, 1901; Cusick, quoted in Schoolcraft, Notes on the Iroquois, p. 478.

108. THE MASSACRE OF THE ANI′-KUTA′NI (p. 392): Swimmer, Ta′gwădihĭ′, Ayâsta, and Wafford all knew this name, which Ayâsta pronounced Ani′-Kwăta′nĭ, but none of them could tell anything more definite than has been stated in the opening sentence. The hereditary transmission of priestly dignities in a certain clan or band is rather the rule than the exception among the tribes, both east and west.

109. THE WAR MEDICINE (p. 393): The first two paragraphs are from Wafford, the rest from Swimmer. The stories are characteristic of Indian belief and might be paralleled in any tribe. The great Kiowa chief, Set-ängya, already mentioned, was—and still is—believed by his tribe to have possessed a magic knife, which he carried in his stomach and could produce from his mouth at will. The Kiowa assert that it was this knife, which of course the soldiers failed to find when disarming him, with which he attacked the guard in the encounter that resulted in his death.

110. INCIDENTS OF PERSONAL HEROISM (p. 394): The incident of the fight at Waya gap is on the authority of the late Maj. James Bryson, of Dillsboro, North Carolina, born in 1818, who had it from his great-uncle, Daniel Bryson, a member of Williamson's expedition.

Speaking of the Cherokee "War Women," who were admitted to the tribal councils, Timberlake says (Memoirs, p. 70): "The reader will not be a little surprised to find the story of Amazons not so great a fable as we imagined, many of the Indian women being as famous in war as powerful in the council."

111. THE MOUNDS AND THE CONSTANT FIRE: THE OLD SACRED THINGS (p. 395): What is here said concerning the mounds, based chiefly upon Swimmer's recital, is given solely

as a matter of popular belief, shaped by tribal custom and ritual. The question of fact is for the archeologist to decide. The Indian statement is of value, however, in showing the supposed requirements for the solemn consecration of an important work.

A note by John Howard Payne upon the sacred square of the Creeks, as observed by him in 1835, just before his visit to the Cherokee, may throw further light on the problem: "In the center of this outer square was a very high circular mound. This, it seems, was formed from the earth accumulated yearly by removing the surface of the sacred square thither. At every Green-corn festival the sacred square is strewn with soil yet untrodden; the soil of the year preceding being taken away, but preserved as above explained. No stranger's foot is allowed to press the new earth of the sacred square until its consecration is complete" (Letter of 1835 in Continental Monthly, New York, 1862, p. 19). See note on the sacred fire.

Conjured with disease—The practice of conjuring certain favorite spots in order to render them fatal to an invading enemy was common to many if not to all tribes. One of the most terrible battles of the Creek war was fought upon the "Holy ground," so called because it was believed by the Indians that in consequence of the mystic rites which had been performed there for that purpose by their prophets, no white troops could set foot upon it and live.

The sacred fire—The method described for producing fire and keeping it constantly smoldering in the townhouse appears to have been that actually in use in ancient times, as indicated by the name given to the plant (*atsil'-sûñti*), and corroborated by the unanimous testimony of the old people. All the older East Cherokee believe that the ancient fire still burns within the mounds at Franklin and Bryson City, and those men who were stationed for a time near the latter place while in the Confederate service, during the Civil war, assert that they frequently saw the smoke rising from the adjacent mound.

The missionary Buttrick, from old Cherokee authority, says: "They were obliged to make new fire for sacred purposes by rubbing two pieces of dry wood together, with a certain weed, called golden rod, dry, between them. . . . When their enemies destroyed the house in which this holy fire was kept, it was said the fire settled down into the earth, where it still lives, though unknown to the people. The place where they lost this holy fire is somewhere in one of the Carolinas" (Antiquities, p. 9).

The general accuracy of Swimmer's account is strikingly confirmed by the description of the New-fire ceremony given more than half a century before by John Howard Payne, the poet, who had gone among the Cherokee to study their ethnology and was engaged in that work when arrested, together with John Ross, by the Georgia guard in 1835. He makes the kindling of the new fire a part of the annual spring festival. At that time, says Payne, "the altar in the center of the national heptagon [i. e. townhouse] was repaired. It was constructed of a conical shape, of fresh earth. A circle was drawn around the top to receive the fire of sacrifice. Upon this was laid, ready for use, the inner bark of seven different kinds of trees. This bark was carefully chosen from the east side of the trees, and was clear and free from blemish." After some days of preliminary purification, sacrifice, and other ceremonial performances, the day appointed for the kindling of the new fire arrived.

"Early in the morning the seven persons who were commissioned to kindle the fire commenced their operations. One was the official fire-maker; the remaining six his assistants. A hearth was carefully cleared and prepared. A round hole being made in a block of wood, a small quantity of dry golden-rod weed was placed in it. A stick, the end of which just fitted the opening, was whirled rapidly until the weed took fire. The flame was then kindled on the hearth and thence taken to every house by the women, who collectively waited for that purpose. The old fires having been everywhere extinguished, and the hearths cleansed, new fires were lighted throughout the country, and a sacrifice was made in each one of them of the first meat killed afterwards by those to whom they respectively belonged."—Payne MS, quoted in Squier, Serpent Symbol, pp. 116–118.

Similar ceremonies were common to many tribes, particularly the southern tribes and the Pueblos, in connection with the annual kindling of the sacred new fire. See Adair, History of the American Indians; Hawkins, Sketch of the Creek Country, quoted by Gatschet, Creek Migration Legend; Bartram, Travels; Fewkes, The New-fire Ceremony at Walpi, in American Anthropologist for January, 1900; Squier, Serpent Symbol. Going beyond our own boundaries it may be said briefly that fire worship was probably as ancient as ritual itself and well-nigh as universal.

Wooden box—The sacred ark of the Cherokee is described by Adair (History of the American Indians, pp. 161–162), and its capture by the Delawares is mentioned by Washburn (Reminiscences, pp. 191, 221), who states that to its loss the old priests of the tribe ascribed the later degeneracy of their people. They refused to tell him the contents of the ark. On this subject Adair says:

"A gentleman who was at the Ohio in the year 1756 assured me he saw a stranger there very importunate to view the inside of the Cheerake ark, which was covered with a drest deerskin and placed on a couple of short blocks. An Indian centinel watched it, armed with a hiccory bow and brass-pointed barbed arrows; and he was faithful to his trust, for finding the stranger obtruding to pollute the supposed sacred vehicle, he drew an arrow to the head, and would have shot him through the body had he not suddenly withdrawn. The interpreter, when asked by the gentleman what it contained, told him there was nothing in it but a bundle of conjuring traps. This shews what conjurers our common interpreters are, and how much the learned world have really profited by their informations."

Such tribal palladiums or "medicines," upon which the existence and prosperity of the tribe are supposed to depend, are still preserved among the plains Indians, the sacred receptacle in each case being confided to the keeping of a priest appointed for the purpose, who alone is privileged to undo the wrappings or expose the contents. Among these tribal "medicines" may be mentioned the sacred arrows of the Cheyenne, the "flat pipe" of the Arapaho, the great shell of the Omaha, and the taime image of the Kiowa (see reference in the author's Ghost-dance Religion and Calendar History of the Kiowa Indians).

White peace pipe—This statement concerning the ancient seven-stem peace pipe carved from white stone is given on the authority of Swimmer, who said that the stone was procured from a quarry near the present town of Knoxville, Tennessee. A certain district of western North Carolina has recently acquired an unenviable reputation for the manufacture of spurious "Indian pipes," ostensibly taken from the mounds, carved from soapstone and having from three to half a dozen stem-holes encircling the bowl.

Turtle drum—This statement is on the authority of Wafford, who had talked with men who claimed to have known those who had seen the drum. He was not positive as to the town, but thought it was Keowee. It is believed that the drum was hidden by the Indians, in anticipation of their speedy return, when the country was invaded by Williamson in 1776, but as the country was never recovered by the Cherokee the drum was lost.

112–115. SHORT HUMOROUS STORIES (pp. 397, 399): These short stories are fairly representative of Cherokee humor. Each was heard repeatedly from several informants, both east and west.

116. THE STAR FEATHERS (p. 399): This story was obtained from John Ax, with additional details from Chief Smith and others, to whom it was equally familiar. It is told as an actual happening in the early days, before the Indian had much acquaintance with the whites, and is thoroughly characteristic of the methods of medicine-men.

The deception was based upon the Cherokee belief that the stars are living creatures with feathers (see number 9, "What the Stars are Like ").

The Indian has always been noted for his love of feather decorations, and more than any from his native birds he prized the beautiful feathers of the peacock whenever it was possible to procure them from the whites. So far back as 1670 Lederer noted of a South Carolina tribe: "The Ushery delight much in feather ornament, of which they have great variety; but peacocks in most esteem, because rare in these parts" (Travels, p. 32, ed. 1891).

117. THE MOTHER BEAR'S SONG (p. 400): The first of these songs was obtained from Ayâsta, and was unknown to Swimmer. The second song was obtained also from Ayâsta, who knew only the verses, while Swimmer knew both the verses and the story which gives them their setting.

The first has an exact parallel among the Creeks, which is thus given in the "Baby Songs" of the Tuggle manuscript:

Ah tan	Down the stream
Ah yah chokese	if you hear
Mah kah cho kofe	chase going
Hoche yoke saw	up the stream
Lit kahts chars,	run,
Lit kahts chars.	run.
A thle poo	Up the stream
Ahyohchokese	if you hear
Mah kah cho kofe	the chase going
Thorne yoke saw	to the high mountain
Lit karts chars,	run,
Lit karts chars.	run.

Translation

If you hear the noise of the chase
Going down the stream
Then run up the stream.

If you hear the noise of the chase
Going up the stream
Then run to the high mountain,
Then run to the high mountain.

118. BABY SONG, TO PLEASE THE CHILDREN (p. 401): This song is well known to the women and was sung by both Ayâsta and Swimmer.

119. WHEN BABIES ARE BORN: THE WREN AND THE CRICKET (p. 401): These little bits of Indian folklore were obtained from Swimmer, but are common tribal property.

120. THE RAVEN MOCKER (p. 401): The grewsome belief in the "Raven Mocker" is universal among the Cherokee and has close parallels in other tribes. Very near to it is the Iroquois belief in the vampire or cannibal ghost, concerning which Schoolcraft relates some blood-curdling stories. He says: "It is believed that such doomed spirits creep into the lodges of men at night, and during sleep suck their blood and eat their flesh. They are invisible" (Notes on the Iroquois, p. 144). On one occasion, while the author was among the Cherokee, a sick man was allowed to die alone because his friends imagined they felt the presence of the Raven Mocker or other invisible witches about the house, and were consequently afraid to stay with him. The description of the flying terror appears to be that of a great meteor. It is a universal principle of folk belief that discovery or recognition while disguised in another form brings disaster to the witch.

The "diving" of the raven while flying high in air is performed by folding one wing close to the body, when the bird falls to a lower plane, apparently turning a somersault in the descent. It seems to be done purely for amusement.

121. HERBERT'S SPRING (p. 403): The subject of this old trader's legend must have been one of the head-springs of Chattooga river, an upper branch of Savannah, having its rise in the southern part of Jackson county, North Carolina, on the eastern slope of the ridge from which other streams flow in the opposite direction to join the waters of the Tennessee. It was probably in the vicinity of the present highlands in Macon county, where the trail from Chattooga river and the settlements on Keowee crossed the Blue ridge, thence descending Cullasagee to the towns on Little Tennessee.

126. PLANT LORE (p. 420): For ceremonies, prayers, and precautions used by the doctors in connection with the gathering and preparation of medicinal roots, barks, and herbs, see the author's Sacred Formulas of the Cherokees, in the Seventh Annual Report of the Bureau of Ethnology, 1891.

Violet—The Onondaga name signifies "two heads entangled," referring, we are told, to "the way so often seen where the heads are interlocked and pulled apart by the stems" (W. M. Beauchamp, in Journal of American Folk-Lore, October, 1888).

Cedar—For references to the sacred character of the cedar among the plains tribes, see the author's Ghost-dance Religion, in the Fourteenth Annual Report of the Bureau of Ethnology, part 2, 1896.

Linn and basswood—The ancient Tuscarora believed that no tree but black gum was immune from lightning, which, they declared, would run round the tree a great many times seeking in vain to effect an entrance. Lawson, who records the belief, adds: "Now, you must understand that sort of gum will not split or rive: therefore, I suppose the story might arise from thence" (Carolina, pp. 345–346, ed. 1860). The Pawnee claim the same immunity for the cedar, and throw sprigs of it as incense upon the fire during storms to turn aside the lightning stroke (Grinnell, Pawnee Hero Stories, p. 126).

Ginseng—For more concerning this plant see the author's Sacred Formulas, above mentioned.

GLOSSARY OF CHEROKEE WORDS

The Cherokee language has the continental vowel sounds *a, e, i,* and *u,* but lacks *o,* which is replaced by a deep *â.* The obscure or short *ŭ* is frequently nasalized, but the nasal sound is seldom heard at the end of a word. The only labial is *m,* which occurs in probably not more than half a dozen words in the Upper and Middle dialects, and is entirely absent from the Lower dialect, in which *w* takes its place. The characteristic *l* of the Upper and Middle dialects becomes *r* in the Lower, but no dialect has both sounds. There is also an aspirated *l;* *k* and *t* have the ordinary sounds of these letters, but *g* and *d* are medials, approximating the sounds of *k* and *t,* respectively. A frequent double consonant is *ts,* commonly rendered *ch* by the old traders (see p. 188, " Dialects ").

a	as in far.
ă	as in what, or obscure as in showman.
â	as in law, all.
d	medial (semisonant), approximating t.
e	as in they.
ĕ	as in net.
g	medial (semisonant), approximating k.
h	as in hat.
i	as in pique.
ĭ	as in pick.
k	as in kick.
l	as in lull.
'l	surd l (sometimes written hl), nearly the Welsh ll.
m	as in man.
n	as in not.
r	takes place of l in Lower dialect.
s	as in sin.
t	as in top.
u	as in rule.
û	as in cut.
ûñ	û nasalized.
w	as in wit.
y	as in you.
'	a slight aspirate, sometimes indicating the omission of a vowel.

A number of English words, with cross references, have been introduced into the glossary, and these, together with corrupted Cherokee forms, are indicated by small capitals.

adâ'lănûñ'stĭ—a staff or cane.

adan'ta—soul.

ada'wehĭ—a magician or supernatural being.

ada'wehi'yu—a very great magician; intensive form of *ada'wehĭ*.

â'gănă—groundhog.

Â'gănstâ'ta—"Groundhog-sausage," from *â'gănă*, groundhog, and *tsistâ'û*, "I am pounding it," understood to refer to pounding meat, etc., in a mortar, after having first crisped it before the fire. A war chief noted in the Cherokee war of 1760, and prominent until about the close of the Revolution; known to the whites as Oconostota. Also the Cherokee name for Colonel Gideon Morgan of the war of 1812, for Washington Morgan, his son, of the Civil war, and now for a full-blood upon the reservation, known to the whites as Morgan Calhoun.

Â'găn-uni'tsĭ—"Groundhogs'-mother," from *â'gănă* and *uni'tsĭ*, their mother, plural of *utsĭ'*, his mother (*etsĭ'*, *agitsĭ'*, my mother). The Cherokee name of a Shawano captive, who, according to tradition, killed the great Uktena serpent and procured the Ulûñsû'tĭ.

Agawe'la—"Old Woman," a formulistic name for corn or the spirit of corn.

agăyûñ'li—for *agăyûñ'lige*, old, ancient.

agidâ'tă—see *edâ'tă*.

agidu'tŭ—see *edu'tŭ*.

Agi'lĭ—"He is rising," possibly a contraction of an old personal name, *Agin'-agi'lĭ*, "Rising-fawn." Major George Lowrey, cousin of Sequoya, and assistant chief of the Cherokee Nation about 1840. Stanley incorrectly makes it "Keeth-la, or Dog" (for *gi'lĭ'*.)

agini'sĭ—see *eni'sĭ*.

agi'sĭ—female, applied usually to quadrupeds.

Agis'-e'gwa—"Great Female," possibly "Great Doe." A being, probably an animal god, invoked in the sacred formulas.

agitsĭ'—see *etsĭ'*.

Agitsta'ti'yĭ—"Where they stayed up all night," from *tsigitsûñ'tihû'*, "I stay up all night." A place in the Great Smoky range about the head of Noland creek, in Swain county, North Carolina. See notes to number 100.

Aguaquiri—see Guaquili.

Ăhălu'na—"Ambush," *Ăhălunûñ'yi*, "Ambush place," or *Uni'hălu'na*, "Where they ambushed," from *ăkălu'ga*, "I am watching". Soco gap, at the head of Soco creek, on the line between Swain and Haywood counties, North Carolina (see number 122). The name is also applied to a lookout station for deer hunters.

ahănu'lăhĭ—"he is bearded," from *ahănu'lăhû*, a beard.

Ahu'lude'gĭ—"He throws away the drum" (habitual), from *ahu'lĭ*, drum, and *akwăde'gû*, "I am throwing it away" (round object). The Cherokee name of John Jolly, a noted chief and adopted father of Samuel Houston, about 1800.

ahyeli'skĭ—a mocker or mimic.

aktă'—eye; plural, *diktă'*.

akta'tĭ—a telescope or field glass. The name denotes something with which to examine or look into closely, from *aktă'*, eye.

akwandu'li—a song form for *akwidu'li(-hû*, "I want it."

Akwan'kĭ—see *Anakwan'kĭ*.

Akwĕ'ti'yĭ—a location on Tuckasegee river, in Jackson county, North Carolina; the meaning of the name is lost. See number 122.

Alarka—see Yalâgĭ.

áligă'—the red-horse fish (*Moxostoma*).

Alkinĭ'—the last woman known to be of Natchez descent and peculiarity among the East Cherokee; died about 1890. The name has no apparent meaning.

ămă'—water; in the Lower dialect, ăwă'; cf. a'mă, salt.

amăyĕ'hĭ—"dwelling in the water," from ămă' (ămă'yĭ, "in the water") and ĕhŭ', "I dwell," "I live."

Ămăye'l-e'gwa—"Great island," from ămăye'lĭ, island (from ămă', water, and aye'lĭ, "in the middle") and e'gwa, great. A former Cherokee settlement on Little Tennessee river, at Big island, a short distance below the mouth of Tellico, in Monroe county, Tennessee. Timberlake writes it Mialaquo, while Bartram spells it Nilaque. Not to be confounded with Long-island town below Chattanooga.

Ămăye'lĭ-gûnăhi'ta—"Long island," from ămăye'lĭ, island, and gûnahi'ta, long. A former Cherokee settlement, known to the whites as Long Island town, at the Long island in Tennessee river, on the Tennessee-Georgia line. It was one of the Chickamauga towns (see Tsĭkăma'gĭ).

amă'yĭnĕ'hi—"dwellers in the water," plural of amăyĕ'hĭ.

Anăda'dûñtăskĭ—"Roasters," i. e., Cannibals; from gûñ'tăskŭ', "I am putting it (round) into the fire to roast." The regular word for cannibals is Yûñ'wini'giskĭ, q. v. See number 3.

anagáhûñ'ûñskŭ'—the Green-corn dance; literally, "they are having a Green-corn dance"; anagáhûñ'ûñsgûñ'yĭ, "where they are having the Green-corn dance"; the popular name is not a translation of the Cherokee word, which has no reference either to corn or dancing.

Anakwan'kĭ—the Delaware Indians; singular Akwan'kĭ, a Cherokee attempt at Wapanaqkĭ, "Easterners," the Algonquian name by which, in various corrupted forms, the Delawares are commonly known to the western tribes.

Anantooeah—see Ani'-Nûn'dăwe'gĭ.

a'ne'tsâ, or a'netsâ'gĭ—the ballplay.

a'netsâ'ûñskĭ—a ballplayer; literally, "a lover of the ballplay."

ani'—a tribal and animate prefix.

ani'da'wehĭ—plural of ada'wehĭ.

a'niganti'skĭ—see dăgan'tú.

Ani'-Gatăge'wĭ—one of the seven Cherokee clans; the name has now no meaning, but has been absurdly rendered "Blind savanna," from an incorrect idea that it is derived from igă'tĭ, a swamp or savanna, and dige'wĭ, blind.

Ani'-Gilă'hĭ—"Long-haired people," one of the seven Cherokee clans; singular, Agilă'hĭ. The word comes from agilă'hĭ (perhaps connected with agĭ'lge-nĭ, "the back of (his) neck"), an archaic term denoting wearing the hair long or flowing loosely, and usually recognized as applying more particularly to a woman.

Ani'-Gilĭ'—a problematic tribe, possibly the Congaree. See page 381. The name is not connected with gĭ'lĭ', dog.

Ani'-Gusă—see Ani'-Ku'să.

a'nigwa—soon after; dine'tlănă a'nigwa, "soon after the creation."

Ani'-Hyûñ'tĭkwălă'skĭ—"The Thunderers," i. e., thunder, which in Cherokee belief, is controlled and caused by a family of supernaturals. The word has reference to making a rolling sound; cf. tĭkwăle'lu, a wheel, hence a wagon; ămă'-tĭkwălelûñyĭ, "rolling water place," applied to a cascade where the water falls along the surface of the rock; ahyûñ'tĭkwălă'stihŭ', "it is thundering," applied to the roar of a railroad train or waterfall.

Ani'-Kawĭ'—"Deer people," one of the seven Cherokee clans; the regular form for deer is a'wĭ'.

Ani'-Kawi'tă—The Lower Creeks, from Kawi'tă or Coweta, their former principal town on Chattahoochee river near the present Columbus, Georgia; the Upper

Creeks on the head streams of Alabama river were distinguished as *Ani'-Ku'să* (q. v.) A small creek of Little Tennessee river above Franklin, in Macon county, North Carolina, is now known as Coweeta creek.

Ani'-Kĭtu'hwagĭ—"Kĭtu'hwă people," from *Kĭtu'hwă* (q. v.), an ancient Cherokee settlement; for explanation see page 182.

Ani'-Ku'să or Ani'-Gu'să—The Creek Indians, particularly the Upper Creeks on the waters of Alabama river; singular, *A-Ku'să*, from Kusa or Coosa (Spanish, Coça, Cossa) their principal ancient town.

Ani'-Kuta'nĭ (also *Ani'-Kwăta'nĭ*, or, incorrectly, *Nicotani*)—a traditional Cherokee priestly society or clan, exterminated in a popular uprising. See number 108.

anină'hilidâhĭ—"creatures that fly about," from *tsĭnai'lĭ*, "I am flying," *tsĭnă'ilidă'hú*, "I am flying about." The generic term for birds and flying insects.

Ani'-Na'tsĭ—abbreviated *Anintsĭ*, singular *A-Na'tsĭ*. The Natchez Indians; from coincidence with *na'tsĭ*, pine, the name has been incorrectly rendered "Pine Indians," whereas it is really a Cherokee plural of the proper name of the Natchez.

Anin'tsĭ—see *Ani'-Na'tsĭ*.

Ani'-Nûn'dăwe'gĭ—singular, *Nûn'dăwe'gĭ;* the Iroquois, more particularly the Seneca, from *Nûndawao*, the name by which the Seneca call themselves. Adair spells it Anantooeah. The tribe was also known as *Ani'-Sĕ'nikă*.

Ani'-Sahâ'nĭ—one of the seven Cherokee clans; possibly an archaic form for "Blue people," from *sa'ka'ni*, *sa'ka'nige'ĭ*, blue.

Ani'-Sa'nĭ, Ani'-Sawahâ'nĭ—see *Ani'-Sawănu'gĭ*.

Ani'-Sawănu'gĭ (singular *Sawănu'gi*)—the Shawano Indians. *Ani'-Sa'nĭ* and *Ani'-Sawahă'nĭ* (see page 380) may be the same.

Ani'-Sĕ'nikă—see *Ani'-Núndăwe'gĭ*.

anisga'ya—plural of *asga'ya*, man.

Anisga'ya Tsunsdi' (-ga)—"The Little Men"; the Thunder Boys in Cherokee mythology. See numbers 3 and 8.

Ani'sgaya'yĭ—"Men town" (?), a traditional Cherokee settlement on Valley river, in Cherokee county, North Carolina.

anisgi'na—plural of *asgi'na*, q. v.

Ani'-Skălâ'lĭ—the Tuscarora Indians; singular, *Skălâ'lĭ* or *A-Skălâ'lĭ*.

Ani'skwa'nĭ—Spaniards; singular, *Askwa'nĭ*.

Ani'-Suwa'lĭ, or Ani-'Suwa'la—the Suala, Sara, or Cheraw Indians, formerly about the headwaters of Broad river, North Carolina, the Xuala province of the De Soto chronicle, and Joara or Juada of the later Pardo narrative.

Ani'ta'gwă—the Catawba Indians; singular, *Ata'gwă* or *Tagwă*.

Ani'-Tsâ'gûhĭ—a traditional Cherokee clan, transformed to bears (see number 75). Swimmer's daughter bears the name *Tsâgûhĭ*, which is not recognized as distinctively belonging to either sex.

Ani'-Tsa'lăgi'—the Cherokee. See "Tribal Synonymy," page 182.

Ani'-Tsa'ta—the Choctaw Indians; singular, *Tsa'ta*.

Ani'-Tsĭ'ksû—the Chickasaw Indians; singular, *Tsĭ'ksû*.

Ani'-Tsi'skwa—"Bird people;" one of the seven Cherokee clans.

Ani'tsu'tsă—"The Boys," from *atsu'tsă*, boy; the Pleiades. See number 10.

Ani'-Wâ'dĭ—"Paint people"; one of the seven Cherokee clans.

Ani'-Wâdihĭ'—"Place of the Paint people or clan"; Paint town, a Cherokee settlement on lower Soco creek, within the reservation in Jackson and Swain counties, North Carolina. It takes its name from the *Ani'-Wâ'dĭ* or Paint clan.

ani'wani'skĭ—the bugle weed, *Lycopus virginicus;* literally, "they talk" or "talkers," from *tsiwa'nihú*, "I am talking," *awani'skĭ*, "he talks habitually." See number 26.

Ani'-Wasa'sĭ—the Osage Indians; singular, *Wasa'sĭ*.

Ani'-Wa'′ya—"Wolf people"; the most important of the seven Cherokee clans.

Ani'-Yu'tsĭ—the Yuchi or Uchee Indians; singular Yu'tsĭ.

Ani'-Yûñ'wiyă—Indians, particularly Cherokee Indians; literally "principal or real people," from yûñwĭ, person, yă, a suffix implying principal or real, and ani', the tribal prefix. See pages 5 and 182.

ANNIE AX—see Sadayĭ'.

AQUONE—a post-office on Nantahala river, in Macon county, North Carolina, site of the former Fort Scott. Probably a corruption of egwânĭ, river.

ARCH, JOHN—see Atsĭ.

asâ'gwălihû'—a pack or burden; asâ'gwăĬlû', or asâ'gwĭ'ĭ', "there is a pack on him." Cf sâ'gwăĬ'.

asčhĭ'—surely.

Asĕ'nikă—singular of Ani'-Sĕ'nikă. See Ani'-Nûndăwe'gĭ.

asga'ya—man.

Asga'ya Gi'găgeĭ—the "Red Man"; the Lightning spirit.

asgi'na—a ghost, either human or animal; from the fact that ghosts are commonly supposed to be malevolent, the name is frequently rendered "devil."

ASHEVILLE—see Kâsdu'yĭ and Unta'kiyasti'yĭ.

âsĭ—the sweat lodge and occasional winter sleeping apartment of the Cherokee and other southern tribes. It was a low-built structure of logs covered with earth, and from its closeness and the fire usually kept smoldering within was known to the old traders as the "hot house."

â'siyu' (abbreviated siyu')—good; the common Cherokee salute; gâ'siyu', "I am good"; hâ'siyu', "thou art good"; â'siyu, "he (it) is good"; âstû, "very good" (intensive).

Askwa'nĭ—a Spaniard. See Ani'skwa'nĭ.

âstû'—very good; âstû tsĭkĭ', very good, best of all. Cf â'siyu'.

Astu'gatâ'ga—A Cherokee lieutenant in the Confederate service, killed in 1862. See page 170. The name may be rendered, "Standing in the doorway" but implies that the man himself is the door or shutter; it has no first person; gatâ'ga, "he is standing"; stu'tĭ, a door or shutter; stuhû', a closed door or passage; stugi'stĭ, a key, i. e. something with which to open a door.

asûñ'tlĭ, asûñtlûñ'yĭ—a footlog or bridge; literally, "log lying across," from asi'ta, log.

ătă'—wood; ata'yă, "principal wood," i. e. oak; cf. Muscogee iti, wood.

Atagâ'hĭ—"Gall place," from ă'tăgú', gall, and hĭ, locative; a mythic lake in the Great Smoky mountains. See number '69. The name is also applied to that part of the Great Smoky range centering about Thunderhead mountain and Miry ridge, near the boundary between Swain county, North Carolina, and Blount county, Tennessee.

ă'tăgû'—gall.

Ătă'-gûĬ'kălû'—a noted Cherokee chief, recognized by the British government as the head chief or "emperor" of the Nation, about 1760 and later, and commonly known to the whites as the Little Carpenter (Little Cornplanter, by mistake, in Haywood). The name is frequently spelled Atta-kulla-kulla, Ata-kullakulla or Ata-culculla. It may be rendered "Leaning-wood," from ătă', "wood" and gûĬ'kălû a verb implying that something long is leaning, without sufficient support, against some other object; it has no first person form. Bartram describes him as "a man of remarkably small stature, slender and of a delicate frame, the only instance I saw in the Nation; but he is a man of superior abilities."

Ata'gwă—a Catawba Indian. See Ani'ta'gwă.

A'tâhi'ta—abbreviated from A'tâhitûñ'yĭ, "Place where they shouted," from gatâ'hiû', "I shout," and yĭ, locative. Waya gap, on the ridge west of Franklin,

Macon county, North Carolina. See number 13. The map name is probably from the Cherokee *wa'ya*, wolf.

ATA-KULLAKULLA—see *Ătă'-gŭl'kălú'*.

â'tălĭ—mountain; in the Lower dialect *á'tărĭ*, whence the "Ottare" or Upper Cherokee of Adair. The form *á'tălĭ* is used only in composition; a mountain in situ is *ătălúñyĭ* or *gatu'sĭ*.

â'tălĭ-gûlĭ'—"it climbs the mountain," i. e., "mountain-climber"; the ginseng plant, *Ginseng quinquefolium;* from *á'tălĭ*, mountain, and *gúlĭ'*, "it climbs" (habitually); *tsĭlăhĭ'* or *tsĭlĭ'*, "I am climbing." Also called in the sacred formulas, *Yûñ'wĭ Usdi'*, "Little Man." See number 126.

a'tălulû'—unfinished, premature, unsuccessful; whence *utalu'lĭ*, "it is not yet time."

Ata'lûñti'skĭ—a chief of the Arkansas Cherokee about 1818, who had originally emigrated from Tennessee. The name, commonly spelled Tollunteeskee, Taluntiski, Tallotiskee, Tallotuskee, etc., denotes one who throws some living object from a place, as an enemy from a precipice. See number 100 for instance.

â'tărĭ—see *á'tălĭ*.

ătăsĭ' (or *ătăsú'*, in a dialectic form)—a war club.

atatsûñ'skĭ—stinging; literally, "he stings" (habitually).

A'tlă'nuwă'—"Tlă'nuwă hole"; the Cherokee name of Chattanooga, Tennessee, (see *Tsatănu'gĭ*) originally applied to a bluff on the south side of the Tennessee river at the foot of the present Market street. See number 124.

A'tsĭ—the Cherokee name of John Arch, one of the earliest native writers in the Sequoya characters. The word is simply an attempt at the English name Arch.

atsi'la—fire; in the Lower dialect, *atsi'ra*.

Atsil'-dihye'gĭ—"Fire Carrier"; apparently the Cherokee name for the will-of-the-wisp. See page 335. As is usually the case in Cherokee compounds, the verbal form is plural ("it carries fires"); the singular form is *ahye'gĭ*.

atsil'-sûñ'tĭ (abbreviated *tsil'-sûñ'tĭ*)—fleabane (*Erigeron canadense*); the name signifies "material with which to make fire," from *atsi'la*, fire, and *gasûñ'tĭ*, (*gatsûñ'tĭ* or *gatlûñ'tĭ*), material with which to make something; from *gasûñ'skú* (or *gatlûñ'skú*), "I make it." The plant is also called *ihyă'ga*. See number 126.

Atsil'-tlûñtû'tsĭ—"Fire panther." A meteor or comet. See notes to number 9.

Atsi'la-wa'ĭ—"Fire ——"; a mountain, sometimes known as Rattlesnake knob, about two miles northeast of Cherokee, Swain county, North Carolina. See number 122.

a'tsĭnă'—cedar; cf. Muscogee, *achena* or *auchenau*.

A'tsĭnă'-k'ta'ûñ—"Hanging cedar place"; from *a'tsină'*, cedar, and *k'taúñ*, "where it (long) hangs down"; a Cherokee name for the old Taskigi town on Little Tennessee river in Monroe county, Tennessee. See number 105.

atsi'ra—see *atsi'la*.

Atsûñ'stă'ti'yĭ (abbreviated *Atsûñ'stă'ti'*)—"Fire-light place," (cf. *atsil·sûñ'·tĭ*), referring to the "fire-hunting" method of killing deer in the river at night. The proper form for Chestatee river, near Dahlonega, in Lumpkin county, Georgia.

ATTAKULLAKULLA—see *Ătă-gûl'kălú'*.

ăwă'—see *ămă'*.

awâ'hĭlĭ—eagle; particularly *Aquila chrysætus*, distinguished as the "pretty-feathered eagle."

a'wĭ'—deer; also sometimes written and pronounced, *ăhăwĭ';* the name is sometimes applied to the large horned beetle, the "flying stag" of early writers.

a'wĭ'-ahănu'lăhĭ—goat; literally, "bearded deer."

a'wĭ'-aktă'—"deer eye"; the *Rudbeckia* or black-eyed Susan.

a'wĭ'-ahyeli'skĭ—"deer mocker"; the deer bleat, a sort of whistle used by hunters to call the doe by imitating the cry of the fawn.

a'wĭ'-e'gwă (abbreviated a'w-e'gwă)—the elk, literally "great deer."

a'wĭ'-unăde'na—sheep; literally "woolly deer."

A'wĭ' Usdi'—"Little Deer"; the mythic chief of the Deer tribe.   See number 15.

Ax, ANNIE—see Sadayĭ'.

Ax, JOHN--see Ităgú'năhĭ.

Ayâ'sta—"The Spoiler," from tsiyă'stihú, "I spoil it"; cf. uyă'ĭ, bad.   A prominent woman and informant on the East Cherokee reservation.

aye'lĭ—half, middle, in the middle.

AYRATE—see e'lădĭ'.

Ayuhwa'sĭ—the proper form of the name commonly written Hiwassee.   It signifies a savanna or meadow and was applied to two (or more) former Cherokee settlements.   The more important, commonly distinguished as Ayuhwa'sĭ Egwă'hĭ or Great Hiwassee, was on the north bank of Hiwassee river at the present Savannah ford above Columbus, in Polk county, Tennessee.   The other was farther up the same river, at the junction of Peachtree creek, above Murphy, in Cherokee county, North Carolina.   Lanman writes it Owassa.

A'yûñ'inĭ—"Swimmer"; literally, "he is swimming," from gayûñinĭ', "I am swimming."   A principal priest and informant of the East Cherokee, died in 1899.

Ayûlsû'—see Dayûlsûñ'yĭ.

BEAVERDAM—see Uy'gilă'gĭ.

BIG-ISLAND—see Ămăye'l-e'gwa.

BIG-COVE—see Kă'lanûñ'yĭ.

BIG-MUSH—see Gatûñ'wa'lĭ.

BIG-WITCH—see Tskĭl-e'gwa.

BIRD-TOWN—see Tsiskwă'hĭ.

BLOODY-FELLOW—see ISKAGUA.

BLYTHE—see Diskwa'nĭ.

BLACK-FOX—see Ină'lĭ.

BOUDINOT, ELIAS—see Gălăgi'na.

BOWL, THE; BOWLES, COLONEL—see Diwa'lĭ.

BRASS—see Ûñtsaiyĭ'.

BRASSTOWN—see Itse'yĭ.

BREATH, THE—see Ûñli'ta.

BRIERTOWN—see Kănu'gă'lă'yĭ.

BUFFALO (creek)—see Yûnsă'ĭ.

BULL-HEAD—see Uskwăle'na.

BUTLER, JOHN—see Tsan'-uga'sĭtă.

CADE'S COVE—see Tsiyă'hĭ.

CANACAUGHT—"Canacaught, the great Conjurer," mentioned as a Lower Cherokee chief in 1684; possibly kanegwă'tĭ, the water-moccasin snake.   See page 31.

CANALY—see hi'gĭna'lĭĭ.

CANASAGUA—see Gănsâ'gĭ.

CANNASTION, CANNOSTEE—see Kăna'sta.

CANUGA—see Kănu'ga.

CARTOOGAJA—see Gatu'gitse'yĭ.

CATALUCHEE—see Gadalu'tsĭ.

CAUCHI—a place, apparently in the Cherokee country, visted by Pardo in 1567 (see page 29).   The name may possibly have some connection with Nacoochee or Nagu'tsĭ', q. v.

CAUNASAITA—given as the name of a Lower Cherokee chief in 1684; possibly for Kanûñsi'ta, "dogwood" (Cornus florida).   See page 31.

CHALAQUE—see Tsă'lăgĭ, under "Tribal Synonymy," page 182.

CHATTANOOGA—see *Tsatănŭ'gĭ*.

CHATTOOGA, CHATUGA—see *Tsatu'gĭ*.

CHEEOWHEE—see *Tsiyă'hĭ*.

CHEERAKE—see *Tsă'lăgĭ*, under "Tribal Synonymy," page 182.

CHEOWA—see *Tsiyă'hĭ*.

CHEOWA MAXIMUM—see *Sehwate'yĭ*.

CHERAQUI—see *Tsă'lăgĭ*, under "Tribal Synonymy," page 182.

CHERAW—see *Ani'-Suwa'lĭ*.

CHEROKEE—see *Tsă'lăgĭ*, under "Tribal Synonymy," page 182; also *Elăwă'diyĭ*.

CHESTATEE—see *Atsŭñ'stă'tĭ'yĭ*.

CHESTUA—see *Tsistu'yĭ*.

CHEUCUNSENE—see *Tsi'yu-gŭnsi'nĭ*.

CHEULAH—mentioned by Timberlake as the chief of Settacoo (*Sĭ'tikŭ*) in 1762. The name may be intended for *Tsu'lă*, "Fox."

CHICKAMAUGA—see *Tsĭ'kăma'gĭ*.

CHILHOWEE—see *Tsŭ'lăñ'we*.

CHIMNEY TOPS—see *Duni'skwa'lgŭñ'ĭ*.

CHISCA—mentioned in the De Soto narratives as a mining region in the Cherokee country. The name may have a connection with *Tsi'skwa*, "bird," possibly *Tsiskwă'hĭ*, "Bird place."

CHOASTEA—see *Tsistu'yĭ*.

CHOPPED OAK—see *Digălu'yătŭñ'yĭ*.

CHOQUATA—see *Itsă'tĭ*.

CHOTA, CHOTTE—see *Itsă'tĭ*.

CITICO—see *Sĭ'tikŭ'*.

CLEAR-SKY—see ISKAGUA.

CLENNUSE—see *Tlanusi'yĭ*.

CLEVELAND—see *Tsistetsi'yĭ*.

COÇA—see *Ani'-Ku'sa*.

COCO—see *Kukŭ'*.

COHUTTA—see *Gahŭ'tĭ*.

COLANNEH, COLONA—see *Kă'lănŭ*.

CONASAUGA—see *Gănsă'gĭ*.

CONNEROSS—see *Kăwăn'-ură'sŭñyĭ*.

COOWEESCOOWEE—see *Gu'wisguwĭ'*.

COOSA—see *Ani'-Ku'sa* and *Kusă'*.

COOSAWATEE—see *Ku'săweti'yĭ*.

CORANI—see *Kă'lănŭ*.

COSSA—see *Ani'-Ku'sa*, Kusa.

COWEE'—see *Kawi'yĭ*.

COWEETA, COWETA—see *Ani'-Kawi'tă*.

COYATEE (variously spelled Cawatie, Coiatee, Coytee, Coytoy, Kai-a-tee)—A former Cherokee settlement on Little Tennessee river, some ten miles below the junction of Tellico, about the present Coytee post-office in Loudon county, Tennessee. The correct form and etymology are uncertain.

CREEK-PATH—see *Ku'să-nŭñnă'hĭ*.

CROW-TOWN—see *Kăgŭñ'yĭ*.

CUHTAHLATAH—a Cherokee woman noted in the Wahnenauhi manuscript as having distinguished herself by bravery in battle. The proper form may have some connection with *gatŭñ'lătĭ*, "wild hemp."

CULLASAGEE—see *Kŭlse'tsi'yĭ*.

CULLOWHEE, CURRAHEE—see *Gălăhi'yĭ*.

CUTTAWA—see *Kĭtu'hwă*.

dăgan'tû—"he makes it rain"; from *aga'skă*, "it is raining," *aga'nă*, "it has begun to rain"; a small variety of lizard whose cry is said to presage rain. It is also called *a'niganti'skĭ*, "they make it rain" (plural form), or "rain-maker." See number 59.

dagûl'kû—the American white-fronted goose (*Anser albifrons gambeli*). The name may be an onomatope. See number 6.

dăgû'nă—the fresh water mussel; also a variety of face pimples.

Dăgûnâ'hĭ—"Mussel place," from *dăgû'nă*, mussel, and *hĭ*, locative. The Muscle shoals on Tennessee river, in northwestern Alabama. It was sometimes called also simply *Tsŭ'stănalûñ'yĭ*, "Shoals place." Cf. *U'stăna'lĭ*.

Dăgû'năwe'lâhĭ—"Mussel-liver place," from *dăgû'nă*, mussel, *uwe'la*, liver, and *hĭ*, locative; the Cherokee name for the site of Nashville, Tennessee. No reason can now be given for the name.

DAHLONEGA—A town in Lumpkin County, Georgia, near which the first gold was mined. A mint was established there in 1838. The name is from the Cherokee *dală'nige'i*, yellow, whence *ate'lă-dalâ'nige'i*, "yellow money," i. e., gold.

daksăwa'ihû—"he is shedding tears."

dăkwă'—a mythic great fish; also the whale. See number 68.

Dăkwâ'Ĭ—"Dăkwă place," from a tradition of a *dăkwă'* in the river at that point. A former Cherokee settlement, known to the traders as Toqua or Toco, on Little Tennessee river, about the mouth of Toco creek in Monroe county, Tennessee. See number 68. A similar name and tradition attaches to a spot on the French Broad river, about six miles above the Warm springs, in Buncombe county, North Carolina. See number 122.

dakwa'nitlastestĭ—"I shall have them on my legs for garters"; from *anitla'stĭ* (plural *dinitla'stĭ*), garter; *d–*, initial plural; *akwă*, first person particle; and *estĭ*, future suffix. See number 77.

da'lĭkstă'—"vomiter," from *dagik'stihú'*, "I am vomiting," *dalikstă'*, "he vomits" (habitually); the form is plural. The spreading adder (*Heterodon*), also sometimes called *kwandăya'hú*, a word of uncertain etymology.

Da'năgâstă—for*Da'năwă-gâsta'yă*, "Sharp-war," i. e. "Eager-warrior"; a Cherokee woman's name.

Da'nawa-(a)sa'tsûñ'yĭ "War ford," from *da'nawa*, war, and *asa'tsûñ'yĭ*, a crossing-place or ford. A ford on Cheowa river about three miles below Robbinsville, in Graham county, North Carolina. See number 122.

Danda'gănŭ'—"Two looking at each other," from *detsi'gănú'*, "I am looking at him." A former Cherokee settlement, commonly known as Lookout Mountain town, on Lookout Mountain creek, near the present Trenton, Dade county, Georgia. One of the Chickamauga towns (see *Tsĭ'kăma'gi*), so called on account of the appearance of the mountains facing each other across the Tennessee river at Chattanooga.

Da'si'giya'gĭ—an old masculine personal name, of doubtful etymology, but commonly rendered by the traders "Shoe-boots," possibly referring to some peculiar style of moccasin or leggin. A chief known to the whites as Shoe-boots is mentioned in the Revolutionary records. Chief Lloyd Welch, of the eastern band, was known in the tribe as Da'si'giya'gĭ and the same name is now used by the East Cherokee as the equivalent of the name Lloyd.

Da'skwĭtûñ'yĭ—"Rafters place," from *daskwĭtûñ'i*, "rafters," and *yĭ*, locative. A former settlement on Tusquittee creek, near Hayesville, in Clay county, North Carolina.

dasûñ'tălĭ—ant; *dasûñ'tălĭ atatsûñ'skĭ*, "stinging ant," the large red cow-ant (*Myrmica?*), also called sometimes, on account of its hard body-case, *nûñ'yunu'wĭ*, "stone-clad," after the fabulous monster. See number 67.

Datle'yăsta'Ĭ—"Where they fell down," a point on Tuckasegee river, a short distance above Webster, in Jackson county, North Carolina. For tradition see number 122.

dâtsĭ—a traditional water monster. See number 122.

Dâtsi′yĭ—"Dâtsĭ place"; a place on Little Tennessee river, near the junction of Eagle creek, in Swain county, North Carolina. See number 122.

Datsu′nălâsgûñ′yĭ—"where there are tracks or footprints," from ulâ′sinûñ′yĭ or ulásgûñ′yĭ, footprint. Track Rock gap, near Blairsville, Georgia. Also sometimes called De′gʌyelûñ′hă, "place of branded marks"; (digăletănûñ′hĭ, branded, or printed). See number 125.

dâ′yĭ—beaver.

Dayûlsûñ′yĭ—"Place where they cried," a spot on the ridge at the head of Tuckasegee river, in Jackson county, North Carolina; so called from an old tradition. See number 80.

dâ′yuni′sĭ—"beaver's grandchild," from dâyĭ, beaver, and uni′sĭ, son's child, of either sex (daughter's child, either sex, uli′sĭ). The water beetle or mellow bug (Dineutes discolor).

Degal′gûñ′yĭ—a cairn, literally "Where they are piled up"; a series of cairns on the south side of Cheŏwa river, in Graham county, North Carolina. See number 122.

De′gătă′gă—The Cherokee name of General Stand Watie and of a prominent early western chief known to the whites as Takatoka. The word is derived from tsitâ′gă, "I am standing," daʻnitâ′gă, "they are standing together," and conveys the subtle meaning of two persons standing together and so closely united in sympathy as to form but one human body.

De′gʌyelûñ′hă—see Datsu′nalâsgûñ′yĭ.

detsănûñ′lĭ—an inclosure or piece of level ground cleared for ceremonial purposes; applied more particularly to the Green-corn dance ground. The word has a plural form, but can not be certainly analyzed.

De′tsătă—a Cherokee sprite. See number 78.

detsinu′lăhûñgû′—"I tried, but failed."

Dida′lăski′yĭ—"Showering place." In the story (number 17) the name is understood to mean "The place where it rains fire." It signifies literally, however, the place where it showers, or comes down, and lodges upon something animate, and has no definite reference to fire (atsi′la) or rain (agăskă, "it is raining"); degaʻláskú′, "they are showering down and lodging upon him."

Dida′skasti′yĭ—"Where they were afraid of each other." A spot on Little Tennessee river, near the mouth of Alarka creek, in Swain county, North Carolina. See number 122.

diga′gwănĭ′—the mud-hen or didapper (Gallinula galeata). The name is a plural form and implies "lame," or "crippled in the legs" (cf. detsi′nigwă′nă, "I am kneeling"), probably from the bouncing motion of the bird when in the water. It is also the name of a dance.

Diga′kati′yĭ—see Gakati′yĭ.

di′gălûñgûñ′yi—"where it rises, or comes up" ; the east. The sacred term is Nûñdâ′yĭ, q. v.

digălûñ′lătiyûñ—a height, one of a series, from galûñ′lătĭ, "above." See number 1.

Digălu′yătûñ′yĭ—"Where it is gashed (with hatchets)" ; from tsilu′yú, "I am cutting (with a chopping stroke)," di, plural prefix, and yĭ, locative. The Chopped Oak, formerly east of Clarkesville, Georgia. See number 125.

Digăne′skĭ—"He picks them up" (habitually), from tsĭne′ú, "I am picking it up." A Cherokee Union soldier in the civil war. See page 171.

digi′găge′ĭ—the plural of gi′găge′i, red.

digû′lanăhi′ta—for digû′lĭ-anăhi′ta, "having long ears," "long-eared"; from gúlĕ, "ear" and gúnahi′ta, "long."

Dihyûñ′dulă′—"Sheaths," or "Scabbards"; singular ahyûñ′dulă′, "a gun sheath," or other scabbard. The probable correct form of a name which appears in Revolutionary documents as "Untoola, or Gun Rod."

diktă'—plural of *aktă'*, eye.

dĭlă'—skunk.

dilsta'ya'tĭ—"scissors"; the water-spider (Dolomedes).

dinda'skwate'skĭ—the violet; the name signifies, "they pull each other's heads off."

dine'tlănă—the creation.

di'nŭskĭ—"the breeder"; a variety of smilax brier. See number 126.

Disgă'gisti'yĭ—"Where they gnaw"; a place on Cheowa river, in Graham county, North Carolina. See number 122.

diskwa'nĭ—"chestnut bread," i. e., a variety of bread having chestnuts mixed with it. The Cherokee name of James Blythe, interpreter and agency clerk.

distai'yĭ—"they are strong," plural of *astai'yĭ*, "strong, or tough." The *Tephrosia* or devil's-shoestring. See number 126.

dista'stĭ—a mill (generic).

dita'stayeskĭ—"a barber," literally "one who cuts things" (as with a scissors), from *tsista'yă*, "I cut," (as with a scissors). The cricket (*tăla'tŭ*) is sometimes so called. See number 59.

Diwa'ᶜlĭ—"Bowl," a prominent chief of the western Cherokee, known to the whites as The Bowl, or Colonel Bowles, killed by the Texans in 1839. The chief mentioned on page 100 may have been another of the same name.

diyâ'hălĭ (or *duyă'hălĭ*)—the alligator lizard (*Sceloporue undulatus*). See number 59.

Diyâ'hăli'yĭ—"Lizard place," from *diyă'hălĭ*, lizard, and *yĭ*, locative. Joanna bald, a mountaiṇ at the head of Valley river, on the line between Cherokee and Graham counties, North Carolina. For tradition see number 122; also number 59.

DOUBLE-HEAD—see *Tăl-tsu'skă'*.

DRAGGING-CANOE—see *Tsi'yu-gănsi'nĭ*.

Dudûñ'leksûñ'yĭ—"Where its legs were broken off"; a place on Tuckasegee river, a few miles above Webster, in Jackson county, North Carolina. See number 122.

Dugilu'yĭ (abbreviated *Dugilu'*, and commonly written Tugaloo, or sometimes Toogelah or Toogoola)—a name occurring in several places in the old Cherokee country, the best known being Tugaloo river, so called from a former Cherokee settlement at that name situated at the junction of Toccoa creek with the main stream, in Habersham county, Georgia. The word is of uncertain etymology, but seems to refer to a place at the forks of a stream.

Dûksa'ĭ, Dûkw'sa'ĭ—The correct form of the name commonly written Toxaway, applied to a former Cherokee settlement in South Carolina, and the creek upon which it stood, an extreme head-stream of Keowee river having its source in Jackson county, North Carolina. The meaning of the name is lost, although it has been wrongly interpreted to mean "Place of shedding tears." See number 123.

Dulastûñ'yĭ—"Potsherd place." A former Cherokee settlement on Nottely river in Cherokee county, North Carolina. See number 122.

dule'tsĭ—"kernels," a goitrous swelling upon the throat.

dulu'sĭ—a variety of frog found upon the headwaters of Savannah river. See number 125.

Duniya'ta'lûñ'yĭ—"Where there are shelves, or flat places," from *aya'te'nĭ*, flat, whence *da'ya'tana'lûñ'ĭ*, a shelf, and *yĭ'*, the locative. A gap on the Great Smoky range, near Clingman's dome, Swain county, North Carolina. See notes to number 100.

Dunidû'lalûñ'yĭ—"Where they made arrows"; a place on Straight creek, a head-stream of Oconaluftee river, in Swain county, North Carolina. See number 122.

Duni'skwa'lgûñ'ĭ—the double peak known as the Chimney Tops, in the Great Smoky mountains about the head of Deep creek, in Swain county, North Carolina. On the north side is the pass known as Indian gap. The name signifies a "forked antler," from *uskwa'lgú*, antler, but indicates that the antler is attached in place, as though the deer itself were concealed below.

Du′stäyalûñ′yĭ—"Where it made a noise as of thunder or shooting," apparently referring to a lightning stroke (*detsistäya′hihá*, "I make a shooting, or thundering, noise," might be a first person form used by the personified Thundergod); a spot on Hiwassee river, about the junction of Shooting creek, near Hayesville, in Clay county, North Carolina. A former settlement along the creek bore the same name. See number 79.

du′stu′—a species of frog, appearing very early in spring; the name is intended for an onomatope. It it is the correct form of the name of the chief noted by McKenney and Hall as "Tooantuh or Spring Frog."

Dutch—see *Tätsĭ′*.

duwĕ′gă—the spring lizard. See number 59.

Eagle dance—see *Tsugidû′ĭ′ Ûlsgi′stĭ*.

Eastinaulee—see *U′stäna′lĭ*.

Echoee—see *Itse′yĭ*.

Echota—see *Itsâ′tĭ*.

Edâ′hĭ—"He goes about" (habitually); a masculine name.

Echota, New—see *Gänsâ′gĭ*.

edâ′tă—my father (Upper dialect); the Middle and Lower dialect form is *agidâ′tă*.

edu′tŭ—my maternal grandfather (Upper dialect); the Middle and Lower dialect form is *agidu′tŭ*; cf *eni′sĭ*.

e′gwa—great; cf *u′tănú*.

egwâ′nĭ—river.

Egwânul′tĭ—"By the river," from *egwâ′nĭ*, river, and *nu′lătĭ* or *nuĭ′tĭ*, near, beside. The proper form of Oconaluftee, the name of the river flowing through the East Cherokee reservation in Swain and Jackson counties, North Carolina. The Cherokee town, "Oconalufte," mentioned by Bartram as existing about 1775, was probably on the lower course of the river at the present Birdtown, on the reservation, where was formerly a considerable mound.

elä—earth, ground.

e′lădĭ′—low, below; in the Lower dialect *e′rădĭ′*, whence the Ayrate or Lower Cherokee of Adair as distinguished from the Ottare (*â′tărĭ*, *â′tălĭ*) or Upper Cherokee.

elanti—a song form for *e′lădĭ*, q. v.

Elätse′yĭ (abbreviated *Elätse′*)—possibly "Green (Verdant) earth," from *elă*, earth, and *itse′yĭ*, green, from fresh-springing vegetation. The name of several former Cherokee settlements, commonly known to the whites as Ellijay, Elejoy or Allagae. One of these was upon the headwaters of Keowee river in South Carolina; another was on Ellijay creek of Little Tennessee river, near the present Franklin, in Macon county, North Carolina; another was about the present Ellijay in Gilmer county, Georgia; and still another was on Ellejoy creek of Little river near the present Maryville, in Blount county, Tennessee.

Eläwâ′diyĭ (abbreviated *Eläwâ′di*)—"Red-earth place" from *elă*, earth, *wâdi*, brown-red or red paint, and *yĭ*, the locative. 1. The Cherokee name of Yellow-hill settlement, now officially known as Cherokee, the postoffice and agency headquarters for the East Cherokee, on Oconaluftee river in Swain county, North Carolina. 2. A former council ground, known in history as Red Clay, at the site of the present village of that name in Whitfield county, Georgia, adjoining the Tennessee line.

Ellijay—see *Elätse′yĭ*.

eni′sĭ—my paternal grandfather (Upper dialect); the Middle and Lower dialect form is *agini′sĭ*. Cf. *edu′tŭ*.

Eskaqua—see Iskagua.

Estanaula, Estinaula—see *U′stäna′lĭ*.

Ĕtăwa'hă-tsistatla'skĭ—"Deadwood-lighter," a traditional Cherokee conjurer. See
    number 100.

e̯'tĭ, or etĭ—old, long ago.

Etowah—see I'tăwă'.

Etsaiyĭ'—see Ûñtsaiyĭ'.

etsĭ'—my mother (Upper dialect); the Middle and Lower dialect form is agitsĭ'.

Euharlee—see Yuha'lĭ.

Feather dance—see Tsugidŭ'lĭ, Ûlsgi'stĭ.

Fighting-town—see Walâs'-unûlsti'yĭ.

Flax-toter— see Tâle'danigi'skĭ.

Flying-squirrel—see Kâ'lahú'.

French Broad—see Unta'kiyasti'yĭ.

Frogtown—see Walâsi'yĭ.

Gadalu'lŭ—the proper name of the mountain known to the whites as Yonah (from
    yânú, "bear"), or upper Chattahoochee river, in White county, Georgia. The
    name has no connection with Tallulah (see Tălulŭ'), and can not be translated.

Gadalu'tsĭ—in the corrupted form of Cataluchee this appears on the map as the name
    of a peak, or rather a ridge, on the line between Swain and Haywood counties,
    in North Carolina, and of a creek running down on the Haywood side into Big
    Pigeon river. It is properly the name of the ridge only and seems to refer to a
    "fringe standing erect," apparently from the appearance of the timber growing
    in streaks along the side of the mountain; from wadălu'yătă, fringe, gadú'tă,
    "standing up in a row or series."

găhăwĭ'sita—parched corn; improperly spelled wissactaw by Hawkins. See note
    under number 83.

Gahûtĭ (Gahú'tă and Gwahú'tĭ in dialectic forms)—Cohutta mountain, in Murray
    county, Georgia. The name comes from gahûtá'yĭ, "a shed roof supported on
    poles," and refers to a fancied resemblance in the summit.

Gakăti'yĭ—"Place of setting free"; sometimes spoken in the plural form, Diga'kăti'yĭ,
    "Place of setting them free." A point on Tuckasegee river about three miles
    above Bryson City, in Swain county, North Carolina. See number 122.

gaktûñ'ta—an injunction, command or rule, more particularly a prohibition or cere-
    monial tabu. Tsiga'te'gú, "I am observing an injunction, or tabu"; adakte'gĭ,
    "he is under tabu regulations."

Gălăgi'na—a male deer (buck) or turkey (gobbler); in the first sense the name is
    sometimes used also for the large horned beetle (Dynastes tityus?). The Indian
    name of Elias Boudinot, first Cherokee editor. See page 111.

găli'sgisidâ'hû—I am dancing about; from găli'sgiă', "I am dancing," and edâhú',
    "I am going about."

gălûñkw'ti'yu—honored, sacred; used in the bible to mean holy, hallowed.

gălûñ'lătĭ—above, on high.

găne'ga—skin.

ganidawâ'skĭ—the campion, catchfly or "rattlesnake's master" (Silene stellata); the
    name signifies "it disjoints itself," from ganidawâskú', "it is unjointing itself,"
    on account of the peculiar manner in which the dried stalk breaks off at the
    joints.

Gănsâ'gĭ (or Gănsâgiyĭ)—the name of several former settlements in the old Cherokee
    country; it cannot be analyzed. One town of this name was upon Tuckasegee
    river, a short distance above the present Webster, in Jackson county, North
    Carolina; another was on the lower part of Canasauga creek, in McMinn county,
    Tennessee; a third was at the junction of Conasauga and Coosawatee rivers,
    where afterward was located the Cherokee capital, New Echota, in Gordon

county, Georgia; a fourth, mentioned in the De Soto narratives as Canasoga or Canasagua, was located in 1540 on the upper Chattahoochee river, possibly in the neighborhood of Kenesaw mountain, Georgia (see page 197).

Gănsa'ti'yĭ—"Robbing place," from *tsina'sahŭñskŭ'*, "I am robbing him." Vengeance creek of Valley river, in Cherokee county, North Carolina. The name Vengeance was originally a white man's nickname for an old Cherokee woman, of forbidding aspect, who lived there before the Removal. See number 122.

Gănsĕ'tĭ—a rattle; as the Cherokee dance rattle is made from a gourd the masculine name, Gănsĕ'tĭ, is usually rendered by the whites, "Rattling-gourd."

gatayûstĭ—the wheel and stick game of the southern tribes, incorrectly called *nettecawaw* by Timberlake. See note under number 3.

Gâtegwâ'—for *Gâtegwâ'hĭ*, possibly a contraction of *Igât(ĭ)-egwâ'hĭ*, "Great-swamp (-thicket place." A high peak southeast from Franklin, Macon county, North Carolina, and perhaps identical with Fodderstack mountain. See number 75.

ga'tsû—see *hatlû'*.

Gatu'gitse'yĭ (abbreviated *Gatu'gitse'*)—"New-settlement place," from *gatu'gĭ* or *sgatu'gĭ*, town, settlement, *itse'hĭ*, new, especially applied to new vegetation, and *yĭ*, the locative. A former settlement on Cartoogaja creek of Little Tennessee river, above Franklin, in Macon county, North Carolina.

Gatuti'yĭ—"Town-building place," or "Settlement place," from *gatu'gĭ*, a settlement, and *yi*, locative. A place on Santeetla creek, near Robbinsville, in Graham county, North Carolina. See number 122.

Gatûñ'lti'yĭ—"Hemp place," from *gatûñ'lătĭ*, "wild hemp" (*Apocynum cannabinum*), and *yĭ*, locative. A former Cherokee settlement, commonly known as Hemptown, on the creek of the same name, near Morganton, in Fannin county, Georgia.

Gatûñ'wa'lĭ—a noted western Cherokee about 1842, known to the whites as "Hardmush" or "Big-mush." *Gatûñ'wa'lĭ*, from *ga'tŭ'*, "bread," and *ŭñwa'lĭ*, "made into balls or lumps," is a sort of mush of parched corn meal, made very thick, so that it can be dipped out in lumps almost of the consistency of bread.

ge'ĭ—down stream, down the road, with the current; *tsâ'gĭ*, up stream.

gese'ĭ—was; a separate word which, when used after the verb in the present tense, makes it past tense without change of form; in the form *hi'gese'ĭ* it usually accompanies an emphatic repetition.

Ge'yăgu'ga (for *Age'hyă-guga*?)—a formulistic name for the moon (*nŭñ'dă'*); it cannot be analyzed, but seems to contain the word *age'hyă*, "woman." See also *nŭñ'dă'*.

gigă—blood; cf. *gi'găge'ĭ*, red.

gi'gă-danegi'skĭ—"blood taker," from *gigă*, blood, and *ada'negi'skĭ*, "one who takes liquids," from *tsi'negiă'*, "I am taking it" (liquid). Another name for the *tsâne'nĭ* or scorpion lizard. See number 59.

gi'găge'ĭ—red, bright red, scarlet; the brown-red of certain animals and clays is distinguished as *wâ'dige'ĭ*.

gi'gă-tsuha'lĭ—"bloody-mouth," literally, "having blood on the corners of his mouth"; from *gi'ga*, blood, and *tsuhănûñsi'yĭ*, the corners of the mouth (*ăha'lĭ*, his mouth). A large lizard, probably the *Pleistodon*. See number 59.

gi'lĭ'—dog; in the Lower dialect, *gi'rĭ'*.

Gi'lĭ'-dinĕhûñ'yĭ—"Where the dogs live," from *gi'lĭ'*, dog, *dinĕhâ'*, "they dwell" (*ĕhâ*, "I dwell"), and *yĭ*, locative. A place on Oconaluftee river, a short distance above Cherokee, in Swain county, North Carolina. See number 122.

Gi'lĭ'-utsûñ'stănûñ'yĭ—"Where the dog ran," from *gi'lĭ'*, dog, and *utsûñ'stănûñ'yĭ*, "footprints made by an animal running"; the Milky Way. See number 11.

ginûnti—a song form for *ginû'tĭ'*, "to lay him (animate object) upon the ground." See number 75.

gï'rï'—see *gï'lï'*.

Gisehûñ'yĭ—"Where the female lives," from *agi'sĭ*, female, and *yĭ*, the locative. A place on Tuckasegee river, a short distance above Bryson City, Swain county, North Carolina. See number 122.

gitlû'—hair (Upper dialect); in the Middle and Lower dialects, *gitsû'*.

gitsû'—see *gitlû'*.

GLASS, THE—see *Ta'gwădihĭ'*.

GOHOMA—A Lower Cherokee chief in 1684; the form cannot be identified. See page 31.

GOING-SNAKE—see *I'nădûna'ĭ*.

GORHALEKE—a Lower Cherokee chief in 1684; the form cannot be identified. See page 31.

GREAT ISLAND—see *Ămăyé'l-e'gwa*.

GREGORY BALD—see *Tsistu'yĭ*.

GUACHOULE—see GUAXULE.

GUAQUILI (*Wakili*)—a town in the Cherokee country, visited by De Soto in 1540, and again in 1567 by Pardo, who calls it Aguaquiri (see pages 25 and 28). The name may have a connection with *wagulĭ'*, "whippoorwill," or with *u-)wă'gĭ'lĭ*, "foam."

GUASULA—see GUAXULE.

GUASILI—see GUAXULE.

GUAXULE—a town in the Cherokee country, visited by De Soto in 1540; variously spelled in the narratives, Guasili, Guachoule, Guasula, Guaxule, Quaxule, etc. It was probably about at Nacoochee mound, in White county, Georgia. It has been suggested that the Spaniards may have changed the Indian name to resemble that of a town in Spain. See pages 26 and 194.

gû'daye'wû—"I have sewed myself together"; "I am sewing," *tsiye'wiă'*; "I am sewing myself together," *gúdayewiû*. See number 31.

gŭgwĕ' (or *g'gwĕ'*)—the quail or partridge; the name is an onomatope.

gŭgwĕ'-ulasu'la—"partridge moccasin," from *gŭgwĕ'* or *g'gwĕ'*, partridge, and *ulasula*, moccasin or shoe; the ladyslipper (*Cypripedium*).

Gûlâhi'yĭ (abbreviated *Gúlâhĭ'*, or *Gúrâhĭ'*, in the Lower dialect)—"Gûlâ'hĭ place," so called from an unidentified spring plant eaten as a salad by the Cherokee. The name of two or more places in the old Cherokee country; one about Currahee mountain in Habersham county, Georgia, the other on Cullowhee river, an upper branch of Tuckasegee, in Jackson county, North Carolina. Currahee Dick was a noted chief about the year 1820.

Gû'lani'yĭ—a Cherokee and Natchez settlement formerly about the junction of Brasstown creek with Hiwassee river, a short distance above Murphy, in Cherokee county, North Carolina. The etymology of the word is doubtful.

gulĕ'—acorn.

gulĕ'-diska'nihĭ'—the turtle-dove; literally, "it cries, or mourns, for acorns," from *gulĕ'*, acorn, and *diska'nihĭ'*, "it cries for them" (*di-*, plural prefix, *-hi*, habitual suffix). The turtle-dove feeds upon acorns and its cry somewhat resembles the name, *gulĕ'*.

gûle'gĭ—"climber," from *tsilahĭ'*, "I climb" (second person, *hĭ'lahĭ';* third person, *gúlahĭ'*); the blacksnake (*Bascanion constrictor*).

Gûl'kăla'skĭ—An earlier name for *Tsunu'lăhûñ'skĭ*, q. v.

gûl'kwá'gĭ—seven; also the mole-cricket (*Gryllotalpa*). See number 59.

gûl'kwá'gine(-ĭ—seventh; from *gûl'kwâgĭ*, seven.

Gûlsădihĭ' (or *Gúltsădihĭ'*?)—a masculine personal name, of uncertain etymology.

GUMLOG—see *Tsilalu'hĭ*.

gûnăhi'ta—long.

Gŭ'năhitûñ'yĭ—"Long place" (i. e., Long valley), from *gănăhita*, long, and *yĭ*, locative. A former settlement, known to the whites as Valleytown, where now is the town of the same name, on Valley river, in Cherokee county, North Carolina. The various settlements on Valley river and the adjacent part of Hiwassee were known collectively as the "Valley towns."

Gûn'-dĭ'gaduhûñ'yĭ (abbreviated *Gûn'-dĭgadu'hûñ*)—"Turkey settlement" (*gû'nă*, turkey), so called from the chief, Turkey or Little Turkey. A former settlement, known to the whites as Turkeytown, upon the west bank of Coosa river, opposite the present Center, in Cherokee county, Alabama.

gû'nĭ'—arrow. Cf. Seneca *ga'na'*.

gûñ'năge'ĭ (or *gûñ'năge*)—black.

Gûñnĕ'hĭ—see *Nûñnĕ'hĭ*.

Gûñskăli'skĭ—a masculine personal name of uncertain etymology.

GUNTERS LANDING, GUNTERSVILLE—see *Ku'să-Nûñnă'hĭ*.

Gûn-tsuskwa''lĭ—"Short arrows,".from *gûnĭ'*, arrow, and *tsuskwa''lĭ*, plural of *uskwa''lĭ*, short; a traditional western tribe. See number 105.

Gûnûñ'da·le·gĭ—see *Nûñnă'hĭ-dihĭ'*.

Gustĭ'—a traditional Cherokee settlement on Tennessee river, near Kingston, Roane county, Tennessee. See number 79. The name cannot be analyzed. Wafford thought it a Cherokee attempt at "Kingston," but it seems rather to be aboriginal.

Gu'wisguwĭ'—The Cherokee name for the chief John Ross and for the district named in his honor, commonly spelled Cooweescoowee. Properly an onomatope for a large bird said to have been seen formerly at infrequent intervals in the old Cherokee country, accompanying the migratory wild geese, and described as resembling a large snipe, with yellow legs and unwebbed feet. In boyhood John Ross was known as Tsan'-usdi', "Little John."

Gwal'gă'hĭ—"Frog place," from *gwal'gû*, a variety of frog, and *hĭ*, locative. A place on Hiwassee river, just above the junction of Peachtree creek, near Murphy, in Cherokee county, North Carolina; about 1755 the site of a village of refugee Natchez, and later of a Baptist mission.

gwehe'!—a cricket's cry. See number 119.

ha!—an introductory exclamation intended to attract attention or add emphasis; about equivalent to *Here! Now!*

ha'-ma'ma'—a song term compounded of *ha!* an introductory exclamation, and *mămă'*, a word which has no analysis, but is used in speaking to young children to mean "let me carry you on my back." See number 117.

HANGING-MAW—see *Uskwă'li-gú'tă*.

ha'nia-lĭl'-lĭl'—an unmeaning dance refrain. See number 24.

HARD-MUSH—see *Gatûñ'wă'lĭ*.

ha'suyak'—a song form for *hasuya'gĭ'*, "(thou) pick it out" (imperative); "I pick it out, or select it," *ga'suyăgiŭ'*; second person, *ha'suyăgiŭ'*. See number 19.

ha'tlû—dialectic form, *ga'tsú*, "where?" (interrogative).

ha'wiye'ĕhĭ', ha'wiye'-hyuwe'—unmeaning dance refrains. See numbers 32 and 118.

hayû'—an emphatic affirmative, about equivalent to "Yes, sir!" See number 115.

hayuya'haniwă'—an unmeaning refrain in one of the bear songs. See number 75.

he-e!—an unmeaning song introduction.

HEMP-CARRIER—see *Tăle'danigĭ'skĭ*.

HEMPTOWN—see *Gatûñlti'yĭ*.

hi!—unmeaning dance exclamation.

hi'gĭna'lĭĭ—"(you are) my friend"; *agina'lĭĭ*, "(he is) my friend." In white man's jargon, *canaly*.

Hickory-log—see *Wane'-asûñ'tlûñyĭ.*

Hightower—see *I'tăwă'.*

hĭla'gû?—how many? how much? (Upper dialect); the Middle dialect form is *hûñgû'.*

hĭlahi'yu—long ago; the final *yu* makes it more emphatic.

hi'lûñnû—"(thou) go to sleep"; from *tsĭ'lihû',* "I am asleep."

hĭ'skĭ—five; cf. Mohawk *wisk.* The Cherokee numerals including 10 are as follows: *să'gwû, tă'lĭ, tsă'ĭ, nûñ'gĭ, hĭ'skĭ, su'tălĭ, gûlʹkwă'gĭ, tsune'la, sañne'la, askă'hĭ.*

Hiwassee—see *Ayuhwa'sĭ.*

hi'yagu'wĕ—an unmeaning dance refrain. See number 32.

Houston, Samuel—see *Kă'lănû.*

hûñgû'—see *hĭla'gû.*

huhu—the yellow-breasted chat, or yellow mocking bird (*Icteria virens*); the name is an onomatope. See number 45.

hûñyahu'skă—"he will die."

hwĭ'lahĭ'—"thou (must) go."

igăgû'tĭ—daylight. The name is sometimes applied to the *ulûñsû'tĭ* (q. v.), and also to the clematis vine.

i'hya—the cane reed (*Arundinaria*) of the Gulf states, used by the Indians for blowguns, fishing rods, and basketry.

ihyă'ga—see *atsil'sûñ'tĭ.*

i'nădû'—snake.

I'nădû-na'ĭ—"Going-snake," a Cherokee chief prominent about eighty years ago. The name properly signifies that the person is "going along in company with a snake," the verbal part oeing from the irregular verb *asta'ĭ,* "I am going along with him." The name has been given to a district of the present Cherokee Nation.

i'năgĕ'hĭ—dwelling in the wilderness, an inhabitant of the wilderness; from *i'năge'ĭ,* "wilderness," and *ĕhĭ,* habitual present form of *ĕhă,* "he is dwelling"; *gĕ'û,* "I am dwelling."

I'năge-utăsûñ'hĭ—"He who grew up in the wilderness," i. e. "He who grew up wild"; from *i'năge'ĭ,* "wilderness, unoccupied timber land," and *utăsûñ'hĭ,* the third person perfect of the irregular verb, *ga'tûñskû',* "I am growing up."

Ină'lĭ—Black-fox; the common red fox is *tsu'lă* (in Muscogee, *chula*). Black-fox was principal chief of the Cherokee Nation in 1810. See page 86.

Iskagua—"Iskagua or Clear Sky, formerly Nenetooyah or the Bloody-Fellow." The name appears thus in a document of 1791 as that of a Cherokee chief frequently mentioned about that period under the name of "the Bloody Fellow." In one treaty it is given as "Eskaqua or Bloody Fellow." Both forms and etymologies are doubtful, neither form seeming to have any reference either to "sky" (*gălûñ'lăhĭ*) or "blood" (*gi'ga*). The first may be intended for *Ik-e'gwa,* "Great-day." See page 69.

Istanare—see *U'stăna'lĭ.*

I'sû'nigû—an important Cherokee settlement, commonly known to the whites as Seneca, formerly on Keowee river, about the mouth of Conneross creek, in Oconee county, South Carolina. Hopeweli, the country seat of General Pickens, where the famous treaty was made, was near it on the east side of the river. The word cannot be translated, but has no connection with the tribal name, Seneca.

Itaba—see *I'tăwă'.*

Ităgû'năhĭ—the Cherokee name of John Ax.

I'tăwă'—The name of one or more Cherokee settlements. One, which existed until the Removal in 1838, was upon Etowah river, about the present Hightower, in Forsyth county Georgia. Another may have been on Hightower creek of

Hiwassee river in Towns county, Georgia. The name, commonly written Etowah and corrupted to Hightower, cannot be translated and seems not to be of Cherokee origin. A town called Itaba, Ytaua or Ytava in the De Soto chronicles existed in 1540 among the Creeks, apparently on Alabama river.

Itsä'tĭ—commonly spelled Echota, Chota, Chote, Choquata (misprint), etc; a name occurring in several places in the old Cherokee country: the meaning is lost. The most important settlement of this name, frequently distinguished as Great Echota, was on the south side of Little Tennessee river a short distance below Citico creek in Monroe county, Tennessee. It was the ancient capital and sacred "peace town" of the Nation. Little Echota was on Sautee (i. e., *Itsâ'tĭ*) creek, a head stream of the Chattahoochee, west of Clarkesville, Georgia. New Echota, the capital of the Nation for some years before the Removal, was established at a spot originally known as *Gänsa'gĭ* (q. v.) at the junction of the Oostanaula and Conasauga rivers, in Gordon county, Georgia. It was sometimes called Newtown. The old Macedonia mission on Soco creek, of the North Carolina reservation, is also known as Itsâ'tĭ to the Cherokee, as was also the great Nacoochee mound. See *Nagu'tsĭ'*.

Itse'yĭ—"New green place" or "Place of fresh green," from *itse'hĭ*, "green or unripe vegetation," and *yĭ*, the locative; applied more particularly to a tract of ground made green by fresh-springing vegetation, after having been cleared of timber or burned over. A name occurring in several places in the old Cherokee country, variously written Echia, Echoee, Etchowee, and sometimes also falsely rendered "Brasstown," from a confusion of *Itse'yĭ* with *ûñtsaiyĭ'*, "brass." One settlement of this name was upon Brasstown creek of Tugaloo river, in Oconee county, South Carolina; another was on Little Tennessee river near the present Franklin, Macon county, North Carolina, and probably about the junction of Cartoogaja (*Gatug-itse'yĭ*) creek; a third, known to the whites as Brasstown, was on upper Brasstown creek of Hiwassee river, in Towns county, Georgia. In Cherokee as in most other Indian languages no clear distinction is made between green and blue (*sa'ka'nige'ĭ*).

i'ya—pumpkin.

iya'-iyu'stĭ—"like a pumpkin," from *iya* and *iyu'stĭ*, like.

iya'-täwi'skage—"of pumpkin smoothness," from *i'ya*, pumpkin, and *täwi'skage*, smooth.

JACKSON—see *Tsek'sĭnĭ'*.
JESSAN—see *Tsĕsa'nĭ*.
JESSE REID—see *Tsĕ'sĭ-Ska'tsĭ*.
JOANNA BALD—see *Diyá'häli'yĭ*.
JOARA, JUADA—see *Ani'-Suwa'lĭ*.
JOHN—see *Tsa'nĭ*.
JOHN AX—see *Itägú'nähĭ*.
JOLLY, JOHN—see *Ahu'lude'gĭ*.
JUNALUSKA—see *Tsunu'lähûñ'skĭ*.
JUTACULLA—see *Tsul'kälû'*.

kâ'gû'—crow; the name is an onomatope.

Kâgûñ'yĭ—"Crow place," from *kâ'gû'*, crow and *yĭ*, locative. See number 63.

ka'ĭ—grease, oil.

Kala'äsûñ'yĭ—"Where he fell off," from *tsĭla'äskú'*, "I am falling off," and *yĭ*, locative. A cliff near Cold Spring knob, in Swain county, North Carolina.

Kâ'lahû'—"All-bones," from *kâ'lû*, bone. A former chief of the East Cherokee, also known in the tribe as *Sawănu'gĭ* (Shawano), and to the whites as Sawnook or Flying-squirrel.

Kâ'lănû—"The Raven"; the name was used as a war title in the tribe and appears in the old documents as Corani (Lower dialect, Kâ'rănû) Colanneh, Colona, etc. It is the Cherokee name for General Samuel Houston or for any person named Houston.

Kâ'lănû Ahyeli'skĭ—the Raven Mocker. See number 120.

Kâ'lănûñ'yĭ—"Raven place," from kâ'lănû, raven, and yĭ, the locative. The proper name of Big-cove settlement upon the East Cherokee reservation, Swain county, North Carolina, sometimes also called Raventown.

kalâs'-gŭnăhi'ta—"long-hams" (gŭnăhi'ta, "long"); a variety of bear. See number 15.

Kâl-detsi'yûñyĭ—"Where the bones are," from kâ'lû, bone, and detsi'yûñyĭ, "where (yĭ) they (de—plural prefix) are lying." A spot near the junction of East Buffalo creek with Cheowa river, in Graham county, North Carolina. See number 122.

kăma'mă—butterfly.

kăma'mă u'tanû—elephant; literally "great butterfly," from the resemblance of the trunk and ears to the butterfly's proboscis and wings. See number 15.

kanahe'na—a sour corn gruel, much in use among the Cherokee and other southern tribes; the tamfuli or "Tom Fuller" of the Creeks.

kănăne'skĭ—spider; also, from a fancied resemblance in appearance, a watch or clock; kănăne'skĭ amăyĕ'hĭ, the water spider.

Kăna'sta, Kănastûñ'yĭ—a traditional Cherokee settlement formerly on the headwaters of the French Broad river near the present Brevard, in Transylvania county, North Carolina. The meaning of the name is lost. A settlement called Cannostee or Cannastion is mentioned as existing on Hiwassee river in 1776. See number 82 and notes.

kanâ'talu'hĭ—hominy cooked with walnut kernels.

Kana'tĭ—"Lucky Hunter"; a masculine name, sometimes abbreviated Kanat'. The word can not be analyzed, but is used as a third person habitual verbal form to mean "he is lucky, or successful, in hunting"; the opposite is u'kwa'legû, "unlucky, or unsuccessful, in hunting." See number 3.

kanegwâ'tĭ—the water-moccasin snake.

Kănu'ga—also written Canuga; a Lower Cherokee settlement, apparently on the waters of Keowee river in South Carolina, destroyed in 1761; also a traditional settlement on Pigeon river, probably near the present Waynesville, in Haywood county, North Carolina. See number 81 and notes. The name signifies "a scratcher," a sort of bone-toothed comb with which ball-players are scratched upon their naked skin preliminary to applying the conjured medicine; de'tsinuga'skû, "I am scratching it."

kănugû'lă (abbreviated nugû'la)—"scratcher," a generic term for the blackberry, raspberry, and other brier bushes. Cf. Kănu'ga.

Kănu'gû'lâyĭ, or Kănu'gû'lûñ'yĭ—"Brier place," from kănugû'lă, brier (cf. Kănu'ga); a Cherokee settlement formerly on Nantahala river, about the mouth of Briertown creek, in Macon county, North Carolina.

kănûñ'năwû'—pipe.

Kâsdu'yĭ—"Ashes place," from kâsdu, ashes, and yĭ, the locative. A modern Cherokee name for the town of Asheville, in Buncombe county, North Carolina. The ancient name for the same site is Unta'kiyasti'yĭ, q. v.

Katâl'stă—an East Cherokee woman potter, the daughter of the chief Yânăgûñ'skĭ. The name conveys the idea of lending, from tsiyatâl'stă, "I lend it"; agatâl'stă, "it is lent to him."

Kăwân'-urâ'sûñyĭ (abbreviated Kăwân'-urâ'sûñ in the Lower dialect)—"Where the duck fell" from kăwâ'nă, duck, urâ'să (ulâ'să), "it fell," and yĭ, locative. A point on Conneross creek (from *Kăwăn'-ură'săñ*), near Seneca, in Oconee county, South Carolina. See number 123.

Kawi'yĭ (abbreviated *Kawi'*)—a former important Cherokee settlement, commonly known as Cowee, about the mouth of Cowee creek of Little Tennessee river, some 10 miles below Franklin, in Macon county, North Carolina. The name may possibly be a contraction of *Ani'-Kawi'yĭ*, "Place of the Deer clan."

KEEOWHEE—see KEOWEE.

KENESAW—see *Găusă'gĭ.*

KEOWEE—the name of two or more former Cherokee settlements. One, sometimes distinguished as "Old Keowee," the principal of the Lower Cherokee towns, was on the river of the same name, near the present Fort George, in Oconee county, South Carolina. Another, distinguished as New Keowee, was on the headwaters of Twelve-mile creek, in Pickens county, South Carolina. According to Wafford the correct form is *Kuwăhi'yĭ*, abbreviated *Kuwăhi'*, "Mulberry-grove place"; says Wafford, "The whites murdered the name, as they always do." Cf. *Kuwă'hĭ.*

Ke'sĭ-ka'gămû—a woman's name, a Cherokee corruption of Cassie Cockram; *ka'gămû* is also the Cherokee corruption for "cucumber."

KETOOWAH—see *Kĭtu'hwă.*

KITTUWA—see *Kĭtu'hwă.*

Kĭtu'hwă—An important ancient Cherokee settlement formerly upon Tuckasegee river, and extending from above the junction of Oconaluftee down nearly to the present Bryson City, in Swain county, North Carolina. The name, which appears also as Kettooah, Kittoa, Kittowa, etc., has lost its meaning. The people of this and the subordinate settlements on the waters of the Tuckasegee were known as *Ani'-Kĭtu'hwagĭ* and the name was frequently extended to include the whole tribe. For this reason it was adopted in later times as the name of the Cherokee secret organization, commonly known to the whites as the Ketoowah society, pledged to the defense of Cherokee autonomy. See also historical notes 1 and 47.

kiyu'ga—ground-squirrel; *te'wa*, flying squirrel; *sălă'lĭ*, gray squirrel.

KLAUSUNA—see *Tlanusi'yĭ.*

KNOXVILLE—see *Kuwandă'tă'lăñ'yĭ.*

kû!—an introductory exclamation, to fix attention, about equivalent to "*Now!*"

kukû'—"cymling"; also the "jigger weed," or "pleurisy root" (*Asclepias tuberosa*). Coco creek of Hiwassee river, and Coker postoffice, in Monroe county, Tennessee, derive their name from this word.

Kŭlsetsi'yĭ (abbreviated *Kŭlse'tsi*)—"Honey-locust place," from *kŭlse'tsĭ*, honey-locust (*Gleauschia*) and *yĭ*, locative; as the same word, *kŭlse'tsĭ*, is also used for "sugar," the local name has commonly been rendered Sugartown by the traders. The name of several former settlement places in the old Cherokee country. One was upon Keowee river, near the present Fall creek, in Oconee county, South Carolina; another was on Sugartown or Cullasagee (*Kulse'tsi*) creek, near the present Franklin, in Macon county, North Carolina; a third was on Sugartown creek, near the present Morganton, in Fannin county, Georgia.

KUNNESEE—see *Tsi'yu-gănsi'nĭ.*

Kŭnstŭtsi'yĭ—"Sassafras place," from *kŭnstŭ'tsĭ*, sassafras, and *yĭ*, locative. A gap in the Great Smoky range, about the head of Noland creek, on the line between North Carolina and Sevier county, Tennessee.

kûnu'nŭ (abbreviated *kănun'*)—the bullfrog; the name is probably an onomatope; the common green frog is *wală'sĭ* and there are also names for several other varieties of frogs and toads.

Kusă'—Coosa creek, an upper tributary of Nottely river, near Blairsville, Union county, Georgia. The change of accent from Ku'să (Creek, see *Ani'-Ku'su*) makes it locative. See page 383.

Ku′să-nûñnă′hĭ—"Creek trail," from *Ku′să*, Creek Indian, and *nûñnă′hĭ*, path, trail; cf. *Suwă′lĭ-nûñnă′hĭ*. A former important Cherokee settlement, including also a number of Creeks and Shawano, where the trail from the Ohio region to the Creek country crossed Tennessee river, at the present Guntersville, in Marshall county, Alabama. It was known to the traders as Creek-path, and later as Gunter's landing, from a Cherokee mixed-blood named Gunter.

Ku′săweti′yĭ (abbreviated *Ku′săweti′*)—"Old Creek place," from *Ku′să*, a Creek Indian (plural *Anĭ′-Ku′sa*), *uwe′tĭ*, old, and *yĭ*, locative. Coosawatee, an important Cherokee settlement formerly on the lower part of Coosawatee river, in Gordon county, Georgia. In one document the name appears, by error, Tensawattee. See page 382.

Kuwâ′hĭ—"Mulberry place," from *ku′wă*, mulberry tree, and *hĭ*, locative; Clingman's dome, about the head of Deep creek, on the Great Smoky range, between Swain county, North Carolina, and Sevier county, Tennessee. See also KEOWEE.

Kuwandâ′taʻlûñ′yĭ (abbreviated *Kuwandâ′taʻlûñ*)—"Mulberry grove," from *ku′wă*, mulberry; the Cherokee name for the present site of Knoxville, in Knox county, Tennessee.

Kwa′lĭ, Kwalûñ′yĭ—Qualla or Quallatown, the former agency for the East Cherokee and now a postoffice station, just outside the reservation, on a branch of Soco creek, in Jackson county, North Carolina. It is the Cherokee form for "Polly," and the station was so called from an old woman of that name who formerly lived near by; *Kwa′lĭ*, "Polly," *Kwalûñ′yĭ*, "Polly's place." The reservation is locally known as the Qualla boundary.

kwandăya′hû—see *da′lĭkstă′*.

lâ′lû—the jar-fly (*Cicada auletes*). See number 59.
LITTLE CARPENTER, LITTLE CORNPLANTER—see *Ătă′-gûlʻkălû′*.
LLOYD—see *Da′sĭʻgiya′gĭ*.
LONG-HAIR—a Cherokee chief living with his band in Ohio in 1795. See page 79. The literal Cherokee translation of "Long-hair" is *Gitlû′-gúnăhi′ta*, but it is not certain that the English name is a correct rendering of the Indian form. Cf. *Anĭ′-Gilă′hĭ*.
LONG ISLAND—see *Ămăyeʻlĭ-gúnăhi′ta*.
LOOKOUT MOUNTAIN TOWN—see *Danda′gănú′*.
LOWREY, MAJOR GEORGE—see *Agĭʻlĭ*.

MAYES, J. B.—see *Tsă′wă Gak′skĭ*.
MEMPHIS—see *Tsudă′tălesûñ′yĭ*.
MIALAQUO—see *Ămăyeʻl-e′gwa*.
MORGAN—see *Âganstă′ta*.
MOSES—see *Wă′sĭ*.
MOYTOY—a Cherokee chief recognized by the English as "emperor" in 1730. Both the correct form and the meaning of the name are uncertain; the name occurs again as *Moyatoy* in a document of 1792; a boy upon the East Cherokee reservation a few years ago bore the name of Ma′tayĭ′, for which no meaning can be given.
MUSCLE SHOALS—see *Dăgú′năhĭ*.

NACOOCHEE—see *Na′guʻtsĭ′*.
Na′dû′lĭ′—known to the whites as Nottely. A former Cherokee settlement on Nottely river, close to the Georgia line, in Cherokee county, North Carolina. The name cannot be translated and has no connection with *na′tûʻlĭ*, "spicewood."
Naguʻtsĭ′—a former important settlement about the junction of Soquee and Santee rivers, in Nacoochee valley, at the head of Chattahoochee river, in Habersham county, Georgia. The meaning of the word is lost and it is doubtful if it be of

Cherokee origin. It may have some connection with the name of the Uchee Indians. The great mound farther up Sautee river, in White county, was known to the Cherokee as *Itsâ'tĭ*, q. v.

năkwĭsĭ' (abbreviated *năkw'sĭ*)—star; also the meadow lark.

năkwĭsĭ' usdi'—"little star"; the puffball fungus (*Lycoperdon?*).

Nă'nă-tlu'gûñ'yĭ (abbreviated *Nă'nă-tlu'gûñ'*, or *Nă'nă-tsu'gûñ'*)—"Spruce-tree place," from *nă'nă*, spruce, *tlu'gûñ'ĭ* or *tsu'gûñ'ĭ*, a tree (standing) and *yĭ*, locative. 1. A traditional ancient Cherokee settlement on the site of Jonesboro, Washington county, Tennessee. The name of Nolichucky river is probably a corruption of the same word. 2. *Nănă-tsu'gûñ*, a place on Nottely river, close to its junction with Hiwassee, in Cherokee county, North Carolina.

NANEHI—see *Nûñně'hĭ*.

NANTAHALA—see *Nûñdăye''lĭ*.

NASHVILLE—see *Dagú'năwe'lăhĭ*.

NATCHEZ—see *Aniˈ-Naˈtsĭ*.

Naˈts-asûñ'tlûñyĭ (abbreviated *Naˈts-asûñ'tlûñ*)—"Pine-footlog place," from *naˈtsĭ*, pine, *asûñ'tlĭ* or *asûñtlûñ'ĭ*, footlog, bridge, and *yĭ*, locative. A former Cherokee settlement, commonly known as Pinelog, on the creek of the same name, in Bartow county, Georgia.

naˈtsĭ—pine.

na'tsĭkû'—"I eat it" (*tsĭ'kiú'*, "I am eating").

na'tû'lĭ—spicewood (*Lindera benzoin*).

Nayě'hĭ—see *Nûñně'hĭ*.

NAYUNUWI—see *Nûñyunu'wĭ*.

nehanduyanû'—a song form for *nehadu'yanú'*, an irregular verbal form denoting "conceived in the womb." See number 75.

NELLAWGITEHI—given as the name of a Lower Cherokee chief in 1684. See page 31. The correct form and meaning are both uncertain, but the final part seems to be the common suffix *dihĭ'*, "killer," Cf. *Ta'gwădihĭ'*.

NENETOOYAH—see ISKAGUA.

NEQUASSEE—see *Nĭ'kwăsĭ'*.

NETTECAWAW—see *gatayú'stĭ*.

NETTLE-CARRIER—see *Tâle'danigi'skĭ*.

NEW ECHOTA, NEWTOWN—see *Itsâ'tĭ*.

NICKAJACK—see *Nĭkutse'gĭ*.

NICOTANI—see *Aniˈ-Kuta'nĭ*.

Nĭkwăsĭ' (or *Nikw'sĭ'*)—an important ancient settlement on Little Tennessee river, where now is the town of Franklin, in Macon county, North Carolina. A large mound marks the site of the townhouse. The name appears in old documents as Nequassee, Nucassee, etc. Its meaning is lost.

Nĭkutse'gĭ (also *Nŭkătse'gĭ*, *Nikwătse'gĭ*, or abbreviated *Nĭkutseg'*)—Nickajack, an important Cherokee settlement about 1790 on the south bank of Tennessee river at the entrance of Nickajack creek, in Marion county, Tennessee. One of the five Chickamauga towns (see *Tsĭkăma'gĭ*). The meaning of the word is lost and it is probably not of Cherokee origin, although it occurs also in the tribe as a man's name. In the corrupted form of "Nigger Jack," it occurs also as the name of a creek of Cullasagee river above Franklin, in Macon county, North Carolina.

NILAQUE—see *Ămăyě'l-e'gwă*.

NOLICHUCKY—see *Nă'nă-tlu'gûñ'yĭ*.

NOTCHY—a creek entering Tellico river, in Monroe county, Tennessee. The name evidently refers to Natchez Indian refugees, who formerly lived in the vicinity (see *Aniˈ-Naˈtsĭ*).

NOTTELY—see *Na'dû'lĭ'*.

nû—used as a suffix to denote "and," or "also"; *ú'lĕ-ʹnû*, "and also"; *nɐ'skĭʹ-nú'*, "and that," "that also."

Nucassee—see *Nĭkwăsĭ'*.

nu'dûññelû'—he did *so and so;* an irregular form apparently connected with the archaic forms *adûñni'ga*, "it has just become so," and *udûñnú'*, "it is matured, or finished." See number 118.

nûñ'dă'—the sun or moon, distinguished as *nûñ'dă' igĕ'hĭ*, "*nûñ'dă'* dwelling in the day," and *nûñ'dă' súñnâ'yĕhĭ*, "*nûñ'dă'* dwelling in the night." In the sacred formulas the moon is sometimes called *Gĕʹyăgu'ga*, q. v., or *Su'tălidihĭ'*, "Six-killer," names apparently founded upon myths now lost.

nûñ'dă'-dikaʻnĭ—a rare bird formerly seen occasionally in the old Cherokee country, possibly the little blue heron (*Floridus cerulea*). The name seems to mean "it looks at the sun," i. e., "sun-gazer," from *nûñ'dă'*, sun, and *da'kaʻnă'* or *detsi'kaʻnă*, "I am looking at it." See number 35.

Nûñ'dâgûñ'yĭ, Nûñdâ'yĭ—the Sun land, or east; from *nûñ'dă'*, sun, and *yĭ*, locative. Used in the sacred formulas instead of *di'gălûñgûñ'yĭ*, "where it rises," the common word.

Nûñ'dăyeʻlĭ—"Middle (i. e. Noonday) sun," from *nûñdă'*, sun and *ayĕ'lĭ*, middle; a former Cherokee settlement on Nantahala river', near the present Jarrett station, in Macon county, North Carolina, so called from the high cliffs which shut out the view of the sun until nearly noon. The name appears also as Nantahala, Nantiyallee, Nuntialla, etc. It appears to have been applied properly only to the point on the river where the cliffs are most perpendicular, while the settlement itself was known as *Kanu'gúʻlá'yĭ*, "Briertown," q. v. See number 122.

Nugătsa'nĭ—a ridge sloping down to Oconaluftee river, below Cherokee, in Swain county, North Carolina. The word is an archaic form denoting a high ridge with a long gradual slope. See number 122.

nûñ'gĭ'—four. See *hĭ'skĭ*.

nugûʻla—see *kănugûʻla*.

Nuhnayie—see *Núñnĕ'hĭ*.

nu'nă—potato; the name was originally applied to the wild "pig potato" (*Phaseolus*), now distinguished as *nu'nă igătĕhĭ*, "swamp-dwelling potato."

Nûndăwe'gĭ—see *Ani'-Núndăwe'gĭ*.

nûñnâ'hĭ (abbreviated *nûñnâ*)—a path, trail or road.

Nûñnâ'hĭ-dihĭ' (abbreviated *Núñ'nâ-dihĭ'*)—"Path-killer," literally, "He kills (habitually) in the path," from *nûñ'nâhĭ*, path, and *ahihĭ'*, "he kills" (habitually); "I am killing," *tsi'ihú'*. A principal chief, about the year 1813. Major John Ridge was originally known by the same name, but afterward took the name, *Gûnûñ'daʻle'gĭ*, "One who follows the ridge," which the whites made simply Ridge.

Nûñnâ'hĭ-tsune'ga (abbreviated) *Núñnâ-tsune'ga*—"White-path," from *nûñnâ'hĭ*, path, and *tsune'ga*, plural of *une'ga*, white; the form is in the plural, as is common in Indian names, and has probably a symbolic reference to the "white" or peaceful paths spoken of in the opening invocation at the Green corn dance. A noted chief who led the conservative party about 1828. See pages 113, 132.

Nûñnĕ'hĭ (also *Gáñnĕ'hĭ;* singular *Nayĕ'hĭ*)—a race of invisible spirit people. The name is derived from the verb *ĕ'hú'*, "I dwell, I live," *ĕ'hĭ'*, "I dwell habitually," and may be rendered "dwellers anywhere," or "those who live anywhere," but implies having always been there, i. e., "Immortals." It has been spelled Nanehi and Nuhnayie by different writers. The singular form *Nayĕ'hĭ* occurs also as a personal name, about equivalent to *Edâ'hĭ*, "One who goes about." See number 78.

ɐᴜɴaiyu'stĭ—"potato-like," from *nu'nă*, potato, and *iyu'stĭ*, like. A flowering vine with tuberous root somewhat resembling the potato. See number 126.

nûñyû'—rock, stone. Cf. *náyŭ*, sand.

Nûñyû'-gûñwani'skĭ—"Rock that talks," from *nûñyû'*, rock, and *tsiwa'nihú*, "I am talking." A rock from which Talking-rock creek of Coosawatee river in Georgia derives its name. See number 125.

Nûñ'yunu'wĭ—contracted from *Nûñyû-unu'wĭ*. "Stone-clad," from *nûñyû*, rock, and *agwŭnu'wû*, "I am clothed or covered." A mythic monster, invulnerable by reason of his stony skin. See number 67. The name is also applied sometimes to the stinging ant, *dasûñtûlĭ atatsûñskĭ*, q. v. It has also been spelled *Nayunuwi*.

Nûñyû'-tlu'gûñĭ (or *Nûñyû-tsu'gûñ'ĭ*)—"Tree rock." A notable rock on Hiwassee river, just within the North Carolina line. See number 66 and notes.

Nûñyû'-tăwi'skă—"Slick rock," from *nûñyû'*, rock, and *tăwiskă*, smooth, slick; the form remains unchanged for the locative. 1. Slick-rock creek, entering Little Tennessee river just within the west line of Graham county, North Carolina. 2. A place at the extreme head of Brasstown creek of Hiwassee river, in Towns county, Georgia.

OCOEE—see *Uwagá'hĭ*.
OCONALUFTEE—see *Egwânûl'tĭ*.
OCONEE—see *Ukwû'nú*.
OCONOSTOTA—see *Âganstá'ta*.
OLD TASSEL—see *Utsi'dsătă'*.
OOLTEWAH—see *Ultiwă'ĭ*.
OOLUNSADE—see *Ulûñsû'tĭ*.
OOSTANAULA—see *U stăna'lĭ*.
OOSTINALEH—see *U stăna'lĭ*.
OOTHCALOGA—see *Uy'gilá'gĭ*.
OTACITE, OTASSITE—see OUTACITY.
OTARI, OTARIYATIQUI—mentioned as a place, apparently on the Cherokee frontier, visited by Pardo in 1567. Otari seems to be the Cherokee *ătărĭ* or *ătălĭ*, mountain, but the rest of the word is doubtful. See page 28.
OTTARE—see *ă'tălĭ*.
OWASTA—given as the name of a Cherokee chief in 1684; the form cannot be identified. See page 31.
OUGILLOGY—see *Uy'gilá'gĭ*.
OUTACITY—given in documents as the name or title of a prominent Cherokee chief about 1720. It appears also as Otacite, Otassite, Outassatah, Wootassite and Wrosetasatow (!), but the form cannot be identified, although it seems to contain the personal name suffix *dihĭ'*, "killer." Timberlake says (page 71): "There are some other honorary titles among them, conferred in reward of great actions; the first of which is Outacity or Man-killer, and the second Colona or the Raven."
OUTASSATAH—see OUTACITY.
OWASSA—see *Ayuhwa'sĭ*.

PAINT-TOWN—see *Ani'-Wá'dihĭ'*.
PATH-KILLER—see *Nûñnă'hi-dihĭ'*.
PHŒNIX, CHEROKEE—see *Tsule'hisanûñ'hĭ*.
PIGEON RIVER—see *Wáyĭ*.
PINE INDIANS—see *Ani'-Na'tsĭ*.
PINELOG—see *Na'ts-asûñ'tlûñyĭ*.

QUALATCHEE—a former Cherokee settlement on the headwaters of the Chattahoochee river in Georgia; another of the same name was upon the waters of Keowee river in South Carolina. The correct form is unknown.

Qualla—see *Kwalĭ*.

Quaxule—see Guaxule.

Quinahaqui—a place, possibly in the Cherokee country, visited by Pardo in 1567. The form cannot be identified. See page 28.

Quoneashee—see *Tlanusi'yĭ*.

Rattlesnake springs—see *Utsanătiyĭ*.

Rattling-gourd—see *Gănsĕ'tĭ*.

Raventown—see *Kâlănûñ'yĭ*.

Red Clay—see *Elăwă'diyĭ*.

Reid, Jesse—see *Tse'si-Ska'tsĭ*.

Ridge, Major John—see *Nûñnă'hĭ-dihĭ'*.

Ross, John—see *Gu'wisguwĭ'*.

Ross' landing—see *Tsatănu'gĭ*.

Sadayĭ'—a feminine name, the proper name of the woman known to the whites as Annie Ax; it cannot be translated.

Sâgwâ'hĭ, or Sâgwûñ'yĭ—"One place," from *să'gwû*, one, and *hĭ* or *yĭ*, locative. Soco creek of Oconaluftee river, on the East Cherokee reservation, in Jackson county, North Carolina. No satisfactory reason is given for the name, which has its parallel in *Tsăskă'hĭ*, "Thirty place," a local name in Cherokee county, in the same state.

să'gwălĭ', horse; from *asâgwălihú*, a pack or burden, *asâgwăĭlú'*; "there is a pack on him."

să'gwălĭ dĭgû'lanăhi'ta—mule; literally "long eared horse," from *să'gwălĭ*, horse, and *digû'lanăhi'ta*, q. v.

Sâkwi'yĭ (or *Suki'yĭ*; abbreviated *Săkwi'* or *Suki'*)—a former settlement on Soquee river, a head-stream of Chattahootchee, near Clarkesville, Habersham county, Georgia. Also written Saukee and Sookee. The name has lost its meaning.

sălă'lĭ—squirrel; the common gray squirrel; other varieties are *kiyu'ga*, the ground squirrel, and *tewa*, the flying squirrel. *Sălă'lĭ* was also the name of an East Cherokee inventor who died a few years ago; *Sălă'lăni'ta*, "Young-squirrels," is a masculine personal name on the reservation.

săligu'gĭ—turtle, the common water turtle; soft-shell turtle, *u'lănă'wă;* land tortoise or terrapin, *tûksĭ'*.

sălikwâ'yĭ—bear-grass (*Eryngium*); also the greensnake, on account of a fancied resemblance; the name of a former Cherokee settlement on Sallacoa creek of Coosawatee river, in Gordon county, Georgia.

Sa'nigilâ'gĭ (abbreviated *San'gilă'gĭ*)—Whiteside mountain, a prominent peak of the Blue ridge, southeast from Franklin, Macon county, North Carolina. It is connected with the tradition of U'tlûñ'ta (see number 66 and notes).

Santeetla—the present map name of a creek joining Cheowa river in Graham county, North Carolina, and of a smaller tributary (Little Santeetla). The name is not recognized or understood by the Cherokee, who insist that it was given by the whites. Little Santeetla is known to the Cherokee as *Tsunda'nilti'yĭ*, q. v.; the main Santeetla creek is commonly known as *Nâyu'hĭ geyûñ'ĭ*, "Sand-place stream," from *Nâyu'hĭ*, "Sand place" (*nâyŭ*, sand), a former settlement just above the junction of the two creeks.

Sara—see *Ani'-Suwa'lĭ*.

sa'sa'—goose; an onomatope.

Sautee—see *Itsâ'tĭ*.

Savannah—the popular name of this river is derived from that of the Shawano Indians, formerly living upon its middle course, and known to the Cherokee as *Ani'-Sawănu'gĭ*, q.v., to the Creeks as *Savanuka*, and to some of the coast tribes of Carolina as *Suwanna*. In old documents the river is also called *Isundiga*, from *I'sŭ'nigŭ* or *Seneca*, q.v., an important former Cherokee settlement upon its upper waters. See number 99.

Sawănu'gĭ—"Shawano" (Indian); a masculine personal name upon the East Cherokee reservation and prominent in the history of the band. See *Anĭ'-Sawănu'gĭ* and *Kă'lahŭ'*.

SAWNOOK—see *Kă'lahŭ'*.

Sehwate'yĭ—"Hornet place, from *se'hwatŭ*, hornet, and *yĭ*, locative. Cheowa Maximum and Swim bald, adjoining bald peaks at the head of Cheowa river, Graham county, North Carolina. See number 122.

selu—corn; sometimes called in the sacred formulas *Agawe'lu*, "The Old Woman." See number 126.

sel-utsĭ' (for *selu-utsĭ'*)—"corn's mother," from *selu*, corn and *utsĭ'*, his mother (*etsĭ'* or *agitsĭ'*, my mother); the bead-corn or Job's-tears (*Coix lacryma*). See number 126.

SENECA—see *Anĭ'-Nŭn'dăwe'gĭ* (Seneca tribe), and *I'sŭ'nigŭ* (Seneca town).

SEQUATCHEE—see *Sĭ'gwetsĭ'*.

SEQUOYA—see *Sikwăyĭ*.

Sĕ͗tsĭ—a mound and traditional Cherokee settlement on the south side of Valley river, about three miles below Valleytown, in Cherokee county, North Carolina; the name has lost its meaning. See number 79. A settlement called *Tăsĕ͗tsĭ* (*Tassetchie* in some old documents) existed on the extreme head of Hiwassee river, in Towns county, Georgia.

SEVIER—see *Tsan'-usdi'*.

SHOE-BOOTS—see *Da'sĭ͗giya'gĭ*.

SHOOTING CREEK—see *Du'stăya'lŭñ'yĭ*.

Sĭ'gwetsĭ'—a traditional Cherokee settlement on the south bank of the French Broad river, not far from Knoxville, Knox county, Tennessee. Near by was the quarry from which it is said the stone for the white peace pipes was obtained. See number 111 and notes. Sequatchee, the name of the river below Chattanooga, in Tennessee, is probably a corruption of the same word.

sĭ'kwă—hog; originally the name of the opossum, now distinguished as *sĭ'kwă utset'stĭ*, q. v.

sĭ'kwă utset'stĭ—opossum: literally "grinning hog," from *sĭ'kwă*, hog, and *utset'stĭ*, "he grins (habitually)." Cf. *sĭkwă*.

Sikwă'yĭ—a masculine name, commonly written Sequoya, made famous as that of the inventor of the Cherokee alphabet. See page 108. The name, which can not be translated, is still in use upon the East Cherokee reservation.

Sikwi'ă—a masculine name, the Cherokee corruption for Sevier. See also *Tsan-usdi'*.

SINNAWAH—see *tlă'nuwă*.

Sĭ'tikŭ' (or *sŭ'tăgŭ'*, in dialectic form)—a former Cherokee settlement on Little Tennessee river at the entrance of Citico creek, in Monroe county, Tennessee. The name, which can not be translated, is commonly spelled Citico, but appears also as Sattiquo, Settico, Settacoo, Sette, Sittiquo, etc.

siyu'—see *ă'siyu'*.

skĭntă'—for *skĭn'tăgŭ'*, understood to mean "put a new tooth into my jaw." The word can not be analyzed, but is derived from *găntkă'* (*ganta͗gă* in a dialectic form) a tooth in place; a tooth detached is *kăyu͗gă*. See number 15.

Skwan'-digŭ͗gŭñ'yĭ (for *Askwan'-digŭ͗gŭñ'yĭ*)—"Where the Spaniard is in the water [or other liquid]". A place on Upper Soco creek, on the reservation in Jackson county, North Carolina. See number 122.

SLICK ROCK—see *Nŭñyŭ'-tăwi'skă*.

SMITH, N. J.—see *Tsalădihĭ'*.

SNOWBIRD—see *Tuti'yĭ*.

Soco CREEK—see *Ságwä'hĭ*.
Soco GAP—see *Ăhălu'na*.
SoQÚEE—see *Săkwi'yĭ*.
SPRAY, H. W.—see *Wĭlsĭnĭ'*.
SPRING-FROG—see *Du'stu'*.
STANDING INDIAN—see *Yûñwĭ-tsulenûñ'yĭ*.
STAND WATIE—see *De'gatâgă*.
STEKOA—see *Stikâ'yĭ*.
ste'tsi—your daughter; literally, your offspring; *agwe'tsĭ*, "my offspring"; *uwe'tsĭ*, "his offspring"; to distinguish sex it is necessary to add *asga'ya*, "man" or *age'hya*, "woman."
Stikâ'yĭ (variously spelled Stecoe, Steecoy, Stekoah, Stickoey, etc.)—the name of several former Cherokee settlements: 1. On Sticoa creek, near Clayton, Rabun county, Gorgia; 2. on Tuckasegee river at the old Thomas homestead just above the present Whittier, in Swain county, North Carolina; 3. on Stekoa creek of Little Tennessee river, a few miles below the junction of Nantahala, in Graham county, North Carolina. The word has lost its meaning.
STRINGFIELD—see *Tlâge'sĭ*.
stugi'stĭ, stui'stĭ—a key; see page 187 and under *Astu'gatâ'ga*.
SUCK, THE—see *Ûñ'tiguhĭ'*.
SUGARTOWN—see *Kûlse'tsi'yĭ*.
sû'năwă'—see *tlă'nuwă*.
sûnĕstlâ'tă—"split noses"; see *tsunú'liyû' sûnĕstlá'tă*.
sûñgĭ—mink; also onion; the name seems to refer to a smell; the various mints are called generically, *gaw'sûñ'gĭ*. See number 29.
Suki'yĭ—another form of *Săkwi'yĭ*, q. v.
su'lĭ'—buzzard; the Creek name is the same.
SUN LAND—see *Núñdá'yĭ'*.
su'-să'-sai'—an unmeaning song refrain. See number 66.
su'tălidihĭ'—see *nûñ'dă'*.
Suwa'li—see *Ani'-Suwa'lĭ*.
Suwa'lĭ-nûñnă'hĭ (abbreviated *Suwa'lĭ-nûñnă'hĭ*)—"Suwali trail," the proper name for the gap at the head of Swannanoa (from *Suwa'lĭ-Nûñ'nă*) river, east of Asheville, in Buncombe county, North Carolina. Cf. *Ku'să-nûñnă'hĭ*. See pages 194 and 379, also *Ani'-Suwa'lĭ*.
Suwa'nĭ—a former Cherokee settlement on Chattahoochee river, about the present Suwanee, in Gwinnett county, Georgia. The name has no meaning in the Cherokee language and is said to be of Creek origin. See page 382.
Suye'ta—"The Chosen One," from *asuye'ta*, "he is chosen," *gasu'yeú*, "I am choosing"; the same form, *suye'ta*, could also mean mixed, from *gasu'yăhú*, "I am mixing it." A masculine name, at present borne by a prominent ex-chief and informant upon the East Cherokee reservation.
SWANNANOA—see *Suwa'lĭ-nûñnă'hĭ*.
SWIM BALD—see *Sehwate'yĭ*.
SWIMMER—see *A'yûñ'inĭ*.

tadeyâ'statakûhĭ'—"we shall see each other." See number 75.
TAE-KEO-GE—see *Ta'ski'gĭ*.
ta'gû—the June-bug (*Allorhina nitida*), also called *tu'ya-dĭskalaw'stĭ'skĭ*, "one who keeps fire under the beans." See number 59.
Ta'gwa—see *Ani'ta'gwa*.
Ta'gwădihĭ' (abbreviated *Ta'gwădi'*)—"Catawba-killer," from *Ata'gwa* or *Ta'gwa*, Catawba Indian, and *dihihĭ'*, "he kills them" (habitually) from *tsi'ihú'*,

"I kill." An old masculine personal name, still in use upon the East Cherokee reservation. It was the proper name of the chief known to the whites about 1790 as "The Glass," from a confusion of this name with *adakĕ″tĭ*, glass, or mirror.

Tagwâ'hĭ—"Catawba place," from *Ata'gwa* or *Ta'gwa*, Catawba Indian, and *hĭ*, locative. A name occurring in several places in the old Cherokee country. A settlement of this name, known to the whites as Toccoa, was upon Toccoa creek, east of Clarkesville, in Habersham county, Georgia; another was upon Toccoa or Ocoee river, about the present Toccoa, in Fannin county, Georgia; a third may have been on Persimmon creek, which is known to the Cherokee as *Tagwă'hĭ*, and enters Hiwassee river some distance below Murphy, in Cherokee county, North Carolina.

TAHKEYOSTEE—see *Unta'kiyasti'yĭ.*

TAHLEQUAH—see *Tălikwă'.*

TAHCHEE—see *Tătsĭ'.*

TAKATOKA—see *De'gătă'gă.*

tă'lădŭ' (abbreviated *tăldŭ'*)—twelve, from *tă'lĭ*, two. Cf. *tăla'tŭ*, cricket.

Tă'lasĭ'—a former Cherokee settlement on Little Tennessee river, about Talassee ford, in Blount county, Tennessee. The name has lost its meaning.

TALASSEE—see *Tă'lasĭ'.*

tăla'tŭ—cricket; sometimes also called *dita'staye'skĭ* (q. v.), "the barber." Cf. *tă'lădŭ'*, twelve.

Tâle'danigi'skĭ (*Utâle'danigi'sĭ* in a dialectic form)—variously rendered by the whites "Hemp-carrier," "Nettle-carrier" or "Flax-toter," from *tâle'ta* or *utâle'ta*, flax (*Linum*) or richweed (*Pilea pumila*), and *danigi'skĭ*, "he carries them (habitually)." A former prominent chief on Valley river, in Cherokee county, North Carolina. See number 95 and notes.

TALIHINA—given as the name of the Cherokee wife of Samuel Houston; the form cannot be identified. See page 223.

Tălikwă' (commonly written Tellico, Telliquo or, in the Indian Territory, Tahlequah)—the name of several Cherokee settlements at different periods, viz: 1. Great Tellico, at Tellico Plains, on Tellico river, in Monroe county, Tennessee; 2. Little Tellico, on Tellico creek of Little Tennessee river, about ten miles below Franklin, in Macon county, North Carolina; 3. a town on Valley river, about five miles above Murphy, in Cherokee county, North Carolina; 4. Tahlequah, established as the capital of the Cherokee Nation, Indian Territory, in 1839. The meaning of the name is lost.

Tali'wă—the site of a traditional battle between the Cherokee and Creeks about 1755, on Mountain (?) creek of Etowah river in upper Georgia. Probably not a Cherokee but a Creek name from the Creek *ta'lua* or *ita'lua*, town. See pages 38 and 384–385.

TALKING-ROCK—see *Năñyŭ'-gŭñwani'skĭ.*

TALLULAH—see *Tălulŭ'.*

Tăl-tsu'skă'—"Two-heads," from *tă'lĭ*, two, and *tsu'skă'*, plural of *uskă'*, (his) head. A Cherokee chief about the year 1800, known to the whites as Doublehead.

talulĭ—pregnant; whence *alulĭ'*, (she is) a mother, said of a woman.

Tălulŭ' (commonly written Tallulah, and appearing in old documents, from the Lower dialect, as Taruraw, Toruro, Turoree, etc.)—a name occurring in two or more places in the old Cherokee country, viz: 1. An ancient settlement on the upper part of Tallulah river, in Rabun county, Georgia; 2. a town on Tallulah creek of Cheowa river, in Graham county, North Carolina. The word is of uncertain etymology. The *dulu'sĭ* frog is said to cry *tălulŭ'*. See number 125. The noted falls upon Tallulah river are known to the Cherokee as *Ugăñ'yĭ*, q. v.

TALUNTISKI—see *Ata'lŭñti'skĭ.*

Tama'li—a name, commonly written Tomotley or Tomatola, occurring in at least two places in the old Cherokee country, viz: 1. On Valley river, a few miles above Murphy, about the present Tomatola, in Cherokee county, North Carolina; 2. on Little Tennessee river, about Tomotley ford, a few miles above Tellico river, in Monroe county, Tennessee. The name can not be translated, and may be of Creek origin, as that tribe had a town of the same name upon the lower Chattahoochee river.

Tănăsĭ'—a name which can not be analyzed, commonly spelt Tennessee, occurring in several places in the old Cherokee country, viz: 1. On Little Tennessee river, about halfway between Citico and Toco creeks, in Monroe county, Tennessee; 2. "Old Tennessee town," on Hiwassee river, a short distance above the junction of Ocoee, in Polk county, Tennessee; 3. on Tennessee creek, a head-stream of Tuckasegee river, in Jackson county, North Carolina. Tanasqui, visited by Pardo in 1567 (see page 29), may have been another place of the same name. See number 124.

Tanasqui—see Tănăsĭ'.

Ta'ski'gi (abbreviated from Ta'skigi'yĭ or Da'skigi'yĭ, the locative yĭ being commonly omitted)—a name variously written Tae-keo-ge (misprint), Tasquiqui, Teeskege, Tuscagee, Tuskegee, etc. derived from that of a foreign tribe incorporated with the Cherokee, and occurring as a local name both in the Cherokee and in the Creek country. 1. The principal settlement of this name was on Little Tennessee river, just above the junction of Tellico, in Monroe county, Tennessee; 2. another was on the north bank of Tennessee river, just below Chattanooga, Tennessee; 3. another may have been on Tuskegee creek of Little Tennessee river, near Robbinsville, Graham county, North Carolina. See page 29 and number 105.

Tasquiqui—see Ta'ski'gi.

Tassel, Old—see Utsi'dsătă'.

Tătsĭ'—"Dutch," also written Tahchee, a western Cherokee chief about 1830. See page 141.

tatsu'hwă—the redbird.

tawa'lĭ—punk.

Tawa'lĭ-ukwanûñ'tĭ—"Punk-plugged-in," from tawa'lĭ, punk; the Cherokee name of a traditional Shawano chief. See number 100.

tăwi'skă, tăwi'skage—smooth, slick.

Tăwi'skălă—"Flint"; a Cherokee supernatural, the personification of the rock flint; tăwi'skălăñ'ĭ, tăwi'skălă, flint, from tăwi'skă, smooth, slick; cf. Iroquois Tăwiskaroñ. See number 25 and notes.

Tayûnksĭ—a traditional western tribe; the name can not be analyzed. See number 105.

Tellico—see Tălikwă'.

telûñ'lătĭ—the summer grape (Vitis æstivalis).

Tensawattee—see Ku'săweti'yĭ.

Terrapin—see Tûksi'.

tewa—flying squirrel; sălă'lĭ, gray squirrel; kiyu'ga, ground squirrel.

Thomas, W. H.—see Wil-usdi'.

Tĭkwăli'tsĭ—a name occurring in several places in the old Cherokee country, viz: 1. Tuckalegee creek, a tributary of War-woman creek, east of Clayton, in Rabun county, Georgia; 2. the Tĭkwăli'tsĭ of the story, an important town on Tuckasegee river at the present Bryson City, in Swain county, North Carolina; 3. Tuckalechee cove, on Little river, in Blount county, Tennessee, which probably preserves the aboriginal local name. The name appears in old documents as Tuckarechee (Lower dialect) and Tuckalegee, and must not be confounded with Tsĭksi'tsĭ or Tuckasegee. It can not be translated. See number 100 and notes.

Timossy—see Tomassee.

Tlăge′sĭ—"Field"; the Cherokee name for Lieutenant-Colonel W. W. Stringfield of Waynesville, North Carolina, one of the officers of the Cherokee contingent in the Thomas Legion. It is an abbreviated rendering of his proper name.

tlâge′sitûñ′—a song form for *tlâge′sĭ a-stûñ′ĭ*, "on the edge of the field," from *tlâge′sĭ*, or *tsâge′sĭ*, field, and *astûñ′ĭ*, edge, border, etc; *ăma′yăstûñ′*, "the bank of a stream." See number 24.

tla′mehă—bat (dialectic forms, *tsa′mehă, tsa′wehă*). See page 187.

tlanu′sĭ′—leech (dialectic form, *tsanu′sĭ′*). See page 187.

Tlanusi′yĭ (abbreviated *Tlanusi′*)—"Leech place," a former important settlement at the junction of Hiwassee and Valley rivers, the present site of Murphy, in Cherokee county, North Carolina; also a point on Nottely river, a few miles distant, in the same county. See number 77 and notes. The name appears also as Clennuse, Klausuna, Quoneashee, etc.

tlă′nuwă′ (dialectic forms, *tsă′nuwă′, sú′năwă′, "sinnawah"*—Adair)—a mythic great hawk. See numbers 35, 64, 65, also page 187.

tlă′nuwă′ usdi′—"little tlă′nuwă′"; probably the goshawk (*Astur atricapillus*). See number 35.

Tlă′nuwă′-atsiyelûñ′ĭsûñ′yĭ—"Where the Tlă′nuwă cut it up," from *tlă′nuwă′*. q. v., and *tsiyelûñ′iskú′*, an archaic form for *tsigûñilûñ′iskú′*, "I am cutting it up." A place on Little Tennessee river, nearly opposite the entrance of Citico creek, in Blount county, Tennessee. See number 64 and notes.

Tlă′nuwa′ĭ—"Tlă′nuwă place," a cave on the north side of Tennessee river a short distance below the entrance of Citico creek, in Blount county, Tennessee. See number 64 and notes.

tlay′kŭ′—jay (dialectic form, *tsay′kú′*). See page 187.

tlûñti′stĭ—the pheasant (*Bonasa umbella*), called locally grouse or partridge.

tlutlŭ′—the martin bird (dialectic form, *tsutsŭ′*). See page 187.

tlûñtû′tsĭ—panther (dialectic form, *tsûñtú′tsĭ*). See page 187.

Tocax—a place, apparently in the Cherokee country, visited by Pardo in 1567 (see page 29). It may possibly have a connection with Toxaway (see *Dúksa′ĭ*) or Toccoa (see *Tagwá′hĭ*).

Toccoa—see *Tagwá′hĭ*.

Toco—see *Dăkwá′ĭ*.

Tollunteeskee—see *Ata′lûñti′skĭ*.

Tomassee (also written *Timossy* and *Tymahse*)—the name of two or more former Cherokee settlements, viz: 1. On Tomassee creek of Keowee river, in Oconee county, South Carolina; 2. on Little Tennessee river near the entrance of Burningtown creek, in Macon county, South Carolina. The correct form and interpretation are unknown.

Tomatola, Tomotley—see *Tama′lĭ*.

Tooantuh—see *Du′stu′*.

Toogelah—see *Dugilu′yĭ*.

Toqua—see *Dăkwá′ĭ*.

Toxaway—see *Dúksa′ĭ*.

Track Rock gap—see *Datsu′nalăsgûñ′yĭ*.

Tsăga′sĭ—a Cherokee sprite. See number 78.

tsâ′gĭ—upstream, up the road; the converse of *ge′ĭ*. See number 117.

Tsaiyĭ′—see *Ûñtsaiyĭ′*.

Tsa′lădihĭ′—Chief N. J. Smith of the East Cherokee. The name might be rendered "Charley-killer," from *Tsalĭ*, "Charley," and *dihĭ′*, "killer" (in composition), but is really a Cherokee equivalent for Jarrett (*Tsalădĭ′*), his middle name, by which he was frequently addressed. Cf. *Tagwădihĭ*.

tsâl-agăyûñ′li—"old tobacco," from *tsâlú*, tobacco, and *agăyûñ′li*, or *agáyûñ′lige*, old, ancient; the *Nicotiana rustica* or wild tobacco. See number 126.

Tsa'lăgĭ' (Tsa'răgĭ' in Lower dialect)—the correct form of Cherokee. See page 182, "Tribal Synonymy."

Tsa'lĭ—Charley; a Cherokee shot for resisting the troops at the time of the Removal. See page 131.

tsâliyu'stĭ—"tobacco-like," from tsâlú, tobacco, and iyu'stĭ, like; a generic name for the cardinal-flower, mullein and related species. See number 126.

tsâlû or tsâlûñ (in the Lower dialect, tsârú)—tobacco; by comparison with kindred forms in other Iroquoian dialects the meaning "fire to hold in the mouth" seems to be indicated. Lanman spells it tso-lungh. See number 126 and page 187.

tsa'mehă—see tla'mehă.

tsă'nadiskâ'—for tsăndiskâĭ' "they say."

tsana'sehâ'ĭ'—so they say, they say about him. See number 118.

tsâne'nĭ—the scorpion lizard; also called gi'gă-danegi'ski, q. v. See number 59.

Tsanĭ—John.

Tsantăwû'—a masculine name which can not be analyzed.

Tsan-uga'sĭtă—"Sour John"; John Butler, a halfbreed Cherokee ball captain, formerly living on Nottely river. See number 122.

Tsan-usdi'—"Little John"; the Cherokee name for General John Sevier, and also the boy name of the chief John Ross, afterward known as Gu'wisguwĭ', q. v. Sĭkwi'ă, a Cherokee attempt at "Sevier," is a masculine name upon the East Cherokee reservation.

tsanu'sĭ'—see tlanu'sĭ'.

tsă'nuwă'—see tlă'nuwă'.

Tsa'răgĭ'—Cherokee; see page 182, "Tribal Synonymy."

tsârû—see tsâlú.

Tsasta'wĭ—a noted hunter formerly living upon Nantahala river, in Macon county, North Carolina; the meaning of the name is doubtful. See number 122.

Tsatănu'gĭ (commonly spelled Chattanooga)—the Cherokee name for some point upon the creek entering Tennessee river at the city of Chattanooga, in Hamilton county, Tennessee. It has no meaning in the Cherokee language and appears to be of foreign origin. The ancient name for the site of the present city is A'tlă'nuwă, q. v. See number 124. Before the establishment of the town the place was known to the whites as Ross' landing, from a store kept there by Lewis Ross, brother of the chief John Ross.

Tsatu'gĭ (commonly written Chattooga or Chatuga)—a name occurring in two or more places in the old Cherokee country, but apparently of foreign origin (see page 382). Possible Cherokee derivations are from words signifying respectively "he drank by sips," from gatu'giă', "I sip," or "he has crossed the stream and come out upon the other side," from gatu'gĭ, "I have crossed" etc. An ancient settlement of this name was on Chattooga river, a head-stream of Savannah river, on the boundary between South Carolina and Georgia; another appears to have been on upper Tellico river, in Monroe county, Tennessee; another may have been on Chattooga river, a tributary of the Coosa, in northwestern Georgia.

Tsă'wă Gakskĭ—Joe Smoker, from Tsâwă, "Joe," and gakskĭ, "smoker," from ga'giskú, "I am smoking." The Cherokee name for Chief Joel B. Mayes, of the Cherokee Nation west.

Tsăwa'sĭ—a Cherokee sprite. See number 78.

tsa'wehă—see tla'mehă.

tsay'kû'—see tlay'kú'.

Tsek'sĭnĭ'—the Cherokee form for the name of General Andrew Jackson.

Tsĕsa'nĭ—Jessan, probably a derivative from Jesse; a masculine name upon the East Cherokee reservation.

Tsĕ'sĭ-Ska'tsĭ—"Scotch Jesse"; Jesse Reid, present chief of the East Cherokee, so called because of mixed Scotch ancestry.

tsetsäni′lĭ—"thy two elder brothers" (male speaking); my elder brother (male speaking), *ûñgini′lĭ*. See note to number 63.

Tsgâgûñ′yĭ—"Insect place," from *tsgâyă*, insect, and *yĭ*, locative. A cave in the ridge eastward from Franklin, in Macon county, North Carolina. See number 13.

tsgâyă—insect, worm, etc. See page 308.

Tsĭkăma′gĭ—a name, commonly spelled Chickamauga, occurring in at least two places in the old Cherokee country, which has lost any meaning in Cherokee and appears to be of foreign origin. It is applied to a small creek at the head of Chattahoochee river, in White county, Georgia, and also to the district about the southern (not the northern) Chickamauga creek, coming into Tennessee river, a few miles above Chattanooga, in Hamilton county, Tennessee. In 1777 the more hostile portion of the Cherokee withdrew from the rest of the tribe and established here a large settlement, from which they removed about five years later to settle lower down the Tennessee in what were known as the Chickamauga towns or Five Lower towns. See page 54 and number 124.

tsĭkĭ—a word which renders emphatic that which it follows: as *ă′stû*, "very good," *ástû′ tsĭkĭ*, "best of all." See number 75.

tsĭkĭkĭ′—the katydid; the name is an onomatope.

tsĭ′kĭlilĭ′—the Carolina chickadee (*Parus carolinensis*); the name is an onomatope. See number 35.

Tsĭksi′tsĭ (*Tûksi′tsĭ* in dialectic form; commonly written Tuckasegee)—1. a former Cherokee settlement about the junction of the two forks of Tuckasegee, above Webster, in Jackson county, North Carolina (not to be confounded with *Tĭkwăli′tsĭ*, q. v.). 2. A former settlement on a branch of Brasstown creek of Hiwassee river, in Towns county, Georgia. The word has lost its meaning.

Tsĭ′nawĭ—a Cherokee wheelwright, perhaps the first in the Nation to make a spinning wheel and loom. The name can not be analyzed. See page 214.

tsĭne′û—I am picking it (something long) up; in the Lower and Middle dialects, *tsĭnigi′û*.

tsĭnigi′û—see *tsĭne′û*.

tsiska′gĭlĭ—the large red crawfish; the ordinary crawfish is called *tsistû′na*. See number 59.

tsi′skwa—bird.

tsiskwa′gwă—robin, from *tsi′skwa*, bird.

Tsiskwâ′hĭ—"Bird place," from *tsi′skwa*, bird, and *hĭ*, locative. Birdtown settlement on the East Cherokee reservation, in Swain county, North Carolina.

tsiskwâ′yă—sparrow, literally "principal bird" (i. e., most widely distributed), from *tsi′skwa*, bird, and *yă*, a suffix denoting principal or real.

Tsilalu′hĭ—"Sweet-gum place," from *tsila′lŭ′*, sweet-gum (*Liquidambar*), and *hĭ*, locative. A former settlement on a small branch of Brasstown creek of Hiwassee river, just within the line of Towns county, Georgia. The name is incorrectly rendered Gumlog (creek).

Tsiskwunsdi′-adsisti′yĭ—"Where they killed Little-bird," from *Tsiskw-unsdi′*, "Little-birds" (plural form). A place near the head of West Buffalo creek, southeast of Robbinsville, in Graham county, North Carolina. See number 122.

Tsistetsi′yĭ—"Mouse place," from *tsistetsĭ*, mouse, and *yĭ*, locative; a former settlement on South Mouse creek, of Hiwassee river, in Bradley county, Tennessee. The present town of Cleveland, upon the same creek, is known to the Cherokee under the same name.

tsistu—rabbit.

tsistû′na—crawfish; the large horned beetle is also so called. The large red crawfish is called *tsiska′gĭlĭ*.

tsist-uni′gĭstĭ—"rabbit foods" (plural), from *tsi′stu*, rabbit, and *uni′gĭstĭ*, plural of *agi′stĭ*, food, from *tsiyĭ′giû* "I am eating" (soft food). The wild rose.

Tsistu′yĭ—"Rabbit place," from *tsistu*, rabbit, and *yĭ*, locative. 1. Gregory bald, high peak of the Great Smoky range, eastward from Little Tennessee river, on the boundary between Swain county, North Carolina and Blount county, Tennessee. See number 75 and notes. 2. A former settlement on the north bank of Hiwassee river at the entrance of Chestua creek, in Polk county, Tennessee. The name of Choastea creek of Tugaloo river, in Oconee county, South Carolina, is probably also a corruption from the same word.

Tsiyâ′hĭ—"Otter place," from *tsiyú*, otter, and *yĭ*, locative; variously spelled Cheowa, Cheeowhee, Chewohe, Chewe, etc. 1. A former settlement on a branch of Keowee river, near the present Cheohee, Oconee county, South Carolina. 2. A former and still existing Cherokee settlement on Cheowa river, about Robbinsville, in Graham county, North Carolina. 3. A former settlement in Cades cove, on Cove creek, in Blount county, Tennessee.

Tsi′yu-gûnsi′nĭ—"He is dragging a canoe," from tsi′yŭ, canoe (cf. *tsi′yú*, otter) and *gûnsi′nĭ*, "he is dragging it." "Dragging-canoe," a prominent leader of the hostile Cherokee in the Revolution. The name appears in documents as Cheucunsene and Kunnesee. See page 54.

Tskĭl-e′gwă—"Big-witch," from *atskĭlĭ′*, or *tskĭlĭ′*, witch, owl, and *e′gwa*, big; an old man of the East Cherokee, who died in 1896. See page 179. Although translated Big-witch by the whites, the name is understood by the Indians to mean Big-owl (see number 35), having been originally applied to a white man living on the same clearing, noted for his large staring eyes.

tskĭlĭ′ (contracted from *atskĭlĭ′*)—1. witch; 2. the dusky horned owl (*Bubo virginianus saturatus*). See number 35.

TSOLUNGH—see *tsălú*.

tskwâ′yĭ—the great white heron or American egret (*Herodias egretta*).

Tsudă′tălesûñ′yĭ—"Where pieces fall off," i. e. where the banks are caving in; from *adătăle′ú*, "it is falling off," *ts*, distance prefix, "there," and *yĭ*, locative. The Cherokee name for the present site of Memphis, Tennessee, overlooking the Mississippi, and formerly known as the Chickasaw bluff.

Tsuda′ye′lûñ′yĭ—"Isolated place"; an isolated peak near the head of Cheowa river, northeast of Robbinsville, in Graham county, North Carolina. See number 79 and notes. The root of the word signifies detached, or isolated, whence Uda′ye′lûñ′yĭ, the Cherokee outlet, in the Indian Territory.

Tsu′dinûñti′yĭ—"Throwing-down place"; a former settlement on lower Nantahala river, in Macon county, North Carolina. See number 122.

Tsugidû′lĭ ûlsgi′stĭ (from *tsugidû′lĭ*, plural of *ugidû′lĭ*, one of the long wing or tail feathers of a bird, and *ûlsgi′stĭ* or *ûlsgi′ta*, a dance)—the feather or eagle dance. See number 35.

tsûñgili′sĭ—plural of *ûñgili′sĭ*, q. v.

tsûñgini′sĭ—plural of *ûñgini′sĭ*, q. v.

Tsukilûñnûñ′yĭ—"Where he alighted"; two bald spots on a mountain at the head of Little Snowbird creek, near Robbinsville, in Graham county, North Carolina. For tradition, see number 122.

tsûñkina′tlĭ—"my younger brothers" (male speaking).

tsûñkită′—"my younger brothers" (female speaking).

tsu′lă—fox; cf. *tsă′lú*, kingfisher and *tlutlŭ′* or *tsutsŭ′*, martin. The black fox is *iná′lĭ*. The Creek word for fox is *chula*.

tsula′skĭ—alligator: the name is of uncertain etymology.

Tsŭ′la′wĭ—see *Tsŭ′lûñwe′ĭ*.

Tsulâ′sinûñ′yĭ—"Footprint place." A place on Tuckasegee river, about a mile above Deep creek, in Swain county, North Carolina. See number 122.

Tsul′kălú′—"Slanting-eyes," literally "He has them slanting" (or leaning up against something); the prefix *ts* makes it a plural form, and the name is under-

stood to refer to the eyes, although the word eye (*aktă′*, plural *diktă′*) is not a
part of it. Cf. *Ătă′-gûʿkălú′*. A mythic giant and ruler of the game. The name
has been corrupted to Jutaculla and Tuli-cula. Jutaculla rock and Jutaculla
old fields about the head of Tuckasegee river, in Jackson, North Carolina, take
their name from him. See number 81 and notes.

Tsule′hisanûñ′hĭ—"Resurrected One," from *di′gwăle′hisanûñ′hĭ*, "I was resurrected,"
literally, "I was down and have risen." *Tsa′lăgĭ′ Tsule′hisanûñhĭ*, the Cherokee
title of the newspaper known to the whites as the Cherokee Phœnix. The
Cherokee title was devised by Worcester and Boudinot as suggesting the idea of
the phœnix of classic fable. The Indian name of the recent "Cherokee Advocate" is *Tsa′lăgĭ Asdeli′skĭ*.

Tsulʿkălû′ tsunegûñ′yĭ—see *Tsunegúñ′yĭ*.

tsulie′na—the nuthatch (*Sitta carolinensis*); the word signifies literally "deaf" (a
plural form referring to the ear, *gûlĕ′*), although no reason is given for such a
name.

tsûʿlû—kingfisher. Cf. *tsuʿlă*.

Tsûʿlûñweʿĭ (abbreviated *Tsûʿlûñ′we* or *Tsúla′wĭ*, possibly connected with *tsûʿlă*,
kingfisher)—Chilhowee creek, a north tributary of Little Tennessee river, in
Blount county, Tennessee.

Tsundaʿnilti′yĭ—"Where they demanded the debt from him"; a place on Little
Santeetla river, west of Robbinsville, in Graham county, North Carolina. The
creek also is commonly known by the same name. See number 122.

Tsundige′wĭ—"Closed anuses," literally "They have them closed," understood to
refer to the anus; from *dige′wĭ*, plural of *ge′wĭ*, closed, stopped up, blind; cf.
Tsuʿkălú′; also *Gúlisge′wĭ*, "Blind, or closed, ears," an old personal name.
See number 74.

tsun′digwûn′tskĭ (contracted from *tsun′digwúntsuʿgĭ*, "they have them forked,"
referring to the peculiar forked tail; cf. *Tsuʿkălú′*)—a migratory bird which once
appeared for a short time upon the East Cherokee reservation, apparently, from
the description, the scissortail or swallow-tailed flycatcher (*Milvulus forficatus*).
See number 35.

Tsunegûñ′yĭ (sometimes called *Tsuʿkălú′ Tsunegûñ′yĭ*)—Tennessee bald, at the
extreme head of Tuckasegee river, on the east line of Jackson county, North
Carolina. The name seems to mean, "There where it is white," from *ts*, a prefix indicating distance, *une′gă*, white, and *yĭ*, locative. See number 81 and
notes.

Tsunilʿkălû—the plural form for *Tsuʿkălú*, q. v.; a traditional giant tribe in the
west. See number 106.

tsunûʿliyû′ sûnĕstlâ′tă—"they have split noses," from *agwaʿliyû′*, "I have it," and
unĕstlââ′, "it is cracked" (as a crack made by the sun's heat in a log or in the
earth); the initial *s* makes it refer to the nose, *kăyăsă′*. See number 76 and
notes.

tsunĭs′tsăhĭ—"(those) having topknots or crests," from *ustsăhú′*, "having a topknot," *ustsăhĭ′*, "he has a topknot" (habitual). See number 76 and notes.

Tsuniya′tigă—"Naked People"; literally "They are naked there," from *uya′tigă*,
naked (singular), with the prefix *ts*, indicating distance. A traditional western
tribe. See number 105.

tsunsdi′—contracted from *tsunsdi′ga*, the plural of *usdi′ga* or *usdi′*, small.

Tsunu′lăhûñ′skĭ—"He tries, but fails" (habitually), from *detsinu′lăhûñ′gû′* (q. v.),
"I tried, but failed." A former noted chief among the East Cherokee, commonly known to the whites as Junaluska. In early life he was called *Gûʿkă-
la′skĭ*, a name which denotes something habitually falling from a leaning position
(cf. *Ătă-gûʿkălú′* and *Tsuʿkălú′*.) See page 164.

tsûñ-ka′wi-ye′, tsûñ-sĭkwa-ya′, tsûñ-tsuʿla-ya′, tsûñ-waʿya-ya′—" I am (*tsûñ* or *tsi*, verbal prefix) a real (*yă*, *ye*, noun suffix) deer" (*kawĭ'*, archaic for *a'wĭ'*); opossum, *sĭ'kwa;* fox, *tsu'lă;* wolf, *wa'ya.* Archaic song forms. See number 15.

Tsûsginâ'Ĭ—"the Ghost country," from *asgi'na*, "ghost," *ĭ*, locative, and *ts*, a prefix denoting distance. The land of the dead; it is situated in *Usûñhi'yĭ*, the Twilight land, in the west. See number 5.

tsuskwa'lĭ—plural of *uskwa'lĭ*, short.

Tsuskwănûñ'năwa'tă—"Worn-out blanket," from *tsuskwănûñ'nĭ*, blanket (the word refers to something having stripes), and *uwa'tă*, "worn out." James D. Wafford, a prominent Cherokee mixed-blood and informant in the Western nation, who died about 1896. See page 236.

Tsûta'ga Uweyûñ'Ĭ—"Chicken creek," from *tsûta'ga*, chicken, and *uweyûñ'ĭ*, stream. An extreme eastern head-stream of Nantahala river, in Macon county, North Carolina. See number 122.

Tsuta'tsinasûñ'yĬ—"Eddy place." A place on Cheowa river at the mouth of Cockram creek, in Graham county, North Carolina. For tradition see number 122.

tsutsŭ'—see *tlutlŭ'*.

tsûñtû'tsĭ—see *tlûñtû'tsĭ*.

tsuwă'—the mud-puppy or water-dog (*Menopoma* or *Protonopsis*). See number 59.

Tsuwa'tel'da—a contraction of *Tsuwa'teldûñ'yĭ;* the name has lost its meaning. Pilot knob, north from Brevard, in Transylvania county, North Carolina. See number 82 and notes.

Tsuwă'-uniyetsûñ'yĬ—"Where the water-dogs laughed," from *tsuwă'* (q. v.), "water-dog," *uniye'tsû*, "they laughed" (*agiyet'skú*, "I am laughing"), and *yĭ*, locative; Tusquittee bald, near Hayesville, in Clay county, North Carolina. For story see number 122.

Tsuwe'năhĬ—A traditional hunter, in communication with the invisible people. See number 83. The name seems to mean "He has them in abundance," an irregular or archaic form for *Uwe'năĭ*, "he has abundance," "he is rich," from *agwe'năĭ'*, "I am rich." As a masculine name it is used as the equivalent of Richard. See number 83.

Tuckalechee—see *Tĭkwăli'tsĭ*.

Tuckasegee—see *Tsĭksi'tsĭ*.

Tugaloo—see *Dugilu'yĭ*.

tugalŭ!—the cry of the *dagŭl'kú* goose.

tugălû'nă—a variety of small fish, about four inches long, frequenting the larger streams (from *gălŭ'nă*, a gourd, on account of its long nose). See number 39 and notes.

tûksĭ'—the terrapin or land tortoise; also the name of a Cherokee chief about the close of the Revolution. *Săligu'gĭ*, common turtle; soft-shell turtle, *u'lănă'wă*.

Tûksi'tsĭ—see *Tsĭksi'tsĭ*.

Tuli-cula—see *Tsul'kălû'*.

tûlsku'wa—"he snaps with his head," from *uskă'*, head; the snapping beetle.

Tunâ'Ĭ—a traditional warrior and medicine-man of old Itsâ'tĭ; the name can not be analyzed. See number 99.

Turkeytown—see *Gûn-di'gaduhûñ'yĭ*.

Turniptown—see *U'lûñ'yĭ*.

Tuskegee—see *Ta'ski'gĭ*.

Tusquittee bald—see *Tsuwă'-uniyetsûñ'yĭ*.

Tusquittee creek—see *Daskwĭtûñ'yĭ*.

tu'sti—for *tusti'gă*, a small bowl; larger jars are called *diwa'lĭ* and *ûñti'yă*.

tûñ'tăwû'—a small yellow night-moth. The name comes from *ahûñ'tú*, a word implying that something flits into and out of the blaze. See number 59.

tu'tĭ—snowbird.

Tuti'yĬ—"Snowbird place," from *tu'tĭ*, snowbird, and *yĭ*, locative. Little Snow-bird creek of Cheowa river, in Graham county, North Carolina.

tû'tsahyesĭ'—"he will marry you."

tu'yă—bean.

tu'yă-dĭskalaw'sti'skĭ—see *ta'gŭ*.

tû'yahusĭ'—"she will die."

TYMAHSE—see TOMASSEE.

Uchee—see *Ani'-Yu'tsĭ*.

udâ'hale'yĭ—"on the sunny side."

udâ'ĭ—the baneberry or cohosh vine (*Actæa?*). The name signifies that the plant has something long hanging from it.

uda'lĭ—"(it is) married"; the mistletoe, so called on account of its parasitic habit.

U'dăwagûñ'ta—"Bald." A bald mountain of the Great Smoky range, in Yancey county, North Carolina, not far from Mount Mitchell. See number 51.

Udsi'skală—a masculine name.

uga'sĭtă—sour.

ûñgidă'—"thy two elder brothers" (male speaking). See notes to number 63.

ûṉ̃ili'sĭ (plural, *tsûñgili'sĭ*)—"my daughter's child." See note to number 66, and cf. *ûñgini'sĭ*.

ûñgini'lĭ—"my elder brother" (female speaking). See notes to number 63.

ûñgini'sĭ (plural *tsûñgini'sĭ*)—"my son's child." See note to number 66, and cf. *ûñgili'si*.

u'giskă'—"he is swallowing it; from *tsĭkiû'*, "I am eating." See number 8 and notes.

u'guku'—the hooting or barred owl (*Syrnium nebulosum*); the name is an onomatope. See also *tskĭlĭ'* and *wa͏'huhu'*.

ugûñste'lĭ (*ugûñste'lû* in dialectic form)—the hornyhead fish (*Campostoma*, stone roller). The name is said, on doubtful authority, to refer to its having horns. See number 59.

Ugûñ'yĭ——Tallulah falls, on the river of that name, northeast from Clarkesville, in Habersham county, Georgia; the meaning of the name is lost. See number 84.

UILATA—See *U'tlûñ'tă*.

uk-ku'sûñtsûtĕtĭ'—"it will twist up one's arm." See number 115.

Uk-ku'sûñtsûtĭ—"Bent-bow-shape"; a comic masculine name. Cf. *gûltsû'tĭ*, bow. See number 115.

uk-kwûnăgi'stĭ—"it will draw down one's eye." See number 115.

Uk-kwûnăgi'ta—"Eye-drawn-down"; a comic masculine name. See number 115.

uksu'hĭ—the mountain blacksnake or black racer (*Coluber obsoletus*); the name seems to refer to some peculiarity of the eye, *aktă'; uksuhă'*, "he has something lodged in his eye." See number 53 and notes.

Ukte'na—"Keen-eyed (?)" from *aktă'*, eye, *akta'tĭ*, to examine closely. A mythic great horned serpent, with a talismanic diadem. See number 50 and notes.

Ukte'na-tsuganûñ'tatsûñ'yĭ—"Where the Uktena got fastened." A spot on Tuckasegee river, about two miles above Bryson City, in Swain county, North Carolina. See number 122.

Uktena-utansi'nastûñ'yĭ—"Where the Uktena crawled." A rock on the north bank of Tuckasegee river, about four miles above Bryson City, in Swain county, North Carolina. See number 122.

Ukwû'nû (or *Ukwû'nĭ*)—a former Cherokee settlement, commonly known to the whites as Oconee, on Seneca creek, near the present Walhalla, in Oconee county, South Carolina.

Ula͏'gû'—the mythic original of the yellow-jacket tribe. See number 13. The word signifies "leader," "boss," or "principal one," and is applied to the first yellow-jacket (*d͏'ska'ĭ*) seen in the spring, to a queen bee and to the leader of a working squad.

u'lănă'wă—the soft-shell turtle; the etymology of the word is uncertain. See also *săligu'gĭ* and *tûksĭ'*.

ulasu'la—moccasin, shoe.

ûlĕ′—and; ûlĕ-′nú′, and also.

Ûñli′ta—"(He is) long-winded," an archaic form for the regular word, gûñli′ta; an old masculine name. A chief about the year 1790, known to the whites as "The Breath."

ûlskwûlte′gĭ—a "pound-mill," a self-acting water-mill used in the Cherokee mountains. The name signifies that "it butts with its head" (uskă′, head), in allusion to the way in which the pestle works in the mortar. The generic word for mill is dista′stĭ.

ulstĭtlû′—literally, "it is on his head." The diamond crest on the head of the mythic Uktena serpent. When detached it becomes the Ulûñsú′tĭ.

Ultiwâ′Ĭ—a former Cherokee settlement about the present Ooltewah, on the creek of the same name, in James county, Tennessee. The name has the locative form (ĭ suffix), but cannot be translated.

ulûññi′ta—domesticated, tame; may be used for persons as well as animals, but not for plants; for cultivated or domesticated plants the adjective is gûnutlûñ′ĭ (or gûnusûñ′ĭ).

Ulûñsû′tĭ—"Transparent"; the great talismanic crystal of the Cherokee. Spelled Oolunsade by Hagar. See number 50 and notes.

ulûñ′ta—"it has climbed," from tsilahĭ′, "I am climbing"; the poison oak (Rhus radicans). See number 126.

U′lûñ′yĭ—"Tuber place," from U′lĭ′, a variety of edible tuber, and yĭ, locative. A former settlement upon Turniptown (for U′lûñ′yĭ) creek, above Ellijay, in Gilmer county, Georgia.

Unacala—see Une′gădihĭ′.

U′nadanti′yĭ—"Place where they conjured," the name of a gap about three miles east of Webster, in Jackson county, North Carolina, and now transferred to the town itself. See number 122.

unăde′na—woolly, downy (in speaking of animals); uwă′nú, wool, down, fine fur (detached from the animal).

u′năhŭ′—see unăhwĭ′.

unăhwĭ′—heart; in Middle and Lower dialects, unăhŭ′. See page 187.

Unaka—see une′gă and Unicoi.

unatlûñwe′hitû—"it has spirals"; a plant (unidentified) used in conjurations. See number 126.

une′gă—white.

une′guhĭ—"he is (was) mischievous or bad"; tsúne′guhĭ′yu, "you are very mischievous" (said to a child). See number 118.

une′gutsătû′—"(he is) mischievous"; a′gine′gutsătú′, "I am mischievous."

Une′lănûñ′hĭ—"The Apportioner"; "I am apportioning," gane′laskú′; "I apportion" (habitually), gane′laskĭ. In the sacred formulas a title of the Sun god; in the Bible the name of God.

une′stălûñ—ice.

Unicoi—the map name of the old Unicoi turnpike (see page 87), of a gap on the watershed between Chattahoochee and Hiwassee rivers, in Georgia, and of a county in eastern Tennessee. Probably a corruption of une′gă, white, whence comes also Unaka, the present map name of a part of the Great Smoky range.

uni′gistĭ—foods; singular, agi′stĭ.

Uniga′yata′ti′yĭ—"Where they made a fish trap," from uga′yatûñ′ĭ, fish trap, and yĭ, locative; a place on Tuckasegee river, at the mouth of Deep creek, near Bryson City, in Swain county, North Carolina. See number 100 and notes.

Uni′hăluna—see Ăhălu′na.

Unika′wĭ—the "Townhouse dance," so called because danced inside the townhouse; the name does not refer to a townhouse (gati′yĭ) and can not be analyzed, but may have some connection with the archaic word for deer. Cf. Ani′-Kawĭ′.

Une′gă-dihĭ′—"White-man-killer"; from *une′ga*, "white," for *yûñ′wune′ga*, "white person," and *dihĭ′*, a noun suffix denoting "killer" ("he kills them" habitually). A Cherokee chief, whose name appears in documents about 1790 as White-man-killer, or, by misprint Unacala. It is an old masculine name, existing until recently upon the reservation. Cf. *Ta′gwădihĭ′*.

u′niskwetu⁗gĭ—"they wear a hat"; *ûlskwe′tăwă′*, hat, from *uskă′*, head. The may-apple (*Podophyllum*). See number 126.

unistilûñ′istĭ—"they stick on along their whole length"; the generic name for "stickers" and burs, including the Spanish needle, cockle bur, jimson weed, etc. See number 126.

uni′tsĭ—her mother; *agitsĭ′*, my mother.

Uniyâ′hitûñ′yĭ—"Where they shot it," from *tsiyă′ihû*, "I shoot," and *yĭ*, locative. A place on Tuckasegee river a short distance above Bryson City, in Swain county, North Carolina. See number 100.

Untoola—see *Dihyûñ′dulă′*.

Unta′kiyasti′yĭ—"Where they race," from *takiya′tă*, a race, and *yĭ*, locative; locally corrupted to Tahkeyostee. The district on the French Broad river, around Asheville, in Buncombe county, North Carolina. The town itself is known to the Cherokee as *Kâsdu′yĭ*, "Ashes place," (from *kâsdu*, ashes, and *yĭ*, locative), which is intended as a translation of its proper name. See number 122.

Untlasgâsti′yĭ—"Where they scratched"; a place at the head of Hyatt creek of Valley river, in Cherokee county, North Carolina. For tradition see number 122.

UNTOOLA—see *Dihyûñ′dulă′*.

unûñ′tĭ—milk.

usdi′gâ (abbreviated *usdi′*), small; plural *tsunsdi′gă*, *tsunsdi′*.

usga′sĕ⁗ti′yu—very dangerous, very terrible; intensive of *usga′sĕ⁗ti*.

Uskwăle′na—"Big-head," from *uskă′*, head; a masculine name, perhaps the original of the "Bull-head," given by Haywood as the name of a former noted Cherokee warrior.

Uskwâ′lĭ-gû′tă—"His stomach hangs down," from *uskwâ′lĭ*, his stomach, and *gû′tă*, "it hangs down." A prominent chief of the Revolutionary period, known to the whites as Hanging-maw.

U⁗stăna′lĭ (from *u⁗stănală′hĭ* or *uni′stăna′lă* (a plural form), denoting a natural barrier of rocks (plural) across a stream)—a name occurring in several places in the old Cherokee country, and variously spelled Eastinaulee, Eastanora, Estanaula, Eustenaree, Istanare, Oostanaula, Oostinawley, Ustenary, etc. One settlement of this name was on Keowee river, below the present Fort George, in Oconee county, South Carolina; another seems to have been somewhere on the waters of Tuckasegee river, in western North Carolina; a third, prominent during and after the Revolutionary period, was just above the junction of Coosawatee and Conasauga rivers to form the Oostanaula, in Gordon county, Georgia, and adjoining New Echota (see *Gănsâ′gĭ*). Other settlements of the same name may have been on Eastanollee creek of Tugaloo river, in Franklin county, Georgia, and on Eastaunaula creek, flowing into Hiwassee river, in McMinn county, Tennessee. Cf. *Tsu⁗stănalûñ′yĭ*, under *Dăgunâ′hĭ*.

u′stûtĭ—see *utsu′gĭ*.

Ustû′tlĭ—a traditional dangerous serpent. The name signifies having something on the calf of the leg or on the heel, from *ustûtûñ′ĭ*, (his) calf of the leg (attached). It is applied also to the southern hoop-snake (*Abastor erythrogrammus*). See number 54.

Usûñhi′yĭ—the "Darkening land," where it is always getting dark, as at twilight. The name used for the west in the myths and sacred formulas; the common word is *wude′ligûñ′yĭ*, "there where it (the sun) goes down." In number 63 the word used is *wusûhihûñ′yĭ*, "there where they stay over night." See also *Tsûsginâ′ĭ*.

u'tănû—great, fully developed. Cf. e'gwa.

utawâ'hilû—"hand-breadth," from uwâ'yi, hand. A figurative term used in the myths and sacred formulas.

U'tăwagûn'ta—"Bald place." A high bald peak of the Great Smoky range on the Tennessee-North Carolina line, northeastward from Big Pigeon river. See number 51.

Ûñ'tiguhĭ'—"Pot in the water," from ûñti'yă or ûñti', pot, and guhĭ', "it is in the water" (or other liquid—habitually). The Suck, a dangerous rapid in Tennessee river, at the entrance of Suck creek, about eight miles below Chattanooga, Tennessee. See number 63 and notes.

U'tlûñ'tă—"He (or she) has it sharp," i. e., has some sharp part or organ; it might be used of a tooth, finger-nail, or some other attached portion of the body, but in the story is understood to refer to the awl-like finger. Ten Kate spells it Uilata. A mythic half-human monster. See number 66 and notes.

U'tlûñtûñ'yĭ—"U'tlûñ'tă place;" see U'tlûñ'tă. A place on little Tennessee river, nearly off Citico creek, in Blount county, Tennessee. See number 66 and notes and number 124.

U'tsălă—"Lichen"; another form of utsăle'ta. A Cherokee chief of the Removal period. See page 157.

utsăle'ta—lichen, literally "pot scrapings," from a fancied resemblance.

Ûñtsaiyĭ' (also Etsaiyĭ' or Tsaiyĭ', the first syllable being almost silent)—"Brass." A mythic gambler. See number 63 and notes. The present rendering, "brass," is probably a modern application of the old myth name, and is based upon the resemblance of the sound to that produced by striking a sheet of metal.

utsa'nătĭ'—rattlesnake; the name is of doubtful etymology, but is said to refer to the rattle.

Utsa'nătĭ'yĭ—"Rattlesnake place." Rattlesnake springs, about two miles south from Charleston, Bradley county, Tennessee. See page 132.

utset'stĭ—"he grins" (habitually). See sĭ'kwă utset'stĭ.

utsĭ'—her (his) mother; etsĭ', agitsĭ', my mother.

Utsi'dsătă'—"Corn-tassel," "Thistle-head," etc. It is used as a masculine name and was probably the Cherokee name of the chief known during the Revolutionary period as "Old Tassel."

utsu゛gĭ—the tufted titmouse (Parus bicolor); also called u'stûtĭ, "topknot, or tip," on account of its crest. See numbers 35 and 66.

û'tsûtĭ'—fish. Cf. u'tsûtĭ, many.

ûñwădâ'lĭ—store-house, provision house. See number 3 and notes.

Uñ'wădâ-tsu゛gilasûñ'—"Where the storehouse (ûñwâdâ'lĭ) was taken off." Either Black rock or Jones knob, northeast of Webster, on the east line of Jackson county, in North Carolina. See number 122.

Uwagâ'hĭ (commonly written Ocoee)—"Apricot place," from uwa'gă, the "apricot vine," or "maypop," (Passiflora incarnata), and hĭ, locative. A former important settlement on Ocoee river, near its junction with Hiwassee, about the present Benton, in Polk county, Tennessee.

uwâ'yĭ—hand, paw· generally used with the possessive suffix, as uwâye'nĭ, "his hand."

uwe'la—liver.

uwe'năhĭ—rich; used also as a personal name as the equivalent of Richard. Cf. Tsuwe'năhĭ.

Uw'tsûñ'tă—"Bouncer" (habitual); from k゛tsĭ, "it is bouncing." A traditional serpent described as moving by jerks like a measuring worm, to which also the name is applied. See number 55.

Uyâhye'—a high peak in the Great Smoky range, probably on the line between Swain county, North Carolina, and Sevier or Blount county, Tennessee. See number 75 and notes.

Uy'gilâ'gĭ—abbreviated from Tsuyu'gilâ'gĭ, "Where there are dams," i. e., beaver dams; from gu'gilú'ûñskú', "he is damming it." 1. A former settlement on Oothcaloga (Ougillogy) creek of Oostanaula river, near the present Calhoun, in Gordon county, Georgia; 2. Beaverdam creek, west of Clarkesville, in Habersham county, Georgia.

VALLEYTOWN—see Gú'nahitûñ'yĭ.
VENGEANCE CREEK—see Gănsa'ti'yĭ.

WACHESA—see Watsi'sŭ.
wadâñ'—thanks!
wâ'dĭ—paint, especially red paint.
wâ'dige-askâ'lĭ—"his head (is) brown," i. e., "brown-head," from wâdige'ĭ, brown, brown-red, and askâ'lĭ, possessive of uskŭ', head; the copperhead snake.
Wadi'yăhĭ—A feminine name of doubtful etymology. An expert basket-making woman among the East Cherokee, who died in 1895. She was known to the whites as Mrs Bushyhead. See page 179.
VAFFORD—see Tsuskwanûñ'năwa'tă.
Wa'gĭnsĭ'—The name of an eddy at the junction of the Little Tennessee and main Tennessee rivers, at Lenoir, in Loudon county, Tennessee. The town is now known to the Cherokee by the same name, of which the meaning is lost. See number 124.
wagulĭ'—whippoorwill; the name is an onomatope; the Delaware name is wekolis (Heckewelder).
WAHNENAUHI—see Wani'năhĭ.
wa'huhu'—the screech-owl (Megascops asio); see also tskĭlĭ' and uguku'.
wa'ka—cow; from the Spanish vaca, as is also the Creek waga and the Arapaho wakúch.
walâ'sĭ—the common green frog; there are different names for the bullfrog (kûnu'nŭ, q. v.) and for other varieties; warts are also called walâ'sĭ.
Walâsi'yĭ—"Frog place." 1. A former settlement, known to the whites as Frogtown, upon the creek of the same name, north of Dahlonega, in Lumpkin county, Georgia. 2. Le Conte and Bullhead mountains in the Great Smoky range on the North Carolina-Tennessee line, together with the ridge extending into Sevier county, Tennessee, between the Middle and West forks of Little Pigeon river. See number 51 and notes.
walâs'-unûl'stĭ—"it fights frogs," from walâ'sĭ, frog, and unûl'stĭ, "it fights" (habitually); gú'lihú', "I am fighting." The Prosartes lanuginosa plant. See number 126.
Walâs'-unûlsti'yĭ—"Place of the plant walâs'-unûl'stĭ," commonly known to the whites as Fightingtown, from a translation of the latter part of the name; a former settlement on Fightingtown creek, near Morganton, in Fannin county, Georgia. See number 125.
Walinĭ'—a feminine name, compounded from Walĭ, another form of Kwalĭ, "Polly," with a suffix added for euphony.
Wane'-asûñ'tlûñyĭ—"Hickory footlog place," from wane'ĭ, hickory, asûñtlûñ'ĭ (q.v.), footlog, bridge, and yĭ, locative. A former settlement, known to the whites as Hickory-log, on Etowah river, a short distance above Canton, in Cherokee county, Georgia.
Wani'năhĭ'—a feminine name of uncertain etymology; the Wahnenauhi of the Wahnenauhi manuscript.
WASHINGTON—see Wa'sitú'nă.
Wâ'sĭ—the Cherokee form for Moses.

Wa′sitû′nă, Wa′sûñtû′nă (different dialectic forms)—a CheroKee known to the whites as Washington, the sole survivor of a Removal tragedy. See page 158. The name denotes a hollow log (or other cylindrical object) lying on the ground at a distance; the root of the word is *asi′ta*, log, and the *w* prefixed makes it at a distance.

Wa′sulû′—a large red-brown moth which flies about the blossoming tobacco in the evening.

Watâ′gĭ (commonly written Watauga, also Watoga, Wattoogee, Whatoga, etc.)—a name occurring in two or more towns in the old Cherokee country; one was an important settlement on Watauga creek of Little Tennessee river, a few miles below Franklin, in Macon county, Tennessee; another was traditionally located at Watauga Old Fields, about the present Elizabethton, on Watauga river, in Carter county, Tennessee. See page 21. The meaning of the name is lost.

WATAUGA—see *Watá′gĭ*.

Watsi′să—a prominent old Cherokee, known to the whites as Wachesa, a name which cannot be translated, who formerly lived on lower Beaverdam creek of Hiwassee river, below Murphy, in Cherokee county, North Carolina. From the fact that the Unicoi turnpike passed near his place it was locally known as the Wachesa trail.

wa′ya—wolf; the name is an onomatope, intended as an imitation of the animal's howl; cf. the Creek name, *yähä*.

Wa′yâ′hĭ—"Wolf place," i. e. place of the Wolf clan; the form *Ani′- Wa′yâ′hi* is not used. Wolftown settlement on upper Soco creek, on the East Cherokee reservation, in Jackson county, North Carolina.

WAYA GAP—see *A′tâhi′ta*.

WAYEH—see *Wâyĭ*.

Wâyĭ—"Pigeon"; the modern Cherokee name for Big Pigeon river in western North Carolina; probably a translation of the English name. It appears also as Wayeh.

WELCH, LLOYD—see *Da′sĭ̆giya′gĭ*.

wesă—cat; a corruption of "pussy."

WHITE-PATH—see *Nûñnâ′hĭ-tsune′ga*.

WILLSTOWN—a former important settlement, so called from the halfbreed chief known to the whites as Red-headed Will, on Will's creek below Fort Payne, in Dekalb county, Alabama. The settlement was frequently called from him *Wili′yĭ*, "Will's place," but this was not the proper local name.

Wĭlsĭnĭ′—the Cherokee name for H. W. Spray, agent and superintendent for the East Cherokee reservation; an adaptation of his middle name, Wilson.

Wil-usdi′—"Little Will," from *Wilĭ′*, Will and *usdi′ga* or *usdi′*, little. The Cherokee name for Colonel W. H. Thomas, for many years the recognized chief of the eastern band.

WISSACTAW—see *găhăwĭ′sita*.

WOLFTOWN—see *Wa′yâ′hĭ*.

WOOTASSITE }
WROSETASATOW } —see ÒUTACITY.

Wude′ligûñ′yĭ—the west; literally "there where it (the sun) goes down" (*w* prefixed implies distance, *yĭ*, locative). See also *Usûñhi′yĭ* and *wusûhihûñ′yĭ*.

Wuliga′nătûtûñ—excelling all others, either in good or bad; it may be used as equivalent to *wastûñ*, "beyond the limit." See page 232.

wusûhihûñ′yĭ—"there where they stay over night," i. e. "the west." An archaic term used by the narrator of the story of Ûñtsaiyĭ′, number 63. The common word is *wude′ligûñ′yĭ*, q. v., while the term in the sacred formulas is *Usûñhi′yĭ*, q.v.

XUALA—see *Ani-Suwa′lĭ*.

-yă—a suffix denoting principal or real, as *tsiskwa'yă*, "principal bird," the sparrow; *Ani'-Yûñwiyă'*, "principal or real people," Indians.

YAHOOLA—see *Yahulá'ĭ*.

Yahulâ'ĭ—"Yahu'la place," from *Yahu'la*, a Cherokee trader said to have been taken by the spirit people; *Yahu'la* seems to be from the Creek *yoho'lo*, a name having reference to the song (*yoholo*), used in the "black drink" ceremony of the Creeks; thus *a'si-yoho'lo*, corrupted into Osceola, signified "the black drink song"; it may, however, be a true Cherokee word, *yahu'lú* or *yahu'lă*, the name for a variety of hickory, also for the "doodle-bug"; *Ûñyahu'lă* is a feminine name, but can not be translated. Yahoola creek, near Dahlonega, in Lumpkin county, Georgia. See number 86 and notes.

Yalâ'gĭ—Alarka creek of Little Tennessee river, above the junction of Tuckasegee, in Swain county, North Carolina; the meaning of the name is lost.

yañdaska'ga—a faultfinder. See number 61.

Yân-e'gwa—"Big-bear," from *yânú*, bear, and *egwa*, great, large. A prominent chief about the year 1800; the name occurs in treaties as Yonah, Yohanaqua and Yona-hequah. See page 164.

yâ'nû—bear.

Yâ'nû-dinĕhûñ'yĭ—"Where the bears live," from *yânú*, bear, *dinĕhú'*, "they dwell" (*ĕ'hú*, "I dwell, I live"), and *yĭ*, locative. A place on Oconaluftee river, a short distance above the junction with Tuckasegee, in Swain county, North Carolina. See number 122.

Yânûgûñ'skĭ—"The bear drowns him" (habitually), from *yânú*, bear, and *tsigûñ'-iskă'*, "I am drowning him." A noted East Cherokee chief, known to the whites as Yonaguska or Drowning-bear. See page 162.

Yâ'nû-u'nătawasti'yĭ—"Where the bears wash" (from *yânú*, bear, and *yĭ*, locative); a former pond in the Great Smoky mountains, about the extreme head of Raven fork, in Swain county, North Carolina. See number 122.

yân'-utse'stû—"the bear lies on it"; the shield fern (*Aspidium*). See number 126.

Yawâ'ĭ—"Yawă place"; a place on Yellow creek of Cheowa river, in Graham county, North Carolina. See number 122.

YELLOW-HILL—see *E lăwâ'diyĭ*.

YOHANAQUA—see *Yân-e'gwa*.

yoho-o!—an unmeaning song refrain. See number 75.

YONAGUSKA—see *Yâ'nûgûñ'skĭ*.

YONAH—1. (mountain) see *Gadalu'lă*. 2. An abbreviated treaty form for the name of the chief Yân-e'gwa.

YONAHEQUAH—see *Yân-e'gwa*.

YTAUA, YTAVA—see *I'tăwă'*.

Yu!—an unmeaning song refrain and interjection.

Yuha'lĭ—Euharlee creek, of lower Etowah river, in Bartow county, Georgia. The name is said by the Cherokee to be a corruption of Yufala (Eufaula), a well-known Creek local name. See number 105.

yûnsû'—buffalo; cf. Creek *yĕna'sa*, Choctaw *yanash*, Hichitee *ya'nasi*.

Yûnsâ'ĭ—"Buffalo place"; West Buffalo creek of Cheowa river in Graham county, North Carolina; the site of a former Cherokee settlement. See number 122.

yu'wĕ-yuwĕhe'—an unmeaning song refrain. See number 118.

yûñ'wĭ—person, man; cf. Mohawk *oñgwe'*.

Yûñ'wĭ Amă'yĭnĕ'hĭ—"Water-dwelling People," from *yûñ'wĭ*, person, and *ămă'-yĭnĕ'hĭ*, plural of *ămăyĕ'hĭ*, q. v.; a race of water fairies. See number 78.

Yûñ'wĭ-dĭkatâgûñ'yĭ—see *Yûñ'wĭ-tsulenûñ'yĭ*,

Yûñ'wĭ Gûnăhi'ta—"Long Man"; a formulistic name for the river, personified as a man with his head resting on the mountain and his feet stretching down to the lowlands, who is constantly speaking to those who can understand the message.

Yûñ'wini'giskĭ—"Man-eaters," literally, "They eat people" (habitually), from *yûñ'wĭ*, person, man, and *uni'giskĭ*, "they eat" (habitually), from *tsĭkiŭ'*, "I am eating"; the Cherokee name for a distant cannibal tribe, possibly the Atakapa or the Tonkawa. See number 105. Cf. *Anădă'dûñtăskĭ*.

Yûñ'wĭ-tsulenûñ'yĭ—"Where the man stood," originally *Yûñ'wĭ-dĭkatăgûñ'yĭ*, "Where the man stands," from *yûñ'wĭ*, person, man, *tsĭtă'gă*, "I am standing," and *yĭ*, locative; Standing Indian, a high bald mountain at the head of Nantahala river, in Macon county, North Carolina. See number 122.

Yûñ'wĭ Tsunsdi'—"Little People," from *yûñ'wĭ*, person, people, and *tsunsdi'gă* or *tsunsdi'*, plural of *usdi'gă* or *usdi'*, little; the Cherokee fairies. See number 78.

Yûñ'wĭ Usdĭ'—"Little Man." A formulistic name for the ginseng, *ă'tălĭ-gúlĭ'*, q. v.

Yûñ'wĭ-usga'sĕ'tĭ—"Dangerous Man, Terrible Man"; a traditional leader in the westward migration of the Cherokee. See page 99.

Yûñ'wiyă'—"Indian," literally, "principal or re 1 person," from *yûñ'wĭ*, person and *yă*, a suffix denoting principal or real. See pages 15 and 181.

INDEX TO PART 1

NOTE: The references to pages with roman numerals are not applicable to the Dover edition and should be ignored. They refer to an administrative report which appeared with the original text and is here omitted.

INDEX

Page

O

A CATALOG OF SELECTED

DOVER BOOKS

IN ALL FIELDS OF INTEREST

A CATALOG OF SELECTED DOVER
BOOKS IN ALL FIELDS OF INTEREST

CONCERNING THE SPIRITUAL IN ART, Wassily Kandinsky. Pioneering work by father of abstract art. Thoughts on color theory, nature of art. Analysis of earlier masters. 12 illustrations. 80pp. of text. 5⅜ x 8½.   23411-8 Pa. $3.95

ANIMALS: 1,419 Copyright-Free Illustrations of Mammals, Birds, Fish, Insects, etc., Jim Harter (ed.). Clear wood engravings present, in extremely lifelike poses, over 1,000 species of animals. One of the most extensive pictorial sourcebooks of its kind. Captions. Index. 284pp. 9 x 12.   23766-4 Pa. $12.95

CELTIC ART: The Methods of Construction, George Bain. Simple geometric techniques for making Celtic interlacements, spirals, Kells-type initials, animals, humans, etc. Over 500 illustrations. 160pp. 9 x 12. (USO)   22923-8 Pa. $9.95

AN ATLAS OF ANATOMY FOR ARTISTS, Fritz Schider. Most thorough reference work on art anatomy in the world. Hundreds of illustrations, including selections from works by Vesalius, Leonardo, Goya, Ingres, Michelangelo, others. 593 illustrations. 192pp. 7⅛ x 10¼.   20241-0 Pa. $9.95

CELTIC HAND STROKE-BY-STROKE (Irish Half-Uncial from "The Book of Kells"): An Arthur Baker Calligraphy Manual, Arthur Baker. Complete guide to creating each letter of the alphabet in distinctive Celtic manner. Covers hand position, strokes, pens, inks, paper, more. Illustrated. 48pp. 8¼ x 11.   24336-2 Pa. $3.95

EASY ORIGAMI, John Montroll. Charming collection of 32 projects (hat, cup, pelican, piano, swan, many more) specially designed for the novice origami hobbyist. Clearly illustrated easy-to-follow instructions insure that even beginning papercrafters will achieve successful results. 48pp. 8¼ x 11.   27298-2 Pa. $3.50

THE COMPLETE BOOK OF BIRDHOUSE CONSTRUCTION FOR WOODWORKERS, Scott D. Campbell. Detailed instructions, illustrations, tables. Also data on bird habitat and instinct patterns. Bibliography. 3 tables. 63 illustrations in 15 figures. 48pp. 5¼ x 8½.   24407-5 Pa. $2.50

BLOOMINGDALE'S ILLUSTRATED 1886 CATALOG: Fashions, Dry Goods and Housewares, Bloomingdale Brothers. Famed merchants' extremely rare catalog depicting about 1,700 products: clothing, housewares, firearms, dry goods, jewelry, more. Invaluable for dating, identifying vintage items. Also, copyright-free graphics for artists, designers. Co-published with Henry Ford Museum & Greenfield Village. 160pp. 8¼ x 11.   25780-0 Pa. $10.95

HISTORIC COSTUME IN PICTURES, Braun & Schneider. Over 1,450 costumed figures in clearly detailed engravings–from dawn of civilization to end of 19th century. Captions. Many folk costumes. 256pp. 8⅜ x 11¾.   23150-X Pa. $12.95

STICKLEY CRAFTSMAN FURNITURE CATALOGS, Gustav Stickley and L. & J. G. Stickley. Beautiful, functional furniture in two authentic catalogs from 1910. 594 illustrations, including 277 photos, show settles, rockers, armchairs, reclining chairs, bookcases, desks, tables. 183pp. 6½ x 9¼. 23838-5 Pa. $9.95

AMERICAN LOCOMOTIVES IN HISTORIC PHOTOGRAPHS: 1858 to 1949, Ron Ziel (ed.). A rare collection of 126 meticulously detailed official photographs, called "builder portraits," of American locomotives that majestically chronicle the rise of steam locomotive power in America. Introduction. Detailed captions. xi + 129pp. 9 x 12. 27393-8 Pa. $12.95

AMERICA'S LIGHTHOUSES: An Illustrated History, Francis Ross Holland, Jr. Delightfully written, profusely illustrated fact-filled survey of over 200 American lighthouses since 1716. History, anecdotes, technological advances, more. 240pp. 8 x 10¾. 25576-X Pa. $12.95

TOWARDS A NEW ARCHITECTURE, Le Corbusier. Pioneering manifesto by founder of "International School." Technical and aesthetic theories, views of industry, economics, relation of form to function, "mass-production split" and much more. Profusely illustrated. 320pp. 6⅛ x 9¼. (USO) 25023-7 Pa. $9.95

HOW THE OTHER HALF LIVES, Jacob Riis. Famous journalistic record, exposing poverty and degradation of New York slums around 1900, by major social reformer. 100 striking and influential photographs. 233pp. 10 x 7⅞. 22012-5 Pa. $10.95

FRUIT KEY AND TWIG KEY TO TREES AND SHRUBS, William M. Harlow. One of the handiest and most widely used identification aids. Fruit key covers 120 deciduous and evergreen species; twig key 160 deciduous species. Easily used. Over 300 photographs. 126pp. 5⅜ x 8½. 20511-8 Pa. $3.95

COMMON BIRD SONGS, Dr. Donald J. Borror. Songs of 60 most common U.S. birds: robins, sparrows, cardinals, bluejays, finches, more–arranged in order of increasing complexity. Up to 9 variations of songs of each species.
Cassette and manual 99911-4 $8.95

ORCHIDS AS HOUSE PLANTS, Rebecca Tyson Northen. Grow cattleyas and many other kinds of orchids–in a window, in a case, or under artificial light. 63 illustrations. 148pp. 5⅜ x 8½. 23261-1 Pa. $4.95

MONSTER MAZES, Dave Phillips. Masterful mazes at four levels of difficulty. Avoid deadly perils and evil creatures to find magical treasures. Solutions for all 32 exciting illustrated puzzles 48pp. 8¼ x 11. 26005-4 Pa. $2.95

MOZART'S DON GIOVANNI (DOVER OPERA LIBRETTO SERIES), Wolfgang Amadeus Mozart. Introduced and translated by Ellen H. Bleiler. Standard Italian libretto, with complete English translation. Convenient and thoroughly portable–an ideal companion for reading along with a recording or the performance itself. Introduction. List of characters. Plot summary. 121pp. 5¼ x 8½. 24944-1 Pa. $2.95

TECHNICAL MANUAL AND DICTIONARY OF CLASSICAL BALLET, Gail Grant. Defines, explains, comments on steps, movements, poses and concepts. 15-page pictorial section. Basic book for student, viewer. 127pp. 5⅜ x 8½. 21843-0 Pa. $4.95

FRANK LLOYD WRIGHT'S HOLLYHOCK HOUSE, Donald Hoffmann. Lavishly illustrated, carefully documented study of one of Wright's most controversial residential designs. Over 120 photographs, floor plans, elevations, etc. Detailed perceptive text by noted Wright scholar. Index. 128pp. 9¼ x 10¾. 27133-1 Pa. $11.95

THE MALE AND FEMALE FIGURE IN MOTION: 60 Classic Photographic Sequences, Eadweard Muybridge. 60 true-action photographs of men and women walking, running, climbing, bending, turning, etc., reproduced from rare 19th-century masterpiece. vi + 121pp. 9 x 12. 24745-7 Pa. $10.95

1001 QUESTIONS ANSWERED ABOUT THE SEASHORE, N. J. Berrill and Jacquelyn Berrill. Queries answered about dolphins, sea snails, sponges, starfish, fishes, shore birds, many others. Covers appearance, breeding, growth, feeding, much more. 305pp. 5¼ x 8¼. 23366-9 Pa. $8.95

GUIDE TO OWL WATCHING IN NORTH AMERICA, Donald S. Heintzelman. Superb guide offers complete data and descriptions of 19 species: barn owl, screech owl, snowy owl, many more. Expert coverage of owl-watching equipment, conservation, migrations and invasions, etc. Guide to observing sites. 84 illustrations. xiii + 193pp. 5⅜ x 8½. 27344-X Pa. $8.95

MEDICINAL AND OTHER USES OF NORTH AMERICAN PLANTS: A Historical Survey with Special Reference to the Eastern Indian Tribes, Charlotte Erichsen-Brown. Chronological historical citations document 500 years of usage of plants, trees, shrubs native to eastern Canada, northeastern U.S. Also complete identifying information. 343 illustrations. 544pp. 6½ x 9¼. 25951-X Pa. $12.95

STORYBOOK MAZES, Dave Phillips. 23 stories and mazes on two-page spreads: Wizard of Oz, Treasure Island, Robin Hood, etc. Solutions. 64pp. 8¼ x 11. 23628-5 Pa. $2.95

NEGRO FOLK MUSIC, U.S.A., Harold Courlander. Noted folklorist's scholarly yet readable analysis of rich and varied musical tradition. Includes authentic versions of over 40 folk songs. Valuable bibliography and discography. xi + 324pp. 5⅜ x 8½. 27350-4 Pa. $9.95

MOVIE-STAR PORTRAITS OF THE FORTIES, John Kobal (ed.). 163 glamor, studio photos of 106 stars of the 1940s: Rita Hayworth, Ava Gardner, Marlon Brando, Clark Gable, many more. 176pp. 8⅜ x 11¼. 23546-7 Pa. $12.95

BENCHLEY LOST AND FOUND, Robert Benchley. Finest humor from early 30s, about pet peeves, child psychologists, post office and others. Mostly unavailable elsewhere. 73 illustrations by Peter Arno and others. 183pp. 5⅜ x 8½. 22410-4 Pa. $6.95

YEKL and THE IMPORTED BRIDEGROOM AND OTHER STORIES OF YIDDISH NEW YORK, Abraham Cahan. Film Hester Street based on Yekl (1896). Novel, other stories among first about Jewish immigrants on N.Y.'s East Side. 240pp. 5⅜ x 8½. 22427-9 Pa. $6.95

SELECTED POEMS, Walt Whitman. Generous sampling from *Leaves of Grass*. Twenty-four poems include "I Hear America Singing," "Song of the Open Road," "I Sing the Body Electric," "When Lilacs Last in the Dooryard Bloom'd," "O Captain! My Captain!"—all reprinted from an authoritative edition. Lists of titles and first lines. 128pp. 5³⁄₁₆ x 8¼. 26878-0 Pa. $1.00

PERSPECTIVE FOR ARTISTS, Rex Vicat Cole. Depth, perspective of sky and sea, shadows, much more, not usually covered. 391 diagrams, 81 reproductions of drawings and paintings. 279pp. 5⅜ x 8½. 22487-2 Pa. $7.95

DRAWING THE LIVING FIGURE, Joseph Sheppard. Innovative approach to artistic anatomy focuses on specifics of surface anatomy, rather than muscles and bones. Over 170 drawings of live models in front, back and side views, and in widely varying poses. Accompanying diagrams. 177 illustrations. Introduction. Index. 144pp. 8⅜ x11¼. 26723-7 Pa. $8.95

GOTHIC AND OLD ENGLISH ALPHABETS: 100 Complete Fonts, Dan X. Solo. Add power, elegance to posters, signs, other graphics with 100 stunning copyright-free alphabets: Blackstone, Dolbey, Germania, 97 more–including many lower-case, numerals, punctuation marks. 104pp. 8⅛ x 11. 24695-7 Pa. $8.95

HOW TO DO BEADWORK, Mary White. Fundamental book on craft from simple projects to five-bead chains and woven works. 106 illustrations. 142pp. 5⅜ x 8. 20697-1 Pa. $4.95

THE BOOK OF WOOD CARVING, Charles Marshall Sayers. Finest book for beginners discusses fundamentals and offers 34 designs. "Absolutely first rate . . . well thought out and well executed."–E. J. Tangerman. 118pp. 7¾ x 10⅝. 23654-4 Pa. $6.95

ILLUSTRATED CATALOG OF CIVIL WAR MILITARY GOODS: Union Army Weapons, Insignia, Uniform Accessories, and Other Equipment, Schuyler, Hartley, and Graham. Rare, profusely illustrated 1846 catalog includes Union Army uniform and dress regulations, arms and ammunition, coats, insignia, flags, swords, rifles, etc. 226 illustrations. 160pp. 9 x 12. 24939-5 Pa. $10.95

WOMEN'S FASHIONS OF THE EARLY 1900s: An Unabridged Republication of "New York Fashions, 1909," National Cloak & Suit Co. Rare catalog of mail-order fashions documents women's and children's clothing styles shortly after the turn of the century. Captions offer full descriptions, prices. Invaluable resource for fashion, costume historians. Approximately 725 illustrations. 128pp. 8⅜ x 11¼. 27276-1 Pa. $11.95

THE 1912 AND 1915 GUSTAV STICKLEY FURNITURE CATALOGS, Gustav Stickley. With over 200 detailed illustrations and descriptions, these two catalogs are essential reading and reference materials and identification guides for Stickley furniture. Captions cite materials, dimensions and prices. 112pp. 6½ x 9¼. 26676-1 Pa. $9.95

EARLY AMERICAN LOCOMOTIVES, John H. White, Jr. Finest locomotive engravings from early 19th century: historical (1804–74), main-line (after 1870), special, foreign, etc. 147 plates. 142pp. 11⅜ x 8¼. 22772-3 Pa. $10.95

THE TALL SHIPS OF TODAY IN PHOTOGRAPHS, Frank O. Braynard. Lavishly illustrated tribute to nearly 100 majestic contemporary sailing vessels: Amerigo Vespucci, Clearwater, Constitution, Eagle, Mayflower, Sea Cloud, Victory, many more. Authoritative captions provide statistics, background on each ship. 190 black-and-white photographs and illustrations. Introduction. 128pp. 8⅞ x 11¾. 27163-3 Pa. $13.95

PIANO TUNING, J. Cree Fischer. Clearest, best book for beginner, amateur. Simple repairs, raising dropped notes, tuning by easy method of flattened fifths. No previous skills needed. 4 illustrations. 201pp. 5⅜ x 8½. 23267-0 Pa. $6.95

A SOURCE BOOK IN THEATRICAL HISTORY, A. M. Nagler. Contemporary observers on acting, directing, make-up, costuming, stage props, machinery, scene design, from Ancient Greece to Chekhov. 611pp. 5⅜ x 8½. 20515-0 Pa. $12.95

THE COMPLETE NONSENSE OF EDWARD LEAR, Edward Lear. All nonsense limericks, zany alphabets, Owl and Pussycat, songs, nonsense botany, etc., illustrated by Lear. Total of 320pp. 5⅜ x 8½. (USO) 20167-8 Pa. $6.95

VICTORIAN PARLOUR POETRY: An Annotated Anthology, Michael R. Turner. 117 gems by Longfellow, Tennyson, Browning, many lesser-known poets. "The Village Blacksmith," "Curfew Must Not Ring Tonight," "Only a Baby Small," dozens more, often difficult to find elsewhere. Index of poets, titles, first lines. xxiii + 325pp. 5⅝ x 8¼. 27044-0 Pa. $8.95

DUBLINERS, James Joyce. Fifteen stories offer vivid, tightly focused observations of the lives of Dublin's poorer classes. At least one, "The Dead," is considered a masterpiece. Reprinted complete and unabridged from standard edition. 160pp. 5³⁄₁₆ x 8¼. 26870-5 Pa. $1.00

THE HAUNTED MONASTERY and THE CHINESE MAZE MURDERS, Robert van Gulik. Two full novels by van Gulik, set in 7th-century China, continue adventures of Judge Dee and his companions. An evil Taoist monastery, seemingly supernatural events; overgrown topiary maze hides strange crimes. 27 illustrations. 328pp. 5⅜ x 8½. 23502-5 Pa. $8.95

THE BOOK OF THE SACRED MAGIC OF ABRAMELIN THE MAGE, translated by S. MacGregor Mathers. Medieval manuscript of ceremonial magic. Basic document in Aleister Crowley, Golden Dawn groups. 268pp. 5⅜ x 8½. 23211-5 Pa. $8.95

NEW RUSSIAN-ENGLISH AND ENGLISH-RUSSIAN DICTIONARY, M. A. O'Brien. This is a remarkably handy Russian dictionary, containing a surprising amount of information, including over 70,000 entries. 366pp. 4½ x 6⅛. 20208-9 Pa. $9.95

HISTORIC HOMES OF THE AMERICAN PRESIDENTS, Second, Revised Edition, Irvin Haas. A traveler's guide to American Presidential homes, most open to the public, depicting and describing homes occupied by every American President from George Washington to George Bush. With visiting hours, admission charges, travel routes. 175 photographs. Index. 160pp. 8¼ x 11. 26751-2 Pa. $11.95

NEW YORK IN THE FORTIES, Andreas Feininger. 162 brilliant photographs by the well-known photographer, formerly with *Life* magazine. Commuters, shoppers, Times Square at night, much else from city at its peak. Captions by John von Hartz. 181pp. 9¼ x 10¾. 23585-8 Pa. $12.95

INDIAN SIGN LANGUAGE, William Tomkins. Over 525 signs developed by Sioux and other tribes. Written instructions and diagrams. Also 290 pictographs. 111pp. 6⅛ x 9¼. 22029-X Pa. $3.95

THE INFLUENCE OF SEA POWER UPON HISTORY, 1660–1783, A. T. Mahan. Influential classic of naval history and tactics still used as text in war colleges. First paperback edition. 4 maps. 24 battle plans. 640pp. 5⅜ x 8½. 25509-3 Pa. $12.95

THE STORY OF THE TITANIC AS TOLD BY ITS SURVIVORS, Jack Winocour (ed.). What it was really like. Panic, despair, shocking inefficiency, and a little heroism. More thrilling than any fictional account. 26 illustrations. 320pp. 5⅜ x 8½. 20610-6 Pa. $8.95

FAIRY AND FOLK TALES OF THE IRISH PEASANTRY, William Butler Yeats (ed.). Treasury of 64 tales from the twilight world of Celtic myth and legend: "The Soul Cages," "The Kildare Pooka," "King O'Toole and his Goose," many more. Introduction and Notes by W. B. Yeats. 352pp. 5⅜ x 8½. 26941-8 Pa. $8.95

BUDDHIST MAHAYANA TEXTS, E. B. Cowell and Others (eds.). Superb, accurate translations of basic documents in Mahayana Buddhism, highly important in history of religions. The Buddha-karita of Asvaghosha, Larger Sukhavativyuha, more. 448pp. 5⅜ x 8½. 25552-2 Pa. $12.95

ONE TWO THREE . . . INFINITY: Facts and Speculations of Science, George Gamow. Great physicist's fascinating, readable overview of contemporary science: number theory, relativity, fourth dimension, entropy, genes, atomic structure, much more. 128 illustrations. Index. 352pp. 5⅜ x 8½. 25664-2 Pa. $8.95

ENGINEERING IN HISTORY, Richard Shelton Kirby, et al. Broad, nontechnical survey of history's major technological advances: birth of Greek science, industrial revolution, electricity and applied science, 20th-century automation, much more. 181 illustrations. ". . . excellent . . ."–*Isis.* Bibliography. vii + 530pp. 5⅜ x 8¼. 26412-2 Pa. $14.95

DALÍ ON MODERN ART: The Cuckolds of Antiquated Modern Art, Salvador Dalí. Influential painter skewers modern art and its practitioners. Outrageous evaluations of Picasso, Cézanne, Turner, more. 15 renderings of paintings discussed. 44 calligraphic decorations by Dalí. 96pp. 5⅜ x 8½. (USO) 29220-7 Pa. $4.95

ANTIQUE PLAYING CARDS: A Pictorial History, Henry René D'Allemagne. Over 900 elaborate, decorative images from rare playing cards (14th–20th centuries): Bacchus, death, dancing dogs, hunting scenes, royal coats of arms, players cheating, much more. 96pp. 9¼ x 12¼. 29265-7 Pa. $11.95

MAKING FURNITURE MASTERPIECES: 30 Projects with Measured Drawings, Franklin H. Gottshall. Step-by-step instructions, illustrations for constructing handsome, useful pieces, among them a Sheraton desk, Chippendale chair, Spanish desk, Queen Anne table and a William and Mary dressing mirror. 224pp. 8⅛ x 11¼. 29338-6 Pa. $13.95

THE FOSSIL BOOK: A Record of Prehistoric Life, Patricia V. Rich et al. Profusely illustrated definitive guide covers everything from single-celled organisms and dinosaurs to birds and mammals and the interplay between climate and man. Over 1,500 illustrations. 760pp. 7½ x 10⅛. 29371-8 Pa. $29.95

Prices subject to change without notice.

Available at your book dealer or write for free catalog to Dept. GI, Dover Publications, Inc., 31 East 2nd St., Mineola, N.Y. 11501. Dover publishes more than 500 books each year on science, elementary and advanced mathematics, biology, music, art, literary history, social sciences and other areas.